DICKENS STUDIES ANNUAL

Essays on Victorian Fiction

DICKENS STUDIES ANNUAL

Essays on Victorian Fiction

DICKENS STUDIES ANNUAL

Essays on Victorian Fiction

VOLUME
44

Edited by
Stanley Friedman, Edward Guiliano,
Anne Humpherys, Natalie McKnight, and Michael Timko

AMS PRESS, INC.
New York

Dickens Studies Annual
ISSN 0084-9812
e-ISSN 2167-8510

Dickens Studies Annual: Essays on Victorian Fiction welcomes essay- and monograph-length contributions on Dickens and other Victorian novelists and on the history of aesthetics of Victorian fiction. All manuscripts should be double-spaced and should follow the documentation format described in the most recent MLA Style Manual. The author's name should appear only on a cover-page, not elsewhere in the essay. An editorial decision can usually be reached more quickly if two copies of the article are submitted, since outside readers are asked to evaluate each submission. If a manuscript is accepted for publication, the author will be asked to provide a 100- to 200-word abstract and also a disk containing the final version of the essay. The preferred editions for citations from Dickens's works are the Clarendon and the Norton Critical when available, otherwise the Oxford Illustrated or the Penguin.

Please send submissions to The Editors, Dickens Studies Annual, Ph.D. Program in English, The Graduate Center, CUNY, 365 Fifth Avenue, New York, NY 10016-4309. Please send inquiries concerning subscriptions and/or availability of earlier volumes to AMS Press, Inc., Brooklyn Navy Yard, 63 Flushing Ave.–Unit #221, Brooklyn, NY 11205-1073.

Dickens Studies Annual: Essays on Victorian Fiction is published in cooperation with Queens College and the Graduate Center, CUNY.

International Standard Book Number
Series ISBN: 978-0-404-18520-6

Vol. 44 Cloth ISBN: 978-0-404-18944-0
Vol. 44 e-ISBN: 978-0-404-90044-1

All AMS books are printed on acid-free paper that meets the guidelines for performance and durability of the Committee on Production Guidelines for Book Longevity of the Council on Library Resources.

AMS PRESS, INC.
Brooklyn Navy Yard, 63 Flushing Avenue–Unit #221
Brooklyn, NY 11205-1073, USA
www.amspressinc.com

Manufactured in the United States of America

CONTENTS

Preface

[N]ine hundred and ninety-nine people out of every thousand, never read a preface at all.

—Preface to the Second Series, *Sketches by Boz*

The essays in this issue offer fresh perspectives that focus on various features in Dickens's art. Although works from throughout Dickens's long career are discussed, a number of these studies give attention to the earlier novels, his beginnings.

We are grateful to Robert C. Hanna for his edition of Wilkie Collins's play *The Storm at the Lighthouse*, first published in this volume and now readily accessible for the first time, with an introduction describing the importance of this drama's themes and action for both Collins and Dickens.

In 2011 the impressive quantity of Dickens-related publications, stimulated in part by anticipation of the bicentennial, made choosing essays and books to read especially difficult. We thank Elizabeth Bridgham for providing an extremely inclusive, thorough, and insightful survey that offers useful guidance in selecting items to examine.

We thank all of the authors who submitted their essays, and we deeply appreciate the generous assistance of our outside readers, whose detailed reviews are of great value to us and also to our contributors.

For practical assistance, we acknowledge our debt to various academic administrators: President William P. Kelly, Provost Chase Robinson, Ph.D. Program in English Acting Executive Officer Carrie Hintz, and Nancy Silverman, Assistant Program Officer, Ph.D. Program in English, all of The Graduate Center, CUNY; and President James L. Muyskens, Acting Dean of Arts and Humanities William McClure, and Department of English Chair Glenn Burger, all of Queens College, CUNY.

We also express our appreciation to John O. Jordan, Director of The Dickens Project at the University of California, Santa Cruz; JoAnna Rottke, Project Coordinator for The Dickens Project; and Jon Michael Varese, the Project's Director of Digital Initiatives, for placing on the Project's website the tables of contents for volumes 1–27 of *DSA*, as well as abstracts for subsequent volumes. (These items can be found on the Project's website: <http://dickens.ucsc.edu>. Click "Resources" to find the link, at the left, to *Dickens Studies Annual*.)

We express gratitude to Gabriel Hornstein, President of AMS Press, for his continued confidence and active interest; to Jack Hopper, retired Editor-in-Chief at AMS Press, for his skilled assistance; and to David Ramm, Editor-in-Chief at AMS Press, for impressive problem-solving and resourceful advice. Finally, we thank our editorial assistant, Julia Fuller, a doctoral student at the Graduate Center, CUNY, for valuable work during the early phases of preparing this volume, and her successor, Erin Spampinato, also a doctoral student at the Graduate Center, CUNY, for effective help with the middle and final stages.

—The Editors

Notes on Contributors

KATTIE M. BASNETT is a Ph.D. candidate studying Victorian Literature at Rice University. Her special interests include period science, animal studies, and women, gender, and sexuality studies. She is a member of Rice's Center for Women, Gender, and Sexuality Studies and is currently completing her dissertation, "Animal Remainders, Remaining Animal: Cross-Species Collaborative Encounters in Victorian Literature."

ELIZABETH BRIDGHAM is Associate Professor of English at Providence College, in Providence, RI, where she specializes in Victorian literature and culture. She is the author of *Spaces of the Sacred and Profane: Dickens, Trollope, and the Victorian Cathedral Town* (Routledge, 2008) and is bibliographer for *Dickens Quarterly*. Her current scholarly projects concern adaptations and appropriations of Dickens in contemporary literary fiction and film and representations of national space in the popular culture of the Victorian period and today.

MONICA F. COHEN is Adjunct Assistant Professor of English at Columbia University and an Instructor in the English Department at Barnard College. She is author of *Professional Domesticity in the Victorian Novel: Women, Work and Home* (Cambridge UP, 1998) and numerous essays on topics significant to the nineteenth-century novel. She is currently working on a book about nineteenth-century literary piracy and pirate narratives.

CHRISTINE L. CORTON formerly worked in publishing, most recently as a director of Boxtree Books. She is a graduate of London University and earned her M.A. in Victorian Studies from Birkbeck College, University of London, while working full time. She was awarded a Ph.D. by the University of Kent for the dissertation "Metaphors of London Fog, Smoke and Mist in Victorian and Edwardian Art and Literature." She is currently working on a book that continues the story on to the 1956 Clean Air Act. She has recently established a very successful branch of the Dickens Fellowship in Cambridge and is a senior member of Wolfson College, Cambridge.

JUSTIN EICHENLAUB is a Lecturer in the English Department at UC Berkeley, where he is teaching courses in Victorian literature, the novel, and animal studies. He is currently working on two projects, including a cultural history of the suburbs' origins in nineteenth-century Britain and a second project that uses particular sites of multi-species encounter to investigate constructions of "the human" and of "the animal" in the nineteenth century.

TIMOTHY GILMORE has recently completed his doctoral studies in the English Department of the University of California at Santa Barbara, where his research focused primarily on Romanticism, environmental literature, and film. He is currently researching the importance of anxiety in regard to contingency for nineteenth-century and contemporary representations of the natural world.

ROBERT C. HANNA is Professor of English and Chair of the English Department at Bethany Lutheran College, Mankato, Minnesota. His most recent publications include "Before Boz: The Juvenilia and Early Writings of Charles Dickens, 1820–1833" in *Dickens Studies Annual* (2009), "Selection Guide to Dickens's Amateur Theatricals, Parts I and II" in the *Dickensian* (2011, 2012), and *Dickens's Uncollected Magazine and Newspaper Sketches as Originally Composed and Published 1833–1836* (2012). He is currently preparing an upper-division course on Charles Dickens's life and writings.

LAUREN ELLIS HOLM is an adjunct assistant professor at Bentley University, where she teaches writing and literature courses on adaptation and nineteenth-century literature. She has a Ph.D. from Brandeis University and works on Victorian stage adaptations of novels by Charles Dickens, Wilkie Collins, Charlotte Brontë, Elizabeth Braddon, and others.

MARIA IOANNOU earned her Ph.D. from the University of Exeter on Victorian literature and nineteenth-century gender studies. She has served as Visiting Lecturer at the University of Cyprus, where she currently works as a researcher. Her research and publications focus on Victorianism, gender, and the cultural, historical, and material forces and practices that shape personhood and literary production.

PRITI JOSHI is Professor of English at the University of Puget Sound, where she teaches courses in nineteenth-century British literature and culture and post-colonial literatures. She has published essays on Chadwick, Dickens, the Brontës, Frances Trollope, Henry Mayhew, masculinity, and empire, and is currently working on a book about an English-language newspaper published in India in the mid-nineteenth century.

JOHN B. LAMB is an associate professor of English at West Virginia University and the editor of *Victorian Poetry*. He has published previously on *A Tale of Two Cities* and *Oliver Twist* in *Dickens Studies Annual*.

REBECCA RICHARDSON is a graduate student in the Stanford University English department, where she is completing her dissertation, titled "Narrative Ambition: Victorian Self-Help and Competition." The project investigates how the popular nineteenth-century narrative of self-help structured ambition in the novel, concentrating on works by Samuel Smiles, Dinah Mulock Craik, William Makepeace Thackeray, Charles Dickens, and Anthony Trollope. Her work has also appeared in the *Fortnightly Review* and is forthcoming in *ELH*.

MELISSA A. SMITH is a fourth-year Ph.D. student in the Department of English at the University of Texas at Austin. She earned her B.A. in English at the University of Rochester and her M.A. from UT-Austin. Her article, "At Home and Abroad: Éowyn's Twofold Figuring as War Bride in The Lord of the Rings," appeared in *Mythlore*, a peer-reviewed journal published by the Mythopoeic Society, in 2007. Her dissertation will examine feminine discourses of stewardship in the Victorian novel.

DEBORAH A. THOMAS is Professor of English at Villanova University. She is the author of *Thackeray and Slavery*, *Dickens and the Short Story*, and Hard Times: *A Fable of Fragmentation and Wholeness*. She is also editor of *Charles Dickens: Selected Short Fiction* (Penguin).

ERIN WILSON is Assistant Teaching Professor and Postdoctoral Fellow at the University of Missouri. She received her M.A. from the University of Tulsa and her Ph.D. from the University of Missouri, where she studied nineteenth-century British literature, gender studies, and film studies.

The Infrastructural Uncanny:
Oliver Twist in the Suburbs and Slums

Justin Eichenlaub

Oliver Twist *foregrounds the interconnections of the suburbs and the slums and places them into dramatic and formal tension through a version of the "architectural uncanny." This essay explores the ties between the rise of the slums and the building of suburban housing with the movements of characters between these zones in the London of the novel. To read the novel with the suburb and slum plot in the foreground is to see the text critiquing a deeply flawed system of classed spaces and their ambiguous, mutable interrelations. This approach allows us to revisit the role of urban space in the novel in a new way, demonstrating Dickens's early engagement and concern with suburban spaces, and the ways in which the interplay of urban and suburban zones function much like the "systems" that are considered hallmarks of his later novels.*

In Dickens's *Oliver Twist* (1837–39), labyrinthine city settings contrast with the less constricted and less defined spaces of suburbs and countryside villages. On one hand are the slums of Spitalfields, Field Lane, Whitechapel, and Bethnal Green. On the other are the suburbs and quasi-suburbs of Islington, Pentonville, Twickenham, and Chertsey. The set-piece horrors of these slums and predictable comforts of their suburban and rural counterparts in the novel have obscured the complex and powerful circuit that characters' movements between these realms create.[1] Their movements construct a symbolic, metaphorical, and social network of knotted spaces that is as much a product of Dickens's allegorical imagination as it is of the realities of urban space in nineteenth-century London.

Dickens Studies Annual, Volume 44, Copyright © 2013 by AMS Press, Inc. All rights reserved.   DOI 10.7756/dsa.044.001.1-27

The city's suburbs and slums were economic and social doubles; the size and comforts of suburban housing were inversely related to the cramped shapes and discomforts of slum tenements. These zones were doubles in two ways: their relationship *symbolically* registered extreme economic inequities, and, second, they were *literally* doubles, since the suburbs were built to allow escape from proximity to the slums, a process that we will see generated more slums and worse conditions in them. In light of this linked relationship, it is possible to claim that, in a figurative sense, "the slums were built in the suburbs" (Dyos, *Victorian Suburb*, 13), a provocative way to characterize the causal link between class inequities and perverse distinctions in the built environment.

Such a provocative, figurative way to describe the relationship of the suburbs and the slums is germane to *Oliver Twist*. The story and discourse of the novel alternate between these spaces that co-create one another—alternations that are most often correlated with the location of the novel's protagonist. Beginning with his first entrance to London—entering at suburban Islington, he makes his way to slummy Field Lane—Oliver travels back and forth between middle and low places repeatedly. His movements between them are rarely clean breaks, instead creating symbolic and literal superimpositions of them. Alexander Welsh and others have pointed out the ways in which Dickens's "good" characters may be *in* the city, but not *of* it (118). Oliver challenges this formula. He is a character *of* the slums *and* the suburbs, and this duality is a key source of his own ambiguity as a character and of much of the novel's tension. Oliver's position and movements, straddling two strata of urbanized space, trace the economic, symbolic, and aesthetic connections of the real suburbs and the slums of nineteenth-century London, a historical and social referent that makes its way into a novel most easily and often read as allegorical and "generic" (Steven Marcus 63).

I approach the novel with the historical, material environs of London in the foreground, following others such as Sharon Marcus in her book *Apartment Stories*. Marcus draws on the architectural patterns used to construct the space inside urban and suburban middle-class houses and also considers a range of literary, periodical, and architectural texts, in order to point toward two discursive sites (the rhetoric of "domestic complaint" and the haunted house stories of the 1850s to 1870s) that break down the constructed division between detached, "middle-class homes" and urban tenements (89). The rhetoric and aesthetics of the suburb-slum circuit that is so predominant in *Oliver Twist* should be seen as another such site, one that casts an even wider net—taking into account both the design of individual homes as in Marcus's sites but also of neighborhoods, even regions, and their intimate material connections.[2]

The importance of London in *Oliver Twist* is well-trod critical terrain. In this essay I show how a novel category of uncanny aesthetics enjoins us to revisit the novel and its urban (as well as most often overlooked *suburban*) infrastructure in new ways. What I call the "infrastructural uncanny" pervades the novel's settings, plot, and narrative—to extend the metaphor, the infrastructural uncanny is the electricity running through the novel's slum-suburb circuits. By this term I mean an aesthetic, psychological, and quasi-material effect similar to what Anthony Vidler calls "the architectural uncanny," a category he uses to point to the inter-weaving of unsettling affects with particular spaces. Vidler explains that what he means by the architectural uncanny is not the same as a "literary or psychological uncanny":

> certainly no one building, no special effects of design can be guaranteed to provoke an uncanny feeling. But in each moment of the history of representation of the uncanny, and at certain moments in its psychological analysis, the buildings and spaces that have acted as the sites for uncanny experiences have been invested with recognizable characteristics [i.e., Gothic]. (11)

Vidler's account of the architectural uncanny captures the subtle tension between the essential subjectivity of uncanny experience and the possibility for uncan-niness to inhere in certain physical spaces. He writes, distilling these theoreti-cal and methodological issues, that the "architectural uncanny invoked in this book is necessarily ambiguous, combining aspects of its fictional history, its psy-chological analysis, and its cultural manifestations" (11). The actual, "uncanny" buildings he discusses do not "themselves possess uncanny properties, but rather [are "uncanny"] because they act, historically or culturally, as representations of estrangement" (12).

This detailed and careful framework for thinking and reading spaces and the uncanny guides my investigation of the infrastructural uncanny in the industrial-izing city's suburbs and slums at a particularly charged moment in their evolution. The suburb has been, and was during its modern origin in the early nineteenth century, one of our most visible "representations of estrangement"—from a stan-dard critical viewpoint, the suburbanite is estranged from the life of the city, the space in which politics and economics actually "happen," and this detachment is reaffirmed by the spatial and temporal journey that he or she makes from suburb to city and back each day. Suburban estrangement may be experienced not just by individuals but by whole groups, sometimes even whole classes of persons. What I term the infrastructural uncanny is a more social and collective category than the architectural uncanny. (It is important to emphasize that this mode of the uncanny does still share with Vidler's concept a physical and spatial grounding, against a merely psychological conception of the uncanny.) The infrastructural uncanny is not associated with a single Gothic building for a subject or two to occupy, but manifests itself through a network of buildings, neighborhoods, and zones that cannot be occupied in a single moment by a single person or a group of people. Likewise, in the novel the infrastructural uncanny is not only, or primar-ily, located in single scenes or moments, but appears (both for characters within the novel and for its readers) as an effect with an extended duration. It is this aesthetic and its function in *Oliver Twist* that compels us to return to this novel and its representations of the city, taking previous readings of the novel and accounts of urban London in the 1830s and 1840s in new and sometimes unexpected directions—toward seeing the early importance of the suburbs in Dickens's fiction, the surprising systematicity of space in *Oliver Twist* that presages Dickens's later "systems" in novels like *Our Mutual Friend* and *Bleak House*, and toward rethinking the unstable hierarchy of infrastructure and character in the novel.

If we approach the novel through its deep engagement with the uncanny relationship that distinct urban zones and neighborhoods may engender when placed in dramatic tension, other traditional readings of the novel recede in importance or are completely inverted. The novel's suburb and slum plot reaffirms but also competes with the always-threatening logic of prison and the noose, the props of the novel's "Newgate" plot. To read the Newgate plot as primary and in the foreground of the novel is to see the text exploring and critiquing a codified and deeply flawed system of criminality and the administration of official, swift, often voyeuristic justice. To read the novel with the suburb and slum plot in the foreground is to see the text thinking through an uncodified, deeply flawed system of classed spaces and their ambiguous, mutable, and often violent superimpositions. This latter plot is a deeper and more pervasive one than the novel's Newgate plot. The infrastructural uncanny points not just toward new conceptions of the novel's "plot" but also of the direction of its allegorical reference. As I observe later, by paying attention to the interplay of urban sites and the return of repressed infrastructures (i.e., the dilapidated Whitechapel tenement that was formerly a wealthy family's home), we can see that Oliver's life often actually is an allegory for the status of buildings and neighborhoods in the changing urban landscape.

The other major intervention this essay makes is to demonstrate the early, sustained, and complex role of suburbia in Dicken's fiction. His first literary products, those preceding *Oliver Twist*, were often set in the suburbs and concerned with lower-middle-class suburban life. The pieces of literary journalism that Dickens wrote between 1833 and 1836 and that were collected in *Sketches by Boz* (1836–37) are predominantly suburban in setting and concern—from the "suburban parish" setting of the first seven sketches to his brilliant observations on the new transport technologies like the omnibus that would come to make large scale suburban living possible ("Scenes" 7). Dickens's first published work, "A Dinner at Poplar Walk" (1833),[3] is a story about a middle-aged gentleman, Mr. August Minns, who has to visit his estranged cousin in the outer suburbs of London near Stamford Hill—a place with a "front garden, and the green railings, and the brass knocker, and all that" (309).[4]

Yet the *Sketches* do not really show the urban-suburban interface with any depth. As Deborah Nord writes, "The relationship between the middle-class reader and the urban underclass is never fully resolved in Sketches, and at times Boz is at pains to isolate, to cordon off, the disturbing realities of city life" (50).

Nord's book is particularly perceptive of efforts to isolate and "quarantine" the less attractive elements of urban life. She writes that in the 1820s the metaphor of the "theater of the street" in writers like Lamb and DeQuincey allowed the middle-class urbanite to be in the city but still maintain necessary distance from low and potentially disgusting objects and persons (30). In the 1830s and particularly in the following decades urban quarantine would come to be understood as a relationship of suburb to slum, a starker, infrastructural segregation compared to its theatrical forerunner. *Oliver Twist* is a transitional work in both Dickens's writing about the city and in the social and cultural understanding of the city that Nord points toward. The city is no longer a free and relatively fluid space for the spectator but on its way toward the more dangerous, Victorian city. The city, however, is not yet an "urban jungle" with its ragged and centralized poor figured as colonized and foreign subjects at the very center of the empire (McLaughlin 1); instead, Oliver, the thieves, and their upper-middle-class pursuers partake of a newly threatening city flimsily divided by the real and imagined contours of interlinked urban zones. This relationship is first given a charged dramatic and literary form in *Oliver Twist*.

In the first part of this essay I focus on several of the novel's literal slum and suburb "itineraries"[5] and show how in them Dickens uses the aesthetic and literary techniques of montage, the uncanny, narrative alternation, and allegory to dramatize these spaces' relationship. In the second part I move to a related but more figurative and fantastic kind of slum-and-suburb experience in the novel. These later encounters and patterns double and deepen the novel's innovations in dramatizing the increasing segmentation of urban residential patterns.[6] The aesthetics of the uncanny deployed in these scenes helps to bridge the suburb and slum itineraries of the novel's first half (which often tap into the everyday uncanniness of this infrastructure) and the less realistic events of the second.[7] It is in these scenes in the second half of the novel that the radical connection of the suburbs and the slums finds its full realization.

From the Country to the Slum: Mudfog to Field Lane via Islington

Oliver Twist follows the trials of its eponymous character, beginning with his illegitimate birth in a rural parish workhouse. Oliver escapes the parish of his birth, which Dickens named Mudfog only in the first serial publication of the novel, when he walks in chapter 8 to London. Guided into the city by a young thief, Oliver is taken in and trained (unsuccessfully) for the position of pickpocket and street criminal. Oliver is later captured by the police after a dramatic chase through the streets of Field Lane, and finds himself in the care of a middle-class gentleman named Mr. Brownlow, a character who is instrumental in his eventual rehabilitation and "saving." Brownlow's relationship to Oliver is just one of the many, extraordinary coincidences in the novel—he was the best friend of Oliver's father. With the introduction of these two parties, the slum-dwelling thieves (this group will come to include Oliver's older, bitter step-brother, Monks) and the suburbanite Brownlow (others will join his camp, including the Maylie family), the novel stages a contest between them for Oliver's body and soul.

In going from his rural parish birthplace of Mudfog to the innermost slums of London, Oliver walks the Great North Road that connects York to London. On the seventh day of his travels, he reaches Barnet, about ten miles north of the city. Barnet, an important coaching station with a good number of public houses, was close enough to the city to attract urban criminals, and it is here that Oliver meets Jack Dawkins. Dawkins, or the Artful Dodger, easily convinces the boy to follow him to London with promises of lodging and fellowship at Fagin's, and the two make their way to the city, where the first line of suburb-to-slum travel is traced in the novel:

> As John Dawkins objected to their entering London before nightfall, it was nearly eleven o'clock when they reached the turnpike at Islington. They crossed from the Angel into St. John's road, struck down the small street which terminates at Sadler's Wells theatre, through Exmouth street and Coppice row, down the little court by the side of the workhouse, across the classic ground which once bore the name of Hockley-in-the-hole, thence into Little Saffron hill, and so into Saffron hill the Great, along which, the Dodger scudded at a rapid pace, directing Oliver to follow close at his heels. (63; bk. 1, ch. 8)

Passages like these invite us to delineate pathways and map routes in nineteenth-century London—to describe and read fictionalized itineraries through real places on the map (fig. 1).

Slum to Suburb: Field Lane to Pentonville

Once inside Fagin's Field Lane lair, Oliver is kept in the house for days. When he does leave, it is to venture out with Dodger and Charley Bates to Clerkenwell, in central London, where the dramatic chase after Oliver begins. Taken to the police station for questioning, Oliver is exonerated by a bookstall keeper who witnessed the other boys' attempted robbery. Handed over to the man his comrades attempted to rob, Mr. Brownlow, Oliver is taken to this gentleman's home in a fashionable suburb, just a few miles from Fagin's slum lair in, Field Lane:

> The coach rattled away down Mount Pleasant and up Exmouth street, over nearly the same ground as that which Oliver had traversed when he first entered London in company with the Dodger,—and, turning a different way

when it reached the Angel at Islington, stopped at length before a neat house in a quiet shady street in Pentonville. (86; bk. 1, ch. 12)

Oliver is put to bed, ill and unconscious, and the text describes him remaining unconscious for many days. When he does awake, his first words register his shock at his change of place: "What room is this?—where have I been brought to?' said Oliver. 'This is not the place I went to sleep in'" (87; bk. 1, ch. 12). Oliver has no idea where he is, no sense of how he has come to be here, and yet the change in place is total. Oliver is not aware of his specific coordinates, but he easily recognizes that this new place is different than his previous one—his sense of his new place is a *negative* one, "This place is *not* where I was before." But as readers we do know, in precise and positive terms, how he has come to be here, and his path is significant. The coach that takes Oliver to Pentonville "rattled ... over nearly the same ground as that which Oliver had first traversed when he

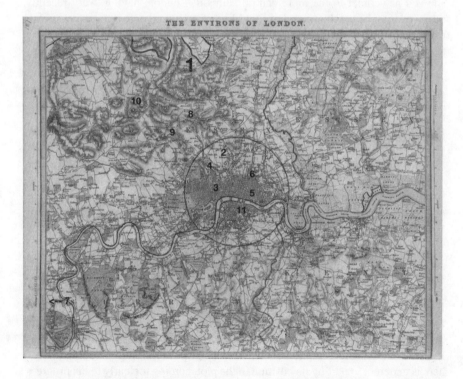

Figure 1. The Environs of London (1832), Society for the Diffusion of Useful Knowledge, drawn and engraved by H. Waters. 1 Barnet, 2 Islington, 3 Field Lane, 4 Pentonville, 5 Whitechapel, 6 Bethnal Green, 7 Chertsey, 8 Highgate, 9 Hampstead, 10 Hendon, 11 Jacob's Island, Bermondsey

first entered London in company with the Dodger." The novel has just made its first of many complete circuits from suburb to slum and back to suburb again.

The novel portends that another trip along the circuit of the suburb and the slum is immanent as the settings of chapters 12 through 15 alternate between Brownlow's suburban home and the thieves' lairs in the slums. Chapter 12 is set at Brownlow's (*suburb*); chapter 13, in Fagin's lair (*slum*); chapter 14, back at Brownlow's (*suburb*); chapter 15 begins "In the obscure parlour of a low public-house, situated in the filthiest part of Little Saffron Hill,—a dark and gloomy den" (*slum*) (116; bk. 1, ch. 15). From here Sikes and Nancy will venture forth to intercept Oliver in the streets of Clerkenwell, the site where his previous, reverse transition from *slum* to *suburb* began after the chase. In chapter 15 not only does the narrative return to the slum, but Oliver does as well.

The preparations for this double reversion of both the protagonist and the narrative to the slum from the suburb are laid in chapter 13. The thieves conspire to send Nancy to the police station to inquire after Oliver's whereabouts because she is a newcomer to the more central slums of London, having "very recently removed into the neighborhood of Field-Lane from the remote but genteel suburb of Ratcliffe" (101; bk.1, ch. 13). At a superficial level, this off-hand reference to the "gentility" of Ratcliffe is merely sarcastic—in *Sketches by Boz* Dickens wrote of Ratcliffe as "that reservoir of dirt, drunkenness, and drabs" (*Sketches by Boz* 212). At a deeper level, however, it plays on the strange conjunctions and interpenetrations of suburbs and slums in the suburban imagination that applied to people's perceptions of London and the fictionalized version of it in *Oliver Twist*. Ratcliffe *is* suburban: it is remote and geographically distinct from more central districts of the city, but it is *not* "genteel." Dickens is not just being sarcastic here: he is hinting at the ways in which the relationship between geographical terms of proximity and distance ("removed" and "remote") and terms that define class relationships in urban and suburban space ("genteel") were variable and fluctuated. The word "suburb" itself was still in flux in the 1830s and 1840s, but it was starting to solidify around its contemporary, middle-class connotations—"As always, language lagged behind reality. It was not until the 1840s that the word 'suburb' lost its older, primarily plebeian associations and became firmly attached to the middle-class residential neighborhood" (Fishman 62–63).

Nancy and Bill recapture Oliver while he is on an errand to return books for Brownlow and Grimwig. When he is apprehended by the thieves, who pretend to be his proper family, Oliver tries to claim his newfound suburban home as his own and proper place—"I live at Pentonville" (122; bk. 1, ch. 15). Oliver's meaningful claim to being a suburbanite when in the grips of the slum-dwelling thieves here is undercut in part by its position in the plot, coming too early in his progress toward middle-class respectability. Nancy takes Oliver to another of Fagin's lairs, this one in Whitechapel.

Oliver's recapture is a basic part of the plot—the thieves want him back so that he does not turn them over to the authorities—but at a more abstract and figurative level, Oliver is something like an "allegorical pawn" (John 136) in the repeated montage of suburb and slum in *Oliver Twist*. The structure of that montage "is [also] the structure of bourgeois society" (Eisenstein 234). The society that gives its form to these structures was one engaged in the battle beginning to be waged between the slums and the suburbs for real estate and space in the city and at its periphery, with the middle classes bound to be the winners. Not just a "pawn," Oliver is a site for the machinations of slum and suburb to meet; through him, their co-dependence crystallizes and its psychological effects propagate.

Slum to Suburb: Bethnal Green to Chertsey

After some time at the Whitechapel house, Oliver joins Bill Sikes for a long journey to Chertsey. Chapter 21 recapitulates and reverses the journey Oliver takes in chapter 8, from the country to the city. The chapter's "expedition" begins at Sikes's lair in the slums of Bethnal Green. Dickens begins the chapter with an involved description of the street, a bare scene devoid of any human presence apart from Oliver and Bill—"for the windows of the houses were all closely shut, and the streets through which they passed noiseless and empty" (170; bk.1, ch. 21). Into this "quarter of town," the day begins to fill with a range of vectors passing through the eastern slums on their way to City and suburb:

> By the time they had turned into the Bethnal Green road the day had fairly begun to break. Many of the lamps were already extinguished, a few country wagons were slowly toiling on towards London, and now and then a stage-coach, covered with mud, rattled briskly by, the driver bestowing, as he passed, an admonitory lash upon the heavy waggoner, who, by keeping on the wrong side of the road, had endangered his arriving at the office a quarter of a minute after his time. Then came the straggling groups of labourers going to their work; then men and women with fish-baskets on their heads, donkey-carts laden with vegetables, chaise-carts filled with live-stock or whole carcasses of meat, milkwomen with pails, and an unbroken concourse of people trudging out with various supplies to the eastern suburbs of the town. (170–71; bk. 1, ch. 21)

This scene is interesting because in it Dickens takes a rare moment in the novel to give explicit details about the travel of others in the novel besides the main characters. The narrative focalizes its space and location not through Oliver or Bill here, but through the location itself—Bethnal Green. It is only the neighborhood itself that is capacious enough to "notice" and contain all of these details, itineraries, and routes that are tangential to the protagonist's course from Bethnal Green to the city and beyond.

The vast majority of the people described in this paragraph are heading toward
the suburbs, a detail that represents the historical fact that more central parts of the
city were beginning to supply and service suburban neighborhoods, but that also
has relevance to the narrative. These minor characters' movements between city
and suburb play a role in the symbolic topography of the novel's urban circuitry.
They add social relief to the more prominent paths traced by the novel's protagonist and antagonists between suburbs and slums.

Oliver and Sikes travel from the slums of Bethnal Green in the East End of
London, through the city, out of it through the West End, and past a number
of river villages: "Kensington, Hammersmith, Chiswick, Kew Bridge, Brentford,
were all passed" (172; bk. 1, ch. 21). Finally, they reach a "solitary house all ruin-
ous and decayed," "dark, dismantled, and to all appearance uninhabited" (175; bk.
1, ch. 21). The novel will return to this house later, as the second of two seemingly
uninhabited houses (the first is the Whitechapel house) that uncannily bring the
logic of suburb and slum home to Oliver.

The same night that they reach the house, the botched robbery of the Maylie
family's Chertsey home ends with Oliver left in a ditch, wounded by a gunshot,
and evidently close to death. As Catherine Robson points out, the novel in both its
serial and volume forms leaves Oliver in this ditch for an inordinate amount of time
(between Oliver's being left in the ditch and his return to the text, three months and
five chapters elapsed for the novel's original serial readers). Robson argues, convincingly, that this "temporal kink" in the narrative (the "kink" is not only delay,
but also the analeptic device the novel uses to return to Oliver in chapter 28) allows
Oliver to die a symbolic death as one kind of child and be reborn as another, when
he drags himself up onto the steps of the Maylies' home (64). Robson also argues
that once Oliver is taken in by the Maylies, the second time he is taken in by a
middle-class family, he is tucked into the "boring bosom of middle-class respectability" (74), where vice and crime can now only look at but not touch him. While it
is clear that Oliver's adoption by the Maylies signifies his adoption into the middle
classes, it is not clear that Oliver is completely free from the lingering and persistent
force of the slum. These are supposed to be the new boundaries—Oliver's suburban
and rural residences and his middle-class protectors should keep him safe. But the
force of the slum overflows these bounds, and it is an overflow that is bound to happen if we recognize the ways in which the nineteenth-century slum is the economic,
social, and symbolic double of the suburb. Though Oliver will never return to the
slum from this point on in the novel, the slum will return to him, in Chertsey and
elsewhere. In addition to our generalized sense of Oliver's time in various parts of
the city, it is useful to consider more specifically the amounts of time that Oliver and
the novel spend in various quarters of the city, suburb, and countryside.

The first of the three charts below maps the location of each chapter's setting
(chart 1). As it shows, the novel moves between suburb and slum no less than ten
times. These are direct moves between two chapters either from the suburb to the
slum or vice versa. Oliver himself makes only four transitions between the suburbs

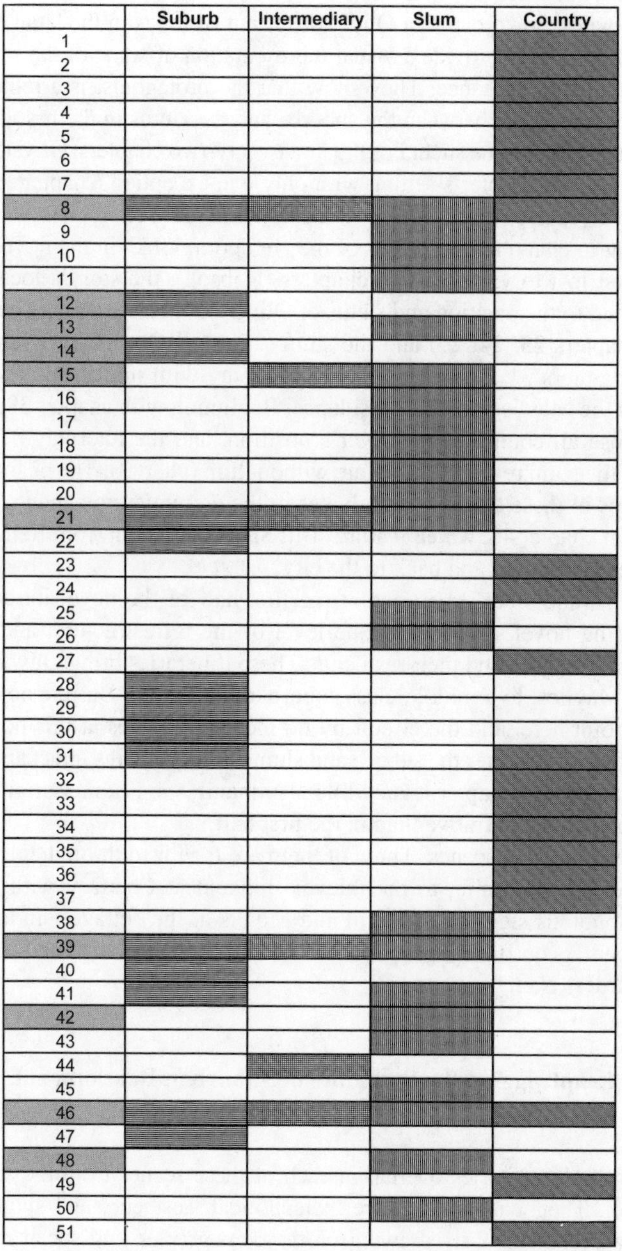

	Suburb	Intermediary	Slum	Country
1				▓
2				▓
3				▓
4				▓
5				▓
6				▓
7				▓
8	▓	▓	▓	▓
9			▓	
10			▓	
11			▓	
12	▓			
13			▓	
14	▓			
15		▓	▓	
16			▓	
17			▓	
18			▓	
19			▓	
20			▓	
21	▓	▓	▓	
22	▓			
23				▓
24				▓
25			▓	
26			▓	
27				▓
28	▓			
29	▓			
30	▓			
31	▓			▓
32				▓
33				▓
34				▓
35				▓
36				▓
37				▓
38			▓	
39	▓	▓	▓	
40	▓			
41	▓		▓	
42			▓	
43			▓	
44		▓		
45			▓	
46	▓		▓	▓
47	▓			
48			▓	▓
49				▓
50			▓	
51				▓

Chart 1. The location of the chapter's setting irrespective of Oliver's position. Gray chapter cells mark chapters of transition between suburb and slum.

and the slums, and these all occur in the first half of the novel (chart 2). These charts confirm the well-known fact that Oliver drops out of focus in the latter half of the novel. In addition they provide a visual representation of some of the subtleties of Oliver's diminished presence. They show that the protagonist is a reliable track-ing agent for transitions between the suburbs and the slums in the first third of the novel but then ceases to be such. For the first twenty-two chapters, Oliver's location determines a given chapter's setting with only one exception, chapter 13, the first hint that the discourse will eventually trace a suburb-slum circuit *without* Oliver.

Beginning in chapter 23, the start of the "temporal kink" in the novel in which Oliver is first lost to view for five chapters (Robson), the story's location is no longer hitched to the position and status of Oliver but is free to range between the country (chapters 23, 24, 27) and the slum (25, 26).[8] Once Oliver returns from the ditch, chapters 31 through 37 follow and stay with him in the countryside, centered on the Maylies' country residence. Beginning with chapter 38, story and discourse lose all contact with Oliver's position, and the interplay between the suburb and the slum resumes, this time without him (chart 3). The charged circuit that develops in these chapters culminates in the dramatic movements among all four zones in chapter 46, which features Bill Sikes on the run from Bethnal Green to Hampstead, Hendon, and back to the city.

The suburb and slum itineraries of the first half of the novel introduce both Oliver and the novel's readers to one level of the infrastructural and narrative circuit of these spaces and their residents. These itineraries bring Oliver to Chert-sey, to the Maylies, to a middle-class suburban household. But the novel is only at its mid-point here, and the circuit by no means dissolves at this point. In the second half of this chapter the suburb and slum circuit remains intact and active at a formal, chapter-by-chapter level while also manifesting in more figurative and uncanny ways in the narrative than in the first half.

I consider four such scenes. Three of them are focalized through Oliver (at the Whitechapel lair, returning to the thieves' hideout at Chertsey with Losberne, and his ambiguous sighting of Fagin and Monks at the cottage window), while the fourth centers on Bill Sikes's errant ramblings in the suburbs and countryside after he murders Nancy.

Leapfrogging the Dynamics of Suburban Development

Slum and suburb territories overlap in each of these scenes from the second half of the novel. Their conjunctions are metaphorical, aesthetic, and symbolic—yet Dickens was simultaneously drawing on the demographic and social referents of nineteenth-century London. One of the most relevant aspects of that referent is the "leapfrogging" of suburbs over slums in a London that was rapidly expanding. Leapfrogging describes the complex maneuvers of the upwardly mobile to avoid

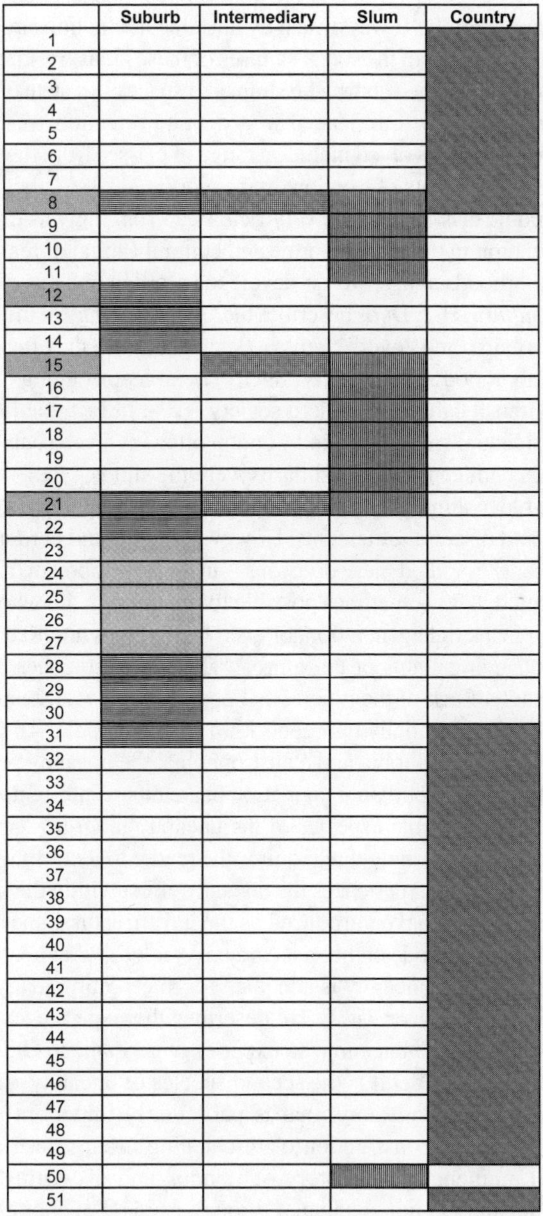

	Suburb	Intermediary	Slum	Country
1				▓
2				▓
3				▓
4				▓
5				▓
6				▓
7				▓
8	▓	▓	▓	
9			▓	
10			▓	
11			▓	
12	▓			
13	▓			
14	▓			
15		▓		
16			▓	
17			▓	
18			▓	
19			▓	
20			▓	
21	▓	▓	▓	
22	▓			
23	▓			
24	▓			
25	▓			
26	▓			
27	▓			
28	▓			
29	▓			
30	▓			
31	▓			▓
32				▓
33				▓
34				▓
35				▓
36				▓
37				▓
38				▓
39				▓
40				▓
41				▓
42				▓
43				▓
44				▓
45				▓
46				▓
47				▓
48				▓
49				▓
50			▓	
51				▓

Chart 2. The location of Oliver in each chapter and those in which he moves from suburb to slum or vice versa denoted by gray chapter cell. Light gray chapters 23–27 represent his time in suburban Chertsey but in the ditch.

living near to or with the lower classes in unfashionable zones, zones whose status was often changing rapidly. It was driven by unstable fluctuations in both neighborhoods and parallel changes in the social statuses of these areas' residents. The spaces involved were, of course, the suburb, the slum, and spaces in a state of indeterminate hybridity between the two (but headed in a definite direction—i.e., toward slum conditions). The persons involved include a range of classes from the most impoverished and homeless residents of London, to the working classes, the various permutations of the middle classes, and the very rich. Leapfrogging was driven in part by a frenzied speculation in the real and projected cultural capital of real estate situated in certain neighborhoods and yet-to-be-developed areas in and out of the city.

In *Victorian Suburb*, H. J. Dyos describes the "leapfrogging" of the middle classes from suburb to suburb (and "over" slums) to keep pace with the often rapid changes in a given neighborhood's desirability. Such "social leapfrogging" made the suburb "one of the transit camps of modern society" (23). In fact, the first step toward middle-class residential suburbs around London often involved such a jump—since prior to the nineteenth century "the suburbs were the slums," the "new suburb had leapfrogged the older slum" (Dyos and Reeder 362). Such "jumps" suggest a series of clean breaks and discrete settlements. However, the limited perdurability of suburban encampments muddied these divisions—in the development of new suburban lands and housing it "was sometimes possible to run through the whole gamut from meadow to slum in a single generation, or even less" (Dyos and Reeder 364).

The rapidly changing status of these urban and suburban zones is fecund territory for the uncanny. Each of the itineraries I consider below is steeped in uncanny experience, "the quintessentially bourgeois kind of fear" (Vidler 4). Often linked to "spatial fear[s]" like agoraphobia and claustrophobia, the uncanny proved a powerful force for shaping the suburban imagination in the nineteenth century and beyond (Vidler 4). There are two main species of the uncanny in *Oliver Twist*—the traditional, Freudian, fictive uncanny that requires the reader to identify with an "anchor character" in the text who experiences the uncanny effect within the fictional world, and a second kind, what I have introduced as the infrastructural uncanny, an extension of but also a distinct mode of theorist Anthony Vidler's "architectural uncanny."

Freud's account of the uncanny is adequate for interpreting many of the scenes and (re)occurrences in *Oliver Twist*. He describes the experience of involuntary repetition as a source of the uncanny, an experience germane to Oliver's travels in the first half of the novel. Yet it is the second species of uncanny effects in *Oliver Twist*, the infrastructural uncanny, that is particularly important as it mediates and intervenes in a new construction of threatening urban space and aesthetics at a transitional moment in the history of London and of writing about it. The infrastructural uncanny is not channeled through a single anchor character but is a product of what Arnold Kettle calls the "objective profundity" of the depressing and perverse world in which we find Oliver (119). The most "objective" aspect of this world is its architecture and infrastructure. Each of the four scenes I read below contributes to and fleshes out this aesthetic's work in the novel.

Dickens was surely aware of the social and physical facts of suburban growth. But his interpretation of them—the account and world he constructs out of these pieces in the novel—is not a neutral, aesthetic, and documentary one. Too much is at stake for Dickens in his construction of multiple positions within the middle classes, their values, and where they are to live to let the suburbs go without a deliberate, purposeful, and *political* reconstruction in the novel. The suburbs are clearly a problematic, still urban, zone for Dickens, but they are still one possible and important landing pad for the middle classes in their escape from the city. In light of this subtle and complex problem, Dickens's representation of the suburbs in *Oliver Twist* and in many other novels strikes a middle position by locating middle-class control of the working classes in the suburb while making the countryside the ultimate safe haven, where many protagonists ultimately find themselves.

The Slums Were the Suburbs: Whitechapel

When Nancy and Bill recapture Oliver, they remove him from the suburbs and bring him to an abandoned house in a former middle-class suburban neighborhood, Whitechapel:

> It was a very dirty place; but the rooms up stairs had great high wooden mantel-pieces and large doors, with paneled walls and cornices to the ceilings, which, although they were black with neglect and dust, were ornamented in various ways; from all of which tokens Oliver concluded that a long time

Suburb	Intermed	Slum	Country		Suburb	Intermed	Slum	Country
		■		38				■
■	■	■		39				■
■		■		40				■
■		■		41				■
		■		42				■
		■		43				■
	■			44				■
		■		45				■
■	■	■	■	46				■
■				47				■
		■		48				■
			■	49				■
		■		50			■	
			■	51				■

Chart 3. Detail of chapters 38 through 51, the narrative's location (left) and the location of Oliver (right) side-by-side.

ago, before the old Jew was born, it had belonged to better people, and had perhaps been quite gay and handsome, dismal and dreary as it looked now. (145; bk. 1, ch. 18)

It is clear that the house has seen better days—"great" and "large" architectural details (including "cornices to the ceilings") signify that "it had belonged to better people." Dickens does not explicitly blame suburban development for the house's decay, but with the attention he pays to describing a realistic scenario of a middle-class home degenerating into a slum lair, he makes it easy to connect the Whitechapel location to the predominant spatial framework of the novel. Of the Whitechapel lair, Phillip Horne notes in his edition of *Oliver Twist,* "With the changes in fashion and growth of such suburbs as Pentonville, formerly grand residences in such areas as Whitechapel, in and around the City, had fallen into decline" (505). This is an important outcome of Dyos's "leap-frogging": "It was no accident that the worst slums were generally found in places where large houses were vacated by the middle classes in their trek to the further suburbs" (Dyos and Reeder 361).

There is a twofold significance to this setting. On the one hand, the house plays into the novel's already-developed circuit. Here we find the double of Brownlow's suburban home, an upper-middle-class house in a formerly fashionable neighbor-hood that is now a slum, a breeding zone for the thieves and low-lifes that threaten Oliver and middle-class comfort at the same time. For Oliver, however, his time spent locked by himself in the house is an opportunity and an awakening. It is the first time that *he* comes to some awareness of the suburb-to-slum-to-suburb circuit that he has been tracing from the time that he arrives in London—"This passage marks Oliver's transition to an active search in the *external* world for the meaning of his plight and for the identity and security he obscurely seeks" (Miller 52). Miller reads the Whitechapel lair's architecture and its domestic history as allegorical and metaphorical parallels to Oliver's own life, a treasure chest of clues: "[The house] also contains the decayed signs, almost the archaeological remains, of another way of life. Oliver sees unmistakable evidence of a happy existence once lived within the very walls of his prison" (53).

This reading is not far from my interpretation of the scene, but I do disagree with Miller on one very important point. In his reading, the house has these qualities because Oliver's life has them. The house responds to the needs of Oliver's redemption plot as if in the mode of a pathetic fallacy. This causation runs throughout Hillis Miller's argument—the city and suburban scenes follow from and parallel Oliver's various states and positions. Spaces and places allegorize Oliver's life, his "progress" itself already an allegory. I see a different direction in the novel's allegorical reference.

I argue that it is Oliver and the story of his "progress" that allegorizes the real and historically describable loop of the suburbs to the slums. Read in this way, it is the infrastructure that becomes the protagonist, and it is the Whitechapel house that is the real enigma. Like Oliver, it has a dubious mixture of high and low elements, a complicated past and unclear present—and in many ways the house is a more interesting character than Oliver. The house is then not so much a clue to Oliver's past as Oliver's travels in the suburb-slum circuits of the novel are a clue to the *house*'s past. Perhaps it should not be surprising that an author who was so interested in infrastructure as a sanitarian, one writing at the start of an era that would likewise obsess over urban infrastructure, would write a novel not just about an orphaned boy, but also about the fate of dilapidated and orphaned buildings as about an orphaned boy.

The Suburbs Were the Slums: The Cherstey Humpback

In chapter 9 of book 2, after a period of rest and recovery at the Maylies' Chertsey house, Oliver expresses a desire to return to the Brownlows and reinstate his name with them. The Chertsey doctor, Mr. Losberne, agrees to take him and they depart for the city. As they are leaving Chertsey, a strange, extended scene stalls their journey. Oliver and Losberne encounter an unstable, unknown man who says he lives in a riverside hovel near the Maylies' Chertsey house, a hovel that Oliver believes he recognizes as the thieves' stopover place in Chertsey.

This scene has received little comment, and for many readers it is easily forgotten. Nevertheless, the scene is pivotal, occurring just after the novel's midpoint. The encounter with the "mad humpback" in Chertsey is enigmatic, uncanny, and surreal, and because it is the scene that most disturbs the narrative's realism it demands more attention than it has received. This episode, bordering on the anti-realistic, catalyzes a major shift in the protagonist's location and sphere of inter-action—after the encounter the Maylies move Oliver to the countryside where he will stay for all remaining chapters except one—making it as important, if not more so, than the novel's other primary turning points.

Losberne approaches the "deserted tenement" and "began kicking at the door like a madman," only to find a literal madman on the other side of the door, a "little ugly hump-backed man" (258; bk. 2, ch. 9):

> The hump-backed man stared as if in excess of amazement and indignation; and, twisting himself dexterously from the doctor's grasp, growled forth a volley of horrid oaths, and retired into the house. Before he could shut the door, however, the doctor had passed into the parlour without a word of parley. He looked anxiously round: not an article of furniture, not a vestige of anything, animate or inanimate, not even the position of the cupboards, answered Oliver's description! (258; bk. 2, ch. 9)

The house does not fit the description; its contents are out of their "proper" places. The house itself seems out of place, and Losberne, so well-known in the parish, and so knowledgeable of the area himself, has somehow never come across this place or its inhabitant before. This fact suggests that the humpback is an anti-realistic, metaphorical displacement of the slum into the suburbs, a striking moment of the infrastructural uncanny.

In this scene the surprising, disturbing, and uncanny interposition of slum into suburb takes over. The humpback's poverty, madness, and ugliness interject the slum into the comfortable, middle-class village life of Chertsey. His presence is at once anti-realistic and surreal, but it is also historically and realistically grounded. As cited previously, the "suburbs were the slums" (Dyos and Reeder 362) prior to the development of the middle-class suburbs of the nineteenth century. While Chertsey itself was not historically known as a slum, the humpback can be read as a representative of the historical slum-dwellers that occupied many of London's suburbs prior to their development by and for the middle classes. In this scene, those repressed and built-over slums return to haunt and trouble the suburban village.

Two weeks after the return of Oliver and Mr. Losberne from this short London trip and the encounter with the humpbacked man, the Maylies are on the move, this time further out from London, as if in an attempt to escape the reminders and remnants of Oliver's tainted, urban past. Such escapes are a recurring motif in Dickens's novels, and the suburbs are often cited as one such space for safe retreat in readings of Dickens. I do not think the suburbs are allowed to play such a role in *Oliver Twist*. At one level in Dickens the suburbs become a space of ideal retreat, ideal in the sense that they can be the site for a fantasy of social existence outside of class distinctions, as if their residents could be "above the social universe altogether" (Moretti 120). In *Oliver Twist* this attempt to place the middle classes outside the city in the safe haven of the suburb or rural retreat is menaced by the uncanny returns and remainders of the slum. In *Oliver Twist*, the ultimate safe haven, if one ever really exists in the novel, is pushed well beyond the suburban rim of the metropolis. At the novel's close, Oliver, the Maylies, and even Losberne must leave Chertsey and their countryside cottage for an unspecified parsonage in the north of England.

Specters of the Slum: Monks and Fagin

At the Maylies' country cottage Oliver carries on, adapting to his pastoral environment, including studying in a back room of the cottage where one day a sleeping vision penetrates the Maylies' seemingly secure zone: "Suddenly the scene changed, the air became close and confined, and he thought with a glow of terror that he was in the Jew's house again. There sat the hideous old man in his accustomed corner pointing at him, and whispering to another man with his face averted, who sat beside him" (281–83; bk. 2, ch. 11). Oliver does not just feel

Fagin's *presence*: he feels as if he were back "in the Jew's house again," superimposing the slummy lair onto the middle-class, country cottage. The text describes Oliver waking and seeing the two men standing at the window, while Cruikshank's drawing shows the two men in the window, Oliver's eyes still closed.

> 'Hush, my dear!' he thought he heard the Jew say; 'it is him, sure enough. Come away.' Good God! What was that which sent the blood tingling to his heart, and deprived him [Oliver] of voice or power to move! There—there at the window—close before him—so close, that he could have almost touched him before he started back—with his eyes peering into the room, and meeting his—there stood the Jew—It was but an instant, a glance, a flash before his eyes, and they [Fagin and Monks] were gone. (283; bk. 2, ch. 11)

Again, the gaze of the slum meets Oliver's nascent middle-class gaze, and again, like the encounter with the humpback, the presence of Fagin and Monks outside the window is an experience for the memory to take up, keep, and return to: "But they had recognized him, and he them, and their look was as firmly impressed upon his memory as if it had been deeply carved in stone, and set before him from his birth. He stood transfixed for a moment, and then, leaping from the window into the garden, called loudly for help" (283; bk. 2, ch. 11). But this time Oliver demonstrates that he has learned the logic of the suburb and the slum, or at least one of their logics—if the slum pursues him, then he can turn back around and pursue it—he leaps from the window, after the invaders. Chapter 11 of book 2 ends with Oliver leaping out the window after the men, calling for help. The next chapter begins with Oliver struggling to tell his friends what he has seen, "scarcely able to articulate the words 'The Jew! the Jew!'" (284; bk. 2, ch. 12). This is an important moment of confirmation—Jonathan Grossman points out that it is in this moment, when Oliver demonstrates that he has learned to label Fagin as Other from his middle-class keepers, that Oliver "claims his place" among the middle classes (40).

The Maylies' search for the criminals is intense, thorough, and lasts several days. The intensity of their search seems to confirm Grossman's argument that Oliver has successfully and officially joined the middle classes. As with the scene at the humpback's hovel, the details of Fagin's and Monk's *absence* are fascinating and prominent: "There were not even the traces of footsteps to be seen. They stood now on the summit of a little hill, commanding the open fields in every direction for three or four miles" (285; bk. 2, ch. 12). There is no sign of them, but the search continues: "Still, in no direction were there any appearances of the trampling of men in hurried flight. The grass was long, but was trodden down nowhere save where their own feet had crushed it. The sides and brinks of the ditches were of damp clay, but in no one place could they discern the print of men's shoes, or the slightest mark which would indicate that any feet had pressed the ground for hours before" (285; bk. 2, ch. 12).

Of this scene, John Bayley writes that "It is a dream from which Oliver awakes to find it true, even though no footprints of the pair can be found" (52). Again, traces of the slum uncannily disturb the middle-class topographies of the supposedly safe country cottage. Oliver's reported sighting is enough to ignite the group's best effort to root out the slum wherever it impinges on the middle-classes' zones of security and comfort. The final itinerary that I trace brings these efforts and the tensions of the slum-suburb circuits of the novel to a head. In it Bill Sikes will be "found out," but his death is at best a pyrrhic victory in the suburb's struggle with the slums.

A Violent Course—from Slum, to Suburb, to Country, and Back

The shapes of the suburb-slum circuits traced in *Oliver Twist* range from the particular and realistic to the abstract and the figurative. The final "itinerary" that moves between these two zones is of the latter type—Bill Sikes's frenetic and disjointed ramble in the suburbs and countryside of London after he murders Nancy is the most intense and abstract representation of these urban entanglements. Sikes's crime is the obvious finale of the Newgate plot but his remaining actions also bring the suburb and slum narrative of the novel to its climax. Both of these finales are accomplished through figurative and anti-realistic elements—the "public" magically materializes to hound Sikes toward his death, and Sikes's itinerary in his final chapter is increasingly antipodal. Sikes's journey traces a fantastic shape that overlays and retraces many of the paths already taken in the novel.

When Sergei Eisenstein read these alternating and overlapping paths in the novel he posited their relationship to filmic montage. He describes montage as "the explosion of the shot ... when the tension within the shot reaches its peak and can mount no further, then the shot explodes, splitting into two separate pieces of montage" (quoted in Tambling, "Dangerous Crossings" 51). If we follow his reading of the novel and his analogy to filmic form, then the climactic violence Eisenstein describes in montage is most apparent in this final itinerary, where the "explosive" violence of montage finds an equal match in the restrictive violence of architecture. This distinction in the "mode of violence" depends on film and architecture's formal differences. In film, montage can be accomplished by having "parallel scenes intercut into one another" (Eisenstein 217), which is how Eisenstein also describes the literary montage of *Oliver Twist*. But architecture's form is less fluid, its dominant mode spatial rather than temporal, and this spatial boundedness leads to a distinct kind of violence as we will see below—rather than a temporal intercutting, people rush into the buildings on Jacob's Island only to be pushed against the walls, on the very point of being crushed and suffocated by their own collective density.

Leaving the scene of his crime in Bethnal Green, Sikes sets a northwest course, passing yet again through Islington, Oliver's entry point into London at the start of the novel:

> He went through Islington; strode up the hill at Highgate, on which stands the stone in honour of Whittington; turned down to Highgate Hill, unsteady of purpose, and uncertain where to go; struck off to the right again almost as soon as he began to descend it, and taking the foot-path across the fields, skirted Caen Wood, and so came out on Hampstead Heath. Traversing the hollow by the Vale of Health, he mounted the opposite bank, and crossing the road which joins the villages of Hampstead and Highgate, made along the remaining portion of the heath to the fields at North End, in one of which he laid himself down under a hedge and slept. (398; bk. 3, ch. 10)

It is as if a power surge hits the suburb-slum circuit here, and the normal fluctuations in the current have become more rapid. Dickens's description continues:

> Where could he go, that was near and not too public, to get some meat and drink? Hendon. That was a good place, not far off, and out of most people's way. Thither he directed his steps,—running sometimes, and sometimes, with a strange perversity, loitering at a snail's pace, or stopping altogether and idly breaking the hedges with his stick.... He wandered over miles and miles of ground, and still came back to the old place; morning and noon had passed, and the day was on the wane, and still he rambled to and fro, and up and down, and round and around, and still lingered about the same spot. At last he got away, and shaped his course for Hatfield. (398–99; bk. 3, ch. 10)

Sikes's desperate attempt to escape from his crime rehearses the repetitive, back-and-forth movements of the novels' characters to this point, but condensed and in fast forward—"not far into the country, but back toward London by the high-road-then back again—then over another part of the same ground as he had already traversed —then wandering up and down in the fields, and lying on ditches' brinks to rest ... and ramble on again" (398; bk. 3, ch. 10). The errant rambling without a destination recapitulates to an extent Oliver's first long walk to London, a journey with only a slight sense of a destination; Sikes's resting in ditches recalls Oliver's time in the ditch in Chertsey. "The Flight of Sikes" distills the logic of the suburbs and the slums, and the tight circuit from which they do not allow escape. London casts its net far into the suburban and rural countryside, leaving no choice but to return to the city.

Suddenly, he took the desperate resolution of going back to London (406; bk. 3, ch. 10). Choosing "the least frequented roads [he] began his journey back," toward his destination of London's Jacob's Island (406; bk. 3, ch. 10). From Hampstead Heath and the Vale of Health to one of the worst and most decrepit slums in London—this is Sikes's determined course. This circuit has kept the thieves' lives in tenuous balance for much of the novel, but this binary of classed, built spaces has lost its protective function for them. Like the slum's buildings that function as the setting for the novel's finale, the circuit is on the verge of collapse. Sikes succeeds in making it back to the slum, temporarily reestablishing the circuit, but at the cost of his life.

"To reach this place, the visitor has to penetrate through a maze ..."

Sikes resolves to return to London at the end of chapter 11 of book 3. After a chapter describing conversations between Brownlow and Monks, the novel returns to Sikes's journey. The first several pages of chapter 12, "The Pursuit and Escape," begin with a description and exploration of Jacob's Island, a Southwark waterside slum based on a real place of the same name. The island, also connected to "chancery suits," seems to be a far worse slum than Tom-All-Alone's or Fagin's Whitechapel lair—"The houses have no owners; they are broken open, and entered upon by those who have the courage, and there they live and there they die" (418; bk. 3, ch. 12). In the scene at Jacob's Island, a public materializes as if out of nowhere and finds its form and contours as it infiltrates, fills, and packs the ruined and empty dwellings of the island; this mob chases and hounds Sikes into this hole:

> On pressed the people from the front—on, on, on, in one strong struggling current of angry faces, with here and there a glaring torch to light them up and show them out in all their wrath and passion. The houses on the opposite side of the ditch had been entered by the mob; sashes were thrown up, or torn bodily out; there were tiers and tiers of faces in every window, and cluster upon cluster of people clinging to every house-top. Each little bridge (and there were three in sight) bent beneath the weight of the crowd upon it; and still the current poured on to find some nook or hole from which to vent their shouts, and only for an instant see the wretch. (425; bk. 3, ch. 12)

These putrid and underpopulated clusters of ruined buildings, many of them teetering and on the brink of destruction, are suddenly jammed with an eager and vengeful crowd. Dickens's description of this fantastic packing of people into uninhabited *and* derelict infrastructure—even the "little bridges bent beneath the weight of the crowd upon it"—is a surrealistic image of an ephemeral population surge in this forgotten and abandoned slum. This scene is a paradigmatic instance of the infrastructural uncanny: it is a perhaps disturbing and deeply morbid take on slum "improvement" with its goal of restoring a productive population to ruined areas. The scene also dramatizes what I referred to earlier as the "violence of architecture." Such violence is found both in the ruined buildings' potential to kill their inhabitants, and in Dickens's grotesque description of the buildings as a kind of "packaging" for a rabid and dense crowd. This crowd, as the quotation below shows, verges on suffocating itself in its "crushing and striving" (426; bk. 3, ch. 12). The passage quoted above is rife with architectural reference—there are "*tiers* and *tiers* of faces" and "*cluster* upon *cluster* of people" who seek "some *nook* from which to *vent*" (emphasis added). This scene is still obviously about a broad social denunciation of Sikes's crime and the quest for swift justice. But the spatial dynamics, architectural details, and *demographics* of the scene are peculiar and pronounced enough to signal that the novel's spatial circuit and its uncanny aesthetics drives the mob (at one point above referred to as a "current") to fill this slum. The crowd serves to reactivate and to enact the return of the Island's repressed infrastructure.[9]

> There was another roar. At this moment the word was passed among the crowd that the door was forced at last, and that he who had first called for the ladder had mounted into the room. The stream abruptly turned as this intelligence ran from mouth to mouth, and the people at the windows, seeing those upon the bridges pouring back, quitted their stations, and, running into the street, joined the concourse that now thronged pell-mell to the spot they had left, each man crushing and striving with his neighbour, and all panting with impatience to get near the door and look upon the criminal as the officers brought him out. The cries and shrieks of those who were pressed almost to suffocation, or trampled down and trodden under foot in the confusion, were dreadful; the narrow ways were completely blocked up; and at this time, between the rush of some to regain the space in front of the house and the unavailing struggles of others to extricate themselves from the mass, immediate attention was distracted from the murderer, although the universal eagerness for his capture was, if possible, increased. (426; bk. 3, ch. 12)

The crowd expends as much if not more focus on "getting into a good position" to see Sikes's capture, to the point that "immediate attention was distracted from the murderer." Even at such a moment, one in which *character* would seem to be the center of both the narrative's and the crowd's attention, the architectural and infrastructural details of the setting compete for narrative focus with the characters at the center of the plot. The surge of social outcry and quest for justice in this scene is also a "surge" in the suburb and slum circuits of the novel. All of the mundane and more figurative itineraries of the novel coalesce and return here, breaking the tenuous balance of the circuit, broken and overwhelmed by its inherent violence. That the architectural and social apocalypse of Jacob's Island is the grotesque and anti-triumphant setting of justice for Bill Sikes is the interest to be paid for the imagined separation of suburb and slum in the novel and in the suburban ideal, a payment which the novel suggested would be due throughout as its characters traced their itineraries between Field Lane, Pentonville, Hampstead Heath, Whitechapel, and Chertsey.

* * *

Dickens's novels contribute to the production of suburb and slum space at the same time that the suburbs and the slums shape the narrative and fictional world of the author's novels. *Oliver Twist* dramatizes and captures the causal integration of these spaces through both its linear, itinerary-based plotting and through uncanny and mysterious points of contact among suburb and slum. In this closed and repetitive framework, *Oliver Twist* is just as much a novel with a "system" as the later, traditionally "systemic" works like *Bleak House* and *Our Mutual Friend*.

The system of *Oliver Twist*, a logical circuit of repeated movement and control, is not signified in the same way that the system is in *Bleak House*. In *Bleak House* the system, Chancery, is frequently apostrophized and discussed *as* a system. Chancery is completely objectified—and while the suburbs and the slums are objective and never just a subjective projection in *Oliver Twist*, they are not crystallized to the point that Chancery is in the later novel. They are a more implicit but no less controlling and pernicious force in *Oliver Twist*.

The system in *Oliver Twist* is closer to that of *Our Mutual Friend*. In Dickens's waterside masterpiece, receptacles and containers for waste, whether the Thames or the dust heaps, are a pervasive literal and figurative presence. I suggest that we think of the suburbs and the slums when we think of *Oliver Twist* just as much as we do about the river and the dust heaps when we talk about *Our Mutual Friend*. The river and the dust-heaps are of course deeply metaphorical and symbolic, but they are also literal infrastructure and often function as such in the novel. In *Oliver Twist's* spatial system we can discern the beginnings of Dickens's fascination with the potential for infrastructural determinants not just of real and implied human lives but also of narration, plotting, and fiction itself.

NOTES

1. I use the word "circuit" throughout because several of this word's uses and definitions illustrate the concept I have in mind for describing the connection of the slums and the suburbs. In the nineteenth century, "circuit" was used to describe the route of itinerant travelers following a relatively fixed path between one site and another, between various performance sites, for instance. Also relevant is the electrical circuit, the path that current follows between two poles of a battery. Such circuits are *looped* networks; they have a point of contact and connection rather than simply a gap or division between two

poles. This detail makes the metaphor of the circuit even more appropriate and accurate for the suburb-slum relationship.

2. A number of critics have placed emphasis on the materiality of urban space in their readings of culture and literature in the nineteenth century. Deborah Nord brings the physicality and embodiment of actual street life into her readings of texts and cultural changes in urban life. Moretti's *Atlas* pays close attention to urban spaces as *geographical* locations, in addition to the cultural geography of whole regions and nations. The most recent study to approach real urban space and its relationship to the literary is Jeremy Tambling's *Going Astray*. Tambling's statement of method at the start of his book is one that also describes well my approach in this essay: "For the novels I have discussed, each chapter has a desire to relate the texts to London, another, to see how foregrounding London locales shapes a reading, and an interest in critical theory. The city can be seen empirically, but every reading must have a theoretical aspect; much of what needs to be said cannot be seen empirically" (10). This essay's key concept of the infrastructural uncanny, which I introduce below, is both a "theoretical aspect" *and* "empirical" phenomenon; it is a product of my reading of both the novel and of the urban infrastructure of early nineteenth-century London.

3. This sketch was later retitled "Mr. Minns and His Cousin" and collected in *Sketches by Boz* as chapter 2 of the "Tales."

4. *Oliver Twist* pays no attention to such standard aesthetic critiques of the suburbs but much to the suburbs' interdependence with the slums. After the *Sketches*, Dickens's account of the suburbs shifts from a traditional and hackneyed critique of the suburbs' "gardenesque" aesthetics, or stories that present tidy boundaries between the suburbs and other areas to a subtler look at the way the suburbs sought to divide and segregate classes. In these later views, the predominant aesthetic is the uncanny.

5. I borrow the term "itineraries" to describe these courses through the city and suburbs of London from Jeremy Tambling (*Going Astray*). In some cases the routes traced by characters in the novel are planned, like real itineraries, but in many cases they are not. Nevertheless, the term still works. The "unplanned" routes are at least planned and plotted by the author.

6. Lynda Nead writes that "Mid-Victorian London was shaped by the forces of two urban principles: mapping and movement" (13). Movement and its uncanny aesthetic affects, registered more in circuits than by mapping in *Oliver Twist*, presage such shaping. *Oliver Twist* of course confirms Nead's claim that "the nature of London's modernity ... seemed to obey the spatial logic of the maze rather than of the grid or étoile" (5).

7. *Oliver Twist* is a novel that, as John Bowen describes Dickens's *The Haunted Man*, "both explores and in some sense attempts to be, a knowledge simultaneously canny and uncanny" (81).

8. When the narrative diverges from Oliver's location at any point throughout the novel, he is either in the suburbs or the countryside. If Oliver is in the slum, so is the narrative discourse, as if the narrative must stay with him at these points.

9. The reality of the situation in Jacob's Island would continue to occupy a place in

Dickens's arguments for reform more than a decade later. His preface to the 1850 Cheap Edition of *Oliver Twist* centers on mistaken claims by Sir Peter Laurie that Jacob's Island was a fictional place and had no reality outside of Dickens's imagination. Dickens's preface lampoons Laurie for supposedly thinking that any place or person described in a work of fiction is therefore wholly fictional.

WORKS CITED

Bayley, John. "*Oliver Twist*: 'Things as They Really Are.'" *Dickens and the Twentieth Century*. Ed. John J. Gross. and Gabriel Pearson. Toronto: U of Toronto P, 1962. 49–64.

Bowen, John. "Uncanny Gifts, Strange Contagion: Allegory in the Haunted Man." *Contemporary Dickens*. Ed. Eileen Gillooly and David Deirdre. Columbus: Ohio State UP, 2009. 75–92.

Dickens, Charles. *Oliver Twist*. Ed. Phillip Horne. New York: Penguin, 2003.

———. *Sketches by Boz*. Ed. Dennis Walder. New York: Penguin, 1995.

Dyos, H. J. *Victorian Suburb: A Study of the Growth of Camberwell*. Leicester: Leicester UP, 1961.

Dyos, H. J. and D. A. Reeder. "Slums and Suburbs." *The Victorian City: Images and Realities*. Ed. Dyos. Boston: Routledge & Kegan Paul, 1976. 360–88.

Eisenstein, Sergei. *Film Form: Essays in Film Theory*. Trans. Jay Leyda. San Diego: Harcourt Brace, 1977.

Fishman, Robert. *Bourgeois Utopias: The Rise and Fall of Suburbia*. New York: Basic Books, 1987.

Grossman, Jonathan H. "The Absent Jew in Dickens: Narrators in *Oliver Twist, Our Mutual Friend,* and *a Christmas Carol*." *Dickens Studies Annual* 24 (1996): 37–57.

John, Juliet. "Twisting the Newgate Tale: Dickens, Popular Culture and the Politics of Genre." *Rethinking Victorian Culture*. Ed. Juliet John and Alice Jenkins. Basingstoke: St. Martin's, 2000. 126–45.

Kettle, Arnold. *An Introduction to the English Novel*. 2nd ed. London: Hutchinson, 1967.

Marcus, Sharon. *Apartment Stories: City and Home in Nineteenth-Century Paris and London*. Berkeley: U of California P, 1999.

Marcus, Steven. *Dickens: From Pickwick to Dombey*. New York: Basic Books, 1965.

McLaughlin, Joseph. *Writing the Urban Jungle: Reading Empire in London from Doyle to Eliot*. Charlottesville: UP of Virginia, 2000.

Miller, J. Hillis. *Charles Dickens: The World of His Novels*. Bloomington: Indiana UP, 1969.

Moretti, Franco. *Atlas of the European Novel, 1800–1900*. New York: Verso, 1998.

Nead, Lynda. *Victorian Babylon: People, Streets, and Images in Nineteenth-Century London*. New Haven: Yale UP, 2000.

Nord, Deborah Epstein. *Walking the Victorian Streets: Women, Representation, and the City*. Ithaca: Cornell UP, 1995.

Robson, Catherine. "Down Ditches, on Doorsteps, in Rivers: *Oliver Twist's* Journey to Respectability." *Dickens Studies Annual* 29 (2000): 61–82.

Tambling, Jeremy. "Dangerous Crossings: Dickens, Digression, and Montage." *Yearbook of English Studies* 26 (1996): 43–53.

———. *Going Astray: Dickens and London.* New York: Pearson Longman, 2009.

Vidler, Anthony. *The Architectural Uncanny: Essays in the Modern Unhomely.* Cambridge, MA: MIT P, 1992.

Welsh, Alexander. *The City of Dickens.* Oxford: Clarendon, 1971.

"No Certain Roof but the Coffin Lid": The Melodramatic Body and the Semiotics of Syphilis in *Oliver Twist*

Erin Wilson

This essay centers on Oliver Twist's *Nancy, considering her development as a collaboration of the "melodramatic body," as theorized by Martha Stoddard Holmes and others, and the medical body. It is my contention that Dickens composes Nancy in a manner that suggests, without stating outright, that she is suffering from late-stage syphilis and I further contend that this apparent affliction performs crucial political and formal work in the space of the novel. The essay traces the pervasive discourses surrounding venereal disease and the body of the prostitute in the nineteenth century, indicating that Dickens's treatment of Nancy vividly deviates from those popular conceptions. The essay goes on to suggest that Dickens's ability to manipulate the paradox of the melodramatic body, specifically the tension between hyper-visibility and invisibility, allows him to generate a realistic pathological narrative that intersects with and fundamentally alters the primary narrative. It is the final assertion of the essay that the novel's resolution, often noted for its adherence to melodramatic tropes, is hosted in medical realism via the case study of Nancy's symptomatolgy and her physical deterioration.*

With its impossible coincidences and caricatured cast of characters, *Oliver Twist* stands as one of Dickens's most classically melodramatic pieces. In the melodramatic mode, as explained by such theorists as Peter Brooks and Ben Singer,

Dickens Studies Annual, Volume 44, Copyright © 2013 by AMS Press, Inc. All rights reserved. DOI 10.7756/dsa.044.002.29-42

29

characters are hyperbolically constructed as figurative models for abstract notions
of virtue and villainy. In *Oliver Twist*, such models are quite evident; Monks and
Sikes are unrepentantly evil, while Rose Maylie and Mr. Brownlow are unflinch-
ingly kind and good. These rather flat figures stand in contrast to the richer character studies of Dickens's later works like *Great Expectations* and *Bleak House*.

Out of *Oliver Twist*'s menagerie of archetypes and stereotypes emerges Nancy,
the prostitute with a heart of gold. Fallen women and prostitutes are fairly frequent in melodrama, typically functioning as objects of mockery or disgust. However, while Dickens shapes other characters in *Oliver Twist* from melodramatic
frames—the Jew, the criminal, the domestic angel—he deviates from this trope
with Nancy, and adamantly so, as he wrote to his friend John Forster: "I hope to
do great things with Nancy" (Chittick 87).[1] She has the overwrought emotions and
tragic end of a melodramatic heroine, but her emotional growth, torturous history,
and ambivalence toward Oliver, Sikes, and her criminal companions make her
much more complex than the stock characters she's cast alongside. This complexity is noted both by Dickens's contemporaries and modern scholars of his work,[2]
who see Nancy as an exceptional Dickensian creation, particularly as he is often
criticized for his treatments of women. With her, Dickens engages with both the
conventions of melodrama and the principles of realism.

Critical treatments of Nancy have largely treated her in abstract terms, often
simplifying hers as a story of melodramatic victimhood, a conversion from evil
to good, and of a conventional death for a fallen woman.[3] In other words, despite
acknowledgment that Nancy is unique in the world of *Oliver Twist*, she remains
within the realm of simplified melodrama because of her excessive passion, emotional outbursts, and horrific end. I propose we revisit Nancy's complexity in
an entirely new vein—through the combination of melodrama and medicine. I
contend that Dickens uses Nancy, specifically her body, to invest the "melodramatic body"[4] with the realistic symptomology of syphilis, blending melodramatic
pathos with medical realism and social commentary. Nancy's sickness extends
the various agendas of this social problem novel, offering a portrait of a diseased
woman that pushes against popular medical discourse. In this way, Dickens's
novel blurs the generic lines between melodrama and realism, giving melodrama
a social conscience and clinical sensibility while investing realism with high feeling. Through Nancy's sporadically presented symptoms, Dickens composes a
narrative of illness that both reinforces the novel's reformist agendas and lays the
foundation for the novel's conclusion.

Nancy exhibits numerous symptoms of syphilis throughout the novel, ranging
from the palpable to the obscure. These symptoms have likely gone unnoticed
due to their relative subtlety and diffuseness, particularly as *Oliver Twist* is not
known as one of Dickens's more understated narratives. Nonetheless, the Nancy
passages are laden with curious and otherwise inconsequential details that, when
taken together, comprise what is essentially the case study of a progressing malady. For instance, Nancy repeatedly shivers, indicating an unshakable fever: "the

girl beat her hands upon her knees, and her feet upon the ground; and, suddenly stopping, drew her shawl close round her: and shivered with cold" (141; ch. 20). Later in the novel, Sikes, Nancy's domestic partner, also comes down with a fever: "Mr. Sikes, being weak from the fever, was lying in bed, taking hot water with his gin to render it less inflammatory." As Nancy cares for him, she is said to be, once again, "shivering" (263; ch. 39). It is also worth noting that no one else in regular contact with Nancy or Sikes—Fagin, Charley Bates, or the Artful Dodger—is said to have fevers or be shivering, indicating that the lovers are sharing the same malady, and that their intimate relationship is complicit in the progressing inflammation. These occurrences are fairly negligible in a narrative sense, serving no purpose in the motion of the plot. Nevertheless, Dickens took time to describe Nancy in this manner more than once, thus her persistent shivering becomes a resolute fixture in the composition of her character, much like her eyes—the feature that Dickens grants the most textual weight.

Nancy's eyes have been the subjects of many perceptive analyses, particularly their ability to haunt Sikes after her death. Little has been said about them, however, when she is alive, despite the fact that Dickens takes great pains in emphasizing them. They are said to, at various times, be "swollen and red" (299; ch. 44) and she exhibits sensitivity to light: "'Put down the light,' said the girl, turning away her head. 'It hurts my eyes'" (141; ch. 20). While the eyes are powerful symbolic devices after her death, they take on new meaning when considered as a symptom of disease as eye-related problems, including photophobia and progressive blindness, are common to late-stage syphilis (Harsin 76). Readers of William Blake might recall the "Harlot's curse" in "London" that is said to blind newborn babies. In addition, Nancy is said to stare, ignorant of her surroundings: "Nancy apparently fearful of irritating the housebreaker, sat with her eyes fixed upon the fire, as if she had been deaf to all that passed" (135; ch. 19). While Nancy may simply be musing or reflecting on her current state, the staring could also indicate paresis, the state in which the spirochetes that cause syphilis create lesions on the brain (Podair 12). Or, indeed, both could be occurring at the same time. As her symptoms become more evident and advanced, Nancy the complicit criminal converts into the source of Oliver's liberation. As it relates to her vision, the literal change in her ability to see links figuratively with how she sees her companions, Oliver, and her own fate. This change in vision is, of course, what will ultimately compel her to seek out Rose Maylie and Mr. Brownlow, an action that consequently triggers the narrative momentum of the novel's final chapters.

The most telling symptoms of syphilis are her manic and sometimes violent fits, as it was popularly known that syphilis causes madness, particularly in the tertiary stage.[5] Her first outburst comes almost immediately after Oliver is returned to Fagin. Sikes remarks, "The girl's gone mad, I think," as Nancy's fit begins. Dickens writes: "The girl laughed again: even less composedly than before; and, darting hasty looks at Sikes, turned her face aside and bit her lip until the blood came" (114). After an impassioned speech detailing her life on the streets, her fit escalates: "The girl said nothing more; but tearing at her hair and dress in a transport of frenzy, made such a rush at the Jew as would probably have left signal marks of her revenge on him, had not her wrists been seized by Sikes at the moment; upon which, she made a few ineffectual struggles: and fainted" (116). Nancy's cohort is not alarmed by her heightened emotional state, attributing her furor, essentially, to her womanliness. Fagin tells her she's "acting beautifully" after she snatches the club from his hands. After her fit, Fagin shakes off the incident, telling Charley Bates, "It's the worst to do with women" (117). Fagin can readily dismiss the incident because Nancy, being female, is prone to weakness, occasional madness, and melodramatic spells. To an extent, Fagin echoes discourse on women and their capacity for disease, drawn from what Mary Spongberg calls the perceived inferiority of the female body (2). This perceived weakness allows Nancy's other frenzied episodes to go relatively unnoticed. The first episode with Fagin initiates a pattern of manic, arguably mad, outbursts that are essentially devoid of the emotional charge of the first incident. Just before Oliver is taken to the attempt at robbery, Nancy "rocked herself to and fro; caught her throat; and, uttering a gurgling sound, struggled and gasped for breath" (141). When Oliver shows concern, she immediately collects herself, saying, "I don't know what comes over me sometimes" (142). Much later in the novel, Dickens writes "she rocked herself to and fro; tossed her head; and after a little time, burst out laughing" (299). Like the fever and descriptions of her eyes, these moments cannot be connected directly to the actions of other characters, nor can they be attributed to affected performativity. In most of her episodes, Nancy is not in the throes of an argument or a struggle, nor is she engaged in emotional contact with anybody. She's nearly cut off from all around her, literally folding into herself and her maddening state.

Nancy's own words, in her lucid moments, provide some of the most revealing evidence that something organic is driving her deterioration, as she seems to be entirely aware that she is in the grips of a terminal malady. There are multiple instances in the novel where Nancy alludes to her impending demise, despite multiple attempts to save her. Apparently, there is something about Nancy that inherently disqualifies her from salvation, as she continuously rejects any possibility of rehabilitation while repeatedly alluding to imminent death. In other words, Nancy's inability to return from fallenness is connected not with unsavory morality, but with a confrontation with her mortality. After all, Dickens certainly believed that prostitutes could be redeemed, as evident in his work at Urania Cottage and his "An Appeal to Fallen Women." Rose Maylie pleads with Nancy to escape from her life on the streets, in language that echoes Dickens's in his "Appeal." Yet Nancy declines assistance, cryptically declaring, "if I had heard them [kind words] years ago, they might have turned me from a life of sin and sorrow; but it is too late—it is too late!" (270). Later, when Rose attempts again to save her, she tells her: "You can do nothing to help me. I am past all hope, indeed," stating that she has "no certain roof but the coffin-lid and no friend in sickness or death but the hospital nurse" (309). Critics have largely used these cryptic comments to claim

that Nancy is either suicidal or somehow prophetic about her death. This proph-
ecy, however, would only be fulfilled if she died in a hospital, as she describes.
Suicide, too, seems unlikely because she begs Sikes not to kill her. Facing certain
death at the hands of her lover, Nancy is not resigned to dying at this moment, but
she continues to allude to a later death. She pleads with him: "the gentleman, and
that dear lady, told me to-night of a home on some foreign country where I could
end my days in solitude and peace ... It is never too late to repent. They told me
so—I feel it now—but we must have time—a little, little time!" (316). Just before
her murder, she speaks of a different impending death. Nancy, it would seem, is
beyond hope, but not because of her murder. She asks for "a little time," which
implies she knows her time is nonetheless fairly limited.

The layers of symptoms and coded language seem contradictory to what scholars and critics of Dickens tend to acknowledge about his work, specifically, that
he is a meticulous and perhaps obsessive recorder of details. In the most practical
sense, though, the sexual dimension of syphilis would necessitate such coding, as
Dickens was likely concerned about alienating his audience with frank mention
of such a scandalous subject. It was, however, evidently important to him that he
explore the obscured dimension of this disease that is so often thought of in terms
of visibility. We may recall that the women of Hogarthian caricature have venereal disease, but the surface rendering gives viewers little sense of its devastating
reality, namely, the physical suffering and mental turmoil it brings to the afflicted.
Nancy's experience is, essentially, the unseen side of a disease that permeated
the nineteenth century. Moreover, this is not the only time Dickens shies away
from naming the diseases that afflict his characters.[6] While most critics accept
that Esther Summerson of *Bleak House* contracts smallpox in the novel, Dickens
never makes this explicit. We never know what mysterious illness claims David
Copperfield's mother and infant brother, or his first wife, Dora, and it is unclear
what is slowly killing Tiny Tim in *A Christmas Carol*. Alice Marwood of *Dombey
and Son* also dies of an unspecified malady that both Patricia Ingham and Deborah
Epstein Nord relate to syphilis (Ingham, 58; Nord, 362–63). Her death scene, like
Nancy's, is notably fixated on descriptions of her eyes. In each of these examples,
the character's trials living through illness feed into the primary narrative, often
fundamentally changing the course of the novel's trajectory. Rather than adopting the clinical language of diagnostics, Dickens favors a descriptive language
as it pertains to medical matters.[7] In other words, it seems it is not the *cause* but
the *experience* of illness that interests Dickens, as the explicit identification of a
disease does less in informing the primary narrative than the narrative life of a
disease has in potentially transforming it.

Coding may also seem contrary to melodrama's "desire to express all" (Brooks
4). However many theorists of melodrama have noted the curious tendency in this
mode to withhold and suppress rather than express. Despite its evocative nature,
melodrama, according to Christine Glendhill, employs a dual operation, both exposing and suppressing levels of discourse: "Melodrama deals with what cannot be said

in the available codes of social discourse; it operates in the fields of the unknown and familiar, but also attempts to short-circuit language to allow the 'beneath' or 'behind'—the unthinkable and repressed—to achieve material presence" (45). While the impetus of melodrama is expression, it must nonetheless negotiate the inexpressible, and it does so through bodies. The melodramatic body is both the site of this short-circuitry, and the material presence achieved through expression. Grappling with the conflict between expression and suppression, the body generates gestures and markers that serve as codes for discovery. In other words, bodies in melodrama become texts that, when read, uncover layers of hidden meaning.

While on the one hand, the body in melodrama is hyperexpressive, both Martha Stoddard Holmes and Peter Brooks propose that the melodramatic body is the primary site for coding Glendhill's "unthinkable and repressed" (Glendhill 45). Holmes asserts that impairments, defects, and disabilities in melodramatic characters are typically coded "with references to the flow of vision and places them within the dynamics of looking and knowing (or failing to know)," indicating that meaning is made from what can be seen rather than heard (17). This concept is related to Brooks's "text of muteness" in which the body in melodrama performs meanings that elude articulation. Brooks describes the pervasiveness of muteness in melodrama, describing the ways in which hidden truths are both concealed and suggested by the body, proposing that a melodramatic text's most important truths are coded.[8] According to Brooks, the body speaks to the audience, suggesting the unutterable yet crucial elements threaded throughout a given melodramatic text.

Like the melodramatic body, the body of the fallen woman, and more specifically the prostitute, was conceived of in this paradoxical play between revealing and concealing in the eighteenth and nineteenth centuries. On the one hand, certain women were thought to be more vulnerable to fallenness and prostitution than others, and certain visual signs could predict such a fate. Furthermore, the prostitute, the definitive fallen woman, possesses an excess of signifiers, becoming a kind of self-caricature. At the same time, the prostitute engaged in a coded body language designed to express everything from advertising of services to concealed contagious infection. Within Victorian popular print and visual culture, the prostitute was easily identified by her flamboyant dress and sexually suggestive mannerisms: "Observers were affronted by the 'painted creatures' sauntering down the thoroughfares and byways of the city with their 'gaudy dress' and aggressive gaze" (Walkowitz, *City of Dreadful Delight* 371). The prostitute was said to be a walking caricature of depravity, whose brazen flaunting of immorality disgusted the upstanding Victorian citizen. She could be recognized by her painted face, bonnetless head, and cheap clothing, and citizens reportedly complained often about prostitutes publicly advertising services through suggestive body language such as baring their ankles or sucking their thumbs (Walkowitz, *City of Dreadful Delight* 373). In this way, the prostitute was seen to embody and enact the hidden transgression of the body, as passersby can recognize these relatively benign gestures as a signal of something licentious. The "wicked glances" and gaudy dress are explicit visual signifiers of a fallen status. At the same time, they are engaging in a visual language only accessible to those trained to read it; not all nineteenth-century people could easily recognize a prostitute. Those residing outside the city, for example, might be less likely to read the signs. Readers of Frances Burney's *Evelina* will perhaps remember the title character's interaction with a pair of prostitutes, completely unaware of what they are. Through the use of dress codes and body language, both in exposing and playing coy in withholding, the prostitute engages in a visual and corporeal conversation with her customers that polite society may not recognize.

This somewhat comical and theatrical characterization of the prostitute's dual nature had more sobering implications with the growing threat of venereal disease, the cause of which was placed squarely at the feet of prostitutes. The threat of prostitution moved beyond gaudy aesthetics and the dictates of sexual morality. Throughout the century, the prostitute was characterized as the conduit of deadly diseases, and her body became the very symbol of contamination and plague. In relation to the visibility of these diseases, the attitudes about the prostitute's body were essentially contradictory. On the one hand, the prostitute bears, and indeed is, the visual signifier of diseases like syphilis. Meanwhile, much of the biomedical discourse focuses on the cunning ability of the prostitute to conceal her infected state from unsuspecting customers. With this contradiction, the prostitute embodies the paradox of the melodramatic body, both excessive in expression and obscure in meaning: "The prostitute was perceived both as one of the visible causes of miasma and as the invisible infection itself" (Nead 21). Thus, usually, the prostitute's body is already a melodramatic body, conducive to a melodramatic reading.

Venereal diseases, particularly syphilis and gonorrhea, were a major public health concern for the Victorians. Marilyn French proposes astronomical numbers for rates of infection during the nineteenth century, as high as one in five men (155). More conservative numbers are still alarming; French physician Alfred Fournier thought that thirteen percent of all Parisians were infected with syphilis (Harsin 74). A. N. Wilson also reports high numbers of infection among patients admitted to major London hospitals: "Among the surgical outpatients at Bartholomew's Hospital in London, one half had venereal disease, mostly the deadly syphilis—at Guy's it was 43 per cent" (308). For the Victorians, venereal disease was seen as evidence of the depravity and filth of the seedy urban underbelly, and many feared its influence would seep into the upper echelons of society. Syphilis was seen as particularly dangerous because of its obscure nature. Known as "The Great Imitator," it may go undetected in its early stages, or symptoms are minute, and can often be attributed to other, more benign pathology. The decline is slow, thus the possibility of infecting others is quite high. While it is possible to be a carrier of the infection without succumbing to it, and as many as a third of those infected recover spontaneously, contracting syphilis generally meant a slow and painful death before the discovery of penicillin.

As rates of syphilis contraction increased, biomedical discourse on containment was focused entirely on the policing of women's bodies, believed to be the source of disease, with the prostitute as the primary target. As Mary Spongberg explains: "Men are consistently represented as the victims of disease, women as its source. For the most part, medical advice was written for the male sufferer, with women being confined to the role of contaminator" (2). According to these medical experts, the deviant woman is a vessel for the spread of pestilence: Until much later in the century, with the work of people like Florence Nightingale and Josephine Butler among others, there was little indication that the clientele of prostitutes would be complicit in infection, or that they continued the chain of contamination by taking the disease home to their wives. The belief that women's bodies carried an inherent deviance went to absurd lengths at times, as Spongberg indicates: "Doctors agreed that it was possible even for virgins to transmit venereal disease," but she does contend, "It was the prostitute who was the obvious symbol of sexual excess and the easiest target for sexual regulation" (6).

There was a tremendous fear among middle- and upper-class Victorians that the prostitute's body was essentially a Pandora's box of contagion. The symptoms of most venereal disease manifest differently in men and women for purely physiological reasons. Men present symptoms sooner than women for the sole reason that they have external genitalia. This difference was not attributed to anatomy, but was instead attributed to the inherent deceptiveness of the woman's body: "The lack of symptoms in women no longer meant that they were less dangerous but rather that they were more dangerous, because the disease was hidden" (Spongberg 5). However, it was held as a truism that infected prostitutes could be identified based on their physiognomy, specifically that sores on the body could tip off both potential patrons and the police. In Victorian print culture, and in circulating reprints of eighteenth-century illustrations and prints, we see this operating primarily through images of prostitutes with facial sores, for example in reproductions of eighteenth-century works like Hogarth's *Rake's Progress* and *Harlot's Progress*. *Oliver Twist*'s illustrator, George Cruikshank, engages in this visual tradition, producing the image "Norfolk Dumplings or Grace Before Meat," which shows three positively grotesque prostitutes, complete with facial sores. Both Nead and Spongberg assert that the condemnation of venereal disease and the condemnation of the prostitute are one and the same, explaining that the diagnosis brought an automatic assumption of degeneracy. The syphilitic prostitute, then, faces double condemnation both as a sexual deviant and as someone infected with a fatal and highly transmittable disease.

Nead notes that as signifiers of disease marked the prostitute's body and face, her entire body became the very mark of contagion: "Prostitution itself *is* the infection. The prostitute is described as a 'pestilence', a 'sore', a cancerous growth, contaminating and destroying society" (122). Walkowitz concurs, and notes that the prostitute's association with blights and sores is a symptom of her larger association with what she calls "The Great Unwashed": "they identified the prostitute literally and figuratively as the conduit of infection to respectable society—a 'plague spot,' pestilence, a sore" (*City of Dreadful Delight* 22). In this paradigm, the prostitute is robbed of the coy and extravagant body play she engaged in previously. She becomes an emblem of all of the ills of a decadent society in moral decline, and such a simplified characterization is ripe for melo-dramatic rendering.

Dickens was certainly aware of the common discourse related to prostitutes, as they made fairly frequent appearances in his early work. From a young age, Dick-ens saw streetwalkers soliciting customers, and many passages in his *Sketches by Boz* refer to them. Incidentally, these sketches paint prostitutes in agreement with popular representations. In "The Prisoner's Van," Dickens describes two young prostitutes, "The progress of these girls in crime will be as rapid as the flight of a pestilence, resembling it too in its baneful influence and wide-spreading infec-tion" (317). Like the popular discourse, Dickens associates prostitutes with pes-tilence. He also notes that the eldest girl is "branded" in the face: "two additional years of depravity had fixed their brand upon the elder girl's features as legibly as if a red-hot iron had seared them" (316). The reference to hot iron branding recalls a medieval practice of branding women believed to be carriers of venereal disease and banishing them from their towns (Spongberg 1). Only a few years later, Dick-ens moved from the panoramic observations of *Sketches* to the individualized portrait of the prostitute in *Oliver Twist*. It seems plausible that this change was caused, at least in part, by his visits to London hospitals. Scholars have speculated that Dickens's accuracy with treating disease and medicine in his fiction is con-nected with his frequent visits to hospitals,[9] one of which is described in detail in "The Hospital Patient" in *Sketches by Boz*. Dickens treats the patients he describes in this sketch with the deepest sympathy, particularly a young victim of domes-tic violence who may serve as a model for Nancy. It seems entirely plausible that Dickens's descriptions of disease throughout his works are based largely on observations he made during these visits, which was undoubtedly accompanied by a level of intimacy and personal connection that extended into his novels.

After *Sketches* and *Oliver Twist*, the prostitute is cast less and less in his fiction, although the more domestically-bound "fallen woman" is an occasional feature.[10] What makes Nancy distinct is the nature of her fall, which Dickens treats with a level of compassion that is rarely granted to fallen women in his other novels. Fallen, or at least questionable, women are rendered with considerably less sym-pathy than Nancy, who is fairly consistently treated as a victim. Patricia Ingham describes Nancy's characterization as emblematic of the dueling sides of the pros-titute—she is somewhat complicit in her life of crime, but is ultimately a victim of dastardly influence. She commits horrible acts in the course of the novel, most notably her participation in the recapturing of Oliver, but she's obviously not of the criminal caliber of Fagin or Sikes. In addition, the glimpses into her back-ground illuminate her circumstances, and add new depth to her character. Accord-ing to Nancy, she did not choose prostitution because of inherent deviance or an overactive libido. She claims to have been forced into prostitution by Fagin: "It is my living; and the cold, wet, dirty streets are my home; and you're the wretch that drove me to them long ago" (116). The idea that Nancy was forced into prostitution serves a critical function in her characterization. It was a commonly held belief among the Victorians that prostitutes were "sexual pariahs," and "abnormal women who could be regarded as less than human" (Spongberg 6). In Nancy's case, Dickens makes it clear that she has not chosen this life; she's essentially a prisoner, a victim of rape or sexual coercion. Prostitution reform activists, as Dickens became in the 1840's,[11] drew upon the theory that prostitutes were victims of the white slave trade to gain sympathy from those who saw prostitutes as complicit in their lifestyles. Walkowitz describes the theory of the kidnapped slave-prostitute: "She was not the innocent victim of middle-class seduction and betrayal; she was a mere child dragged and entrapped into prostitution by white slavers" ("Prostitution, Social Disease, and Venereal Disease" 13). Regardless of whether or not the white slave trade was a legitimate concern, it seems that Dickens had this notion of forced prostitution in mind when he constructed Nancy. However, he does not make as much of this background as he could for melodramatic pathos. Even if Nancy was helplessly drawn into this life, she remains in it largely of her own free will. We never see her asking for help; on the contrary she turns down help when it is offered, and she makes the clear choice to remain in this world, mostly to remain with Bill Sikes. Dickens, therefore, isn't reversing the status of the prostitute, moving her from perpetrator to victim. Rather, he's complicating her position in either of those categories.

Dickens continues to complicate social positioning through the use of disease with Monks, who at least one critic believes has syphilis. While I argue that Nancy has syphilis, its manifestation is vastly different from the caricatures of Hogarth and Cruikshank. The facial lesions that "mark" the faces of Hogarthian prostitutes, the markers of sexual depravity, may instead mark the face of a man, and a supposed gentleman no less. Mr. Brownlow indicates that Monks bears the markers of disease on his face: "you, who from your cradle were gall and bitterness to your own father's heart, and in whom all evil passions, vice, and profligacy, festered till they found a vent in a hideous disease which has made your face an index even to your mind" (330). Fred Kaplan suggests that Dickens is actually implying that Monks has syphilis, an assertion that I find both provocative and persuasive.[12] While Monks suffers from a seizure earlier in the novel, this "vent" cannot be connected to a seizure disorder like epilepsy. To begin with, epilepsy has no visual signifiers; there is nothing in biomedical discourse indicating that we can empirically identify an epileptic. Secondly, while being strongly connected with madness, epilepsy is not connected with vice. Mr. Brownlow speaks of this "hideous disease" in the same breath as he describes Monks's "evil passions, vice, and profligacy." Furthermore, it is possible that the seizure is caused by the neurological deterioration that accompanies syphilis, rather than epilepsy. If this assessment is correct, Dickens is rendering this disease rather unconventionally as this is not a prostitute; this isn't even a woman. The idea of the facial "index" of one's degeneracy is, as Spongberg asserts, most frequently ascribed to women. In this case, it is the male body that is inscribed. Dickens uses this degenerate physiognomy to further highlight Monks's deviance, making him the vessel for disease rather than the victim.

The displacement of facial lesions from a woman to a man is valuable both for how we understand the operation of the melodramatic body and how we understand Nancy's possible illness working in this novel. The melodramatic body relies on visibility for voicing the unsaid. In the novel, with the absence of an embodied stage presence, the ability to see what the body gestures toward translates into an ability to read the codes imbedded in lengthy character description. Nancy's symptoms span the narrative, forcing us to read passages from disparate portions of the novel alongside one another. Naturally, visualization would make meaning simpler to ascertain, and part of the reason the diagnosis I present is elusive is that Nancy's illness lacks visualization. The absence of this visualization serves a dual function in *Oliver Twist*. To begin with, the visual indicators would likely detract from a sympathetic rendering of Nancy because facial sores were so intimately linked with vice and depravity. To put it simply, if we "saw" sores on Nancy, we would inevitably read her as a deviant. Secondly, the absence of facial sores actually makes Dickens's rendering more realistic. The lesions that Hogarth depicts, while common in the early stages of the disease, disappear completely by the final stages of the disease. While, as I've previously observed, representations and conceptualizations of syphilitic prostitutes would have the public believe that women do not suffer from this disease, that they merely inflict, Dickens's rendering of Nancy presents an alternative vision, one more closely aligned with reality.

Nancy's apparent illness strengthens what Sally Ledger calls *Oliver Twist*'s radical social agenda. Ledger focuses her discussion of *Oliver Twist* on Dickens's critique of the New Poor Law of 1834, also proposing rather persuasively that Nancy and Sikes are based on the highly publicized murder of Elizabeth Beesmore by her lover Thomas Bedworth in 1815.[13] With the incorporation of political critique, the Newgate novel, medical realism, and classical melodrama, Dickens engages in what Singer claims is the inherently intertextual nature of melodrama. In *Melodrama and Modernity*, he argues that the structure of modern cinematic melodrama, particularly early serial films, necessitates intertextual engagement, but claims that this is a decidedly modern phenomenon. However, I would propose that the structure of *Oliver Twist* develops on a similar intertextuality. Dickens's novel is one of textual hybridity, mining from the realm of the real and the realm of performative representation. In the character of Nancy, realism, specifically medical realism, blends with melodrama, and indeed the language of both modes is required to read her and perhaps to realize fully the work of Dickens's novel. Nancy's affliction is more than a collection of symptoms. It constitutes its own narrative that intermingles with and fundamentally reroutes the primary narrative. It is Nancy's declining physical condition that pushes her to contact Rose Maylie, an event that ignites the hectic action and eventual resolution of the novel's final chapters—the murder of Nancy, the pursuit of Sikes, the capture of Fagin and Monks, and Oliver's reclamation of his birthright. While the novel's climax and resolution often serve as further evidence of the novel's melodramatic slant, the energy behind it is solidly situated in the realm of the clinical case study and a realistic narrative of disease. Nancy's apparent illness, in other words, serves as the seed of the novel's synthesis. Her development indicates a level of both social and generic sophistication that this early novel is often not given credit for. As early as 1837, we can now see Dickens grappling with the complicated literary construction of interior suffering and emotional complexity that writers of high realism, many years later, will continue to negotiate. The melodramatic body of the prostitute, for all its paradox and disharmony, serves as a multifaceted political and formal device in *Oliver Twist* as its degeneration from disease renders a shadow narrative that, ultimately, provides the gateway to the synchronization of the novel's central plot. Consequently the entire novel, in a sense, mimics the melodramatic body in its persistent play with concealing and revealing, and in the strategic exploitation of affect and authenticity.

NOTES

1. Chittick quotes from Dickens's letter to Forster, Volume I, dated November 3, 1837.
2. John Forster praised the work he did with Nancy, and Dickens's friend and fellow novelist Wilkie Collins called her "the finest thing he ever did. He never afterwards saw all sides of a woman's character—saw all round her" (Slater 221).
3. These critics include Tom Winnifrith, who writes, "Nancy and Alice Marwood are lost beyond redemption, even though the former has a heart of gold," and calls her death "the conventional early and unhappy death reserved for erring females" (100). George J. Worth characterizes Nancy and Charley Bates as "evildoers who repent of their wickedness" (39), and Sally Ledger calls her "a melodramatic victim" (69).
4. The term "melodramatic body" is largely attributed to Martha Stoddard Holmes, although she builds her definition from the extensive work of Brooks and others on the role of the body in melodrama.
5. Harsin reports that a third of those with untreated syphilis will succumb to dementia in the final stages of the disease (76).
6. A few exceptions include Sir Leicester in *Bleak House*, who suffers from gout, and Richard in the same novel, who dies of consumption.
7. Dozens of articles appearing in medical journals throughout the twentieth century that attest to the accuracy with which Dickens describes diseases ranging from leukemia to supranuclear palsy.
8. Brooks's "text of muteness" is very effectively outlined in the third chapter of *The Melodramatic Imagination*.

9. Physician John Markel, for example, describes Dickens's "fine eye for medical diagnosis" (409), proposing that he visited hospitals and shadowed physicians in order to realistically describe various diseases.
10. *David Copperfield* has two fallen women—Martha Endell and Little Em'ly. *Dombey and Son*'s Alice Marwood falls as well, eventually dying of a mysterious illness.
11. In the late 1840s, along with philanthropist Angela Burdett Coutts, Dickens helped to found Urania Cottage, which served as a refuge for fallen women and prostitutes. In 1849, Dickens distributed his "An Appeal to Fallen Women" in London jails, urging prostitutes to seek help at Urania, where they could be rehabilitated and sent to Australia for potential marriage.
12. In his footnote to the aforementioned passage, Fred Kaplan writes: "Probably syphilis, which sometimes produces disfiguring sores on the face" (*Oliver Twist*, 330n2).
13. The same year as the murder, William Hone produced the Newgate novel *The Power of Conscience Exemplified in the Genuine and Extraordinary Confession of Thomas Bedworth*.

WORKS CITED

Brooks, Peter. *The Melodramatic Imagination: Balzac, Henry James, and the Mode of Excess*. New Haven: Yale UP, 1976.
Brown, William J., et al. *Syphilis and Other Venereal Diseases*. Cambridge: Harvard UP, 1970.
Chittick, Kathryn. *Dickens and the 1830's*. Cambridge: Cambridge UP, 1990.
Cruikshank, George. *Norfolk Dumplings or Grace Before Meat*. Etching on Paper. 1814. London: British Museum.
Dickens, Charles. "An Appeal to Fallen Women." *Oliver Twist*. Ed. Fred Kaplan. Norton Critical Edition. New York: Norton, 1993. 381–83.
———. "The Hospital Patient." *Sketches by Boz*. Ed. Dennis Walder. New York: Penguin, 1995. 277–82.
———. *Oliver Twist*. Ed. Fred Kaplan. Norton Critical Edition. New York: Norton, 1993.
———. "The Prisoner's Van." *Sketches by Boz*. Ed. Dennis Walder. New York: Penguin, 1995. 314–16.
French, Marilyn. *From Eve to Dawn: A History of Women in the World*. Volume 3: *Infernos and Paradises: The Triumph of Capitalism in the Nineteenth Century*. New York: Feminist at the City University of New York, 2002.
Gledhill, Christine. "Christine Gledhill on 'Stella Dallas' and Feminist Film Theory." *Cinema Journal* 25.4 (1986): 44–48.
Harsin, Jill. "Syphilis, Wives, and Physicians: Medical Ethics and the Family in Late Nineteenth-Century France." *French Historical Studies* 16 (1989): 72–95.
Holmes, Martha Stoddard. "Melodramatic Bodies." In *Fictions of Affliction: Physical Disability in Victorian Culture*. Ed. David T. Mitchell and Sharon L. Snyder. Ann Arbor: U of Michigan P, 2007. 16–33.

Ingham, Patricia. "Fallen Girls." *Dickens, Women and Language*. Toronto: U of Toronto P, 1992. 39–61.

Ledger, Sally. *Dickens and the Popular Radical Imagination*. Cambridge Studies in Nineteenth-Century Literature and Culture. 56. Cambridge: Cambridge UP, 2007.

Markel, Howard. "Charles Dickens and the Art of Medicine." *Annals of Internal Medicine* 101 (1984): 408–11.

Nead, Lynda. *Myths of Sexuality: Representations of Women in Victorian Britain*. New York: Blackwell, 1988.

Nord, Deborah Epstein. "The Urban Peripatetic: Spectator, Streetwalker, Woman Writer." *Nineteenth-Century Literature* 46 (Dec. 1991): 351–75.

Podair, Simon. *Venereal Disease: Man against a Plague*. Palo Alto: Fearon, 1966.

Singer, Ben. *Melodrama and Modernity: Early Sensational Cinema and Its Contexts*. New York: Columbia UP, 2001. Film and Culture 18.

Slater, Michael. "'Sketches by Boz' to 'Martin Chuzzlewit'." *Dickens and Women*. London: Dent, 1983. 221–42.

Spongberg, Mary. *Feminizing Venereal Disease: The Body of the Prostitute in Nineteenth-Century Medical Discourse*. New York: NYU P, 1997.

Strachan, Charles G. "The Medical Knowledge of Charles Dickens: Gargery's Illness." *British Medical Journal* 2.3330 (1924): 780–82.

Walkowitz, Judith. *City of Dreadful Delight: Narratives of Sexual Danger in Late-Victorian London*. Chicago: U of Chicago P, 1992. Women in Culture and Society 21.

———. "Prostitution, Social Disease, and Venereal Disease." *Prostitution and Victorian Society: Women, Class, and the State*. Cambridge: Cambridge UP, 1980. 11–66.

Wilson, A. N. *The Victorians*. New York: Norton, 2003.

Winnifrith, Tom. "Dickens." *Fallen Women in the Nineteenth-Century Novel*. New York: St. Martin's, 1994. 93–112.

Worth, George J. "*Oliver Twist* and *Nicholas Nickleby*." *Dickensian Melodrama: A Reading of the Novels*. Lawrence: U of Kansas P, 1978. 39–66.

Making Piracy Pay:
Fagin and Contested Authorship in
Victorian Print Culture

Monica F. Cohen

In light of Dickens's professional struggle with literary piracy wherein the claims of exclusive ownership encountered the claims of democratic access, Fagin—one of his most notorious villains—emerges as a site through which Dickens imagines the criminalization of a practice common in the Victorian entertainment industry: unauthorized adaptation. From the crowd of characters vying to author Oliver Twist's story, Fagin stands out for his successful manufacture of criminal identities through the control of public words, which culminates in his production of Nancy's murder through the savvy publication of a fake story. This paper argues that through Fagin Dickens mounted an anti-piracy campaign whose primary objective was to win the hearts and minds of literary consumers hitherto unconcerned with brand loyalty.

Although he bears only a single name, Charles Dickens's Fagin can be called many things: the first "of Dickens's great villains" (Lane 94); one of the most famous Jews in all of English literature (Rosenberg 4); a reference to the period's noted fence, Ikey Solomons (Rosenberg 134–35); a recreation of Bob Fagin, the older boy who befriended the young Dickens during his infamous stint working at the blacking warehouse (Johnson 38; Marcus 483–84; Rosenberg 120); a misspelling of the historical Robert Fegen's name (Rowland 14); a repository

Dickens Studies Annual, Volume 44, Copyright © 2013 by AMS Press, Inc. All rights reserved.   DOI 10.7756/dsa.044.003.43-54

of anti-Semitic archetypes current in the 1830s (Lane 94); an allegory for the evil urban forces that wait to ensnare the innocent child (Lane 100; Lankford 23); an allusion, albeit oblique, to a child prostitution ring leader (Wolff 227); a stage scoundrel replete with Oriental costuming, the stock red hair of a devil, and the slapstick routines of music hall theater (Lane 95; Rosenberg 119); a sinister compilation of those traits of "otherness" that constitute the nineteenth-century monster (Halberstam 335, 337); a counter-cultural father figure who provides a poor orphan with food, shelter, and companionship (Miller 48–49); an illustration of how *homo economicus* engenders economic parasitism and virtual cannibalism (Rosenberg 133). To this epic catalogue of what and how Fagin means, I want to propose that we add "author"—not merely in the sense of he or she who invents a story, but in the sense of the person who feigns the manufacture of a story by stealing and controlling the circulation of information. This is to say, I would like to consider Fagin as a figuration of the nineteenth-century literary pirate.

Beginning with its title page, *Oliver Twist* takes shape as a story whose metaphorical ownership is contested by an ambivalent allusion to both allegory and anti-allegory: the subtitle, "A Parish Boy's Progress" refers at once to John Bunyan, whose *A Pilgrim's Progress* (1678) provides a masterplot for much of nineteenth-century Anglo-American narrative in Christian's journey from the fallen city to the celestial city of divine redemption, as well as to William Hogarth, whose pictorial series *A Harlot's Progress* (1731) and *A Rake's Progress* (1735) recast the Christian plot in the ironic terms of urban corruption and devolution. In this initiatory gesture, the novel announces itself as borrowed wares, albeit not in any radical departure from Victorian fiction generally, where late-coming and leftovers so often serve as creative strategies.

Although the novel invites readers to apprehend the crux of its story as the battle between Oliver's innocent nature and the environmental corruption of the institutional life into which he is born at the workhouse (not to mention the mock institutional life into which he is indoctrinated in Fagin's den of thieves), this struggle for Oliver's soul occurs as a struggle for controlling the ownership of his story: for the first two volumes, nearly every character vies to tell the story of Oliver Twist. By insisting several times that "that boy will be hung" (27; ch. 2; 55; ch. 7), the "gentleman in white waistcoat" on the Parish Board mobilizes the sociolect of an emergent criminology whereby poverty breeds crime. By insisting that Oliver's mother at the time of her death was on her way to either prison, transportation, or the gallows (52; ch. 6), Noah Claypole depicts a tabloid Fallen Woman, to which Mr. Bumble refers when he concludes she came from a bad family as evidenced by her having walked so far in physical affliction and exhaustion (57; ch. 7). By calling "Stop Thief!" after Oliver dashes from the bookstall (73–74; ch. 10), Dodger and Bates stage the fiction that Oliver is a Fugitive from the Law, thereby inciting the rabble to group violence as if in uncanny anticipation of twentieth-century fascistic crowd control. By fabricating answers for a fainting Oliver in the courtroom on arraignment, Mr. Fang's officer renames

Oliver "Tom White" and recasts his social identity with such words as, "'He lives where he can'" (79; ch. 11), conveying a sense of customary dereliction and irreverence wholly out of character for the boy we have seen thus far. By demanding "a full, true, and particular account of the life and adventures of Oliver Twist" (101; ch. 14), Mr. Grimwig categorizes Oliver as the protagonist of an eighteenth-century novel. When the telling of this picaresque story is deferred by Oliver's errand to the bookstall, this storyline, too, is threatened by Nancy's crime fiction: disguised as Oliver's sister, she tells another story to yet another eager and believing crowd-turned-audience: "'he ran away near a month ago from his parents, who are hard-working and respectable people, and joined a set of thieves and bad characters and almost broke his mother's heart'" (107; ch. 15). Juxtaposed to the hardworking parents, the thankless son conjures associations to The Prodigal Son as it echoes through so much Victorian stage melodrama, recycling the parable but with menacing intent. Later on, Rose Maylie challenges Nancy's fiction by projecting her own sentimental story of orphanhood, despair, repentance, and redemption: "'think that he may never have known a mother's love, or even the comfort of a home, and that ill-usage and blows, or the want of bread, may have driven him to herd with the men who have forced him to guilt'" (197; ch. 30). And although her rendering serves as a prelude to Oliver's recounting of his own true "simple history," Mr. Losberne makes it clear that Oliver's story in a court of law would look quite different:

"On his own showing, you see, he has been the companion of thieves for some time past; he has been carried to a police-office on a charge of picking a gentleman's pocket, and is taken away forcibly from that gentleman's house to a place which he cannot describe or point out, and of the situation of which he has not the remotest idea. He is brought down to Chertsey by men who seem to have taken a violent fancy to him, whether he will or no, and put through a window to rob a house, and then, just at the very moment when he is going to alarm the inmates, and so do the very thing that would set him all to rights, there rushes into the way that blundering dog of a half-bred butler and shoots him, as if on purpose to prevent his doing any good for himself." (204; ch. 31)

As if charging a phantom jury, Mr. Losberne summarizes the novel's main action by recounting an undeniable sequence of events that criminalizes Oliver. That this fake story may be told so persuasively catalyzes the vigilante justice that forms the novel's final plot sequence in Monks's arraignment before a mock court populated by Oliver's friends, that band of a happy few, a staple of the Victorian novel that, for all its alleged genuflection to a mature jurisprudential culture, nevertheless fantasizes about renegade forms of justice. Because Oliver's account is so easily perverted, his friends (Mr. Brownlow, Mr. Losberne, the Maylies) must take justice into their own hands and they do so with a zeal worthy of Henry V's troops at Agincourt.

All of the stories circulated about Oliver share three features: firstly, they all incriminate him—make him into the latest Newgate Calendar pin-up; secondly, each of the stories is overdetermined by a prior generic discourse, whether criminology, yellow journalism, melodrama, or crime fiction; and thirdly, each of the stories is false—not at all a true, authentic account of the eponymous hero— false in the sense that each departs from the single characteristic that insistently defines Oliver for the narrator, that is, his uncontestable and unrelenting moral innocence. In this sense, the proliferation of inauthentic stories coincides with modes of incrimination.

Enter Fagin. What is so frightening about Fagin, and the urban imaginary world he comes to embody, is his ability to manufacture identities that are themselves as potentially arbitrary as the alphabetical naming that Mr. Bumble uses to produce "Oliver Twist" in the second chapter, a name that inexplicably sticks even after the names of Oliver's birth parents materialize. Monks, who allegedly provides Fagin with a motivation for his own Oliver plot, makes it clear that Fagin trades not only in handkerchiefs, but in people: "'Why not have kept [Oliver] here among the rest, and made a sneaking, sniveling pickpocket of him at once? ... Why, do you mean to say you couldn't have done it if you had chosen? ... Haven't you done it with other boys scores of times?'" (178; ch. 26). Like the stolen handkerchiefs whose owners are effaced when their monograms are picked out by novices like Oliver, similarly featureless "scores" of boys are repackaged as pickpockets in Fagin's workshop, the virtually archetypal story of urban corruption thereby attributed to Fagin himself. These manufactured identities are arbitrary in the sense that they bear no connection to the prior subjects they represent—like the "old suit of clothes" that Master Bates miraculously returns to Oliver upon his recapture (117; ch. 16). For Oliver, the terror of the wrong clothes' return derives from both the threat of the identity theft at stake in Fagin's den as well as from the revelation of its machinery—a recycling network whereby what he had thrown out as rummage at Mr. Brownlow's passes through an underground community of Jewish used goods dealers and hence back into Fagin's grasping hands.

The shocking return of the old suit of clothes, however, repeats the novel's first illustration of the inexorable power of institutional life to shape an identity that is inescapably defined by social and, for Dickens, deforming forces. At the end of the first chapter, the newly born Oliver is dressed:

And what an excellent example of the power of dress young Oliver Twist was! Wrapped in a blanket which had hitherto formed his only covering, he might have been the child of a nobleman or a beggar;—it would have been hard for the haughtiest stranger to have fixed his station in society. But now he was enveloped in the old calico robes, that had grown yellow in the same service; he was badged and ticketed, and fell into his place at once—a parish child— the orphan of a workhouse—the humble, half-starved drudge—to be cuffed and buffeted through the world, despised by all, and pitied by none. (19; ch. 1)

The passage's pleasure in human potential—he "might have been"—is checked by assembly-line badging and ticketing—verbs that occur here in the shape of past actions working grammatically as adjectival modifiers ("enveloped," "badged and ticketed," "cuffed," "buffeted"), a rhetorical move that represents processes that are external to the subject as intrinsically identifying; Oliver emerges from the sentence's conveyer belt with a social identity incongruent with something prior and more authentic. But this theme is characteristic of the Dickensian imagination: individual subjectivity precedes and either withstands or is destroyed by the corruptions of institutional life. What is interesting here, however, is that this theme, that institutional life corrupts individuals, occurs through sartorial motifs that in the Fagin plot stand for the circulation of false stories: while the swaddling clothes tell a false story about Oliver's innate moral superiority and hidden class status (he is in the end, after all, the son of a gentleman), the old suit of clothes that he sheds at Mr. Brownlow's tells a false story about the identity Fagin intends to publish. The return of these clothes during Oliver's second sojourn with Fagin thus aligns the economy of false stories with Dickens's signature Romantic individualism and commitment to social protest.

Much of the history of the nineteenth-century fight for copyright protection revolves around the distinction between piracy, which is stealing the property belonging to others, and reprinting, which is circulating what belongs to everyone (Claybaugh 441; McGill 113)—that is, what Pettitt calls the conflict between "fixed identity" (ownership) and "dispersal" (alienation), made all the more pressing by technological advances that facilitated democratic access (5). Of course, we relive this same conflict today as the literary, musical, and cinematic marketplace reorganizes in response to the phenomenally democratic dissemination made possible by the Internet. While the American refusal to sign any kind of international copyright agreement throughout the nineteenth century threatened English authors with a "culture of reprinting" whereby American publishers rarely and only voluntarily paid royalties to English authors, English authors at home remained equally unprotected in practice against unauthorized reprinting and in law against unauthorized theatrical dramatizations from which they received no profit shares and over which they had no artistic control. Well before *Oliver Twist* had even finished its serialization, for example, a renegade stage version appeared at Saint James's Theatre, only to be followed the next year by five more (Douglas-Fairhurst 308), one of which famously left Dickens writhing in protest on the floor of his box after the first scene (Johnson 141). From the vantage point of Dickens's career as a professional writer, the Victorian literary marketplace looks like a bargain basement of knock-offs and imitations: Edward Lloyd's *Oliver Twiss* by "Bos" features a good-hearted prostitute named Polly and a juvenile ruffian named Knowing Cove (Douglas-Fairhurst 308); *Oliver Twiss* by "Poz" renames the beadle Bumble as Fumble and the undertaker Sowerberry as Merryberry and includes the death of Oliver's father in a workhouse and the suicide of his mother (Douglas-Fairhurst 309); Henry Mayhew's 1858 novel *Paved With*

Gold retells *Oliver Twist* with a "cut-and-paste" technique that nevertheless culminates in a runaway boy's inevitable urban corruption (Douglas-Fairhurst 352).
These examples illustrate how piracy often went beyond the free-for-all reprinting
that enabled Dickens's sketches to appear during the 1830s without his permission in at least 140 different newspapers and periodicals in Britain and the United
States (Schlicke 2) and underscore Dickens's experience of artistic assault as well
as financial loss.

A favorite puzzle of nineteenth-century fiction asks, for what, precisely is
Fagin hanged: even an unreformed penal code does not account for how pick-
pocketing and receiving stolen goods would qualify as capital crimes (Sutherland
54). As most readers would agree, the answer emerges in chapter 9 of book 3,
entitled "Fatal Consequence," the scene in which Fagin invents Nancy's murder through the crafty rhetoric that turns Sikes into his homicidal puppet. The
scene demonstrates and villainizes what has been the nature of Fagin's power
all along: information and language. When Nancy argues with him, Fagin makes
it clear that intellectual and linguistic power trumps physical force: "'Listen to
me, you drab! Listen to me, who with six words can strangle Sikes as surely as
if I had his bull's throat between my fingers now'" (175; ch. 26). The words are
so few—why only six?—because so powerful, so powerful because they would
putatively convey information about Sikes's crimes—they would be "peaching"
words, to use the cant of the novel. But the metaphorical substitution of words
for strangling fingers elides the instrument of strangulation itself, the gallows that
haunt everyone in Fagin's gang no less so than when they use their ubiquitous and
symbolically fraught handkerchiefs to rehearse death by hanging. I have more to
say about these handkerchiefs later. The point here is that Fagin's boast makes
the circulation of words central to the exercise of power, its uses and its abuses.

Whereas Fagin's threat aligns power with the circulation of true stories about
Sikes's crimes, the novel depicts him actually using that power only in the circulation of fake stories. In "Fatal Consequences," Fagin's pivotal motivational speech
begins with an ascending series of imperative subjunctives deployed in Socratic
method: with drum-like rhythm he challenges Sikes to repeatedly "'Suppose'"—
suppose the feckless Noah Claypole had betrayed the group to the authorities
without any motivation other than his own pleasure, "'what then?'" Suppose it
had been he, Fagin. Suppose it had been "'Charley, or the Dodger, or Bet, or—'"
(31; ch. 47). And here Fagin, instead of disclosing Nancy's identity, follows the
elliptical dash with an eyewitness testimony of overheard words—inadmissible
evidence—known as hearsay—in an English court of law if not in the court of
opinion implicit in the novel's jurisprudential plot. Or, to put it more accurately,
Fagin details a distorted account of Nancy's conversation with Oliver's friends,
one that Claypole/Bolter corroborates until forced to reveal in his own words the
act that would be most personally abhorrent to Sikes, the fact that Nancy had
drugged him on the night she met with the band of happy few. And, predictably,
in keeping with the page's running header, "Goading the Wild Beast," which

Dickens added to the 1867 edition, Sikes responds with violent illustrations of grinding skulls and beating out brains (313; ch. 47) until he rushes out to bludgeon fatally the good-hearted Nancy, under the heading, "The Wild Beast Springs."

My point here is that Fagin not only authors the murder in his role as a stand-in for Dickens, who infamously relished performing Fagin in the lucrative public readings of "Sikes and Nancy" he would perform, but he authors it through information that he has distorted and circulated: similar to the children's game of "Telephone," the story Fagin conveys to Sikes is an unauthorized version of the story that Claypole/Bolter told Fagin, which is an unauthorized version of what was said on the bridge, which itself refers to the previous and private conversation between Rose and Nancy in which the details of Monks's plot to capture and ruin his half-brother Oliver are revealed. The fact that Nancy had remained loyal to Sikes, standing by her man to the bitter end—a definitive trait of the prostitute Dickens imagines, remains omitted in the retelling that Fagin orchestrates. What gets told is something like what Dickens's novel has narrated, but a misrepresentation of it—just like the various versions of *Oliver Twiss* that misrepresent Dickens's original novel. Insofar as Fagin hangs for goading Sikes to murder Nancy, he hangs for a goading that relies on circulating fake stories. That this circulation of fake stories is indistinguishable from the circulation characteristic of oral culture (gossip comes immediately to mind) underscores the fanaticism of its villainization in the novel and suggests that it represents something more than what it names, something perhaps like the unauthorized circulation of print, something in fact like the circulation of the pirated text.

Interestingly, the original Oliver story in this sequence, and the one authorized by the novel itself—what Nancy tells Rose Maylie—is metaphorically paid for by Rose's handkerchief, an exchange that suggests, as John Jordan has so shrewdly put it, that "the handkerchief has story value of its own" (589), or at least that it has become a metonymy for literary circulation. Indeed, Jordan has persuasively argued that the insistent ubiquity of handkerchiefs in the novel represents textual circulation. Due to Thomas Bell's invention of the roller printing machine, printed textiles, particularly handkerchiefs, could be mass-produced, featuring not only decorative patterns, but all sorts of commemorative motifs, poems, statistical tables, maps, and texts—an article Dickens features in *Nicholas Nickleby* when a weeping boy rubs his face with "the Beggar's Petition in printed calico" (45; ch. 4); in *Dombey and Son* when "the Strangers' Map of London" appears on pocket handkerchiefs (79; ch. 6)[1]; and in *Pickwick Papers* when the Reverend Mr. Stiggins laments Tony Weller's refusal to support the missionary project of supplying "infant negroes in the West Indies with flannel waistcoats and moral pocket handkerchiefs" that "combine amusement with instruction" (402; ch. 27).

That the handkerchiefs in *Oliver Twist* stand not only for texts but for stolen texts emerges most forcefully in the setting of Fagin's den in Field-lane, a narrow, crime-ridden alley famous for shops selling stolen silk handkerchiefs, an alley that Dickens elsewhere uses analogically to describe a literary marketplace dominated by pirates; in complaining to the editor of *Monthly Magazine* in a letter of October 1834 about the unauthorized and unacknowledged dramatic adaptation of his short story "A Bloomsbury Christening" by John Baldwin Buckstone at the Adelphi Theatre, Dickens protests:

> I celebrated a christening a few months ago in the *Monthly*, and I find that Mr. Buckstone has officiated as self-elected godfather, and carried off my child to the Adelphi, for the purpose, probably, of fulfilling one of his sponsorial duties, viz., of teaching it the vulgar tongue.
>
> Now as I claim an entire right to do 'what I like with my own', and as I contemplated a dramatic destination for my offspring, I must enter my protest against the kidnapping process.
>
> It is very little consolation to me to know, when my handkerchief is gone, that I may see it flaunting with renovated beauty in Field-lane; and if Mr. Buckstone has too many irons in the fire to permit him to get up his own 'things', I don't think he ought to be permitted to apply to my chest of drawers. (*Letters* 42)

Abandoning the initial metaphor in which a kidnapped child stands for a stolen story, Dickens explicitly settles on the figure of a stolen handkerchief as a vehicle for representing the stolen text.

The context of the analogy and the reception climate surrounding it, however, complicate the moral outrage Dickens proposes to incite. What Dickens has used in the discovery of his stolen handkerchief for resale in Field-lane is a metaphor for the discovery of his stolen short story repackaged at the Adelphi Theatre. The editors of his letters, however, do not fully corroborate Dickens's claim: "In fact," they demur, "only the title, the type of name given to the godfather (in CD, Dumps; in Buckstone, Grum) and some jokes and phrases were borrowed" (42n). While the editors' "only" stands as a gesture of dismissal, the list (title, type of name, jokes, and phrases) surely substantiates Dickens's objection, an apparent contradiction that draws attention to the potential ambiguities at issue when we talk about the public ownership of ideas. The editors then go on to note that Dickens published a favorable and good-natured review of Buckstone's play in the *Morning Chronicle* (42n), thereby seeing in his collegiality some measure of exoneration. And indeed the tone of Dickens's complaint does admit a playfulness alongside its protest: the letter likens the crime to a nefarious kidnapping, but the criminal to a humorously self-elected godfather (the opposite in fact of the reluctant and curmudgeonly godfather center stage in both the short story and the play) and certainly does not cast the event in the black paint generally characteristic of Dickens's most castigating prose.

The episode as it takes shape in 1834 when Dickens and Buckstone are writing, and even as it registers in 1965 when Dickens's letters are edited, suggests a surprising moral ambiguity attendant on the unauthorized circulation of intellectual properties in what we must consequently recognize as an evolving philosophical climate—one in which the claims of exclusive ownership coexist with the realities, creative opportunities, and even excitements of artistic borrowing. Whereas Dickens accuses Buckstone of being nothing more than a fence for stolen objects, his audience did not distinguish between owners; in his joyful praise, a *Court Journal* reviewer demonstrates that consumers did not necessarily share Dickens's discriminations: "'We remember laughing at two or three of these sketches when they first appeared in a contemporary, and we roared at the 'Christening' as introduced by Mr Buckstone at the Adelphi'" (Schlicke 4). While the 1834 letter uses the stolen handkerchief to dramatize Dickens's reclaiming ownership of the stolen story, it also seems pitched to reeducate literary consumers who do not care whether their entertainment hails from Dickens or Buckstone. In light of this campaign to reeducate consumers, it is not surprising that Nicholas Nickleby, the eponymous hero of the novel Dickens writes just after *Oliver Twist*, explicitly calls unauthorized theatrical adaptors handkerchief stealers (598; ch. 48).

In this sense, the letter discloses a dimension of nineteenth-century literary piracy consistent with Dickens's tangled portrayal of Fagin: to the extent that Fagin's villainy takes shape in the terms of literary piracy, we are reminded that Fagin plays both *Oliver Twist*'s villain and Oliver Twist's first provider—of food, of shelter, of companionship, and, importantly, of entertainment. In training the boys to pick pockets, Fagin stages a virtual slapstick routine that occasions the first if not the only instance of Oliver's laughter: "[Fagin] would look constantly round him, for fear of thieves; and keep slapping all his pockets in turn, to see that he hadn't lost anything; in such a very funny and natural manner, that Oliver laughed till the tears ran down his face" (70; ch. 9). As Dickens most likely sensed, many consumers generally do not share with artists (and the professionals invested in them) a robust belief in the criminalization of artistic piracy. The promise of entertainment is just too tempting.

It is therefore not surprising that the scene in which the novel illustrates how handkerchiefs get stolen in the first place occurs at a bookstall where Mr. Brownlow is victimized, too absorbed in the entertainment of reading to protect his own property let alone the property of others. Here Mr. Brownlow seems to abuse the very concept of browsing:

> He had taken up a book from the stall, and there he stood, reading away as hard as if he were in his elbow-chair in his own study. It was very possible that he fancied himself there, indeed; for it was plain, from his utter abstraction, that he saw not the book-stall, nor the street, nor the boys, nor, in short, anything but the book itself, which he was reading straight through, turning over the leaves when he got to the bottom of a page, beginning at the top line of the next one, and going regularly on with the greatest interest and eagerness. (73; ch. 10)

Perversely, it is the model reader—the one consumed by the text, physically and intellectually abstracted by the reading experience—who unwittingly constructs the scene of the crime, the stealing of a handkerchief that is itself fraught with textual significance. Indeed Mr. Brownlow's behavior as a consumer of books ironically refuses the book's status as a consumer good, as an object that must be paid for. The atmosphere that colludes in the stealing of his handkerchief is the same one that enables him to show up in the courthouse holding an inadvertently stolen book. One stolen text (the handkerchief) leads to another (the book). It is no wonder then that Oliver is himself stolen on his way to return some books to the bookseller, his story thereby again molested by the unauthorized rerouting characteristic of a book trade governed by inveterate piracy and populated by abstracted readers.

Whether we accept the legal plot in which Fagin hangs for inciting Nancy's murder or the archetypal one in which he is scapegoated in order for the urban community to heal itself, the hanging rehearses the fate with which Dickens threatened potential literary pirates elsewhere. In "The Nickleby Proclamation" that Dickens nailed to his next novel by advertising it in Part V of the 1838 Chapman Hall reissue of *Sketches by Boz*, he warned:

> This is to give Notice,
> Firstly,
> To Pirates
> That we have at length devised a mode of execution for them, so summary and terrible, that if any gang or gangs thereof presume to hoist but one shred of the colours of the good ship NICKLEBY, we will hang them on gibbets so lofty and enduring, that their remains shall be a monument of our just vengeance to all succeeding ages ... (*Nicholas Nickleby*, Appendix 1)

Though the days of real pirates paying for their crimes on Execution Dock were long gone, Dickens resurrects them here in a rhetorical move that serves several purposes. As wish fulfillment, the fantasy avenges his perceived experience of victimization in the literary marketplace. As a means of elevating the novel, still a relatively debased aesthetic form, the figure of the "good ship NICKLEBY" appropriates associations with English nautical supremacy. As part of an anti-piracy campaign, the near-hysterical warning aspires to spread the belief, if not in fact to create it, that pirating is wrong. Ironically, however, the notice is also an advertisement: what better way to recommend a piece of fiction than to suggest that it is worth stealing in the first place! Thus piracy might in the end pay, but in more ways than one.

That Dickens's Fagin played an instrumental role in the exacting of this payment was not lost on Victorian readers: the May 29, 1847 issue of *Punch* mock-praised the American publisher George Putnam, recently accused in the English press of publishing unauthorized reissues of a critically acclaimed biography of Jeremy Taylor, as an "example to be followed by 'the Fagins of letters'" ("English Authors" 178). It would seem that by the 1840s, "Fagin" did indeed name the literary pirate—at least to the Victorian readers who consumed *Punch*, a humor magazine.

NOTE

1. These two examples are both drawn from Jordan (584–85).

WORKS CITED

Buckstone, John Baldwin. *The Christening; A Farce in One Act.* London: William Strange, 1836.

Claybaugh, Amanda. *The Novel of Purpose: Literature and Social Reform in the Anglo American World.* Ithaca: Cornell UP, 2007.

Dickens, Charles. "The Bloomsbury Christening." *Sketches by Boz.* http://www.gutenberg.org/ebooks/882.

———. *Dombey and Son.* Ed. Andrew Sanders. London: Penguin, 2002.

———. *The Letters of Charles Dickens.* Ed. Madeline House and Graham Storey. Vol. 1. Oxford: Clarendon Press, 1965.

———. *Nicholas Nickleby.* Ed. Mark Ford. London: Penguin Classics, 1999.

———. *Oliver Twist.* Ed. Fred Kaplan. New York: Norton, 1993.

———. *The Pickwick Papers.* Ed. James Kinsley. Oxford: Clarendon, 1986.

Douglas-Fairhurst, Robert. *Becoming Dickens.* Cambridge, MA: Harvard UP/Belknap, 2011.

"English Authors—American Booksellers." *Punch* 8 May 1847: 178. *19th Century UK Periodicals.* Web. 12 Oct. 2012.

Halberstam, Judith. "Technologies of Monstrosity: Bram Stoker's *Dracula.*" *Victorian Studies* 36 (1993): 333–52.

Johnson, Edgar. *Charles Dickens: His Tragedy and Triumph.* New York: Penguin, 1986.

Jordan, John O. "The Purloined Handkerchief." *Oliver Twist.* Ed. Fred Kaplan. New York: Norton, 1993. 580–93.

Lane, Lauriat. "Dickens' Archetypal Jew." *PMLA* 73.1 (1958): 94–100.

Lankford, William T. "The Parish Boy's Progress: The Evolving Form of Oliver Twist." *PMLA* 93 (Jan. 1978): 20–32.

Marcus, Steven. "Who Is Fagin?" *Oliver Twist.* Ed. Fred Kaplan. New York: Norton, 1993. 478–95.

McGill, Meredith. *American Literature and the Culture of Reprinting, 1834–53.* Philadelphia: U of Pennsylvania P, 2003.

Miller, J. Hillis. *Charles Dickens and the World of His Novels*, Cambridge, MA: Harvard UP, 1959.

Pettitt, Clare. *Patent Inventions: Intellectual Property and the Victorian Novel.* Oxford: Oxford UP, 2005.

Rosenberg, Edgar. *From Shylock to Svengali: Jewish Stereotypes in English Fiction.* Stanford: Stanford UP, 1960.

Rowland, Peter. "No sich a person: In Search of the Original Fagin." *Times Literary Supplement* 21 Jan. 2011: 14.

Schlicke, Paul. "'Risen Like A Rocket': The Impact of *Sketches by Boz.*" *Dickens Quarterly* 22 (Mar. 2005): 3–17.

Sutherland, John. *Can Jane Eyre Be Happy? More Puzzles in Classic Fiction.* Oxford: Oxford UP, 1997.

Wolff, Larry. "'The Boys are Pickpockets, and the Girl is a Prostitute': Gender and Juvenile Criminality in Early Victorian England from *Oliver Twist* to *London Labour.*" *New Literary History* 27 (1996): 227–49.

Reversing Domestication in Dickens: Forging Masculine and Domestic Types through the Cross-Species

Kattie M. Basnett

Located at the forefront of Dickens's domestic imaginary, animals are integral to the formation of normative masculine and domestic types in his early novels. Although Dickens's animals are often read as metaphorical figures for marginal human populations rather than as animals imbued with distinctly nonhuman forms of significance and agency, Dickens employs a domestic triad—composed of human male, human female, and animal—in his early work to insist that the agency of the animal as an animal is necessary for creating and sustaining domestic and masculine typologies. This cross-species triad facilitates Dickens's reimagination of human-animal power dynamics so that animals are represented not merely as the passive objects of symbolic domestication, but as capable of reversing traditional power hierarchies and exercising reverse domestication on their primarily male interactants. Dickens's method of rethinking domestic power as something wielded by humans and animals across species divides is significant for understanding the domestic politics and ethics of his early novels as he carves a path toward radically challenging Victorian assumptions about masculinity, domesticity, the cross-species, and the ethics of animal representation.

Dickens Studies Annual, Volume 44, Copyright © 2013 by AMS Press, Inc. All rights reserved.   DOI 10.7756/dsa.044.004.55-83

[M]y reproach is that Fielding has not attempted to
differentiate between dog-kind and mankind, and
that he does not seem aware that it is necessary to do
so, not even in his own mind ... [On the other hand,]
Dickens's description of the burglar's dog [Bull's-eye]
shows that the writer had observed dogs and was in
sympathy with their instincts.—George Moore[1]

I. Introduction

In the first installment of *Household Words* Charles Dickens expresses his desire
to "live in the Household affections, and to be numbered among the Household
thoughts" of his Victorian audience (1–2). As this editorial mission statement
makes clear, Dickens situates himself, almost like a domestic dog, centrally at the
hearth, and views himself as its "prophet" and as a "purveyor of cozy domestic
bliss" (Waters, "Gender, Family" 120). Yet, in Dickens's fiction, domestic bliss
is never readymade and, for that matter, rarely achieved. Instead, the novels are
replete with "fractured" or dysfunctional relationships characterized often by low-
class status and male domestic abuse, while "idealised 'happy families'" haunt
the texts' margins, or are simply nonexistent (Waters, *Politics of Family* 28).
What ties these otherwise very disparate functional and dysfunctional "families"
together, along with the texts that house them, is the presence of an animal, typically a domestic one. Dickens, in fact, signals that such animals are the focal point
of his own domestic space in an 1844 letter to F. W. Powell: "When you came
in[to my home], I should have shewn you an Eagle (a real Eagle, you know, no
nonsense or make believe), a Raven and a very small white dog" he explains (*Letters*). Just as Dickens distinguishes animals as the most defining points of his own
home in his letter to Powell, animals and animal agency are imperative in creating
and defining domestic spaces and domestic relations in Dickens's novels. Located
centrally in the domestic space—much like Dickens, the "domestic prophet," at
the hearth—the domestic animal is integral to the formation of masculine and
domestic types in novels spanning Dickens's career. Here, however, I focus on
three of Dickens's early novels (*Oliver Twist*, *The Old Curiosity Shop*, *Barnaby
Rudge*) and *David Copperfield*. I do so because these novels cohere around a
project of normative domesticity constituted through particular constellations of
cross-species relations that Dickens reconfigures as he transitions from the normatively structured domestic imagined in his early work to a domestic—imagined
in late texts—that no longer assumes normativity as its driving force.[2]

Unlike many scholars who have written on domesticity and the animal in early
Dickens novels, I do not treat animals in these texts *merely* as metaphorical or
metonymic figures for the disenfranchised domestic individual of choice—the
woman, often one subject to male domestic abuse.[3] This is only one facet, albeit

an important one, of the animal in Dickens's representational schema. On a deeper and less explored level, he portrays animals and humans as having reciprocities beyond the symbolic and analogical vagaries of the Victorian cultural imagination. Dickens's portrayal of animal-human relations is radical, moving outward from the conventional depiction of the animal as a symbolic stand-in for a marginalized human group, to a focus on the co-constitutive nature of humans and their nonhuman others, and the ways in which zones of contact both shape and are shaped by these interacting cross-species entities. This mode of thinking about the human and animal is significant in that it necessarily grants animals more inherent value—significance in and of themselves—in addition to more power in their relationships with humans than is traditionally recognized. Dickens takes seriously the idea of species "co-evolving" in his work, reimagining human-animal power dynamics on a path toward radically changing our "constructions of ourselves" as human beings by recognizing that "'[h]uman nature is an interspecies relationship'" (Nash 93; Haraway 218).

Dickens's engagement with the phenomenon of species co-evolution is expressed through his imagining of a series of cross-species encounters in which animals are not merely the subjects of symbolic domestication, but actually have the power to exercise reverse domestication on their primarily male interactants as they construct gendered identities and domesticity. For Dickens, the power of the animal originates, as Nash puts it, through the animal's co-participation in a "governing logic of interdependence that runs counter to the long-accepted doctrine of dominion, under which one species of animal domesticates another in the form of divinely sanctioned subordination" (93). In Dickens's texts, the reverse domestication of males, particularly from the lower class, by the animals they are codependent on performs the function of allowing men to rehearse masculine typologies that are subsequently extended into the realm of heterosexual relations and the shared space of domesticity. Ultimately, Dickens stages the inadequacy of violent, lower-class males who abuse both wife and animal, or who fail to gain a spouse at all, as a failure on the part of these men to "properly" domesticate, and be reciprocally domesticated by, the animals they encounter. Such men cannot achieve the middle-class domesticated masculinity that Dickens ultimately champions: a masculinity predicated upon the radical values of cross-gender and cross-species companionship and codependency that finds its origins in a visionary ethics in which human subjectivity is forged through a heterogeneous assemblage of empowered gendered and speciated agents.[4]

II. The Case for Reversing Domestication in Dickens

It has traditionally been tempting to read the distinction between particular humans and animals as entirely "blur[red]" in Dickens's novels, and Victorian

fiction at large (Ritvo 3). This is due to a pervasive Victorian cultural logic of
dominance and subordination in which the "animal kingdom, with humanity
in a divinely ordained position at its apex, represented, explained, and justified
the hierarchical human social order" (Ritvo 14–15). The Victorian penchant for
symbolically aligning human and animal via the issues of domestic violence and
animal abuse has been well documented by scholars such as Lisa Surridge who,
in *Bleak Houses: Marital Violence in Victorian Fiction*, points to a significant
link between the institution of the Royal Society for the Prevention of Cruelty to
Animals (RSPCA), the Parliamentarian Richard Martin's 1820's animal cruelty
legislation, the rise of the "wife-assault debates," and Robert Peel's 1828 Offense
Against the Person Act (Surridge 6–9). And, moreover, it has been well documented by Surridge as well as historians such as Harriet Ritvo, how animal abuse,
like spousal abuse, was culturally coded as an issue plaguing the lower-classes.[5]
Woven or "knotted" together by intricately overlapping threads of socially con-
doned forms of domination, victimization, suffering, and violence, the class-laden
issues of animal and spousal abuse are structured around a "symbolic economy"
in which the body of the female becomes aligned with that of the animal (Haraway 4; Wolfe, *Animal Rights* 8).[6]

In making such connections between the ethico-political issues of spousal and
animal abuse, these literary and historical scholars have gestured, at least in part,
to what Haraway means when she speaks of the "doubleness" which characterizes intra- and cross- species interactions (4–5). But where such arguments do
not go, and where Haraway's work ultimately points, is to the recognition of
a lesser explored notion of human-animal reciprocity existing beyond the traditional symbolic coding of the animal as the double for, or representative of, a
particular classed or gendered marginal human group. Rather than merely being
the convenient site on to which the human and human concerns can be offloaded,
nonhuman animals are, for Haraway, "meaning-making beings" that are "consequent" in shaping the human through a "dance of encounters" that transcends
disingenuous species hierarchies and the logic of exclusion (4–5). Humans and
nonhuman animals are "knotted" together into an "unpredictable kin[d] of 'we'"
as they engage in embodied interaction facilitated by the locus of a shared space,
what Haraway calls a "contact zone" (4). Defined as any space shared by humans
and animals that gives rise to the possibility of "world-making," a process that
entails "species interdependence" and "becoming with" the animal through forms
of "regard and respect," the contact zone in Dickens's corpus is often the domestic space, and that is the zone this essay addresses (Haraway 4, 19). If domestic
spaces in Dickens's texts are contact zones defined by meaningfully situated and
interacting human and animal bodies, then it becomes clear that Dickens's animals are not only meant to be symbolic twins for women in a domestic dyad
(man-woman), but have agency and significance beyond such twinning.

In fact, the problematic nature of the ubiquitous practice of twinning animal
identities and human ones in order to confirm the Victorian hierarchical social

order is showcased in an *All The Year Round* article, "A Parenthesis or Two," in which a miserly former bachelor comments: "'Love me, Love my dog.' A wise adage, I dare say. I don't at all mind their loving me, but I have the strongest objection to their loving my dog—when, as in this instance, my dog is represented by my wife" (106). Disconcerted by the way his male friends exploit the blurring of the positions of wife and dog, the former bachelor attributes his failure of masculinity and domestic control to the way in which his wife, "warming her feet by the fire," is petted and coddled by other males as if she were a domestic dog at the hearth (106). While the strategy of consolidating the positions of woman and animal is meant to perform the function of managing and cleaning up what Haraway, for example, might characterize as the "messiness" of embodiment in a cross-species world, the former bachelor's commentary makes it clear that this strategy effects the removal of one sort of mess at the cost of creating others. In fact, the cultural imaginary produced through the conflation of woman and dog entails a symbolic promiscuity that legitimates the sexual promiscuity of the former bachelor's pretty wife and male friends. The wife's inhabitation of the representational position of "my dog" thereby leads to the disintegration of masculinity and normative domesticity, rather than serving its intended purpose: the consolidation of middle-class heteronormative domestic relations as well as entrenched Victorian gender and species hierarchies. Just as the former bachelor rearticulates the practice of equating woman and animal as dangerous rather than socially productive, Dickens offers his own radical counternarrative that often gets obscured in readings that assume a more customarily casual blurring of human and animal identity in his work.

The traditional Victorian rhetorical strategy of collapsing human and animal, along with the traditional scholarly reading that is its companion, is held in strong tension with Dickens's more radical representations of human-animal relations—namely, relations in which the animal occupies the role of a coparticipant in establishing meaning as staged through the related issues of masculinity and domesticity formation. As in "A Parenthesis or Two," where the promiscuous symbolic exchange between woman and animal occasions the disruption of the former bachelor's masculinity and domestic arrangements, in Dickens's texts the formation of ideal masculine and domestic types is dependent on the existence and agency of an animal *as an animal,* while dysfunction arises when the animal is symbolically overwritten by or overwrites human identities. Dickens materializes this conviction by eschewing the traditional domestic dyad in which woman and animal occupy the same relational space, an arrangement that is cross-species only in the sense of animal-as-woman, or in the former bachelor's words, arrangements in which "my dog is represented by my wife." Dickens opts instead for a radical cross-species domestic triad in which the human male and female are partners with a nonhuman animal that occupies its own distinct space in a triadic relationship, rather than being, as Grace Moore has argued, the figure through which the identities of male and female domestic partners can be simultaneously triangulated.[7] I maintain that Dickens's reorientation to a cross-species domestic triad in which the animal itself is an agent in domestic arrangements contradicts the notion, proffered implicitly by Moore and explicitly by Ivan Kreilkamp, that animals cannot be significant characters within Victorian texts because their "'essential formal position'" is one of "subordinate beings who are delimited in themselves while performing a function for someone else" (Kreilkamp 83, 82).[8]

Animals in Dickens's texts do fit into this character schema in the sense that they "perform[] a function for someone else," emerging as the site from which male characters can rehearse their masculine and domestic types (Kreilkamp 82). However, the animal for Dickens is far too complicated, robust, and full of cross-species agency to be easily demarcated as minor. Although domestic animals in Dickens's novels might be supposed to be "subordinate" to, and present only to "perfor[m] a function" for, the males who attempt to domesticate them, it is the case that in Dickens's most functional domesticities the act of domestication is *not* the traditionally imagined arrangement in which the human male exerts his gender and species superiority over an animal that merely plays the role of malleable and passive receptacle or symbolic wife (82). Instead, Dickens actively rewrites the parameters of domestication so that it is no longer a stubbornly linear, hierarchical exchange of power and is represented, instead, as a dynamic cross-species arrangement entailing a cyclical exchange of power originating in the human male and reciprocated by the domestic animal and the female domestic partner. In this cyclical rather than linear cross-species power arrangement, the force of domestication is usurped by the animal and returned to the male and to the larger domestic arrangement in the form of reverse domestication exercised by animals themselves. Centered upon a notion of "harmony" and "companionship" tied *specifically* to masculinity[9] ideal domesticity in Dickens's texts requires that the male be reciprocally guided by animals who occupy a role similar to, but distinct from, the role of the companion female through whom men can achieve a form of masculinity conducive to idealized middle-class domesticity (Surridge 20; Francis 639).[10] Animals, it seems, are not minor at all. Dickens's reimagination of the politics of domestic power across species categories extends to animals a very significant role in the formation of ideal cross-gender and cross-species domestic relations. To be a middle-class male with an idealized middle-class home, the male must not only deal out, but must also be willing to receive unto himself, the force of domestication from the animal, who is "a feature of that constellation of cultural equipment and social constructions that characterize bourgeois identity" (Brown 33).

III. (un)Domesticating Masculinity in Dickens

For Dickens, imagining a diverse array of possible masculinities across a range of texts becomes integral to a process of parsing out a middle-class gender and

domestic project that is also, simultaneously, a project of cross-species collaboration. In Dickens's assemblage of imagined masculinities, dysfunctional masculinities occur with the greatest frequency. Dysfunctional males in Dickens's
works often suffer from problematic relationships with their animal others. Many
of these men breed lower-class, violent, and otherwise un-ideal domesticities by
being too wedded to rigid gender and species hierarchies to surrender the power of
domestication temporarily to the animals and women through whom they might
become ideally masculinized, while others deny animals their domestic influence
by forcibly marginalizing them via the promiscuous symbolic exchange between
human and animal identified in "A Parenthesis or Two" as problematic to normative gender and domestic types. Paradoxically, men such as Sikes in *Oliver Twist*,
Quilp in *The Old Curiosity Shop*, and Barnaby in *Barnaby Rudge* practice both
of these strategies of animal marginalization. Unlike the two ideally masculine
characters I will discuss as test cases for the functionality of reverse domestication
at the close of this essay—David of *David Copperfield* and Kit of *The Old Curiosity Shop*—these dysfunctional men champion linear power dynamics analogous
to the dynamics of patriarchal masculinity while, simultaneously, consolidating
multiple distinct human and animal subjectivities into one symbolic domestic
identity that disrupts the tripartite structure of ideal cross-species domesticity.
Indeed, these dysfunctional men and the texts that house them demonstrate three
distinct instances of dysfunctional masculinity, with each successive dysfunctional male I discuss below revealing a more profound desire to encroach upon
and subsume the distinct subjectivities and domesticating agencies of animal and
female members of the ideal cross-species domestic triad.

The specific representational function of Bull's-eye in Dickens's early novel
Oliver Twist has been discussed at length. However, rather than viewing Bull's-
eye as a violently marginalized animal participant in a dysfunctional domestic
arrangement spearheaded by Sikes—a low-class, abusive, criminal—the bulldog
has been read either as Nancy's symbolic twin (and by extension as representing all abused women) or as a figure through which male and female domestic
identities in the novel can be triangulated.[11] Neither of these interpretations pays
attention to Bull's-eye himself as an animal in interaction with Sikes and Nancy
because his animal identity is too completely and continuously overwritten by the
human identities that surround him. There is good reason why literary scholars
have tended to read Bull's-eye in this way. It is the strategy of reading that Sikes
adopts toward the close of the novel before accidentally hanging himself in an
attempt to evade a mob of men that has mobilized to hold him accountable for
the murder of his domestic partner, Nancy: "looking behind him on the roof, [he]
threw his arms above his head, and uttered a yell of terror. 'The eyes again!' he
cried.... Staggering as if struck by lightning, he lost his balance and tumbled over
the parapet. The noose was on his neck ... he hung" (412).

As in "A Parenthesis or Two" where the conflation of the subjective positions of wife and dog entails an unintended corruption of accepted hierarchies

and norms, Sikes suffers the ultimate corruption—death—for enacting what Surridge has characterized as a "grotesquely concrete" transfiguration of Bull's-eye into Nancy, such that Sikes sees *"Nancy's eyes* looking out of the *dog's body"* (Surridge 43). Even when Sikes removes Nancy's literal body from the domestic equation, he persists in symbolically mapping wife onto dog, effectively using Bull's-eye as the vehicle for Nancy's posthumous re-embodiment by overwriting Bull's-eye's identity as an animal with Nancy's identity as human wife. For Sikes, who participates in the Victorian imaginary in which abused animal and abused spouse occupy symbolically identical positions, the bodies of Nancy and Bull's-eye become metonymically collapsed into one another so completely that, for the remainder of the text, Bull's-eye is continuously misread by Sikes as human rather than as an animal. Bull's-eye's animal form, his physical animality, seems to disappear entirely for Sikes only to be recalled and reaffirmed through the perspectives of other, functional males as related by the narrator. Unlike Sikes, who reads "The eyes again!" as the eyes of Nancy rather than the eyes of Bull's-eye, the men who crowd together to watch the scene unfold are able to read the visual and auditory information that Bull's-eye offers them—his physical form and howl—apart from the symbolic register that Sikes depends upon, and which contributes to his death. As the narrator explains, "each man [was] crushing and striving with his neighbor, and all panting with impatience to get near the door, and look upon the criminal," and, after Sikes hangs, they see "A dog, which had lain concealed till now, run backwards and forwards on the parapet with a dismal howl" (411–12; ch. 50). Whereas Sikes looks at Bull's-eye and actually sees particular physical traits of Nancy, for the crowd of men the only things to be seen are a (soon to be) hanged man and a howling dog—the very pieces of visual data represented in the scene's accompanying illustration. If Nancy is anywhere in the scene, she is present only as the unembodied and unillustrated specter of injustice and domestic dysfunction that these men convene to appease.

Although most literary interpretations of *Oliver Twist* replicate Sikes's strategy of reading women and animals as interchangeable, his reading strategy is a flawed one. That Sikes's perspective is not the perspective Dickens endorses, nor the "proper" perspective for the reader to emulate, is denoted by Sikes's identity as a lower-class criminal and his concomitant failure to embody a masculinity conducive to the formation of idealized middle-class domesticity through collaboration with an animal agent. The alternative we are left with is the perspective activated by the men in the crowd who watch Sikes fall prey to, and die because of, the ubiquitous Victorian tendency to blur human and animal identity to the point that actual bodies can become overwritten by the qualities of other bodies, even those of other species. As harbingers of justice who are outraged at Sikes's violation of ideal middle-class domesticity, these men become the true carriers of public and political opinion,[12] as well as the only individuals capable of recognizing Bull's-eye *as an animal*—one who might, through loyalty, compassion, and self-sacrifice, have had the power to domesticate even Bill Sikes. By putting the interpretive voice of the narrator behind the group of men while allowing Sikes to speak for himself through his violent erasure of Bull's-eye's doggishness—"'The eyes again!'"—Dickens makes his own position on animal representation and the cultural imaginary clear: a parallel between domestic violence and animal abuse exists, but it is not a parallel that should be sustained through the metonymic eradication of the animal. Instead, it must involve an awareness of the import of each individual interacting human and animal body, and the recognition that to erase one of these bodies either literally or symbolically, as Sikes does, is to commit an act of violence that violates the domestic politics of the novel and effectively undermines the very normative cultural values which are meant to be reified.

It is not only the case that males misread their female partners as interchangeable with animals to the detriment of domestic relations; sometimes the males perform the more insidious act of actively misreading themselves as animal in order to destabilize their species identities and, consequently, their domestic arrangements. Demonstrating a permutation of the pernicious symbolic alignment of human and animal performed by Sikes, Quilp, the monkey-faced dwarf in *The Old Curiosity Shop*, perversely disavows both his humanity and what would otherwise be considered an ideal domesticity in an effort to "become-animal," a process that he fundamentally misunderstands and, consequently, fails to achieve.[13] Quilp is perpetually in the process of becoming a cur—a mean, mongrely dog— who "snarl[s]" and bites without provocation like the wharf dog he warns Mr. Brass about, which "'bit a man last night, and a woman the night before, and last Tuesday he killed a child'" (468; ch. 62). Similar to the undomesticated wharf dog whose home-space is uncertain and shifting—"'He lives on the right hand ... but sometimes he hides on the left, ready for a spring'"—Quilp is fascinated by, and repeatedly imagines himself to be one among, the aggressive dogs who emblemize unattained or dysfunctional domesticities like the "broken" domesticity he shares with his wife (468; 169).

In a telling moment of cross-species interaction, Quilp

> [h]ad like to have met with a disagreeable check, for, rolling very near a broken dog-kennel, there leapt forth a large fierce dog, who, but that his chain was of the shortest, would have given him a disagreeable salute. As it was, the dwarf remained ... in perfect safety, taunting the dog with hideous faces ... hissing and worrying the animal till he was nearly mad. (169–70; ch. 21)

Quilp does not treat the dog as a domesticated or domesticateable animal. Instead, he chooses to antagonize it until "*he* goes nearly mad," a phrase whose ambiguous pronoun, "he," is able to travel across species groups to indicate that, perhaps, Quilp's violent behavior produces madness not only in the dog, but also in himself (170; ch. 21; emphasis mine). Associated with rabies,[14] the dog's and Quilp's proximities to a state of "mad[ness]" in the wake of Quilp's instigations points to the instability of the domestic-wild binary and the disconcerting way in which domestic animals or domestic men, through infection or other means, might revert to a violent undomesticated state in which women and children— principal domestics—would become possible victims: "'last Tuesday he killed a child'" (468; ch. 62). Quilp embodies this potential to revert as he rolls his ape-like form across the wharf—as though willfully abandoning the human capacity for upright bipedal movement—and into the dog's path, becoming a source of infection as he communicates his violence and domestic dysfunction to the dog whose "broken" home space and "shortest" chain signal its special susceptibil-ity to Quilp's disease: domestic unease. The dog and Quilp are both chained— literally by metal or symbolically by the law—to domestic arrangements they deem unnatural, restrictive, and inhospitable, both yearning instead for the violent and spatially shifting state of existence of the wharf dog, which Quilp describes as an "agreeable freedom from the restraints" of domestication (375; ch. 50). The domestic chafing that Quilp and the dog share gives birth to a retaliatory violence which acts to consolidate their representational positions. Just as the chained dog "worr[ies]" Quilp as a means of retaliating against domestication and the working-class man or woman who has subjected him to it, Quilp actively worries his wife—"inflict[ing]" her with "pinches" and sleep deprivation—in order to dismantle the idealized, middle-class home that his undomesticated masculinity rejects (107; ch. 13).

Quilp, who, from the outset, occupies a questionable position in the species hierarchy because of his ape-like appearance, undergoes an uneasy reversion from domesticated man to undomesticated animal, as indicated by the words that frame his illustration: "Man" and "Beast" (448). Through their vertical align-ment on the page the terms "Man" and "Beast" visually embody an accepted cultural hierarchy of social and evolutionary "progress" in which domesticated man is the ultimate state of development and undomesticated beast is the primi-tive subsidiary. Quilp actively defies this hierarchy in his effort to become animal, but he misunderstands the terms of the very process of becoming animal he puts into motion. Rather than miring himself between these strongly delineated spe-cies categories—man and beast—in an effort to become the complex, undefined, and multiplied subject that a becoming-animal truly entails, he retains his identity as a singularity by merely swapping one identity for another (Bruns 703–04). Indeed, Quilp trades his position as a human male in an ideal domestic state in order to subsume, rather than cohabit with, the alternative identity of the wharf dogs who actively combat domestication and members of the domestic space, such as the killed child and bitten woman. Quilp's desire to inhabit a singular animal identity at the cost of abandoning an ideally multiple position could, in part, be due to the fact that Quilp faces special challenges in regards to attaining an identity as a fully humanized male figure because of his animalizing physical features. What Quilp yearns for is the reinstatement of an *animal remainder*[15] that he hopes will constitute for him a new, more palatable, animal identity that he imagines as having a greater reciprocity with his own physiology and psychology than a human one. Rather than desiring either to progress normatively forward toward fully actualized humanity or to fully follow through on the destabilizing and "anarch[ical]" process of becoming-animal, Quilp merely fixates on a new singular identity, undomestic dog, which he hopes will fully transcend and overwrite a human identity he has never seen himself as fit or desirous to own. Quilp stages this violent dismissal of one identity and its replacement by another by way of decentering domestic values through his interactions with the dog he nearly drives mad, his valorization of the child-killing undomesticated wharf dog, and violent interactions with his own wife. But, ultimately, the solidification of Quilp's desire to become-undomesticated animal comes when he finally abandons domesticity altogether.

Quilp is not interested in middle-class domesticity or its requirements, nor is he particularly interested in being domesticated through the influence of his loving and patient wife or through the animals he encounters in the text who demonstrate to him the unhappy fruits of his particular breed of (un)domestication. While in *Oliver Twist*, Sikes resorts to violence due to a mistaken, lower-class belief that it will allow him to create and sustain domestic relations, Quilp's violent, masculine orientation to the domestic demonstrates an added layer of dysfunction as it is meant to achieve a complete dissolution of his marriage and the surprisingly ideal domestic space his wife has created for him. Quilp repeatedly imagines escaping from idealized middle-class domesticity and his domestic responsibilities as a male, either by fantasizing about his wife's death, or by fantasizing about reverting to a "Robinson Crusoe" state of isolation and bachelorhood at the wharf among the undomesticated wharf dogs (373; 375; ch. 50). Quilp makes this latter fantasy a reality toward the close of the novel when he is overcome with a "mad ... rage" similar to the madness he earlier causes in the chained dog, demanding in the wake of this diseased feeling of madness that his wife "'ask no questions about me, make no search for me, say nothing concerning me. I'll not be dead, mistress, and that'll comfort you'" (507; ch. 67). Failing to domesticate himself and his masculine orientation to the middle-class domestic space, Quilp abolishes his domestic ties in an effort to finally consolidate his identity with the wharf dogs' in the mistaken belief that to surrender his human identity in order to assume an animal one will be a productive rather than destructive act.

Similar to Bull's-eye, whose physical animality becomes subsumed within the identity of Nancy, Quilp exploits the latent animality written on to his physiognomy in an effort to actually become-animal. Quilp, however, can only assume an uneasy hybridized identity rather than accomplish becoming a full-fledged animal precisely because in his attempt to animalize himself he continues to privilege the human subject—a human subject which finds its origins in a hubristic human fantasy in which the human is *imagined* as having complete access to, and mastery over, the particular mode of being-in-the-world embodied by specific nonhuman animals. In relying on this fantasy of an all-knowing human subject, Quilp fails to understand the distinct identities of the *actual animals* in question, instead only having access to animals as he imagines them to be from his particular human perspective.[16] In so doing, Quilp is guilty of an act of symbolic sacrifice, a sacrifice entailing the failure to pay attention and respect to cross-species similarity *and difference*.[17] In mistakenly assuming that he has a full understanding of, and consequently the ability to subsume the identities of, the undomesticated dogs, Quilp fails to recognize his own resistantly domestic *human* identity as distinct enough from the dogs' *animal* ones to put in motion the necessary process of dynamic cross-species domestication, a failure which ultimately contributes to his demise. Quilp's steady belief in singularity and his concomitant belief that he can trade in one identity and merely replace it with a different animal one, demonstrates that he cannot fully understand the unique mode of being-in-the-world of these animals, nor understand fully his own subjective position. Consequently, Quilp encroaches upon the dogs' territory as animals within the tripartite domestic arrangement to such an extent that he both forecloses their ability to perform reverse domestication on him and permanently forecloses his own access to an identity as human male.

Quilp's failure to respect and understand the autonomy and difference of the animals he encounters makes him blind to his "proper" function as a domestic and a domesticator, since he fails to attend to the dogs as they mirror back to him his own violence and dysfunction and offer him a cautionary glimpse of the danger that arises outside of the domestic space and, in particular, the danger posed by the non-domestic animals he is so desperately trying to become. Despite the assurances Quilp offers his wife that he will "not be dead," his efforts to become-animal at the cost of abandoning an ideal domestic arrangement and potential identification as a representative of middle-class masculinity cause him to share in Sikes's fate: violent and premature death (507).

The undomesticated dogs that Quilp incompletely models himself on become, like Bull's-eye, agents in his death, emerging as sirens who call to him in a language he cannot, finally, truly understand or use as a guide for his own behavior, precisely because he is not really one of them: "He stood listening intently ... Nothing was to be heard in that deserted place, but at intervals the distant barking of dogs. The sound was far away—now in one quarter, now answered in another—nor was it any guide" (509). As Quilp stumbles across the wharf, the unintelligibility of the dogs' barks makes it impossible for him to reorient himself to his makeshift domestic space, for he is excluded from communication with the dogs as they call out to, and answer, one another in a language he has only imagined himself as fluent in:[18]

[H]e staggered and fell; and next moment was fighting with the cold, dark water ... he could hear the knocking at the gate again—could hear a shout that followed it—could recognize the voice ... [he knew] they were close at hand, but could not make an effort to save him; that he himself had shut and barred them out. He answered the shout—with a yell ... It was of no avail. (509; ch. 67)

It is only in the moments he spends submerged in water and on the verge of drowning that Quilp appears to comprehend his folly in abandoning ideal domesticity and a functional *human* position within it and, concomitantly, the undesirability of attempting to reconstitute oneself according to the terms defining another's singularity.

While the barking of the dogs cannot "guide" Quilp to safety, he realizes that the sound of the human hand, knocking against the gate of his alternative domestic space at the wharf, could have. Moreover, unlike the voices of the dogs which Quilp can neither decipher nor respond to, he "c[an] recognize the voice" of the human male calling for him and can respond to it. Even as Quilp calls out to the man for help, however, he realizes that he cannot be saved. Quilp's recourse to an inarticulate "yell" that falls somewhere between the barking of the dogs and the language constructions of man signals his occupation of a subjective state so mired in an already doomed process of radical species-identity transformation that he can never be fully recovered either as a singular human identity or a multiplied human-animal one. In his inattention to and disrespect for difference, Quilp has effectively "shut and barred ... out" this man, all men, even his own identity as a human male in a failed attempt to construct for himself a subjectivity contiguous with that of the undomesticated animal (509). The resounding knocks on Quilp's alternative domestic space at the wharf revivify his discarded identity as a domesticated human male and open up the possibility for the constitution of a multiplied identity, but only fleetingly, as the act of calling out to another human being "seemed to make the hundred fires that danced before his eyes tremble and flicker as if a gust of wind had stirred them" (509). This is the final resurgence of Quilp's human identity before he surrenders to the death he has chosen for himself: that of a man who cannot speak or bear witness to either of the species communities his identity is naturally (human) or artificially (canine) carved from (509; ch. 67).[19]

The dysfunctional male Barnaby, of *Barnaby Rudge,* not only replicates the process of becoming-animal showcased by Quilp but, in the process, demonstrates an extra layer of dysfunction. Unlike Quilp who is content to encroach only upon the identity of the animal, or Sikes, who retains his masculine identity while consolidating Nancy and Bull's-eye, Barnaby reimagines the gender- and species-heterogeneity of the ideal domestic triad as a mono-species *and* mono-gender triadic assemblage in which human males subsume the individuated subjectivities of domestic animals *and* women. Identified, much like Quilp, as occupying a subjective position that is fraught with death or the threat of death, Barnaby falls largely outside of the normal parameters of humanity and domestication. Although his "features [are] good," he is described as "terrible" in the text due to his "absence of soul," a lack which not only denotes his perceived subhuman status, but even a subanimal one (35; ch. 3). Lacking the "noblest powers" of the human soul, Barnaby is viewed by functional males in the text as simultaneously akin to nonhuman animals who are poor in soul, and to the soulless dead (35).[20] Barnaby's deathli-

ness is not occasioned by any desire on his part to actively spurn a soulful identity
as human male in an effort to become-animal, as Quilp does. Instead, Barnaby's
soullessness and questionable status as human or man, living or dead, is a product
of his innate, biological "idio[cy]" that makes him incapable of understanding and
embodying domesticated humanity (390). Barnaby, who "wander[s] abroad from
dawn of day ... into night" with the only companions that can keep up with him, "a
score of vagabond dogs," inhabits a space and participates in a set of relations outside of ideal, middle-class domesticity (371). Only his mother's tales, which "she
would repeat, as a lure to keep him in her sight ... within doors," are capable of
temporarily holding him to the domestic as he flits between two subjective states
that are not naturally conducive to it: undomesticated animality and death (371).

Even though mentally limited, Barnaby recognizes at some level the way in
which he and other animalized men, such as the "centaur" figure Hugh, are separated from mankind and traditional domestic arrangements and collapsed with the
animal (622). When Mr. Chester gives Barnaby, whom he calls "'a strange creature'" (94), money for delivering a message for him, Barnaby excitedly exclaims:
"For Grip [the raven], and me, and Hugh to share among us ... Grip one, me two,
Hugh three; the dog, the goat, the cat—well, we shall spend it pretty soon'" (96).
Barnaby *appears* at a quick glance to vocalize two distinct triadic relationships
in this moment: first, an ideal interspecies one—Grip, me, and Hugh—that seemingly replicates the triadic cross-species structure of ideal domesticity and, second, an undesirably homogenized, interspecies (or interanimal) one—dog, goat,
and cat. However, if Barnaby's two triadic structures are viewed as two sides of
one algebraic equation, it becomes apparent that in Barnaby's symbolic imaginary, each side is numerically equivalent and, therefore, the sum and parts of both
sides are identical. The sum of Barnaby's equation is, in fact, "we," the word he
uses to effect a violent consolidation of the two triads into one, such that the dog,
goat, and cat become un-individuated from the individuals who precede them (96;
ch. 10). If in Barnaby's algebraic formula Grip, the triad's figurehead, is equivalent to the preeminent domestic animal, the dog, then his two other animalized,
human male constituents make up the remaining two positions. Hugh, whom John
Willet describes as having all of his human faculties save for imagination and an
uncommonly "small" bit of soul (111), maps readily on to the lesser domestic,
the cat, while Barnaby, as the most animalized figure in the triad because of his
idiocy and soullessness, can undoubtedly be mapped on to the figure of the goat,
a "dumb" beast that, unlike the dog and cat, lives on the border of the domestic
space rather than being a functional member in it.

Barnaby's domestic equation is dysfunctional, then, because it is doubly
homogenous: structured initially by the gender homogeny of the triad he com-
pletes with Grip and Hugh and the species homogeny of the goat, dog, and cat
triad, Barnaby produces a second layer of homogeny when he violently equates
the individuated species-identities of the dog, goat, and cat with those of human
males and Grip. Barnaby's triads, and his violent act of consolidating them under

the language of "we," marks a return to a more traditional, linear power dynamics of domestication that excludes the sharing of power across gender and species boundaries, precisely because those boundaries are continuously encroached upon by an exclusively male group which excludes one set of domestic others—women—while usurping the identities of another—the animal. Reverse domestication of the male by animals and women is impossible in Barnaby's domestic imaginary because representative individuals from those groups are either not included in the triad at all, or they have been symbolically consolidated with the males to such an extent that they occupy all three places in the triad: Barnaby's relational structure is a purely masculinized one and a purely animalized one.

Barnaby's homogenous triadic relational structure pervades the novel and contributes directly to the destruction of its functional domestic spaces, as well as to the imprisonment and deaths of it dysfunctional male practitioners. Framing the action of the novel are the Gordon Riots of 1780, spurred on by the anti-Popery rhetoric of Lord George Gordon. Ironically, the creaturely and primitive mob that mobilizes to oppose Catholic emancipation in England, destroying functional Catholic homes in the process, are unaware that they have much in common, structurally, with a processional model of the Trinity associated with some forms of Catholicism. Although the Trinity, composed of the Father, Son, and Holy Spirit, is described as having an ostensibly male,[21] three-person, one-substance structure across Christian traditions, some Catholic interpretations of the Trinity imbue the Father with an exalted position as the originator of its other two members. Replicating the power structure embodied in this model of the Trinity, the men who participate in the Gordon Riots mobilize around an all-male triad composed of Hugh, Barnaby, and Dennis, with Barnaby singled out as occupying a position of symbolic, if not actual, power for the rioters. As in Barnaby's imagined triad with Hugh and Grip in which power flows unilaterally from the male animal, Grip, to animalized men in an inversion of the "divinely ordained" Victorian species hierarchy, the mob reinscribes what Mary Daly has characterized as the "patriarchal patterning" of power relations implicit in the "paradigm of the trinity" (Ritvo 14–15; Daly 38). Through their replication of a processional structure, the mob consolidates symbolic power in one animalized male individual, Barnaby, whose position of power within the processional schema makes him a figure beyond the reach of other forces of domestication, such as women and actual animals.

As the symbolic representative of the anti-Popery movement, the undomesticated Barnaby and his homogenous triad structure emerge as the model on which the mob of men come to constitute a new set of relations that are antithetical to the normative middle-class domestic space. Because predicated upon a unilateral movement of power achieved through gender and species homogeny, the alternative relations born out of Barnaby as Trinitarian figurehead demand not only that rioting men become-animal, but that they reformulate the normative heterosexual desire of ideal middle-class domesticity into the homosocial desire implicit in the Trinity, which,

Daly notes, idealizes "male monogender mating" in the service of realizing "the perfect all-male marriage, the ideal all-male family" inscribed by patriarchy (Daly 38). Just as the all-male Trinity demands a male, rather than female, practitioner as its "proper" desiring subject, the animalized mob of men participating in the riots must sublimate traditional heterosexual desire into a desire for other animalized men. The men of the mob renounce fully humanized identities and heterosexual desire—"'You an't in love I hope, brother? That an't the sort of thing for us, you know'" (405)—and, instead, reconstitute love in the form of a homosocial brother-hood focalized through the animalized male triad composed of Barnaby, Hugh, and Dennis the hangman—the mob's unholy Trinity.

In the wake of Lord Gordon's inflammatory rhetoric, the homosocially oriented mob of men combine to actively destroy the material marker of functional gender and species heterogeneity—the domestic space—in the service of consolidating an "all-male family" born outside the parameters of domesticity (*Barnaby Rudge* 465; ch. 55, 462; ch. 55, Daly 38):

> The besiegers being now in complete possession of the house, spread themselves over it from garret to cellar, and plied their demon labours fiercely. While some smaller parties kindled bonfires underneath the windows, others broke up the furniture and cast the fragments down to feed the flames below ... they hurled out tables, chests of drawers, beds, mirrors, pictures, and flung them whole into the fire; while every fresh addition to the blazing masses was received with shouts, and howls, and yells. (460; ch. 55)

By reducing functional homes to "heaps of ruins" and murdering domestic animal companions such as the caged canaries that they "cast into the fire alive," Dennis and the other mobbing males attempt to expose gender and species heterogeneity as the middle-class domestic space's point of weakness and offer their homoso-cial and animalized arrangement as the better alternative (461; ch. 55; 552; ch. 66). Unlike even a lesser functional domestic male, Mr. Haredale, who mourns the loss of his home, the surging mass of men who "danc[e] and trampl[e]" on beds of flowers, while yelling and howling as the domestic space and its animal constituents burn, foreclose the possibility for normative domesticity by replacing and then eradicating actual animals but, also, by excluding women. The mob's policy of exclusion is reinforced, in part, by the act of destroying the very domes-tic spaces that would provide women the opportunity for forging companionate relationships with males: as Dennis says, love and marriage "'tan't the sort of thing for'" them (405; ch. 49). Even when female figures, such as Dolly Varden and Emma Haredale, are introduced into the body of mobbing men for the purpose of completing heterosexual couplings through (forced) marriage, the men regress from the domestic ideal of heterosexual desire into a desire to reinstate homoso-ciality through gender-bending. The men, in fact, move from desiring the women in marriage to desiring *to be them*: "Who could look on and see her [Dolly's] lavish caresses and endearments, and not desire to be in Emma Haredale's place; to be either her or Dolly; either the hugging or the hugged? Not Hugh. Not Dennis" (495; ch. 59). However, just as in the Trinity where the Holy Spirit is coded as "He" but also as "feminine," in this moment of potential gender-bending, Hugh and Dennis implicitly subsume the feminine into an otherwise monogender male structure, just as they have earlier subsumed animality only to burn up and disenfranchise actual animals (Daly 38). As Daly notes, "male made-up femininity has nothing to do with women" as they actually are; the all-male Trinitarian model seeks to include women only by interpreting them through, and subsuming them in, the male—whether that male be the "He" of the Holy Spirit or Dennis and Hugh (Daly 38).

By identifying as and desiring to be women and animals, men such as Barnaby, Hugh, and Dennis enact a *doubly* promiscuous and violent consolidation of identities that effectively dismantles any potentiality for a "properly" heterogeneous and heterosexual domestic triad involving the exercise of reverse domestication by animal *and* women companions. Grip, who perhaps understands the way in which he has been disenfranchised by the mob's Trinitarian brotherhood of animalized men, becomes an informant rather than a domesticator as he works secretly to uncover the brotherhood's theft of the domestic space's riches—"Golden cups, spoons, candle-sticks, coined guineas—all the riches were revealed"—as if, in the process, attempting to recover his own treasured status as a domestic animal (478; ch. 57). Grip, in this moment of revelation, exposes the fact that the ideal middle-class domestic space offers domesticated males a life of material comfort, while simultaneously demonstrating how the alternative masculinity assumed by the homosocial and animalized brotherhood of rioters offers no material, no comfort, and no chance at freedom and continued life. As if in confirmation of Barnaby's status as soulless and deathly, the unholy Trinity of men who take Barnaby as their processional Trinitarian figurehead have, as Dennis explains, "'got into bad company'" and reap the consequences—imprisonment and death by hanging—of sharing in Barnaby's dysfunctional masculinity and the criminal homogenization of the human and animal, male and female, constituents of ideal middle-class domesticity (619; ch. 74). Only Barnaby, the figurehead, is spared a deadly fate, his madness allowing him to be rehabilitated and reincorporated into the domestic by his mother, who perhaps continues only to have a tenuous hold on him, much like that occasioned by the tales she previously told him to keep him "within doors" (371; ch. 45).

In Dickens's later novel, *David Copperfield*, the class, gender, and species dynamics of masculinity and the domestic space operate in a way distinct from the lower-class and dysfunctionally animalized masculinities evidenced in *Oliver Twist*, *The Old Curiosity Shop*, and *Barnaby Rudge*. This is most notably the case, not only because the male protagonist, David, undergoes a series of class transitions—moving from middle-class boy, to working-class orphan, before finally returning to his middle-class origins as an adult—but because he makes a transition from dysfunctional domestic male to functional male within the scope of the bildungsroman narrative through domestication by the dog, Jip. David prefigures his initially dysfunctional relationship to Jip in his descriptions of his childhood domestic space. David's childhood home is oddly emptied of its animal constituents, characterized by "a pigeon-house ... without any pigeons," and a "great dog-kennel ... without any dog," while also missing the rooks that lend the home its name: The Rookery (25; ch. 2). David's youthful domestic situation is one pregnant with absence: absent a domesticating male, due to his father's death, and various domestic animals, David grows and develops without "proper" masculinity and cross-species domestication modeled for him. Moreover, even when these roles in the domestic triad are filled by a stepfather, Mr. Murdstone, and a dog, the newly introduced masculine and animal triad members embody dysfunction. The dog which fills the "empty dog-kennel" is "a great dog—deep mouthed and black-haired," which "sprung out to get at David," signaling the failure of David's step-father, Mr. Murdstone, to successfully domesticate the dog and, consequently, the foreclosure of reverse domestication for Murdstone himself and the promise of dysfunctional domesticity for David and his mother.

Murdstone, demonstrating a similarity to Sikes, Quilp, and other dysfunctional men in Dickens's works, resorts to violence not only in his interactions with "obstinate horse[s] or dog[s]" but preeminent human domestics such as spouses and children, viewing David as a "creature" whom he will "conquer" and control by making him "wince and smart" with beating (57). Sent to school for biting Murdstone, David's creaturely-ness is concretized through his consolidation with the abused domestic dog of his childhood, for he must wear a sign around his neck that proclaims him to be nothing more than a bad dog: "*Take care of him. He bites*" (90; ch. 5). Admitting that, "I positively began to have a dread of myself, as a kind of wild boy who did bite," David's interaction with a dysfunctional mas-culine type, Murdstone, leads to confusion about his own identity as human male as he wonders if, instead, he might really be a "wild boy" or a dog (90; ch. 5). It is this very confusion that causes David to fail to relate to nonhuman animals, such as Jip, in a way productive of middle-class domesticity because he is unable, initially, to understand the domesticating influence that Jip, Dora's lap dog, offers to him as he begins his courtship of Dora. Conditioned from youth to expect that animals will either be absent or violent toward him, and to think that he is one of them, David reads Jip's antagonism as typical rather than instructional, and undergoes confusion about the distinctly speciated but co-shaping roles he and Jip are meant to perform for one another. David's various layers of confusion ultimately cause him to commit to a failed first marriage with Dora before consti-tuting an ideal domesticity with Agnes.

Jip proclaims David an unfit suitor for Dora when he responds to David's first indications of love for Dora by "show[ing] his whole set of teeth" and "snarl[ing]!" in order to ward off the "least familiarity" (401; ch. 26). Jip, as Dora's lifelong companion, has insight into her character, capacities, and needs that David does not and that David ignores Jip's attempts at masculine domestication cause the dog to find the marriage, as well as the wedding cake, "disagreeable" (639; ch. 43). In fact, many of the trials and tribulations that the couple encounters once married are issues that Jip identifies as problematic during their courtship. When Jip "stands upon" the cookbook that David buys for Dora prior to their marriage, Jip is actively communicating to David that Dora will never use the book, and that she will never be capable of making David the "nice Irish stew" his future self might desire from her (612; ch. 41). Moreover, that the pencil case David buys in the hopes of teaching Dora "accounts" and housekeeping is made by Jip into a chew toy rather than used by Dora as a practical instrument of homemaking signals that Dora will never know how to buy David's hypothetical "shoulder of mutton for dinner" from a butcher's shop without getting cheated or going over the household budget (611–12). In such moments of seeming un-domestication and bad behavior Jip performs something akin to what Susan McHugh has described as "intelligent disobedience" in seeing-eye dogs that "refuse[] (no matter what the consequences) to bring the guided person into danger" (McHugh 53). David is, indeed, much like a blind man and Jip much like his seeing-eye dog when it comes to domestic matters, but David continually violates the cross-species power dynamics of this relationship in failing to recognize when to surrender himself to the dog's "leadership" (McHugh 53). David is too "undisciplined" to recognize Jip as an empowered agent capable of intelligent disobedience and capable, also, of fulfilling the role of a guide to domestic happiness, leaving David to enmesh himself blindly within a domestic relationship with Dora that ultimately proves dysfunctional (704; ch. 48).

In his marriage with Dora, David has "no partner" and must perform the "toils and cares" of a domestic arrangement that seems to accrete and expand its dysfunction as it attracts drunken and thieving servants, cheating shop keepers, and even criminals to its coal cellar (654; 646–47). Jip, who "positively refused to adapt himself to circumstances," and who is physically sickened by the "wedding cake" he eats, is distanced, even after marriage, from the couple and the dysfunctional domestic situation they've originated, refusing to be an active animal constituent of their domestic triad (610; 639). In fact, Jip's distance from the dysfunctional domesticity of David and Dora is reinforced by the couple through their very inability to perform the material duties of the household, as they buy an overly-large alternative domestic space for Jip, a "Chinese house … with little bells on top," in lieu of "a kitchen fender and meat-screen" meant to enhance the comfort and functionality of their own home (633; ch. 43). That Jip lives, to some extent, outside the bounds of the couple's domestic space leaves him open to facilitate a functional cross-species domestic triad between David and the female companion, Agnes, who is more fit to be the "comfortable" wife that David feels Dora is not (643; ch. 44). When Jip interacts with Agnes, he displays an affection and acceptance of her that he routinely denies to David, Aunt Betsey, and other visitors to the domestic space. Whereas David and Aunt Betsey meet with

Jip's antagonism for their shared history of poorly chosen spouses and domestic discord, Agnes has long been a fit homemaker, entrusted by her father with the housekeeping keys and the duties of the household for most of her life. Jip intuits, through "her manner of making acquaintance" with him, Agnes's capacity to play the role of functional female in a domestic triad and "respond[s] instantly" to her domestic ideality by receiving her into his good graces as the long-missing constituent of David's domestic triad (617). David's profound awareness of Jip's open approval and preconception of the ideal match he could make with Agnes allows Jip to play the role of animal domesticator in the couple's triad, even though his death and Dora's precede the couple's union. Jip's efforts at domesticating David—sitting atop the cookbook and chewing pencil cases—become retroactively effective as David begins to understand what Jip has, from the start, been conditioning him to understand: "'There can be no disparity in marriage like unsuitability of mind and purpose'" (671).

In much the same way that David must have his masculinity domesticated and, in some sense, rehabilitated by Jip before being capable of forging an ideal domesticity with Agnes, in the earlier novel *The Old Curiosity Shop*, Dickens pits the young, lower-class male Kit against a pony with a penchant for misbehaving to create a scenario in which a nonviolent, nonbestial masculinity is deployed effectively to achieve not only the domestication of a truly hard-to-manage animal, but normative middle-class domesticity forged through reciprocal, cross-species domestication.[22] Kit is regularly described in the text as a source of domestic order, sustainability, and creation. He assumes masculine control and surveillance over little Nell's domestic space when her grandfather abandons her in the evenings to gamble, and when Quilp seizes the home that little Nell shares with her grandfather, Kit offers his own "'poor one'" to them as a return to normal domestic life sans Quilp (87; ch. 10; 96; ch. 11). Although Kit is never able to see his offer realized in the way of introducing Nell and her grandfather into the home he shares with his mother and siblings, one can imagine that if Nell had in fact come to live with Kit that the outcome might have been a functional domestic triad, most notably because Kit partially fulfills his promise of a home to Nell by taking in her bird, which Nell is sure will "by some means fall into the hands of Kit who would keep it for her sake" (101; ch. 12). Just as Dickens makes the link between ideal domesticity and animal relations clear by describing the veritable animal menagerie that defines his home in the letter to F. W. Powell, Kit's functional masculinity and potential for creating an ideal, middle-class domestic space is predicated upon the relationships he forges with domestic animals like Nell's bird and Whiskers, the goodnatured but rather headstrong and independent pony owned by the Garland family (*Letters*).

The Garland household is largely ideal in that Mr. and Mrs. Garland, and Abel seem to constitute a loving, charitable, felicitous, and surprisingly functional family unit. However, their domesticity is constantly disrupted by the family pony, Whiskers, who seems more often than not to invert traditional power relations by "'mak[ing] the family go where he will'" in much the same way that the raven Grip exerts a hierarchy-inverting mastery over Barnaby and his movements in *Barnaby Rudge* (61; ch. 6). Upon Kit's introduction into the family as the Garlands' servant, it is notable that the disorder caused by Whiskers is significantly reduced, not through Kit's application of violence or other forms of antagonism and abuse, but by his ability to forge a relationship of respect and mutual dependence with the pony, while other characters, such as the Garlands and the insidious Mr. Chuckster, fail to do so. While the Garlands, who chase after Whiskers as he "dodged the family round a small paddock in the rear, for one hour and three-quarters," fail to exert mastery over and even seem to surrender domestic mastery to the pony, Mr. Chuckster threatens to "'break'" Whiskers and seeks recourse in the Victorian species hierarchy and the linear exchange of domesticating power written into that hierarchy as he wishes to "asser[t] the supremacy of man over the inferior animals" (174; ch. 22; 289; ch. 38). By contrast, Kit treats Whiskers as though he were a true "'Christian,'" a relationship of mutual respect and shared moral obligation that not only allows Kit to domesticate and shape the pony to his will or, rather, that of the Garland family, but allows for Whiskers ultimately to facilitate Kit's transition into heterosexual marriage and normative domesticity (427; ch. 57). Whiskers, who has "such a remarkable partiality for" Kit, and who, "from being the most obstinate and opinionated pony on the face of the earth" went to being "the meekest and most tractable of animals," fosters the burgeoning heterosexual relations and ultimately ideal domesticity of Kit and Barbara (288; ch. 38).

Toward the close of the novel, Dickens inserts Barbara into the Whiskers-Kit dyad, creating a functional cross-species and cross-gender domestic triad in which none of the members—whether man, woman, or animal—is symbolically consolidated into the identity of any other member of the triad. Although Kit, Whiskers, and Barbara are autonomous and heterogeneous individuals, it is clear that all three individuals are necessary components in the formation of an ideal domestic state. Although cross-species and cross-gender dyadic relations between Kit and Whiskers, Kit and Barbara, and Barbara and Whiskers persist in the early parts of the novel, "proper" domesticity arises only when the individuals are unified into one heterogeneous triad upon Kit returning from jail after being (intentionally) wrongly accused of theft. That functional domesticity could not occur for Kit and Barbara in the absence of their third member, Whiskers, points to the significance of the pony within the domestic relations of the couple. In fact, it is the respectful bond that the human male and female form with the pony that ultimately brings them together, their union significantly staged not within an existent domestic space but in the peripheral space, the stable, of the domesticating animal:

> Kit takes the first opportunity of slipping away and hurrying to the stable ... and when Kit goes up to [the pony to] caress and pat him, the pony rubs his nose against his coat, and fondles him more lovingly than ever pony fondled man.... But how comes Barbara to trip in there?... How comes Barbara in the stable, of all places in the world? Why, since Kit has been away, the

pony would take his food from nobody but her.... It may be that Kit has caressed the pony enough; it may be that there are even better things to caress than ponies. He leaves him for Barbara.... Was it natural that at that instant, without any previous impulse or design, Kit should kiss Barbara? He did it, whether or no ... [and] the pony kicked up his heels and shook his head, as if he were suddenly taken with convulsions of delight. (515; ch. 68)

Although Laura Brown has argued that sexualized physical exchanges between humans and animals, such as Kit's "caress[es]," express an "immoderate love" that ultimately speaks to the animal's displacement of appropriate human rela-tions—whether familial or romantic—it is clear that Whiskers's relationship with Kit is formative of, rather than destructive to, Kit's burgeoning domestic relations with Barbara (Brown 37; *OCS* 515; ch. 68). Dickens effectively shows how Kit signals to Barbara his domesticated masculinity by transferring the companion-ate relational structure and physical intimacies he indulges with the pony—the "caress[es]" and "fondl[ings]"—to Barbara who signals her reciprocally ideal sta-tus as domestic partner through the functions she performs for the pony, which are transferrable to Kit and to the domestic space.

In fact, whereas in *David Copperfield* Jip demonstrates Dora's unsuitability for marriage by signaling, via the cookbook, that she is incapable of nourishing her domestic partner, Whiskers is able to endorse Barbara with "convulsions of delight" precisely because she proves equal to this task while Kit is away and unable to nourish Whiskers himself. Unlike Dora, who is "no partner" and forces her husband to per-form the "toils and cares" of the domestic by himself, Barbara demonstrates through the domestic function she performs for Whiskers—feeding him and otherwise caring for him—that she will make Kit a "comfortable" wife, much like Agnes is a "com-fortable" wife for David (654; ch. 44; 643; ch. 44). Both Kit and Barbara, then, ulti-mately must prove their domestic suitability for one another by first rehearsing their domestic potentials in their interactions with Whiskers, who acts less as an uncom-plicated symbolic double or replacement for Barbara than as a matchmaker whose approval the couple needs in order to move toward a happy domestic. Ultimately, the Kit-Whiskers-Barbara triad confirms that animal agents as reverse domesticators are imperative to the formation of the middle-class masculine and domestic values so integral to the domestic politics and ethics of Dickens's novel.

IV. Conclusion: Reverse Domestication and Dickens's Ethics of Cross-Species Representation

Dickens's ostensible goal in his early novels—parsing out a normative domestic-ity predicated on a middle-class masculine ideal—is achieved through a represen-tational multiplicity in which a host of competing classed masculinities emerge

as social constructions that find their origins in the cross-gender, but most importantly, the cross-species bonds men form within the realms of domestication and
domesticity. In this sense, it becomes clear that, for Dickens, "[h]uman nature is
an interspecies relationship" and that animals are meaningful as representational
subjects in literature apart from their traditional function as symbolic representatives of marginalized human populations (Haraway 218). In so representing the
animal, Dickens marks the animal as an ethical subject in a way that is drastically
divergent from the predominant stance on animal rights in the Victorian period:
namely, that animals must be protected because violence against animals is a
stepping stone to violence against other humans (Ritvo 131). According to this
humanist ethics, of course, the latter violence against the human is the real ethical
dilemma, and the violated human the true ethical subject. Dickens, in resisting
the ubiquitous literary practice of promiscuously collapsing human and animal
identities, also resists this flawed ethical system. The period's prevalent animal
rights discourse, in seeking to determine the ethical weight of the animal in direct
proportion to its ability to prefigure or correspond to ethical infractions against
human individuals, operates in much the same vein as the symbolic erasure of the
animal and its agency in period literature, which formal practice is carried out in
the service of privileging the representational value of *human* over animal subjectivity. Dickens, in order to escape these mutually reinforcing systems of animal
erasure and human exceptionality, consequently radicalizes his representational
practices in order to actively rewrite this logic, ultimately recognizing animals in
his novels as powerful partners within a domestic triad characterized by relations
of cross-species companionship and co-constitution.

In so doing, Dickens imagines a set of relations in which animals are placed
alongside humans as significant subjects of moral and political power, as well
as ethical consideration. Dickens achieves a radical ethics by imagining animal
agency in the domestic as a marker of normative middle-class homes and men, but
also as constitutive of what McHugh has described in twentieth-century literature
as a "relational ethics" in which assemblages of humans and nonhumans work
together to produce a phenomenon greater than the "sum of [their] individual
efforts" (5). In this way, Dickens asks readers to think of a new representational
and cultural ethics in which the animal is not only an entity empowered enough to
facilitate its own and humans' needs and desires—however much these needs and
desires might look suspiciously heteronormative and middle-class in Dickens's
rendering of them—but in which the animal and human must combine in order
to achieve a more ethical outcome that would not be possible in the absence of
such cross-species cooperation. This is precisely because, as empowered agents
who resist the "substitutive logic of" symbolic erasure, animals in Dickens's texts
are able to challenge the notion of the human as a privileged site of "singularity" within the nation's ethical system and a tradition of literary representation
that both take the human as, finally, the only "proper" subject of consideration
(McHugh 8). To these ends, it seems no coincidence that it is men over whom

the animals in *Oliver Twist*, *The Old Curiosity Shop*, *Barnaby Rudge*, and *David Copperfield* must exercise their power of reverse domestication, not only to establish normative class, gender, and political values but, in order to gain status as ethical subjects themselves. Dickens, through animals endowed with the power of reverse domestication, challenges the role of Victorian men as the ultimate or "singular" subjects of ethical consideration as well as the ultimate engineers, via judicial enforcement and parliamentary legislation, of the nation's ethical investments. Instead, he ultimately envisions the goal of establishing a more ethical balance within the domestic and without as dependent upon the joining of powerful nonhuman animal and male agents who, in coming together and domesticating each other, constitute new communities and new, more functional, ways of being in the world.

NOTES

1. Moore 78; ch. 19.
2. As Robert Patten notes, that "Clara isn't mistress of her home, Dora can't keep house, Peggotty can't keep her buttons on, Traddles has a harem, and Agnes points to heaven, not the kitchen or the bedroom" signals *David Copperfield* as the terminating point for Dickens's preoccupation with representing domestic normativity (Patten, personal communication). *David Copperfield* marks a transitional moment for Dickens as he discovers that normative domesticity "isn't working" in his early novels and, consequently, goes on in his later career to problematize and reformulate the domestic, ultimately renegotiating the representational possibilities of the animals and cross-species relations he places at the forefront of a domestic situation no longer structured around normativity.
3. Although the practice of reading animals in Dickens's texts as metaphorical stand-ins for marginal human populations is ubiquitous in Dickens scholarship—see, for example, Kreilkamp and Moore—there are of course notable exceptions, such as publications by scholars like Natalie McKnight and A. J. Larner, as well as the earlier book by George Moore, *Avowals*, which records a conversation between Moore and Edmund Gosse on literature and criticism.
4. My argument is not that their gender or species empowers them, but rather, irrespective of their gender or species and irrespective of Victorian cultural norms, members of various gender and species groups become empowered through reverse domestication.
5. According to Hammerton, middle- and upper-class domestic abuse received little to no visibility in the service of protecting an idealized middle-class value system in which instances of male violence against women existed only as "embarrassing aberrations" (274). Animal abuse was similarly coded as a lower-class phenomenon. William Gull, for example, proclaimed that animal cruelty laws were "for the ignorant, and not for the best people," while a textbook produced by the RSPCA in 1885 was designed to

"include kindness to animals in 'the system of education among the poorer classes,'" which happened to be the class most often recorded as offenders in RSPCA reports (Harrison 791, 810).

6. Peter Singer argues that humans and nonhumans are equally deserving of protection from physical and psychological pain due to their shared capacity for suffering, while Cary Wolfe, in *Animal Rights*, draws on Jean-Francois Lyotard's *The Differend* to suggest that because animals are incapable of "bearing witness," the animal represents a "paradigm of the victim" on to which other silenced groups can be mapped (and vice versa)—in this case, women (61–62).

7. My definition of the domestic triad is distinct from the "triangular relationship" in *Oliver Twist*, discussed in Grace Moore's article. Moore interprets the animal figure, in this case Bull's-eye, as carrying the representational weight of both the male and female domestic partners—Nancy and Bill Sikes. Rather than the human or animal characters having distinct, autonomous identities all human figures are triangulated through the symbolic animal such that none of the figures—human or animal—is ever free from symbolic collapse. I am arguing beyond this triangulation of human identity through a symbolic nonhuman animal to suggest that the animal itself forms one unit in a triadic relationship of which it is a necessary, autonomous, and non-symbolic component.

8. In evaluating the animal as such, Kreilkamp is drawing on Alex Woloch's character schema in which minor characters are analogous to *"the proletariat of the novel."* Kreilkamp suggests that because animals are representationally subordinate even to minor characters, that they are the "sub-proletariat" or, as I rephrase it for clarity, "subminor." He confirms the minor state of the animal by arguing that animals, especially domestics, are "represented, but only in passing," are given no "true markers of identity" and "posses[s] no solid claim to recognition or memory" (82).

9. Much scholarship on Victorian gender has focused on either homosocial masculinities or the "conflict *between* masculine and feminine"; I consider conflict *within* literary representations of masculinity by focusing on the "competition among" a multiplicity of socially constructed functional and dysfunctional masculine types (Sussman 367, 372). My treatment of domestic masculinities is in keeping with the historical work done by Martin Francis, James Hammerton, and John Tosh and suggests men were very significant in the domestic space and that scholars "might need to pay more attention than hitherto to the male presence" in the domestic (Francis 638–39).

10. Defined by Hammerton as "both partners ... work[ing] together in the interests of harmonious companionate marriage.... This [conception of domesticity] ... impose[d] a more direct responsibility on men for the success of the companionate partnership. It required a considerate husband who took an interest in and ... shared the domestic burdens of his wife.... The husband's primary concern remained the public sphere, but there was greater stress on his entry into domestic matters in a more supportive and intimate way.... The messages directed at men focused on the male virtues necessary for a harmonious marriage: on patience, tenderness, consideration, forbearance" (281).

11. See Moore.

12. Some may want to resist viewing the mob of men who pursue Sikes and witness his

death so benevolently, but that Mr. Brownlow, the good angel to Fagin's bad one, offers the men a reward of "fifty pounds" for taking Sikes *alive* makes him a participant in the proceedings and suggests a more positive reading of the mob by association. That he offers the men a reward as motivation to seek justice rather than the exercise of extra-legal revenge indicates that the mob is at least indirectly motivated to deliver Sikes up to a courtroom, judge, and proper justice (411; ch. 50).

13. Deleuze and Guattari describe becoming-animal as a state involving the "fascination" of the human by a "demonic" animal. The fascination with the demonic, wild, pack animal—the nondomestic—allows for a radical transformation of human subjectivity by moving beyond thinking of the animal only in terms of an Oedipal pet whose animal identity is overwritten entirely to reflect the human, human culture, and its desires. The goal of becoming-animal is not to lose one's identity as human in order to take over the identity of an Other defined species of animal but, instead, to embrace the anomic, or "the condition in which standards of definition and practice lose their application or are placed in suspension," or, in other words, to seek a situation in which one "avoid[s] all forms of incarceration" by moving from a state of unity, to a state of multiplicity and increased complexity (Bruns 706, 709, 704). Becoming-animal facilitates the human's occupation of a state of in-betweeness and non-identity, a state of a more ambiguous and multiple personhood (versus identity as human) to which the animal is always subject (Bruns 713–15).

14. See Walton or Festa, among others.

15. "Animal remainder" is the term I use elsewhere to describe the remnant of an animal biological heritage that cannot finally be purged, even though this is the ostensible goal of progressive theories of human evolution as manifested in species hierarchies.

16. In *The Beast and the Sovereign*, Derrida argues that Deleuze and Guattari's concept of becoming-animal must be critiqued because it is "always only about man, about the becoming-animal of man, the history and stories of man in his becomings-animals, in other words, of the becoming-anthropomorphically-animal of man, and not about the animal and the beast, as it were, themselves" (196). However, it is well to note that McHugh reinterprets stories of becoming-animal, insisting that they are "key points of ethical negotiation across artistic and scientific models of species and social life" (14).

17. As Derrida explains in "The Animal That Therefore I Am (More to Follow)" and elsewhere, we must respect similarities and differences across types of animals and among individual members of those types. To elide either the similarities or differences of particular nonhuman and human animals is to do a fundamental violence. This violence is akin to that which Derrida indentifies in the use of the term "'the Animal' in the singular" to erect a divide between humans and all other animals via a disingenuous erasure not only of the human's shared status as animal, but also of the differences among various types of nonhuman animals (400).

18. As Richard Nash has noted, "as we listen to dogs, we must know that we cannot hear as well" on account of linguistic and other species-based difference (93). And, as Cary Wolfe explains, the ability to listen to what nonhumans are really telling us necessitates that we "have our own modes of perception,... habits of knowledge,... [and] own

prerogatives of power, interrogated by taking seriously *the radical alterity of other*, nonhuman, ways of being in the world" ("Speciesism" 103, italics mine).

19. In this instance, Quilp is doubly incapable of speaking his imminent death because his status in the process of transitioning to a singular animal identity has closed him off from both available species communities that might have remained open to him if he had adopted a multiplied identity, such as Freud's Wolf Man, whom Deleuze and Guattari recuperate in *A Thousand Plateaus* by reading him as an ideally "multiplied and depersonalized subject," a "single assemblage" produced through "multiplicities of multiplicities," "packs," or "collective agents" (34–38).

20. In *Of Spirit: Heidegger and the Question*, Derrida elucidates (and ultimately critiques) Heidegger's philosophical work on the animal. As Derrida explains, for Heidegger the animal must occupy a status as "poor in world" due to the fact that animals are lacking the "spirit" or soulfulness which he associates directly with humanity and fully actualized being or living.

21. Women are excluded from the Trinity, according to Mary Daly, who argues that the "classic answer [to Christian women] has been: 'You're included under the Holy Spirit. He's feminine'" (38).

22. Horses were viewed by Victorians as one of the preeminent domesticates, but also one of the more wild, spirited, and hard-to-tame ones (Dorre 10–11, 26).

WORKS CITED

Brown, Laura. "The Lady, the Lapdog, and Literary Alterity." *Eighteenth Century* 52 (2011): 31–45.

Bruns, Gerald L. "Becoming Animal (Some Simple Ways)." *New Literary History* 38 (2007): 703–20.

Daly, Mary. *Gyn/ecology: The Metaethics of Radical Feminism*. Boston: Beacon, 1990.

Deleuze, Gilles, and Felix Guattari. *A Thousand Plateaus: Capitalism and Schizophrenia*. Minneapolis: U of Minnesota P, 1987.

Derrida, Jacques. "The Animal That Therefore I Am (More to Follow)." *Critical Inquiry* 28 (2002): 369–418.

———. *The Beast and the Sovereign*. Vol. 1. Trans. Geoffrey Bennington. Chicago: U Chicago P, 2009.

———. *Of Spirit: Heidegger and the Question*. Trans. Geoffrey Bennigton and Rachel Bowlby. Chicago: U of Chicago P, 1991.

Dickens, Charles. *Barnaby Rudge*. Ed. John Bowen. New York: Penguin, 2003.

———. *David Copperfield*. Ed. Jeremy Tambling. New York: Penguin, 2004.

———. Letter to F. W. Powell. 13 Mar. 1844. *The Letters of Charles Dickens: 1820–1870*. Ed. Madeline House, Graham Storey, and Kathleen Tillotson. Vol. 4. 1977. Electronic Edition.

———. *The Old Curiosity Shop*. Ed. Elizabeth M. Brennan. New York: Oxford UP, 1999.

————. *Oliver Twist*. Ed. Kathleen Tillotson. New York: Oxford UP, 2008.

————. "A Preliminary Word." *Household Words* 1.1 (30 Mar. 1850): 1–2.

————, ed. "A Parenthesis or Two." *All the Year Round* 45 (26 Jan. 1867): 106–08.

Dorre, Gina M. *Victorian Fiction and the Cult of the Horse*. Burlington, VT: Ashgate, 2006.

Festa, Lynn. "Person, Animal, Thing: The 1796 Dog Tax and the Right to Superfluous Things." *Eighteenth-Century Life* 33 (2009): 1–44.

Francis, Martin. "The Domestication of the Male? Recent Research on Nineteenth- and Twentieth-Century British Masculinity." *Historical Journal* 45 (2002): 637–52.

Hammerton, A. James. "Victorian Marriage and the Law of Matrimonial Cruelty." *Victorian Studies* 33 (1990): 269–92.

Haraway, Donna J. *When Species Meet*. Minneapolis: U of Minnesota P, 2008.

Harrison, Brian. "Animals and the State in Nineteenth-Century England." *The English Historical Review* 88.349 (1973): 786–820.

Kreilkamp, Ivan. "Dying Like a Dog in *Great Expectations*." *Victorian Animal Dreams: Representations of Animals in Victorian Literature and Culture*. Ed. Deborah Denenholz Morse and Martin A. Danahay. Burlington, VT: Ashgate, 2007. 81–94.

Larner, A. J. "Dickens and Monboddo." *The Dickensian* 100 (2004): 36–41.

McHugh, Susan. *Animal Stories: Narrating Across Species Lines*. Minneapolis: U of Minnesota P, 2011.

McKnight, Natalie. "Dickens and Darwin: A Rhetoric of Pets." *Dickens Quarterly* 102 (June 2006): 131–43.

Moore, George. *Avowals*. Edinburgh: Edinburgh UP, 2004 (1919).

Moore, Grace. "Beastly Criminals and Criminal Beasts: Stray Women and Stray Dogs in *Oliver Twist*." *Victorian Animal Dreams: Representations of Animals in Victorian Literature and Culture*. Ed. Deborah Denenholz Morse and Martin A. Danahay. Burlington, VT: Ashgate, 2007. 201–14.

Nash, Richard, et al. "Speciesism, Identity Politics, and Ecocriticism: A Conversation with Humanists and Posthumanists." *Eighteenth Century* 52.1 (2011): 87–106. DOI 10.1353/ecy.2011.0004.

Patten, Robert. Email to the author. 30 June 2011.

Ritvo, Harriet. *The Animal Estate: The English and Other Creatures in the Victorian Age*. Cambridge: Harvard UP, 1987.

Singer, Peter. "All Animals are Equal." *Animal Rights: A Historical Anthology*. Ed. Andrew Linzey and Paul Barry Clarke. New York: Columbia UP, 2004.

Surridge, Lisa. *Bleak Houses: Marital Violence in Victorian Fiction*. Athens: Ohio UP, 2005.

Sussman, Herbert. "The Study of Victorian Masculinities." *Victorian Literature and Culture* 20 (1992): 366–77.

Tosh, John. *A Man's Place: Masculinity and the Middle-Class Home in Victorian England*. New Haven: Yale UP, 1999.

Wahrman, Dror. "'Middle-Class' Domesticity Goes Public: Gender, Class, and Politics from Queen Caroline to Queen Victoria." *Journal of British Studies* 32 (1993): 396–432.

Walton, John K. "Mad Dogs and Englishmen: The Conflict over Rabies in Late Victorian England." *Journal of Social History* 13 (1979): 219–39.

Waters, Catherine. *Dickens and the Politics of Family.* New York: Cambridge UP, 1997.

———. "Gender, Family, and Domestic Ideology." *The Cambridge Companion to Charles Dickens.* Ed. John O. Jordan. New York: Cambridge UP, 2001. 120–35.

Wolfe, Cary. *Animal Rites.* Chicago: U of Chicago P, 2003.

———, et al. "Speciesism, Identity Politics, and Ecocriticism: A Conversation with Humanists and Posthumanists." *The Eighteenth Century* 52 (2011): 87–106. DOI 10.1353/ecy.2011.0004.

Not Too Cheery:
Dickens's Critique of Capital in
Nicholas Nickleby

Timothy Gilmore

As the power and avarice of those who seek to profit at the expense of society increases wildly with each passing year, it is important to look once more to Dickens, one of our most trenchant critics of the human cost of capitalist exploitation. Dickens's early novel Nicholas Nickleby *has been criticized repeatedly for being a melodramatic narrative without strong focus and purpose, but this article argues that such an assessment misses the deeper unity beneath the "muddle" of scenes that compose the novel. As a sustained critique of the capitalist mode of production and the reification intrinsic to the logic of commodification, the novel gains a structural integrity otherwise missing if we try to locate it in some other aspect of the narrative, such as its protagonist. The novel astutely investigates the ways that reification, by beguiling everything within a commodity calculus, affects the quality of social relations and restricts individuals' life potential. This essay posits that the novel is best understood as a kind of allegory of capital detailing the deleterious effects of reification upon social and personal life. Close attention to the novel's critique of capitalism reveals that there is no such thing as a good capitalist and usurious activity is the rule.*

Dickens Studies Annual, Volume 44, Copyright © 2013 by AMS Press, Inc. All rights reserved.   DOI 10.7756/dsa.044.005.85-109

A Question of Structure

Nicholas Nickleby presents itself as a novel with the loosest of structures. Held together by a series of episodes that seem to come one after the other more from authorial whim than narrative exigency, and following the "exploits" of a protagonist who has the consistency of pasteboard, the novel cannot be strictly classified as picaresque because, while it loosely accords with the genre's episodic lack of unity of action, its protagonist is not a rogue and, arguably, not even particularly likeable. Moreover, the novel may follow the progress of a young man seeking his fortune in the world, but his lack of depth and development as a character rules out categorizing the novel as a bildungsroman. The genre in which the novel fits best and which accounts for its episodic structure is that of melodrama. As a melodrama, the loose structure of the novel as a succession of scenes in which often overblown and contrived actions are performed by characters varying from very good to very bad, with none of the moral ambiguity of the excluded middle to be noted, may find an organizing principle. However, it is an organizing principle that does little organizing because melodrama is concerned more with the depiction of dramatic and passionate extremes in tableau-like scenes than with considerations of well-wrought story.

It would seem, then, that we must accept the fact, argued by such critics as Edgar Johnson and John Lucas, that *Nickleby* is a jumbled, patchy, quilt of scenes meant more to entertain its readership than to offer a sustained story that probes such things as the depths of character and society. Of course, the pressures of serial publication forced Dickens to write at a pace that would explain the novel's apparent failings, but as we know post post-structuralism, more speaks through the author than he or she knows in the process of composition. As Lacan would say, we know more than we know. If such is the case, can we not read the novel with different eyes—eyes that look not at the novel as a product of the author's intention but as a largely unconscious production of a particular conjuncture? Such a reading's gaze discovers a novel whose real protagonist is the capitalist mode of production and which, despite its lack of structure on the level of action, gains coherence on the level of allegory. Viewed from this perspective, the melodramatic character of the novel, with its monochromatic characters, seems to invite an allegorical reading.

My reading of the novel participates in a critical literature, including work by Steven Marcus, John Bowen, and Tatiana Holway, which seeks to redeem the novel from its estimation as an "incoherent muddle" (Lucas 55). In particular, my reading is in dialogue with the excellent critiques by Joseph Childers and Paul Jarvie of Dickens's often contradictory depictions of capital in the novel. For Childers, it is an issue of the Doux Commerce presented as an ideal in the novel and how the novel acts to undermine that ideal. Jarvie extends this critique, one centered on the problematic character of the Cheerybles and their philanthropic benevolence, to show how, despite his attempts, Dickens was unable to extricate his work from the logics of commodification and marketing that he was forced to employ in order to develop his critique of them. Jarvie reads this fissure at the heart of the novel as a sign of Dickens's own ambivalence about the logic of capital and his inability to find a viable solution from within its boundaries. Insightful as their readings may be, the problems that both Childers and Jarvie see at work in the novel are more adequately addressed when placed within the framework of the process of reification intrinsic to the commodity logic of capital, which organizes the material world of the novel and the interactions between its characters. The novel is best understood as a kind of allegory of capital detailing the deleterious effects of reification upon social and personal life.

An allegorical reading such as that proposed, therefore, offers an organizational principle for the novel that structures the narrative as a progressive depiction of the effects of the capitalist mode of production on human relations and possibilities. If we follow Nicholas through the novel, stopping along with him at particular important points in order to analyze their figural dimensions, a three-part structure can be determined for the novel: Part 1 involves Nicholas's encounter with the exploitative structure of capitalism at Squeers's school; part 2 concerns his move from the darkness of the school into the light of the theater as an alternative economic system; and the final part of the novel follows him through London and the working out of a viable mode of life within the system. The guiding theoretical concept of reification serves as a mediation between the figural and literal levels of the narrative facilitating the analysis and revealing a depth of complexity that will aid in rehabilitating the novel for critical appreciation. Our current economic woes resulting from the logic of reification driving finance capital make it all the more important that we attend to the critique of usurious capital Dickens offers us in *Nicholas Nickleby*.

Squeers's School of Scandal

Like a secular version of Spenser's Redcrosse Knight journeying forth into the world for the first time and destined to stray into the cave of Errour, Nicholas ventures forth full of idealized notions of what awaits him at Dotheboys hall; however, his romantic notions are quickly dispelled upon continued exposure to the master of the hall. We first meet Mr. Wackford Squeers as he waits in the hope of garnering more pupils for his school. Bemoaning the lack of business, he soliloquizes to himself: "At Midsummer ... I took down ten boys; ten twenty's— two hundred pound. I go back at eight o'clock tomorrow morning, and have only three—three oughts an ought—three twos six—sixty pound" (44; ch. 4). Aside from being evidence of Squeers's mathematical acuity, his mumbled complaint to himself reveals that for him the existence of his pupils (and the class of all potential pupils) is bound up with their status as a value of 20 pounds. This reduction of the pupil to a monetary value bound up in a system of exchange constitutes the process whereby the particularity of an object (in this case a human being) is obscured by its reduction to an abstract unit of exchange. Squeers's calculations are an example of the commodification of the human and reveal the source of his brutal treatment of his pupils.

In his analysis of the commodity form, Marx shows how the calculation of value based upon the abstract, socially necessary labor time involved in the production of any product reduces that product to the status of a commodity divested of any indication of the real labor involved in its production and of any use-value. The commodity exists as an abstract value to be exchanged and "the relationships between the producers, within which the social characteristics of their labors are manifested, take on the form of a social relation between the products of labour" (Marx, *Capital* 164). Marx's theory of commodity fetishism explains the way in which the reduction to an abstract value eliminates the content of the commodity and reduces it to an empty form. Peter Stallybrass explains this reduction well when he writes that, "The fetishism of the commodity inscribes *im*materiality as the defining feature of capitalism" (184). The commodity form reduces everything to immaterial value, including the workers who, by selling their labor-power as if it were an object in their possession, are placed on the market and commodified.

The theory of reification, as developed by Georg Lukács, takes up Marx's analysis of the fetishism of commodities and generalizes it into a theory of the commodity structure of capitalist society. As Lukács states:

> The divorce of the phenomena of reification from their economic bases and from the vantage point from which alone they can be understood, is facilitated by the fact that the [capitalist] process of transformation must embrace every manifestation of the life of society if the preconditions for the complete self-realisation of capitalist production are to be fulfilled. (95)

The mystification that the commodity produces extends beyond the sphere of commodity exchange as a strictly economic activity into all aspects of capitalist society, and, in fact, "It stamps its imprint upon the whole consciousness of man" (Lukács 100). If Lukács is correct, and the reign of the commodity form is total in capitalist society, then the effects of reification extend through all human social relations and can be discovered at work within them. What allows Squeers, then, to reduce his pupils to the status of things bearing a value of twenty pounds is the pervasive logic of the commodity, which states that even human beings can be treated as things bearing a value; he may do this in good conscience because the very forms of consciousness within which he lives promote the activities of assessing, valuing, and reducing to immateriality. Even the dominant ethical theory of the period, Utilitarianism, which Dickens so trenchantly was to assault in *Hard Times*, promoted the notion that ethics was a question of calculation and of subsuming the individual to

the greater good of a population, of reducing considerations of individual specificity and action to rational calculations of abstract populations. Timothy Bewes
describes the functioning of reification well when he says that "Reification refers
to the moment that a process or relation [I would add individual] is generalized into
an abstraction, and thereby turned into a 'thing'" (3).

Squeers may be read, then, as a kind of allegorical figure of the capitalist in general. His exploitation of his pupils mirrors that of the working classes by the capitalists and his school is a figure of the factory, replete with disciplinary regimens and
whistles signaling changes in activity. Disciplinarity is a strategic form of control
that subjects the mind and body to a rationalized regimen of thought and behavior, which serves the end of streamlining or mass-conditioning individuals and thus
reduces them to uniform machines. The first teacherly act of Squeers's that Nicholas
witnesses is the feeding of breakfast to the newly impressed pupils. The meager
repast is subjected to a regimen reminiscent of rationalized production:

> "When I say number one ... the boy on the left hand nearest the window may
> take a drink; and when I say number two the boy next him will go in, and so
> till we come to number five, which is the last boy. Are you ready?"
>
> "Yes, sir" cried all the little boys with great eagerness.
>
> "That's right," said Squeers, calmly getting on with his breakfast; "keep
> ready till I tell you to begin. Subdue your appetites, my dears, and you've
> conquered human natur. This is the way we inculcate strength of mind, Mr
> Nickleby," said the schoolmaster, turning to Nicholas, and speaking with his
> mouth very full of beef and toast.
>
> ...
>
> "Number one may take a drink."
>
> Number one seized the mug ravenously, and had just drunk enough to
> make him wish for more, when Mr Squeers gave the signal for number two,
> who gave up at the same interesting moment to number three, and the process
> was repeated till the milk and water terminated with number five.
>
> "And now," said the schoolmaster, dividing the bread and butter for three
> into as many portions as there were children, "you had better look sharp with
> your breakfast, for the horn will blow in a minute or two, and then every boy
> leaves off." (58; ch. 5)

"Nicholas was considerably startled by these very economical arrangements" (59;
ch 5), as we should be because they reveal the economic logic behind Squeers's
feeding of the boys (the same profit-driven logic that led capitalists to calculate
wages based on subsistence for the worker), as well as the disciplinary technique
that inscribes the body and its desires within a rigid mechanism that forces it to
work within specific parameters of motion (space) and order (time) and leaves the
individual thus reified as a unit within the system longing for more with the knowledge that more is always denied. Not only does Squeers hide his avarice behind the

ideological ruse of conquering human nature in order to build strength of mind; he also numbers the boys, thus abstracting away from their existential specificity. We could say, then, with Lukács, that, "mechanisation makes of them isolated abstract atoms whose work [in this case, life activity] no longer brings them together directly and organically; it becomes mediated to an increasing extent exclusively by the abstract laws of the mechanism which imprisons them" (90). The boys eat not like little boys—predominantly for enjoyment—but like machines that need to refuel and have no ability to enjoy in their machinic survival.

On the road to Dotheboys, Squeers is asked by a lady whether the little boys traveling with him are all brothers, and Squeers's response is doubly significant. He says, "'In one sense they are, ma'am,' ... 'They are all under the same parental and affectionate treatment. Mrs Squeers and myself are a mother and father to every one of 'em" (67; ch. 6). On one hand, this is an interesting example of the conflation of the boys to a group constituted by similarity and thus of their reification, but, on the other hand, his response evokes the bourgeois myth of the paternal capitalist as master looking out for his workers or "hands" (we find Dickens attempting to use this myth later in the novel in a positive manner in regard to the paternalistic and benevolent Cheerybles). In both cases, the family illusion serves to sell something while hiding the truth that these two ideological families mask very harsh relations of exploitation. The boys that Nicholas finally meets upon his arrival at Dotheboys reveal the effects of the "parental and affectionate treatment" they have endured:

> But the pupils—the young noblemen! ... Pale and haggard faces, lank and bony figures, children with the countenances of old men, deformities with irons upon their limbs, boys of stunted growth, and others whose long meagre legs would hardly bear their stooping bodies, all crowded on the view together; there were the bleared eye, the hare-lip, the crooked foot, and every ugliness or distortion that told of unnatural aversion conceived by parents for their offspring [an ironical description when brought into relation with that of Squeers previously quoted], or of young lives which, from the earliest dawn of infancy, had been one horrible endurance of cruelty and neglect. (97; ch. 8)

And the description continues on in a metonymic cataloguing that cannot help but evoke comparison with contemporary descriptions, such as those given by Engels in his *Condition of the Working Class in England*, of the often horrible effects of factory labor and subsistence wages upon the men and women who worked in them but also on the "children with the countenances of old men" who toiled and lived in the same conditions. It is commonplace now to see the triad of school/military/factory as the three most intensive institutions of discipline, and thus it does not take a great leap to read the school at Dotheboys as embodying the same logic of reification as the factory and its structure as zone of production and exploitation.

By extension, then, what Nicholas is faced with at Dotheboys is not the exception but the very essence of capitalism; for, as Lukács tells us, "The internal organisation of a factory [or school] could not possibly have such an effect [namely the reduction of workers to atoms or things] were it not for the fact that it contained in concentrated form the whole structure of capitalist society" (90). The school, run as a venture of capitalist accumulation, produces value via the same commodity logic, if not the same material means, as the factory. In addition, the narrator refers to the school as a prison because of the horrible conditions to which the boys are subjected. While the factory, school, and prison all perform discrete functions in society, what unifies them all as modern institutions is the disciplinary logic controlling the bodies of those forced to inhabit them.[1] These institutions depend for their functioning upon a control of human motility and potentiality made possible by the quantification of experience characteristic of the capitalist mode of production, where all life is captured by the abstract calculus of profit. In such a system, all institutions contain something of the carceral, and little boys are rendered equivalent to pounds and pence.

The little boys file one after the other to be fed a vile treacle substance purported to bolster their resistance to illness but which in fact is meant to keep them from wanting to eat and thus can only lead to a suppression of their immune systems. In similar fashion, the workers are fed an ideology that keeps them striving in poverty and misery, while the capitalist and his family live without want just like the Squeerses, whose little boy is the beneficiary of all the food that should go to the pupils and of their expropriated possessions. The pupils must even watch as Squeers reads their letters from home and pockets the gifts sent them by their families. And if these examples of exploitation are not enough to support the analogy, their manner of sleeping portrays their reification through figuring them as akin to rodents and lacking in individuality:

> It needed a quick eye to detect from among the huddled mass of sleepers, the form of any given individual. As they lay closely packed together, covered, for warmth's sake, with their patched and ragged clothes, little could be distinguished but the sharp outlines of pale faces, over which the sombre light shed the same dull heavy colour, with here and there a gaunt arm thrust forth: its thinness hidden by no covering, but fully exposed to view in all its shrunken ugliness. (149; ch. 13)

This description, in its rat warren imagery of huddled sleeping bodies, raises the specter of the often crowded homes of the poor, forced to sleep together for warmth and for lack of space. The image of the shrunken arm fully exposed seems to call out for recognition, to resist being subsumed back into the mass.

Before we leave this scandalous school with Nicholas, let us linger with this defiant arm for a moment and remember Squeers's assertion of the brotherhood of the boys. The negative brotherhood forced upon the boys by the exploitation of Squeers, which reduces them to a homogeneous group of characterless atoms, also contains a potential positive power. A figure for all groups constituted out of oppression, the boys take power from their enforced unity and revolt after Squeers is sentenced to be transported. It is significant, however, that they take control of the school only after the paternal figure of authority has been eliminated and are quickly dispersed when John Browdie enters as a kind of repressively tolerant authority. The success of the pupils, their joyously enacted retribution upon the Squeers family, and their liberation from the school has a shadow cast on it by Dickens's description of what becomes of them post-Dotheboys. Like too many revolts in which the oppressed finally rise up to seek vengeance and freedom, the success they achieve is undermined by the fact that those who have been subjected to strict discipline may be externally freed but internally remain subjected and may even attempt to recreate in some manner the external conditions of their subjection. Thus, we find that some boys simply disappear, others do not survive, and some even return to the hall until they are removed. Regardless of what becomes of them, the breakup of Dotheboys suggests that the elimination of a symptom does not necessarily cure the disease and that what at the time bears much potential power for change eventually becomes "only spoken of as among the things that had been" (774; ch. 64).

The Problem with Theater

Nicholas's flight from the school with Smike draws him back into the world in search of a position. After the school destroys his opportunistic illusions of meeting a young nobleman who would be his ticket to fortune and society, he is left instead with knowledge of the brutalities of his society and with Smike, who embodies those brutalities and their effects upon a human being. Smike becomes a living reminder and figure of the oppressed; his fortunes are inextricably bound up with our genteel everyman, and his fate will indicate just how effective bourgeois society is at incorporating the reality he embodies. But, before we move farther down the path of the narrative, we must consider the significance of the next micro-world that Nicholas and Smike enter.

If Dotheboys represents a figuration of the horrors of capitalist exploitation and the reification of social relations and the human that facilitate those horrors, then the theater troupe of Crummles serves as a kind of antipode to the school. The troupe functions as an alternative model of both the family and of economic activity. Whereas at Dotheboys we find the rhetoric of family being used ideologically to mask the abusive economic exploitation of the pupils, an exploitation that allows the Squeers family to prosper and little Wackford to grow fat while the pupils starve, the theater company gives us a model of an organic family that acts as a cohesive unit without the need to present itself as such with overt rhetoric.

Ironically, it is the theater, where illusion is business, that provides an example of authentic human relations, replete with all the normal strife, intrigue, and posturing of everyday life, where the only real exploitation is self-exploitation.

From the moment Nicholas meets Crummles, he is treated with respect and candor. Unlike Squeers, who is always "on the make" and revealing (through his attempts to conceal) his self-interest, Crummles makes no attempt to hide that he thinks primarily in terms of self-interest. More important, though, is that the self-interest of Crummles is intimately bound up with that of his compatriots, unlike the narrow self-interest of Squeers. As a result, Crummles's attempts at furthering his interests also function to further those of the people around him. An example of this comes when Crummles dissuades Nicholas from seeking service at sea. Crummles is obviously out to acquire both Nicholas and Smike as new attributes of his theater, but in doing so he not only offers them jobs that will support them well and provide entry into a community, but saves them from the rigors of life at sea, which at the time of the narrative was far from easy and by no means the fast track to fortune and social position—not to mention the fact that it most likely would have killed a person of Smike's constitution.

The coincidence of interests indicated by the former example illustrates a form of social interaction in which the social relations of the individuals involved form a sustainable community of common interests in which no one individual or group is exploited for the benefit of another. Another example of the functioning of this community of interests is the bespeak of Miss Snevellicci. According to Crummles, her bespeak is "[h]er benefit night, when her friends and patrons bespeak the play" and, interestingly, "even if it should not work up quite as well as we expect, why it will be her risk, you know, and not ours" (295; ch. 24). The bespeak, then, is the devotion of a night of performance to the economic benefit of one particular member of the troupe; it is a way to celebrate that member, to whom a large percentage of the proceeds of the night are given. Such a promotion of a particular member of the troupe serves a dual purpose: it promotes the individual actor and thus the troupe as a whole, and it is a communal generosity in which the interests of the individual are willingly placed above that of the group, with the knowledge that it will benefit the group overall even if on that night the rest of the troupe loses money. When Crummles states that it is her risk if the show falls flat, he is not simply being selfish because either way he is not making the profit he would have normally. Rather, he is referring to the fact that if Nicholas's performance bombs, it will only affect one member rather than the whole troupe, hence his use of the possessive plural "ours." Nicholas's assertion that the proper pronoun for Crummles to use is the singular possessive (the quotation above continues: "'Yours, you mean,' said Nicholas. 'I said mine, didn't I?' returned Mr. Crummles") points to the fact that, as leader of the troupe, it is Crummles who benefits the most on a regular basis from the theater's performances (and also that Nicholas does not view their interests as connected quite as closely as Crummles does—prefiguring his eventual departure). While this may be true, Crummles is not so much a figure of the capitalist as he is of the patriarch and even of the master craftsman.

His position as master craftsman figures the troupe itself as a model of the pre-capitalist economic mode of craft that was rapidly becoming eliminated by the mass production logic of capitalism. Lukács points out that:

> At every stage of its development, the ceaselessly revolutionary techniques of modern production turn a rigid and immobile face towards the individual producer. Whereas the objectively relatively stable, traditional craft production preserves in the minds of its individual practitioners the appearance of something flexible, something constantly renewing itself, something produced by the producers. (97)

The "rigid and immobile face" of modern production, which we will return to in regard to Ralph Nickleby, is discomposed, made fluid, by the self-renewing activity of the craft producer and in the present case is exemplified by the bombastic performativity of the theater as a site of exaggerated bodily and facial gestural expressivity, as well as a dynamic site of production where the performance of the play is constantly being made anew from night to night by virtue of the unstable nature of live theatrical performance. The theater, then, may be read as a pre-capitalist formation of community and craft production and thus as an economic alternative to the exploitative capitalist model found at Dotheboys, a place whose very name suggests horrible acts committed against innocent humanity.

In connection with the troupe viewed as a pre-capitalist economic formation, it is not surprising to find another mode of more or less economic activity that, while itself alive and well within capitalism, provides a model of a non-exploitative economic logic, namely that of the gift. Arjun Appadurai, in his analysis of forms of exchange, shows us that

> Gifts, and the spirit of reciprocity, sociability and spontaneity in which they are typically exchanged, usually are starkly opposed to the profit-oriented, self-centred and calculated spirit that fires the circulation of commodities. Further, where gifts link things to persons and embed the flow of things in the flow of social relations, commodities are held to represent the drive— largely free of moral or cultural constraints—of goods for one another, a drive mediated by money and not by sociality. (81)

Admittedly, Appadurai goes on to state that this opposition is an oversimplified one because it assumes that gift exchange is devoid of economic calculation, a notion he shows to be naïve, since all exchange involves calculation of return and gain over time. Despite this qualification, it is still evident that there may be cases in which gain is not a consideration, though recognition of interpersonal debt may still be. Such a case is that of Nicholas's gifts to the Crummles family upon his final farewell meeting with them before their departure to America. We are told that: "He availed himself of this interval [before dinner with the Crummles family] to buy a silver snuff-box—the best his funds would afford—as a token of remembrance for Mr Crummles, and ... purchased besides a pair of ear-rings for Mrs Crummles, a necklace for the Phenomenon, and a flaming shirt-pin for each of the young gentlemen ..." (595; ch. 48). It is important to note that Nicholas can have no thought of anything but remembrance of him to result from his gifts since the troupe plans to leave England for good, and he spends as much money as he can afford on the gifts. In addition, he buys Crummles a gift that is perfectly suited to him as an individual, with his ubiquitous snuffbox, because his act of gift-giving has only symbolic value for him—a recognition of the value he sees in the Crummleses and the time he spent with them.

This value of the individual is directly tied to the value of the group, of community, that the theater company represents. When Nicholas gives his gifts and parts with Crummles for what may be the last time, we find that

Not a jot of [Crummles's] theatrical manner remained; he put out his hand with an air which, if he could have summoned it at will, would have made him the best actor of his day in homely parts, and when Nicholas shook it with the warmth he honestly felt, appeared thoroughly melted.

"We were a very happy little company, Johnson," said poor Crummles. "You and I never had a word. I shall be very glad tomorrow morning to think that I saw you again, but now I almost wish you hadn't come." (600; ch. 48)

This moving farewell scene portrays the depths of human feeling that can be nurtured by living within "a very happy little company" and which are either squashed altogether by social relations of exploitation or perverted into doggish fixation and dependency as in Smike's case. However internally troubled the troupe may have been, as with the strife between Nicholas and Mr. Lenville, it managed to maintain an internal integrity and remain a positive community of interests in which every individual, like Nicholas, could "be useful ... in a hundred ways" (278). Everything that has been said thus far about the troupe as an economic unit should show that it functions according to a non-reified logic. In fact, if it is characteristic of the logic of reification that it obscures the individual relations and forces of production, and in a sense eliminates the faces of the individuals engaged in commodity production just as the faces of the individual pupils vanished in their atomization, then I would like to suggest that the very structure of the theater resists such reification. This resistance resides in the fact that one cannot help but be confronted by the faces of the actors in performance because theatrical performance forces the spectator to read the faces of the actors as they engage in their craft. Marx's comment that, "the social relations between individuals in the performance of their labour appear at all events as their own personal relations, and are not disguised as social relations between things, between the products of their labour" could be seen to apply very well in relation to the theater, especially when one recognizes that the performance and product of labor in the theater are one and the same, and thus producer and product cannot be separated and placed in a relation of opposition and alienation (*Capital* 170).

If the theater is such a wonderful place then why does Nicholas not stay within it? A partial answer to this is given by the narrator:

> There were graver reasons, too, against his returning to that mode of life [other than that his mother would have a fit]. Independently of those arising out of its spare and precarious earnings, and his own internal conviction that he could never hope to aspire to any great distinction, even as a provincial actor, how could he carry his sister from town to town, and place to place, and debar her from any other associates than those with whom he would be compelled, almost without distinction, to mingle? "It won't do," said Nicholas, shaking his head; "I must try something else." (426–27; ch. 35)

While financial considerations are a factor in his decision, his main concern is the fact that the social position theater offers is far from the bourgeois ideal of afflu-ent gentility to which he and his family aspire to return. Nicholas cannot return for the same reason that the Crummleses must retire to America, that land of promise. As a residual economic form, the theater represents an economic struc-ture fast becoming obsolete and untenable as a lucrative mode of activity, both in terms of economic and cultural capital. Knowing that they will struggle to sup-port themselves with another child on the way and their best days behind them, the Crummleses exit stage left and cross the pond to find land and a future in America. Meanwhile, Nicholas, upon parting with Crummles the first time, does what any self-respecting young gentleman without means would do—he heads to the big city to face his future and protect his family, and it is to London that we must follow him.

Models of Capital

It is in the "wilderness of London" that Nicholas must seek the means of restoring his family to a society more amenable to them than the "happy little company" of the theater troupe (429; ch. 35). But because the story is essentially a comic one, his eventual success and inevitable marriage must first be postponed by a block-ing character: Ralph and his double, Gride. The machinations of the pair serve the plot, giving it the necessary dramatic tension and villainous intervention, but they also allow a structural binary to arise within the text, which foregrounds, through opposition, two models of capitalist activity. These two models, represented by the pairs Ralph/Gride and Cheeryble/Cheeryble, may be termed the appropriative/

usurious and the benevolent/philanthropic. For convenience sake, we may adopt a subtle distinction appearing in the novel between the "capitalist" Ralph and the "merchant" Cheerybles (25; ch. 2; 430; ch. 35). When we meet Ralph, we find that he

> was not, strictly speaking, what you would call a merchant: neither was he a banker, nor an attorney, nor a special pleader, nor a notary. He was certainly not tradesman, and still less could he lay any claim to the title of professional gentleman; for it would have been impossible to mention any recognised profession to which he belonged. (21; ch. 2)

Ralph's occupation seems to be a difficult one for the narrator to pin down, and thus he presents it negatively through telling us what it is not. Similar to negative determinations of God seeking to accentuate God's transcendence of the very systems of signification meant to define it, the negative determination of Ralph's occupation through a metonymic list of socially accepted professions that do not apply to him strongly suggests that there is a certain aberrant character to his unrecognized profession. This odd assertion of the financial speculator and usurer as outside the system of capitalist society immediately sets Ralph off as unnatural and villainous, as a kind of excremental element in need of sanitizing. The excremental, like Kristeva's conception of the abject, is "what disturbs identity, system, order. What does not respect borders, positions, rules" and as such must be (r)ejected, repressed, and re-contained in order to maintain the stability and integrity of a system (Kristeva 4). In its expulsion from a system, however, the excremental affirms the boundaries of that system and thus its own central place within it as a necessary element of its structure. Ralph becomes a figure, then, for the "unfortunate" potential of capitalist activity to promote exploitation and thus of the dark side of capitalism. Ralph, himself, describes his own activity and its motivations best:

> How many proud painted dames would have fawned and smiled, and how many spendthrift blockheads done me lip-service to my face and cursed me in their hearts, while I turned that ten thousand pounds into twenty! While I ground, and pinched, and used these needy borrowers for my pleasure and profit, what smooth-tongued speeches, and courteous looks, and civil letters they would have given me! The cant of the lying world is, that men like me compass our riches by dissimulation and treachery, by fawning, cringing, and stooping. Why, how many lies, what mean and abject evasions, what humbled behaviour from upstarts who, but for my money, would spurn me aside as they do their betters every day, would that ten thousand pounds have brought me in! (693–94; ch. 56)

This bit of invective reveals Ralph as a demonic, tempter-figure who seems to engage in business primarily in order to have power over others and to revel in

debasing others in order to make himself feel superior. While the demonic figure
he presents suggests that he is unnatural and intrinsically evil, his assertion that
the fault lies not on the part of the usurer but on that of the used points to the fact
that usury and speculation are not aberrant and unnatural activities within capitalism but rather fundamental structural elements of it—we need only remember that
the maligned individual usurer has now become the corporate creditor so important to the "health" of the economy. Furthermore, Marx discusses interest-bearing
capital as the most developed form of reification:

> In interest-bearing capital, therefore, this automatic fetish, self-expanding
> value, money generating money, is brought out in its pure state and in this
> form it no longer bears the birth-marks of its origin. The social relation is
> consummated in the relation of a thing, of money, to itself. Instead of the
> actual transformation of money into capital, we see here only form without
> content.... [I]t appears now, on the contrary, as though interest were the
> typical product of capital, the primary matter, and profit, in the shape of
> profit of enterprise, were a mere accessory and by-product of the process
> of reproduction. Thus we get a fetish form of capital, and the conception of
> fetish capital. (Qtd. in Lukács 94)

The functioning of credit promotes the fetishization of money insofar as money
generates money in an economic vacuum consisting only of numerical abstractions and completely devoid of all reference to or connection with the human
productive activity from which the value of money as a form of capital derives.

As excremental villain, Ralph illustrates, then, the effects of reification; in fact, he
is an embodiment of the dehumanization of reification. "Stern, unyielding, dogged,
and impenetrable," he is a man who "cared for nothing in life, or beyond it, save
the gratification of two passions: avarice, the first and predominant appetite of his
nature, and hatred, the second" (536; ch. 44). His fixation upon the acquisition of
money has replaced his humanity with cold hatred and contempt. The only thing
that even partially awakens some human feeling in him is the distress of his niece,
whom he has used as a pawn in his schemes, but even that fails ultimately to break
through his cold composure and calculating self-interest. We are told,

> He thought of what his home might be if Kate were there ... he strewed
> his costly rooms with the hundred silent tokens of feminine presence and
> occupation; he came back again to the cold fireside and the silent dreary
> splendour; and in that one glimpse of a better nature, born as it was in selfish
> thoughts, the rich man felt himself friendless, childless, and alone. Gold, for
> the instant, lost its luster in his eyes, for there were countless treasures of the
> heart which it could never purchase.
>
> A very slight circumstance was sufficient to banish such reflections from
> the mind of such a man. (384; ch. 31)

"The mind of such a man" has been so infused with the effects of reification that he is incapable of valuing anything other than money, which means that what he values is nothing at all, insofar as money is nothing but the abstract embodiment of abstract exchange value. He lives a kind of death-in-life, his heart "rusting in its cell, beating only as a piece of cunning mechanism, and yielding not one throb of hope, or fear, or love, or care, for any living thing" (128; ch. 10). He is the rei-fied man of rational activity, an example of the negative potential of the Kantian ideal of the individual who acts only according to reason devoid of all inclina-tion. Ralph, then, is the figure of the capitalist as demonic, rationalizing economic force seeking only its own growth.

The troubling character of Ralph as the negative, reified aspect of capitalism is accentuated by his pairing with Arthur Gride. It doesn't take much of a hom-onymic leap to read his name and thus his character as a figure for greed. Greed is both product and producer of reification. The effects of reification upon capitalist society facilitate the functioning of greed as a motivational force that places finan-cial acquisition over and above that of the community of interests of humanity as an ideal to be pursued, and the pursuit of the satisfaction of greed, through its necessary reduction of the world to an economics of abstract value, furthers the emptying out of the human from the world characteristic of reification.

The mask-like cold indifference of Ralph's face that often exhibits a sneering contempt, reveals its inner truth in the face of his fellow usurer, for whom "the whole expression of the face was concentrated in a wrinkled leer, compounded of cunning, lecherousness, slyness, and avarice" and "in whose face there was not a wrinkle, in whose dress there was not one spare fold or plait, but expressed the most covetous and griping penury" (577, 578; ch. 47). Gride's whole character is representative of the twisted distortion of the human that greed, that unnatural obsession with accumulation for its own sake, creates. His character serves to accentuate Ralph's insofar as we are given an alternate model of avarice that develops upon its nature in a way that reveals its pathetic side without rendering Ralph pathetic, which would detract from his main narrative function as villain.

The attempt on the part of Gride to marry Madeline Bray exemplifies both the pathetic nature of his character and the extent to which reification has infested his consciousness. Indeed, the reification of consciousness that allows his attempt to marry Madeline is that which makes him pathetic in its reduction of him to a sniveling, cowardly cretin of a man, who is incapable of gaining a wife outside of an economic transaction and who needs a go-between to compensate for his inadequacies—a situation that furthers his characterization as a pathetic, malad-justed man through its parody of the comic scenario of the inept, shy lover. But money gives him power and has the ability to conjure away his pathetic quality. As Marx astutely points out, "Money is the *pimp* between man's need and the object.... I *am* ugly, but I can buy for myself the most *beautiful* of women. There-fore I am not *ugly*, for the effect of *ugliness*—its deterrent power—is nullified by money" (*Economic and Philosophic Manuscripts* 165, 167). This marital farce dramatizes the reduction of the human to an object to be acquired in an economic exchange, the commodification of the human, and of the woman as an object in marital exchange whose feelings do not matter. Gride desires her in the way that he would desire to acquire any other commodity and as a result is blind to the effect his proposal has upon her. He is unable to see the torment that Nicholas sees in her face, but he also reveals a kind of palsied human desire, akin to that evoked in Ralph by his interaction with Kate, for the human companionship from which their narrow, acquisitive economic activities have kept them.

Economic activity that seeks accumulation as an end in itself and gives little or nothing back to promote the circulatory health of the system is generally referred to as "hoarding." In the matrix of the novel, hoarding is used to accentuate the message that accumulation as end in itself promotes stagnation, immobility, and death-in-life. The hoarder's entire existence becomes oriented around the central goal of accumulation. In his chapter on hoarding in *Capital*, Marx writes,

> The hoarding drive is boundless in its nature. Qualitatively or formally considered, money is independent of all limits, that is it is the universal representative of material wealth because it is directly convertible into any other commodity. But at the same time every actual sum of money is limited in amount, and therefore has only a limited efficacy as a means of purchase. This contradiction between the quantitative limitation and qualitative lack of limitation of money keeps driving the hoarder back to his Sisyphean task: accumulation. (230–31)

The hoarder is driven by the recognition of the power that is derived from possession of things, of commodities of all kinds that can be translated into money; however, he is driven on ever harder by the recognition of the limited power of what he has, just as Ralph reflects on the power he lost with the £10,000 and of the even greater power that £20,000 would have given him. Hoarding can become an obsession and like all obsessions has the unfortunate effect of overcoming the psychic well-being of the possessed, making him into a mere functionary of his own obsession, a means to the obsession's end. We can see this complex at work in the description we are given of Gride's house:

> In an old house, dismal dark and dusty, which seemed to have withered, like himself, and to have grown yellow and shrivelled in hoarding him from the light of day, as he had in hoarding his money, lived Arthur Gride. Meagre old chairs and tables of spare and bony make, and hard and cold as misers' hearts, were ranged in grim array against the gloomy walls; attenuated presses, grown lank and lantern-jawed in guarding the treasures they enclosed, and tottering, as though from constant fear and dread of thieves, shrunk up in dark corners, whence they cast no shadows on the ground, and seemed to hide and cower from observation. (629; ch. 51)

This description, which continues in a similar fashion making the objects of the house anthropomorphic reflections of Gride's singularly decrepit condition, illustrates, with its image of the house hoarding Gride from the light, the fact that the hoarded turns back upon the hoarder and becomes like a prison. Hoarder and hoarded mutually imprison each other and decay in the obsessive embrace, always in fear of separation. The description also reinforces the message in the narrative about the model of capital to which the hoarder Gride contributes, namely that accumulation for its own sake is death-in-life. The objects accumulated become dead through their removal from circulation and use-value, and the hoarder engages in an activity of self-immolation. Like the dragon of legend sleeping on its hoard of treasure, both guardian and guarded, hoarder and hoarded exist in a life-stasis out of touch with the vibrant world of social and economic circulation.

The connection of hoarding with the economic theory associated with mercantilism connects Ralph and Gride to a residual economic system and would seem to support a reading, such as that previously considered, of the appropriative/usurious model of capital as an excremental byproduct capable of sanitization. However, excrement, something to which the bourgeoisie of the nineteenth-century were quite averse, is a permanent reality that may be hidden but never gotten rid of for good. As Marx shows,

> In order that the mass of money actually in circulation may always correspond to the saturation level of the sphere of circulation, it is necessary for the quantity of gold and silver available in a country to be greater than the quantity required to function as coin. The reserves created by hoarding serve as channels through which money may flow in and out of circulation, so that the circulation never overflows its banks. (*Capital* 231–32)

It would seem, indeed, that hoarding is a necessary structural element of capitalism, which would mean that it cannot be done away with if the sewer is not to overflow and send the value of money plummeting into it. If such is the case, we must face the fact that capitalism cannot be separated from its dark matter, that the Ralphs and Grides are not aberrant but intrinsic to the system. Nonetheless, it is clear that they are meant in the novel to represent a negative "capitalist" dimension of capitalism and one which needs to be balanced by a more positively valorized "merchant" model, such as that offered by the Cheerybles.

If Ralph and Gride represent the evil blocking characters and the dark side of capitalism that the narrative seeks to expel, then the Cheerybles are the benevolent facilitators of Nicholas's good fortune and the positive, valorized "merchant" form of capitalism. When Nicholas meets Charles Cheeryble for the first time, he is mesmerized by his face:

> ... what principally attracted the attention of Nicholas, was the old gentleman's eye,—never was such a clear, twinkling, honest, merry, happy eye, as that.

And there he stood ... his hat a little more on one side than his head, (but that was evidently accident; not his ordinary way of wearing it,) with such a pleasant smile playing about his mouth, and such a comical expression of mingled slyness, simplicity, kind-heartedness, and good-humour, lighting up his jolly old face, ... and there were so many little lights hovering about the corners of his mouth and eyes, that it was not a mere amusement, but a positive pleasure to look at him. (427–28; ch. 35)

Charles Cheeryble's face presents itself to Nicholas as a thing alive with goodness and in an almost perpetual state of glowing and twinkling flux, unlike the fixed, cold composure of Ralph and the sniveling death-mask of Gride. This radiating face of goodness mesmerizes Nicholas in a fashion similar to the way a shiny new product or the phantasmagoria of the magic lantern would hold someone spellbound. Charles Cheeryble's hat even indicates an openness and lack of rigidity that contrasts with the description of Ralph's tight, crabbed dress. The brothers function in the narrative as an opposing force and principle to that of Ralph and embody a vision of the merchant as philanthropic angel, whose purpose is not the acquisition of money for its own sake but rather for the end of keeping society moving well through the circulation of capital. It is important that we know little of their business other than the fact that they deal in textiles and are an international concern. Paul Jarvie has read this absence of specific information regarding the business of the Cheerybles as a sign of the failure of Dickens to resolve his own ambivalence about the possibility of a position within the capitalist mode of production that remains untainted by commodification. What we do see much of in the novel, instead, is their extreme philanthropy. Not only does brother Charles take Nicholas on (after checking his references, of course), giving him a job in his time of need, but one of the first acts he performs in Nicholas's presence is that of giving money to a charitable cause, even though his brother Ned has already done so.

What is odd about the Cheerybles is the fact that they are identical twins and even seem to think exactly alike. It may be that the doubling of the Cheerybles shows a kind of life connection, a harmonious bonding of minds or a pair of cherubim. In such a view, they would represent the idealized vision of business as a partnership going beyond the goal of material gain (they are certainly no Scrooge and Marley) and striving after a filial ethics of charity, a Christian use of business for higher ends. On the other hand, the harmonious unity of this bizarre pair could be viewed as a representation of the identity of money with itself. Normally, the appearance of a figure identical to another in fiction, especially the Romantic, Gothic fiction circulating so abundantly in the period before the writing of the novel, would be used to evoke what Freud would describe as "the uncanny." In *The Uncanny*, Freud comments that, in addition to the physical likeness, the doppelganger "relationship is intensified by the spontaneous transmission of mental processes from one of these persons to the other ... so that the one becomes co-owner of the other's knowledge, emotions and experience," which is precisely the case with the Cheerybles—they not only look but think exactly alike (141–42; ch. 12). While not doppelgangers in the strict sense, they are more one person than two individuals, and I would like to suggest that this doubling indicates something odd and disturbing about the twins. Unlike the typical story of the uncanny double in which the effect depends upon a significant difference, as, for example, in Bulwer-Lytton's "Monos and Daimonos," the disturbing quality of the Cheerybles resides precisely in the degree to which the narrative insists on their sameness. Freud goes on to explain, "The double was originally an insurance against the extinction of the self, or, as Rank puts it, 'an energetic denial of the power of death'" (142). If such is the case, then the Cheerybles may be read as the figure of the eternality of the abstract unity of money with itself, as representatives of the life of capital as the constant circulation of commodities. If one dismisses their uncanny dimension, then it is possible to view what they represent in a positive manner. They counterbalance the death-in-life of capital stagnation, speculation, and hoarding that Ralph and Gride embody as blocking characters. The activity of the Cheerybles keeps the narrative moving by giving Nicholas a job, providing his family with a home, and by using their power to overcome the machinations of Ralph.

However, is all as cheery as it seems? Or, just as the dark activities of Ralph/ Gride were shown to be necessary and thus "positive" elements of capitalism, can the positive, benevolent activities of the Cheerybles be shown to have a dark side? If we consider the investigative surveillance activity they employ to bring down Ralph and Gride as situating them firmly within the disciplinary repression of the state, then yes. If we consider the job they give Nicholas within the counting-house as a kind of middle-class clerical drudgery, becoming more and more the common fate in the Victorian period, and the manner in which Tim Linkinwater tests him for fitness and then proclaims him fit when he manifests acceptable behavior—a technique that mirrors that of Tim—as an indication of the streamlining of action and thought in the business world, then yes. We should read the bird in the cage as a symbol for the clerk in the counting-house.

Paul Jarvie argues forcefully that the Cheerybles exhibit a "mania for control" exhibited in their management of the "marriage arrangements at the end of the novel, their insistence on making decisions for all those in their sphere, and their subtle but constant moves to ensure social control throughout their sphere" (Jarvie 38). But, most important of all, if we return to the assertion that the Cheerybles represent a figure of self-reflective money, of M-M, now the doubling effect evoking the transcendence of death may be read as truly uncanny in the horrific sense of the word, because what the double Cheeryble/Cheeryble represents as a model of capital is the assertion of its eternality and its objective, non-individual character. Their doubling effaces individuality in favor of the replication of the type "merchant" as the objective face of a benevolent and caring capitalism. They represent a system claiming its own eternality and pitying the very individuals it uses its power to crush. They engender the movement toward a future situation in which, as Bewes writes, "Capitalism creates 'its own monstrous ghosts', in the form of the mystical inevitability of its own expansion. The violence of capital, observes Žižek, 'is no longer attributable to concrete individuals and their "evil" intentions; it is purely "objective", systemic, anonymous'"[2] (68). The uncanniness of the Cheerybles resides, then, in their being the phantasmagoric, hypnotizing, self-reflecting face of the system drawing us in, remaking us, like Nicholas, in its image, and doing its best to conceal and sanitize those excremental villains who always threaten to put a face to its monstrosity.

The truth of the Cheerybles, unintended by Dickens but resulting from his inability to find a strong, viable solution to the rapaciousness of capitalism, is that they are only a more palatable, but no less insidious, form of the capitalist than that represented by Ralph/Gride. It becomes a question, even, as to whether or not Dickens himself ultimately understood the rotten core of the Cheerybles when he recast their unquestioned rags to riches story in *Hard Times,* using it as a means to exemplify the hypocrisy of Bounderby. In addition, while Dickens may have believed in the potential and benevolence of philanthropy early in his career, it would seem that by the time of *Bleak House* and Mrs. Jellyby he had begun to understand that most philanthropic activities, while alleviating specific cases of hardship, facilitate mass suffering by allowing the system causing that suffering to go unquestioned. The Cheerybles embody the logic of philanthropy, in which specific benevolent actions cleanse the conscience of those with power and serve to legitimate that power. While Joseph Childers does not specifically argue that they are sinister characters, he did believe a strong case could be made for it and emphasizes "the incredible power that accrues to them through the effects of their philanthropic steamrolling as they gleefully force their good will on everyone who lies in their path" (62).

Despite the dichotomy set up in the novel between capitalist and merchant, the merchant, no matter how benevolent, is still a type of capitalist and the two pairs of doubles are peas in a commodified pod. If we follow the *OED*, and a definition current in Dickens's time, a capitalist is "one who has accumulated capital; one who has capital available for employment in financial or industrial enterprises." According to this definition, Ralph, Gride, and the Cheerybles are capitalists, but there is an even stronger connection between all of them. Ralph is considered a capitalist because he engages in speculative financial scams, such as the United Metropolitan Improved Hot Muffin and Crumpet and Punctual Delivery Company, and usury—both activities that produced nothing but rather use money to produce more money through parasitic means. This kind of parasitic activity was anathema to Dickens, who had to struggle early in his career for control not only of his own intellectual property but for a reasonable percentage of the profit resulting from his labor. Because the Cheerybles are merchants engaged in the production and/or trade of textiles, it seems that Dickens found their form of business one of positive value contrasted with the empty parasitic activity of usury.

While the Cheerybles may make their profit from the circulation of tangible commodities, the textiles involved are nonetheless bound up in the reification intrinsic to the market. But, more importantly, as an international concern, the business of the Cheerybles is dependent on maritime trade. A glance into the history of the indemnity practices of maritime trade reveals that the business of the Cheerybles is far from untarnished by the kind engaged in by Ralph. The irony here is that, as John Hare has shown in his paper "The Omnipotent Warranty: England *v* The World," the modern institution of insurance originated with maritime trade and the necessity to get around a thirteenth-century Papal ban on usury. Maritime trade's inherent risk had been, under the new name of insurance, dealt with through the extension of loans on interest in order to protect the owner of the goods from complete loss. It turns out, then, that insurance is essentially usury by another name and with ever more elaborate rules and terms. Dickens tries to situate the source of the trouble with capitalism in usury as an aberrant form of activity in need of sanitization, but as the history of maritime insurance shows, usury is the very force that drives the system. Financial parasitism in the form of the loan has always been at the very heart of the circulation of capital, and there can be no capitalist mode of production without it, as well as no Cheerybles. Given these considerations, the prospect of a future (already arrived) of a "benevolent" capitalism run by the clones of the Cheerybles is none too cheery.

Two Sides of a Coin

Nonetheless, despite the equivocal nature of the Cheerybles and that which they represent, they perform the very necessary narrative function of facilitating the comic resolution of the novel. Their activities allow Nicholas to establish himself in the world and to replace the lost landed wealth and status with a more suitable bourgeois merchant prosperity, which in the end allows him to regain the old family country home. It is in this reappropriation of the lost home that the utopian and regressive symbolic act of the novel's conclusion is expressed, insofar as the return to the country home resolves the tension within the narrative between the city as seat of industry and business and the country as privileged site of family bliss and memory.

We are told at the end of the novel that his merchant prosperity allows him to buy the old house and that "As time crept on, and there came gradually about him a group of lovely children, it was altered and enlarged, but none of the old rooms were ever pulled down, no old tree was rooted up, nothing with which there was any association of bygone times was ever removed or changed" (777; ch. 65). This description of the nostalgic maintenance of the house, which may be expanded to accommodate the new family but never altered in its connection to the past, is indicative of a glorification of the past and of the attempt on Nicholas's part to preserve that past into the future. The utopian dimension of this nostalgia resides in the fact that it represents a desire to forget the present in the memorialization of the past, in order to cover over the source of the wealth that allowed him to regain the house as an emblem of the past and thus of the moribund ideal of country gentility and landed wealth. Within the shrine of the house and property, Nicholas and his family live a bucolic idyll that allows them to forget the chaos of the city and the industrialized society it embodies. The reversion to country time negates the fast-paced time of the city and attempts to escape the circulatory system that supports their idyll. What is most disturbing about this conclusion is that, while it represents a regressive tendency and a desire to revert to "simpler" times when people had a closer relation to the land, it promotes a stasis and nostalgia that will reappear in much less valorized terms in the figure of Miss Havisham in *Great Expectations*.

However, the symbolic resolution is undermined earlier in the text in two ways. To begin with, the idealization of the country as site of memory and a more dense life of quality as opposed to the city is undercut humorously by the garrulous exertions on the part of Tim Linkinwater to prove by example and anecdote that there is just as much density of life and quality of experience, if not more, to be found in the city than in the country. Unlike Nicholas's detached nostalgia, Tim's appreciation of the city asserts a life of active engagement with urban life. What Tim proves is that it is not the place but the life lived in it and the manner in which that life is lived that make of a place what it becomes for an individual. This understanding of place ties into the other element that undermines the symbolic resolution in that it recalls the fact that we are told while Nicholas's family is living in the outskirts of London,

> Many and many a time in after years did Nicholas look back to this period of his life, and tread again the humble quiet homely scenes that rose up as of old before him.... the glee with which Smike would start from the darkened corner where he used to sit, and hurry to admit her, ... every little incident, and even slight words and looks of those old days, little heeded then, but well remembered when busy cares and trials were quite forgot, came fresh and thick before him many and many a time, and, rustling above the dusty growth of years, came back green boughs of yesterday. (602; ch. 49)

It would seem that this oddly haunting proleptic passage indicates the absence that exists at the heart of the conclusion. There can be no coincidental connection between the tone of this passage with its image of Smike gleefully coming out of his "darkened corner" and the fact that the final words and image of the novel remind us of his absence. The real domestic bliss of the Nickleby family would seem to reside not in the future of the conclusion but rather in the future anterior of this passage, representing as it does the bliss that is only retroactively constructed. The shadow over Smike and his eventual death reveal his status within the narrative as a kind of necessary sacrifice. Insofar as he is connected to the school and the abuse coincident with it, Smike is a figure of the excremental saint. Within the allegory of the novel, he functions as an ambiguous figure of the degraded humanity of the lower classes and the guilty conscience of the bourgeoisie who must sacrifice them for their own gain. The darkness attached to Smike and his withering away as a result of his recognition of his inability to truly fit into the Nicklebys' world renders problematic this proleptically recollected domestic bliss, even as this domestic scene serves to suggest that the Nicklebys' real pleasure as a family resided with them as a happy little company regardless of where they lived.

The problem with the domestic ideal in question is that it is undercut by its form of presentation as well as by the troubling nature of Smike's position within the family—he seems to reside both inside and outside at the same time. Even at the end of the novel, Smike's grave with the children shedding tears over it suggests that there is an absence, an unresolvable problem residing with the family, and understood in terms of the allegory being explored, this problem is that the family as a figure of community of interests is tainted in some way by its implication within the capitalist social formation—as a type of the bourgeois family unit, their treatment of Smike figures that of the lower classes in general, who must remain in the position of subordination that philanthropy reinforces in its partial gesture of the hand-out, which leaves one begging rather than achieving the means of self-subsistence. They offer Smike a marginal place within the family but cannot offer him what he really desires and needs to survive.

In order to locate a more viable positive ideal for life activity in the novel, focus must shift from the tainted Nicklebys to John Browdie. The character of Browdie, with his rough country manners and speech, remains a marginal figure throughout the novel, but he is shown to contain all the virtues that Nicholas lacks and to dwell on the periphery in a way that keeps him from being contaminated by the reification that permeates so many of the other characters' relations. Browdie is a small-town householder whose job as a corn-factor situates him as well-to-do but not wealthy and as a kind of small-scale merchant involved in the agrarian life of his community. His actions throughout the novel show him as a good-humored individual who acts to help people altruistically and without violence; indeed, he intercedes on behalf of the Squeers family at the breakup of Dotheboys, preventing them from further harm. Nicholas's esteem for Browdie, and his going all the way to see the Browdies just to share his happiness with them, shows that their relationship is an ideal, insofar as it is a social bond that has nothing to do with economic gain but is rather based upon respect. Therefore, in a novel that reveals the pervasive effects of reification upon human relations and character, such a seemingly inconsequential and perhaps even unnecessary relationship such as that of Nicholas's with Browdie presents the reader with a model for untainted human relations and gestures toward the character of Browdie as the real ideal of the novel and the model for a viable life within the social formation of the novel.

Read allegorically with an eye for the functioning of reification, *Nicholas Nickleby* gains a formal coherency and complexity of content that recuperates the novel from its fragmented, episodic structure. Such a reading does justice to the complexity of the novel and seeks to reside with its contradictions, ambiguities, and ideological longings and to think them through in order to restore integrity to the narrative. The surface fragmentation of the novel replicates formally the violence done to reality by rationalization and reification and serves to distract us through melodramatic entertainment from the fundamental social reality exposed, analyzed, and questioned by the narrative.

NOTES

1. Leona Toker argues convincingly in this regard that "[t]he principle on which they are kept in Squeers's institution is also the principle that underlies the economics of concentration camps: maximum profit and minimum expenditure, with the basic needs of the human body redefined in ways that turn hygiene, privacy, autonomy, and nourishment into their opposites ..." (22); see esp. 21–25.
2. This quote appears in Žižek (15).

WORKS CITED

Appadurai, Arjun. "Commodities and the Politics of Value." *Interpreting Objects and Collections.* Ed. Susan M. Pearce. New York: Routledge, 1994.

Bewes, Timothy. *Reification or the Anxiety of Late Capitalism.* London: Verso, 2002.

Bowen, John. "Performing Business, Training Ghosts: Transcoding *Nickleby.*" *ELH* 63.1 (1996): 153–75.

Bulwer, Edward. "Monos and Daimonos." *The Vampyre and Other Tales of the Macabre.* John Polidori. Ed. Robert Morrison & Chris Baldick. Oxford: Oxford, 1997. 53–62.

Childers, Joseph W. "*Nicholas Nickleby's* Problem of *Doux Commerce.*" *Dickens Studies Annual* 25 (1996): 49–66.

Dickens, Charles. *Nicholas Nickleby.* Ed. Mark Ford. New York: Penguin, 1999.

Freud, Sigmund. *The Uncanny.* Trans. David Mclintock. New York: Penguin, 2003.

Hare, John. "The Omnipotent Warranty: England v The World." *University of Cape Town Marine and Shipping Law.* 29 Oct. 2011. <http://web.uct.ac.za/depts/shiplaw/imic99.htm>.

Holway, Tatiana. "The Game of Speculation: Economics and Representation." *Dickens Quarterly* 9.3 (1992): 103–14.

Jarvie, Paul A. *Ready to Trample on All Human Law: Financial Capitalism in the Fiction of Charles Dickens.* New York: Routledge, 2005.

Kristeva, Julia. *Powers of Horror: An Essay on Abjection.* Trans. Leon S. Roudiez. New York: Columbia UP, 1982.

Lucas, John. *The Melancholy Man: A Study of Dickens's Novels.* London: Methuen, 1970.

Lukács, Georg. *History and Class Consciousness.* Trans. Rodney Livingstone. Cambridge: MIT P, 2002.

Marcus, Steven. *Dickens: from Pickwick to Dombey.* London: Chatto & Windus, 1965.

Marx, Karl. *Capital.* Trans. Ben Fowkes. New York: Vintage, 1977.

———. *The Economic and Philosophic Manuscripts of 1844.* Trans. Martin Milligan. New York: International, 1969.

Stallybrass, Peter. "Marx's Coat." *Border Fetishisms.* Ed. Patricia Speyer. New York: Routledge, 1998.

Toker, Leona. "*Nicholas Nickleby* and the Discourse of Lent." *Dickens Studies Annual* 38 (2007): 19–33.

Žižek, Slavoj. *The Fragile Absolute, or, Why Is the Christian Legacy Worth Fighting For?* London: Verso, 2000.

Drowning in the Fog:
The Significance of Quilp's Death in
The Old Curiosity Shop

Christine L. Corton

The Old Curiosity Shop *is viewed by many critics as a text which was largely improvised and written with "less consciousness of design" according to John Forster than any other work by Charles Dickens. This article suggests that the novel is, in fact, much more tightly constructed and planned than has often been thought. John Bowen has recently argued this point, with reference to the figure of the garland. I examine other figures used in the novel: the interconnected metaphors of smoke, mist, and fog. The death of Quilp, through the element of a natural fog, as opposed to the man-made "London particular" of* Bleak House, *is linked with themes that recur throughout the novel. Quilp is presented as a representation of industrialism punished by elements of the natural world. The juxtaposition of the natural with the industrial world throughout the novel indicates a high degree of planning and coherence in the novel's composition.*

I

Many commentators have devoted a good deal of space to analyzing the metaphorical uses of fog in the famous opening passage of *Bleak House* (1851–53).

Dickens Studies Annual, Volume 44, Copyright © 2013 by AMS Press, Inc. All rights reserved.   DOI 10.7756/dsa.044.006.111-126

But this is far from being Dickens's only deployment of fog for metaphorical purposes. In particular, the significance of fog in *The Old Curiosity Shop* (1841) has largely been ignored, but the fog that appears in chapter 67 is closely linked to themes which recur throughout the novel. Dickens's biographer John Forster wrote of this work that there was "less direct consciousness of design on his own part than I can remember in any other instance throughout his career" (vol. 1, 117). Elizabeth M. Brennan refers to *The Old Curiosity Shop* as "Dickens's only improvised novel" (xii). I want to suggest, however, that the metaphorical uses of fog in the novel point to a far greater degree of planning and structural design than has often been thought.

The formlessness of fog lends itself to a wide variety of representations and metaphorical usages, perhaps even more so than other, comparable phenomena like mud or dust. Fog has been used by writers as a metaphor for the dissolution of contour and form in human society, the moral order, and the urban world. Fog's dissolution of clarity and definition also had a linguistic dimension. Fog, mist, haze, and smoke could merge into one another, defying easy categorization. Before the nineteenth century, "fog" was in fact very much synonymous with "mist." John Kersey's *English Dictionary* of 1702 substitutes tautology for definition by describing fog as "A fog or mist" and mist as "A mist or fog." In the same dictionary, smoke is detached from both fog and mist, being defined purely as "Smoke, and to smoke." But later, Francis Grose, in his 1785 dictionary, equates fog with smoke, although under "smoke" there is no mention of "fog" (Grose, under fog). Slightly later, in Humphrey Potter's 1795 cant dictionary, "fog" is also defined as "smoke." In Dickens's hands, terminological confusion and ambiguity provide the opportunity to develop a rich pattern of metaphorical representation.

Although the phenomenon of fog proved difficult to pin down linguistically, London has often been viewed in the terms of this, its major pollution problem. It became known colloquially as the "smoke," or the "great" or "big" smoke, especially by country people. The first reference to this usage is from John Hotten's *Slang Dictionary* of 1874. The earlier editions of the dictionary do not include a reference to the "smoke," but his text indicates earlier, and frequent, usage: "Country-people, when going to London, frequently say they are on their way to the SMOKE, and LONDONERS, when leaving for the country, say they are going out of the smoke" (298). This would be appropriate to a city that was often obscured by the dense cloud of smoke which hung over it. In a similar way writers often described London, especially from a distance, as purely a vapor—rendered to almost obscurity by its polluted haze. Charles Dickens often employed this image. For example, when London is viewed from afar, he describes it as quite insubstantial, quite formless. In *Barnaby Rudge* (1841) London is "a mere dark mist—a giant phantom in the air" (308; ch. 31). In *Martin Chuzzlewit* (1843–44) London, on first viewing, is "a city in the clouds" (180; ch. 8). In *David Copperfield* (1849–50) London appears as a vapour: "I saw all London lying in the distance like a great vapour, with here and there some lights twinkling through it"

(350; ch. 20). *The Old Curiosity Shop* is no exception. When Nell and her grand-father look back on London in the early stage of their wanderings, they see "old Saint Paul's looming through the smoke, its cross peeping above the cloud (if the day were clear) and glittering in the sun" (173; ch. 15)—almost the exact phrasing of Dickens's own remembrance of viewing London as a child as told to Foster: "at the cupola of St. Paul's looming through the smoke" (14).

Pierre-Jean Grosley (1718–85), one of many foreign travelers to complain of London's smoke, summed up the general view succinctly, on his visit to London in 1765: "If we add to the inconveniency of the dirt, the smoke, which, being mixed with a constant fog, covers London, and wraps it up intirely,... This smoke, being loaded with terrestrial particles, and rolling in a thick, heavy atmosphere, forms a cloud, which envelopes London like a mantle; a cloud which the sun pervades but rarely" (1: 47–48). London's geographical position gave rise to its foggy atmosphere. Peter Cunningham hypothesized in his guide to London that this was the main source of London's atmospheric problems:

> The unwholesome fogs that prevail around London originate in the lamentably defective drainage of the neighbouring lands, as the numerous stagnant pools, open ditches, and undrained marshes in the east, and cold clay lands along the banks of the Thames, Colne, Lea, Wandle, &c. When these spots are thoroughly drained, the fogs will cease, and London will become the most healthy city in the world. (30)

Cunningham omits to mention that the naturally foggy atmosphere mixed with the smoke from the increasing number of industrial and domestic chimneys caused London to live under a gloomy black canopy which often moved nearer to the ground and created what Dickens would later popularize as a "London particular" in *Bleak House* and which would much later be termed a smog. Fog's obvious origins lie not just in nature on the one hand, or human agency on the other, but also, often, in a synthesis of the two. This has encouraged representations that pit nature against culture.

II

It is this relationship between the natural fog of London and the smoke generated by coal fires that is understood by Dickens in *The Old Curiosity Shop* and which is used metaphorically in a number of important ways. The villain of the novel, the evil dwarf Quilp, is associated with man-made smoke—cigar-smoke, pipe-smoke, chimney-smoke. He shares the characteristics of the polluting industrial town. Chimney-smoke does not cause him the discomfort people usually experi-ence; in fact, he appears to enjoy it:

Mr Quilp once more crossed the Thames, and shut himself up in his Bachelor's Hall, which, by reason of its newly-erected chimney depositing the smoke inside the room and carrying none of it off, was not quite so agreeable as more fastidious people might have desired. Such inconveniences, however, instead of disgusting the dwarf with his new abode, rather suited his humour; so, after dining luxuriously from the public-house, he lighted his pipe, and smoked against the chimney until nothing of him was visible through the mist but a pair of red and highly inflamed eyes, with sometimes a dim vision of his head and face, as, in a violent fit of coughing, he slightly stirred the smoke and scattered the heavy wreaths. (469–70; ch. 50)[1]

Quilp is constantly trying to impede vision through his smoke, suggesting his desire to conceal his stratagems with obfuscatory tactics. Here he uses the smoke to make himself virtually invisible. Quilp even adds one form of artificial vapor (the coal smoke) to another (his self-produced cigar smoke), creating an "atmosphere, which must infallibly have smothered any other man" (470; ch. 50).

Quilp is indelibly associated with tobacco. He uses smoke to discomfort other people—especially his lawyer Samuel Brass, for "tobacco-smoke always caused him great internal discomposure and annoyance" (137; ch. 11). This fact has obviously not escaped Quilp's attention: "Quilp looked at his legal adviser, and seeing that he was winking very much in the anguish of his pipe, that he sometimes shuddered when he happened to inhale its full flavour, and that he constantly fanned the smoke from him, was quite overjoyed and rubbed his hands with glee" (139; ch. 11).

Quilp's association with the polluting horrors of industry is made explicit by Dickens's description of a city dominated by "tall chimneys, crowding on each other and presenting that endless repetition of the same dull, ugly form, which is the horror of oppressive dreams, poured out their plague of smoke, obscured the light, and made foul the melancholy air" (424; ch. 45). Quilp's ugly, smoke-emitting form may not be tall like the chimneys; but he too is the stuff of "oppressive dreams," as Nell, the innocent heroine of the book, finds out when she tries to sleep after having caught sight of him near Mrs. Jarley's caravan: "she could get none but broken sleep by fits and starts all night, for fear of Quilp, who throughout her uneasy dreams was somehow connected with the wax-work, or was wax-work himself, or was Mrs Jarley and wax-work too" (278–79; ch. 27). In the same way as the chimneys crowd "on each other," Nell feels "as if she were hemmed in by a legion of Quilps, and the very air itself were filled with them" (278). The smoke from the chimneys obscures the light, just as the smoke from Quilp's cigar does. Quilp's threat to "blaze away all night" till the end of his cigar has gone "a deep fiery red" (82; ch. 4) is associated with the factory chimneys in chapter 45 whose "smoke was changed to fire" (424; ch. 45) at night. Quilp represents the horrors of industrialization in the novel.

The factory described in this chapter of the book is seen as a hell-like environment: "In this gloomy place, moving like demons among the flame and smoke, dimly and fitfully seen, flushed and tormented by the burning fires ... a number of men laboured like giants" (417; ch. 44). Nancy K. Hill suggests: "The industrial, material thrust of the changing society seems in *The Old Curiosity Shop* to be turning many into grotesques. The new industrialism forces men to act like giants, to work in situations scarcely human" (109). The dwarf, Quilp, whose "head and face were large enough for the body of a giant" (65; ch. 3), belongs to this world of grotesques, and, like the "burning fires" of the factory, he too torments his victims. The factory workers are described as moving "like demons," and Quilp is likened to "an evil spirit" (159; ch. 13) earlier in the book, and later he seems "like some familiar demon invisible to all eyes" (454; ch. 48) but Kit Nubbles's. Quilp's association with smoke emphasizes his devilish, almost supernatural qualities, accentuated by his red eyes gleaming through the murk. Later in the book, the night fog has the same effect on the light from Quilp's counting-house as the smoke had on Quilp's eyes; it makes the house seem "inflamed and red ... as though it suffered from it like an eye" (562; ch. 62). Quilp displays the same restless, smoky, and diabolical energy as the industrial environment. He represents the uncontrolled and manic face of the new industrial society.

III

The events in chapter 67 of the book are concerned with retribution visited on Quilp for his crimes. He is pursued by the representatives of the law and is drowned as a consequence. The evil dwarf has plagued his own wife, as well as Nell and her grandfather. He has also caused Kit Nubbles to be sent to prison on a trumped-up charge of theft. Quilp is finally brought to justice, not from the legal proceedings of the state, but from two great natural elemental forces—the water of the river Thames and the fog of London. Retribution is made complete through fire, another natural element. As E. D. H. Johnson states in his introduction to Dickens's novels: "Increasingly, the natural world is pictured as embodying principles of moral order which do not so much reflect as stand in judgment on human activities" (153). In the end, the unnatural and polluting Quilp is thoroughly punished by the elements of the natural world.

The chapter opens with a direct reference to the fact that justice, pursued through the state, is about to be done: "It was the day next after Mr Brass's confession, and consequently that which threatened the restriction of Mr Quilp's liberty" (612; ch. 67). Samuel Brass, Quilp's legal advisor, has been caught by the authorities and has informed them of Quilp's crimes. But Quilp has "no intuitive perception of the cloud which lowered upon his house" (613; ch. 67). The cloud is a part of the natural world which is threatening to bring Quilp to justice. In addition to being an atmospheric metaphor, it is also a literary allusion—to Shakespeare's character Richard III—"all the clouds that lour'd upon our house/In the deep bosom of the ocean buried"(1.1.3). It is commonly recognized that parallels between Quilp and Richard III are made throughout the novel. Both are characters deformed in body and spirit; each is determined "to prove a villain" (1.1.30) of himself. They both delight in evil, for its own sake as much as for material gain. Richard III is often described as a rooting hog (1.111.228); Quilp screeches and howls like an animal to vary his "monotonous routine." Just as Shakespeare's clouds are temporarily buried in the ocean, the link between vapor and water runs through Dickens's representations of Quilp as well. The allusion is further reinforced when we remember that fog itself is a combination of water and vapor.

In *The Old Curiosity Shop,* retribution for Quilp's crimes is brought about by both the water of the Thames and the cloud of fog which covers London: "The day, in the highest and brightest quarters of the town, was damp, dark, cold and gloomy. In that low and marshy spot, the fog filled every nook and corner with a thick dense cloud" (613; ch. 67). Given the atmospheric conditions usually necessary for fog or mist—a temperature inversion in which high ground is in clear sunlight, and the water vapor is trapped in a layer clinging to the ground—it seems on the face of it implausible that the high ground could have been "damp, dark, cold and gloomy" (613; ch. 67). The gloom has to be taken as metaphorical. Its thickness and density add to the idea that there is no escape from retribution. Earlier, Quilp had been shown to be comfortable with fog. We are told that he sleeps "amidst the congenial accompaniments of rain, mud, dirt, damp, *fog,* and rats" (472; ch. 51, my italics).

Dickens builds up the atmosphere of an extremely foggy day around the river: "Every object was obscured at one or two yards' distance. The warning lights and fires upon the river were powerless beneath this pall and but for a raw and piercing chillness in the air, and now and then the cry of some bewildered boatman as he rested on his oars and tried to make out where he was, the river itself might have been miles away" (613; ch. 67). The "warning lights and fires" are powerless because Quilp does not heed their message, unlike his almost instant reaction to a warning note from Sally Brass, informing Quilp of her brother's confession, which leads Quilp to his death. The obscuration of the fog and the deception it creates over distances alert the reader to the possibility of an accidental drowning in the river. We are told that "the river itself *might* have been miles away" (613, my italics). Indeed it proves to be all too near. But the obscuration also supplies the tension in the chapter. A foggy day could give criminals cover to escape should they be discovered. Will the fog be used by Quilp to escape justice?

Up to this point in the novel, both fog and cloud are viewed interchangeably. In the next paragraph, the fog changes to mist, as it takes on a personal, spiritual, and supernatural character: "The mist, though sluggish and slow to move, was of a keenly searching kind. No muffling up in furs and broad-cloth kept it out. It seemed to penetrate into the very bones of the shrinking wayfarers, and to rack them with cold and pains" (613; ch. 67). The metaphorical allusion to justice is here suddenly intensified. Justice has not been particularly speedy in its pursuit of Quilp. After all, we are told, in connection with Quilp's accomplice, that it is already "the day next after Mr Brass's confession." But Dickens assures us that justice always wins through. There is no escape because it is "of a keenly searching kind." Just as, earlier on, both the highest and lowest quarters are subject to its power, so neither the furs of the rich nor the broad-cloth of the poorer classes can be used as a shield from it. The rack, an instrument of torture, causes "pains" in an obvious metaphor that is virtually a cliché; but behind it is a second meaning, unavoidable in this context, for the verb "to rack" also refers to "clouds driven before the wind in the upper air as well as a driving mist or fog" (*OED*). The supernatural quality of the mist is intensified because it causes such a chill to the bones.

The only antidote to the mist and fog is the hearth. It is "the warm blaze alone" that defies the fog. When Kit Nubbles, who was imprisoned wrongly through the evil machinations of Quilp, is freed and returns to his family, his home is described as containing "lighted rooms, bright fires, cheerful faces, the music of glad voices, words of love and welcome, warm hearts, and tears of happiness" (622; ch. 68). To reinforce the idea of the hearth as a place of protection as well as a source of family companionship, Dickens has already told us that Quilp, who is "by no means insensible to the comfort of being indoors," prefers "to have a fireside to himself" (613; ch. 67). Quilp perverts Dickens's own image of the hearth through his selfishness in trying to deny his wife the comfort of his fire so concerned is he to protect himself (614–15; ch. 67).

The emphasis in the final part of this chapter is on the darkness and obfuscation created by the cloud: "It was about eight o'clock; but the dead of the darkest night would have been as noon-day, in comparison with the thick cloud which then rested upon the earth and shrouded everything from view." The passage has a biblical feel of retribution, reminiscent of the darkness that descended over the Egyptians in the book of Exodus, an allusion that would have been obvious to Victorian readers, steeped as they were in the narratives of the Bible (Exodus 10:22). Yet Quilp misinterprets the fog. He views it more as an ally, just as earlier he had seen fog as congenial, remarking: "'It will be a good night for travelling anonymously'" (617; ch. 67).

Fog was an obvious cloak under which criminals could ply their trade. But the blackness of the night proves to be as false a friend as Brass, whose confession has led the authorities to Quilp: "A good, black, devil's night this, to have my friend here. If I had but that wish, it might, for anything I cared, never be day again" (619; ch. 67). His wish is ironically granted, since he will indeed not see the day again. Quilp moves outside and darts forward "as if into the mouth of some dim, yawning cavern" (619; ch. 67). The simile emphasizes the darkness created by the fog but also gives the passage a cannibalistic air through the personification of the cavern yawning, which reflects the savagery of Quilp's own eating habits, as well as his reluctant dismissal of cannibalism in himself: "'I don't eat babies; I don't like 'em'" (223; ch. 21).

In *The Victorians and the Visual Imagination,* Kate Flint refers to "anxieties about the condition of England which were expressed through the dread of what lay under the earth." She goes on to quote Patrick Brantlinger, who has commented in relation to late Victorian imperial gothic fiction of "the nightmare of being swallowed by the world's dark places" in which "characters are swallowed up or temporarily entombed in chasms, tunnels, crypts, and caves" (155–56). The image of fog creating a cavernous environment can be perceived as a manifestation of this fear. Caverns are traditionally depicted as homes for ogres and dwarves in fairy tales. In fact earlier, Quilp appears "to have risen out of the earth" (276; ch. 27) when Nell spots him by an old gateway of the town in which she and Mrs. Jarley stay. To middle-class Victorians, this underground world housed the poorest and most dangerous people; there was a constant fear that the denizens of this "nether world" would move out from their underground dwellings and invade more respectable areas (for more, see Jones 12–16). The ultimate literary expression of this phenomenon is in H. G. Wells's *The Time Machine* (1895), in which the Morlocks emerge from their underground home to devour the Eloi—representatives of the elite. Dwarves were often associated with the Underworld, and this included the dark recesses of the mind: "Coming from it and remaining linked to it, they symbolize those dark forces which are within us and which can so easily take monstrous shape" (Chevalier 321). The representation of Quilp being swallowed up by the fog taps into Victorian psychological fears and hints that he is being taken into the underworld.

On reading the news of Brass's disclosures to the authorities, Quilp had threatened the traitor with drowning. His description of Sampson Brass's death prefigures his own: "Drowning men come to the surface three times, they say. Ah! To see him those three times, and mock him as his face came bobbing up,—oh, what a rich treat that would be!" (616; ch. 67). The death Quilp had promised for Sampson Brass becomes his own death. His fall into the river is sudden. The final paragraphs, a dramatic description of a man fighting for his life in the water, show Dickens's fascinated horror at the physicality of death. They also contradict Mr. Humphrey's earlier view "that drowning was not a hard death, but of all means of suicide the easiest and the best" (44; ch. 1). At the point of death, Quilp achieves a clear awareness and understanding of what is happening. He had enjoyed being the master of manipulation; he now understands that his actions are leading to his own death, for he realizes that he has destroyed his only hope of being saved by having locked the gate to frustrate his pursuers. The fog, for which he had been grateful earlier as a means of escape, will prevent him from being seen and rescued. This realization is made more terrifying by the repetition and rhythm of the passage:

> [H]e could hear the knocking at the gate again—could hear a shout that
> followed it—could recognise the voice. For all his struggling and splashing,
> he could understand that they had lost their way, and had wandered back to

the point from which they started; that they were all but looking on while he was drowned; that they were close at hand, but could not make an effort to save him; that he himself had shut and barred them out. (620; ch 67)

Another portent of Quilp's death is in the knocking at the gate—the Shakespearean signal to so many of the significant deaths in Dickens's novels.[2]

Retribution is heightened further by the elements, whose punishments parallel Quilp's own cruelty in life. If "the strong tide filled his throat," so too had his own lusty drinking habits; he had repeatedly attempted to cause pain to people by making them drink spirits too strong to enjoy (226; ch. 21) and too hot to endure (567; ch. 62). His "yell" and his "wild and glaring eyes" (620; ch. 67) all emphasize his grotesque animal character in life as well as in death. Even when the river has given up toying with its catch, the notion of games, so enjoyed by Quilp in his life, is reinforced as his "hair, stirred by the damp breeze, played in a kind of mockery of death—such a mockery as the dead man himself would have revelled in when alive" (620; ch. 67).

Fog and water are not the only natural elements that punish Quilp. Another element, fire, destroys Quilp's hermitage. Again, it is Quilp who had caused this through his own clumsiness, when he had left his favored haunt and knocked over the stove. This is not entirely unexpected, since the reader had also been given signs that this might happen when earlier Quilp showed Sampson Brass the figurehead, which he thought looked like Kit Nubbles. The dwarf beat and poked it with a red-hot poker, and announced: "I mean to burn him at last" (566; ch. 62). Just as Quilp's promise to drown Brass only ends up with his own death, so his threat to burn the figure-head turns upon himself and his own property.

The final few lines complete the description of Quilp's punishment. The fog, now that it has pursued Quilp to his death, seems to have disappeared but it is as though the whole of nature has been revolted by his crimes: "The sky was red with flame, and the water that bore it there had been tinged with the sullen light as it flowed along" (620; ch. 67). Nature's revulsion also makes this a hell-like picture and indicates that Quilp is destined for the inferno. The red tinge of the scene shows the path to hell from sky to water. But it also recalls the "lurid glare hanging in the dark sky; the dull reflection of some distant fire" (416; ch. 44) in the earlier industrial scene. On the point of death Quilp loses his identity as a human being—there is a repeated emphasis on "corpse" and "carcase"; his body is no more than "ghastly freight," which is referred to, no longer as "he," but as "it," in a phrase reminiscent of Nell's earlier encounter with the kindly furnace stoker, who is initially degraded by the text into a thing: "as if to show that *it* had no desire to conceal itself or take them at an advantage" (416; ch. 44, my italics). Even when the form is shown to be a man, he is never given a name, as Nell shamefacedly recalls (426; ch. 45). The savage nature of Quilp's death is, of course, in direct contrast to the peaceful rest into which Nell falls three chapters later and which is not narrated directly but described at second hand. Quilp's death is reported in the present, emphasizing the horror of it. His body is left a "deserted carcase." Nell's body is left as if she were still alive, and when she is discovered, unlike Quilp, she is not reduced to an "it" but her humanity, even in death is emphasized: "She seemed a creature fresh from the hand of God, and waiting for the breath of life; not one who had lived and suffered death" (652; ch. 71).

Reluctant to die, Quilp struggles for life in the water, showing his determination to fight for his life. Nell acquiesces in death: "She felt a hopelessness of their ever being extricated together from that forlorn place, a dull conviction that she was very ill, perhaps dying; but no fear or anxiety. A loathing of food" (426; ch. 45). And indeed, whereas Quilp carries on eating and drinking right up to the point of death, Nell stops desiring food early on. As Garrett Stewart notes, "Nell's death is the apotheosis of all her faint quiescence throughout the book, just as Quilp's death, for all its surprise and horror, is a kind of epitomizing moment, almost a sarcastic triumph ... Nell's wished peace *is* a suicide, and Quilp would have given anything to live the few more hours needed to laugh at it"(99). Quilp is denied the right to die in bed, mirroring his pleasure in denying Nell her bed back in London.[3]

In his introduction to the Penguin edition of the novel, Malcolm Andrews writes that when Quilp "is eventually brought to heel he is punished not as a result of the inevitable logic of plot within the novel, but by an arbitrary end whose brutality can be seen as a part-reflection of Dickens' revenge for the death of Nell" (18). Michael Steig has claimed that "Quilp's death is accidental, almost arbitrary" (177). But, as we have seen, Quilp's end is far from arbitrary. His death by drowning is foreshadowed by many indications in the text, as I have indicated. In this chapter alone there are many portents of death. Tom Scott, Quilp's servant, is described "rattling his feet ... like a Banshee" (615; ch. 67), a spirit whose shrieks traditionally foretold death. The fog is a "pall" (613; ch. 67)—a cloth spread over a coffin, usually black or purple. Later, the cloud has "*shrouded* everything from view" (619; ch. 67).

His punishment and death, through the natural elements of fog, water, and fire, is completely appropriate in thematic terms, since Quilp is so associated with man-made smoke, the industrial condition, and the denial of nature. As Andrews also states,

[Quilp] is in many ways a microcosm of Dickens' London, the city whose ferocious and destructive energy is at once repulsive and fascinating, and whose individual features become grotesquely disproportionate when assembled to make a whole entity. On these terms the novel might be read as an indictment of industrialization, its blighting influence on men and their environment. (19)

The death of Quilp in a natural fog shows nature reasserting itself by ridding the world of an unnatural pollutant.

IV

The appropriateness of Quilp's death through the elements of fire and water has often been noted by literary critics. In his introduction to the Everyman edition of the novel, Peter Washington alludes to the "demonic Quilp, whose proper element is fire and who therefore dies appropriately by water" (xvii). No commentator, however, has noted the appropriateness of the natural fog which brings about the drowning, except in terms of its impeding visibility. Quilp is often associated with the dark, whereas Nell's association is with the light. Garrett Stewart notices

> How careful Dickens is to have them die "together." Quilp drowns in a preternaturally black night at the end of the sixty-seventh chapter ... and two days later the search party arrives to find that the child has been dead for those same two days. "She died soon after daybreak" on the morning (so we discover by working backward) just after Quilp's death, with the first coming of light after his black terror.... After the stage is set in each case, the lighting is all-important. The fragile child, willing and even glad, "faded like the light upon a summer's evening." This dimming and flickering out at dawn (although compared with day's end) is in exact contrast to that "good black devil's night" on which Quilp is drowned, blinded by the hideous brilliance of "the hundred fires that danced before his eyes."(98)

Quilp's identification with the dark ties in with the description of the darkness of the factory floor, the obscuration of the day by the smoke from the factory chimneys—"black vomit, blasting all things living or inanimate, shutting out the face of day, and closing in on all these horrors with a dense dark cloud" (424; ch. 45). Later, another type of cloud, one composed of fog, will shut out the horror, which is Quilp, and lead to his death.

Quilp perverts the idea of the natural in the novel. As John Lucas notes, "Quilp's 'bachelor hall' is a debasing parody of pastoral values ... His summer-house provides the anti-pastoral element of the novel, and that this should be so reinforces the concept of Quilp as supremely unnatural, which his deformity and grotesque manners also indicate" (86). Quilp is hunted out by the fog; it is nature's way of revenging itself on him. Lucas goes on to remark how it is "tempting to see Dickens playing with an anti-pastoralism; this river does not purify or return the body to the processes of nature." But the text tells us that the body was left "there to bleach." Surely, through a process of whitening, the body is being purified by nature; at the very least, it can be seen as part of nature's retribution to whiten the corpse of the man who so reveled in the dark and whose "complexion was one of that kind which never looks clean or wholesome" (65; ch. 3).

The illustration by Hablot Knight Browne (Phiz) shows Quilp entwined by the grasses and wilderness of the area where his body comes to rest; it is as if the grasses are snakes or worms preventing his escape and taking his body back to themselves. This can be seen to refer back to chapter 16, when the sight of the clergyman's horse eating the grass leads Dickens's narrator to expound on the religious idea "that this was what all flesh came to" (180; ch. 16). In the background the swirling fog recedes, having completed its task. The fog represented in *The Old Curiosity Shop* is part of the natural world and indicates a desire that nature will reimpose itself on the urban spaces of London, in the same way that nature, through its fog, wreaks vengeance on Quilp as an emblem of industrial pollution.

Two chapters after Quilp's death struggle has been narrated, Nell's dead body is discovered. Garrett Stewart is one of many critics who highlight the contrasts between the two deaths. However, there are also some significant similarities that illustrate the ways in which Dickens wanted the reader to see the relationship between the two deaths. The weather, in the later chapter, is not used as a means of retribution. It is dark, as it is when Quilp dies, but this is the natural darkness of night, not the darkness imposed by the fog. Yet there are still portents of death. The snow on the ground creates "a solemn stillness.... The life of their progress seemed to be slowly hushed, and something death-like to usurp its place" (640; ch. 70). It is not the foggy world of the previous chapter but vision is still dimmed.

Fig. 1: Quilp Lies Dead (621; ch. 67).

Kit is forced to shade his eyes from the snow "which froze upon their lashes and obscured his sight" (640; ch. 70). Even the sights he passes are "turned into dim illusions" (640; ch. 70) resembling the effect of a fog. Kit, Mr. Garland, and the single gentleman leave the coach driver behind to awaken the innkeeper while they walk on impatiently, trying to find Nell and her grandfather. They hear the coachman's knocking at the inn door as they make their way through the snow and it disturbs them: "The knocking, which was now renewed, and which in that stillness they could plainly hear, troubled them. They wished the man would forbear, or that they had told him not to break the silence until they returned" (641; ch. 70). This echoes the knocking at the gate of Quilp's pursuers—the last sound Quilp hears as he drowns, signaling his death. Here, they are another indication that Little Nell has died. Nell's bed is covered with "some winter berries and green leaves" (652–54; ch. 71). These have been placed by her at her request: "'When I die, put near me something that has loved the light, and had the sky above it always'" (654; ch. 71). In his letter to the illustrator George Cattermole, Dickens shows how complete the picture of Nell's death is in his imagination: "It is winter time, so there are no flowers; but upon her breast, and pillow, and about her bed, there may be slips of holly, and berries, and such free green things" (*Letters* 2:172). The red of the berries and the green of the leaves, according to the symbolic meaning of these colors, are a "symbolic interplay of alternations" (Chevalier 451). "Green is the colour of plant life rising afresh from the regenerating and cleansing WATERS to which baptism owes all its symbolic meaning," and "red is the colour of fire, and this is why humanity has always instinctively felt a relationship between these two colours on a par with human life and being" (Chevalier 451). The green leaves reinforce the idea of the resurrection of Nell by providing a symbolic meaning of regeneration and baptism; but the dark red of the winter berries is reminiscent of blood and is also related to the womb (Chevalier 793) and reminds us of the children that Nell will never bear. When Quilp struggles to survive the water, he experiences a "hundred fires that danced before his eyes" (620; ch. 67) and, of course, his own bachelor home has been destroyed by fire. The symbolism of the winter berries and green leaves refers back to Quilp's punishment. The grasses that surround Quilp's body (as shown in fig. 1 and discussed above) seem to entwine and entrap him, whereas Nell's body is surrounded by "free green things," which suggest a voluntary association with nature in a more comforting and peaceful scene.

V

Many critics quite correctly distinguish between the optimism of the earlier works by Dickens and the pessimism of the later ones. In his introduction to a recent edition of *Our Mutual Friend,* Andrew Sanders notes: "The tired, dreary, sprawling

London in which the novel is located is not the vibrant, dismaying, multifarious city of Dickens' early fiction" (xiv). As Robert Alter remarks:

> The key to Dickens's searching vision of the cityscape is his use of figurative language. After Shakespeare, he is probably the greatest master of metaphor in the English language. Through the radical originality of his metaphors [Dickens] registers a profound perception that the mushrooming metropolis of the nineteenth century constitutes a fundamental, and worrisome, alteration of the nature of urban existence, that the growth of the city may be running out of control. (48)

The fog represented in *The Old Curiosity Shop* is part of the natural world in London. It is not the same oily and greasy fog of the later books, which Dickens for the most part used as a metaphorical representation of the troubling meanings of the new urban reality of London. It provides an apt source of retribution against Quilp, an emblem of smoke pollution. It is this smoke that transformed the natural fog into the smoke-fogs (later termed smogs) that turned London's days into darkness during the nineteenth and twentieth centuries.[4] Nell, by contrast, is associated with light and with the same natural world which generates the fog. Quilp himself notes: "Such a fresh, blooming, modest little bud" (125; ch. 9). Nell's identification with the country and the natural world creates a tension that is in opposition to the values which Quilp represents. It is Quilp's attempts to blight the life of the innocent Nell that lead to his own death.

The Old Curiosity Shop is described by Andrew Sanders as a novel which "will never again be held to be Dickens's supreme achievement" because "there is no getting away from the fact that [it] stands and falls on the account of Nell's fate" (65). And for most readers, it falls because of the sentimentality of Nell's death. Yet, surely the novel is as much about Quilp, his demonic energy, and his death as it is about Nell. Mario Praz refers to "chance retribution" in *The Old Curiosity Shop*, but he does admit that it "has all the violence of a natural phenomenon, against which human energies avail nothing" (162). The circumstances of Quilp's death are not chance or accidental, but the gathering together of natural forces to seek retribution for his crimes. John Bowen writes that, "*The Old Curiosity Shop* is a more significant and sophisticated text than is often recognized" (1). He is one of the very few critics who see the construction of the novel in this way. Quilp's death illustrates Dickens at the height of his creative powers, not only because of the powerful way it is described but also the way in which it links themes which recur throughout the novel. These metaphorical resonances illustrate that this early novel of Dickens was much more tightly constructed than critics have suggested.

NOTES

1. All citations to *Curiosity Shop* are to the edition by Andrews and Easson, unless otherwise indicated.
2. An example is the porter in *Macbeth* who sees himself as a gatekeeper to hell (2. 3. 1).
3. The importance of dying in bed is discussed in Friedman, 71–86.
4. H. A. Des Voeux coined the term "smog." See the London *Times* 27 Dec. 1904: 11, col. a.

WORKS CITED

Alter, Robert. *Imagined Cities: Urban Experience and the Language of the Novel*. New Haven: Yale UP, 2005.

Bowen, John. "A Garland for *The Old Curiosity Shop*." *Dickens Studies Annual* 37 (2006): 1–16.

Chevalier, Jean, and Alain Gheerbrant. *The Penguin Dictionary of Symbols*. London: Penguin, 1996.

Cunningham, Peter. *Hand-book of London: Past and Present*. London: John Murray, 1850.

Des Voeux, H. A. *Times* [London] 27 Dec. 1904: 11, col. a.

Dickens, Charles. *Barnaby Rudge*. Ed. Gordon Spence. London: Penguin, 1986.

———. *David Copperfield*. Ed. Trevor Blount. London: Penguin, 1988.

———. *The Letters of Charles Dickens*. Pilgrim Edition. Ed. Madeline House, Graham Story, and Kathleen Tillotson. Oxford: Clarendon, 1965–2002. 12 vols.

———. *The Life and Adventures of Martin Chuzzlewit*. Ed. P. N. Furbank. London: Penguin, 1987.

———. *The Old Curiosity Shop*. Ed. Malcolm Andrews and Angus Easson. London: Penguin, 1984.

———. *The Old Curiosity Shop*. Ed. Peter Washington. London: David Campbell, 1995.

———. *The Old Curiosity Shop*. Ed. Elizabeth M. Brennan. Oxford: Oxford UP, 2008.

———. *Our Mutual Friend*. Intro. Andrew Sanders. London: David Campbell, 1994.

Flint, Kate. *The Victorians and the Visual Imagination*. Cambridge: Cambridge UP, 2000.

Forster, John. *The Life of Charles Dickens*. London: Dent, 1969. 2 vols.

Friedman, Alan Warren. *Fictional Death and the Modernist Enterprise*. Cambridge: Cambridge UP, 1995.

Grose, Francis. *A Classical Dictionary of the Vulgar Tongue*. London: S. Hooper, 1788.

Grosley, Pierre-Jean. *A Tour to London: or, New Observations on England, and Its Inhabitants*. Trans. Thomas Nugent. London: Lockyer Davis, 1772. 2 vols.

Hill, Nancy K. *A Reformer's Art: Dickens' Picturesque and Grotesque Imagery*. Athens: Ohio UP, 1981.

Hotten, John. *The Slang Dictionary: Etymological, Historical, and Anecdotal*. London: Chatto & Windus, 1874. (Earlier editions date from 1859 and 1860.)

Johnson, E. D. H. *Charles Dickens: An Introduction to His Novels*. New York: Random House, 1969.

Jones, Gareth Stedman. *Outcast London: A Study in the Relationship between Classes in Victorian Society*. London: Penguin, 1984.

Kersey, John. *A New English Dictionary or, a Compleat Collection of the Most Proper and Significant Words, Commonly Used in the Language, with a Short ... Exposition of Difficult Words*. London: n.p., 1702.

Lucas, John. *The Melancholy Man: A Study in Dickens's Novels*. London: Methuen, 1970.

Potter, Humphrey Tristam. *A New Dictionary of all the Cant & Flash Language*. London: J. Downes, 1795.

Praz, Mario. *The Hero in Eclipse in Victorian Fiction*. Trans. Angus Davidson. Oxford: Oxford UP, 1956.

Sanders, Andrew. *Charles Dickens Resurrectionist*. London: Macmillan, 1982.

Shakespeare, William. *King Richard III*. Ed. E. A. Honigmann. London: Penguin, 1968.

———. *Macbeth*. Ed. Kenneth Muir. The Arden Shakespeare. London: Methuen, 1979.

Simpson, J. A., and E. S. C. Weiner, eds. *Oxford English Dictionary*. Oxford: Clarendon, 1989. 20 vols.

Steig, Michael, "The Grotesque and the Aesthetic Response in Shakespeare, Dickens, and Günter Grass." *Comparative Literature Studies* 6 (1969): 167–81.

Stewart, Garrett. *Dickens and the Trials of Imagination*. Cambridge: Harvard UP, 1974.

Wells, Herbert G. *The Time Machine: An Invention*. London: Dent, 1993.

The Wax Girl: Molding Little Nell in
The Old Curiosity Shop

John B. Lamb

This essay explores Dickens's use of the waxwork figure and the waxwork tableau in The Old Curiosity Shop *as visual tropes for melodrama's engagement with the body. By portraying Little Nell as the wax girl, Dickens attempts to obscure Nell's narrative history and with it forestall both her maturity and her mortality. In so doing, the author seeks to maintain Nell's status as a melodramatic heroine, as a figure of unchanging virtue and purity—the "Good Angel of the race." But this attempt and the melodramatic impulse that sustains it are undermined by the waxwork effigy's origin in death and by the irresolvable tension in the novel between the ideal fixity of tableau and the relentless forward movement and temporality of narrative, a narrative that, in the case of* The Old Curiosity Shop, *ironically both begins and ends with Nell's death.*

All narrative may be in essence obituary.

Peter Brooks, *Reading for the Plot* (95)

Before Master Humphrey exits Dickens's *The Old Curiosity Shop*, he inaugurates melodrama's function as a matter of seeing and hints at the visual and scoptic regime by which Nell Trent, the "wax girl," will be known. Long before Nell and her grandfather take up with Mrs. Jarley and her "stupendous collection of real wax-work" (207; ch. 27), Humphrey notes in the grandfather the "delicate mould which [he] had noticed in the child" (13; ch. 1). "Mold" has a long history

Dickens Studies Annual, Volume 44, Copyright © 2013 by AMS Press, Inc. All rights reserved.   DOI 10.7756/dsa.044.007.127-142

and a longer morphology; both noun and verb, it implies the notions of character, construction, and corruption so central to the creation and display of wax effigies. Furthermore, since a "mold" is the wire frame on which pulp is spread to make sheets of paper, Dickens's narrative links the waxwork's preservation of the corpse with the corpus, with the act of writing itself. If the body of Nell is represented and exposed through the figure of the waxworks, the reader of *The Old Curiosity Shop* assumes the voyeuristic glance of Humphrey himself whose "curiosity and interest" (12; ch.1) in Little Nell cause him to pass and re-pass her grandfather's house, unable either to tear himself away or to solve the enigma of Nell and her grandfather's nightly perambulations.

The relationship between melodrama and waxwork display is not as fanciful as, at first, it might appear. Both melodrama and Madame Tussaud's have their origin in the French Revolution and in an "aesthetics of embodiment," a narrative and visual process by which the body becomes an "intelligible sign" and where the most important meanings have to be inscribed "on and with the body" (Brooks, *Body Work* 54, 55). As Peter Brooks points out, melodrama was *the* genre of the French Revolution, and many of Madame Tussaud's first wax figures were of revolutionary leaders like Robespierre and Jean-Paul Marat.[1] If the waxwork figure functions as a visual trope for melodrama's engagement with the body in *The Old Curiosity Shop*, it also announces the strange metaleptic drift of Dickens's narrative which moves from Nell's effigy to her dead body, the very dead and molding body which is, ironically, the precondition for the molded and scripted image of the wax girl.

Such a narrative drift should suggest to us that *The Old Curiosity Shop* commences in the repeated recognition of Nell's death—"She was dead" (538; ch. 71)—and in the image of her on her deathbed and not with the "lonely figure of the child" in her grandfather's shop surrounded by the "grim objects that are about her bed when her history is first foreshadowed," as Dickens insists in his 1848 preface (8).[2] For it is in that deathbed scene that Nell's history is truly prefigured, a history which moves from her death to a scripted and scriptural narrative that invites the reader to participate in an act of cultural wish-fulfillment, a melodramatic fantasy which sees Nell's life as the journey of a child "fresh from God" (12; ch. 1) to one of God's angels. It is a journey that while tracking Nell's travels seeks to obscure the narrative history of her travails, particularly the predatory sexuality she is often threatened by. But in the mortuary turn of the novel, in its dual fascination with death and preservation, if Nell's corpse "effaces all traces of death's inscription in life," her deathbed scene is the founding moment of the novel's narrative—of its "commemorative stories"—and the originary moment of her figurative transformation into the wax girl (Bronfen 89). Nell's death at the end of the novel is the precondition for the "narrative monument" which replaces her body with the allegorical figure of an angel (Bronfen 89, 90), just as her deathbed tableau is a funereal monument to her virtue—"so young, so beautiful, so good" (543; ch. 72). As Hilary Schor notes, Dickens's preface invites us to get "caught up in Nell's wanderings, which become the peregrinations of the novel itself"

(32). That preface also invites a particularly "speculative gaze ... centered on Nell's own body" (Schor 36). But the novel's and Nell's pilgrimage from place to place often thwart that speculative gaze, just as Nell's own body seems, at times, to refuse to answer the look of the reader as spectator, thereby destabilizing the moral trajectory that very journey implies.

What is significant about melodrama is the persistence of the body as the privileged term in its visual economy; what is noticeable in *The Old Curiosity Shop* is the waxwork effigy's and waxwork tableau's function as paradigms for corporeal display in the novel. As Kelly Hager suggests, "the novel itself is a gallery of wax-work figures" (223), and the most important of these is Little Nell herself. Dickens's depiction of Nell as the wax girl seeks both to preserve her status as a melodramatic heroine and to forestall narrative temporality and the body's mutability, occluding the history of Nell's incipient maturity and inevitable mortality. But the waxwork's origin in death, its implicit recognition of the corruption which underwrites the effigy's preservation of the corpse and its safeguarding of the meanings Dickens attempts to assign to it, often undermines the novel's melodramatic impulse, its desire to represent and retain Nell as an unstained symbol of virtue. At the moment that waxwork tableau and the gaze it engenders seek to construct and secure a Nell who is outside of time and time's vicissitudes, the wax girl refuses to acknowledge the insistent gaze of the novel and its readers. She refuses to return a look.

*

Dickens's melodramatic fascination with the spectacle of Nell's body, in which the surrounding people and objects or her recumbent pose must always allude to her death, might encourage us to turn to that other space for death on display that held such a fascination for Dickens and his readers, the Paris Morgue. While the principle function of display in the Paris Morgue was identification of corpses, the morgue also served as a form of popular theater, clearly linking its sensationalism with other types of nineteenth-century exhibition like Madame Tussaud's wax museum. Revolutionary politics and sensational crime were at the heart of Tussaud's exhibition and point to the ways in which waxwork displays, like the display of bodies at the morgue, encourage a form of spectatorship rooted in the detection of political, sexual, and criminal deviance. It is this very resemblance between morgue and waxworks that Dickens's Uncommercial Traveller notes in "Some Recollections of Mortality." Although written more than twenty years after the publication of *The Old Curiosity Shop*, "Some Recollections of Mortality" nonetheless provides a useful template for investigating some of the narrative and visual tensions—between corpse and catalogue, spectator and spectacle—so central to Dickens's novel and Dickens's art.

Alerted by a rush of spectators and an "angry procession" that "it was a Body coming to the Morgue," the Traveller in "Some Recollections of Mortality" follows the crowd into the building, his curiosity to know the cause of death becoming "quite ravenous": "Was it river, pistol, knife, love, gambling, robbery, hatred, how many stabs, how many bullets, fresh or decomposed, suicide or murder?" (220, 221). The Traveller's questions concerning the mystery of the "Body's" demise, resemble Master Humphrey's own attempts to answer the "strange mystery" of Nell and her grandfather, a mystery which leads him recollect urban tales of "dark and secret deeds" that have gone undetected (20; ch. 1). But just as such tales prove fruitless in the case of Nell and her grandfather, the Traveller's sensational queries are ill-adapted to the case at hand. For it is not a criminal or suicide but merely the body of a "poor old man" struck dead by a falling stone. Significantly, Dickens's narrator notes that the old man has "nothing about him to lead to his identification" ("Recollections" 221) and ruminates whether his fellow spectators may have guessed "what kind of sight they were looking at": "And there was a much more general, purposeless, staring at it—like looking at a waxwork, without a catalogue, and not knowing what to make of it. But all these expressions concurred in possessing the one under-lying expression of *looking at something that could not return a look*" (223, emphasis added).

Like the waxwork figure, the body in the morgue has a history and a story that at first cannot be told, despite the potential narratives the Traveller alludes to. As Paul Vita remarks of this episode, "without identity the tragedy of death is reduced to spectacle and speculation," and without a catalogue the spectator "cannot retrace the narrative that led to the cause of death" (244). More importantly, the corpse's or, by analogy the waxwork figure's, refusal to answer the spectator's look undermines an important interpellative moment of visual hailing in which the observed body confirms a sceptic and narrative regime which pathologizes its subjects as victims of urban crime or self-inflicted moral downfall. Thus, this moment in the Paris Morgue thwarts what Peter Brooks identifies as the "fundamental premise" of narrative and melodramatic display, the assertion that character and identity can, indeed, be made visible, and it forestalls the telling of the body's story—it's passage "into the realm of the letter, into literature." In melodrama, as Brooks observes, the body marked by death and desire is a "hieroglyph, a sign that can eventually, at the right moment of the narrative, be read" (*BW* 22).[3]

But melodrama, Brooks insists, needs both "document and vision" (*Melodramatic Imagination* 9); it needs both a corpse and a catalogue. It requires a compensatory and interpretive mechanism to overcome the lacunae of reading, a mechanism to surmount those moments in the narrative when the body resists interpretation, when it will not "return a look." In "Some Recollections of Mortality" such an interpretive moment comes a few pages later in the remembrance of a similar display seen years earlier at a "certain open-air Morgue" that the Traveller had come upon in his wandering about London in "the hard winter of 1861." There, as "darkness thickens fast and soon" ("Recollections" 224), he gazes on the body of a woman who has apparently drowned herself in the canal at the north end of Regent's Park. This moment recalls Master Humphrey's speculation about those passersby—especially those of "a very different class"—who crossing the Thames look down upon the river and seem to remember that "drowning was not a hard death, but of all means of suicide the easiest and best" (*OCS* 11; ch. 1). It is worth noting that if the identity of the old man in the Paris Morgue remains unknown, his history unnarratable, and the trauma it implies unseen, the woman's body is eminently legible:

> Looking over ... I saw, lying on the towing-path, with her face turned up towards us, a woman, dead a day or two, and under thirty, as I guessed, poorly dressed in black. The feet were lightly crossed and the ankles, and the dark hair, all pushed back from the face, as though that had been the last action of her desperate hands, streamed over the ground. (224)

Reviving the scene in his memory, the Traveller recalls seeing on the face of a passing costermonger the same expression he finds on the faces of his fellow visitors to the Paris Morgue, "that stare at it which I have likened to being at a waxwork exhibition without a catalogue" (224). For the costermonger, too, we must imagine that this is an act of "looking at something that could not return a look." But now Dickens's narrator possesses the cultural catalogue—a way of defining the body and organizing the world around it—that allows him retrospectively to read and identify the woman and the woman's "storied" body:[4] "So dreadfully forlorn, so dreadfully sad, so dreadfully mysterious, this spectacle of our dear sister here departed!" (224); and his reading of the corpse is "representative of his role as the reader's versatile exhibition guide" (Drew 129).

In this morgue-like moment, the public display of the body in Regent's Park mimics a standard trope in the representation of the Paris Morgue to British readers: the "public display of the body serve[s] as a sort of Dantesque punishment for illicit love and deviant behavior" (Vita 243). The woman's body, like early waxwork effigies, seems to enact a symbolic punishment and betrays in death the signs of both her passion and her ruin—of her representativeness. She is simply "another nature dragged down to perdition" (224), and we need only go so far as the very author Dickens pays homage to in that 1848 preface, Thomas Hood, to find many of the elements of the catalogue that makes of the woman's body a hieroglyph. In Hood's 1844 poem, "The Bridge of Sighs," the auburn hair "Escaped from the comb," the "dark arch" and "black flowing river," and the "Dreadfully staring" eyes create the impression of a woman morally lost and ruined, what Dickens calls "forlorn." Hood's entreaty to the men who tend to the woman's body in "The Bridge of Sighs" to "compose" her limbs exposes the textual and melodramatic operation at work in his poem and in Dickens's novel, an operation which seeks to claim that "All that remains of her / Now is pure womanly" (317–20).

The conjunction between "remains" and "pure" in Hood's poem highlights the disjunction so central to waxwork representation in *The Old Curiosity Shop*, just as the conjunction of "pure" and "womanly" highlights the tension in the novel's representation of Little Nell. The waxwork body is a literal and material relic, a surviving remnant or trace, both remainder and reminder. The waxwork effigy represents a long-lasting and significant bodily vestige of a now dead and missing person that survives beyond death; and such traces of the absent body "allow the wax figures to evoke their source body" (Sandberg 63), to recall their transitoriness and mortality. In the case of *The Old Curiosity Shop*, such figures serve to remind us that "She is dead." Just as all tableaus have a prehistory in medieval religious display, so too the waxwork effigy is linked to religious iconography and Christian reliquary. The waxwork effigy, like the preserved bodies of saints, is incorruptible and immaculate, visually spotless and morally stainless. Unmarked both literally and figuratively, the incorruptible body symbolizes an unspotted and "pure" soul and thus achieves a kind of corporeal apotheosis. It is also a body situated ironically outside of temporality. Yet those remains (or the waxwork reminder of them) are essentially corrupt and decaying. As Maria Warner points out "Waxworks exude the spirit of life and death equally. In the embalmer's art of the dead and the verisimilitude of Tussaud's popular art both morbidity and the promise of immortality co-exist" (186). The waxwork figure is the reminder that if something remains, something is lost. In *The Old Curiosity Shop*, like countless other nineteenth-century narratives, "the motif of 'death and the maiden' combines the eroticism and beauty of the feminine body in full bloom with bodily decay, ephemerality, and the abrupt termination of a life of pleasure" (Bronfen 98). Preserved from decomposition the body becomes ready for composition, and in some sense Nell's deathbed tableau at the close of *The Old Curiosity Shop* becomes the origin of all corporeal display. It is the "staged" moment or primal scene in which the living body is transformed in the nonliving work of art,[5] the moment when the body yields itself to narrative and "'reality' assumes narratability" (Brooks, *Reading for Plot* 96). The scene of Nell's death is, ironically, the "event that allows the narrative to unfold" (Lukacher 36).[6]

Stanley Fish's observations on the rhetorical strategies at work in Freud's discovery of the originary, or primal, scene in "From the History of Infantile Neurosis" can be helpful here in determining the structuring power of *The Old Curiosity Shop*'s ending, which retrospectively gives order and significance to the narrative actions that precede it. Fish likens the narrative pattern of Freud's "History" to a story of detection, a story in which "an absolutely omniscient author distributes clues to a master meaning of which he is fully cognizant and toward which the reader moves uncertainly but always under the direction of a guide who builds the narrative structure and structure of understanding at the same time" (936).[7] Just as Dickens's Traveller functions as our exhibition guide to the spectacle of the drowned woman, so too the narrator who takes over for Humphrey in *The Old Curiosity Shop* fashions a catalogue, a text of understanding, that moves inevitably and knowingly toward the novel's end, toward its inaugural scene, the scene of Nell's death. This is the moment of full disclosure toward which melodrama tends, the moment that reveals the sacrifices which must be made for Nell to remain pure and virtuous. According to Fish, even though the originary scene is the "last thing to be put in place, it immediately becomes the anchor and explanation of everything that precedes it." In *The Old Curiosity Shop*, then, the scene of the wax girl's death, like the originary scene in Freud's narrative, "emerges triumphant as both the end of the story and its self-authenticating origin" (Fish 938). Furthermore, as Lee Edelman points out in his reading of Freud's "History," the logic of the narrative construction of the originary scene is metalepsis—"the rhetorical substitution of cause for effect or effect for cause" (100).

But something of the mystery of identity remains, and the catalogue that allows the waxwork body to be read juxtaposed to the very waxwork body which refuses to acknowledge the spectator's gaze and "return a look" points to the fundamental tension implicit in the melodramatic way of seeing and in the scoptic regime at the heart of *The Old Curiosity Shop*. For Nell's is a body that is constantly read, but constantly refuses to look back, that does not return a look. It is a body which in motion eludes identification and one which at rest seems at times to refuse the interpellation of the melodramatic catalogue at the heart of Dickens's novel and Victorian culture. Part of that narrative tension is implicit in the workings of melodrama itself. As a moral economy, melodrama revolves around a set of essential conflicts, and melodrama polarizes the world into a Manichean universe of moral absolutes—good versus evil, pure versus impure, spiritual versus carnal. But as a form of corporeal representation, melodrama depicts bodies in excess, bodies that seem to transgress the narrative and scoptic regime at the heart of melodrama. Waxwork and melodrama alike reveal a disturbing uncanniness which not only "trouble[s] the boundaries between the living and the dead" (Bowen 152), but also the line between narrative progress and visual stasis. If the melodramatic body finds its representative form in the waxwork figure, then it is a body whose very uncanniness often disrupts the fixed identity on which melodrama's moral economy essentially depends.

The close connection in the nineteenth century between the morgue and the wax museum "strengthens the case for wax as a form of recording." Waxwork mannequins "implicitly acknowledge wax as a preservative form of realistic representation by substituting a wax effigy for the badly decaying corpse" (Sandberg 48). In addition, that connection and the ways in which both forms of corporeal display were linked to melodramatic and sensational literature expose the uneasy relation between the "frozen moments" of wax display and the relentless temporal drift of the narrative supplements or catalogues that out of necessity accompanied the waxwork tableau. Since wax preserves by sealing the material body from air, it appears to "bring about imperishability, to stall the passage of time, and prevent its mark" and to "symbolically challenge the corruption of the flesh and seem to overcome death" (Warner 186, 187). However, as Mark Sandberg argues, despite the waxwork's ability to "preserve, immortalize, and liberate the body from the confines of time and space" (37), the visual narrative implied in the waxwork tableau, provides "only a partial sense of story" and the ubiquitous written guide or catalogue is needed to "fill in the gaps" in the narrative, because the wax tableau came up short "in its ability to create narrative effects and plot" (79, 82). If the waxwork figure is haunted by a kind of "semantic emptiness" (Warner 196), that emptiness can be corrected not only by a narrative catalogue but also by placing the figure in an increasingly more detailed tableau and by surrounding it with objects, accessories, and ornaments that add to the figure's authenticity and create the illusion of reality. As Lillian Craton remarks in her discussion of Mrs. Jarley's display in *The Old Curiosity Shop*, the waxwork's message and appeal "depend on a balance between image and narrative, as the commentary and context of the collection bring meaning to individual bodies" (50).

Unsupplemented, all wax figures are "dead," but they acquire a life and a history through a complex of relational structures—props and postures, costumes and catalogues. But that life and history, like the waxwork figure itself, are haunted by the sense of loss and absence and the trauma of death and decomposition that are at the core of the wax figure and of all corporeal display. The wax effigy is inevitably linked to the dead body both through the properties of wax itself which make it suitable for representing deathly pallor and through the predilection for death scenes in wax museums themselves. Indeed, Maria Warner's analysis of the Sleeping Beauty, the oldest surviving waxwork in Madame Tussaud's museum and one of the three such figures she originally inherited from Ernst Curtius,[8] combined with *The Old Curiosity Shop*'s illustrations of a reclining sleeping or dead Nell, should remind us of how often Nell appears as what Warner calls a "secular tomb effigy," whose relaxed posture represents "a wishful fiction about death" (185). The languorous repose of the Sleeping Beauty and the "aesthetic confusion of erotic femininity and narcotic catalepsy" (Warner 185) it provokes, should remind us as well that, as many critics have noted, in *The Old Curiosity Shop* "sexuality is everywhere present and nowhere stated" (Ackroyd 315). Indeed, as Elizabeth Bronfen argues:

> The fascination engendered when the wax cast depicts a feminine body has to do with the fact that the two enigmas of western culture, death and female sexuality, are here "contained" in a way that exposes these two conditions to a sustained and indefinite view, but does so in such a way that the real threat of both, their disruptive and indeterminate quality, has been put under erasure.

Wax casts "served to cover, distance and control both sexuality and death by rendering the mutable, dangerously fluid, destabilized feminine body in a cleansed, purified immobile form" (Bronfen 99). Like the woman in Regent's Park, the narrative of Nell's flight from London is the story of her mobility and mutability, and her transformation into a waxwork effigy ultimately attempts to render her "fixed and changeless" (*OCS* 537; ch. 71), to erase both her sexuality and her mortality.[9]

*

As Elizabeth Campbell reminds us, Dickens often thinks in "iconographic terms" (79), and central to the tension between *The Old Curiosity Shop*'s frozen moments of corporeal display and the "never-ending restlessness" (*OCS* 9; ch. 1) and relentlessness of its narrative progress is the significance of the oft-repeated words "trace" and "track." Like the visitors to the Paris Morgue, Dickens's readers need a catalogue to trace the history of Nell and her grandfather. As a noun, "trace" is a track or a trail and a sign or a mark, a course of conduct or action as well as a vestigial reminder of something formerly present but now absent. As a verb, "trace" is to draw or outline a figure and to write; it is an act which both deciphers and makes clear what is obscure. "Tracks" are imprints the body makes, signs of its presence and the direction of its movement.

Nell Trent is a particularly fugitive character to trace or track, one whose very etherealness and elusiveness leave no imprint to guide either her pursuers or Dickens's readers, who are left at novel's end like her grandfather, claiming, "I have oft tried to track the way she had gone, but her small fairy footstep left no footprint upon the dewy ground, to guide me" (*OCS* 535–36; ch. 71). Impelled by the narrative logic of Nell and her grandfather's flight, it is the business of the novel and its narrators to trace her, to find the clues to both her whereabouts and her identity, but that attempt often occurs "without success" (*OCS* 359; ch. 47). Only when the novel pauses in the frozen moments of tableau can we begin to decipher what is often obscure in Nell's character, and it is telling that Dickens's analogy for such moments of discernment is decidedly visual:

> If you have seen the picture-gallery of any one old family, you will remember how the same face and figure—often the fairest and slightest of them all—come upon you in different generations; and how you trace the same sweet girl through a long line of portraits—never growing old or changing—the Good Angel of the race—abiding them in all reverses—redeeming all their sins—. (525; ch. 69)

If there is a kind of *bildungstableau* logic here, it is the logic of the same. What Dickens stresses here is a timeless moral quality preserved in common physical lineaments—"never growing old or changing"—a palimpsest or "trace" of the "Good Angel" of which Nell is the epitome.

Master Humphrey is the first to attempt to trace Little Nell, and his night-time perambulations and voyeuristic occupation allow him "greater opportunity of speculating on the characters and occupations of those who fill the streets" (*OCS* 9; ch. 1). "Speculate" points to the predominantly visual nature of his investigations as well as to their personal libidinal investment. From the outset the reader is inclined, if not invited, to consider Humphrey's visual preoccupation with Nell as a form of transgressive spectatorship that reveals his voyeuristic intentions: "the beholding of the forbidden, often sexual objects or acts" from a secret vantage point (Mitchell 7). Indeed, Humphrey would have us believe that the furtive "glimpse" by night is far superior to the "full revelation in daylight." But his speculation into the life and character of Nell is unsuccessful, and he rejects both the "hundred different explanations" (12; ch. 1) of his own musing and the available narrative frames or the novel as cultural catalogue—"all the strange tales ... of dark and secret deeds committed in great towns and escaping detection"—as insufficiently adapted to the mystery of Nell and her grandfather, a mystery which he claims, "only became more impenetrable, in proportion as I sought to solve it" (20; ch. 1). Only when he leaves off pacing before the Curiosity Shop and returns home does he begin to "picture" Nell to himself and that figuration is based largely on a vision of Nell surrounded by external objects, or "visible aids," which help to define her and bring "her condition palpably" before him. Humphrey's search for the knowledge of Nell's history is particularly voyeuristic, and that voyeurism marks Nell's body as a site for signification, as a "place for the inscription of stories." Since Humphrey's speculations about Nell seem to be firmly rooted in and on her body, the "region on which [he] was little disposed to enter" as he imagines her "in her future life" must surely allude to her maturation—to marriage and to motherhood—and to her sexuality (22; ch. 1). For even the grandfather, whose vision of Nell is essentially static for most of the novel, knows she "would be a woman soon" (412; ch. 44).

In their ability to create a "palpable" Nell who, figuratively speaking, can be touched, the objects in the shop function metonymically for Nell's body itself and recall the macabre history of dismemberment that haunts all waxworks figures. These are the same "still and motionless" (78; ch. 9) objects that Nell later will be compared to, and they reinforce the notion that such tableaus resist the forward drive of the narrative, just as they presage Nell's identity with the still and silent waxwork figures at Jarley's. These are the objects that crowd the shop itself—"musty treasures" hidden "from the public eye." The image of the grandfather as part antiquarian, part grave-robber groping "among old churches and tombs" (13; ch. 1) links these objects (and Nell as well) with the twin aspects of death and preservation central to waxworks and also prepares the reader for Nell's presentation in the first of the novel's waxwork-like tableaus. In Dickens's novel, the curiosity shop—especially as pictured in the woodcuts "The Old Curiosity Shop," "The Child in Her Gentle Slumber," and "Little Nell as Comforter"—represents the post-sacral world of melodrama, a heterogeneous mixture of modern and medieval elements, the detritus of the sacred systems and symbologies so evident in the novel's closing illustrations.

Samuel Williams's illustration of "The Child in Her Gentle Slumber" forces the reader to "pause and contemplate" the tableau, arresting the forward movement of the verbal narrative. As Dawn Kelly observes, the illustration "enables us to peep back voyeuristically at the shop and at Nell," and also "hints ahead" to those illustrations of Nell's death at the end of the novel (138). As a complement to Humphrey's narrative catalogue and as a visual element in its own right, the tableau of Nell asleep is, like the objects that surround her, a "visible aid" or a help to the "fancy" of both Master Humphrey and the reader, the former of whom is led on by these visual prompts to declare: "'It would be a curious speculation,' said I, after some restless turns across and across the room, 'to imagine her in her future life, holding her solitary way among a crowd of wild grotesque companions; the only pure, fresh, youthful object in the throng. It would be curious to find—'" (22; ch. 1). But Humphrey checks himself, because "the theme was carrying [him] along with it at a great pace" (22; ch. 1). This "curious speculation" into Nell's future life will be the stuff of the narrative itself, despite Humphrey's exit from the novel some two chapters later only to be replaced by a narrator, very like the Uncommercial Traveller, who will serve as our exhibition guide to the continued spectacle of Little Nell. Humphrey will, figuratively speaking, return to the novel in chapter 34 in the guise of the single gentleman, Nell's great-uncle, whose self-appointed task is to find Nell and her grandfather and whose "chief delight," after Nell's death, is "to travel in the steps of the old man and the child (so far as he could trace them from her last narrative)" (554; ch. "The Last"). Since the single gentleman only finds Nell on her deathbed, that journey, we must imagine, is backwards, from the village church to the old curiosity shop, and, like the narrative and its narrators, it moves from corpse to effigy. *The Old Curiosity Shop*, like Humphrey's pacing in his room, turns restlessly "across and across" between Nell's death and her "palpable" representation as the wax girl. If the figure of the sleeping Nell surrounded by what John Forster called "the quaint grotesque figures of the old curiosity warehouse" (124) is, as Humphrey insists, to be seen as an emblem or a "kind of allegory" (22; ch. 1), then it is an allegory of the molded and molding body. It is the "allegory of the body become a subject for literary narrative—a body entered into writing" (Brooks, *Body Work* 3). Faced with the conundrum that is Little Nell, it is her body that Master Humphrey first both fixates on and speculates about. If, like the old man at the morgue, there is nothing about Nell that helps to establish her identity, there is an engraving in the novel and there are tokens or objects within that engraving. At the very moment that Nell becomes an object for speculation, she becomes a subject for the ensuing narrative.

That allegory is made all too clear when Nell and her grandfather join Mrs. Jarley's caravan and her waxwork menagerie. When Nell meets Mrs. Jarley that female impresario claims that her waxworks is "calm and classical ... always the same, with a constantly unchanging air of coldness and gentility; and so like life" (208; ch. 27).

It is apparent that when the caravan stops in the town that Nell is "supposed to be an important item of the curiosities" (216; ch. 28) and that she quickly becomes the "chief attraction" of the show, the figure "on which all eyes were fixed" (221; ch. 29). With their "death-like faces" and their "great glassy eyes" the figures may be "grim," but their "stillness and silence" recalls the earlier description of Nell and the inanimate occupants of the curiosity shop. More importantly, the waxwork figures all stand "with their eyes wide open": "all the ladies and gentleman were looking intensely nowhere, and *staring with extraordinary earnestness at nothing*" (218;

ch. 28, emphasis added). The waxwork figures, and by analogy Nell herself, take on the appearance of the corpse in the Paris Morgue that Dickens will describe later in "Some Recollections of Mortality" as "something that could not return a look." As the novel progresses and Nell moves closer to her death, her features will more and more tell "their silent tale," the tale of the waxworks, and confirm Mrs. Jarley's claim that while waxworks are not "quite like life," life is "exactly like wax-work" (208; ch. 27).

When Master Humphrey abandons his quest for Little Nell and his need to decipher the mystery of her identity, he surrenders his glance for the novel's gaze, for a melodramatic catalogue that scripts a body "free from the trace of pain, so fair to look upon," a body "waiting for the breath of life; not one who had lived and suffered death" (538; ch. 71). In so doing, one form of knowledge is occluded in favor of another. Where were the "traces of her early cares, her sufferings, and fatigues?" the novel asks. "All gone" is the reply: "Sorrow was dead indeed in her, but peace and perfect happiness were born; imaged in her tranquil beauty and profound repose" (540; ch. 71). The reader/spectator is invited to participate in this epiphany, a moment of viewing that eclipses the body and the glance, which Norman Bryson defines as that "furtive and sideways look ... which is capable of carrying unofficial *sub rosa* messages of hostility, collusion, rebellion, and lust" (94). The glance is separated out, repressed, and as it is repressed, it "is also constructed as the hidden term on whose disavowal the whole system depends" (121). As Bryson notes, "Against the Gaze, the Glance proposes desire, proposes the body, in the durée of its practical activity" (122). The glance is the ungovernable and mobile look of Quilp, whose myriad and fluctuating postures and poses point to another way in which the body resists the order of the narrative catalogue and requires "some new language; such, for power of expression, as was never written, read, or spoken" (507; ch. 67). The glance, we may suspect, is also the nighttime glimpse of Master Humphrey as well.[10]

But the moment of the gaze, Bryson insists, is "outside of duration"; the vision of the gaze is "vision disembodied, vision decarnalized," and the activity of the gaze is "prolonged, contemplative, yet regarding the field of vision with a certain aloofness and disengagement, across a tranquil interval." The gaze "arrests the flux of phenomena, contemplates the visual field from a vantage-point outside of the mobility of duration, in an eternal moment of disclosed presence" (94). Like the wax tableau, with the gaze "What is removed from the world is its duration: the bodily postures and gestures are frozen" (95). With the gaze the act of viewing is "constructed as the removal of space and time" and as the "disappearance of the body" (96). The gaze steps "outside of the flux of sensations ... to call into being the realm of transcendent forms" (122). In freezing narrative time and the time of the body, the gaze seeks to repress "desire . . . the body, [and] the desire of the body" (123).

The wax girl is outside of duration as well, and wax is an erasive medium which seeks to cover its own tracks, to cover the traces of body and the body's suffering, leaving Nell "unaltered in this change" (*OCS* 540; ch. 71). Wax is a medium that seeks to arrest the flux of phenomena that always haunts the narrative catalogue. The gaze contemplates the drama of Little Nell from the perspective of the novel's last act when Nell will be honored after her death by her apotheosis. The novel's gaze, then, is commensurate with the grandfather's unchanging vision of Nell; we are to be content reading "the book of her heart from the page first presented to [us], little dreaming of the story that lay hidden in its other leaves" (76; ch. 9). But at the moment that the deathbed narrative and its accompanying illustration encourage Dickens's reader to see Little Nell as the good angel, the wax girl truly "cannot return a look," and so confounds both the aims of the melodramatic narrative and the melodramatic gaze. In the end, Dickens's body art is an art that is always trying to shake off the body, to rub out the signs that make the body legible. Ironically, it is an art that quite often fails.

*

As Peter Brooks argues, melodrama has recourse to tableau "at moments of climax and crisis, where speech is silenced and narrative arrested in order to foster a fixed and visual representation" (*Melodramatic Imagination* 61). The use of tableaus in *The Old Curiosity Shop* is evident in the motif of waxwork effigy and exhibition, which function as paradigms of corporeal display in the novel, and in the illustrations that punctuate Dickens's text, both of which serve to dislocate the verbal narrative. While tableau is linked to both the history of art and the history of dramaturgy, especially the melodrama, the art of tableau is distinct from the art of narrative composition. Tableau functions to isolate a particular scene in a kind of "immovable fixation." Concealing history and suspending temporality, the tableau engages in the illusion of timelessness in which the "transitoriness of the real world is magically transformed into an ideal of fixity" (Caplan 18). Arousing the eager look of the reader and arresting that look in the framing of a specific scene, tableau encourages a special concentration of meaning, inviting the spectator to participate in a kind of melodramatic reading, in a search for the body's significance. Furthermore, that framing accomplishes a complete closure of the text from the reality that surrounds it, a closure free from the restless and relentless forward drive of the narrative. Tableau introduces a "kind of parenthesis in the narrative order where a spatial mode of representation prevails, and it organizes the represented material in a finite image governed by specific compositional devices" (Tygstup 212). Presenting scenes of arrested life, the tableau, like the waxwork, creates the illusion of stasis, the illusion that bodies don't change, that they don't mature, decay, and die. Forced to acknowledge loss, if only implicitly, tableaus are always in search of some compensatory gesture; they represent "both a loss and a desire to compensate for that loss" (24). While disclosing that loss the tableau, particularly the waxwork tableau, nonetheless, attempts to promise some future redemption, promises a future "without loss, without suffering, even without death" (25). Yet, as Jay Caplan reminds

us, the tableau is "also a *tombeau*, a tomb and it inevitably recalls the sacrifices that
have been made for a virtuous cause" (25).

In *The Old Curiosity Shop* that sacrifice is the life and history of Little Nell.
Gaze and tableau collude at novel's end in a melodramatic and ideal fixity. Nell
is both literally and figuratively entombed. If the wax girl loses all the traces of
her suffering, the history of her travails, like the curiosity shop itself, is at best
a fading memory, as the narrator acknowledges: "Such are the changes which a
few years bring about, and so do things pass away, like a tale that is told" (556;
ch. "The Last"). The waxwork effigy is the epitome of the preserved body, and
the waxwork tableau is the representative of its particular form of visibility. As
a preserved body, Dickens's wax girl is a signifier "for an arrested and eternal-
ized moment countering all notions of mutability" and "suggests that the eternal
stasis of the displayed body is used by the narrative as a moment where the narrative, in its conjunctions with temporality and change, can be cut off" (Bronfen
102). If melodrama and melodramatic narrative inscribe the body with meaning,
The Old Curiosity Shop would appear to enact a moment when the body's inevitable meanings become unbearable and the narrative needs to be cut off. But, in
its strange metaleptic drift, in its movement from corpse to catalogue, Dickens's
novel and Dickens's heroine are victims of the paradox of all melodramatic display—arrested development. If the motif of the waxwork seeks to "fix" Nell's
identity and to see the figure of Nell as the representation of ideal virtue, it ultimately invokes the transitoriness of the real world that is the stuff of her narrative.
If "She was dead" is ultimately both the novel's prelude and is coda, both its end
and origin, tableau and waxwork ultimately fail to close off the history of sexuality, poverty, criminality, and mortality that haunt the nineteenth-century morgue,
wax museum, and *The Old Curiosity Shop*.

NOTES

1. Billie Melman gives an interesting account of the relation between Tussaud's wax museum
   and the British perception of the French Revolution. See *The Culture of History*, 29–65.
2. The claim that Nell's narrative actually begins at the moment of her death and in the
   repeated phrase "She was dead" certainly coincides with that other inaugural moment
   of *The Old Curiosity Shop*, the death of Dickens's sister in-law, Mary Hogarth, in 1837.
3. Although melodrama (the subject of his earlier *The Melodramatic Imagination*) is not
   the subject of *Body Work* per se, Brooks does claim, "During the revolution, the new
   popular genre of melodrama provides a literalistic realization of this new importance
   of the body as the site of signification" (56), and he devotes chapter 3, "Marking Out
   the Modern Body: The French Revolution and Balzac," to the melodramatic body.
   Melodramatic narrative is simply one of the ways the body gets into and is represented
   in writing (54–87).

4. In *Body Work* Brooks maintains that "The prostitute's body is by definition a storied body, itself enacting and creating narratives of passion, lust, and greed, as it passes through the social economy" (70).
5. In answer to the question "What makes a scene Primal?" Harold Bloom writes, "A scene is a setting as seen by a viewer, a place where action, whether real or fictitious, occurs or is staged. Every Primal Scene is necessarily a stage performance" (47).
6. Like Lukacher, I do not use the term "primal scene" to evoke the conventional psycho-analytic sense of the expression, which he aptly summarizes as "A child's witnessing of a sexual act that subsequently plays a traumatic role in his or her psycho-sexual life" (24). Like Fish, Lukacher, and Brooks (*Reading for the Plot* 264–81), I employ the term to indicate both a particular narrative and rhetorical strategy and a scenic construction or reconstruction.
7. In *Reading for the Plot*, Brooks, too, likens Freud's "History" to a detective story.
8. Maria Warner identifies the three women as the Princess de Lamballe, Madame du Barry, and Madame de Saint Amaranthe, all of whom were victims of the guillotine (185). It is not clear which of three figures later became known as the Sleeping Beauty.
9. Laurie Langbauer notes the connection between Nell's mobility and her inherent sexuality and argues that her death is necessary to put end to such motion and deny that sexuality.
10. In the novel's first illustration, Humphrey is represented as a crouched and furtive figure hidden in the shadows and standing in the doorway in a pose quite similar to one often assigned to Quilp.

WORKS CITED

Ackroyd, Peter. *Dickens*. New York: Harper Collins, 1990.
Bloom, Harold. *A Map of Misreading*. New York: Oxford UP, 1980.
Bowen, John. *Other Dickens: Pickwick to Chuzzlewit*. Oxford: Oxford UP, 2000.
Bronfen, Elisabeth. *Over Her Dead Body: Death, Femininity and the Aesthetic*. Manchester: Manchester UP, 1992.
Brooks, Peter. *Body Work: Objects of Desire in Modern Narrative*. Cambridge, MA: Harvard UP, 1993.
———. *The Melodramatic Imagination: Balzac, Henry James, Melodrama, and the Mode of Excess*. New Haven: Yale UP, 1995.
———. *Reading for the Plot: Design and Intention in Narrative*. New York: Knopf, 1984.
Bryson, Norman. *Vision and Painting: The Logic of the Gaze*. New Haven: Yale UP, 1983.
Campbell, Elizabeth A. *Fortune's Wheel: Dickens and the Iconography of Women's Time*. Athens: Ohio UP, 2003.
Caplan, Jay. *Framed Narratives: Diderot's Geneology of the Beholder*. Minneapolis: U of Minnesota P, 1980.
Craton, Lillian. *The Victorian Freak Show: The Significance of Disability and Physical Difference in Nineteenth-Century Fiction*. Amherst, NY: Cambria, 2009.

Dickens, Charles. *The Old Curiosity Shop*. Ed. Norman Page. New York: Penguin, 2000.

———. *The Uncommercial Traveller and Other Papers 1859–70*. Ed. Michael Slater and John Drew. Columbus, Ohio: Ohio State UP, 2000.

Drew, John M. L. "Voyages Extraordinaires: Dickens's 'Travelling Essays' and *The Uncommercial Traveller* (Part Two)." *Dickens Quarterly* 13 (Sept. 1996): 127–50.

Edelman, Lee. "Seeing Things: Representation, the Scene of Surveillance, and the Spectacle of Gay Male Sex." *Inside/Out: Lesbian Theories, Gay Theories*. Ed. Diana Fuss. New York: Routledge, 1991. 93–116.

Fish, Stanley. "Withholding the Missing Portion: Power, Meaning and Persuasion in Freud's 'The Wolfman.'" *Times Literary Supplement* 29 Aug. 1986: 935–38.

Forster, John. *The Life of Charles Dickens*. Vol. 1. London: Dent, 1948. 2 vols.

Hager, Kelly. "Jasper Packlmerton, Victorian Freak." *Victorian Literature and Culture* 34 (2006): 209–32.

Hood, Thomas. *Selected Poems of Thomas Hood*. Ed. John Clubbe. Cambridge: Harvard UP, 1970.

Kelly, Dawn P. "Image and Effigy: The Illustrations to *The Old Curiosity Shop*." *Imagination on a Long Rein: English Literature Illustrated*. Ed. Joachim Moller. Marburg: Jonas Verlag, 1988. 136–47.

Langbauer, Laurie. "Dickens's Streetwalkers: Women and the Form of Romance." *ELH* 53 (1986): 411–31.

Lukacher, Ned. *Primal Scenes: Literature, Philosophy, Psychoanalysis*. Ithaca: Cornell UP, 1986.

Melman, Billie. *The Culture of History: English Uses of the Past 1830–1853*. New York: Oxford UP, 2006.

Mitchell, W. J. T. "Tableau and Taboo: The Resistance to Vision in Literary Discourse." *CEA Critic* 51.1 (1988): 4–10.

Sandberg, Mark B. *Living Pictures, Missing Persons: Mannequins, Museums, and Modernity*. Princeton: Princeton UP, 2003.

Schor, Hilary M. *Dickens and the Daughter of the House*. New York: Cambridge UP, 1999.

Schwartz, Vanessa R. "The Morgue and the Musée Grévin: Understanding the Public Taste for Reality in Fin-de-Siècle Paris." *Spectacles of Realism: Body, Gender, Genre*. Ed. Margaret Cohen and Christopher Prendergast. Minneapolis: U of Minnesota P, 1995. 268–93.

Tygstup, Frederick. "The Textual Tableau: Models of Human Space in the Novel." *Reinventions of the Novel: Histories and Aethetics of a Protean Genre*. Ed. Karen-Margrethe Simonsen, Marianne Ping Huang and Mad Rosendahl Thomsen. New York: Rodolpi, 2004. 211–26.

Vita, Paul. "Returning the Look: Victorian Writers and the Paris Morgue." *Nineteenth Century Contexts* 25 (2003): 241–56.

Warner, Maria. "Waxworks and Wonderlands." *Visual Display*. Ed. Lynne Cook and Peter Wollen. Seattle: Bay, 1995. 178–201.

Dora Spenlow, Female Communities, and Female Narrative in Charles Dickens's *David Copperfield* and George Eliot's *Middlemarch*

Maria Ioannou

The article argues that Dickens's David Copperfield *and Eliot's* Middlemarch *pose the problem of a story which is non-narratable in female terms, while at the same time trying to articulate it within the main narrative, in what becomes a commentary on the central story. The two novels, though different in many respects, have one similarity: a certain characteristic of the way the narrator of each novel describes events, which makes it possible to register conflicting interpretations of experience. This is especially so concerning the voices of women characters, particularly women whose positions within the social structure seem problematic, women who have been judged as having failed in their wifely roles, or women who have been defined by one single attribute. These women exist in a space that forms a female narrative and enables the creation of female community. This way, a female-centered explanation of the questions pertaining to female belonging in Victorian society begins to emerge.*

"Is she [Mrs. Casaubon] very clever?" asks Rosamond Vincy of Will Ladislaw, only to get the condescending reply, "I never thought about it.... When one sees a perfect woman, one never thinks of her attributes ..." (409; bk. 5, ch. 43). Yet *Mid-*

Dickens Studies Annual, Volume 44, Copyright © 2013 by AMS Press, Inc. All rights reserved.
DOI 10.7756/dsa.044.008.143-164

dlemarch (1871–72) is precisely asking us to "think of" Dorothea's "attributes"; and the fact that these have no currency within male-dominated social structures and the male point of view (here exemplified by Will) is one of the major themes of the novel. Conversely, Dorothea's attributes and abilities are exactly what Rosamond wishes to know more about; the relationship between Rosamond Vincy and Dorothea Brooke in *Middlemarch* constructs a female way of thinking about women that attempts to remedy the inadequacies of patriarchal social norms and structures. Similarly, in Dickens's *David Copperfield* (1849–50), the female community made up of Dora Spenlow, Agnes Wickfield, and Miss Betsey Trotwood alerts readers to a female world that reassesses Victorian constructions of proper femininity and proper female "attributes." This way, both novels trace the development of a female narrative which acts as an interpretive adjunct to the dominant (and dominating) male-centered ideology of domesticity and the doctrine of separate spheres; this article argues that the two novels not only pose the problem of a story which is non-narratable in female terms, but that they also try to articulate this female-centered story within the main narrative, in what becomes an interesting commentary on the primary story. As the women in *David Copperfield* and *Middlemarch* attempt to formulate their stories, they create a site where woman is acknowledged as a relational being, not to men, as daughter, wife, or mother, but, importantly, to other women.

Comparing *David Copperfield* and *Middlemarch*

To the best of my knowledge, an extensive comparison or a comparative study of *David Copperfield* and *Middlemarch* has not so far been made. Therefore, I will begin by explaining what has led me to draw an explicit parallel between the two novels. This will also serve as a form of theoretical approach that will unify the examination of the texts and their common theme—that is, the construction of a female-centered narrative within the dominant narrative.

Admittedly, there are basic differences between *David Copperfield* and *Middlemarch*. In terms of theme, for instance, Eliot's novel has broader concerns; for example, the political climate surrounding the first Reform Bill, the relationship between scholarship and theorizing about life with actual life and living, the relationship between art and life. *David Copperfield* is more obviously a bildungsroman.

Further, the lot of women is more directly engaged in *Middlemarch*. There is no comment from David Copperfield to match the *Middlemarch* narrator's remark about women's life being a road which led nowhere (26; bk. 1, ch. 3). Most of the time, the central women characters of *David Copperfield* are seen in relation to David and his life-story; they are, notably, seen by David, who has the sole responsibility of recording their actions and lives.

This brings us to the question of narration in the two novels. Mode of narration is, I argue, a fundamental difference and, at the same time, a source of similarity when it comes to the theme of women and narratives within narratives in the text. Narration constitutes a fundamental point of difference for reasons that seem obvious. In *David Copperfield,* the narration is in the first person, carried out by the eponymous hero, and is accompanied by the strengths and weaknesses that can be found in nearly any first-person narration: authenticity and immediacy are examples of the former, while a restricted point of view and a more obvious mediation of reality are examples of the latter. *Middlemarch,* on the other hand, is told in the words of an omniscient third-person narrator, who moves from character to character and story to story in a way that the *David Copperfield* narrator is unable to do. The *Middlemarch* narrator can pause in the middle of a sentence and shift the focus from one character to another, an action that significantly alters the text that follows immediately after.[1] Therefore, *Middlemarch* might appear to be more inclusive, though both novels deal with multiple characters and complex, intersecting story-lines. The action is more dispersed in *Middlemarch,* while in *David Copperfield* it is more focused, proceeding toward the eventual union of David and Agnes, which ends his journey and confirms the disciplining of his heart.

Thus, another obvious difference in narration concerns the gender of the narrator in each text. *David Copperfield* is the story of a male hero, spoken in his own words; one of the goals of the text is to establish David as an exemplary middle-class man.[2] As a result, actions and characters are assessed by their contribution or relation to this goal. Clara Copperfield and her tragic destiny, for instance, are represented in terms of the manner in which they influenced the life of the boy David; the story of Dr. Strong and his much younger wife Annie is told from the point of view of an admiring pupil for his teacher—it would probably have sounded remarkably different had it been told by the narrator of *Middlemarch.*

Nevertheless, the question of the gender of the narrator in *Middlemarch* is not settled. J. Hillis Miller suggests that the *Middlemarch* narrator is male (68), and, apart from a concern with women's issues, there are not too many other indications as to what can be a definitive answer to this. In fact, there is an obvious concern with masculinity and the masculine destiny that balances, though it does not outweigh, the concern with womanhood. We may like to think here of the ways Casaubon's bookishness and late marriage, as well as Ladislaw's feminine attributes (such as curly-haired beauty, pettishness, and economic dependence),[3] interrogate dominant concepts of masculinity in the Victorian era and with what degree of success; whether, also, Lydgate's efforts to fulfill the Victorian heterosexual destiny constitute a critique of that destiny. Caleb Garth and Mr. Farebrother are also images of masculinity that can be problematized. This is, however, beyond the scope of the present article, which merely suggests that the *Middlemarch* narrator seems to be interested in the general formation of gender in the Victorian era, and not only with women and femininity (though the emphasis on femininity, women, and their destiny, is greater).

Notably, what makes narration a source of similarity between *David Copperfield* and *Middlemarch* is not the narrator him/herself, but a certain characteristic of their ways of describing events, a certain aspect of their voice. Both narrators have the capacity of registering opposite points of view, conflicting interpretations of experience—the *Middlemarch* narrator more obviously, the *David Copperfield* narrator more covertly. Though Gareth Corderoy has called *David Copperfield* "David's panoptic prison,"[4] I consider this claim to hold true only so far as the ideology of domesticity and heterosexual fulfillment in marriage are concerned. It is not altogether accurate when it comes to the existence of a variety of voices that David is not able to contain. Intentionally or not,[5] Dickens has made David's narration multifaceted and ambiguous. Victorian reviewers sensed this characteristic of the novel when they called it "an all-containing treasure house" of Victorian society (Matthew Arnold 269).

Though the narrators of the two novels seem different in many ways, there is a specific machinery of the narration which allows us to examine the novels on the basis of aspects of the stories that spring from the narration. This is not to say that differences do not exist; it is merely to say that there is an area of intersection in the way narration records voices and events.

There are similarities between the two novels also in terms of theme. Both *Middlemarch* and *David Copperfield* deal with marriage failure and remarriage. Dorothea's claim that the marriage stays with us like a murder (749; bk. 8, ch. 81) can be very well used to describe David's marriage to Dora also. Of course, it does not apply to David only; it applies to Dora's character and story as well. As I will be suggesting later in this article, the way the second marriage remedies the restlessness of the first is under scrutiny in both novels, while both marriage and remarriage seem to share a problematic nature.

However, the most important parallel between *Middlemarch* and *David Copperfield* remains a result of the way narration works to record conflicting experiences, explicitly in *Middlemarch*, less so in the Dickens novel. This produces, in both novels, a female-centered narrative that is adjacent to the main story and operates as a critical perspective on it. The female narrative develops along the same plot-lines as the main narrative and shares its themes. In the case of Eliot's novel, it develops in relation to the Casaubon and Lydgate marriages and the theme of marriage failure; in the case of *David Copperfield*, in relation to David's marriage to Dora (and Clara's earlier marriage to Murdstone). The female narrative is, in both cases, a re-writing of the ideology that supports the main narrative, an ideology of domesticity, saintly wifehood, and male dominance. Let us first consider the emergence of this ideology in *David Copperfield*.

Masculine and Feminine Values in *David Copperfield*

The novel records David's journey inside the masculine, competitive, often hostile world, and the way he makes himself fit to survive in that world; even if, as

Virginia Carmichael has noted, David seeks to recover the mother he has lost (129), this recovery is done in terms of the masculine, dominant structure.

Accordingly, Agnes is the proper wife, because she is the nourishing, idealized, and spiritual side of the lost mother—a figure in a stained glass window. However, the novel also records the formation of a female-centered discourse that constructs a femininity outside of official narratives; alongside the masculine, disciplinarian world, the novel develops an alternative world of women, which is a transformative reflection of the masculine world. In the female community of *David Copperfield*, societal judgments and classifications surrounding women are shown as inadequate descriptions of the female experience.

This is precisely what makes Dora, Aunt Betsey, and Agnes a "community" for the purposes of this article: the development, which can be traced to their relationship, of a specific narrative thread on the subject of domesticity, or a narrative version of domesticity. The figure of the domestic woman, and woman's domestic destiny, constituted the dominant framework of middle-class female experience in the Victorian era and the story of Dora, Aunt Betsey, and Agnes forms a subversive commentary on that framework.

In *Communities of Women*, Nina Auerbach's exposition of the fellowship of sisterhood, a female community can be defined by various factors. For example, in Jane Austen's *Pride and Prejudice* (1813) and Louisa May Alcott's *Little Women* (1868–69), the constitutive parts of a female community are family and what these women do or can teach each other (Auerbach 35–37). In Elizabeth Gaskell's *Cranford* (1851), it is that the women are "beyond the years of waiting. The hunt has failed, their mothers are dead, and they are in possession of themselves ..." (Auerbach 79). Thus, these women exemplify stability and strength, and a "cohesion against the world" (Auerbach 80). The girls' boarding school in Charlotte Brontë's *Villette* (1853) makes a community because it creates a space where "passive female essence can be discarded." The women forming a female community in *Villette* are those who, prompted by seclusion, free their masculine instincts—that is, Mme Beck, Ginevra Fanshawe and, obviously, Lucy Snowe herself (Auerbach 98). For Auerbach, a community of women is a tradition in the novel "that does allow women an independent life beyond the saga of courtship and the settlement of marriage ... a furtive, unofficial, often underground entity" (11).

Therefore, a female community can be defined in terms of types of bond and bonding, blood relation, or creating a space in the novel that can be set up as an alternative to some of the novel's themes. This last component or defining characteristic is what seems to apply in the cases of *David Copperfield* and *Middlemarch* (for *Middlemarch*, see below). The element which posits Dora Spenlow, Aunt Betsey, and Agnes Wickfield as a community is the ability of their relationship to form a commentary on the saga of courtship and marriage. When I mention the term "narrative thread," I mean a formulation of narrative that runs through the dominant narrative in accordance with a common theme. This sort of narrative is not so much an embedded text (a story that can be new and complete and explain or resemble the primary story [Bal 52–53] as an "other narrative that can be *constructed in response* to [the basic story] or *perceived as related* to it (Smith 144, emphasis original). It is a narrative version, an account "told from a particular or partial perspective." This version is a "retelling" of a particular prior narrative text (Smith 139). Thus, Dora, Aunt Betsey, and Agnes are selected as a community because of their "retelling" of David's primary narrative, which is the narrative of the adjustment to domesticity—the narrative of a man fulfilling his middle-class destiny. I do not claim that there cannot be any other communities of women in the novel. For example, Little Emily and Rosa Dartle may adumbrate a particular combination of versions of the figure of the fallen woman; Rosa Dartle and Mrs. Steerforth may be read to form a community in terms of the construction of a narrative on female repressed passion and female confinement. These communities are potent and certainly part of the gender dynamics of the novel. However, they are beyond the scope of this article, which is concerned with domesticity and angelic wifehood, and a female-centered version of these themes, that exists in tandem with the main, or basic, narrative.

The key figure in the female community of *David Copperfield* is Dora Spenlow, primarily because of the marked antithesis between how David interprets her and her actions after she becomes his wife, and the way Aunt Betsey and Agnes interpret her or, rather, refuse to interpret her. The love, acceptance, and understanding with which Dora is regarded and surrounded by in this small community of females speaks of a female capacity to appreciate and comprehend other women, which is far wider than any system of Victorian categorization of women would allow.

Women perceive Dora differently than David does, and more favorably, a phenomenon usually read as a reflection on David's character and role as narrator[6] and, more recently, as revelatory of a depth and resolve in Dora that needs to be discussed in terms of her own understanding of her marriage situation: "wisdom in the guise of foolishness seems to be Dora's chief characteristic," writes Kelly Hager (138). For Dora, death is "an escape from marriage, an escape for which she is eager, perhaps even more eager than David" (Hager 136). Indeed, Hager calls Dora's death "a self-willed flight from the unbearable" (140).

This article suggests that another function of the stories of the women is to explain David's inadequacies as narrator: in fact, the female narrative of *David Copperfield* shows that David cannot be *anything* but an inadequate narrator, because he is being conditioned, as a young man and head of a family, to think in a specific way. Women are better narrators than men when it comes to the woman's story, and this is precisely the point.

The woman's story, in *David Copperfield*, is constructed by the three women themselves (Dora, Agnes, Aunt Betsey) and does not acknowledge the dominant definitions of womanhood as the only framework within which a female subjectivity can be developed. Female subjectivity in the novel is relational between the women themselves and belongs to no binary distinctions. As a wife, Dora often behaves selflessly, and Agnes looks beautiful and is admired for her beauty. If any person inside the novel behaves as a proper husband should to Dora, this is Aunt Betsey. She "courted Jip ... never attacked the Incapables ... went wonderful distances on foot to purchase, as surprises, any trifles that she found out Dora wanted; and never came by the garden ... but she would call out, at the foot of the stairs, in a voice that sounded cheerfully all over the house: 'Where's Little Blossom!'" (656; ch. 44). Aunt Betsey straddles all categories, both male and female. Still, John Forster described her as "a gnarled and knotted piece of female timber, sound to the core," "perfect womanhood" (429). Both nurturing and authoritative, tender and decisive, Aunt Betsey is head of a household, and at one stage has a man and a boy under her protection.

Thus, Dickens put the "female timber" to good use when constructing *David Copperfield*. To read from the text to the culture it represented is to appreciate *this female narrative, or narrative of females*. Within the female community, Dora's girlish beauty is no longer a means of interpretation, and no longer a judgment on her character. In the context of the female triad formed by Dora herself, Agnes, and Aunt Betsey, frivolity, girlishness, and an inability to fulfill the traditional wifely role of housekeeper are not the grave offenses they are defined to be by the male-centered world of angelic domesticity, where the wife is responsible for counseling and redeeming the man.

The way the female community negotiates an appreciation of woman based on individuality and on a recognition of the right to be appreciated on the grounds of that individuality would obviously run counter to the strictures of Victorian household and conduct manuals, which both preached and constructed angelic wifehood. For example, Sarah Stickney Ellis had written that the objectives of the true wife were to make her husband happy, raise his character, give dignity to his house, and train his children on the path of wisdom (Ellis, *Wives* 59), tasks at which Dora Spenlow does not altogether succeed. The mistress of the home must endeavor to make those under her roof happy, wrote both Ellis and Mrs. Beeton (Beeton 11; Ellis, *Women* 45, 63, 73), making no mention of the wife's own right to happiness and respect as a person with wants, fallibilities, and needs.

Rather than following or reflecting conduct books and domestic manuals, *David Copperfield* investigates the implications of Ellis's idea that "the greatest calamity in woman's history [is perhaps] the loss of her husband's love" (Ellis, *Daughters* 186) and the actual impact this has on the wife herself. David's viewpoint is not the only conceivable one (Brown 207), and the masculine world of competition (with male self-assertion depending on the fulfillment of the heterosexual destiny of having a leisured woman maintaining the household) to which David belongs never completely aborts Dora and the form of female belonging weaved around her character. This is avoided in ways I will proceed to examine.

The Memories of Dora's Sexual Allure

An important reason why the female-centered world survives inside disciplinarian, male-centered society is Dora's sexual allure, which remains strong in
David's memory. As Maia McAleavey has recently pointed out, "it would be hard
to determine if David does cease loving ... Dora by the time he marries Agnes"
(203). In fact, it is clear that David the narrator (happily married to Agnes) has not
erased Dora's sexual allure from his mind and thoughts. Dora, even as a memory,
continues to excite in him sensations which Agnes never does. He still remembers, in sexual terms, their encounter in the garden the first day they met: "I had
not been walking long ... when I met her. I tingle again from head to foot as my
recollection turns that corner, and my pen shakes in my hand" (402; ch. 26). It
seems that David has never experienced in his second marriage the love he has
had with Dora, despite the happy union with Agnes. Following Dora's phaeton on
horseback, the narrator David says: "I shall never have such a ride again. I have
never had such another" (489; ch. 33). David does not stop loving Dora in a sexual
manner. His first gift to her as a young lover was a ring made of Forget-me-nots,
"a pretty little toy ... so associated in my remembrance with Dora's hand, that
yesterday, when I saw such another ... on the finger of my own daughter, there
was a momentary stirring in my heart, like pain!" (495; ch. 33).

Notably, David's and Agnes's daughter is also called Dora. The repetition
of the name has the double function of, first, renewing Dora's presence inside
the narrative and, second, of establishing a continuity between Dora and Agnes.
The similarities between the two women form an inclusive site that accumulates
versions of womanhood, in order to examine them in a female-centered manner.

Dora Spenlow and Agnes Wickfield

It is not only Aunt Betsey's notable association with Dora and Agnes and
appreciation of Dora on the basis of her goodness and ability to love that
draws attention to the community of women in *David Copperfield*; it is also
the association between Dora and Agnes themselves. Competent household
management aside, what makes the two women seem so different from each
other is merely David's often erroneous perception of them (angel, useful
woman/coquette, decorative woman).

In fact, Dora's thought that she might have learnt from Agnes what
she cannot learn from David (651; ch. 44) hints at David's inability to see the
two women clearly. It also shows the female community as a world where
relationships between women are established over the gaps opened by the male-
centered world. For Hager, Dora does reproach David for his behavior toward

her, tries to talk to him seriously about their incompatibility, and wonders why
he did not fall in love with Agnes (137–38). Sharon Marcus has argued that
the Dora-Agnes association "establishes each woman's femininity as a matter
of same-sex relations" (89). With this, Marcus does not seem to me to imply a
homoerotic attachment between Dora and Agnes, though her book does center
around female same-sex desire. What Marcus seems to suggest here is that female
identity between Dora and Agnes is, to an extent, formed as a matter of their
relationship to each other. The two women love each other, and this underscores
Agnes's womanly virtue, and Dora's potential for improvement (89). Dora "states
a desire she shares with her husband: to have chosen Agnes as her first spouse,"
says Marcus (89). Agnes incorporates Dora, and is identified with her (89–90).
The choice of the word "spouse" may seem odd only if taken out of the context
of *Between Women*; Marcus's wider argument in this book is that bonds between
women in the Victorian period did not function "as the antithesis of heterosexual
relations" (19). Emotional and loving friendships between women were "central
to lives organized around men" (19). Thus, when it comes to Dora and Agnes,
Marcus explains: "[a]fter her wedding, Dora conjectures that a longer friendship
with Agnes would have made her a better helpmate" (89). Significantly, the two
women redeem the notion of forming a woman's mind, by removing the cruelty
and condescension men associate with that endeavor. In fact, the forming of a
woman's mind (nightmarish and brutish when undertaken by men) is reimagined
by Dora as fruitful and productive, if a competent and intelligent woman like
Agnes were going to undertake it.

Between themselves Agnes and Dora combine everything Dickens found
lovable in a woman (Slater 371). Beth Newman also points out that the contrast is
not clear-cut in all areas. Both are beautiful; both are modest; both sing and play
music in front of an audience of family or friends (62–63). The little we learn
of Dora's behavior during her and David's wedding ceremony has to do with
Agnes. Dickens closely associates Dora and Agnes, and this cannot be accidental,
meaningless, or fortuitous, in a novel where, as Jeremy Tambling indicates,
"identities are made to flow into each other" (xxxii). In fact, Dickens himself had
insisted on the meticulousness of the composition of *David Copperfield*; writing
to the Reverend James White (writer and contributor to *Household Words*),
he expresses his pleasure that it was being received so well, and adds: "I have
carefully planned out the story, for some time past, to the end, and am making out
my purposes with great care" ("The Letters of Charles Dickens" [126]).

What is more, the elements which David acknowledges in Dora are those
he fails to acknowledge in Agnes, and vice versa. That is, the playful elements of
Agnes go unnoticed by David, and the same happens with the nurturing elements
in Dora. For instance, Dora's efforts at housekeeping are repudiated by David, so
that her tender attempts to take care of him are usually unacknowledged. When
David said he would have liked some fish, Dora says, "I went out myself, miles
and miles, and ordered it, to surprise you" (644; ch. 44). This is not, of course, to

say that Dora is as adept as Agnes at housekeeping. It is merely to indicate that she does make efforts that are all read by David in a very negative manner. For example, he admits that Dora had been very kind, so that he did not "mention" on that day that she bought more salmon than they could afford (however, he does mention it, albeit on a later day). David constantly and systematically misreads Dora's abilities as wife, saying that she is "as merry as if we had been keeping a baby-house, for a joke" (655; ch. 44).

This is David's view of things, not Dora's; Dora's interpretation of events is quite different, for the love she has for David is constant and sincere. It is a part of the complexity of Dora's characterization, and one of the ways in which it becomes possible to free her from David's dominating gaze, that her behavior exhibits self-knowledge and an ability to evaluate a situation with accuracy. Consequently, I cannot agree with John Lucas's idea that Dora is regarded as "a pretty toy or plaything" because "there is nothing else she can be" (62). Dora's characterization is part of the dialectic that unites women in the novel.

In fact, the ease with which Dora fits in the community of women in the novel refutes Lucas's claim, and suggests that there are alternative ways of belonging, even within tight patriarchal positioning. Dora indeed reveals what Margaret Flanders Darby calls a self which is "beyond her narrator's understanding" (155). Alongside the placement or interpellation of women effected by the male protagonist and narrator, the novel forms an initiative toward understanding women that is effected by the women themselves.

For it is not only Dora's nurturing (Agnes) side that is unnoticed by David and the majority of critics; so is Agnes's erotic (Dora) side. Agnes is the image of her mother, who had been passionate and capable of strong feelings (847; ch. 60). John Kucich reads Agnes as "perfected internal conflict," defining conflict as a shifting relation between passion and repression (146). For Robert R. Garnett, asexuality is not an inherent quality in Agnes, since Uriah Heep certainly lusts for her in a sexual way (221).

Though Slater believes that it would take a bold critic to redeem Agnes as a character, he does admit that the story narrated from Agnes's point of view might give us an insight into the struggle going on inside her heart (250). As it is, we only see Agnes through David's eyes. He subjects her to what Simon Edwards calls "the dazzlingly persuasive power of narration" (72).

This is not to say that Agnes was even intended by Dickens to have been as sexually exciting as Dora or Clara Copperfield; however, her manner can be flirty and emotional, even playful at times. Hilary Schor alerts us to this feature of *David Copperfield:* "Women's stories throughout the novel carry a special emotional significance ... and cast a sceptical gaze over David's ... narrative powers" (10). Only David sees Agnes without passion, interest, or desire (Schor 12). "Is Agnes really a legless angel? asks Peter Gay. To David, Agnes is "an icon, a superhuman superego." But, as Gay has rightly pointed out, this is, after all, "his problem, not hers." John Carey was more colorful, whimsically saying that Agnes is pointing not upwards, "but towards the bedroom"; her instincts are "perfectly normal" (171).

Importantly, it is because Agnes has a passionate and amorous side that she is able to wait for so many years for David to reciprocate her love. The marriage between David and Agnes happens not only because now David can look clearly inside his heart, but also because Agnes's feelings are lasting and strong.

Woman's Own: Dora, Agnes, and Communities of Women

If, as Nina Auerbach observes, female communities evolved as a literary myth that "sweeps across official cultural images of female submission, subservience and fulfillment in a bounded world" (6), this article seeks to demonstrate how the presence of a female community inside a text can form a commentary on the main story that is elaborate enough to produce another version of the story itself. While David assures his aunt that he had "no other intention than to speak [to Dora] tenderly ... about our own home affairs" (644; ch. 44), she reminds him of his own home during his mother's marriage to Murdstone, and explains that marriage requires patience, for "Rome was not built in a day, nor in a year" (645; ch. 44).

Inside the female community, Dora's belonging is secure; the bonding and relations among the women are not grounded on disciplining, silencing, and crime, as happens in the male-dominated community. While the masculine world of middle-class professionalism is perhaps productive of stability, it is a carceral, disciplinarian world, as the Uriah Heep plot clearly shows: Heep carries the work ethic to an extreme that shows its potential for criminality. The novel suggests that, at least as far as woman is concerned, what works better is not categorization, typecasting, and the allocating of roles, but a community (shown in the novel) capable of subsisting and functioning without the obstacles imposed by categories . Importantly, the household established by the Claras Peggotty and Copperfield also functioned well, and is remembered by David as a haven of happiness and nurture. What destroyed that household was perhaps not sexuality per se, but Murdstone's sadistic form of disciplining.

What ensures the survival of the female-centered viewpoint within patriarchal domesticity is the strength and inclusiveness of the female community that lies in its refusal to define itself according to the masculinist code and in its ability to exist in narratives which, though less than official, are integrated into the main narrative—the narratives of memory, friendship, and the varying, sometimes silenced, sides of the women characters.

David Copperfield indicates that categorizations of women are constantly under negotiation. Thinking in terms of those categories, Dora is afraid that Agnes will not approve of her; Agnes wins Dora over by means of facial expression

(Dora is attracted by Agnes's goodness, shown in her face), physical proximity, and emotion (the two women embrace and thus begin to love each other [616–17; ch. 42]. As far as Agnes herself is concerned, her love for David is neither angelic (i.e., other-worldly and totally spiritual) nor cold. These definitions do not readily apply to Agnes, in that she loves David in an erotic manner, which is what enables her to wait all those years. Not allowed to love in this manner, but pushed instead into artificial definitions, Dora withers and dies.

In *David Copperfield* Dickens has recorded a female world that is adjacent to the patriarchal world. The relationship is both cooperative and antagonistic, but never destructive. The formation of female identity happens, in the novel, within a collective of women, who define themselves through their ability to love, accept, and understand each other. A similarly peculiar and female-centered examination of the questions pertaining to female belonging in Victorian society occurs in *Middlemarch*.

Rosamond Vincy in *Middlemarch*

Rosamond Vincy, the blonde, failed wife from *Middlemarch*, was seen as a temptress and destroyer of men by Victorian critics. Enthusiastic editor John Blackwood had observed that "Lydgate had very great merit in not taking a stick to Rosamond," who was a "heartless ... obstinate devil" (293; bk. 3, ch. 32). In the *Revue des Deux Mondes*, Th. Bentzon was distressed to note that Lydgate becomes "the plaything and victim of a woman without heart or intelligence, ignorant of the harm she does" (58–59). Henry James saw Rosamond as "gracefully vicious" (66), Lydgate's "miserable little wife" (65). Traditionally, Rosamond is still being read as a foil to saintly Dorothea,[7] and, for feminist critics, she is seen to enact anger against the stifling and constraining institution of marriage.[8]

I continue the feminist tradition of examining Rosamond as a complex and multifaceted element in the novel and argue that she is a character whose story is by no means the dark side to Dorothea's, but a commentary on, and useful adjunct to, Dorothea's story. What makes Dorothea and Rosamond a "community" of women is, just as in the case of *David Copperfield*, the nature of the narrative which is formed between them. This narrative is a rereading of dominant narratives of domesticity; though it does not replace the narrative of domesticity, it is one of the main reasons why the latter is able to survive inside the novel. The female-centered narrative is sustained by Dorothea and Rosamond, and it sustains the two women characters as a community—a sum of women who can, and do, attempt to say, or say in a manner which is more comprehensible to them, what has not been deemed as sayable about women by the dominant, male-orientated discourse that determines their lives.

Interestingly, both women begin *Middlemarch* by having no woman-orientated explanation for their lives and experiences. Let us put it "at its crudest," states Lawrence Lerner. "If Dorothea ... could have become a doctor or a teacher, she wouldn't have needed Sir James Chettam's help to build the cottages; and she wouldn't have married Casaubon" (243–44). The same can well apply to Rosamond. For Gillian Beer, the theme of the unfit preparation of women for life's opportunities is "as crucial for understanding Rosamond as it is for understanding Dorothea" (159). Thus, if Rosamond could have become a musician or could have had a wider social life, she would not have married Lydgate. Mrs. Lemon was proud that Rosamond's "musical execution was quite exceptional" (89; bk. 1, ch. 11). As Rosamond tells Lydgate, "our organist at St Peter's is a good musician, and I go on studying with him" (149; bk. 2, ch. 16). The narrator verifies that this organist was indeed "excellent" (150; bk. 2, ch. 16), and Rosamond cultivated her talent with care: "Rosamond played admirably.... A hidden soul seemed to be flowing forth from her fingers" (150; bk. 2, ch. 16). Lydgate comes to the point where he sees his wife as someone with the "shallowness of a waternixie's soul" (611; bk. 7, ch. 64); but it is music that brings out the soul in Rosamond, not marriage. Phyllis Weliver argues that it is only Lydgate who hears a "hidden soul" in Rosamond's music: in reality, Rosamond is imitating the performance of her music teacher (208; bk. 2, ch. 22). However, the "hidden soul" comment seems to belong to the narrator and not Lydgate; and it is placed inside a paragraph on Rosamond's musical abilities.

The story which surrounds Rosamond is that of a young woman with a trained talent for music; however, *Middlemarch* plainly suggests that this story must remain untold, and is unnarratable in available, official female terms. It can be told in terms of "accomplishments," of wifely ability to make the home a shelter for the husband—that is, in terms of the dominant (male-centered) discourse of domesticity. However, it has very little meaning in terms of a woman's life and potential for development. Unlike Lydgate, Rosamond has never been to Paris to listen to "the best singers. I have heard very little: I have only once been to London" (149; bk. 2, ch. 16). Yet Rosamond stubbornly practices her music until the end of the novel proper, and music forms a refuge for her (rather than for Lydgate) as marital troubles deepen. What *Middlemarch* shows is that the story of her musical talent lacks a core of meaning—it is a story that cannot become meaningful in terms of Rosamond herself. In the case of Dorothea, this lack of a meaningful core to which the story can refer is exacerbated. Rosamond has a calling, music; Dorothea has none. Despite her abilities, kindness, and eagerness, Dorothea can find no real outlets in a professional sense (though in a personal sense her life gains value after she marries for the second time). If Rosamond's narrative of a failed marriage is built against a narrative of a woman gifted with musical and social skills, Dorothea's is built upon the ghostly narrative of an absent calling, of attributes, leading her nowhere.

Dorothea and Rosamond both face what Eliot calls "the stifling oppression of [the] gentlewoman's world" (257; bk. 3, ch. 28). Both Dorothea and Rosamond are subjected to men's interpretation and domination. Kathleen Blake wonders whether Will Ladislaw differs from Casaubon to any considerable extent. The qualities he seems to love most about Dorothea are her "innocent shortsightedness and her inaccessibility" (308). On the face of it, Will Ladislaw seems to be the exact antithesis of Mr. Casaubon. Unlike Casaubon, Will is young, attractive, and often impulsive and emotional; certainly Dorothea's second marriage is based on feeling, physical attraction, and compatibility in terms of age. Blake's question here, however, refers to the extent to which Ladislaw's stance toward women differs to any great degree from that of Casaubon, and whether marriage to him has altered Dorothea's dreams of "reforming a conventional life" (785; bk. 8, finale). As Dorothea Barrett points out, "Will is a dilettante": his flirtation with Rosamond has implications for Rosamond, the community, and Dorothea as well, Since his light gallantry to Rosamond seems "rather brutal" (135). All in all, he is "a figure who cannot be seriously contemplated as the appropriate partner of Dorothea's scope" (134). As Lydgate does with Rosamond, Will drapes Dorothea in fancy and fantasy. She is his sovereign, he is a worshipper (204; bk. 2, ch. 22). When Dorothea remarks that she is sure she could never produce a poem, Ladislaw's reply seems inevitable: "You are a poem" (209; bk. 2, ch. 22). Dorothea's weak reference to a vocation is immediately thwarted; from the potential position of subject she is immediately assigned the position of object, and Ladislaw's product. The stories that center on the women themselves fade as the stories their partners write for them take priority.

Rosamond and Dorothea

However, an important scene in *Middlemarch* records female belonging as an open and honest dialogue between women. During their climactic meeting, Dorothea's manner toward Rosamond is caring, maternal: "Dorothea ... came forward and with her face full of sad yet sweet openness, put out her hand. Rosamond ... could not avoid putting her small hand into Dorothea's, which clasped it with gentle motherliness" (745; bk. 8, ch. 81). Rosamond is unmothered; she lacks female guidance, companionship, and friendship.

As in *David* Copperfield, the female community in *Middlemarch* has the ability to straddle dominant categories; both women have elements of the "other"—the failed wife, the basil plant—in their composition; and if prevailing social mores could not articulate this form of womanly experience, *Middlemarch* suggests that women themselves could and did articulate it.

Dorothea, observes Blake, produces a movement of human fellowship in Rosamond: "She understands [Rosamond's] troubles as specifically a woman's"

(304). The narrator is explicit about how much their encounter differs from conventionality and role-playing. "[T]here had been between them too much serious emotion for them to use the signs of it superficially." Rosamond will keep Dorothea's generosity "in religious remembrance"; for Dorothea "had come to her aid in the sharpest crisis of her life" (782; bk. 8, finale). Marcus sees the Dorothea/Rosamond relationship as providing a hopeful glimpse "of two very different people speaking openly about what separates and unites them" (86); this in a novel about "community and its fissures" (85). Amity converts rivalry into a sense of connection, which also provides a model of how men and women can resolve differences (86).

Further, exemplary fellow feeling is shown in this scene as plainly female in origin. Rosamond gives Ladislaw a note, indicating that she has told Dorothea the truth: "I told her because she came to see me and was very kind" (755; bk. 8, ch. 82). Both Rosamond and Dorothea, writes Hilary Franklin, express "the rejection of the idealized nineteenth-century Englishwoman's uncompromising submission" (31).

Lydgate had thought that Rosamond would be a woman "who would reverence her husband's mind after the fashion of an accomplished mermaid, using her comb and looking-glass and singing her song for the relaxation of his adored wisdom alone" (547; bk. 6, ch. 68). What does the mermaid see inside the looking-glass? The man does not wish to know; the mermaid looks inside the glass and then sings a song of reverence. Perhaps it is her husband she is seeing in the looking-glass. Perhaps she is seeing nothing. From the male point of view, the looking-glass reveals only the female's absence from herself, her subservience to male-defined roles, and male-constructed structures of being.

In the encounter between Dorothea and Rosamond, the mirror no longer reflects a male-constructed image of woman: each woman becomes the other's looking-glass, and reflects a yearning to understand and make whole. In *Middlemarch*, as in *David Copperfield*, two women mirroring each other produce a deeper truth. Continuity in the Dickens novel is ensured because Agnes is not the asexual, other-worldly creature patriarchal categorizations of women would have her be; her relationship to Dora, and Dora's relationship to Aunt Betsey create an alternative story, which challenges these patriarchal categorizations of women and renders them problematic. In *Middlemarch,* Dorothea becomes the medium through which Rosamond learns about feelings Lydgate experienced but never shared with her: "And he felt he had been so wrong not to pour out everything about this to you" (746; bk. 8, ch. 81). It is only through Dorothea that Lydgate can fully express himself as a husband; Dorothea takes upon her the function of the good husband, something Aunt Betsey was doing in relation to Dora in *David Copperfield*. The female figure is here able to straddle the husband/ wife dyad, and become the mouthpiece of the husband in front of his wife. What she has to say puts things in the right, because more realistic, perspective. Rather than plague Rosamond with saccharine and idealized versions of marriage as a haven, where the wife selflessly but willingly labors to make the husband happy, Dorothea will say, "There is something awful in the nearness [marriage] brings.... [T]he marriage stays with us like a murder—and everything else is gone" (748–49; bk. 8, ch. 81).

Female power to heal is stronger than the male power to wound. Dorothea's arms around her make Rosamond wish "to free herself from something that oppressed her as if it were blood guiltiness" (749; bk. 8, ch. 81). As she confesses everything to Dorothea, Rosamond gathers "the sense that she was repelling Will's reproaches, which were still like a knife-wound within her" (750; bk. 8, ch. 81).

Middlemarch suggests that this problem of women's lives can be, to an extent, resolved through female agency. Dorothea's words to Rosamond rewrite the narrative of marriage as female-centered: "[I]t hurts [your husband] more than anything, that his misfortunes must hurt you" (747; bk. 8, ch. 81). The husband is no longer a person with the ability to command obedience; he is weakened by love for his wife. Lydgate did not share his troubles not because he felt that Rosamond did not have a right to know, but "because he feels so much more about your happiness than anything else" (746–47; bk. 8, ch. 81). The woman now holds central place in marriage: "Your husband depends on you for comfort" (750; bk. 8, ch. 81). Dorothea transcends the essence/otherness division, the ideal and the non-ideal, explaining as she does how the husband too can be self-sacrificing (748; bk. 8, ch. 81) and how marriage, far from being a male-centered heaven of music and repose, places terrible duties upon both parties (748–49; bk. 8, ch. 81).

Importantly, Dorothea's words strengthen and comfort Rosamond (748–49; bk. 8, ch. 81), and Eliot suggests that Dorothea is right to view her interference as a sort of female quest (she wants to "rescue" Rosamond, 747; bk. 8, ch. 81). Rosamond's beauty now signifies her loss of pride and her honesty in front of Dorothea: "her eyes met Dorothea's as helplessly as if they had been blue flowers" (748; bk. 8, ch. 81). Rosamond works in tandem with Dorothea to propose a female-centered narrative, where coercive social structures are recycled to allow women to find hope and aspiration. Now the woman's story is able to re-write the stories of men, albeit in a still limited manner. The character of Rosamond does not only suggest that *Middlemarch* "attempts to imagine ways in which a woman can adjust to Victorian culture without being tied to normative ideologies" (Jean Arnold 284); the implication is also that any such adjustment must examine components and figurations of the non-ideal, and that indeed the non-ideal might be essential in the formation of a female-centered explanation of life and events that will be fruitful and productive.

Therefore, the female narrative in *Middlemarch* must be taken into consideration, if we are not to make complete failures not only of Lydgate's life, but of Rosamond's, and perhaps also even Dorothea's. Of course, in the novel, failure is an important aspect that which has been given due and extensive consideration.[9] Nevertheless, the female rewriting of the story elements discussed above suggests that it is not against success that failure must be measured in the novel, but against the aspects of personality, the social context, and the historical moment which define the concepts of failure and success, and make them possible. Thus, the narrator's final comment about Dorothea's effect on others, and about "the growing good of the world" being "partly dependent on unhistoric acts" (785; bk. 8, finale), refers to the novel's particular rendition of success and failure, especially *female* success and failure. Dorothea's life has certainly contributed to the common good; nevertheless, "we insignificant people with our daily words and acts are preparing the lives of many Dorotheas, some of which may present a far sadder sacrifice than the Dorothea whose story we know" (785; bk. 8, finale). Though Dorothea's life has ultimately been limited in scope, the novel asks its readers to question their own notions of society in relation to personal failure and success and place them within their appropriate context(s), at the same time implying that every man or woman has a responsibility for the failure or success of their fellow human beings.

The masculine narrative is purportedly life-significant—the men in *Middlemarch* are engaged with discoveries in medicine, with philosophical enquiries, and developments in literature and in politics. All the same, what actually shapes life is the female world. The female narrative is life-shaping, even while it is about life's restrictions. The restrictions that shape the life of the women become a ground for them to express and discuss their common lot. Eventually, it is left to the women to make sense of the male-defined world, and find viable terms and definitions with which to articulate the narrative of their (women's and men's) interrelated lives.

In *David Copperfield* and *Middlemarch*, gaps in the understanding of experience are fruitfully filled by female perception and the positive action of women; a caring nature and sensitivity are practical attributes. Most importantly, female perception and a female explanation of experience (necessary to complete and make sense of the male-centered official world) are a matter of relationship between the women themselves. D. A. Miller has spoken of a "non-narratable base" in *Middlemarch*, a novel that is imagined but not realized, the novel "of what might have been" (93). This article shows that the female community in the Eliot and Dickens novels works out a female-centered revision of the structuring of their lives, and succeeds not to transform those lives, or write the novel of what might have been, but rewrite elements of the novels we have before us from the might-have-been perspective, which is thus given validity. The network, or community, or narrative of, the women, constructs a site where the limitations of patriarchal ideology are recognized and discussed, and uses these limitations to draft a story that makes the women's lives seem more meaningful. This site neither dismisses nor denies patriarchal ideology, but it is undoubtedly feminist, in that it criticizes it, and depicts the women as far more able than the men to appreciate the subtle workings of that ideology.

The female networks of *David Copperfield* and *Middlemarch* constitute the role and function of women as, to an extent, a matter of association and verbal exchange between women, an exchange which involves the interpretation and appropriation of available narratives, so as to produce viable meaning. Admittedly, the aspirations of the two groups of women differ in important ways. Dora and Agnes are orientated toward marriage, while the suggestion for Dorothea and Rosamond is that they could have succeeded in a world beyond the household, where they could have developed their talents and have acted as agents in their own right. What is common between the treatment of those two groups of women, however, is a female-generated examination of the male-centered, dominant narratives that have defined the lives of those women. In other words, it is not common aspirations that form the basis of similarity between the female narratives of *David Copperfield* and *Middlemarch*—it is a similar formation of a response to the limitations imposed on women by male explanations of the female experience.

Thus, relationship and exchange between women moves to reread subtly the norms, values, and demands framing a woman's destiny. Woman's place in society is not only a matter of debate, but also a matter continually revised on the basis of female relationship, and a female rendering of attitudes, ideologies, and norms.

NOTES

1. "One morning some weeks after her arrival at Lowick, Dorothea—but why always Dorothea? Was her point of view the only possible one with regard to this marriage?" (261; bk. 3, ch. 19). The narrator then shifts the focus to Mr. Casaubon and his own reasons for marrying so that, by the time a letter from Ladislaw reaches Dorothea, readers have been afforded a sympathetic look into Mr. Casaubon's actions and thoughts.
2. See, for example, Vanden Bossche 32.
3. But for a discussion of how Ladislaw is feminized yet freer than a woman, see Gillian Beer. As Beer argues, Ladislaw "exactly focuses what is peculiar to women's predicament by sharing many of their conditions, and yet living a liberated life. This liberation depends upon his being a man" (159).
4. Cordery (81) notes that David's story records his own disciplining into social norms and regulations (71). See also D. A. Miller's discussion of the same subject.
5. Whether the existence of viewpoints antithetical to David's can be traced directly to Dickens's intentional acts is difficult to ascertain. The novel is evidently autobiographical; moreover, Dickens cannot easily be called a feminist. As Slater has shown, Dickens thought that women were fit only for "the quiet domestic life"—any other occupation was destructive of this (315–16, 324). Yet strands of feminist thought, outlook, and ideas do run through most of his novels. In addition, Dickens portrayed Victorian society with an acumen and an insightfulness that continue to impress critics, theorists and writers today (see, for example, Regenia Gagnier 76, Judith Flanders xxiii, and Peter Ackroyd 308). Dickens criticized as

well as affirmed domesticity, and was remarkably able to portray disillusion. It is possible that the feminist undercurrent was inserted into the novel as part of what Ackroyd has called "the very image of his own time," which Dickens managed to portray (308). A subtext may exist in a text without the author's being aware of its existence (Morris 16). While incorporating the polyphonic voices from culture inside his work, Dickens also incorporated the voices of women speaking for themselves, and women speaking to each other.

6. See, for example, Carl Bandelin and Janet H. Brown.

7. Rosamond is a siren, a type of Victorian female demon, observes Phyllis Weliver (6). For Felicia Bonaparte, Rosamond is vice, while Dorothea is virtue (xvi). According to Rosemary Ashton, the two women "are opposites in their expectations of marriage and their responses to marriage troubles" (viii).

8. See, for example, Sandra Gilbert and Susan Gubar (516).

9. "Dorothea never finds the comprehensive outward energy that she seeks," writes Suzanne Graver. In the end, her spirit breaks, and is spent (203). For Beer, Dorothea Ladislaw and the successful Dr. Lydgate are "mitigated failures" (178). Trotter believes that marriage is not a satisfactory solution, since Ladislaw's presence promises much but yields little (43).

WORKS CITED

Ackroyd, Peter. *Dickens*. Abbreviated ed. London: Vintage, 2002.

Arnold, Jean. "Cameo Appearances: The Discourse of Jewellery in *Middlemarch*." *Victorian Literature and Culture* 30.1 (2002): 265–88.

Arnold, Matthew. "From 'The Incompatibles', *Nineteenth Century*, June 1881, ix, 1034–42." *Dickens: The Critical Heritage*. Ed. Philip Collins. London: Routledge & Kegan Paul, 1971. 267–69.

Ashton, Rosemary. Introduction. *Middlemarch*. By George Eliot. London: Penguin, 1994. vii–xxii.

Auerbach, Nina. *Communities of Women: An Idea in Fiction*. Cambridge: Harvard UP, 1998.

Bal, Mieke. *Narratology: Introduction to the Theory of Narrative*. 2nd ed. Toronto: U of Toronto P, 1997.

Bandelin, Carl. "David Copperfield: A Third Interesting Penitent." *SEL* 16.4 (1976): 601–11.

Barrett, Dorothea. *Vocation and Desire: George Eliot's Heroines*. London: Routledge, 1989.

Beer, Gillian. "*Middlemarch* and 'The Woman Question.'" *Middlemarch: Contemporary Critical Essays*. Ed. John Peck. Houndmills, UK: Macmillan, 1992. New Casebook Series. 155–81.

Beeton, Isabella. *Mrs Beeton's Book of Household Management*. Ed. Nicola Humble. Oxford: Oxford UP, 2000.

Bentzon, Th. "*Revue des Deux Mondes*, February 1873." *George Eliot,* Middlemarch: *A Casebook.* Ed. Patrick Swinden. Houndmills, UK: Macmillan, 1972. Casebook Series. 56–60.

Blackwood, John. "To George Eliot." 29 July 1872. *The Letters of George Eliot.* Ed. Gordon S. Haight. Vol. 5. London: Oxford UP, 1956. 293–94.

Blake, Kathleen. "*Middlemarch* and the Woman Question." *Nineteenth Century Fiction* 31.3 (1976): 285–312.

Bonaparte, Felicia. Introduction. *Middlemarch.* By George Eliot. Oxford: Oxford UP, 1996. vii–xxxviii.

Brown, Janet H. "The Narrator's Role in *David Copperfield,*" *Dickens Studies Annual* 2 (1972): 197–207.

Burgis, Nina. Introduction. *David Copperfield.* By Charles Dickens. Oxford: Oxford UP, 1982. vii–xv.

Carey, John. *The Violent Effigy: A Study of Dickens's Imagination.* 2nd ed. London: Faber, 1991.

Carmichael, Virginia. "'In Search of Beein': Nom/Non Du Per in *David Copperfield.*" David Copperfield *and* Hard Times: *Contemporary Critical Essays.* Ed. John Peck. London: Macmillan, 1995. New Casebooks. 125–40.

Cordery, Gareth. "Foucault, Dickens and *David Copperfield.*" *Victorian Literature and Culture* 26.1 (1998): 71–85.

Darby, Margaret Flanders. "Dora and Doady." *Dickens Studies Annual* 22 (1993):155–69.

Dickens, Charles. *David Copperfield.* Ed. Jeremy Tambling. London: Penguin, 2004.

———. Letter to Rev. James White, 13 July 1850. "The Letters of Charles Dickens." *The Dickens Page.* n.d. Web. 2 Aug. 2008. < http://www.lang.nagoya-u.ac.jp/~matsuoka/CD-Letters.pdf>.

Edwards, Simon. "David Copperfield: The Decomposing Self." David Copperfield *and* Hard Times: *Contemporary Critical Essays.* Ed. John Peck. London: Macmillan, 1995. New Casebooks. 58–80.

Eliot, George. *Middlemarch.* Ed. David Carroll. Oxford: Oxford UP, 1996.

Ellis, Sarah Stickney. *The Women of England: Their Social Duties and Domestic Habits.* London, 1839.

———. *The Daughters of England: Their Position in Society, Character and Responsibilities.* London, 1842.

———. *The Wives of England: Their Relative Duties, Domestic Influence and Social Obligations.* London, 1843.

Flanders, Judith. *The Victorian House: Domestic Life from Childbirth to Deathbed.* London: Harper Perennial, 2003.

Flint, Kate. *Dickens.* Brighton, UK: Harvester, 1986.

Forster, John. *The Life of Charles Dickens.* London: Chapman and Hall, 1893.

Franklin, Hilary. "Self-(Un)Conscious Narrative of the Female Body: Dorothea's and Rosamond's 'Finger Rhetoric' in Eliot's *Middlemarch.*" *The Haverford Journal* 2.1 (2006): 30–40.

Gagnier, Regenia. *Idylls of the Marketplace: Oscar Wilde and the Victorian Public.* Stanford: Stanford UP, 1986.

Garnett, Robert R. "Why Not Sophy? Desire and Agnes in *David Copperfield.*" *Dickens Quarterly* 14.4 (1997): 213–31.

Gay, Peter. "The Legless Angel of *David Copperfield:* There's More to Her Than Victorian Piety." *New York Times on the Web* 22 Jan. 1995. Web. 2 Mar. 2008.

Gilbert, Sandra M., and Susan Gubar. *The Madwoman in the Attic: The Woman Writer and the Nineteenth-Century Literary Imagination.* 2nd ed. New Haven; Yale Nota Bene; Yale UP, 1979.

Graver, Suzanne. "Organic Fictions: *Middlemarch.*" Middlemarch: *Contemporary Critical Essays.* Ed. John Peck. Houndmills, UK: Macmillan, 1992. New Casebooks. 95–105.

Hager, Kelly. *Dickens and the Rise of Divorce: The Failed Marriage Plot and the Novel Tradition.* Farnham, UK: Ashgate, 2010.

Jackson, Arlene M. "Agnes Wickfield and the Church Leitmotif in *David Copperfield.*" *Dickens Studies Annual* 8 (1978): 53–65.

James, Henry. "*Galaxy* March 1873." *George Eliot,* Middlemarch: *A Casebook.* Ed. Patrick Swinden. Houndmills, UK: Macmillan, 1972. Casebook Series. 60–68.

Kucich, John. "Self-Conflict in *David Copperfield.*" David Copperfield *and* Hard Times: *Contemporary Critical Essays.* Ed. John Peck. London: Macmillan, 1995. New Casebooks. 141–54.

Lerner, Lawrence. "Dorothea and the Theresa-Complex (1967)." *George Eliot,* Middlemarch: *A Casebook.* Ed. Patrick Swinden. Houndmills, UK: Macmillan, 1972. Casebook Series. 225–47.

Lettis, Richard. "The Names of *David Copperfield.*" *Dickens Studies Annual* 31 (2002): 67–86.

Lucas, John. *Charles Dickens: The Major Novels.* London: Penguin, 1992. Penguin Critical Studies.

Marcus, Sharon. *Between Women: Friendship, Desire and Marriage in Victorian England.* Princeton: Princeton UP, 2007.

McAleavey, Maia. "Soul-mates: David Copperfield's Angelic Bigamy." *Victorian Studies* 52.2 (2010): 191–218.

Miller, D. A. "George Eliot: The Wisdom of Balancing Claims." Middlemarch: *Contemporary Critical Essays.* Ed. John Peck. Houndmills, UK: Macmillan, 1992. New Casebooks. 84–94.

Miller, J. Hillis. "Optic and Semiotic in *Middlemarch.*" Middlemarch: *Contemporary Critical Essays.* Ed. John Peck. Houndmills, UK: Macmillan, 1992. New Casebooks. 65–83.

Morris, Pamela. *Literature and Feminism: An Introduction.* Oxford: Blackwell, 2000.

Myers, Margaret. "The Lost Self: Gender in *David Copperfield.*" David Copperfield *and* Hard Times: *Contemporary Critical Essays.* Ed. John Peck. London: Macmillan, 1995. New Casebooks. 108–24.

Newman, Beth. *Subjects on Display: Psychoanalysis, Social Expectation and Victorian Femininity.* Athens: Ohio UP, 2004.

Schor, Hilary. *Dickens and the Daughter of the House*. Cambridge: Cambridge UP, 1999.

Slater. Michael. *Dickens and Women*. London: Dent, 1983.

Smith, Barbara Herrnstein. "Narrative Versions, Narrative Theories." *The Narrative Reader*. Ed. Martin Mcquilan. London: Routledge, 2004. 138–45.

Tambling, Jeremy. Introduction. *David Copperfield*. By Charles Dickens. London: Penguin, 2004. xi–xxxix.

Tosh, John. *A Man's Place: Masculinity and the Middle-Class Home in Victorian England*. New Haven: Yale UP, 1999.

Trotter, David. "Space, Movement and Sexual Feeling in *Middlemarch*." *Middlemarch in the Twenty-First Century*. Ed. Karen Chase. Oxford: Oxford UP, 2006. 37–63.

Vanden Bossche, Chris R. "Cookery not Rookery: Family and Class in *David Copperfield*." "The Lost Self: Gender in *David Copperfield*." AU: Is latter article also in this collection and somehow combined with the former? Clarify? David Copperfield *and* Hard Times: *Contemporary Critical Essays*. Ed. John Peck. London: Macmillan, 1995. New Casebooks. 31–57.

Weliver, Phyllis. *Women Musicians in Victorian Fiction, 1860–1900: Representations of Music, Science and Gender in the Leisured Home*. Aldershot: Ashgate, 2000.

Vibrations in the Memory:
Bleak House's Response to
Illustrations of Becky in *Vanity Fair*

Deborah A. Thomas

As indicated by evidence in Bleak House, *Dickens was more aware of Thackeray's* Vanity Fair *than has been commonly recognized. Dickens's response to that widely acclaimed work by his contemporary and rival reflects an interest in the concept of the double and takes the form of splitting and rewriting* Vanity Fair's *multifaceted Becky Sharp. In* Bleak House, *Esther, Lady Dedlock, and Hortense can each be seen as embodying a particular facet of Becky suggested in certain of Thackeray's illustrations that appear to have triggered Dickens's imagination. Although he may have misunderstood* Vanity Fair, *his reworking in* Bleak House *of aspects of Thackeray's Becky displayed in these pictures illuminates important differences between these two great novels. Dickens's response also reminds us that discussions of intertextuality should consider visual as well as verbal dimensions of texts.*

> The picture of the mind revives again
>
> —William Wordsworth, "Lines Composed a Few
> Miles above Tintern Abbey"

"I'll be shot if it ain't very curious how well I know that picture!" Guppy blurts out in astonishment in chapter 7 of *Bleak House* upon seeing the portrait of Lady Dedlock for the first time in the drawing-room at Chesney Wold (82). As

Dickens Studies Annual, Volume 44, Copyright © 2013 by AMS Press, Inc. All rights reserved.   DOI 10.7756/dsa.044.009.165-193

readers of this 1852–53 Dickens novel know, Guppy soon connects his unexpected sense of pictorial recognition to a realization that the portrait resembles Lady Dedlock's unacknowledged daughter, Esther Summerson, with whom the gauche young law clerk has become romantically smitten. His clumsy detective work to ferret out an explanation for the resemblance is an important thread in the complex web of this great book. Yet, among people in the real world as well as characters in fiction, Guppy is by no means alone in experiencing a sense of déjà vu, which—as in Guppy's case—may actually derive from a genuine memory haunting the edges of one's mind.[1] As Wordsworth suggests in "Tintern Abbey," pictorial memories can be powerful, especially for someone (like both Wordsworth and Dickens) with a vivid visual imagination. Moreover, tracing the presence of such a memory in Dickens's case can bring us into contact with what Rosemarie Bodenheimer has called "the revealing and concealing intelligence that lurks ... in Dickens's writing" (2). As I shall argue, *Bleak House* reveals Dickens's concealed recollection of particular pictures of Becky in Thackeray's *Vanity Fair* (1847–48). Dickens's reworking of these visual images in his written text not only demonstrates his use of the idea of the double and his critical response to Thackeray's novel but also casts a spotlight on some important artistic differences between *Bleak House* and *Vanity Fair*.

Peter Ackroyd has observed about Dickens and Thackeray that "after the publication of *Vanity Fair*, the two writers were always being compared and contrasted, by friends or enemies or critics" (542).[2] Nevertheless, there has been surprisingly little critical discussion of the potential relationship between Thackeray's *Vanity Fair* and Dickens's *Bleak House*, although these two great social satires—both published in monthly installments by Bradbury and Evans—appeared only five years apart. Even Jerome Meckier's valuable exploration of *Hidden Rivalries in Victorian Fiction* focuses on other literary rivalries, while mentioning the Dickens-Thackeray relationship only in passing.[3] Some of the reason for the paucity of critical examination of the tantalizing question of what *Bleak House* might owe to or intentionally reject in Thackeray's *Vanity Fair* undoubtedly stems from the fact that, after the latter much-acclaimed work had made Thackeray famous, Dickens apparently made a point of not commenting specifically on Thackeray's novels. For example, in a letter of 9 January 1848, when *Vanity Fair* had been appearing for a year and Thackeray's celebrity was growing, Dickens thanked Thackeray for a letter Thackeray had written in praise of *Dombey and Son*, which Dickens was then serializing. In turn, Dickens complimented Thackeray on a short sketch, "The Curate's Walk," which the latter had published in *Punch* in November 1847, but Dickens declared, "I am saving up the perusal of Vanity Fair until I shall have done Dombey" (*Letters of Charles Dickens* 228).[4]

Nonetheless, Thackeray believed that Dickens had not only read *Vanity Fair* but had also been subtly influenced by it. In a letter of 4 May 1849 to his close friend Jane Brookfield, Thackeray wrote about Dickens's *David Copperfield:*

It has some of his very prettiest touches—those inimitable Dickens touches wh. make such a great man of him. And the reading of the book has done another author a great deal of good. In the first place it pleases the other Author to see that Dickens who has long left off alluding to his the O A's works has been copying the O A, and greatly simplifying his style and foregoing the use of fine words. By this the public will be the gainer and David Copperfield will be improved by taking a lesson from Vanity Fair. (*Letters and Private Papers* 531)[5]

After Thackeray's death, Dickens himself insisted to a person who had tried to praise him at Thackeray's expense, "The author of *Vanity Fair* was a very great genius" (Storey 15).[6] However, a more significant explanation for this inattention by critics to the issue of possible responses to *Vanity Fair* within *Bleak House* may be the fact that no one, to my knowledge, has investigated potential links between certain of Thackeray's illustrations—"the Author's own candles" as Thackeray's "Manager of the Performance" calls them in "Before the Curtain" (xv)—and what Dickens subsequently wrote in *Bleak House*.[7] Yet the pictorial dimension of *Vanity Fair*, as a number of Thackeray scholars have emphasized, is very much a part of the meaning of this novel, and Dickens had a very keen eye.[8] According to Dickens's daughter Kate, her father had the ability to "remember with distinctness any face he may have seen for however short a time" (qtd. in Ackroyd 462). In fact, close examination of *Vanity Fair* and *Bleak House* reveals certain intriguing details from *Vanity Fair*—particularly some featured in a handful of notable illustrations of Becky—that seem revised through the technique of character splitting in *Bleak House*'s text.[9]

Dickens's fascination with the concept of the double in his writings is well known, as is his particular use of the idea of doubleness in *Bleak House*, both in terms of the dual narrative method of this novel and in terms of characters who serve as surrogates for one another within it.[10] However, critics who have dealt with doubling in *Bleak House* have tended to focus either on this novel alone, or in conjunction with other works by Dickens. In such other works, there is ample evidence that the creative possibilities offered by the idea of the double were very much on Dickens's mind at the time of *Vanity Fair*'s appearance. While focusing on Mrs. Gamp/Mrs. Harris in *Martin Chuzzlewit*, Goldie Morgentaler has recently pointed out that "Dickens created an abundance of female doubles in his fictions of the 1840s" (5). Dickens also made use of the notion of the double in his treatment of the character of Redlaw, haunted by a lookalike phantom and paired with a savage child, in the Christmas Book for 1848, *The Haunted Man*. Furthermore, Dickens's interest in doubles was not confined to his work alone. He is on record as thinking specifically about the figure of the double, or doppelgänger, in connection with a book by Catherine Crowe in 1848. In February of that year, he wrote in an *Examiner* review of Crowe's *The Night Side of Nature*, "This Doppelgänger, it appears, is so common among learned professors and studious men in Germany, that they have no need of the Kilmarnock weaver's prayer for grace to see themselves as others see them, but enjoy that privilege commonly" (*Amusements of the People* 85).[11] When a reader looks at *Vanity Fair* through the lens of the double, as Dickens might have done in 1848, a new perspective on *Bleak House* suddenly comes into view, suggesting a splitting and rewriting on Dickens's part of Thackeray's famous figure of Becky Sharp. In particular, the three prominent women in *Bleak House*, whom critics have viewed as surrogates or alter egos of one another—Esther, Lady Dedlock, and Hortense—can each be seen as echoing and revising a significant aspect of Becky.[12] Evidence of these links is suggested by a close comparison of both texts as they relate to a group of illustrations featuring Becky, drawn by Thackeray, in *Vanity Fair*.[13]

Esther as orphan heroine is perhaps the most obvious point of connection between *Bleak House* and *Vanity Fair*. The superficial parallels between Esther and Becky (Rebecca) are striking. Not only do these major female protagonists bear the names of strong women from the Hebrew Bible, but each of these fictional characters, who might arguably be called a heroine, is paired with a weaker friend—Ada in *Bleak House* and Amelia in *Vanity Fair*. Most conspicuously of all, both Esther and Becky are orphans who have trained as pupil-teachers at a boarding school in preparation for a career as a governess. (A small sign of Dickens's interest in doubling at the time of writing *Bleak House* can be seen in the fact that, while each of the boarding schools attended by Esther and Becky is operated by two sisters, the Miss Donnys in charge of Esther's school at Reading are twins [26; ch. 3]). Indeed, Meckier insightfully suggests, in passing, that *Bleak House* "may have begun ... in conscious repudiation of *Vanity Fair*," since both works contain near their beginning a situation where "an orphan leaves finishing school for a new residence and possibly marriage" (245). Of course, the idea of an orphan embarking on life is hardly unique to *Vanity Fair* and *Bleak House* (see Reed, *Victorian Conventions* 250–67). Critics have pointed to similarities and differences between Esther and the orphaned heroine of Charlotte Brontë's *Jane Eyre* (e.g., see Moers 22; Shatto 7, 45–47, 225). However, it is worth looking beyond this 1847 novel by Brontë to *Vanity Fair*, the publication of which overlapped that of *Jane Eyre*. One result of this chronological overlap was a frequent comparison by contemporary readers of *Vanity Fair*'s and *Jane Eyre*'s major female characters, although Richard A. Kaye (723–39) has shown that Thackeray made a deliberate effort to emphasize the contrast between his Becky and Brontë's Jane.[14]

Careful attention to Esther's description of her doll in chapter 3 of *Bleak House* demonstrates the value of considering *Vanity Fair*, including its illustrations, as a possible springboard for some of *Bleak House*'s details. Susan Shatto has pointed out that Esther's remarks about "My dear old doll" (17; ch. 3) are suggestive of Jane's description of her love for her doll near the beginning of *Jane Eyre* (Shatto 45–46). Yet it is important to remember that Becky also engages in doll-play in chapter 2 of *Vanity Fair*, in an episode highlighted in one of Thackeray's illustrations, although Becky's mocking treatment of her dolls as caricatures of Miss Pinkerton and the latter's sister Miss Jemima is a far cry from Jane Eyre's and Esther's use of their dolls as objects of affection. Moreover, like Becky—and unlike Jane Eyre—Esther carries on imaginary conversations with her doll. According to the omniscient narrator of *Vanity Fair*, after a visit to the school at Chiswick Mall, Becky "used to go through dialogues with" the doll representing Miss Pinkerton (13). After a subsequent visit, Becky adds a second doll, representing Jemima, to her repertoire. Thackeray's woodcut shows Becky in a sitting position—apparently on a floor cushion—with a smug expression on her face, playing with the Pinkerton and Jemima dolls as hand puppets before a delighted audience of her father and his friends (fig. 1). In contrast, in beginning her first-person part of the double narrative of *Bleak House*, Esther recounts how she used to place her doll "propped up in a great arm-chair" (17; ch. 3) and habitually, "when I came home from school of a day, to run up-stairs to my room, and say, 'O you dear faithful Dolly, I knew you would be expecting me!' and then to sit down on the floor, leaning on the elbow of her great chair, and tell her all I had noticed since we parted" (17; ch. 3). The details in Esther's description here seem reminiscent of those portrayed—both verbally and visually—by Thackeray in his depiction of Becky's play with her puppet-dolls. Both girls sit on, or almost on, the floor, and both girls converse with their dolls. Nevertheless, Esther's humble (and private) position, with herself on the floor and her doll in the chair, differs from the more comfortably reclining Becky's audience-oriented theatricality. Esther's self-abasing, emotionally-conflicted insistence that "I know I am not clever" (17; ch. 3) also differs strikingly from the precocious "wit" (12; ch. 2) of which Becky's "lazy, dissolute, clever" (13; ch. 2) father is so proud.

The parallels, as well as the contrasts, are even more marked in a symptomatic event as Esther and Becky leave school. In a famous episode at the end of *Vanity Fair*'s chapter 1, as Becky and her friend Amelia Sedley depart from Chiswick Mall, kind-hearted Miss Jemima unofficially hands Becky the school's customary parting gift of Samuel Johnson's *Dictionary* that Becky has earlier been denied by the loftier Miss Pinkerton. However, Becky throws the book back at Jemima. Thackeray's full-page illustration, entitled "Rebecca's Farewell," unforgettably captures the moment as the dictionary flies through the air toward the astonished Jemima (fig. 2). The narrator's description of this scene is also memorable:

"Stop!" cried Miss Jemima rushing to the gate with a parcel.

"It's some sandwiches, my dear," said she to Amelia. "You may be hungry you know—and Becky—Becky Sharp—Here's a book for you that my sister—that is I,—Johnson's Dixonary you know—you mustn't leave us without that. Good bye. Drive on, coachman. God bless you!" And the kind creature retreated into the garden overcome with emotions.

But lo, and just as the coach drove off—Miss Sharp put her pale face out
of the window—and actually flung the book back into the garden. (7; ch. 1)

In *Bleak House*, Esther's departure from her school at Reading interestingly
echoes that of Becky from Chiswick Mall in the sense that, in both cases, someone from the school comes rushing with a farewell gift as the orphan heroine is
about to depart in a coach. As Esther describes this leave-taking:

And when the two Miss Donnys grieved as much to part with me, as the least
among them; and when the maids said, "Bless you, miss, wherever you go!"
and when the ugly lame old gardener, who I thought had hardly noticed me
in all those years, came panting after the coach to give me a little nosegay of
geraniums, and told me I had been the light of his eyes—indeed the old man
said so!—what a heart I had then! (28; ch. 3)

Esther's appreciative acceptance of the offered gift and her overall affectionate attitude are strikingly different from Becky's callousness. In similar fashion, the loving
attitude of the school's population toward Esther differs from the fact that "nobody
cried for leaving" (7; ch. 1) Becky Sharp. Indeed, the extensive description of the
widespread "weeping" (28; ch. 3) elicited by news of Esther's departure suggests
the "hugging and kissing and crying" with which "All the servants ... all the dear
friends—all the young ladies—the dancing master who had just arrived" (7; ch. 1)
at the school at Chiswick take leave not of Becky but of the weaker (and, to many
modern eyes, wimpy) Amelia. To the extent that Dickens is recollecting and rewriting the departure scene of Becky and Amelia in chapter 1 of *Vanity Fair*, his point
seems to be that a female protagonist may be a strong woman like Becky but, unlike
Becky, she can inspire affection in others and have a loving heart.

In thus responding to the orphan-heroine-facing-the-world aspect of Becky,
Dickens also seems to be addressing a major objection raised by his friend and literary confidant John Forster in a 22 July 1848 review of *Vanity Fair* in the *Examiner*. According to Forster, Thackeray's view of human nature and society in this
novel was unduly negative. Forster emphatically complained that *Vanity Fair* is
flawed by "a preponderance of unredeemed selfishness in the more common-place
as well as the leading characters," and "we feel that the atmosphere of the work is
overloaded with these exhalations of human folly and wickedness. We gasp for a
more liberal alternation of refreshing breezes of unsophisticated honesty" (rev. of
Vanity Fair 468). In the somewhat simplistic terms of Forster's review, Esther is a
breath of "unsophisticated honesty" and unselfishness. By making Esther the first-
person narrator of approximately half of *Bleak House* and having Esther move—
with her kindness, good sense, and generosity intact—through a seriously flawed
society that so greatly needs remediation, Dickens appears to be trying to express
the opinion (in contrast to what Forster perceived as the "grave defect" [468] of
Vanity Fair) that although the world may be bad it is not wholly wicked.

Even the rather strange suggestion that Esther's beauty may return at the end of *Bleak House* can be seen as a response to Thackeray's picture of a rejuvenated Becky in his ironic, concluding full-page illustration, "Virtue rewarded. A booth in Vanity Fair" (fig. 3). Like the ending of *Vanity Fair*, where the narrator replaces his puppets in their box yet the vanities of the world go on, the ending of *Bleak House*—with its unfinished last sentence by Esther—is indeterminate.[15] Nevertheless, the message behind these two indeterminate endings is very different. If Thackeray is suggesting with the graphic depiction of Becky's youthful face at the end of his novel that the ruthless selfishness she embodies will endure in society without change, Dickens may be suggesting with the possible return of Esther's good looks that the social illness anatomized in *Bleak House* will not forever scar the innocent.

Fig. 1. William Thackeray. Depiction of Becky with her father and his friends.
From chapter 2 of *Vanity Fair*.

Fig. 2. William Thackeray. "Rebecca's Farewell."
From chapter 1 of *Vanity Fair.*

Like Esther, her mother—Lady Dedlock—recalls certain aspects of *Vanity Fair*'s Becky, although the parallel here involves achievement in Lady Dedlock's case and aspiration in Becky's. In particular, Lady Dedlock accomplishes the marriage to a much older baronet that the energetically social-climbing Becky so greatly desired. In Thackeray's *Vanity Fair*, Becky's marital ambitions are frustrated because, before she receives a marriage proposal from the elderly Sir Pitt Crawley, she has already secretly married the baronet's younger son, Rawdon. In Dickens's subsequent *Bleak House*, to achieve her socially elevated position as wife of the baronet Sir Leicester Dedlock, Esther's mother renounces the lover whom she should have married, Esther's father, Captain Hawdon. Not only do these details of plot and the similarity of the names "Hawdon" and "Rawdon" suggest a connection between the two novels, but there are other affinities as well. Sir Pitt's recently deceased wife (his second), who is named Rose, is "an iron-monger's daughter" (79; ch. 8), while Lady Dedlock's maid Rosa loves—and is loved by—an ironmaster's son. Much later, in chapter 51 of *Vanity Fair*, Thackeray's narrator describes the precarious social success achieved by Becky—still married to Rawdon but temporarily under the patronage of the powerful Marquis of Steyne: "Becky has often spoken in subsequent years of this season of her life, when she moved among the very greatest circles of the London fashion. Her success excited, elated, and then bored her" (503). Becky's eventual boredom in this fashionable world may be echoed in Lady Dedlock's complaint in *Bleak House*'s chapter 2 (titled "In Fashion") that "she has been 'bored to death'" (11) at the Dedlock estate of Chesney Wold. A more visual point of connection, however, can be seen in subtle echoes of one of Thackeray's illustrations, as well as a bit of its associated context, in Dickens's verbal sketch in chapter 2 concerning Lady Dedlock's marriage and consequent social position.

The relevant picture is Thackeray's eye-catching woodcut at the conclusion of *Vanity Fair*'s chapter 14, depicting Sir Pitt on his knees in order to make a "reglar" (152) declaration of marriage to Becky while Becky stands before him with an expression of surprise and chagrin (fig. 4). The placement of this illustration at the end of the chapter (and the end of the fourth monthly installment in the original serial version) seems calculated to highlight the idea of Becky's grief, further underscored by the narrator's brief concluding commentary following the illustration:

> Rebecca started back a picture of consternation. In the course of this
> history we have never seen her lose her presence of mind; but she did now,
> and wept some of the most genuine tears that ever fell from her eyes.
> "Oh, Sir Pitt!" she said. "Oh, Sir—I—I'm *married already*." (152)

Becky's emphatic grief at her absolute inability (for legal as well as cultural reasons) to accept Sir Pitt's offer at this point suggests the kind of raw ambition that might cause a woman, like the one who becomes Lady Dedlock in *Bleak*

Fig. 3. William Thackeray. "Virtue rewarded. A booth in Vanity Fair."
From chapter 67 of *Vanity Fair.*

House, to abjure the father of her out-of-wedlock child—a child believed to have died at birth—in order to make a more advantageous match. The description of Lady Dedlock by *Bleak House*'s omniscient third-person narrator makes clear that ambition was indeed part of her character when she married Sir Leicester: "she had beauty, pride, ambition, insolent resolve, and sense enough to portion out a legion of fine ladies" (12; ch. 2).[16] Moreover, Becky's tears, suggested by her facial expression in Thackeray's illustration and emphasized in his narrator's commentary after the picture, take inverted form in the account by *Bleak House*'s third-person narrator of Lady Dedlock's marital composure:

How Alexander wept when he had no more worlds to conquer, everybody knows—or has some reason to know by this time, the matter having been

Fig. 4. William Thackeray. Depiction of Sir Pitt Crawley's proposal to Becky.
From chapter 14 of *Vanity Fair.*

rather frequently mentioned. My Lady Dedlock, having conquered *her* world, fell, not into the melting, but rather into the freezing mood. An exhausted composure, a worn-out placidity, an equanimity of fatigue not to be ruffled by interest or satisfaction, are the trophies of her victory. (12–13; ch. 2)

In these details about her ambitious marriage and subsequent lack of tears, Dickens's verbal depiction of Lady Dedlock's marital achievement parallels yet significantly diverges from Thackeray's verbal/visual portrayal of Becky's acute disappointment.

Other possible links between Sir Pitt's proposal in *Vanity Fair* and *Bleak House*'s description of the Dedlock marriage can be seen in the span of years associated with the two men as well as the implications of the pictures in the background of Thackeray's illustration. In making his pitch to Becky, Sir Pitt assures her, "I'm good for twenty years" (152; ch. 14), while "Sir Leicester is twenty years, full measure, older than my Lady" (12; ch. 2). In addition, the pictures on the wall in the background of Thackeray's woodcut, presumably representing ladies of the Crawley family, remind the reader (as do those at which Becky gazes in an earlier illustration at the start of chapter 8) that Becky has no place by birth in the aristocratic world to which she yearns to belong. Similarly, the third-person narrator of *Bleak House* explains about Lady Dedlock that "A whisper still goes about, that she had not even family; howbeit, Sir Leicester had so much family that perhaps he had enough, and could dispense with any more" (12; ch. 2). In such respects, Dickens's overview of the Dedlock marriage at the beginning of *Bleak House*'s chapter 2 reveals small but significant reflections of Thackeray's depiction, both verbally and graphically, of the scene of Sir Pitt's proposal of marriage to Becky in *Vanity Fair*.

However, between Sir Pitt Crawley's proposal and Sir Leicester Dedlock's marriage there is one especially important difference—Sir Leicester's genuine love for his wife. The boorish Sir Pitt's attraction to Becky is largely lecherous, an attitude indicated by Thackeray's words leading into the illustration—"the old man fell down on his knees and leered at her like a satyr" (152; ch. 14). Sir Pitt's lecherous desire is perhaps also suggested in the picture by the arrangement of his hands, one of which is positioned in his pocket, while the other reaches outward in the direction of Becky's knee. In contrast, the courtly Sir Leicester's love for Lady Dedlock is both idealistic and sincere. *Bleak House*'s third-person narrator indicates Sir Leicester's true "gallantry to my Lady" (12) in the initial description of him in chapter 2 and emphasizes the sincere nature of this love at the end of chapter 54 (see 653–54) when Sir Leicester has just learned of his wife's former relationship with a man by whom she had a child. Dickens further underscores the genuine nature of Sir Leicester's love when the physically and emotionally suffering baronet sends detective Bucket searching for Lady Dedlock with the message of her husband's "Full forgiveness" (669; ch. 56). Sir Leicester certainly has his faults. The third-person narrator introduces him as "obstinate ... intensely prejudiced, perfectly unreasonable" (12; ch. 2), and the ramifications of Sir Leicester's prejudices form a large part of what Dickens satirizes as wrong in the society of *Bleak House*. Nonetheless, Sir Leicester is also "honourable ... [and] truthful" (12; ch. 2). His love for his wife is an important part of that honor and truth. In other words, while Lady Dedlock's marriage may echo the marriage that *Vanity Fair's* Becky wanted to make, the characterization of Lady Dedlock's husband once again suggests Dickens's agreement with Forster's criticism that *Vanity Fair* is "overloaded with ... exhalations of human folly and wickedness" and that, as Forster also explained in his review, these "stifling ingredients are administered by Mr Thackeray to excess, without the necessary relief" (468). In a seriously ill society where government is paralyzed while Doodle and Coodle squabble (495; ch. 40) and where innocent children die while "Right Reverends and Wrong Reverends of every order" (572; ch. 47) ignore them, Sir Leicester's love for his lady provides— as does the character of Esther to a much greater degree—"necessary relief."

A third prominent woman in *Bleak House*, the French maid Hortense, also parallels an important aspect of *Vanity Fair's* Becky—in this case, her murderous side. Scholars have commonly assumed that Dickens based Hortense on the real-life character of Maria Manning, who, with her husband, committed a widely publicized murder and was hanged in 1849 in a public double execution attended by a huge number of spectators including Dickens (Collins, *Dickens and Crime* 235–37; Slater 298–99). It is likely that Dickens did indeed have the notorious Mrs. Manning to a great extent in mind in his depiction of Hortense, who murders the lawyer Tulkinghorn, in *Bleak House*. However, in terms of possible connections between Becky and the murderess in *Bleak House*, it is worth noting that Maria Manning (although a French speaker) was Swiss, while the background of both Becky (on her mother's side) and Hortense is French. More importantly, although Thackeray is famously ambiguous on the question of whether Becky does, in fact, murder Joseph Sedley at the end of *Vanity Fair*, the novel repeatedly suggests that she is capable of murder.[17] At a charade in chapter 51, Becky triumphantly plays the role of Clytemnestra (who—with her lover—killed her husband, Agamemnon, according to Greek legend). After this performance, in which Becky electrifies the partygoers at Gaunt House by raising a dagger over the figure representing the sleeping Agamemnon as the light illuminating the charade-tableau goes out, Lord Steyne roars over the applause of the crowd, "By ___, she'd do it too," and he subsequently jokes, "Mrs. Rawdon Crawley was quite killing in the part" (511). Much later, the ominous illustration that Thackeray captioned "Becky's second appearance in the character of Clytemnestra" (fig. 5) and its context in chapter 67 strongly hint that Becky actually kills the unfortunate Jos Sedley to obtain her share of "the two thousand pounds for which his life was insured" (687).[18] Thackeray's text, both verbally and visually, is not explicit on the question of whether Becky is literally a killer. Nevertheless, in his review of *Vanity Fair*, Forster (468) had no doubt. He saw Becky as clearly a murderess, albeit a very attractive one:

It is ... impossible to escape being charmed with the indomitable buoyancy, self-possession, and *applomb* [sic] of the little adventuress, Becky, even while we are conscious of her utter depravity. She commits every conceivable wickedness; dishonours her husband, betrays her friend, degrades and embrutes herself, and finally commits a murder; without in the least losing those smart, good-tempered, sensible manners and ways, which ingratiate her with the reader in spite of all her atrocities.

Forster further adds, "In this we may think the art questionably employed, but it is not to be denied that it *is* very extraordinary art" (rev. of *Vanity Fair* 468). Dickens's treatment of the last scene involving Hortense in *Bleak House* suggests a determination to employ his own art in a contrary direction.

In particular, a fundamental contrast, as well as some intriguing similarities, can be seen in a close comparison of *Vanity Fair*'s depiction of "Becky's second appearance in the character of Clytemnestra" and *Bleak House*'s description of the arrest of Hortense. The similarities warrant attention first. One analogous feature in the pages associated with these two episodes is a sense of mystery. *Vanity Fair* remains ultimately mysterious about whether Jos Sedley's death is truly the result of murder, while *Bleak House*—although clear that Tulkinghorn has been killed—is initially mysterious concerning who the perpetrator of that murder might be. Chapter 54 of *Bleak House* ("Springing a Mine") deliberately builds up this impression of mystery before discharging it with Hortense's arrest. Bucket first tells Sir Leicester, "I have now completed it [the case], and collected proof against the person who did this crime." Then, a few lines later (after indicating that an earlier suspect, George, is no longer believed to be the perpetrator), Bucket informs Sir Leicester, "It was a woman" (637). Next, Bucket moves to an extended discussion—interrupted and amplified by the Smallweed-Chadband entourage—of Lady Dedlock ("the pivot it all turns on," according to Bucket [638]). After eventually getting rid of the interruption, Bucket informs Sir Leicester, "The party to be apprehended is now in this house" and adds, "I'm about to take her into custody in your presence" (646). Finally, in the next paragraph, Hortense enters, to be "take[n] ... into custody" by Bucket several paragraphs later "on a charge of murder" (648).

While the gradual build-up of suspense leading to Hortense's arrest can be seen as Dickens's variation on Thackeray's ambiguity concerning Becky's guilt, a more tangible analogous feature in Hortense's definite and Becky's possible crime is the role played by knives in the suspicions regarding both women. In her first appearance in *Vanity Fair* as Clytemnestra—in the charade at Gaunt House—Becky is armed with a dagger, and Thackeray depicts this weapon as an enormous knife in his relevant illustration, "The Triumph of Clytemnestra" (fig. 6). In his illustration of her "second appearance," Becky—with a sinister expression on her face—again holds something that the allusion to Clytemnestra in the caption indicates may be a murder weapon. In this second case, the

Fig. 5. William Thackeray. "Becky's second appearance in the character of
Clytemnestra." From chapter 67 of *Vanity Fair*.

ominous but indistinguishable object is perhaps a gun or a bottle of poison. However, the Clytemnestra reference suggests that whatever is in Becky's hand might also be a knife. Significantly, in *Bleak House*, although Hortense kills Tulkinghorn by shooting him with a pistol, it is the sight of this woman holding a knife that first gives Bucket the idea of her guilt. He explains to Sir Leicester, when arresting Hortense in chapter 54, that the Frenchwoman has been lodging in Bucket's house for several weeks (possibly to blind him to her involvement in the crime that she intends to commit). As Bucket describes his discovery, when he goes home on the night after the murder, "By the living Lord it flashed upon me, as I sat opposite to her at the table and saw her with a knife in her hand, that she had done it!" (649).

Other details suggesting a connection between Thackeray's picture of Becky's "second appearance" and Dickens's account of Hortense's arrest are the similar placement in each scene of the three central figures—Dobbin, Joseph Sedley, and Becky on the one hand and Bucket, Sir Leicester, and Hortense on the other. In Thackeray's illustration, Dobbin stands before an enfeebled Joseph Sedley, who sits in a chair. According to the narrator of *Vanity Fair*, Dobbin is trying to persuade Jos "to break off a connexion [with Becky] which might have the most fatal consequences to him" (687; ch. 67), but the illustration shows that Becky, who is supposed to be absent, is eavesdropping on their conversation from behind a curtain. In *Bleak House*'s chapter 54, although he does at one point "take a seat" (638) at Sir Leicester's request, Bucket also apparently stands or walks about for much of the scene—from his opening of the door in response to the Smallweed disturbance (640) to his mockingly friendly declaration to the arrested Hortense that "I'll sit down by you" (650) on the sofa. His movements on his feet are particularly emphasized at the crucial point when Hortense enters the room. Contrary to Bucket, Sir Leicester (who is suffering from gout and "comes slowly to his easy-chair" [636] at the beginning of the chapter) remains, like Jos Sedley, in a chair, except for one feeble and ultimately unsuccessful attempt to stand during the discussion with Hortense (650). Sir Leicester leaves the chair only after the departure of Bucket and the now handcuffed Hortense, when the baronet "rises unsteadily to his feet, pushes back his chair ... walks a few steps" (653), and collapses, apparently due to a stroke. Furthermore, the high point of this chapter—Hortense's entrance into the room—again seems to echo details of Thackeray's picture, in this case in terms of Becky's position. The perspective in this part of Thackeray's illustration is a bit confusing, but it appears that Becky—concealed behind a curtain but visible to the reader—is just inside the door (indicated by a fanlight) of the room in which Dobbin and Jos converse. In chapter 54 of *Bleak House*, however, it is Bucket who conceals himself just inside the room, behind its door, in order to trap Hortense. As the third-person narrator explains, "Mr. Bucket rings, goes to the door, briefly whispers Mercury [a footman in the Dedlock household], shuts the door, and stands behind it with his arms folded. After a suspense of a minute or two, the door slowly opens, and a French woman enters.

Mademoiselle Hortense" (647). Bucket then "claps the door to, and puts his back against it" so that when Hortense turns to leave the room, "Her step towards the door brings her front to front with Mr. Bucket" (647). The positioning of the three main figures in *Bleak House*'s chapter 54, especially the proximity of Hortense to the door and the concealment of Bucket behind it, thus seems reminiscent of Thackeray's illustration—with the significant difference that the murderess in Dickens's novel is clearly identified and caught.

Fig. 6. William Thackeray. "The Triumph of Clytemnestra."
From chapter 51 of *Vanity Fair*.

Finally, a particularly intriguing point of connection between these episodes in the two novels may be the presence of two classical allusions in quick succession at the end of chapter 54 of *Bleak House*. Unlike Thackeray—who received a so-called gentleman's education, emphasizing the classics, at Charterhouse School, followed by Cambridge University—Dickens's formal education was brief. It consisted of about a year and a half at a good school taught by William Giles in Chatham and—after a hiatus that included Dickens's time of child labor in the blacking warehouse—less than three years at a mediocre school run by a Mr. Jones in London. (Dickens was taught to read by his mother and, prior to Mr. Giles's academy, briefly attended a dame school.) To a large extent, through Dickens's own extensive reading, "he may be said to have educated himself," as his father is reputed to have remarked (Forster, *Life* 47). Thus it does not seem surprising that, unlike the wide range of Latin and Greek allusions in Thackeray's writings, there are, in general, far fewer classical references in Dickens's works. Collins has observed that "At Jones's school he had been 'put into Virgil,' but he soon found his way out, and rarely alludes to Ancient literature or mythology" (Collins, "Dickens's Reading" 142). In this context, the inclusion of two references to classical mythology in the last three pages of *Bleak House*'s chapter 54 stands out as unusual.[19] As Bucket explains how Hortense has attempted to cast the blame for her crime on Lady Dedlock, he compliments the latter to Sir Leicester by comparing her appearance to that of "Venus rising from the ocean" (652). Then, shortly afterward, the third-person narrator declares that the way in which Bucket maneuvers the now handcuffed but still defiant Hortense out of the room is as indescribable as Jupiter's visitation in the guise of a cloud enveloping the nymph Io: "It is impossible to describe how Mr. Bucket gets her out, but he accomplishes that feat in a manner peculiar to himself; enfolding and pervading her like a cloud, and hovering away with her as if he were a homely Jupiter, and she the object of his affections" (653).[20] If, as seems likely, Dickens had Thackeray's illustration of Becky's sinister eavesdropping on the conversation between Dobbin and Joseph Sedley in mind at this point, these two classical allusions in rapid sequence as the murderess Hortense is about to depart for jail may be a perhaps unconscious variation on Dickens's part to Thackeray's Clytemnestra reference.[21]

In any case—regardless of Dickens's possible echo here of Thackeray's classical frame of reference—what is important is the striking contrast between how Dickens and Thackeray handle the idea of crime and punishment in these two episodes. Becky may, like Hortense, be guilty of murder, but the issue of Becky's guilt is never clearly resolved. The illustration of her "second appearance in the character of Clytemnestra," along with the picture's context in Thackeray's novel, strongly implies criminal conduct on Becky's part, resulting in Jos's death. Yet not only is she not punished; she ends the novel apparently "very wealthy" and possessed of "a very strong party of excellent people [who] consider her to be a most injured woman" (689; ch. 67). In *Bleak House*, however, Hortense is caught; her guilt is unambiguously explained not only to Sir Leicester but also to the reader, and she is taken away for punishment. In this swift, clear justice, Dickens seems to be agreeing with Forster's opinion that Becky, despite her charming qualities, is a killer as well as demonstrating that someone guilty of murder should not escape scot free. With Bucket's efficient arrest of Hortense, Dickens is also showing that while the Court of Chancery may operate in a blighting fog, with interminable, unresolved proceedings, Common Law dealing with crimes of murder can quickly lead to decisive action.[22]

To be sure, the conclusion that Dickens was replying in *Bleak House* to certain aspects of *Vanity Fair* is inferential. However, in the group of cases I have discussed, where particular *Vanity Fair* illustrations appear to have, consciously or unconsciously, triggered Dickens's thinking about Thackeray's Becky, the evidence for this deduction is very strong. Examination of the connections between Thackeray's pictures and Dickens's words suggests that Dickens was far more aware of Thackeray's 1847–48 novel than has been commonly believed. This close look at the subtle but significant links between *Bleak House* and *Vanity Fair* also suggests that while Dickens himself refrained from public comment on *Vanity Fair*, he privately concurred with the assessment expressed in Forster's *Examiner* review of Thackeray's work. For Forster, "Not Vanity Fair so properly as Rascality Fair is the scene he [Thackeray] lays open to our view; and he never wholly escapes from its equivocal associations, scarcely ever lays aside for a whole page his accustomed sneer" (468). For Dickens—although Esther and Lady Dedlock may stem from particular aspects of Becky (on the one hand, as orphan heroine and on the other, as social climber desiring advancement through marriage to a baronet)—Esther's unselfishness and the forgiving love of Lady Dedlock's husband stand in clear opposition to the "preponderance of unredeemed selfishness" that Forster perceived in *Vanity Fair*. Hortense, the third figure in the trio of female alter egos who play such an important part in *Bleak House*, can also be seen as stemming from an aspect of Becky (in this instance, her capacity for murder). Likewise, Hortense's exposure and arrest again indicate a negative reaction on Dickens's part to a notable feature of *Vanity Fair*—in this case, Becky's lack of punishment for what Forster unequivocally considered to be her crime of murder. As John Reed has pointed out, a concern with justice was characteristic of Dickens, who "was deeply interested in seeing cruelty and vice punished, and arranged his narratives so that this retribution was almost always accomplished" (Reed, *Dickens and Thackeray* 325). In thus responding to *Vanity Fair* while writing *Bleak House*, Dickens seems to have been recalling Thackeray's illustrations as much as his written text—a circumstance serving as a reminder that discussions of intertextuality need to take visual as well as verbal aspects of texts into account.

It is also important to remember that, as Thackeray complained, Forster's review greatly oversimplified *Vanity Fair* and, according to Thackeray, missed its point. In writing to thank another, more favorable reviewer (Robert Bell), Thackeray observed, "my object ... [was] to indicate, in cheerful terms, that we are for the most part an abominably foolish and selfish people 'desperately wicked' and all eager after vanities" (*Letters and Private Papers* 423). Thackeray further explained in this 3 September 1848 letter (referring both to Forster's less complimentary *Examiner* review of *Vanity Fair* and to the despicable Blifil in Fielding's *Tom Jones*), "For instance Forster says After a scene with Blifil, the air is cleared by a laugh of Tom Jones—Why Tom Jones in my holding is as big a rogue as Blifil. Before God he is—I mean the man is selfish according to his nature as Blifil according to his" (*Letters and Private Papers* 424). Although they recognized the greatness of *Vanity Fair*, Dickens and Forster may indeed have missed—or misunderstood—Thackeray's point about pervasive human imperfection. Nevertheless, Dickens's response to what he thought he saw in *Vanity Fair* contributed to his own great achievement in *Bleak House*.

In addition, this response by Dickens not only reveals his agreement with Forster's objections to Thackeray's *Vanity Fair* but also highlights certain general differences—beyond the more particular contrasts already discussed—between *Bleak House* and *Vanity Fair* as distinctive works of art. One fundamental difference between the two novels—a difference sharply illuminated by Dickens's rewriting of Thackeray's Becky as traced in this essay—is *Vanity Fair*'s deliberate deviousness versus *Bleak House*'s clarity of message.[23] With its clear sense of right and wrong, *Bleak House* lacks, for the most part, the carefully nuanced ambiguity—that Thackerayan habit, described by G. H. Lewes, of showing "a soul of goodness in things evil, as well as the spot of evil in things good" (108)— so characteristic of *Vanity Fair* as a whole and so evident in Becky. In this context, Dickens's splitting of Thackeray's Becky into three separate characters may suggest an underlying artistic unwillingness on Dickens's part to conceive of an individual as multifaceted and chameleon-like as "the indomitable little aide-de-camp's wife" (299) as Thackeray's narrator calls Becky in a famously ironic passage in chapter 30 of *Vanity Fair*. Peter K. Garrett has aptly remarked about *Vanity Fair*, "Irony infects every moral stance the narrator and his audience may adopt" (109). An irresolvable uncertainty about how we should, ultimately, assess the character of Becky (or even if we should try) is one of the pleasures of reading *Vanity Fair*. This uncertainty is an important way in which *Vanity Fair* differs from *Bleak House* with its unambiguous message, as Robert Newsom describes it, that Esther "embodies the maxim ... 'charity begins at home,'" in contrast to the lack of care provided by the corruptive and dysfunctional Court of Chancery or "ineffective career philanthropists" such as Mrs. Jellyby and Mrs. Pardiggle (*Charles Dickens Revisited* 120). By dividing Becky into three separate figures, Dickens enables one of them, his heroine, to express and demonstrate this maxim clearly, while making her alter egos—Lady Dedlock and Hortense—bear the weight, in varying degrees, of his readers' moral disapproval.

Two other recognizable differences—a greater social breadth and a greater psychological depth in *Bleak House* than in *Vanity Fair*—are also highlighted by Dickens's use of the Esther-Lady Dedlock-Hortense trio in reaction to Thackeray's Becky. Although Thackeray touches briefly on Becky's childhood poverty in *Vanity Fair*'s chapter 2 and returns her temporarily to a similarly impecunious bohemian existence (a raffish, student-associated life that "Becky liked" [652]) in chapter 65, his emphasis in depicting this incorrigible social climber—as in *Vanity Fair* in general—is on her movements in middle-class, upper-middle-class, and aristocratic circles. In *Bleak House* by contrast, as John O. Jordan and Gordon Bigelow have recently pointed out, "the scope of its social vision is almost uniquely broad" (*Approaches* 1). In his depiction of *Bleak House*'s three variations on Becky—the servant Hortense, the middle-class-by-birth but aristocrat-by-marriage Lady Dedlock (who dies at the gate of the paupers' cemetery where her bygone lover is buried), and the illegitimately born, middle-class Esther (saved from a fate like that of Jo, the street waif, by the cold charity of her aunt and then the more generous charity of Mr. Jarndyce)—Dickens displays a much wider social reach than that of Thackeray. (The interactions of Esther and Lady Dedlock with the impoverished brickmaker's wife, Jenny—whose identity at a crucial point in the novel is confused with that of Esther's mother—further extend this social reach.)

Finally, by splitting and rewriting Thackeray's Becky in the manner that I have traced, Dickens suggests a much deeper psychological dimension than Thackeray does with his own representation of this figure. In general, as Geoffrey Tillotson has observed, Thackeray conceived of character "as static," rather than changing (155). For Thackeray, circumstances simply bring out aspects of an individual's personality latent from the beginning.[24] Thus, although she has grown older and many sides of her nature have emerged in the course of the novel, the "Rebecca, Lady Crawley" who "busies herself in works of piety" (689; ch. 67) to enhance her standing in society at the end of *Vanity Fair* is essentially no different from the Becky who "perform[s] the part of the *ingénue*" near the book's beginning to persuade Miss Pinkerton to accept this seemingly "modest and innocent little child" (12; ch. 2) as an articled-pupil at the school at Chiswick Mall. In contrast, Esther gradually develops from the insecure girl produced by a loveless childhood at the beginning of her narrative to a more confident woman, in Timothy Peltason's words, "capable of declaring and worthy of receiving the love of another" at the novel's end ("The Esther Problem" 72).[25] With Lady Dedlock, who changes over the course of the novel from the ambitiously dry-eyed conqueror of "the world of fashion" (10; ch. 2) to an intentionally houseless wanderer, dying in her own words "of terror and my conscience" (710; ch. 59), and Hortense, whose suppressed rage eventually explodes into murder, Dickens also explores the passions that may well up, churn beneath, and finally break through the socially acceptable surface that once held them in check. As Alexander Welsh has pointed out (68), it would seem more logical if the murder were perpetrated not by Hortense but by Lady Dedlock, since the latter has to fear Tulkinghorn's revelation of her guilty secret while Hortense merely doesn't like him. Welsh argues, in addition, "Displacement in the murder mystery does not stop here, however, for it reaches to a third look-alike, the person only less interested in the secret than her mother, Esther

Summerson" (70) because Esther, for her mother's sake, dreads Tulkinghorn's potential revelations. Yet beyond its effect on "the murder mystery," this kind of projection is a potent psychological tool through which Dickens can suggest the powerful feelings experienced both by Lady Dedlock and, less consciously, by Esther. In a well-known passage in chapter 64 of *Vanity Fair*, Thackeray's narrator declines to show Becky's activities below "the water-line" (638), although he does give a few hints. In *Bleak House*, by contrast, with his three responses to Becky, Dickens repeatedly probes sub-surface emotional depths.

With these three variations on Becky, Dickens—like his character Guppy—seems to have had his thoughts engaged by a pictorial stimulus. Unlike Guppy, however, Dickens had a luminously creative imagination, although he may not always have been fully conscious of how this imagination might respond to stimulation. As Shelley said of music, which "when soft voices die, / Vibrates in the memory," Dickens—perhaps without fully knowing or acknowledging this particular visual vibration in his mind—recalled and wove his responses to Thackeray's depictions of Becky into a grand fictional design that largely conceals the origin of these (like many other) component parts. Julia Kristeva reminds us that "any text is constructed as a mosaic of quotations; any text is the absorption and transformation of another" (37). Unpacking the connections with *Vanity Fair* as I have done in no way lessens Dickens's achievement in *Bleak House*. Rather, this examination brings into sharper focus some of the important differences between these two major nineteenth-century novels. In absorbing Thackeray's visual-verbal text and dividing Thackeray's Becky into Esther, Lady Dedlock, and Hortense, Dickens was guided, I believe, by a recollection of Thackeray's illustrations. Yet this response to *Vanity Fair*, while critical of Thackeray's text, was probably not entirely deliberate. Dickens's reply to Thackeray is likely a case of what a creative consciousness may "half create, / And what perceive," as Wordsworth's "Tintern Abbey" describes the poetic process. The resulting artistic transformation of what Dickens perceived in and then recalled from *Vanity Fair* plays an essential role in the unique masterpiece that is *Bleak House*.

NOTES

1. For an excellent discussion of the recurring sense of déjà vu in *Bleak House*, see Newsom, *Dickens on the Romantic Side of Familiar Things* 44–45 and 50–68. Newsom analyzes the feeling of déjà vu in this novel in terms of Freud's concept of the uncanny and, in *Charles Dickens Revisited*, emphasizes that this "particular form of unwilled repetition known as *déjà vu*.... becomes pervasive and therefore almost normal in the world of *Bleak House*, where we continually have the unsettled experience of returning upon our own tracks without entirely realizing it" (126). My essay, which builds upon Newsom's insight into an important feature of this 1852–53 novel, argues that Dick-

ens's own, to some extent submerged, pictorial memories of *Vanity Fair* (1847–48) played a significant part in what he wrote in *Bleak House*.

2. An example of Ackroyd's remark is the declaration by the reviewer David Masson in 1851:

> Thackeray and Dickens, Dickens and Thackeray—the two names now almost necessarily go together. It is some years since Mr. Thackeray, whose reputation as an author had until then, we believe, been of somewhat limited extent, suddenly appeared in the field of literature already so successfully occupied by Mr. Dickens. But the intrusion, if it may be called such, was made with so much talent, and so much applause followed it, that since that time the two have gone on as peers and rivals. (57)

3. Meckier, who observes briefly that *Bleak House* may have commenced as an intentional rejection of Thackeray's *Vanity Fair* (245), also perceives Dickens and Thackeray as "competitor-allies" (245) in the sense that they "both possessed an essentially satirical frame of mind" (244). Meckier's principal focus in *Hidden Rivals* is on the reactions of George Eliot, Trollope, Gaskell, and Collins to Dickens and Dickens's response to these four rivals, not to Thackeray.

4. This letter is cited by Edgar Johnson as evidence that Dickens "was disagreeably impressed by what seemed to him a flippant cynicism in Thackeray's attitude and seldom read him" (616). However, Harry Stone has demonstrated "that there *is* evidence that Dickens read Thackeray's books, and that Dickens was *not* insensible to Thackeray's genius" (43).

5. In a discussion of the relationship between another novel by Thackeray and *David Copperfield*, Mark Cronin has shown that "Explicitly sustained intersections and parallels between the two novels indicate that Dickens may have shaped characters and events from *David Copperfield* in response to Thackeray's *Pendennis*" (216). However, Cronin does not deal with the *Vanity Fair–Bleak House* relationship that I am discussing here.

6. Among the books in Dickens's library after his death was the 1848 first edition in book form of *Vanity Fair*, "*with illustrations on steel and wood by the Author*" (Stonehouse 110).

7. Citations from *Vanity Fair* in my text are to the Norton edition. Illustrations are reproduced from volume 11 of the Oxford Thackeray edition.

8. On the significance of *Vanity Fair*'s pictorial dimension, see, for example, Gneiting; Stevens ("*Vanity Fair* and the London Skyline" in Norton *VF* 777–97); Stevens ("Thackeray's Pictorial Capitals" 116–19, 125–28, 133, 135–40); and Pickwoad.

9. In her very insightful recent study, Bodenheimer comments that "Character splitting, in which different characters display extreme versions of qualities that more realistically belong to the mixed nature of one character, is ... a well-recognized Dickens strategy" (6), although she does not discuss the particular Esther-Lady Dedlock-Hortense split and its connection with *Vanity Fair* on which I will be focusing in my present discussion. Bodenheimer also makes an intriguing observation about Dickens's fondness for mirrors

in household decoration: "Mirrors were the decorative equivalents of Dickens's imaginative ability to expand, heighten, or double everything he looked at" (146). She points out that at Tavistock House, into which Dickens moved immediately prior to beginning the writing of *Bleak House* and where his study was separated from the adjacent drawing room by a concealed door, "a large mirror taken from Devonshire Terrace was reframed and installed in a recess of the door-bookcase directly opposite the study window, while other mirrors were installed in three recesses on the drawing-room side" (145).

10. In addition to Bodenheimer, a number of recent critics have discussed the idea of doubleness in Dickens's writing (e.g., see Gillman and Patten; Morgentaler; Paganoni), and this idea has also been explored by earlier scholars (e.g., see Lane; Moynahan).

11. Slater's headnote to this review in *The Amusements of the People* (81) points out that Dickens's mention of "the Kilmarnock weaver's prayer for grace to see themselves as others see them" is a reference to Robert Burns's poem "To a Louse." The conjunction between Dickens's facetious 1848 remark about the figure of the doppelgänger in his review of Crowe's book and his use of this technique in the same year in *The Haunted Man* has been pointed out by Bodenheimer (10–12) and Thomas (*Dickens and the Short Story* 59).

12. Among the critics who have called attention to Esther, Lady Dedlock, and Hortense as alter egos, see Newsom (*Dickens on the Romantic Side* 50–51, 88–90; *Charles Dickens Revisited* 194n38), Blain (in Tambling 72, 77), and Gillman and Patten (445–46). See also the discussion of Esther and Lady Dedlock by Schor (101–23).

13. In my reading of *Bleak House*, Becky's husband Rawdon in *Vanity Fair* can be seen, less conspicuously, as split in *Bleak House* into the ruined Captain Hawdon (Nemo) and the more upright ex-cavalry soldier George. In this pair of male alter egos in *Bleak House*, Hawdon's kindness to the young crossing-sweeper Jo and George's later kindness to the same boy, as well as George's friendship with the Bagnet children, seem reflective of Rawdon's affection for his son.

14. Kaye indicates that Brontë's novel "had been published on 16 October 1847" (725)—"after the first nine installments of *Vanity Fair* [containing chapters 1–32] had been serialized" (724–25). In chapter 33 of *Jane Eyre*, "Brontë's highly ethical heroine" (Kaye 726) divides with her three cousins the £20,000 legacy she has received from her uncle, reserving only £5000 as life-time amount for herself. Kaye focuses on the contrast between this action by Jane Eyre and Becky's famous remark in chapter 41 of *Vanity Fair*, "I think I could be a good woman if I had five thousand a year"—a remark that he persuasively contends is a "sly reference to *Jane Eyre*" (726), which was read by Thackeray shortly before writing this chapter (published in the December 1847 installment of his novel). With this allusion, Kaye argues, "Thackeray presents *Vanity Fair* as offering a truer, less sentimentalized depiction of his era's material values ..." (731), and Kaye suggests that Thackeray's "determination to differentiate Becky Sharp from Jane Eyre may have stemmed from his alarm that Brontë's heroine was being read as Becky's fictional twin" (727).

15. Kucich comments about *Bleak House*'s ending, "The instability of any permanent resolution is summed up in the last hanging, unresolved sentence" (155). Jordan takes

the title of his admirable recent book *Supposing* Bleak House from Esther's hanging, final word ("supposing"), and he perceptively suggests that this word, along with the unfinished statement in which it occurs, offers a sign of "[t]he angry, desiring, giddy, critical, eloquent Esther"—who is previously often evident in her narrative but who, in her final chapter, "is almost entirely absent ... hidden behind a coy, self-effacing gender stereotype" (78).

16. Dabney describes Lady Dedlock's "real sin as that of marrying for money and position instead of for love" (82). The reference to Lady Dedlock's "beauty," in the description from chapter 2 (12) quoted in my text, suggests a further link between Thackeray's scene of Sir Pitt's proposal and Dickens's account of the marriage of Sir Leicester and his lady. At the beginning of chapter 15 of *Vanity Fair*, the narrator alludes ironically to the proposal scene depicted visually and verbally at the end of the previous chapter, "what can be prettier than an image of Love on his knees before Beauty?" (153). Then, however, the narrator drops his mock-sentimental tone to explain, "But when Love heard that awful confession from Beauty that she was married already, he bounced up from his attitude of humility on the carpet, uttering exclamations which caused poor little Beauty to be more frightened than she was when she made her avowal" (153). Thackeray's sardonic conjunction here of Love and Beauty is paralleled in a different key in *Bleak House* by the third-person narrator's remarks that not only was Lady Dedlock beautiful at the time of her marriage but that "She has beauty still" (13; ch. 2) and Sir Leicester "married her for love"(12; ch. 2). Notably, there is no mention of any reciprocal love of Lady Dedlock for Sir Leicester.

17. For a possible reason behind some of this ambiguity by Thackeray in connection with Joseph Sedley's death, see Thomas ("Thackeray, Capital Punishment, and the Demise of Jos Sedley").

18. In an appendix to *Supposing* Bleak House, Jordan reproduces and briefly discusses this illustration as an example of the importance of considering an illustrated novel's visual dimension as well as its written text (149–51).

19. The earlier references in chapter 54, as well as elsewhere in *Bleak House*, to a Dedlock footman as "Mercury" do not seem so remarkable. A footman's job included tending the door and informing his employer of the arrival of visitors. The *OED* indicates that the use of "Mercury" as a noun alluding to the Roman messenger god of that name and thus referring to "A messenger; a person who brings news" was current among writers in 1844 and 1864 and that the term had also been previously used in this sense by Shakespeare in *Richard III* 2.1.89 (see "Mercury," Def. I.3b, *Oxford English Dictionary Online*).

Pauline Fletcher has astutely traced a progression in Dickens's treatment of classical references over the course of his career. She shows that "Dickens's use of classical material changes and develops as his art matures and, perhaps more significantly, as his relationship to the dominant culture evolves" (1), although she also observes that—in contrast to many of his contemporaries—"Dickens had not read very widely in the ancients" (17). Fletcher points out that "It is likely that Dickens's interest in the ancient world was stimulated by his year in Italy" (8), where he lived with his family in 1844–45. Thus, she sees Italy, "to which he returned for a second visit in 1853" (8)—

after finishing *Bleak House*—as an important factor in Dickens's growing comfort with "discourse containing classical references [that] would normally be considered the language of the dominant and official culture" (1). However, although Fletcher (12) analyzes Dickens's recurring and increasingly elaborated treatment of the depiction of "Allegory, in Roman helmet and celestial linen" (119; ch. 10) on Mr. Tulkinghorn's ceiling in *Bleak House*, she does not discuss the two classical allusions in the last pages of that novel's chapter 54 with which I am presently concerned.

20. A note in the Norton edition of *Bleak House* glosses the reference to Jupiter in this passage as follows: "Identified with Zeus, the Greek god of the heavens, who assumed various guises in pursuing *objects of his affections* such as the maiden Io, whom he visited in the form of a dark *cloud*" (653n; ch. 54).

21. Jordan convincingly argues that an extended classical allusion—to the story of Orpheus's attempt to rescue his wife, Eurydice, from the underworld—occurs as "a proto-psychoanalytic mythic structure" (44, 57) in chapters 57 and 59, where Esther recounts her journey with Bucket in pursuit of Lady Dedlock (*Supposing* Bleak House 60–66). In this reading, Jordan compares Bucket's relationship with Esther during the journey to that of a "psychoanalyst who accompanies his patient down into the world of the unconscious ... searching for clues that will enable her to escape from the prison of her neurosis" (60), although Jordan concludes that, for Esther, "Bucket's therapeutic intervention is at best only a partial success" (74). While Hortense's arrest in chapter 54 and what Jordan calls "[t]he chase sequence in chapters 57 to 59" (127) appear in different monthly installments (numbers 17 and 18 respectively), the two events are closely linked in terms of plot. After "Springing a Mine" (ch. 54) in the opening chapter of number 17, the remaining two chapters in that installment build toward another climax in chapter 56 with Bucket's commission by Sir Leicester—now partially paralyzed as a result of the information revealed in chapter 54—to find Lady Dedlock and convey her husband's forgiveness and with Bucket's rapid move to enlist Esther to join him in the search. The possible extended allusion to the tale of Orpheus and Eurydice in the chase then detailed in installment 18 may have been at least partly prompted—like the brief allusions to Venus and Jupiter near the end of chapter 54—by Dickens's recollection, while writing the scene of Hortense's arrest, of Thackeray's use of classical reference in one or both of the "Clytemnestra" illustrations.

22. See the useful discussion of the distinction between the Court of Chancery and Courts of Common Law in the Norton *Bleak House* edition's "Introductory Note on Law Courts and Colleges" (xvi–xviii).

23. Dyson describes *Vanity Fair* as "surely one of the world's most devious novels" (76).

24. Geoffrey Tillotson remarks that "Thackeray ... sees his personages as things made so once for all" (153). Kathleen Tillotson concurs with this assessment but observes that Thackeray's presentation of his characters may create the illusion that they change when they actually do not: "His characters are so mixed, so often on a moral borderland, so subject to time, and also so gradually unfolded—often with unpredictable detail—that they do not give the impression of being static. But they are not shown as evolving, nor do they undergo much inward conflict" (239).

25. For a more detailed discussion of Esther's growth process, see Peltason ("Esther's Will" in Tambling 205–27). Other important critical works that examine Esther's struggle for self-identity and have influenced my thinking include the studies by Graver ("Writing in a 'Womanly Way' and the Double Vision of *Bleak House*"); Michie ("'Who is this in Pain?': Scarring, Disfigurement, and Female Identity in *Bleak House* and *Our Mutual Friend*"); Schor (ch. 4 of *Dickens and the Daughter of the House*); and, most recently, Jordan (*Supposing* Bleak House). A significant early discussion of Esther's psychology, which has also contributed to my thinking about this topic, is by Zwerdling ("Esther Summerson Rehabilitated"). Bodenheimer terms Dickens "the Victorian novelist most deeply intrigued by nineteenth-century ideas about the unconscious mind" (6), while Jordan insightfully points out in *Supposing* Bleak House that "Dickens carefully orchestrates Esther's actions and language in ways that allow her to reveal, and us to see, unconscious dimensions of her character" (10).

WORKS CITED

Ackroyd, Peter. *Dickens*. 1990. New York: HarperPerennial-HarperCollins, 1992.

Blain, Virginia. "Double Vision and the Double Standard in *Bleak House*: A Feminist Perspective." *Literature and History* 2 (1985): 31–46. Rpt. in Tambling 65–86.

Bodenheimer, Rosemarie. *Knowing Dickens*. Ithaca: Cornell UP, 2007.

Collins, Philip. *Dickens and Crime*. 3rd ed. New York: St. Martin's, 1994.

———. "Dickens's Reading." *The Dickensian* 60 (1964): 136–51.

Cronin, Mark. "The Rake, The Writer, and *The Stranger*: Textual Relations between *Pendennis* and *David Copperfield*." *Dickens Studies Annual* 24 (1996): 215–40.

Dabney, Ross H. *Love and Property in the Novels of Dickens*. Berkeley: U of California P, 1967.

Dickens, Charles. *The Amusements of the People and Other Papers: Reports, Essays and Reviews, 1834–51*. Dent Uniform Edition of Dickens' Journalism. Vol. 2. Ed. Michael Slater. Columbus: Ohio State UP, 1996.

———. *Bleak House*. Norton Critical Edition. Ed. George Ford and Sylvère Monod. New York: Norton, 1977.

———. *The Letters of Charles Dickens*. Pilgrim Edition. Vol. 5. Ed. Graham Storey and K. J. Fielding. Oxford: Clarendon, 1981.

Dyson, A. E. *The Crazy Fabric*. London: Macmillan, 1965.

Fletcher, Pauline. "Bacchus in Kersey: Dickens and the Classics." *Dickens Studies Annual* 27 (1998): 1–22.

Forster, John. *The Life of Charles Dickens*. Ed. J. W. T. Ley. London: Cecil Palmer, 1928.

[Forster, John]. Rev. of *Vanity Fair: a Novel without a Hero*, by William Makepeace Thackeray. *Examiner* 22 July 1848: 468–70.

Garrett, Peter K. *The Victorian Multiplot Novel: Studies in Dialogical Form*. New Haven: Yale UP, 1980.

Gillman, Susan K., and Robert L. Patten. "Dickens: Doubles:: Twain: Twins." *Nineteenth-Century Fiction* 39 (1985): 441–58.

Gneiting, Teona Tone. "The Pencil's Role in *Vanity Fair.*" *Huntington Library Quarterly* 39 (1976): 171–202.

Graver, Suzanne. "Writing in a 'Womanly' Way and the Double Vision of *Bleak House.*" *Dickens Quarterly* 4 (1987): 1–15.

Johnson, Edgar. *Charles Dickens: His Tragedy and Triumph.* 2 vols. Boston: Little, Brown, 1952.

Jordan, John O. *Supposing* Bleak House. Charlottesville: U of Virginia P, 2011.

Jordan, John O., and Gordon Bigelow, eds. *Approaches to Teaching Dickens's* Bleak House. New York: MLA, 2008.

Kaye, Richard A. "A Good Woman on Five Thousand Pounds: *Jane Eyre, Vanity Fair,* and Literary Rivalry." *SEL* 35 (1995): 723–39. *JSTOR.* Web. 7 Aug. 2008.

Kristeva, Julia. "Word, Dialogue and Novel." *The Kristeva Reader.* Ed. Toril Moi. Oxford: Blackwell, 1986. 34–61.

Kucich, John. *Excess and Restraint in the Novels of Charles Dickens.* Athens: U of Georgia P, 1981.

Lane, Lauriat, Jr. "Dickens and the Double." *The Dickensian* 55 (1959): 47–55.

[Lewes, G. H.]. Review of *Pendennis,* by William Makepeace Thackeray, *Leader,* 21 Dec. 1850. Rpt. in *Thackeray: The Critical Heritage.* Ed. Geoffrey Tillotson and Donald Hawes. London: Routledge, 1968. 105–10.

[Masson, David]. "*Pendennis* and *Copperfield*: Thackeray and Dickens." *North British Review* 15.29 (1851): 57–89. *British Periodicals.* Web. 12 June 2009.

Meckier, Jerome. *Hidden Rivalries in Victorian Fiction: Dickens, Realism, and Revaluation.* Lexington: UP of Kentucky 1987.

"Mercury." Def. I.3b. *Oxford English Dictionary Online.* Oxford UP, 2009. Web. 12 Oct. 2009.

Michie, Helena. "'Who is this in Pain?': Scarring, Disfigurement, and Female Identity in *Bleak House* and *Our Mutual Friend.*" *Novel: A Forum on Fiction* 22 (1989): 199–212. *JSTOR.* Web. 7 Feb. 2011.

Moers, Ellen. "*Bleak House*: The Agitating Women." *The Dickensian* 69 (1973): 13–24.

Morgentaler, Goldie. "Mrs. Gamp, Mrs. Harris and Mr. Dickens: Creativity and the Self Split in Two." *Dickens Quarterly* 26 (2009): 3–14.

Moynahan, Julian. "The Hero's Guilt: The Case of *Great Expectations.*" *Essays in Criticism* 10 (1960): 60–79. Rpt. in *Victorian Literature: Selected Essays.* Ed. Robert O. Preyer. 1966. New York: Harper Torchbooks-Harper, 1967. 126–45.

Newsom, Robert. *Charles Dickens Revisited.* New York: Twayne, 2000.

———. *Dickens on the Romantic Side of Familiar Things:* Bleak House *and the Novel Tradition.* New York: Columbia UP, 1977.

Paganoni, Maria Cristina. *The Magic Lantern: Representation of the Double in Dickens.* New York: Routledge, 2008.

Peltason, Timothy. "The Esther Problem." Jordan and Bigelow 71–78.

———. "Esther's Will." *English Literary History* 59 (1991): 671–91. Rpt. in Tambling 205–27.

Pickwoad, Nicholas. "Commentary on Illustrations." *Vanity Fair*. Ed. Peter L. Shillingsburg. New York: Garland, 1989. 641–47.

Reed, John R. *Dickens and Thackeray: Punishment and Forgiveness*. Athens: Ohio UP, 1995.

———. *Victorian Conventions*. [Athens]: Ohio UP, 1975.

Schor, Hilary M. *Dickens and the Daughter of the House*. Cambridge: Cambridge UP, 1999.

Shatto, Susan. *The Companion to* Bleak House. London: Unwin Hyman, 1988.

Slater, Michael. *Charles Dickens*. New Haven: Yale UP, 2009.

Stevens, Joan. "Thackeray's Pictorial Capitals." *Costerus* ns 2 (1974): 113–40.

———. "*Vanity Fair* and the London Skyline." *Costerus* ns 2 (1974): 13–41. Rpt. in Norton *Vanity Fair* 777–97.

Stone, Harry. "Dickens's Knowledge of Thackeray's Writings." *The Dickensian* 53 (1957): 42–45.

Stonehouse, J. H., ed. *Catalogue of the Library of Charles Dickens from Gadshill, Catalogue of His Pictures and Objects of Art, Catalogue of the Library of W. M. Thackeray and Relics from His Library*. 1935. [Kusatsu City, Shiga], Japan: Takashi Terauchi, 2003.

Storey, Gladys. *Dickens and Daughter*. 1939. New York: Haskell House, 1971.

Tambling, Jeremy, ed. Bleak House*: Charles Dickens*. New York: St. Martin's, 1998.

Thackeray, William Makepeace. *The Letters and Private Papers of William Makepeace Thackeray*. Ed. Gordon N. Ray. Vol. 2. Cambridge: Harvard UP, 1945.

———. *Vanity Fair*. Norton Critical Edition. Ed. Peter Shillingsburg. New York: Norton, 1994.

———. *Vanity Fair*. The Oxford Thackeray. Ed. George Saintsbury. Vol. 11. London: Oxford UP, [1908].

Thomas, Deborah A. *Dickens and the Short Story*. Philadelphia: U of Pennsylvania P, 1982.

———. "Thackeray, Capital Punishment, and the Demise of Jos Sedley." *Victorian Literature and Culture* 33 (2005): 1–20.

Tillotson, Geoffrey. *Thackeray the Novelist*. Cambridge: Cambridge UP, 1954.

Tillotson, Kathleen. *Novels of the Eighteen-Forties*. Oxford: Clarendon, 1954.

Welsh, Alexander. *Dickens Redressed: The Art of* Bleak House *and* Hard Times. New Haven: Yale UP, 2000.

Zwerdling, Alex. "Esther Summerson Rehabilitated." *PMLA* 88 (1973): 429–39.

When Fairy Godmothers Are Men: Dickens's Gendered Use of Fairy Tales as a Form of Narrative Control in *Bleak House*

Melissa A. Smith

This paper explores how Charles Dickens's use of a female narrator in Bleak House *(1853) fundamentally problematizes and undermines his use of the fairy tale's cultural cachet, motifs, and characters to support and project his fantasies of the feminine ideal. More specifically, it examines the effects of the thematic presence of several tale types and stock fairy tale figures on Dickens's ability to prescribe ideal feminine behaviors, such as lack of curiosity and selfless obedience, to both his characters and his female audience. Because Esther's ability to write and her interest in either discovering or constructing her own identity establish her as competitor to the males who attempt to script her life, Dickens tries to control and circumscribe her ability to know and act through her own and other characters' resemblance to traditional fairy tale character types, especially Bluebeard and Griselda. Esther's narrative, however, betrays these unnatural delimitations in telltale interruptions and denials as Dickens attempts to circumvent the constraints he has placed on her voice. Esther's narrative therefore resists but imperfectly overcomes the Victorian male author's scripting of femininity.*

Dickens Studies Annual, Volume 44, Copyright © 2013 by AMS Press, Inc. All rights reserved.

DOI 10.7756/dsa.044.010.195-220

Storytelling makes women thrive.

—Marina Warner[1]

Esther, like the novel in which she appears, is a hybrid. She is certainly, as many critics have argued, the product of Charles Dickens's prolific imagination, desires, and ambivalences.[2] However, Dickens also brings her to life within a specific literary tradition whose politics exert an influence over which he has little control. This tradition, encompassing the genres of folk and fairy tales,[3] has been described by Maria Tatar as an historically powerful means of culturation and socialization, scripting readers' responses and desires—especially Western culture's responses to women's desires for knowledge and power (*Off with Their Heads!* xxvii). Working in this genre proves complicated for Dickens, who, trying to construct an angel (or Cinderella) in the house, is also attempting to portray an expressive, psychologically complex, and realistic voice.[4] Neither Esther nor Dickens, then, can be described as the sole producers of Esther's contributions to *Bleak House* (1852–53).[5] Rather, Esther's idiosyncratic narration, with its constant recursions and (to some) exasperating false modesty, must be viewed in the light of the competition between a Victorian's desires and the fairy tale's spell.

In Western Europe, tale-telling and -collecting, before Charles Perrault's famous project, was a distinctly female way of passing information to members of the community and the next generation (Warner xvi). While old wives' tales could "train children in attitudes and aspirations" (49), they did so informally and usually orally, outside of institutions sanctioned by males (33). As literacy spread, however, these traditionally oral messages began to be transcribed into written forms and, as a result, began to transform in meaning. One reason for this transformation was the new interference of men in the fairy tale's genealogy. The sphere of publication—from which male collectors of the fairy tale like Perrault and the Grimm brothers began to exert their ideological sway—was one in which women had little power, either to alter the content of the tales or produce competing versions. Freezing women into the position of source rather than author,[6] these narrative gender politics condemned women to a state of perpetual mediation by men, who gave themselves unlimited license to interpret and shape women's utterances authoritatively. By the nineteenth century, however, women writers had gained a position in the literary marketplace from which they could contest "male idealizations of a feminized innocence" and "wrest child-texts away from the fantasists who had come to dominate the market" (Auerbach and Knoepflmacher xii). Through this reappropriation, they were able to revive the original spirit and message of the oral folktales.[7] Imagining young girls as their audience (Knoepflmacher xi), male users of enchantment attempted to compete with this female community of storytellers,[8] prescribing their fantasies and idealizations of female innocence and immaturity to a group of readers who had historically been nourished by tales.

Nina Auerbach and U.C. Knoepflmacher, in the introduction to *Forbidden Journeys* (1) and Knoepflmacher in *Ventures into Childland* (5), emphasize the thesis that male Victorian authors used the fairy tale form to freeze their female characters into the endless childhood they fantasized for themselves and their female audience. No less true of Dickens, this paper will examine the effects of the thematic presence of several tale-types and stock fairy tale figures on Dickens's ability to prescribe ideal feminine behaviors, such as lack of curiosity and selfless obedience, to both his characters and audience. For the sake of plot, Dickens must grant Esther the ability to write and an interest in either discovering or constructing her own identity. This power to write her own happy ending, as it were, allows her to inherit her proper place in the female tale-telling tradition. However, this handling of half of the narrative on Esther's terms inadvertently establishes her as a competitor to the males who attempt to "write" her life. Dickens, however, tries to control and circumscribe Esther's ability to know and act by modeling her and other characters on traditional fairy tale character types, especially those found in the stories of Bluebeard and Griselda. Esther's narrative betrays the unnatural delimitation of female-authored fairy tales by male-authored fairy tales in telltale interruptions and denials, which are the natural result of Dickens's attempts to circumvent the constraints he himself has placed on his heroine's voice. Esther's narrative is therefore resistant to but can only imperfectly overcome the Victorian male author's scripting of femininity.

Dickens undoubtedly joins the likes of Lewis Carroll and John Ruskin in projecting a feminine ideal in his own work that reflects his personal predilections for nostalgia and stasis.[9] In 1853, while writing *Bleak House*, Dickens published an essay in *Household Words* tellingly entitled "Where We Stopped Growing." It begins, "Few people who have been much in the society of children, are likely to be ignorant of the sorrowful feeling sometimes awakened in the mind by the idea of a favourite child's 'growing up'" (385). He explains, "Childhood is usually so beautiful and engaging, that ... there is a mournful shadow of the common lot, in the notion of its fading into anything else" (385). Already betraying a yearning to constrain children in eternal immaturity, Dickens soon demonstrates that he can go beyond simply wishing for this impossible feat, for he has the ability to arrest even adults in their growth and send them, piecemeal, back to youth. The tools with which he performs this operation are the literary works of one's childhood. His nostalgia first leads him to consider "whether there were any things as to which this individual We actually did stop growing when we were a child" (385). Much to his relief, Dickens is able to enumerate a long list of these suspensions in his development, each associated with a favorite story whose details retain such a strong hold on his imagination that they have actually prevented him from developing any new conceptions regarding them as he has aged. This power is one way in which, as Dickens wistfully asserts in "Frauds on the Fairies," also published in 1853, "stories help keep us, in some sense, ever young, by preserving through our worldly ways one slender track not overgrown with weeds, where we may walk with children, sharing their delights" (56).

It is clear, however, that Dickens does not just want to walk with children; he also wants to become one, and this same nostalgia worked with a vengeance on the women in his life and books. Shuli Barzilai has theorized that the passing of his sister-in-law, Mary, whose early death allowed her seventeen-year-old self to be eternally "cherished in its changeless purity" in Dickens's mind ("Bluebeard Barometer" 513), inspired in him a feminine ideal that was "an abiding ghost, always youthful, virginal, and fair" (513), much like a Snow White, perfectly preserved in her glass coffin. Indeed, David Parker acknowledges that Dickens "constructed an after-life for [Mary] ... to meet his own emotional needs" (72), keeping her dresses until they rotted and wearing a ring that he had taken from her finger upon her death (Slater 85). Barzilai claims that Dickens's uses of the Bluebeard fairy tale in his novels are ploys that hide the palimpsest of such underlying desires and fantasies. Like other male authors of his day, it is indeed through stories that he would attempt to keep women, not just ever young, but the indefatigable angels of the house who give all and ask nothing in return (Barzilai, "Charles Dickens" 32).[10]

Esther Summerson does not escape Dickens's authorial projection of this desire. In Esther, as Alex Zwerdling asserts, "Dickens is interested in portraying someone who remains trapped between childhood and real maturity" (429). It should come as little surprise, therefore, that when Dickens introduces his first female narrator, he positions her immediately within the fairy-tale tradition. In the third paragraph of Esther's narrative, she begins her own "once upon a time": "I was brought up, from my earliest remembrance—like some of the princesses in the fairy stories, only I was not so charming—by my godmother" (17; ch. 3).[11] From the first, then, Esther is complicatedly both a teller of and an actor in a fairy tale that must negotiate two traditions, one in which, as a female storyteller, she is entitled to an authoritative voice that grants herself, as an actor, agency and options; and another in which Dickens must control her voice to express certain desires, attitudes, and values that a female storyteller could not realistically be expected to communicate.[12] For a Victorian author like Dickens, these narrative politics make his use of a female narrator an almost acrobatic venture,[13] one in which he must bring her to the forefront but always stand in her way, develop her, and yet keep her miraculously stunted. Esther is akin to the female writers of her day competing with the likes of Lewis Carroll, who desired so strongly to keep his "beloved dream child," Alice, "ever enshrined in 'happy summer days' unaffected by change" that he indulged "in fantasies of containment and domination that were totally inimical to [female authors'] own yearning for autonomy and authority" (Auerbach and Knoepflmacher 6).

Dickens is able to perform these gymnastics, however, by making Esther a character, not just in her own narration, but in another's narration as well. By splitting this representation of her, Dickens momentarily silences Esther and makes her subject to larger considerations of genre, plot trajectory, and identity, the terms of which Dickens gets to set and within which her narrative is then forced to operate.

This explains, in part, why the book opens, not with Esther's "portion of these pages" (17; ch. 3), but with the third-person narrator, who irresistibly establishes his authority by employing the same telegraphic style a playwright would use to write stage directions. By being inscribed in this way, Esther is prevented from using the fairy-tale form on her own terms, is prohibited from writing herself as an actor who, as Tatar argues of Jane Eyre, could become "a one-woman crusade and act of resistance to the roles modeled for girls and women in fairy tales" (*Classic Fairy Tales* xvii)—specifically, I would clarify, male-authored fairy tales. Denied the ability to make "productive use of fairy tales by reacting to them, resisting them, and rewriting them" (Tatar, *Classic Fairy Tales* xviii), Esther instead has Dickens's own rewriting imposed upon her. In the words of Brenda Ayres,

> In recognizing the legitimacy and power of women's writing, Dickens also works to contain it within the acceptable bounds of domestic endeavor.... [A]ll the while characters—especially women—are writing, they are being written/controlled by Dickens. Nevertheless, as he constantly tries to enclose women within Victorian boundaries, his narrative—as woman's writing—evinces a struggle against this form of enclosure. (147)

This bind begins to explain the observations of critics who have sought the source of the syntactical hiccups that stilt Esther's narrative. Lisa Ruth Sternlieb's conclusion that Esther can write, but not creatively or imaginatively (104) and Joan D. Winslow's statements that Esther continually denies her imagination as a way of knowing truth (4) merely point out symptoms of Dickens's struggle both to grant and strategically withhold Esther's feminine fairy-tale heritage.

One of the fundamental ways that Dickens inscribes Esther within fairy-tale scripts is by embodying certain stock fairy-tale figures in his characters. Particularly useful to Dickens is the godmother figure or "Benevolent Agent," as Edwin M. Eigner calls her, who was probably modeled on the old wife, the female storyteller.[14] The fairy godmother's descent from the female storyteller explains why, traditionally, the fairy godmother exerts a kind of authorial control over other characters, changing their natures or directing their fates. Importantly, fairy godmothers in folk tales are frequently implicated in what Victorians called the "pious fraud," a lie told for a moral end (Eigner 54), usually to shape or "assess the character of the person being tested" (53). Appropriating this female authorial role for a male, Dickens casts Mr. Jarndyce in the role of fairy godmother, using him to "write," or direct, Esther's life.[15] He magically appears and vanishes several times, most memorably in the carriage carrying young Esther to Greenleaf (24–25; ch. 3), before revealing himself to be the noble benefactor and architect of the "six happy, quiet years" (26; ch. 3) she spent at that school. The novel culminates in his pious fraud, in which he delays telling Esther that he plans to allow her to marry Allan Woodcourt so that her future mother-in-law can have time to observe and be assured of Esther's good character. As Jarndyce puts it, "I would not have my Esther's bright example lost; I would not have a jot of my dear girl's virtues unobserved and unhonoured" (752; ch. 64). As a reward for passing her test, Esther gets to marry the man she loves and inherits a second Bleak House, appointed and prepared by Mr. Jarndyce.

The benevolence of Mr. Jarndyce's deft manipulation of Esther's life at this juncture has been praised by critics, who have lauded him as "one of the best and kindest human beings ever described in a novel" (Nabokov 90), a "moral superman" (qtd. in Barzilai, "Bluebeard Barometer" 514) and a true "fairy god-mother" (515). "Jarndyce is certainly no Bluebeard," Anny Sadrin adds (56), opining that Esther ought to thank her guardian for her sexual liberation (55). His benevolence becomes questionable,[16] however, when we acknowledge, as I have delayed doing, that Jarndyce is not a fairy godmother, but a godfather with matrimonial designs on his "godchild." His patriarchal position of power over Esther alters the dynamics of their relationship, leaving it fraught with the inequalities of social and gender-based power. In his position as fairy godmother/father, Jarndyce acts in the father's domain, which in fairy tales, Tatar tells us, is "[c]ontrol of marriage, and hence the regulation of desire and sexuality," but also usurps the mother's domain, "the organization of the domestic sphere, which also determines the availability and desirability of daughters" (*Off with Their Heads!* 137). His assumption of this maternal duty is plain in Mr. Jarndyce's gift to Esther of the housekeeping keys (65; ch. 6), which transforms her into the "best little housekeeper" (750; ch. 64) and therefore a suitable marriage partner. The keys, however, also have a disciplinary aspect that works to regulate Esther's desires and feelings. Having brought the keys with her to her first interview with her Guardian, she uses them to suppress emotions she knows will make Mr. Jarndyce uncomfortable: "I felt that I was choking again—I tasked myself with it.... But I gave my housekeeping keys the least shake in the world as a reminder to myself, and folding my hands in a still more determined manner on the basket, looked at him quietly" (90; ch. 8). As the keys become reminders of Esther's debt of grati-tude and therefore duty-bound position toward Mr. Jarndyce, they also regulate her desires for knowledge, which are typically expressed in that most feminine of vices (*Off with Their Heads!* 111), curiosity. As if to test her, soon after she is given the housekeeping keys, she is let into Mr. Jarndyce's confidence and is especially charged with discretion with respect to the information he gives her (90; ch. 8). Esther is simultaneously asked if there is anything she would like to know about her past (92; ch. 8). She immediately denies her own desires and defers to his prerogative, suppressing her curiosity by replying, "Nothing! I am quite sure that if there were anything I ought to know, or had any need to know, I should not have to ask you to tell it to me" (92; ch. 8).

Through these means, Esther is made to act like the ideal woman. She becomes, in fact, very much like the most desirable bride that the prince in Perrault's version of Griselda can imagine: "a woman who has never shown / the slightest disobedi-ence: she must be / Of proven patience, modest, lacking pride, / And free from any wishes of her own" ("History of Griselda" 14). In the Griselda story, a king or prince refuses to marry any but the most submissive, humble, and obedient wife. Generally joined in matrimony to a girl from the lower classes who displays such traits (in Perrault's version the bride is a shepherdess), the husband then begins a test, a sort of pious fraud, in which her longsuffering is observed through a series of appalling trials, including abandonment by her husband and separation from her children. Griselda endures with such patience that her husband is won back to her and she is restored to her former enviable position. Mr. Jarndyce's gift of the keys and his pious frauds write Esther into a Griselda story, forcing her to enact the same behaviors as the tale's heroine when faced with similar tests. Consider, for instance, the similarity between Esther's complete deferral to Mr. Jarndyce, above, and Griselda's immediate agreement to the terms of her marriage with the prince:

> "But you must swear, for peace to reign
> Eternally between yourself and me,
> Henceforward to obey my will alone."
> "I swear," she answered; "I have always known,
> Although the man I married might be poor,
> That on all matters he would then decide,
> And I obey with joy; how much the more
> If you, my lord, should take me for your bride!"
> (22)

Further resemblance between Griselda and Esther surfaces when Esther, like Perrault's heroine, is required to pass through a test of her fidelity in the face of her own betrayal. In Perrault's tale, the prince recalls his wife from her banishment to serve the lovely maiden (who also happens to be their daughter) that he has chosen to replace her. The full effect of this test is achieved in *Bleak House* through a constellation of events. Unaware that Mr. Jarndyce was apprised beforehand of the proposal (752; ch. 64), Esther receives a declaration of love from the man she prefers to marry but nevertheless refuses him and begins "very quietly to make such preparations as I thought were necessary" (748; ch. 64) for her impending marriage to Mr. Jarndyce. In addition, just as Griselda is forced to turn over to her usurper all that had once been hers, Esther is asked to offer her advice about Mr. Jarndyce's gift to Woodcourt, a house in which she sees, in all of its appointments, "*my* little tastes and fancies, *my* little methods and inventions ... my odd ways everywhere" (751; ch. 64). This Griseldan sacrifice, in which she is forced to admire and serve where she has been dispossessed, elicits the same reaction from Esther as it does from Griselda. Esther matches Griselda's concern for the potential queen, whom Griselda begs the prince not to mistreat as he has her, with her own concern for Mr. Woodcourt, for she fears the evidences of her housekeeping style might remind him "mournfully of what he believed he had lost" (751; ch. 64).

Esther's actions, then, mimic Griselda's, and just as Griselda becomes the woman in whom the virtue of patience is "shown / In perfect form by her alone" (41), Esther's forbearance causes her to be celebrated as a "pattern young lady" (747; ch. 63). The word "pattern" here denotes both Esther's desirability as a model to be imitated and the artificiality of her construal as such, suggesting that she has been made after a pattern, as indeed she has. For, like Perrault, Dickens has attempted to "enlist the consciousness of [his] readers in the effort to foster patient suffering as the preferred modality of power for women" (*Off with Their Heads!* 108), a moral that could never have sprung from the tradition of female-authored fairy tales. In fact, the Griselda story, in Perrault's telling, is premised on the male desire for authority over the female: "'What I myself am certain of is this,'" declares the prince, "'for there to be a chance of married bliss, / Authority must not be shared by both [spouses]'" (13–14). But while Perrault, whose omniscient third-person narrator has no difficulty in drawing the aphorism, "'These torments are for me ... a test: / My husband makes me suffer in this way / To rouse my virtue, which too long a rest, / I know, would cause to perish and decay. / ... We ought to love the pains we bear: / To suffer brings us future joys'" (27), from the stoic Griselda, Dickens must resort to all sorts of wiles, especially key jingling, to make his female narrator believably compliant during similar moments of trial.

Before I address the idiosyncrasies of Esther's narration in more detail, however, I must address the slippage into the role of husband that Mr. Jarndyce, as a fairy godmother, performed during my discussion of the Griselda tale. As in *Bleak House*, the boundaries between father and husband are demonstrably unstable in fairy tales. "Donkeyskin," "Catskin," and a host of other tales[17] feature fathers who offer marriage to their daughters. In Dickens's novel, Mr. Jarndyce's role as (potential) husband is essential to his ability to play the role of benevolent father, not only because it provides a pretext for his pious fraud, but also because it allows him to reserve Esther in a maturational holding pattern until he, as the godfatherly marriage broker, can see her safely into the right marriage. This dual role is convenient for Dickens, whose resistance to female growth I have already discussed: it precipitates in Jarndyce's tardy release of Esther from their engagement, a move that stalls the fulfillment of her desires and the progress of her development until practically the moment it becomes, because of the marriage plot, inescapable. Esther's ability to endure self-denial is crucial to this scheme. Attentive to the lessons of the keys and following after the pattern of Griselda, Esther submits to this new embarrassment to her desires and does not admit her feelings until sanctioned to do so by Mr. Jarndyce: after bringing her to Mr. Woodcourt's new house, he asks her, "Full of curiosity, no doubt, little woman, to know why I have brought you here?" Esther replies, "Well, guardian, without thinking myself a Fatima, or you a Blue Beard, I am a little curious about it" (749; ch. 64).

It is no accident that Esther alludes to Bluebeard, another fairy tale narrative in which she has been trapped, in this moment of great duress.[18] As Shuli Barzilai observes, "wherever this motif emerges in [Dickens's] writings, and no matter how seemingly humorous or benign the reference, darker atmospheric components may also be found" (29). Under the circumstances, Esther is more a Fatima than a Griselda, admitting, as she does, her desire to understand motives and to gain more control over her own story. If, through the Griselda tale, Dickens strives to make Esther into the angel of the house who serves asking nothing in return, it is through the Bluebeard tale that he tries to keep her innocent and immature, to make her stop growing by putting her in a plot in which examination and knowledge of her own desires for the purposes of increased understanding and romantic fulfillment would terminate in decapitation. It is not a major leap, either, between one husband's masochistic cruelty and another's when the only essential difference is that one intends to reward while the other intends to punish. As a Bluebeardian husband, Mr. Jarndyce is one of the primary agents of Dickens's folkloric forbidding, though he is joined in *Bleak House* by several other Bluebeards who also exert their control over Esther's actions.

Even while these Bluebeards employ a male rendering of the Bluebeard story to carry out Dickens's campaign of infantilization against Esther, they are competing with a female fairy-tale tradition surrounding the tale that was very much present, even in Perrault's version. Clarissa Pinkola Estés, a Jungian analyst, has revitalized the female uses of the Bluebeard story in her *Women Who Run with the Wolves*. In this study, she renews women's access to their storytelling roots, empowering them to use archetypal tales to explore options for healing and making healthy life choices. "Story solutions," she declares, "elicit doses of adrenaline at just the right times, and ... cut doors into walls which were previously blank" (61). She points out the rift between male uses of fairy tales and female uses, which exist even in her field of psychoanalysis:

Some psychological thinkers, including Freud and Bettelheim, have interpreted episodes such as those found in the Bluebeard tale as psychological punishments for women's sexual curiosity. Early in the formulation of classical psychology women's curiosity was given quite negative connotation, whereas men with the same attribute were called investigative.... In reality, the trivialization of women's curiosity ... denies women's insight, hunches, intuitions.... It attempts to attack her most fundamental powers: differentiation and determination. (47–48)

Referring to the key the heroine uses to open the door to the bloody chamber, Estés declares that female uses of the Bluebeard story are able to "[raise] to consciousness the psychic key, the ability to ask any and all questions about oneself, about one's family, one's endeavors, and about all around" (61).[19]

Though the changes made by Perrault to the folk version of the tale tend to divert attention from the extreme violence perpetrated by the blue-bearded husband and to incriminate the wife and deprive her of power, agency, and knowledge, traces of this female tradition are still discernible in his revision.[20] The Bluebeard story's typical elements include a monstrous husband who murders his curious wives after they learn a secret they were forbidden to search out. Its moral is consistently, as Estés affirms, the condemnation of curiosity, which is figured in the tale as a morally dangerous, transgressive pleasure or passion, especially because it admits women's desire—and ability—to gain access to forbidden knowledge. In the tale, in fact, the wife's curiosity becomes the means of detecting, exposing, and condemning the kinds of male cruelty evident in stories like "Griselda." The wife's curiosity, which impels her to open the door her husband warns her never to look behind, reveals the "bodies of several dead women ... all the wives that the Blue Beard had married and murder'd one after another" (Perrault 23).[21] When Fatima is rescued, Blue Beard is killed, and as his heir, Fatima assumes the responsibility for redistributing and managing his wealth. Like Jane Eyre, who can proclaim at the close of her narrative, "Reader, I married him" (552), Fatima's revolution allows her the autonomy to "marry herself" to the man of her choice, to set up her brothers' careers, and to give away her sister in marriage, deciding the fates of herself, her siblings, and the money that has come under her control. By telling the story, not of the wives who are found dead in the bloody chamber, but of the young lady who is rewarded for her curiosity by her husband's death, the tale "reveal[s] possibilities, [and] maps out a different way and a new perception of love, marriage, women's skills, thus advocating a means of escaping imposed limits and prescribed destiny" (Warner 24). Perrault's version scrambles to preclude this reading of the story, appending a moral that reinforces the male reading of the story in unmistakable terms:

> O Curiosity, thou mortal bane!
> Spite of thy charms, thou causest often pain
> And sore regret, of which we daily find
> A thousand instances attend mankind:
> For thou, O may it not displease the fair,
> A flitting pleasure art, but lasting care,
> And always costs, alas! too dear the prize,
> Which, in the moment of possession,
> Dies.
>
> (30)

The potential of "Blue Beard" to reveal the ability of a woman's desire for knowledge to lead her to an autonomous adult life makes it essential for the Bluebeards Esther encounters to keep her from this secret by reinforcing, through overt proscriptions and psychological manipulation, the version of the tale that will keep her from her rightful inheritance of selfhood.

The dangers of feminine desire are recognized by the first Bluebeard that the reader—and Esther—encounters in the novel: Esther's first guardian, her aunt Miss Barbary. Miss Barbary's name not only invokes images of exotic barbarism, such as that thought to exist among Moorish peoples and exhibited in Blue-beard,[22] but also the word "beard" itself, which is rendered *la barbe* in the French tongue. Like Bluebeard, she is the guardian of a secret about the results of female desire, one that she tries to keep from the dependent girl in her charge. For the results of Lady Dedlock's affair with Captain Hawdon were, it seems, not simply the tragic circumstances into which Esther was born, but also the source of enough "pride, ambition, insolent resolve, and sense" to motivate Lady Dedlock to marry a baronet, despite having no connections, and to climb to "the top of the fashionable tree" (12; ch. 2). Indeed, Lady Dedlock implies that the results of her passion taught her self-determination, if only through expediency, when she speaks to Esther for the first and last time: "To hope to do what I seek to do, I must be what I have been for so long. Such is my reward and doom" (452; ch. 36). The secret, guarded by Miss Barbary, is one that Victorian society needs her to keep so that its construct of femininity and masculinity, in which women were "politically, economically, legally, and erotically disempowered" (Gilbert 358) and men were allowed "public power but also ... fatal private knowledge of sexuality" (358), could persist. Because she is female, Miss Barbary, armed with this "fatal private knowledge," has revolutionary potential, nascent "public power" to destabilize her society's construct of male and female desire—and therefore male claims to power. Traditionally, this female caretaker figure would initiate Esther into such knowledge through tale-telling, and Miss Barbary's godmother alias indicates that this should be her role. Dickens, however, is unwilling to give Esther the opportunity to learn and follow the subversive plot lines laid down in women's stories. In typical Bluebeard fashion, Miss Barbary kills the female in herself to keep the secret from spreading, becoming desexualized and desocialized through her rejection of Boythorn's marriage proposal and her self-imposed antisociability. She herself referred to this process as a death, writing to Boythorn "that from the date of that letter she died to him" (533; ch. 43). Repressing and abstaining from personal knowledge of female desire, she becomes a woman "always grave, and strict" (17; ch. 3) and "stiff" (18; ch. 3), one with whom Esther "never could be unrestrained" (18; ch. 3), a vessel, in other words, that cannot be breached, like the bloody chamber locked forever by its master.[23]

At times, as Estés acknowledges, "this keeping a woman in line by her female peers and older women lessens controversy and enhances safety for women who must live under hostile conditions. Under other circumstances, however, this psychologically pitches women into full scale betrayals of one another" (Estés 492n). Miss Barbary's strictness hardly protects Esther. In fact, Miss Barbary wishes her dead, or at least never born (19; ch. 3); Esther, problematically for Miss Barbary, is an uncontainable sign of the secret, especially in her likeness to Lady Dedlock, which, like Fatima's permanently bloodied key, is easily read by the other characters. Miss Barbary, therefore, closely contains Esther, whom she attempts to desocialize by preventing her from forming friendships with her classmates (18; ch. 3) and raising her in secret. This effort is combined with an effort to desexualize Esther—an attempt to replicate the femicide Miss Barbary practices on herself.

Miss Barbary's betrayal closes Esther into the "architectonics" of the male-authored scripts, and Esther is given, instead, incomplete and disrupted narratives about her own social and sexual possibilities. She is raised in an entirely female household devoid of fatherly and masculine influence. In fact, the obsession with mothers, despite its focus on their guilt, produces a declaration from Miss Barbary that practically implies a miraculous, virgin birth: "You are different from other children, Esther, because you were not born, like them, in common sinfulness and wrath. You are set apart" (19; ch. 3). Moreover, Esther is schooled to be appetite-less and passionless; "submission, self-denial, diligent work" (19; ch. 3) are the virtues she is taught to develop. Importantly, however, Esther also learns to deny herself the satisfaction of her curiosity after her questions about her mother are answered with a close-lipped, "Esther, good night!" (18; ch. 3) by Mrs. Rachael, and her pleadings to be told about her past prompt Miss Barbary to reply, "Ask me no more, child!" Her guardian follows up with a terrifying lecture about disgrace and degradation (19; ch. 3). For Esther, Miss Barbary's sermon is not one against sexual deviance, which she knows nothing about, but is a warning not to ask questions.[24] Like Bluebeard, Miss Barbary "forbids the young woman to use the one key that would bring her to consciousness. To forbid [this] strips away ... her natural instinct for curiosity that leads her to discover what lies under" (Estés 47). This key, again, is the "ability to ask any and all questions about oneself ... and about all around" (61). Esther, written into a tale in which to ask questions is equivalent to losing one's head, cannot hope to discover that, as Estés puts it, "by choosing to open the door"—that is, uncover the secret—"she chooses life" (47).

Miss Barbary's death makes the secret about the existence and power of female desire less containable by allowing Esther to circulate socially. It is therefore far more important that Esther internalize a message decrying curiosity—desire for knowledge—than any passive messages she may receive about sexual desire. It is through curiosity that Esther would become aware of the transgressive power she wields to bear testimony of the illegitimacy of Victorian gender ideologies perpetuated by male-authored fairy tales. However, Esther has been well trained to contain the circulation of secrets. She therefore continues Miss Barbary's course of disacknowledging female desire, though not, of course, to purposefully disempower herself as her "godmother" did. The result of this repression is Esther's confused but slavish devotion to "submission, self-denial, diligent work" (19; ch. 3). The direct link between her desire for self-knowledge (curiosity) and her compulsion to repress it through self-denial and work is apparent in a scene that follows Mr. Woodcourt's pre-voyage farewell, when Esther tells her reader, "It would not be worth mentioning for its own sake, but I was wakeful and rather low-spirited. I don't know why. At least I don't think I know why. At least, perhaps I do, but I don't think it matters. At any rate, I made up my mind to be so dreadfully industrious that I would leave myself not a moment's leisure to be low-spirited" (211; ch. 17).

Mr. Jarndyce, as Esther's next Bluebeard incarnation, has only to pick up where Miss Barbary left off. The first thing she is given by this new guard-

ian is a set of keys, the exact object entrusted to Fatima when she becomes
a member of Bluebeard's household. For both women, this trust opens many
doors: Fatima is given access to all the wealth her husband has, and Esther
becomes mistress of a household, the apogee of a Victorian woman's career.
This opportunity to make decisions and accept responsibility could initiate
Esther into womanhood. As has been discussed earlier, however, it has the
opposite effect, becoming a reminder of the bounds within which her knowledge and desires for knowledge must stay. From the first time she defers her
right to knowledge, all her actions in the novel demonstrate that she has inter-
nalized this policy, initially ingrained in her by Miss Barbary and continually reinforced by Mr. Jarndyce, until her refusal of knowledge has become
virtually a reflex. For instance, when Mr. Boythorn's behavior prompts Esther
to ask her guardian if Mr. Boythorn had ever been married, she is answered
no, but venturing to ask if he was supposed to have been, she cannot help
"reddening a little at hazarding what was in [her] thoughts" (110; ch. 9). Her
blush signals that she is alert to some risk in reaching after knowledge, particularly on a topic that has been taboo from her youth, and after a brief and
vaguely informative exchange with Mr. Jarndyce, Esther reports, "I felt, from
my Guardian's manner, that beyond this point I could not pursue the subject
without changing the wind [upsetting Mr. Jarndyce]. I therefore forbore to
ask any further questions. I was interested, but not curious" (111; ch. 9). This
softening of her desire for knowledge[25] is evidently the result of a trying self-
discipline; it is not a coincidence that she "dreamed of the days when I lived
in my godmother's house" that night (111; ch. 9).

By casting Esther as a Fatima and guarding her closely with Bluebeards, Dickens successfully withholds from her the growth and development that could come
with increased understanding about her world, her past, and her possibilities. This
stunting is reflected in the names Mr. Jarndyce assigns to Esther, names that pun
on her stewardship over the keys. His favorite appellation, "little woman," derives
from "the little old woman of the Child's ... Rhyme" (90; ch. 8).[26] Additional
names by which she was thereafter called include Old Woman, Little Old Woman,
Cobweb, Mrs. Shipton, Mother Hubbard, Dame Durden, "and so many names of
that sort, that my own name soon became quite lost among them" (90; ch. 8).
These names, especially "little woman," belittle Esther, effacing her own identity
and diminishing her to a static type or even a pet. Importantly, these identities to
which she is obligated to conform are those of old women, archetypes beyond the
possibility of growth and change and safely beyond desires or being desirable.[27]

Besides Esther's "without thinking myself a Fatima, or you a Blue Beard" (749;
ch. 64), this name-giving operates as one of Dickens's most overt efforts to assign
Esther roles that will stifle her growth. At least one more person in *Bleak House* is
assigned the role of Bluebeard toward Esther, however, and the designation is made
just as overtly as these previous designations. This person is Mr. Bucket, whom
Volumnia Dedlock refers to as "a perfect Blue Chamber" (633; ch. 53), which, in

his delayed revelation of dead female bodies, he indeed is. Esther is placed into Mr. Bucket's hands at the moment when the secret about her mother's indiscretion is made public knowledge. This is a moment when narrative control of Esther is crucial; if Esther were openly to become her mother's daughter, her life options would differ radically from those prescribed by fairy tales like Griselda and Bluebeard. She would become a Cinderella ascending to the throne with the aid of her mother instead of by the condescension of a prince, an heiress after the style of Jane Eyre. She would, in fact, be transferred into female versions of the Bluebeard tale, in which male desires for domination are highlighted as bloody cruelties.[28]

The presence of Mr. Bucket, however, insures that the manner in which the secret is revealed neither teaches Esther how to ask questions nor starts her down the path of self-knowledge. The Inspector requires her presence at his investigation but with Bluebeardian perversity forbids her from asking questions about his methods: "My dear ... don't you fret and worry yourself no more than you can help. I say nothing else at present; but you know me, my dear; now, don't you?" (690; ch. 57). Their journey around London becomes a prolonged "bride-test" that reinforces Esther's blindness and applauds the suppression of her curiosity. Though she suffers mentally and physically from the strain of unanswered questions, she remains obedient: "I could eat nothing, and could not sleep; and I grew so nervous under these delays ... that I had an unreasonable desire upon me to get out and walk. Yielding to my companion's good sense, however, I remained where I was" (686; ch. 57). Her fatigue is strongly contrasted with the energy with which Mr. Bucket's questioning enlivens him: "All this time, kept fresh by a certain enjoyment of the work in which he was engaged, he was up and down at every house we came to; addressing people whom he had never beheld before, as old acquaintances; running in to warm himself at every fire he saw; talking and drinking and shaking hands" (686; ch. 57). In Mr. Bucket, whose name prophesies his containing role, male curiosity is clearly institutionalized and sanctioned.[29] This unmistakable double standard makes his approval of Esther all the more pointed; her finest attribute is perfect obedience: "If you only repose half as much confidence in me as I repose in you, after what I've experienced of you, that'll do. Lord! You're no trouble at all.... When a young lady is as mild as she's game and as game as she's mild, that's all I ask" (704; ch. 59). Inspector Bucket's absolute control over the investigation guarantees his control over the secret, and Sir Leicester's promise of forgiveness has ensured Lady Dedlock a safe return to the patriarchal status quo after she is caught. Esther can make no personal use of the secret for her own empowerment; it is instead carefully contained by a group of authoritative males who have an interest in her continuing to reject it. By the time Mr. Bucket relieves the suspense she has labored under by satisfying her curiosity about her mother's fate, Esther is psychically incapacitated, unable even to attach meanings to words (713; ch. 59). This fact, combined with the death of Lady Dedlock before Esther is able to reach her, makes the insight she gains into her identity a dead end, barring her from the female storyline. The woman who could have been for Esther a genuine fairy godmother is dead.

But Esther cannot be entirely prevented from claiming her right to tell her own story. As a female narrator, she is a de facto participant in the female fairy-tale-telling tradition, and her narrative often betrays the difficulty Dickens had in negotiating the ideologically incompatible worlds of male and female authorship. Esther's narrative often erupts, like *Jane Eyre*'s madwoman in the attic, in rebellious murmurings. For instance, after she expresses so much faith in Mr. Jarndyce's ability to judge the kind of information it is proper for her to know, Esther protests to herself that the interview has left her feeling "quite easy with him, quite unreserved, quite content to know no more, quite happy" (92; ch. 8). This compulsive repetition has an unconvinced anxiety to it that makes apparent to the reader an underlying longing that only repeated attempts could write out of the sentence. Because of her position within a male narrative, Esther apparently has more to say than she is authorized to articulate.

While dwelling obsessively is one rhetorical strategy through which the female narrative obtrudes into Dickens's, Esther's refusal to acknowledge or see her own desires is another common occurrence. The effect of this refusal is to deflect the narrative from these desires, leaving gaps or gasps that thrust the reader's attention more fully upon the denied thing. This act of pretended omission momentarily gives her rhetorical power to circumvent her Bluebeards, to peek behind the door without getting blood on the key.[30] A work attributed to Cicero calls this rhetorical device "praeteritio," but it is often translated as "paralipsis." Of it he says,

> Paralipsis occurs when we say that we are passing by, or do not know, or refuse to say that which precisely now we are saying.... This figure is useful if employed in a matter which it is not pertinent to call specifically to the attention of others, because there is advantage in making only an indirect reference to it.... As a result, it is of greater advantage to create a suspicion by Paralipsis than to insist directly on a statement that is refutable. (321)

One example of Esther's use of paralipsis centers on Mr. Woodcourt: "I have omitted to mention in its place, that there was some one else at the family dinner party. It was not a lady. It was a gentleman.... a young surgeon. He was rather reserved, but I thought him very sensible and agreeable. At least, Ada asked me if I did not, and I said yes" (163; ch. 13). By displacing this mention from its proper chronological place and burying her intended meaning in negatives, Esther's employment of paralipsis has the same effects as what Robyn Warhol-Down has called "unnarration": "In contrast with that which is simply left out, the unnarrated and disnarrated aspects of a text become a vividly *present absence*, existing at a narrative level somewhere between the text and everything that is left out of it" (49). This narrative disruption, then, creates a parallel narrative in which the denied or misplaced thing can exist, allowing Esther to suggest to the reader exactly what she feels without saying it outright. This peculiarly feminine maneuver[31] is at once liberating and punishing: it gives her a power of expression but is simultaneously self-marginalizing. But in the architectonics of a story in which acting on one's desires merits severe punishment, this circumlocution is a form of self-protection that allows others to guess what she feels without incurring the guilt of extensive self-knowledge.

Esther is, nevertheless, punished for her narrative audacity in a way that parallels Perrault's punishing of the subversive, potentially feminist moral of his Bluebeard tale with an authoritative, directly stated patriarchal moral. When she encounters Lady Dedlock near Chesney Wold and sees something in her face "that I had pined for and dreamed of when I was a little child" (448; ch. 36), Esther relates, "I looked at her; but I could not see her, I could not hear her, I could not draw my breath. The beating of my heart was so violent and wild, that I felt as if my life were breaking from me" (449; ch. 36). Knowing he cannot keep Esther from talking in her elliptical way, Dickens creates eclipses in her actual sight, making it more difficult for her to express her desires because she can never see the objects of them clearly. This description of the happy revelation of her parentage and fulfillment of one of her deepest desires tallies closely with how she looks at but does not openly acknowledge her desires for Mr. Woodcourt in the earlier quotation. In fact, when she is first approached by Lady Dedlock in the wood, Esther has uncommon trouble discerning who her visitor is: "The perspective was so long, and so darkened by leaves, and the shadows of the branches on the ground made it so much more intricate to the eye, that at first I could not discern what figure it was ... (she was almost within speaking distance before I knew her)" (448; ch. 36). It should come as no surprise, then, that blindness is Esther's reward for the one moment in the novel when she is able to assert self-knowledge with absolute certainty. As she heads to the brickmaker's cottage to see the feverish Jo, she muses, "I had for a moment an undefinable impression of myself as being something different from what I then was. I know it was then, and there, that I had it" (380; ch. 31). I believe this moment represents a resolution of the identity crisis Esther experiences both before and after this incident. John O. Jordan suggests this is the moment that Esther comes "to the sudden 'unthought' realization of who her mother was and is" (23).

Pushing this observation further, I would like to suggest that this is the moment when Esther realizes who *she* is as the daughter of a living mother. This realization allows her to embrace, if briefly, a matrilineal inheritance[32] that empowers her with a heritage of female storytelling and, through the blood and example of Lady Dedlock, a socially disruptive autonomy. The revelation quoted above and the passage immediately preceding it reflect this fleeting empowerment:

In the north and north-west, where the sun had set three hours before, there was a pale dead light both beautiful and awful.... Toward London, a lurid glare overhung the whole dark waste; and the contrast between these two lights, and the fancy which the redder light engendered of an unearthly fire, gleaming on all unseen buildings of the city, and on all the faces of its many thousands of wondering inhabitants, was a solemn as might be. (380; ch. 31)

Dickens seems unable at this juncture to diminish Esther; the vivid and unbroken style in which he allows her to express herself is a concession he must make to elucidate the mystery of her unusual feeling and to provide a kind of catharsis, without which Esther's self-denials of her parentage and inheritance, in the face of so much evidence, could not long be maintained. However, this concession also becomes an admission that his character is clearly capable of telling her story in terms quite different than those he has constrained her to. For Esther, this level of self- and universal awareness is a sin, and her indulgence in clarity is punished a few pages later by temporary but complete blindness (391; ch. 31).

Like Lewis Carroll, who "at least partially accepts that he can no longer hold out against the possibility of Alice's passage into adulthood" (Knoepflmacher xii) in *Through the Looking Glass*, Dickens is finally forced to allow Esther to leave her "father's" household, to grow up and enter maturity through marriage to a man who equals her in age, love, and sexual viability. But Dickens cannot help including a shadow of the infantilized Esther he fantasized about in the form of Caddy Jellyby's baby. This Esther, sickly when she was born, has begun to grow, "but she is deaf and dumb" (768; ch. 67). The developmental stunting of this projection of Esther Summerson's psyche, who might as well be blind, too, registers Dickens's continued "ambivalence about adult female power" (Knoepflmacher xii).

In fact, this phantom Esther prefigures Dickens's solution to his narrative bind. Dickens never again attempted to use a female narrator in his novels. However, two female narrators appear in a series of stories he published in 1868 in an American magazine, *Our Young Folks*, and in his own *All the Year Round* (Zipes 89). Of these four stories, which were given the collective name of *Holiday Romance* (89), "The Magic Fishbone" purported to have been penned by one Alice Rainbird, aged seven ("Magic Fishbone" 91), and a second tale was written by a younger girl.[33] "The Magic Fishbone" is far from demonstrating the narratological problems from which *Bleak House* suffered. In fact, it complacently founds itself on the most conventional expectations about gender roles: "There was once a King," it begins, "and he had a Queen, and he was the manliest of his sex, and she was the loveliest of hers" (91). The heroine of the story, a princess named Alicia, is the oldest of nineteen children ranging in age "from seven years to seven months" (91), and the seven-year-old princess "took care of them all" (92). One day on his way to the Office, the King is stopped by the Good Fairy Grandmarina, who tells him to invite Princess Alicia to eat some of the salmon he was then purchasing for dinner, and that after she had eaten, to tell her to polish the fishbone that remained on her plate, which would bring her, only once, "whatever she wishes for, PROVIDED SHE WISHES FOR IT AT THE RIGHT TIME" (92). The king delivers his message, Alicia follows the instructions, and the next day she is provided with an opportunity to use her one wish when her mother falls ill. However, Alicia delays using her wish, despite her father's silent and persistent entreaties, until she knows the King has "done his very very best" (97) to provide for his family. Meanwhile, Alicia has capably nursed her mother, entertained and fed the children, and has been as matronly and responsible as a wise woman of seventy, much less a girl of seven. Alice Rainbird's narrative, in other words, casually performs Dickens's own fantasies about womanhood. Princess Alicia is capable in all the domestic arts and happily works to provide for her father's and the rest of the family's comfort. She possesses a sort of prelapsarian wisdom that allows her to perform all of these duties while remaining a child; in contrast, Charley, Esther's maid, who shares a similar experience, wears "an air of age and steadiness that [sits] so strangely on the childish figure" (188; ch. 15). Unlike the "elliptical, subversive, open-ended" fairy tales written by women (Auerbach and Knoepflmacher 8), this one remains untroubled and straightforward in style. Dickens seems to have hit on a way to control the expression of a female narrator: to keep her a child. The childish authorship of the story is a shared joke between Dickens and the reader, humorous because of how conscious we are of suspending our disbelief to agree that Alice Rainbird is the actual author. The childish elements, like Alice's naïveté in believing that nineteen children could be born in the course of seven years, are meant to make the reader fondly dismiss Alice as a serious narrator and collude with Dickens. The story itself becomes a novelty, a stunt that undermines Alice's status as speaker and makes her an obvious mouthpiece for Dickens himself, through which he can freely project and fantasize.

"The Magic Fishbone," published two years before Dickens's own death, probably represents his last policing of female voices. But while he seems to gain control of his puppets in this final attempt, his loss of control in *Bleak House* proves that women must—and will—grow up. Female expression, so painstakingly controlled in his novel, is not, in the end, effectively silenced. Esther, even as she chokes on the articulation of her own hopes, approaches, via curiosity, the realm of her personal possibilities: "I know that my dearest little pets are very pretty, and that my darling is very beautiful, and that my husband is very handsome ... and that they can very well do without much beauty in me—even supposing—" (770; ch. 67). That dash, as eloquent a typographic marker as any word in the text, offers a perpetual threat of rupture to the hopeful signifiers of closure—sometimes a period, sometimes a THE END—with which Dickens and his editors have tried to conclude *Bleak House*. For Esther's last moment of strategic evasion, Warner writes a fitting epitaph: "Women's capacity for love and action tragically exceeded the permitted boundaries of their lives" (393). Nevertheless, even in the bleakest of houses, storytelling has helped women survive—and thrive.

NOTES

1. Warner xv.
2. The impact of Dickens's own psychology on Esther's characterization has been explored by critics like Wilt and Goodman. Wilt opines that the denials, gaps, and refusals of knowledge so often commented upon in Esther's narration are the result of a male author finding himself "committed to the wider complexities of the Self-Other relationship, which are the female's lot in the world" (285). In unfamiliar psychological territory, it is no wonder Dickens had difficulty hiding the seams of his mental effort. As Goodman notes, "One of the reasons [Esther's] characterization is so confusing and can seem at moments so inconsistent is that she fulfills a double function in the novel. She portrays many characteristics of the angel in the house, but also enacts the conflicts, tensions, angers, fears, and hurt of the masculine constructed psyche" (150).
3. Broadly considering Dickens's relationship to the fairy tale, Stone argues that Dickens's writings were "profoundly shaped by his early interest in fairy tales" (3), pointing out two specific ways fairy tales gained ascendency in Dickens's mind. First, Dickens found escape from his deadening experience in the bottle-blacking factory by reading fairy tales (56, 60); second, he derived a sense of power and garnered recognition by telling stories, at which he was particularly adept (48). With this childhood inspiration in the background, Stone charts the increasing presence of magic in Dickens's work as enchantment becomes more sophisticatedly integrated with Dickens's portrayal of "reality," beginning with *Pickwick Papers* and continuing through *David Copperfield* (1850)—in which, Stone argues, Dickens perfected his use of the fairy tale—and concluding with *Great Expectations* (1861). Stone, however, omits *Bleak House* (1853) from his discussion, saying, as one review summarizes it, that the other major works he analyzes "contain a great deal of autobiographical material and have, presumably, more facts, more 'realism' to be used in the fairy tale manner" (Eigner "Review," 317).
4. Slater reports that Dickens queried Grace Greenwood on the verisimilitude of Esther's narration, asking, "Is it quite natural, quite girlish?". He told the same young lady that writing in a woman's voice "cost him no little labor and anxiety" (Slater 255).
5. Such has been implied in the arguments of Zwerdling and Schor. Although Zwerdling's essay was a major turning point in criticism about Esther, his case that Dickens's attitude toward Esther is "essentially clinical" (429) and that "the major aim of her portion of the narrative is to study in detail the short- and long-range effect of a certain kind of adult violence on the mind of a child" (429) seems to make Dickens too knowing about his own intentions regarding Esther and too omnipotent in his control of a character that he admittedly felt a great anxiety about rendering realistically. Schor, on the other hand, seems to regard Esther too wholly as the producer of her text. For example, she reads Esther's narrative hesitations as symptoms of her narrative authority, of her ability to piece together and create her own identity.
6. Tatar reminds us, "Although virtually all of the national collections of fairy tales compiled in the nineteenth century were the work of men, the tales themselves were

ascribed to women narrators," a tradition that she traces back the second century A.D. (x).

7. For examples of female-authored fairy stories, see Auerbach and Knoepflmacher.

8. I refer here to both the traditional female storytellers and the professional women writers Knoepflmacher discusses in *Ventures Into Childland*, all of whom still exerted subversive power. The figure of the old wife spinning yarn by the fireside continued in Victorian fiction, where she was often depicted as a female servant. According to Barzilai, such women were often seen as bringing "sensational and potentially pernicious material within the home" ("Charles Dickens" 22). Stone traces Dickens's own initiation into fantasy literature to the education he received from Mary Weller, a servant in the Dickens house. Mary would entertain and frighten young Dickens with ghoulish, fantastic stories, including one that became the basis for his Bluebeard adaptation, "Captain Murderer" (34).

9. See Knoepflmacher's *Ventures Into Childland*, in which he traces the differences between male and female uses of the fairy tale in the Victorian age by closely examining the fairy tales of John Ruskin, W. M. Thackeray, George MacDonald, and Lewis Carroll, among others.

10. Dickens is aided in this endeavor by several interesting adaptations of his work. In one series published in America called *Dickens' Little Folks*, a volume entitled *Dame Durden: Little Woman from the Bleak House of Charles Dickens* (1878) venerates Esther as an "elder sister" whose excellent example should inspire imitation in those who read of her exploits (preface v). Consisting wholly of Esther's narrative from *Bleak House*, the book visually represents the aspect of Esther's character it wants most to emphasize before the text even begins: an illustration facing the title page shows a modest Esther being presented with her housekeeping keys.

11. The effect of this statement in *Dame Durden* is striking, coming as it does only three paragraphs from the beginning of the book and without having been imbedded in the third-person narrative and its subsequent interruptions.

12. Dickens's difficulty was summed up by George Brimley's review in the *Spectator*, which snidely observes, "Such a girl would not write her memoirs, and certainly would not bore one with her goodness" (qtd. in Fletcher 67).

13. Wilt remarks that, indeed, "the book strove against him rather more than he looked for" (285), citing John Forster's report that Dickens complained uncharacteristically of overwork during the novel's composition (285n1). It appears that Dickens had to take remedial measures against this fatigue; the summer of 1853 found him in Boulogne, where he had arrived "badly overworked," having been "chained to *Bleak House* for a year and a half" (Stone 1).

14. The Benevolent Agent that Eigner describes was a stock figure from the Pantomime. However, as Michael Kotzin notes, "As a child, Dickens may have confronted fairy-tale material in plays, pantomimes, and toy theater productions" (34). The Pantomime was strongly rooted in the fairy-tale tradition.

15. In addition to John Jarndyce, Eigner also numbers the Cheerybles, Aunt Betsey, and Mr. Boffin among Dickens's Benevolent Agents (67).

16. In the literature that I have surveyed, Jarndyce seems rather more applauded than otherwise. However, several scholars have expressed their discomfort with Jarndyce's manhandling of Esther's heart. McKnight, in her observations of Dickensian fathering, remarks, "Seemingly without irony or critique, [Dickens] depicts positive father figures such as John Jarndyce ... exerting complete control over the [life] of [Esther].... Yet modern readers often find these overcontrolling father figures a bit distasteful, if not downright frightening" (136). Slater adds that such readers "are surely right in such a response" (167). It is Esther herself who reveals a darker side of Jarndyce in Gottfried's analysis. According to her reading, "What Esther knows retrospectively (and ... suspected all along) is that ... if [Jarndyce] is not ... the "Incarnation of Selfishness," he is not as selfless and benevolent as her overtext makes him either" (171–72). Esther's emphasis on Jarndyce's fatherly manner in the renunciation scene "obliquely condemns Jarndyce's methods by pointing to his unnecessary and tormenting prolongation of her ignorance" (198). Most recently, Jordan has blamed Jarndyce for "his sentimental, self-indulgent philanthropy," claiming that the novel itself "never whole-heartedly endorses his generosity" (72).

17. Tatar classes these stories as "Cinderella" variants in *The Classic Fairy Tales*. The difference, she writes, is that "Cinderella" tales are "driven by the anxious jealousy of biological mothers and stepmothers"; "Catskin" variants are "fueled by the sexual desire of fathers, whose unseemly behavior drives their daughters from home" ("Introduction: Cinderella" 102). The daughters in "Catskin" tales escape their fathers and endure trials to find a suitable marriage partner.

18. Barzilai's research has revealed that "Blue Beard," extremely popular in England after Perrault's tales were translated into English in 1729 ("Charles Dickens" 159n4), received special attention from Dickens (23), who made references to it in most of his works and even wrote his own parodic version about a man named Captain Murderer (23). Barzilai's *Tales of Bluebeard* is the first study to unearth and closely examine Dickens's overt and frequent references to this bloody fairy tale. While Barzilai demonstrates how this fantasy informs Dickens's depiction of Esther Summerson, who she says passes her Bluebeardian bride-test in *Bleak House* with unflagging loyalty and self-sacrifice, Barzilai's main point in using it is to examine the triangulated relationship resolutions present throughout Dickens's works, resolutions that are a projection of his own "fantasy of incestuous conjugality" ("Bluebeard Barometer" 515).

19. Feminist critics, who were among the first to explore how the fairy tale has informed the social and sexual development of characters in Victorian fiction, have even pointed out ways in which the traditionally female uses of fairy tales can help men in their life choices. Gilbert, in her essay "*Jane Eyre*," suggests that the Bluebeard tale provides a frame in which to interpret "the mystery of male sexuality" (363) posed in the novel. In her argument, the male figures that Rochester and Jane encounter in the course of the book offer "virtuoso variations on the theme of Blue Beard to represent the life options available to Rochester," alternatives that range from "masochistic self-abnegation" to "sadistic passion" (363).

20. Perrault's version of Bluebeard demonstrates how male-authored versions of oral tales could recode what had once been subversive messages about female agency and power. Tatar elaborates on the liberties taken by Perrault, which are subtle but telling. Perhaps of most importance, Tatar asserts, is the fact that "folk versions of the tale do not fault the heroine for her curiosity" ("Introduction: Bluebeard" 142).

21. All references are to the first English translation of Perrault's story, published in 1729.

22. Illustrators often depicted Bluebeard as a Turk or Arab. The beard was indicative of filthiness and lust, and Christians historically associated both beards and lechery with Saracens or Muslims (Warner 242). Such a characterization of Oriental peoples was typical in European thought; Rana Kabbani has noted that the two most common claims Europeans made about the East were that it was a place of "lascivious sensuality" and "inherent violence" (qtd. in Barzilai 160n13).

23. Female Bluebeards are less common but not unknown. In the Grimms' version of the Bluebeard tale, called "Marienkind," the Virgin Mary fills the role of Bluebeard and "savagely punishes the wayward girl who uses the forbidden key" (Warner 244).

24. The two have a long history, however, of being inextricably connected: "The principle sin ... with which the tongue is connected is lust.... The tongue is seduction's tool" (Warner 47). Notably, Eve herself was a victim of a tale-telling serpent.

25. Esther has evidently saddled the word "curiosity" with a negative connotation, a move that is not necessarily a foregone conclusion. The *Oxford English Dictionary*'s entry on "curiosity" divides the fifth sense in which it is used, "Desire to know or learn" (def. 5), according to its "blamable sense" (def. 5a) and its "neutral or good sense" (def. 5b). In its blamable sense, it means "The disposition to inquire too minutely into anything; undue or inquisitive desire to know or learn" (def. 5a). In its neutral sense, however, it is virtually indistinguishable from being interested: "The desire or inclination to know or learn about anything, *esp.* what is novel or strange; a feeling of interest leading one to inquire about anything" (def. 5b).

26. Mr. Jarndyce here quotes the following rhyme: "'Little old woman, and whither so high?'—/ 'To sweep the cobwebs out of the sky'" (90; ch. 8).

27. For corroborating arguments, see Sadrin 52, and Jordan 11.

28. For instance, in Carter's version of Bluebeard, entitled "The Bloody Chamber," it is the "sheer carnal avarice" (11) of the leonine husband that takes center stage, and his brutality is highlighted in the sadistic delight he takes in his bride's sexual innocence, humiliating her on their wedding night. The wife, as narrator, confides that she "could not but flinch from [his] intimate touch" after discovering the bloody chamber, "for it made me think of the piercing embrace of the Iron Maiden and of his lost lovers in the vault" (34). In a subversive twist, it is the girl's mother who rescues her daughter, arriving on horseback to shoot the diabolical groom just as he is about to execute the young woman. Her arrival interrupts his script as Lady Dedlock's survival might have Dickens's: "The puppet master ... saw his dolls break free of their strings, abandon the rituals he had ordained for them since time began and start to live for themselves" (39).

29. Tatar chafes against this bias, in which "female curiosity is ... tainted with evil, while male curiosity is enshrined as a virtue" (*Off with Their Heads!* 111). She condemns

readings of the bloody key as a sign of marital infidelity or the irreversible loss of virginity or innocence as "willfully wrong-headed in [their] effort[s] to vilify Bluebeard's wife" ("Introduction: Bluebeard" 141).

30. Iterations of this argument have been made by several scholars. Jaffe uses a Freudian version of paralipsis, called denegation, to explain the advantage this narratological maneuver gives Esther: "'[D]enegations' derive from judgments about what the ego wishes to take into itself and what it wishes to reject.... Esther's denegations signal her otherness to herself—the presence of material she wishes to distance herself from.... Presenting herself as alienated from her own knowledge, Esther cannot be held responsible for what she knows or says" (qtd. in Sternlieb 76). Sternlieb makes a subtle adjustment to this argument by suggesting that Esther's is a "*conscious* and *retrospective* strategy, one that acknowledges without articulating desire" (76).

31. Following Auerbach and Knoepflmacher, it seems safe to say that there is a distinctively feminine style of storytelling. However, Sadrin makes the following timely caveat:

> To say that Esther's style is recognizably that of a woman does not imply the recognition of "feminine writing" as a universal concept. The general assumption that female writers are less assertive than men, more subtle, more reticent, more evasive in their statements, may well be right, but it does not follow that it is in the nature of women to be so. Let us say, rather, in Estella's words, that it is "in the nature formed within [them]." (51)

Indeed, Carr suggests that the style in which Esther's narrative is written shows that "there is no ready language for what women wish to 'write'" (164).

32. Several scholars of *Bleak House* have pointed out a distinction in the novel between legal male inheritance and the peculiar portion allotted to women. Blain, in noting "what might seem a perverse allocation of material[:] ... giving the telling of Richard Carstone's battle with Chancery to the female narrative voice and the story of Lady Dedlock's guilty secret to the male narrative voice," suggests that the "novel is opening a pathway for a commentary on the male preserve of legal inheritance from a female standpoint, and on the female "preserve" of illicit sexuality (Lady Dedlock) or illegal inheritance (Esther herself)—from the male" (68). Schor has expanded on the implication that a female inheritance is necessarily illegal and qualitatively different from a male inheritance: "It is never clear in *Bleak House* what kind of property the daughter could hope to inherit.... [b]ut the particular form male property takes in this novel (documents, wills, testimonies) has its parallel in the form of separate female property: narrative secrets, contagion, resemblance, a bastard line of property" (110). This bastard's portion is seemingly as empowering as Fatima's inheritance of house and treasury. Schor writes, "[F]or in the dead mother's will ... we see the mother's most powerful, terrifying, alien gift: to scribble, write, crease, direct, dictate; to devise and bequeath, to rewrite and revise; the courage not to stop that process of writing and rewriting" (123) in which Esther is controversially engaged.

33. "The Perfect Country," written by Miss Nettie Ashford, aged half-past-six, describes a country in which adult and child roles are reversed. In the tale, the children throw the adults a party and discuss how exhausting it is to keep them entertained. Miss Ashford ends by sending her "helpless" parents to a sort of boarding school for adults so that she will no longer be troubled with taking care of them. The other two stories, written by Robin Redfort (self-styled Lieutenant-Colonel), aged nine, and William Tinkling (self-styled Esq.), aged eight, deal with more heroic themes. These four tales have been variously collected. See, for instance, *Captain Boldheart and Other Stories* (New York: Macmillan, 1927).

WORKS CITED

Anonymous. Preface. *Dame Durden: Little Woman from the Bleak House of Charles Dickens.* New York: Anderson, 1878.

Auerbach, Nina, and U. C. Knoepflmacher, eds. Introduction. *Forbidden Journeys: Fairy Tales and Fantasies by Victorian Women Writers.* Chicago: U of Chicago P, 1992. 1–10.

Ayres, Brenda. *Dissenting Women in Dickens' Novels: The Subversion of Domestic Ideology.* Westport, CT: Greenwood, 1998.

Barzilai, Shuli. "The Bluebeard Barometer: Charles Dickens and Captain Murderer." *Victorian Literature and Culture* 32 (2004): 505–24.

———. "Charles Dickens and Captain Murderer." *Tales of Bluebeard and His Wives from Late Antiquity to Postmodern Times.* New York: Routledge, 2009. 22–42.

Blain, Virginia. "Double Vision and the Double Standard in *Bleak House*: A Feminist Perspective." *New Casebooks: Bleak House.* Ed. Jeremy Tambling. New York: St. Martin's, 1998. 65–86.

Brontë, Charlotte. *Jane Eyre.* 1847. Ed. Richard Nemesvari. Toronto: Broadview, 1999.

Carr, Jean Ferguson. "Writing as a Woman: Dickens, *Hard Times*, and Feminine Discourses." *Dickens Studies Annual* 18 (1989): 161–78.

Carter, Angela. "The Bloody Chamber." *The Bloody Chamber.* 1979. New York: Penguin, 1993. 7–41.

"curiosity 5a." *The Oxford English Dictionary.* 2nd ed. 1989. *OED Online.* Oxford UP. 28 Mar. 2011. <http://dictionary.oed.com>.

"curiosity 5b." *The Oxford English Dictionary.* 2nd ed. 1989. *OED Online.* Oxford UP. 28 Mar. 2011. <http://dictionary.oed.com>.

Dickens, Charles. *Bleak House.* Ed. George Ford and Sylvère Monod. New York: Norton, 1977.

———. *Captain Boldheart and Other Stories in A Holiday Romance by Charles Dickens.* New York: Macmillan, 1927.

———. "Frauds on the Fairies." *Fantastic Literature: A Critical Reader.* Ed. David Sandner. Westport, CT: Greenwood, 2004. 56–58.

———. "The Magic Fishbone." *Victorian Fairy Tales: The Revolt of the Fairies and Elves*. Ed. Jack Zipes. New York: Methuen, 1987. 91–90.

———. "Where We Stopped Growing." *The Centenary Edition of the Works of Charles Dickens in 36 Volumes*. Ed. B. W. Matz. Vol. 1. London: Chapman & Hall, 1911.

Eigner, Edwin M. *The Dickens Pantomime*. Berkeley: U of California P, 1989.

———. Review of *Dickens and the Invisible World: Fairy Tales, Fantasy, and Novel-Making*, by Harry Stone. *The Yearbook of English Studies* 1982: 317–18.

Estés, Clarissa Pinkola. *Women Who Run with the Wolves: Myths and Stories of the Wild Woman Archetype*. New York: Ballantine, 1995.

Fletcher, LuAnn McCracken. "A Recipe for Perversion: The Feminine Narrative Challenge in *Bleak House*." *Dickens Studies Annual* 25 (1996): 67–89.

Gilbert, Susan M. "Jane Eyre and the Secrets of Furious Lovemaking." *NOVEL: A Forum on Fiction* 31 (1998): 351–72.

Goodman, Marcia Renee. "I'll Follow the Other: Tracing the (M)other in *Bleak House*." *Dickens Studies Annual* 19 (1990): 147–67.

Gottfried, Barbara. "Fathers and Suitors: Narratives of Desire in *Bleak House*." *Dickens Studies Annual* 19 (1990): 169–203.

Jordan, John O. *Supposing Bleak House*. Charlottesville: U of Virginia P, 2011.

Knoepflmacher, U. C. *Ventures Into Childland: Victorians, Fairy Tales, and Femininity*. Chicago: U of Chicago P, 1998.

Kotzin, Michael. *Dickens and the Fairy Tale*. Bowling Green: Bowling Green UP, 1972.

McKnight, Natalie. "Dickens's Philosophy of Fathering." *Dickens Quarterly* 18.3 (2001): 129–38.

Nabokov, Vladimir. "Charles Dickens: *Bleak House*." *Lectures on Literature*. Ed. Fredson Bowers. New York: Harcourt, 1982.

Parker, David. "Dickens and the Death of Mary Hogarth." *Dickens Quarterly* 13.2 (1996): 67–74.

Perrault, Charles. *Histories, or Tales of Past Times*. London, 1729. *Eighteenth Century Collections Online*. Gale. U of Texas at Austin. 8 Dec. 2010.

———. "The History of Griselda." Trans. Christopher Betts. *The Complete Fairy Tales*. Oxford: Oxford UP, 2009. 9–41.

Pseudo-Cicero. *Rhetorica Ad Herennium*. Trans. Harry Caplan. Cambridge: Harvard UP, 1954.

Sadrin, Anny. "Charlotte Dickens: The Female Narrator of *Bleak House*." *Dickens Quarterly* 9.2 (1992): 47–57.

Schor, Hilary M. "Bleak House and the Dead Mother's Property." *Dickens and the Daughter of the House*. Cambridge: Cambridge UP, 1999. 101–23.

Slater, Michael. *Dickens and Women*. Stanford, CA: Stanford UP, 1983.

Sternlieb, Lisa Ruth. *The Female Narrator in the British Novel: Hidden Agendas*. NewYork: Palgrave, 2002.

Stone, Harry. *Dickens and the Invisible World: Fairy Tales, Fantasy, and Novel-Making*. Bloomington: Indiana UP, 1979.

Tatar, Maria. Introduction. *The Classic Fairy Tales*. Ed. Maria Tatar. New York: Norton, 1999. ix–xviii.

————. "Introduction: Bluebeard." *The Classic Fairy Tales*. Ed. Maria Tatar. New York: Norton, 1999. 138–44.

————. "Introduction: Cinderella." *The Classic Fairy Tales*. Ed. Maria Tatar. New York: Norton, 1999. 101–37.

————. *Off with Their Heads!: Fairytales and the Culture of Childhood*. Princeton: Princeton UP, 1992.

Warhol-Down, Robyn. "'What Might Have Been Is Not What Is': Dickens's Narrative Refusals." *Dickens Studies Annual* 41 (2010): 45–59.

Warner, Marina. *From the Beast to the Blonde: On Fairy Tales and Their Tellers*. New York: Noonday, 1996.

Wilt, Judith. "Confusion and Consciousness in Dickens's Esther." *Nineteenth-Century Fiction* 32 (1977): 285–309.

Winslow, Joan D. "Esther Summerson: The Betrayal of the Imagination." *Journal of Narrative Technique* 6 (1976): 1–13.

Zipes, Jack, ed. *Victorian Fairy Tales: The Revolt of the Fairies and Elves*. New York: Methuen, 1987.

Zwerdling, Alex. "Esther Summerson Rehabilitated." *PMLA* 88 (1973): 429–39.

An Old Dog Enters the Fray; or, Reading *Hard Times* as an Industrial Novel

Priti Joshi

Although Dickens had wanted to write an industrial exposé as early as 1838, it was not until 1854 that he published what is widely read as his denunciation of industrial dehumanization, Hard Times. *Had he included in* Nicholas Nickleby *a disquisition on industrial ills as he had considered, he would have been present at the birth of the subgenre; as it is,* Hard Times *appeared during the dying days of—to paraphrase Franco Moretti—the subgenre's life cycle. This essay examines the tropes and conventions of the genre as established by three predecessors, Frances Trollope, Elizabeth Gaskell, and Charlotte Brontë, and argues that Dickens's rehearsal of the established tropes is tinged with fatigue and repetition rather than innovation. As an industrial novel,* Hard Times *marks the last gasp of a subgenre whose literary moment had passed.*

After the phenomenal triumph of *The Pickwick Papers* (March 1836–October 1837) and the success of *Oliver Twist* (February 1837–April 1839), Dickens was hailed as a Fieldingesque talent who was willing to deploy his pen against social ills such as the New Poor Law of 1834. Those who had been working to improve conditions in factories and especially on legislation to protect children hoped Dickens would visit the north so he could see for himself and direct his considerable talent and caustic pen against the atrocities of industrial labor. Dickens visited Birmingham and Manchester and in a 29 December 1838 letter to E. M. Fitzgerald wrote, "I went, some weeks ago, to Manchester, and saw the *worst* cot-

Dickens Studies Annual, Volume 44, Copyright © 2013 by AMS Press, Inc. All rights reserved.   DOI 10.7756/dsa.044.011.221-241

ton mill. And then I saw the *best*. *Ex uno disce omnes*. There was no great difference between them" (*Letters* 1: 483). He planned to return in a few weeks and also to write about what so horrified him; in the same letter he continued: "So far as seeing goes, I have seen enough for my purpose, and what I have seen disgusted and astonished me beyond all measure. I mean to strike the heaviest blow in my power for these unfortunate creatures [child laborers], but whether I shall do so in the 'Nickleby', or wait some other opportunity, I have not yet determined" (*Letters* 1: 484).[1]

Despite his indignation and determination, the "blow" did not quite land: *Nicholas Nickleby* (March 1838–September 1839) and *The Old Curiosity Shop* (April 1840–February 1841) followed and while both novels' protagonists are young and face many challenges, neither Nicholas nor Little Nell (nor even the crushed Smike) are abused by a factory system. Nicholas's nemeses are the thrash-happy Wackford Squeers of Dotheboys Hall and his cold uncle Ralph, while Little Nell is tormented by the grotesque Quilp. Both novels, along with *Oliver Twist*, depict a world in which evil adults scheme against an innocent young person for personal gain and greed. There are no "unfortunate creatures" pounded by industrial labor in Dickens's fiction of the period.[2] The factories, laborers, and critique had to wait fifteen years before they finally claimed Dickens's attention; *Hard Times*, widely regarded as Dickens's denunciation of the dehumanization of industrial conditions, appeared between April and August 1854. It is not entirely clear why Dickens waited so long to strike his "blow" against the conditions of industrial labor. What is clear, however, is that in the intervening years a number of writers entered the fray, and the subgenre of the industrial novel was born. The questions that animate this paper are prompted by Dickens's tardiness to the scene: first, is it fruitful to read *Hard Times*, as it generally has been, from within the framework of the industrial novel?[3] And second, if we read it as an industrial novel, does it mark the genre's apogee or its nadir?

When we speak of the industrial novel, the usual suspects include (in chronological order) Benjamin Disraeli's *Sybil*, Elizabeth Gaskell's *Mary Barton*, Charles Kingsley's *Alton Locke*, Charlotte Brontë's *Shirley*, Dickens's *Hard Times*, and Gaskell's *North and South*.[4] The list indicates that Dickens was a latecomer to the generic scene; indeed, in a longer list of industrial novels, today obscure to most readers, Dickens's tardiness appears even more strikingly.

> Harriet Martineau, *A Manchester Strike* (1832)
> Frances Trollope, *Michael Armstrong, the Factory Boy* (1839–40)
> Charlotte Elizabeth Tonna, *Helen Fleetwood* (1839–40)
> Fredric Montagu, *Mary Ashley* (1839)
> Elizabeth Stone, *William Langshawe, the Cotton Lord* (1842)
> Benjamin Disraeli, *Sybil* (1845)
> Elizabeth Gaskell, *Mary Barton* (1848)
> Charles Kingsley, *Alton Locke* (1849)

Charlotte Brontë, *Shirley* (1849)
Geraldine Jewsbury, *Marian Withers* (1851)
Charles Dickens, *Hard Times* (1854)
Elizabeth Gaskell, *North and South* (1854)
Dinah Mulock Craik, *John Halifax, Gentleman* (1856)

Not all of these novels posited factories or industrial labor practices as requiring reform; Stone's and Craik's novels, for instance, are sympathetic, even defensive, portraits of mill-owners. Even in this expanded cohort, however, *Hard Times* was written closer to the death of the genre than its birth.

In *Graphs, Maps, Trees*, Franco Moretti elaborates his theory of "distant reading" by charting novels published in Britain between 1740 and 1900. Interested in mapping large patterns—unavailable when we perform close readings of single or a few canonical texts—Moretti locates books as points on a graph and discerns that each subgenre of the English novel—the epistolary novel, Oriental tale, the Newgate novel, the nautical novel, the industrial novel, and some three dozen others—emerges and then dies with a surprising regularity. Moretti notices that each has a life cycle of approximately 20 to 30 years. In an effort to explain this phenomenon of fairly constant regularity for almost 45 subgenres across 160 years of the British novel (replicated in French, Italian, Danish, and Japanese novels as well, although Moretti does not elaborate on those), he speculates that "a [sub]genre exhausts its potentialities—and the time comes to give a competitor a chance—when its inner form is no longer capable of representing the most significant aspects of contemporary reality. At which point, either the [sub]genre loses its form under the impact of reality, thereby disintegrating, or it turns its back to reality in the name of form, becoming a 'dull epigone' indeed" (17). To this socio-formal explanation, Moretti adds another: "Books survive if they are read and disappear if they aren't: and when an entire generic system vanishes at once, the likeliest explanation is that *its readers vanished at once*" (20). And why would readers vanish? Moretti's answer is simple: "what most attracts readers is the drama of the day, then, once the day is over, so is the [subgenre of the] novel" (24). To illustrate his points, Moretti offers a reading of the life-cycle of a single trope in a series of "village stories" between 1832 and 1853 ("Maps") and of the "micro-level of stylistic mutations" in British detective fiction between 1891 and 1900 ("Trees"; 91).

While this essay does not attempt the *longue durée* "distant reading" that Moretti advances, his framework offers a fruitful entry-point for our query about *Hard Times* as an industrial novel. I borrow from his insight about the shelf-life of a subgenre and propose, to alter the metaphor, to locate Dickens's novel within its generic strata; in doing so, I hope to illuminate the birth of a number of key tropes of the industrial novel and assess Dickens's novel's contribution in light of his predecessors'. Had Dickens written about the crushing weight of industrial labor on some of the most vulnerable populations as he considered in

1838, he would have been present during the infancy of the subgenre; instead he wrote his industrial novel some fifteen years later during its dying days. Did those fifteen years make a difference? The question is one of those "what-ifs" and difficult to answer. Yet, knowing the arc of Dickens's career, his interests and their development in some detail, we can speculate that whatever he wrote in 1838 or thereabouts would likely have been accomplished—but unlikely to have been as satiric as the 1854 novel is, nor as melancholy. But while we can only conjecture about the phantom 1838 novel, we can answer the question of the difference those fifteen years made by considering the way the novel reads given the shape and developments of other industrial novels in the intervening years. By reading *Hard Times* against key industrial novels that preceded it, we can assess it from within the subgenre of the industrial novel that it helped bring to a finale.

Let us begin with the specific and gradually broaden our scope of inquiry. Specifically: what precipitated Dickens's decision to write an industrial novel in 1854? One suggestion has been the Preston strike and Dickens's visit to the town on 29 January 1854.[5] Yet as Dickens himself wrote on 11 March 1854 to Peter Cunningham—whom he suspected as the author of a news item to this effect—the rumor was "altogether wrong. The title [of the novel] was many weeks old, and chapters of the story were written, before I went to Preston." Dickens added that the "mischief" of such a rumor was that it "localizes" a story that has "reference to the working people all over England, and it will cause ... characters to be fitted on to individuals whom I never saw or heard of in my life" (*Letters* 7: 290–91). The warning, however, has not stopped some from seeking in the months'-long strike at Preston impetus for Dickens's belated turn to industrial conditions.[6]

Others have taken a longer view, tracing Dickens's interest in industrial questions back to *Pickwick Papers* and *The Old Curiosity Shop*, while yet others have pointed to essays in *Household Words* that sometimes critiqued, sometimes celebrated industrial practices.[7] But an interest in industrial questions is one thing, an industrial exposé of the sort some hoped for and Dickens indicated an interest in producing in 1838 is another. As his letter to Fitzgerald above indicates—and as House and Storey confirm—Dickens had considered including a section in *Nicholas Nickleby* about industrial ills and child labor. But he abandoned the idea when he learned that Frances Trollope's *Michael Armstrong*, a meandering novel that exposed both "orphan farms" and industrial child labor, was starting to appear in a few weeks. Put out by the news—in particular an advertisement for Trollope's novel that indicated to Dickens "its doubtfully honest or respectable imitation of Nickleby," a similarity Dickens refused to believe was "unintentional" (diary entry for 8 February 1839 cited in *Letters* 1: 640)—Dickens resorted to his characteristic sarcasm; in a 9 February 1838 letter to Samuel Laman Blanchard he wrote: "I will express no further opinion of Mrs Trollope than that I think Mr Trollope must have been an old dog and chosen his wife from the same species" (*Letters* 1: 507). If this sounds petulant, it was; while even a few years later the point was moot, at the time, as the Trollope scholar Pamela Neville-Sington

writes, "Dickens saw her [Frances Trollope] as a serious rival" (20).[8] The seeming convergence between his and Trollope's novel and her apparent poaching
on "his" territory so upset Dickens that, in a second letter to Blanchard the same
day, he seemed to wash his hands of industrial fiction altogether, declaring that
his next novel, *Barnaby Rudge* (February 1841–November 1841), "has nothing
to do with factories, or Negroes—white, black or parti coloured. It is a tale of the
riots of Eighty, before factories flourished as they did thirty years afterwards, and
containing—or intended to contain—no allusion to cotton lords, cotton slaves, or
anything that is cotton" (*Letters* 1: 507). That Trollope was on his mind is evident by the reference to "Negroes—white, black or parti coloured"; her *Domestic Manners of the Americans* (1832) fulminated against slavery and established
her as a critic of social evils. The comment has led the critic James Simmons to
remark: "This disclaimer might lead one to suspect that Dickens felt that there
was enough literature on the market about factory workers" (347).

Whether Dickens thought so or not, some others certainly did. As early as
August 1839, an *Athenaeum* review of the early numbers of *Michael Armstrong*
rebuked Trollope for being too late: "But we pray Mrs. Trollope to reflect that
this contingency has passed away. A cry, a fanatical cry has been raised on the
subject; the evil is in the hands of the legislature, and fully before the public; for
all purpose of practical good the Factory Boy has come too late" (qtd. in Kestner
51). The 1840s have been called the "Hungry Forties," but it would not be too
fanciful to designate them the "Blue Decade": the sheer volume of royal commissions, Parliamentary reports (bound in blue covers), and media-sponsored or
individually-undertaken investigations launched and publicized during the "long
'40s" is simply staggering. Factory and mine, children's and women's labor,
urban and agricultural conditions, windows and sewers—all came under scrutiny
in this period of pulsating investigative energy, all passed under the "hands of the
legislature ... and before the public." While the *Athenaeum* reviewer was of the
"fiction-as-avant-garde" school, others, as we shall see, believed that novels could
play a more reflective role in engaging social questions. Nonetheless, by the end
of the '40s, the market for industrial fiction was saturated, and the topic seemed
more or less exhausted as the following passage in Kingsley's *Alton Locke* suggests. On his way to a Chartist meeting, Alton meets a fellow-delegate who
denounces factory conditions. Alton, generally indignant about industrial ills and
eager to expose the wealthy, instead dismisses his "rural cousin['s] ... rambling
bitter diatribe on the wrong and sufferings of the labourers; which went on till late
at night, and which I shall spare my readers: for if they have either brains or heart,
they ought to know more than I can tell them, from the public prints" (255; ch. 28;
emphasis added). This 1849 fictional character closely echoes the 1839 reviewer.
In a similar vein, when Dickens invited Harriet Martineau to contribute to *Household Words* in 1850, they both agreed that because "our chief textile manufac-
tures were already familiar to every body's knowledge," Martineau would write
about the manufacture of lesser-known products such as tea-trays and dyed silks

(Fielding and Smith 418; she eventually wrote a series of sanitary tales). While the remark is specific to the textile industry, it indicates that discussion of industrial conditions had reached saturation point. This is not to imply that by 1854 the problems that plagued Britain's entry into industrialism had been "solved"; rather, the *perception* existed that its worst excesses were known and that mechanisms to address its abuses were in place even if they weren't always enforced.[9] Thus, by the time Dickens started to publish *Hard Times* the sense of crisis that had propelled the genre of the industrial novel into existence had passed, suggesting, to use Moretti's terms, that the "drama of the day" had moved elsewhere. If by the 1850s this "drama" had played itself out, it had been ushered to the stage by a well-known concatenation of circumstances in the 1830s: unregulated industrial growth that led to developments such as the Sadler commission, the agitation for the Ten Hours Bill, blue books and journalistic investigations, an assertive working-class press, and Chartism, all of these serving to thrust industrial conditions and relations to the forefront of middle-class consciousness. The fictional form this consciousness took is embodied in the subgenre of the industrial novel. In what follows I trace the development of the genre in three key industrial novels that preceded *Hard Times*: Trollope's *Michael Armstrong*, Gaskell's *Mary Barton*, and Brontë's *Shirley*. I focus on conventions that each introduced or developed that became key tropes of the genre and conclude with an assessment of *Hard Times* in light of these conventions.

Any assessment of *Hard Times* as an industrial novel should take account of the harsh assessments that have been levied against the subgenre as a whole, authored as it was by middle-class writers standing at an ideological remove from their working-class subjects. Philip Collins writes:

> Notoriously no significant Victorian authors, with the solitary exception of Mrs. Gaskell, had a long-term or intimate knowledge of an industrial town: and this must be one reason, though not the only one, for the remarkably sparse and feeble literary response to a phenomenon so evident and momentous as England's becoming the first predominantly industrial and urbanized community in the history of mankind. For, like the Great American Novel, the great industrial novel never got written. Few novelists, and fewer poets, seriously attempted the topic at all; hence the disproportionate attention given to the few who did. Such a lamentable fiction as Mrs. Trollope's *Michael Armstrong, the Factory Boy* (1839–40) would never have been heard of, had it entered a competition more severe than this 'industrial novel' class. (652)

Peter Brooks offers a more generous approach to evaluating "lesser" literary forms such as the industrial novel: "Before 'social realism' could become a watchword—and perhaps with greater effect than was ever achieved by more sober novels—the lurid and melodramatic fiction opens up the social concerns, makes them imaginatively available" (168). That "social concerns" are not a priori social concerns but had to be made "imaginatively available" echoes the point Moretti makes via "distant reading": novelistic genres emerge to help readers grasp a particular "contemporary reality." Industrial novels made the stark world of factories and industrial labor "imaginatively available" to scores of readers for whom they were at best a news item. That process of imaginative labor was messy at times, and Brooks's patience for the "lurid and melodramatic" will hold us in good stead as we plunge into the pioneering texts of the industrial novel.

I begin with the "lamentable" *Michael Armstrong* because it is the first full-fledged industrial novel and also because it develops a number of themes that recur, with variations, in those that follow. Seizing on the stardom she had achieved with the publication of *Domestic Manners of the Americans*, Trollope turned her critical eye to horrors being committed on British soil. She felt compelled to write *Michael Armstrong* because she wished "to drag into the light of day, and place before the eyes of Englishmen, the hideous mass of injustice and suffering to which thousands of infant labourers are subjected, who toil in our monster spinning-mills" (preface). Exposure of hidden ills was a central feature of industrial novels, their incipient raison d'être, and it lends them a starkly polemical air. Drawing on journalistic, blue book, working-class accounts, and a personal visit to Manchester, Trollope attacks the ills of industry in prose that reveals the labor involved in birthing a language to describe this new "contemporary reality." Here is the novel's first description of a mill:

> The ceaseless whirring of a million hissing wheels, seizes on the tortured ear; and while threatening to destroy the delicate senses, seems bent on proving first, with a sort of mocking misery, of how much suffering it can be the cause. The scents that reek around, from oil, tainted water, and human filth, with that last worst nausea, arising from the hot refuse of atmospheric air, left by some hundred pairs of labouring lungs, render the act of breathing a process of difficulty, disgust, and pain.... [T]he whole monstrous chamber, redolent of all the various impurities that 'by the perfection of our manufacturing system,' are converted into 'gales of Araby' for the rich, after passing in the shape of certain poison, through the lungs of the poor. (98; ch. 8)

Trollope's sentences strain as she attempts to capture the sounds and smells that stultified the senses. Her clunky metaphor of the lungs of the poor acting as a filter that transforms not only cotton into textiles but also filth to gold falls flat, as does her allusion to Araby and her derisive citation about industrial progress. Trollope's prose is fueled by her outrage: "Two hundred thousand little creatures, for whose freedom from toil during their tender years the awful voice of nature has gone forth, to be snatched away, living and feeling, from the pure air of heaven ...—taken for ever from all which their Maker has surrounded them for the purpose of completing his own noblest work—taken and lodged amidst stench and stunning, terrifying tumult ..." (274; ch. 23). It was passages such as these that earned her praise from reformers and in the working-class press and vilification from more highbrow reviewers. Her prose is, to use Brooks's language, "lurid and melodramatic," but it is a first, tentative step to make "imaginatively available" a social problem of immense magnitude.[10]

Following close on the heels of industrial exposé is the trope of social awakening. Michael Armstrong, the factory boy who labors in appalling conditions, is rescued by a young heiress, the daughter of the richest mill-owner in town. Mary Brotherton—a character whose name evokes both Carlyle's appeal to "brotherhood" to suture the hostile relations between "rich and poor," and also the Abolitionist slogan of a chained black man asking "Am I Not A Man and Brother?"—awakens from her life of luxury one day to ask "whether, by the nature of things, it is impossible to manufacture worsted and cotton wool into articles useful to man, without rendering those employed upon it unfit to associate with the rest of their fellow-creatures" (137; ch. 11). When Mary learns the horrors of factory conditions and child labor, her anguished cry— "Alas! alas! Is it thus my wealth has been accumulated?" (236; ch. 19)—resonates through the novel and is its moral north. Moments of awakening such as this are the second convention of the industrial novel. If exposé was about bringing the attention of the haves to the plight of the poor, the awakening of the haves was its necessary next step, and Trollope developed the theme at length (it preoccupies almost half the novel).

Exposé, Awakening ... Solution: Trollope stumbled considerably on this last step. The Rev. Bell, a reform-minded clergyman Mary meets during her search for truth, informs her that although he wishes to

"encourage your generous benevolence, I cannot in conscience tell you that it is in your power effectually to assist [factory children]. That you may save your own excellent heart from the palsy of hopeless and helpless pity, by the indulgence of your benevolence in individual cases of distress, I need not point out to you; but that any of the ordinary modes of being useful on a larger scale, such as organising schools, founding benefit societies, or the like, could be of any use to beings so crushed, so toil-worn, and so degraded, it would be idle to hope." (243; ch. 19)

The Rev. Bell counsels her to support the Ten Hours Movement as the only effective response to the atrocities she has witnessed. While Mary initially heeds his advice, she soon proceeds to "indulge her benevolence" by rescuing Michael, his brother, and a young factory girl and fleeing to Germany. Reviewers and critics have lambasted Trollope for her lack of consistency: does she propose legislation or philanthropy focused on rescuing individuals? Legislative change or paternalism? System reform or escape? Should the state enact social change or should private persons intervene? On the one hand, the novel presents the manufacturing process itself as the root of the "evils." (Trollope was unique among industrial novelists in her fierce critique of industrialism itself). On the other, Trollope was a Tory-Radical and took her cues from Shaftsbury and Oastler, who supported Parliamentary reform. On an implausible third hand, the novel could envision only individual, philanthropic intervention as capable of changing the blighted lives of factory workers. A rejection of the system of industrial labor, a defense of state protectionism, and an advocate of paternalistic intervention all at once, *Michael Armstrong* is an unsteady early step in the exploration of the social relations created by industrial labor. Such vacillations regarding solutions, we know in hindsight, are the hallmark of the genre: almost every novel swings between describing and escaping the problems it identifies, offering solutions it evinces little faith in itself.[11] Few pull in so many contradictory directions or are quite as unstable as *Michael Armstrong*.

Michael Armstrong deserves our attention because it highlights the contours of the industrial novel in its early manifestations and lays the groundwork of its central concerns that persisted through the next decade-and-a-half. Gaskell's *Mary Barton* appeared almost a decade later, a decade in which the commentary on industrialism exploded, and in which the working classes became more politically organized and vocal. Gaskell's novel is more sure and sophisticated in its language and plots than Trollope's, drawing on similar themes and tropes even as Gaskell extends them in new directions. Like Trollope, Gaskell exposes industrial ills,[12] but, in her handling, exposé takes second-place to a quasi-ethnographic exploration of workers' everyday lives. Rather than factory or work conditions, Gaskell emphasizes the domestic lives of her working-class characters; indeed, *Mary Barton* contains not a single scene showing a mill in operation and the only mill in the novel burns down early on. As Collins notes, Gaskell's depth of knowledge about working-class lives far surpassed that of any other industrial novelist's.[13] Because Gaskell's focus is primarily on working-class characters, she, unlike Trollope, who painstakingly narrated her upper-class protagonist's slow awakening, is less concerned with unfolding such awakening in her text. While Mary Barton is roused from her fantasy of upward mobility, and John Barton and the senior Carson both arrive at personal transformations, the primary awakening the novel aims for is directed outward—to its middle-class *readers*, who Gaskell hopes will hear the "agony of suffering" of their working-class brethren.[14]

More significantly, Gaskell differed from Trollope in that the former did not represent industrial labor or factories as an inherent evil, nor did she echo almost every journalist and reformer who traced a direct line from, as one critic has called it, "power loom to prostitution" (Zlotnick 149). Gaskell denied that factory work carried a sexual taint; indeed, Mary's aunt, Esther, becomes a prostitute precisely because she considers herself too good for factory work and, aspiring to the condition of a lady, winds up on the streets. Instead, Gaskell went out of her way to celebrate mill workers as independent and intelligent. In the opening pages Mary is presented as a spirited lass, neither bashful nor coy. She does not, of course, work in a mill, but she is a child of Manchester and serves as a contrast to her sickly mother, an agricultural "rustic" (20) with a "deficiency of sense in her countenance, which is likewise characteristic of the rural inhabitants in comparison with the natives of the manufacturing towns" (4). Furthermore, as several critics have pointed out, it is not in a mill but in the genteel profession of dress-making that Mary is exposed both to Sally Leadbitter's dreams of upward mobility and Harry Carson's eye (Nord 150). Neither is industrial labor crippling for men: both Barton and Jem Wilson are prosperous and steady workers who are dignified by their work and earn enough to support their families—in good times, that is. In *Mary Barton* privation comes not from industrial work, but from the lack of work or a depression in wages brought about by fluctuations in the market. When his "gaunt, anxious, hunger-stamped" fellow-workers come to advise John Barton on the eve of his trip to London, their list of grievances begins and ends with the distress brought about by a downturn in trade (see 98, 99, and 101).

Gaskell replaces Trollope's generalized critique of the manufacturing system with another target: the lack of communication and understanding between masters and men in industrial towns. She was by no means the first to identify this gulf or yearn for class reconciliation: Carlyle spent much of his early career developing the theme. In his 1829 "Signs of the Times," he identified the first adverse effect of the Mechanical Age in "the increas[ed] distance between rich and poor" (35), and in the 1839 *Chartism* he insisted that what was needed was "a genuine understanding by the upper classes of society" as to what "torments these wild inarticulate souls." "All battle is misunderstanding," he declared, yet continued more optimistically: "did the parties know one another, the battle would cease" (309). The 1843 *Past and Present* offers the most comprehensive exploration of the theme of class warfare and its detrimental effects, as Carlyle contrasts a medieval monastery in which brotherhood prevailed against the present in which all deny kinship with one another. "It is not to die, or even to die of hunger, that makes a man wretched," he writes, "but it is to live miserable we know not why; to work with a cold universal Laissez-faire: it is to die slowly all our life long, imprisoned in a deaf, dead, Infinite Injustice.... [In the past] sisterhood, brotherhood was often forgotten; but not till the rise of these ultimate Mammon and Shotbelt Gospels did I ever see it so expressly denied" (210).

The turn to "brotherhood" as an antidote to class divisions was one that many in the 1840s and 1850s were drawn to: we saw it in Trollope's swing toward paternalist intervention, and we see it again in Disraeli's *Sybil*. When the protagonist Egremont challenges the belief that "the Privileged and the People formed Two Nations, governed by different laws, influenced by different manners, with no thoughts or sympathies in common; with an innate inability of mutual comprehension," Sybil responds haughtily: "Sir! I am one of those who believe that the gulf is impassable ... utterly impassable" (245–46; bk. 4, ch. 8). The novel's mission, of course, is to prove her wrong, which it does, but only by first acknowledging and then denying the import of class difference: both Sybil and Egremont move seamlessly from an aristocrat's mansion to an agricultural laborer's hovel, and Egremont's plea, "I am a man, Sybil, as well as a noble" (276; bk. 4, ch. 15), replaces class difference with the more "natural" gender difference. And as every reader has complained, the late-breaking news that Sybil is not a commoner after all but an aristocrat hardly bodes well for Disraeli's vision of reconciling the "two nations." That Disraeli's faith in the idea of "brotherhood" to suture class differences crumbles (or was abandoned) part-way through his narrative is in keeping with the genre's instability regarding solutions. But it also underscores the appeal of brotherhood as a trope for uniting the classes.

Gaskell maintains her faith in brotherhood but does not take Disraeli's easy road; rather than produce brotherhood by denying class differences, she acknowledges those differences but insists that there exists a convergence of interests between masters and men. When an order of goods comes in from "a foreign market," the narrator intervenes to explain that manufacturers have to lower wages because rivals on the Continent were poised to snatch the market by producing the goods cheaper. The moral is briskly articulated: "Distrust each other as they may the employers and employed must rise or fall together" (200; ch. 15).[15] Shared interests, however, are merely a lever; Gaskell's larger point is that ignoring their mutual interests causes unnecessary pain and "mute reproach" (199; ch, 14). When Carson Sr. mockingly asks if Barton was "an Owenite; all for equality and community of goods, and that kind of absurdity," Job Legh quietly replies that "John Barton was no fool" but "what hurt him sore, and rankled in him" was that his masters "kept him at arm's length, and cared not whether his heart was sorry or glad" (452–53; ch. 37). Echoing Carlyle, Gaskell presents this lack of sympathy as the tragedy of the industrial age, although, tellingly, the only resolution she is able to narrate to it is pushed to the margins of the text's closure.

As Charlotte Brontë started to plan *Shirley*, her contribution to the subgenre of the industrial novel, she wrote to her publisher, W. S. Williams on 28 January 1848: "Details, situations which I do not understand and cannot personally inspect, I would not for the world meddle with, lest I should make even a more ridiculous mess of the matter than Mrs Trollope did in her 'Factory Boy'" (qtd. in Smith intro.; Brontë x). Instead, she turned to the recent past, the 1811–12 Luddite unrest in Yorkshire, which she researched in the local papers. The historical distance gives *Shirley* the appearance of being distinct from other industrial novels, but it was of the same ilk. Indeed, half-way through writing her novel, Brontë read *Mary Barton* and again wrote Williams on 1 February 1849: "In reading 'Mary Barton' ... I was a little dismayed to find myself in some measure anticipated both in subject and incident" (Smith xi). Despite her concerns, Brontë left her mark on the industrial novel by transforming Gaskell's convergence of interests between masters and men into an argument about the parallel between the position of middle-class women and that of industrial workers.

In contrast to Trollope, Brontë refrains from describing mill conditions and, unlike Gaskell, she shies away from focusing on workers' lives; indeed, readers might be hard-pressed to recall the name of a single mill-worker or rebel in *Shirley*. Instead, Brontë focuses intensively on the lives of Caroline Helstone and Shirley Keeldar, the middle- and upper-class women with whom the novel is primarily concerned. Considering this focus, why, then, is *Shirley* included in the pantheon of industrial novels? Primarily because Brontë uses the historical distance of some three decades to develop a series of parallels between women and workers that reflected on the present: in *Shirley* both workers and middle-class women resist and rebel (one against marriage, the other against the machine); both find themselves out of purposeful work; both are largely invisible to the men who have considerable authority over their lives; and both find themselves facing hunger or starvation (self-imposed in the case of the women, industrially-induced in the lives of workers). Yet, contrary to those who argued that "masters" and men shared interests, Brontë never suggests that the interests of the well-off women and workers are identical or even that they are natural allies. Indeed, as consumers of cloth that they idly transform into fancy-work for the "Jew-basket" and sell at "four or five hundred per cent. above cost price" (112; ch. 7), middle-class women could not be further removed from the problems workers face and are in fact their competition in a small way. But, as commodities in a marriage market, they share the fate of workers: both women and workers in this novel, as Sally Shuttleworth has pointed out, must sell—either their labor or their goods—on an open market (185). The notion that there is a connection between economic and sexual exploitation is one Gaskell had raised in *Mary Barton*—Harry Carson is both the father's dismissive master and the daughter's seducer—and Brontë dilates on this point and makes it the central focus of her novel.

In drawing the analogy between middle-class women and workers, Brontë links two distinct strands of the industrial-novel genre: the crushing effects of industrial labor and the urgent call to bridge the gulf between masters and men. While Gaskell—and Carlyle—bemoaned the gulf between classes introduced by industrial relations, Brontë suggests that underlying this gulf is a commonality shared by some, that physical privation and emotional hunger are equivalents. Thus, at the nadir of the novel, Caroline, devastated because the man she loves is not interested in her, stops eating and wastes away. That the focus of her affections is Robert Moore, the mill-owner who leads the other owners in suppressing the workers' demands, is crucial to Brontë's argument that physical and emotional poverty— one experienced by working men, the other by well-off women—are intertwined. Presenting middle-class women and workers as similarly positioned—in arguing that workers' rebellion and women's passivity are two sides of the same coin— Brontë extends the scope of the industrial novel, utilizing an industrial lens to bring domestic issues that concerned her, the superfluity of women, into focus. Most powerfully, the analogy illuminates both parties, politicizing middle-class women and domesticating the alienated worker.

By 1854 when *Hard Times* started to appear, very little about industrial conditions or workers' lives was unknown, and the conventions of the industrial novel well established. The arc of Dickens's own fictional writings indicates that he had travelled a good distance from the outraged reaction of his 1838 letter to Fitzgerald. Social ills concerned him more than ever, but his scope had broadened considerably, as is evident in *Dombey and Son* (October 1846–April 1848) and, of course, *Bleak House* (March 1852–September 1853). Indeed, after the conclusion of the latter novel in September 1853, Dickens was so spent that he planned to take a short break from fiction. But sales of *Household Words* were languishing, and Dickens's printers prevailed upon him to write a novel for the journal to buoy sales (Ford and Monod intro.; *Hard Times* ix–x). Dickens somewhat reluctantly undertook the project, and *Hard Times* started to appear in April 1854. Thus it was that Dickens not only found himself working on another novel, but this time on a weekly deadline, a particularly taxing schedule and one he had abandoned since *Barnaby Rudge* in 1841. These material factors—the publication schedule and condensed length—might explain why the novel has felt to some critics more like a "menu card" for a meal than one of Dickens's "feasts" (qtd. in Ford and Monod intro.; *Hard Times* ix). Others, such as Anne Humpherys, have argued that Dickens turned such cramped conditions to advantage, producing a text with sharper narrative coherence, a darker ending, and rich figures of speech ("*Hard Times*"; 394–97). Much of the debate in regards to assessments of the novel has swirled around differing emphases in regards to verisimilitude: whether or how well the novel grasps and represents industrial conditions vs. its imaginative vision of social change. My own reading seeks to consider *Hard Times* less in terms of its material context or critical vision and more laterally against its predecessors in the subgenre of the industrial novel and the tropes they introduce. What use, if any, does *Hard Times* make of Trollope's exposé and plot of middle-class awakening, of Gaskell's insistence on brotherhood and a convergence of interests between masters and men, of Brontë's use of the industrial plot to explore an analogy between workers and women? What does Dickens's novel contribute to the genre?

Despite its reputation as an industrial novel[16]—today based not least upon the oft-anthologized "Key-Note" chapter in which Dickens first introduces his fictional industrial town Coketown in deft and inspired images[17]—*Hard Times* contains little in it of factories, machines, trade, market fluctuations, or even workers' lives. We learn nothing about the condition of Bounderby's mills although we are by Stephen Blackpool's side during a work day (see chapters 11 and 12). Workplace injuries, a topic Trollope had fulminated about and that was being angrily written up in *Household Words*, is excised from the novel.[18] The relation between masters and men plays a role in this novel, but with a significant twist. As we have seen, Gaskell interpreted Carlyle's vision of brotherhood as a "convergence of interests"—both economic and emotional—between masters and men. In *Mary Barton*, when John Barton eventually meets Carson, Sr. and witnesses his anguish about his son's death, "The eyes of John Barton grew dim with tears.... The mourner before him was no longer the employer; a being of another race, eternally placed in antagonistic attitude" (431). The veil of class conflict is rent and Barton can finally see. A kind man willing to tend to those in pain, Barton has killed, and for Gaskell his next gesture is equally important: "But who was he, that he should utter sympathy or consolation.... He had forfeited all right to bind up his brother's wounds.... Stunned by the thought, he sank upon the seat, almost crushed with the knowledge of the consequences of his own actions" (431; ch. 35). "Forfeited all right to bind up his brother's wounds": while Barton may have lost the chance, his abject sinking serves as a fable and Gaskell's moral. Dickens recaps the "gulf between masters and men" theme in *Hard Times* on two occasions, one a mechanical rehearsal, the other a more substantial extension. The first is Stephen Blackpool's dying monologue when he declares "If soom ha' been wantin' in unnerstan'in me better, I, too, ha' been wantin' in unnerstan'in them better" (201; bk. 3, ch. 6). An echo of Barton's words, these sound precisely like an echo—hollow—reiterating a familiar refrain in mechanical fashion. (Given his portrayal of Bounderby, Dickens could not seriously be suggesting that Stephen should have tried harder to get along with his blustering master).

But Dickens comes at the convergence-of-interests question from another direction as well, one akin to Brontë's analogy between working-class men and middle-class women. Early in the novel Stephen Blackpool visits his master Bounderby at his home. To readers accustomed to the conventions of the industrial novel, the reason for Stephen's visit comes as a surprise (as it does to Bounderby himself): Stephen comes not regarding work—the grounds on which he and Bounderby share an association—but about his marriage. That Stephen should turn to Bounderby for "advice" (58; bk. 1, ch. 11) about his wife is an explicit expression of the Carlylean exhortation that workers and masters ought to be bound by ties of "love" not just "cash-payment."[19] But even as he endorses the Carlylean vision, Dickens adds a satiric gloss to it that suggests the impossibility of realizing such a vision in a Coketown. In approaching Bounderby, Stephen Blackpool assumes a Carlylean commonality between them. And, indeed, the men *are* linked only, not in the way Stephen supposes: both men are seeking *release* from a woman, Stephen from his wife, Bounderby from his mother. The former's plight constitutes the novel's tragic subplot, the latter's posturing its satiric exposé of the *soi disant* self-made industrialist.

But Dickens, like Brontë, makes a more explicit analogy too, a parallel between workers and the prosperous children: "Is it possible," the narrator wonders, "that there was any analogy between the case of the Coketown population and the case of the little Gradgrinds?" (24; bk. 1, ch. 5). Of course, there is: both are crushed by the Gradgrind-Bounderby regime of facts and statistics; both lack Fancy; both Louisa and Stephen are trapped in unhappy marriages, Stephen's tragic marriage twisted into Louisa's desperate one to Bounderby; Louisa's two conversations with her father mirror Stephen's two conversations with Bounderby; and Stephen's entirely pure relationship with Rachael takes a dangerous turn in Louisa's dalliance with James Harthouse. Even the images of the Coketown Keynote ripple outward from the industry they purport to describe and settle on the novel's middle-class characters: thus, the "painted face of a savage" returns as young Tom in blackface; the coiled serpent as Mrs. Sparsit eavesdropping on Louisa's garden of Eden; and the melancholy head of a mad elephant returns as Mr. Gradgrind's large head that takes a very definite turn toward the melancholy. The middle-class characters, it seems, are as deeply imprinted by industrialism as the working-class ones who work in the Coketown mills.

Yet, even as Dickens develops the parallel, he eventually abandons the plot-line of the crushed worker in lieu of the crushed children's plight. The first encounter between Louisa and Stephen is a case in point. As she follows Stephen to his room, Louisa, following the familiar trope of the industrial novel, has her moment of awakening: "For the first time in her life Louisa had come into one of the dwellings of the Coketown hands; for the first time in her life she was face to face with anything like individuality in connexion with them" (119; bk. 2, ch. 6). If in Trollope's hands Mary Brotherton's awakening leads to engagement, in Dickens's Louisa's encounter leads not to sustained engagement with the social problem, but to the narrator's disquisition on Louisa's inadequate education in anything but Utilitarian principles, the novel's ultimate target. "She knew of their [workers'] existence by hundreds and by thousands. She knew what results in work a given number of them produce in a given space of time," intones the narrator in a syntactic flatness that echoes the flatness inside Louisa. But there appears to be more than form-mirroring-content here: Louisa's numbness and tepid interest in the workers seems to have spread like a virus through the novel. The shift her mind makes at this moment from an individual connection to her rote learning, is surprisingly replicated in the plot's lack of interest in and displacement of workers' lives with those of the industrialist's children's. Humpherys has argued that although Louisa's story threatens to intervene in and disrupt the "father's story" and indeed generates much of the narrative, ultimately "the novel's overt interest is in the father's story and his need for redemption" ("Louisa Gradgrind's Secret" 179). Her reading teases out a narrative thread that is "present intermittently," but never allowed to displace that of Gradgrind's fall and return to grace. It also heightens our attention to the text's other suppressed or unnameable narratives, primarily that of the workers.

The novel's deployment of Sissy Jupe, the antithesis of the Utilitarian principles Dickens attacks, mirrors Louisa's avoidance of connection and engagement with Stephen—and breaks, too, with the analogy trope of the industrial novel that Brontë developed. Gradgrind "rescues" Sissy from a life in the circus—a deliverance promptly challenged by Sleary's counteroffer of an apprenticeship (34; bk. 1, ch. 6)—for largely instrumental purposes: he wishes to use her, he tells Bounderby, "as an example to Louisa, of what this pursuit which has been the subject of vulgar curiosity, leads to and ends in" (31; bk. 1, ch. 6). The novel, of course, trumps his arrogant disregard of the girl: the one who learns any lesson is not so much Louisa, who early doubted the system of education and never embraced it as ardently or self-interestedly as Bitzer or Tom did, but eventually Gradgrind, who humbly acknowledges to Louisa that "some change may have been slowly working about me in this house, by mere love and gratitude: that what the Head had left undone and could not do, the Heart may have been doing silently" (166; bk. 3, ch. 1). In the Gradgrind household Sissy functions as "the Heart," pumping life into its members—but she is also largely "silent," doing the work Gradgrind can't. In a compressed "moral fable," as *Hard Times* as surely is, the elision of a worker is unremarkable; but in light of the text's status as an industrial novel, the repeated suppression of workers' stories for the distorting effects of Utilitarian principles on the minds and lives of middle-class children signals less an analogy between them than a displacement. One cannot help but wonder if Louisa's enervation does not mirror Dickens's own, if descriptions of "the large streets all very like one another" and the "small streets still more like one another, inhabited by people equally like one another," who "went in and out at the same hours, with the same sound upon the same pavements, to do the same work" (22; bk. 1, ch. 5) do not reflect Dickens's own exhaustion about a topic he had put off writing about for fifteen years and now only did so at the behest of his printers.

Moretti writes of the regular pattern in which one subgenre dies and another is born. In *Hard Times* we witness the dying gasps of the industrial novel as Dickens, sometimes mechanically, rehearses the familiar tropes, but also innovates in directions that leave the subgenre behind.[20] I want to end this essay by pursuing another axis on which we might consider *Hard Times*, an axis that Moretti's "distant reading" of genre does not allow for: that of Dickens's own oeuvre. Perhaps nothing better captures the subgenre fatigue of *Hard Times* than a consideration of the death of Jo in *Bleak House*, the novel that preceded *Hard Times*, and that of Stephen Blackpool. The former is Dickens at the heights of his power: from the metaphor of the cart that grows heavier to Jo's "letter" of apology to Esther (the only thing this crushed boy has to bequeath) to his faltering inaccuracies as Woodcourt leads him through the Lord's prayer to the narrator's anguished final words that boys like Jo are "dying thus around us every day," the chapter rises to a crescendo that conveys Dickens's grief and rage, his deep sorrow and shame too, that is ours as well. Stephen's death, by contrast, is talky and labored, lacking dignity or drama, confusedly bringing together pastoral, mine, and mill, drawing on tropes of the industrial novel but unable to infuse them with freshness or make them relevant to this novel. The scene is, in the words of one critic, "feeble beyond belief" (Barnard 376).

More profoundly, *Hard Times*'s "Is it possible there was an analogy" between Coketown and the Gradgrind children echoes *Bleak House*'s "What connexion can there be, between the place in Lincolnshire, the house in town, the Mercury in powder, and the whereabout of Jo ...? What connexion can there have been between many people in the innumerable histories of this world, who, from opposite sides of great gulfs, have, nevertheless, been very curiously brought together?" (235; ch. 16). This is the central preoccupation of Dickens's late career: what connection can there be between the exalted and the abject, forgotten creatures of society? Dickens's answer is that Lady Dedlock and Jo *are* connected, and not merely through the accident of Nemo, but more fundamentally through a responsibility she and the rest of society bear toward his making. Many first-time readers of *Bleak House* expect a late-breaking revelation that Jo is Lady Dedlock's or Jarndyce's or some other rich person's son, much as Smike in *Nicholas Nickleby* was. Activating and then subverting that novelistic convention, Dickens's point is that Jo *is* Lady Dedlock's—or, more broadly, Britain's—"son," if not biologically then materially, the product of, as Dickens put it in a *Household Words* essay, "England's sins and negligences" (4 Jan 1851: 338). One achievement of *Bleak House* lies in Dickens's transformation of the tropes of lineage and lost sons that the eighteen-century novel was preoccupied with into a broader ethical concept that insisted on asking where a community fails and in activating a moral response to that failure. The novel immediately following *Hard Times*, *Little Dorrit*, extends this investigation of the national community into a broader "ecology of local, national, and cosmopolitan identities" (Buzard 413). Sandwiched between these two massive novelistic investigations, *Hard Times* appears as something of a detour, even a throwback or valediction to an earlier time of his career, a time when Dickens was engaged in a searching analysis of the structural interconnectedness of social totalities. Where *Little Dorrit* was to lead readers on a tour of their many forms of self-incarceration, readers of *Hard Times* may have felt imprisoned within the narrower confines of a dying form where good and ill could still be localized and starkly opposed.

NOTES

1. Madeline House and Graham Storey comment: "He postponed the 'blow', although he had prepared for the possibility by placing the Cheerybles' business in Lancashire." (*Letters* 1: 483n4).
2. Chapter 44 of *The Old Curiosity Shop* offers a brief glimpse of a man brought up from childhood to stoke the fires of a factory.
3. The number of critics who have written on it in this vein is long and illustrious: from Raymond Williams to Catherine Gallagher, Rosemary Bodenheimer to Suzan Zlotnick, Louis Cazamian to Joseph Kestner, and many more.
4. While Raymond Williams and Catherine Gallagher include George Eliot's *Felix Holt* (1866) in the pantheon of industrial novels, other critics dispute its inclusion: Rosemarie Bodenheimer calls it a "metafiction of industrialism" (233) and Susan Zlotnick a "postindustrial novel" (224). I contend it is a political coming-of-age novel more than an industrial one.
5. The earliest reference to Preston as the origin of the novel is an *Illustrated London News* story of 4 March 1854 that stated: "The title of Mr. Dickens's new work is 'Hard Times.' His recent inquiry into the Preston strike is said to have originated the title,

and, in some respects, suggested the turn of the story" (qtd. in Ford and Monod's ed. of *Hard Times* 273).

6. See George Ford and Sylvère Monod's selection of documents on Preston in the Norton edition of *Hard Times* or Robert Barnard's discussion of the novel in terms of Preston. John Holloway, while not claiming origination-status for Preston, nonetheless locates it centrally when he writes of the "deliberate falsification of what Dickens knew, from his visit to Preston, to be the facts" (167).

7. Philip Collins offers the most comprehensive analysis of Dickens's attitudes toward the industrial question in his fiction and journalism. See also Patrick Brantlinger. As numerous critics note, Dickens at times supported manufacturers, at others critiqued practices.

8. In a 30 November 1836 letter to Richard Bentley, Dickens called "the show of names" for the prospective journal "excellent" (*Letters* 1: 202); House and Storey identify Frances Trollope as one of the prospective contributors. By 1839 Dickens appears to have been feeling less sanguine: in a fastidiously and one senses mockingly polite letter of 30 January, he declined Trollope's invitation for dinner on account of a friend's visit ("I fear this circumstance—which would not occur with me once in ten years—will deprive me of the happiness of joining your party"; *Letters* 1: 499). Two decades later, when any trace of rivalry between them had been supplanted by Dickens's inimitable status, their relationship took a novelistic turn: in 1858 when Fanny Ternan, Ellen's sister, went to Florence to study voice, Dickens wrote to Trollope who was living there with her eldest son, Thomas Adolphus. In the 20 September 1858 letter he asked Mrs. Trollope "to shew [the bearer of this letter] any aid or attention in your power," adding "if you bestowed it on one of my daughters, it could not be more welcome to me" (*Letters* 7: 667). Trollope must have been assiduous in fulfilling the charge: eight years later, Fanny Ternan married Thomas Adolphus, and in 1895 she published the first biography of Frances Trollope.

9. For instance, the Factory Act of 1844 reduced the hours of children in textile mills and for the first time included women as a protected class; the Act of 1847 limited the working hours of women and children to ten; and the Act of 1850 specified that working hours could only occur between 6 a.m. and 6 p.m.

10. By contrast, a decade later when Alton Locke enters a tailors' workroom, he is assailed by "the combined odours of human breath and perspiration, stale beer, the sweet sickly smell of gin, and the sour and hardly less disgusting one of new cloth" (Kingsley 23). The language—and outrage—is far more restrained and less melodramatic.

11. In his analysis of industrial novels, Raymond Williams writes: "Recognition of evil was balanced by fear of becoming involved. Sympathy was transformed, not into action, but into withdrawal" (109). More specifically, of *Mary Barton* he writes: "Her response to the suffering [of the industrial poor] is deep and genuine, but ... [i]s joined ... by the confusing violence and fear of violence, and is supported, finally, by a kind of writing-off, when the misery of the actual situation can no longer be endured.... A solution within the actual situation might be hoped for, but the solution with which the heart went was a cancelling of the actual difficulties and the removal of the persons

pitied to the uncompromised New World" (91). While withdrawal or violence do not play a role in *Michael Armstrong*, escape does, and Williams's larger point about the instability of solutions offered in industrial novels resonates.

12. In a 1848 letter to Mary Ewart, Gaskell wrote: "I do think that we must all acknowledge ... evils existing in relation to [the manufacturing system] which may be remedied in some degree, although we as yet do not see how; but surely there is no harm in directing the attention to the existence of such evils" (*Letters* 67).

13. In his review of *Mary Barton* Charles Kingsley praised her for just this intimate knowledge: "In spite of blue-books and commissions, in spite of newspaper horrors and parliamentary speeches, Manchester riots and the 10th of April, the mass of higher orders cannot yet be aware of what a workman's home is like in the manufacturing districts" (qtd. in Butwin 63).

14. Gaskell noted in an 1848 letter: "[M]y intention was simply to represent the view many of the work-people take" (*Letters* 67). In writing *Mary Barton* Gaskell did not aim to be even-handed; in a 16 July 1850 letter to Lady Kay-Shuttleworth, she wrote that her urge to write *Mary Barton* was "caused by my feeling strongly on the side which I took.... I know, and have always owned, that I have represented *but one* side of the question.... I believe what I have said in Mary Barton to be perfectly true, but by no means the whole truth.... I do not think it is possible to do this in any *one* work of fiction" (*Letters* 119).

15. Gaskell's *North and South* contains a twist on the notion of masters' and men's shared interests: Bessy Higgins explains to Margaret Hale that she is dying of consumption because both the masters and the workers resist efforts to install a "wheel" to remove fluff from the air, the former because of costs, the latter because the machine would deprive them of matter that fulfills their hunger (102). Here, masters' and men's interests converge to work *against* reform.

16. As Humpherys notes: "The compression of the novel has encouraged a focus on the novel's industrial and utilitarian themes. Dickens himself prompted this concentration by dedicating the first book edition of *Hard Times* to Thomas Carlyle" ("*Hard Times*" 397).

17. The current editions of all three major undergraduate anthologies for Victorian literature in the U.S.—the Norton, Longman, and Broadview—include the opening of "The Key-Note" chapter in their Industrialism-in-context sections.

18. In the manuscript version Dickens included a passage in which Stephen speaks of Rachel's "little sisther ... Wi' her child arm tore off afore thy face." In the proofs, Dickens inserted a footnote to the passage that reads: "See *Household Words* vol. IX page 224, article entitled GROUND IN THE MILL" (Ford and Monod 247, note to 70.27). Neither the passage nor the footnote made it into the published version. Butwin's discussion of the relationship between fiction and journalism at the time provides what is probably the most likely explanation for its excision. He argues that "the novel of social reform exists in a continuum with journalism" (62) and that in *Hard Times* Dickens counted on a readership that had "been trained to respond to journalism" (67). "Within the novel," Butwin continues, "specific complaints of the workers are abbreviated, and attention is diverted from the novel to the journal where the editorial voice suggests action on the part of the middle class rather than the working class" (73).

19. From *Past and Present*: "Love of men cannot be bought by cash-payment; and without love, men cannot endure to be together" (207).

20. In a sensitive essay, Humpherys shifts our attention from the industrial plot to the "father-daughter" plot, particularly the questions of marriage and divorce by which "parts of Louisa's story enter the narrative and vie for center stage with her father's story" ("Louisa Gradgrind's Secret" 180), and more recently, Helena Michie has called it the first "Novel of Divorce." There are a half-dozen other subgenres from which we might read *Hard Times* productively, but that is not the project of this paper.

WORKS CITED

Barnard, Robert. "Imagery and Theme in *Hard Times*." *Hard Times*. Ed. George H. Ford and Sylvère Monod. 2nd ed. New York: Norton, 1990. 367–79.

Brantlinger, Patrick. "Dickens and the Factories." *Nineteenth-Century Fiction* 26.3 (1971): 270–85.

Bodenheimer, Rosemarie. *The Politics of Story in Victorian Social Fiction*. Ithaca: Cornell UP, 1988.

Brontë, Charlotte. *Shirley*. 1849. Ed. Herbert Rosengarten and Margaret Smith. Intro. Margaret Smith. Oxford: Oxford UP, 1981.

Brooks, Peter. *Reading for the Plot*. Cambridge: Harvard UP, 1984.

Butwin, Joseph. "*Hard Times*: The News and the Novel." *Charles Dickens's* Hard Times. Ed. Harold Bloom. New York: Chelsea House, 1987: 61–78. Rpt. from *Nineteenth-Century Fiction* 32.2 (1977): 166–87.

Buzard, James. "'The Country of the Plague': Anticulture and Autoethnography in Dickens' 1850s." *Victorian Literature and Culture* 38.2 (2010): 413–19.

Carlyle, Thomas. *Chartism*. 1839. New York: Wiley and Putnam, 1847.

———. *Past and Present*. 1843. Ed. Richard Altick. New York: NYU P, 1965.

———. "Signs of the Times." *A Carlyle Reader: Selections from the Writings of Thomas Carlyle*. Ed. G. B. Tennyson. Cambridge: Cambridge UP, 1984. 31–54.

Collins, Philip. "Dickens and Industrialism." *SEL* 20.4 (1980): 651–73.

Dickens, Charles. *Bleak House*. Ed. Stephen Gill. Oxford: Oxford UP, 1998.

———. *Hard Times: An Authoritative Text, Backgrounds, Sources, and Contemporary Reactions, Criticism*. 1834. Ed. George H. Ford and Sylvère Monod. 2nd ed. New York: Norton, 1990.

———. "The Last Words of the Old Year." *Household Words* 41 (4 Jan. 1851): 338.

———. *The Letters of Charles Dickens*. Vol. 1: *1820–1839*. Ed. Madeline House and Graham Storey. Vol. 7: *1853–1855*. Ed. Graham Storey, Kathleen Tillotson, and Angus Easson. Oxford: Clarendon Press, 1965; 1993.

Disraeli, Benjamin. *Sybil or The Two Nations*. 1845. Ed. Sheila M. Smith. Oxford: Oxford UP, 1991.

Fielding, K. J., and Anne Smith, *"Hard Times* and the Factory Controversy: Dickens vs. Harriet Martineau." *Nineteenth-Century Fiction* 24.4 (1970): 404–27.

Gallagher, Catherine. *The Industrial Reformation of English Fiction, 1832–1867.* Chicago: U of Chicago P, 1985.

Gaskell, Elizabeth. *The Letters of Mrs. Gaskell.* Ed. J. A. V. Chapple and Arthur Pollard. Cambridge: Harvard UP, 1967.

———. *Mary Barton.* 1848. Ed. and Intro. Edgar Wright. Oxford: Oxford UP, 1998.

———. *North and South.* 1855. Ed. Angus Easson. Intro. Sally Shuttleworth. Oxford: Oxford UP, 1998.

Holloway, John. "Hard Times: A History and Criticism." *Dickens and the Twentieth Century.* Ed. John Gross and Gabriel Pearson. Toronto: U of Toronto P, 1962. 159–74.

Humpherys, Anne. *"Hard Times." A Companion to Charles Dickens.* Ed. David. Paroissien. Oxford: Blackwell, 2008. 390–400.

———. "Louisa Gradgrind's Secret: Marriage and Divorce in *Hard Times.*" *Dickens Studies Annual* 25 (1996): 177–95.

Kestner, Joseph. *Protest and Reform: The British Social Narrative by Women, 1827–1867.* Madison: U of Wisconsin P, 1985.

Kingsley, Charles. *Alton Locke, Tailor and Poet: An Autobiography.* 1850. Ed. Elizabeth A. Cripps. Oxford: Oxford UP, 1987.

Michie, Helena. "Doing Hard Time: The Tenses of History." Keynote lecture delivered at Dickens Universe. 27 July 2008. Santa Cruz, CA.

Moretti, Franco. *Graphs, Maps, Trees: Abstract Models for Literary History.* New York: Verso, 2005.

Neville-Sington, Pamela. "The Life and Adventures of a Clever Woman." *Frances Trollope and the Novel of Social Change.* Ed. Brenda Ayers. Westport, CT: Greenwood, 2002. 11–25.

Nord, Deborah Epstein. *Walking the Victorian Streets: Women, Representation, and the City.* Ithaca: Cornell UP, 1995.

Shuttleworth, Sally. *Charlotte Brontë and Victorian Psychology.* Cambridge: Cambridge UP, 1996.

Simmons Jr., James Richard. "Industrial and 'Condition of England' Novels." *A Companion to the Victorian Novel.* Ed Patrick Brantlinger and William Thesing. Oxford: Blackwell, 2005. 336–51.

Trollope, Frances. *The Life and Adventures of Michael Armstrong, The Factory Boy.* 1840. Ed. Brenda Ayers. Intro. Priti Joshi. London: Pickering & Chatto, 2008.

Williams, Raymond. *Culture and Society, 1780–1950.* New York: Columbia UP, 1958.

Zlotnick, Susan. *Women, Writing, and the Industrial Revolution.* Baltimore: Johns Hopkins UP, 1998.

Book-Snatcher/Body-Snatcher: Adaptation, Resurrection, and *A Tale of Two Cities*

Lauren Ellis Holm

Dickens claimed an intimate relationship with his works by embodying his characters both in his public readings and while writing. This intimacy allowed him to set himself up as the perpetually besieged victim of literary and dramatic pirates. In the case of A Tale of Two Cities, *however, his attempts to claim ownership of his characters were undermined by accusations of plagiarism that called the originality of his characters into question. This ambiguity threatens to collapse the distinction between Dickens and his appropriators that he was eager to maintain. Rather than condemn Dickens for his purported unoriginality, this essay views both Dickens and the pirate dramatists he fought against as sharing a similar desire to bring characters back to life to postpone their final end.*

> *Lorry*: I did intend to have burnt these books with the papers here; but on second thoughts, perhaps it might be as well to bury them.
> *Cruncher*: Meaning to keep 'em snug, Muster Lorry?
> *Lorry*: Yes,—if they're found by the mob, they may involve a great many lives, Jerry.
> *Cruncher*: Then, if I might make bold—meaning no offence, Muster Lorry, sir—I wouldn't bury 'em.

Dickens Studies Annual, Volume 44, Copyright © 2013 by AMS Press, Inc. All rights reserved. DOI 10.7756/dsa.044.012.243-266

> *Lorry*: Why not?
> *Cruncher*: Why, you see, Muster Lorry, I haven't that
>   confidence in burying, in regard to keeping on 'em
>   snug, that is—whether it's books or stiff-uns.
> *Lorry*: Indeed!—you think there may be such a thing
>   as book-snatchers, as well as body-snatchers, eh,
>   Muster Cruncher?
>
> —Tom Taylor, *A Tale of Two Cities*

The scene of my epigraph may seem both familiar and strange to readers of Dickens's *A Tale of Two Cities*. Taken from Tom Taylor's 1860 adaptation produced under the superintendence of Dickens himself, the conversation features Jerry Cruncher, the anti-flopping odd-job man of Tellson's bank, and the bank's living embodiment, Mr. Lorry. In the novel, Cruncher unintentionally exposes his sideline as a resurrection man, as he does in this scene. However, this conversation was not included in the novel, and it seems to have been added only to compare book-snatching to body-snatching. This insertion serves as a jab at the unauthorized adaptors who might be tempted to perform their own resurrections of Dickens's characters in staged dramatizations. Dickens was, in the words of Charles Reade, "steadily defrauded out of his dramatic rights from the first hour he wrote" (213). Inspired by Reade's own legal proceedings and personal counsel, Dickens began, with the publication of *A Tale of Two Cities*, to use more aggressive measures for preventing others from profiting from his work. His collaboration with Tom Taylor to produce the first dramatization of the novel was one such measure. The equation of the book and the body in the scene above additionally provides a way of vilifying the act of unauthorized dramatization by comparing adaptors to grave-robbers.

Though not as popular for stage adaptation as some of his earlier works (*Oliver Twist* or *A Christmas Carol*, for example), *A Tale of Two Cities* marks an important shift in Dickens's relationship to the theater and performance. Appearing at a time when Dickens was formulating a more intimate physical relationship among himself, his works, and his audience through his public readings, the stage plays at the time of the publication of *A Tale of Two Cities* offer an important counterpoint to Dickens's new professional undertaking. Ivan Kreilkamp sees Dickens's public readings as being in competition with the existing "appropriation[s] by rivals" and suggests that "in order to maintain his power as an author, [Dickens] must link writing with performances that he cannot entirely control" (102). His failed efforts to control the dramatization of *A Tale of Two Cities* led him to focus more on preventing unauthorized dramatizations and to turn more eagerly to his own performances in public readings.

Dickens's public readings served several functions (in addition to any pecuniary considerations that may have motivated them). First, they allowed an intimate meeting between author and audience. As Malcolm Andrews compellingly illustrates, "most novelists want celebrity and the widest possible readership. Dickens seems exceptional in wanting not only celebrity but friendship, personal affection, a permanent place in people's lives, and a corner in their homes. Serialization gave him the chance to develop this relationship, and the Readings gave him the chance to confirm it" (25). Although Dickens was performing to vast crowds in huge venues, he used the readings to cultivate intimacy among author, work, and audience.

At the same time, the public readings allowed him some control over the dissemination of his works. He had the opportunity to continue revising existing scenes and to offer, through tone and gesture, interpretive suggestions to his readers. As he put it, to "drop into some hearts, some new expression of the meaning of my books, that would touch them in a new way" (*Letters* 11: 354). However, as Kreilkamp insightfully argues, Dickens's very attempts to use public readings as "a means of controlling, protecting, and in effect copyrighting his writing as speech" indicates his inability to control either the circulation of his works through competing performances or his audience's reactions to and interpretations of his texts (90). The public readings offered Dickens more control than the dramatic adaptations, but I am not as confident as Andrews that these readings "fulfilled [the dream of complete control over the representation of imaginary worlds] by ensuring that he would have at his command a large cast of characters but no acting personnel to shepherd and bring up to scratch" (28). The struggle for control was not only between Dickens and the actors who were usurping his works, but between himself and his text.

In her important discussion of Dickens's relationship to the theater, Deborah Vlock suggests that his public readings were an attempt to control the theatricality of his texts and redirect it into more acceptable channels. "Surely," she suggests, "his own public readings were prompted at least in part by a desire to control the flow of indiscriminate dramatizations of his novels; or, to put it differently, to harness the powerful theatrical impulses in his texts which, if unpoliced, could erupt into dubious adaptations" (61). Dickens's attempt to "harness" the theatricality of *A Tale of Two Cities* by participating in the dramatization was ultimately unsuccessful. His association with a stage version had the opposite effect, drawing his novel into comparison with existing dramas and bringing Dickens's originality into question. His successful public reading career can thus be seen not as a move toward theatricality, but as a retreat from a failed venture in the theater. In Susan Ferguson's view, Dickens's performance as a *reader* rather than an *actor* in his public readings provides "as much evidence of his distance from theatrical performance as of his involvement with it" (733). In my reading, this distance is motivated by Dickens's complicated relationship to the staged dramatizations of his novels.

Though Taylor's dramatization was a financial and critical success, it entangled Dickens in an unpleasant controversy over the source of his ideas. This may have been particularly embarrassing for the novelist because he was so outspoken on the issue of copyright. His efforts to obtain international copyright protection for his works were public and persistent; less visible was his struggle for protection against pirate-dramatists. Nineteenth-century British copyright law did not protect novelists from dramatic adaptation, and as a result it was common for multiple stage versions of a popular novel to be produced simultaneously at different theaters within weeks of a novel's completion. The many dramatizations, abridgments, and pirate editions circulating alongside novels forced authors to assert actively the originality and value of their works while discrediting competing versions.

This issue particularly plagued Dickens. When Frederick Fox Cooper anticipated the ending of *Little Dorrit* in his November 1856 stage adaptation (prior to Dickens's writing of it), the term "original" fails to fully account for the complexities of the Victorian literary marketplace. When Dickens responded to William Thomas Moncrieff's premature adaptation of *Nicholas Nickleby* by writing him into the novel,[1] the boundaries between source and adaptation are blurred. In her important theorization of adaptation, Linda Hutcheon asserts that "to be second is not to be secondary or inferior; likewise to be first is not to be originary or authoritative" (xiii). Hutcheon reminds us that although adaptations come after their source, they are not therefore to be denigrated or deemed unworthy of critical consideration. This is undoubtedly an important premise for critical approaches to adaptation. However, in the examples above and the series that I am about to outline, the very terms "first" and "second" are problematized.

It is commonplace to view Dickens as a perpetual victim of both dramatic and publishing pirates (which he was), but the distinction between that piracy and his own reworking of others' material—what might euphemistically be called influence—is not so great as he or his defenders would have us believe. The scene added to Taylor's *A Tale of Two Cities* to assail book-snatchers couched adaptation as a theft comparable to a bodily violation. Though not its intended effect, the scene's correlation of adaptation and resurrection can also provide a new framework for thinking about a variety of practices, what I will call "intertextual resurrections"[2]— a way of seeing public readings, adaptations, even the act of novel-writing itself, as versions of a similar impulse to bring characters to life. By locating his novels' origins within his body, Dickens attempted to assert his proprietary rights to his material; the force of his insistence itself suggests that those rights were contested. *A Tale of Two Cities* was composed and published amid an intricate exchange between performance and text that will allow us to explore how Dickens established a physical connection between his body and his book as a way of claiming ownership and why such a claim was both necessary and specious.

In my epigraph the parallelism of the phrases "body-snatcher" and "book-snatcher" suggests the interchangeable potential of the words "book" and "body." Dramatizations literally exchange the book for a group of bodies who will stand in for the words on the page or the image created in readers' minds. Not only does dramatization substitute actors' bodies for linguistic signs, but as the product of the author's labor the book and body are already conflated. Within *A Tale of Two*

Cities, writing is literally a product of the author's body when Manette composes his Bastille letter: "these words are formed by the rusty iron point with which I write with difficulty in scrapings of soot and charcoal from the chimney, mixed with blood" (307; bk. 3, ch. 10). Though written with standard ink, *A Tale of Two Cities* the book was also already mediated by Dickens's body. In the preface, he explains conceiving the initial idea for the story: "A strong desire was upon me then, to embody it in my own person.... Throughout its execution, it has had complete possession of me; I have so far verified what is done and suffered in these pages, as that I have certainly done and suffered it all myself" (3). Although this sounds like a description of an actor assuming a role, here embodying the idea in his "own person" refers to the act of writing the novel. The idea inhabited his body, and through his physical exertion gained its verisimilitude. By framing his body as the source for the novel, he asserted his ownership of the material. Indeed, he at times thought of his novels as his offspring. In the preface to the 1869 edition of *David Copperfield*, Dickens refers to each of his books as a "child" of his "fancy" (*DC* 766). Many years before, when completing this novel, Dickens wrote to his friend John Forster on October 21, 1850, "I seem to be sending some part of myself into the Shadowy World" (*DC* 773).

Firsthand accounts of Dickens's writing process confirm this transmission from thought to page through bodily intervention. Dickens's daughter, Mamie, observed his unorthodox composing method:

> my father wrote busily and rapidly at his desk, when he suddenly jumped from his chair and rushed to a mirror which hung near, and in which I could see the reflection of some extraordinary facial contortions he was making. He returned rapidly to his desk, wrote furiously for a few moments, and then went again to the mirror. The facial pantomime was resumed, and then turning toward, but evidently not seeing, me, he began talking rapidly in a low voice. Ceasing this soon, however, he returned once more to his desk, where he remained silently writing until luncheon time.... I knew that with his natural intensity he had thrown himself completely into the character that he was creating, and that for the time being he had not only lost sight of his surroundings, but had actually become in action, as in imagination, the creature of his pen. (49–50)

His recursive movement between the desk and the mirror, between writing and enacting, suggests his physical connection to his characters. "It was," as Philip Collins reflects, "a private 'reading' as an immediate preliminary to writing" (lix). Writing, for Dickens, involved experiencing in his body both the outward appearance of his characters and the dialogue on the page. The text temporarily interceded between Dickens's body and his readership, but the physical enactment of his characters in public readings was anticipated by the "private 'reading'" performed during his writing process.

Dickens began his professional career as a reader of his own works in April 1858. After publication, then, Dickens's works took on a closer corporeal connection through these staged readings in which characters were manifested in his physical performance. Charles Kent observes how, "attending his Readings, character after character appeared before us, living and breathing, in the flesh" (31). Similar to Mamie's account of his composing process, Kent's description shows Dickens's body becoming possessed by his characters, who appeared to inhabit his body during his public readings. Yet at the same time he retained his own presence as author-celebrity and creator of the multitude of characters he impersonated. In her discussion of his public readings, Susan Ferguson illustrates how "Dickens's performances were not simply of his *characters,* but of *himself* or, more accurately, of his public persona as the author of the novels from which the characters came" (731). The public readings gave audiences a chance to encounter both favorite characters and their esteemed creator. As both author and performer, Dickens offered a privileged interpretation of his own works through his readings.

His writing practice and public readings make clear that Dickens saw his relationship to his characters as complex and intimate. For someone else to dramatize his characters, then, was also in some sense to dramatize him. The "book-snatchers" I began with are equated with the worst type of thief, men who would do anything for profit. The word "snatcher" implies not only a thief, but a kidnapper. In his treatise on copyright, Charles Reade claims that if the courts had not "legalized *indirect* swindling of authors, the managers would have been compelled to come to Mr. Dickens for his children instead of suborning kidnappers." He believes that Dickens would prefer to "dramatize his own child instead of letting scribblers mangle it" (214, 125). In this formulation, the personified book is the author's child. The book as offspring is physically connected to the author who birthed it; only he should have the pleasure of introducing his child to the public.

For *A Tale of Two Cities*, Dickens recalls the moment of this child's conception. In the preface to the novel he recounts, "When I was acting, with my children and friends, in Mr. Wilkie Collins's drama of *The Frozen Deep*, I first conceived the main idea of this story" (3). Specifically, the role of Richard Wardour, the hero of *The Frozen Deep* whom Dickens played, held a powerful interest for Dickens that prompted him to revisit the character in his own fiction. In *The Frozen Deep* Wardour, like Carton, is the rejected, degenerate lover who ultimately sacrifices himself to save his rival. In a letter, Dickens sets the scene in which he came up with the novel and gives insight into how *The Frozen Deep* is reenacted in *A Tale of Two Cities*: "Sometimes of late, when I have been very much excited by the crying of two thousand people over the grave of Richard Wardour, new ideas for a story have come into my head as I lay on the ground, with surprising force and brilliancy" (*Letters* 8: 432). In the moment of Wardour's death, Dickens imagines a new fictional life for the character. In *A Tale of Two Cities*, Dickens accomplishes an intertextual resurrection in the character of Sydney Carton.

In the same letter we gain some insight into that transference. He goes on to tell an anecdote about the "very gentle and good little girl," Maria Ternan, who played Clara. In rehearsal, he recounts her "natural emotion" in response to Wardour's death. In the performance,

> when she had to kneel over Wardour dying, and be taken leave of, the tears streamed out of her eyes into his mouth, down his beard, all over his rags—down his arms as he held her by the hair. At the same time she sobbed as if she were breaking her heart, and was quite convulsed with grief. It was of no use for the compassionate Wardour to whisper "My dear child, it will be over in two minutes—there is nothing the matter—don't be so distressed!" She could only sob out, "O! It's so sad, O it's so sad!" and set Mr. Lemon (the softest hearted of men) crying too. (*Letters* 8: 433)

In the final scenes of the novel, Sydney Carton rides to the guillotine in the guise of Charles Darnay with a young woman to whom he reveals his true identity in order to raise her spirits. When he rewrites Wardour in *A Tale of Two Cities*, Dickens writes not a mere repetition of the original character, but a new character combining part and actor, Wardour and Dickens himself.

On stage, Dickens simultaneously played the role of Richard Wardour (who dies at the end of the play) and remained himself, an author coming up with an idea for his next novel and an actor soothing a fellow performer. Similarly, in the novel Sydney Carton plays Charles Darnay on the way to the guillotine, and, to the girl with him whom he comforts, he remains Carton. The narrator tells us that "if he had given utterance" to his thoughts as he rode in the tumbrel they would have been simultaneously of the crowd he saw in front of him and of a fictional future in which he imagines a story (360; bk. 3, ch. 15), much as Dickens imagines *A Tale of Two Cities* while he observes "the crying of two thousand observers over the grave of Richard Wardour." In Dickens's rewriting, the character resurrected is not the Wardour of the script, a character who could be played by any actor, but is specifically Dickens's performed experience of him: a novelist playing a role in front of spectators while imagining novels.

Dickens seemed preoccupied by the character of Richard Wardour long after the final curtain. His absorption in the character can be seen in a mundane letter to Wilkie Collins written during rehearsals of the play that Dickens signed, "Ever Faithfully, R. Wardour" (*Letters* 8: 276). Like the merging of Dickens and character in public readings described earlier, here Dickens becomes his character while remaining himself (the letter is a brief note whose content is unrelated to the play or character). In a letter to John Forster from September 1857, Dickens recounts an "expedition" he and Wilkie Collins have taken into the mountains. Lost on precarious terrain, Collins sprained his ankle. Dickens describes having to carry Collins "melo-dramatically (Wardour to the life!) everywhere; into and out of carriages; up and down stairs; to bed; every step" (*Letters* 8: 440). Describing the same incident in another letter, he writes about carrying Collins about "exactly like Wardour in private life" (*Letters* 8: 442).

For Dickens, Wardour exceeded the part allotted him in *The Frozen Deep* necessitating a new medium for the exploration of his character. In a letter to Wilkie Collins from August 1858, Dickens writes "I miss Richard Wardour's dress, and always want to put it on" (*Letters* 8: 624). It is even probable that he was already imagining not just the writing of *A Tale of Two Cities* but the subsequent dramatization of the character of Sydney Carton when he went on to say, "I think I have a very fine notion of a part." In effect, writing *A Tale of Two Cities* was an opportunity for Dickens to extend his ability to inhabit Richard Wardour's dress. The production of the play of *A Tale of Two Cities* is an anticipated extension of Wardour's life, and of Carton's, a reincarnation of both with the opportunity to continue exploring and recasting their characters.

At the time when he wrote to Collins about missing Wardour's dress, Dickens had just begun embodying his novelistic characters in his professional readings. There may be a few reasons he could not do the same with Wardour. For one thing, although Dickens is often credited with co-authoring *The Frozen Deep*, legally it was Collins's work, not Dickens's. Dickens claimed to have conceived the idea himself. In a letter written during the time of composition, Dickens wrote, "Collins and I have a mighty original notion (mine in the beginning) for another play at Tavistock House" (*Letters* 8: 81). Many critics credit Dickens over Collins for his role in the production both because of his suggestions during the composition and because of his performance of Wardour during which, as Winona Howe puts it, he "made the character ... peculiarly his own" (72). In her study of the collaboration between Collins and Dickens, Lillian Nayder emphasizes Collins's role in the play's composition, even suggesting that he used the conflict between the main characters, Wardour and Frank Aldersley (played by Collins at Tavistock House), to dramatize his own antagonistic relationship with Dickens (64). Collins asserted his authorship of the play by revising it in 1866 (and undoing Dickens's revisions to his initial draft) and preparing a novelized version for his public reading tour in America in 1874.

Although Collins eventually turned the play into a narrative, in 1858 it only existed as a play, and this may be a more important reason why Dickens did not assume Wardour's "dress" in a public reading. His efforts to keep the public readings from becoming too theatrical (no costume changes or sets, no actors but himself) may have prevented him from taking a character from a drama. To establish an intimate engagement with his readership, Dickens had to present his public readings as private and personal, rather than public and dramatic, even though these categories cannot always be kept separate. For both of these reasons, when Dickens chose to continue with the character of Richard Wardour, he did so in a new text (one that was entirely his own) and in a novel.

His description of coming up with the idea while acting in the play is different from the embodiment of character evident in Mamie Dickens's description of his writing process. Though the two are similar, they suggest two different trajectories between drama and story. The process described by Mamie originates in Dickens's mind, is enacted privately in his study, and is later read publicly in a setting that attempts to evoke the intimate family circle reading around the fire. The other, described in Dickens's letters and the preface to *A Tale of Two Cities*, originates in a drama, onstage, and is later returned to the stage as a new drama. Dickens described the process of performing in *The Frozen Deep* as one of composition. Writing to Daniel Maclise in July 1857 about his attendance at *The Frozen Deep*, Dickens explains that "the interest of such a character [as Wardour] to me is that it enables me, as it were, *to write a book in company* instead of in my own solitary room, and to feel its effect coming freshly back upon me from the reader" (*Letters* 8: 357). I would argue that the emergence of *A Tale of Two Cities* out of a shared dramatic experience made it difficult for Dickens to assert control over the novel's "powerful theatrical impulses" (Vlock 61). Although Dickens prepared a version of *A Tale of Two Cities* for public readings, entitled "The Bastille Prisoner," he never performed it. The reading text focuses on the opening scenes when Lucie Manette is reunited with her father at Defarge's wine shop; it does not include Carton.

Instead of the reading set, Sydney Carton took his place on the theatrical stage where he had originated. Dickens considered the possibility of playing Carton on stage himself. In a letter to Mary Boyle from early December 1859, he muses, "I must say that I like my Carton. And I have a faint idea sometimes, that if I had acted him, I could have done something with his life and death" (*Letters* 9: 177). Plans to produce the adaptation at the Lyceum were already underway by December. Dickens's reference to "my Carton" suggests both his ownership of the character and a distinction between the character as Dickens wrote him and as Fred Villiers would soon perform him on the Lyceum stage. Dickens seems to anticipate disappointment in the performance, as though if he does not play the role himself nothing will be done with Carton's "life and death." He wrote to French actor François Regnier that despite giving Madame Celeste permission to stage *A Tale of Two Cities*, he feared her troupe was "a very poor one" (*Letters* 9: 163). Dickens sensed that the character would be better represented by himself. Although reviews of Villiers's Carton are positive, they suggest that his character was overshadowed by Celeste's Madame Defarge. After praising Celeste's performance at length and acknowledging much of the rest of the cast, the reviewer for the *London Illustrated News* hastily notes that "Mr. Villiers and Mr. Forrester acquitted themselves admirably as *Sydney Carton* and *Charles Darnay*" (83). The *Times* reviewer gives Villiers more credit, admiring "some very clever dumb-show" when Carton goes to the guillotine, but offers this compliment only after commenting more extensively on all the other major characters (12).

Although he did not perform Carton on stage, the character grew out of Dickens's performance, originating in his body. His physical intimacy with Carton and all his other characters in *A Tale of Two Cities* seems to give him a special claim to injury when pirate dramatists attempt to appropriate them. In this case, the first unauthorized adaptation on record was written by Frederick Fox Cooper, a frequent adaptor of Dickens's works, for the Victoria Theatre in July 1860.[3] Dickens had collaborated with Tom Taylor early to present the first play to the public in hopes of dissuading other playwrights. Although the issue was debated in several legal cases in the mid-nineteenth century, in 1859 dramatizing one's own novel did not prevent others from doing the same. The only way to gain legal protection against unauthorized adaptations was to publish a version of the novel *first* as a drama, before publishing it as a book. Dickens adopted this practice later that year with the short work *Message from the Sea*, which he coauthored with Wilkie Collins, and again with *Great Expectations*. Although these plays were never performed, the registration of a dramatic version prior to publication allowed Dickens to pursue legal injunctions against pirate adaptors.

His approach with *A Tale of Two Cities* did not allow such legal action to be taken, but did allow him to participate in the dramatic dissemination of his works. It was a practice he had engaged in periodically throughout his career. A decade earlier Dickens had given permission to Mark Lemon and Madame Celeste (who was then manager of the Adelphi with Benjamin Webster) to dramatize "The Haunted Man and the Ghost's Bargain," his Christmas number for 1848. Despite this strategy, copyright law did not require playwrights to justify borrowing from Dickens's novel. Instead, they only had to differentiate their works from each other to show that they were returning directly to the source, rather than copying from other dramas.

The preface to a dramatization of *Tale of Two Cities* attributed to Henry Rivers attempts to do just that. In his opening remarks, Daniel George takes great pains to suggest that Rivers is justified in adapting Dickens's novel and to distinguish Rivers's play from Tom Taylor's. George suggests that if it is unsurprising that Dickens would be struck by "a catastrophe so shockingly unique, as the French Revolution's Reign of Terror," then "that our playwrights should seize upon a story so interesting and so admirably told, is also a very natural consequence" (5). Although the word "seize" here reverberates with the charges of snatching and stealing insinuated in Taylor's adaptation, George frames this act as a "natural" progression. George also places Rivers's work in a larger tradition of dramatization, citing how "Sir Walter Scott was over and over again *'Terry-fied'* by his friend Terry, and the fecundity of Mr. Dickens has furnished food in abundance for the stage." George insists that Rivers is not an anomalous encroacher, but an artist skilled in a long-established practice. He points out how Rivers's adaptation is an improvement over the novel: "however powerfully the novelist, by his unequalled word-painting, may have depicted those appalling times, the histrionic art, aided by its picturesque auxiliaries, scenery, mechanism, and costume, not forgetting music, appeals still more irresistibly to the eye and to the ear" (5–6).

At the same time that George hopes to establish Rivers as a legitimate artist, he wants to distinguish the play he introduces from others on the market. George contrasts Tom Taylor with Henry Rivers, who was "an actor, as well as an author, now playing at the Olympic." His credentials here are an attempt to gain credibility for his version. George highlights the distinction between Taylor's and Rivers's versions (one of the only differences), saying that Taylor is guilty of "*mis*-calling it 'A Tale of Two Cities,'" (for *his* scenes are entirely confined to Paris) instead of 'One' City; a deviation from the original that sadly mars its variety, interest, and effect." On the contrary, "laying the scenes both in London and in Paris, and selecting and arranging them with a keen eye to stage effect. [Mr. Rivers] has rendered the denouement particularly striking" (5). Rivers's use of the London setting in two scenes, though, does not notably demonstrate the importance of the two cities. George tries to draw attention to the few differences, thus deflecting attention from the fact that Rivers borrows a good deal of structure from Taylor.

Having discredited Taylor's version, George needs only to claim priority: "It may not be out of place to observe that this piece was in the possession of the publisher before Mr. Tom Taylor's tale unfolded itself at the Lyceum" (6). He explicitly denies that Rivers's play was influenced by Taylor's. Despite these long and elaborate prefatory remarks, though, there is some question whether this version was ever actually performed or ever had anything to do with Henry Rivers. The script is identical to Frederick Fox Cooper's (itself very similar to Taylor's), and the cast of characters listed comes from Madame Celeste's troupe at the Lyceum. Rivers or George may simply have been seeking quick financial gain by pirating the script without bothering to produce a performance. In light of this fact, George's focus on the relationship between this published edition and Taylor's can be seen as an effort to distract attention from a more damning connection between Rivers's alleged version and Cooper's and from the inconsistencies in the volume's own account of its production history.[4]

Among these convoluted claims to originality, it is interesting to note that both Dickens's novel and Tom Taylor's superintended adaptation use the title "A Tale of Two Cities," while both Cooper and Rivers make the minor adjustment to "*The* Tale of Two Cities." Through that small linguistic change, both Cooper and Rivers present their work as the definitive one. Even more striking, both Cooper's and Rivers's versions retain the scene where Mr. Lorry equates book-snatching with body-snatching. Here the scene seems no longer to refer to what Cooper or Rivers has stolen from Taylor or Dickens, but from what is allegedly being stolen from them.

The standard view would cast Cooper and Rivers as economically motivated thieves while Dickens appears as a victim of gross appropriation. However, we can read Dickens's preface to *A Tale of Two Cities* as participating in a similar undertaking as Daniel George's remarks on the drama: to steer the reception of the work and frame the author as artist and originator against the anticipated allegation that he is neither. If George draws attention to one play while ignoring another, Dickens can be seen to do the same thing in the preface to *A Tale of*

Two Cities. Dickens's preface appeared in November 1859 when the novel was published in a single volume. In it, Dickens mentions both *The Frozen Deep* and Thomas Carlyle's *The French Revolution* as sources for his work. The popularity of Carlyle's work meant that readers would likely draw a comparison between *A Tale of Two Cities* and *The French Revolution* whether Dickens acknowledged it or not. He had no reason to fear an injurious comparison with either text because *A Tale of Two Cities* presents an obvious departure from Carlyle's work (a generic shift from "a history" to a novel) and Collins's (not just the move from drama to novel, but a locational shift from the arctic to the two cities and a temporal shift from the present to the past).

While the preface's clues to the story's origins appear to be a simple statement giving credit to various influences, there may have been less magnanimous reasons for the identification of the sources and conception of the idea for the novel. By acknowledging both Collins and Carlyle in the novel's preface, Dickens, like George, suggests certain connections while discouraging others. Although *A Tale of Two Cities* is often singled out as being unlike Dickens's prior novels, both in length and in its focus on plotting rather than character, it was not so unique in its contemporary market. In early November 1859 (coincident with the final three installments of *A Tale of Two Cities*[5] and the publication of Dickens's preface), Benjamin Webster staged a successful production of Watts Phillips's *The Dead Heart.* Phillips's play was also about the French Revolution and bore a striking resemblance to *A Tale of Two Cities* in many ways, including the wrongly imprisoned man who is released from the Bastille after seventeen years and the self-sacrificing lover's substitution at the guillotine.

Although accusations of plagiarism were initially leveled at Phillips, those claims were countered by Webster, who (in a move familiar from George's preface) revealed that he had the play in his possession for several years before he produced it. He publicly bore witness to the fact that "'The Dead Heart' was written and paid for years before 'The Tale of Two Cities,' or the periodical in which it appeared, was dreamed of" (qtd. in E. W. Phillips 49). Placing the play sequentially before *A Tale of Two Cities* was even "dreamed of," Webster refutes the possibility that the two authors conceived the idea at the same time, but developed their individual treatments at different rates. Furthermore, according to Webster, "*The Dead Heart* had been known to Dickens who had, in fact, attended a reading of the piece given to a number of friends a short time after it was written" (Morley 35). The fact that Dickens knew *The Dead Heart* has never been disproved and suggests that if a similarity exists between the two works Dickens, not Phillips, is the appropriator. Either way, the same copyright law that leaves Dickens helpless to prevent Cooper (or Rivers) from adapting *A Tale of Two Cities* protects Dickens even if it could be proven that he stole ideas for his novel from Phillips. The term *plagiarism* (rather than adaptation) for what Dickens has done points to the fact that, unlike Cooper or Taylor, Dickens concealed the connection between his work and Phillips's. Though Dickens may have wished to prevent dramatizations, at least the dramatists give him credit even if they did so primarily to attract audiences rather than for any benevolent reason.

Webster insisted that Phillips's play was "perfectly original from first to last to my knowledge, not even adapted from a novel, which does not, in my humble opinion, entitle a drama to be styled original" (qtd. in E. W. Phillips 48). The date of this letter to the *Sun*, 18 January 1860, puts it a little more than a week before Taylor's version of *A Tale of Two Cities* appeared. Certainly this is not only an attempt to separate Phillips from Dickens, but also to assert his superiority to Taylor. This proved necessary, as Taylor's adaptation accentuated the similarities between the two plays, particularly in the closing scene. *The Dead Heart* ends with a dramatic tableau in which the "back of stage opens and discovers a view of the guillotine, guarded by Gendarmes and Sectionaires, surrounded by Mob.... In the extreme background, upon scaffold, stands Robert Landry, prepared for the fatal axe. He extends his arms in direction of Countess, as curtain slowly falls" (W. Phillips act 3, scene 2). While Dickens's *A Tale of Two Cities* ends with a similarly melodramatic glimpse of the self-sacrificing hero, the audience is not comprised of the novel's other characters who have already exited the text in a carriage leaving Paris. Tom Taylor's version, like Phillips's, ends with the scene of the execution being viewed by the surviving players. Darnay "goes to windows—raises blinds—the Crowd is seen grouped without along the street, by which the tumbrel passes along, filled with victims—Carton stands erect, his face towards the window." The play ends in a tableau after Carton sees Lucie and Darnay, "smiles, and waves his hand" (Taylor act 2, scene 6). The appearance of *A Tale of Two Cities* on stage at the Lyceum brought attention to the resemblance between Phillips's play and Dickens's novel.

Previously, the similarities were immediately evident to Watts Phillips when he saw the published opening installments of *A Tale of Two Cities*. In a letter to Webster in June 1859, Phillips writes,

> of course, *they will make a play* of Dickens's new tale, 'The Two Cities,' and (if you have read it) you will see how the character of the man 'dug out' of the Bastille will *clash* with the man in 'The Dead Heart,' written more than *three* years ago ... And now, owing to a *delay of years*, Dickens puts into *words* what I had hoped long ago to see you put into *action*. The tone of the resurrection from the Bastille ought to have been *fresh* in my play, not in his story. It's very heartbreaking. (qtd. in E. W. Phillips 46–47)

Phillips's fear of a "clash" suggests that the two stories will be compared to the detriment of each. The desire to present his material as "fresh" and therefore unique is thwarted both by the novel and by Phillips's (accurate) anticipation of a stage version. Phillips specifically complains about Dickens putting "into *words* what I had hoped long ago to see you put into *action*." Partly this is a comment on how long the delay is—*The Dead Heart* was written before *A Tale of Two Cities* was even "dreamed of," and the novel takes longer to create than the play does to stage. The time it takes Dickens to put the novel "in words" would have been sufficient to present Phillips's play "fresh" at the theaters. But, beyond that, once Dickens puts the idea in words, it is no longer sufficient to wait till the memory of a particular performance of a competing play fades from memory; the novel will pose a permanent point of comparison.

Evidence of this can be seen when Henry Irving staged *The Dead Heart* in 1889 (at the Lyceum where *A Tale of Two Cities* was first staged). He "also studied *Tale of Two Cities* intently. He told [Ellen] Terry that he saw in Landry a great deal of Manette ('that same vacant gaze into years gone by when he crouched in his dungeon nursing his wounds')" (Tetens 41). Ellen Terry wrote to her son, who was also participating in the staging, "If you read and study Dickens *Tale of Two Cities* just at present it will be very profitable, for the story of Sydney Carton in that book is the story of *The Dead Heart*, and is of the same period" (qtd. in Tetens 44). In this staging, *The Dead Heart* is viewed as an adaptation of *A Tale of Two Cities*.

Though Dickens probably would have resented his novel being used as a blueprint for Phillips's play, he hoped that the actors performing *A Tale of Two Cities* at the Lyceum would consult his novel as a guide for their performance. In his correspondence with the cast he frequently returned their attention to his text. To Celeste, he wrote, "On the other side, I send you, from my book The Tale of Two Cities, my own fancy of the Carmagnole" (*Letters* 9: 192). To Fred Villiers (who played Carton), he similarly instructed, "I send you a few words (from the Tale itself) to make a better exit for you at the point where you justly felt the want of something. Tomorrow, when you have added them to your part, will you be so kind as to see that Mr. West adds them to his Prompt-book?" (*Letters* 9: 200). His reminders suggest that even under his supervision the dramatization threatened to evade his control and needed corralling back to its source.

Dickens hoped that his involvement with the performance would infuse it with something he found lacking in the theater of the time. As he oversaw the rehearsals at the Lyceum, he reported to Tom Taylor, "the crowd (to which I have given particular attention) is on the whole good and fierce—and not quite conventional" (*Letters* 9: 198). Complaining to Angela Burdett Coutts of his fatigue with the project, he wrote, "I am very hard-worked just now, for, finding that I could not prevent the dramatizing of my last story, I have devoted myself for a fortnight to the trying to infuse into the conventionalities of the Theatre, some thing not usual there in the way of Life and Truth. The result will become manifest tonight. I have some hopes that there is a French populace dancing the Carmagnole, which is not like the languid run of unrealities of that kind" (*Letters* 9: 204).

His ambitions with the dramatization were most likely frustrated by the public response, which focused not on the unusual "Life and Truth" of the piece, but its overwhelming similarity to *The Dead Heart*. John Coleman, a friend of Watts Phillips, wrote in reminiscence, "The two plays 'caught on,' and their resemblance to each other having attracted universal attention, society divided itself into two factions—the Celestites and Dickensites, the Websterites and Phillipsites" (E. W. Phillips 51). Former colleagues at the Adelphi, Celeste and Webster had just ended their professional relationship and set up at opposing theaters. Dickens got caught up in a contest between two rival theater managers and in a complex debate over the originality of his novel. Even if Dickens was partly successful in inhibiting dramatic adaptations of *A Tale of Two Cities* (there were far fewer than there had been with previous works), this reaction to the play that he supervised compromised his position.

Not only was there comparison of *The Dead Heart* and *A Tale of Two Cities*, both Dickens and Phillips were also accused of taking material from Dion Boucicault's play *Genevieve; or the Reign of Terror*, itself an adaptation of Dumas's *Chevalier de la Maison Rouge*, which had been produced in 1853 at the Adelphi with Webster and Celeste in the starring roles (*Letters* 9: 282n). Similarities to both of those texts, Carlyle's *French Revolution*, which both Phillips and Dickens admitted to borrowing from, and even Edward Bulwer-Lytton's *Zanoni* allow most critics to fall back on a shared source theory. In discussing his use of Carlyle, Phillips writes, "my only borrowing was from an incident related in Carlyle's history (concluding chapter of third volume), in which an old man, the Marquis de something, answers to the roll-call in place of his son (who is asleep) and takes *his place in the tumbrel*" (qtd. in E. W. Phillips 44). Phillips downplays his knowledge of Carlyle by botching the marquis's name and treats Carlyle's text as merely one treatment of the event by referring to it as "an incident related" by Carlyle. If the ideas that make up both *The Dead Heart* and *A Tale of Two Cities* are in general circulation then Dickens is pardoned of the charge of plagiarism, but his claim to being robbed when others take them up appears less justified.

Whether any of the charges of plagiarism are valid or not, the preface to Dickens's *A Tale of Two Cities* demonstrates his need to establish the originality of his own idea and to differentiate his version from competing ones. In this, he is like the playwrights who adapted his novel. To attract audiences to *their* version and avoid accusations of copyright violation, these adaptors needed to advertise their unique contributions. Dickens's only claim may be that *A Tale of Two Cities* presents this story as a novel. It is a testament to the enduring power of print that his novel is the only piece in this series of related texts that remains in popular memory. But even his novel's lasting interest may be, at least in part, due to the dramatizations that periodically return it to public awareness. *The Only Way*, an adaptation famously starring John Martin-Harvey as Sydney Carton, was responsible for renewed interest in Dickens's novel at the turn of the twentieth century. Most recently, *A Tale of Two Cities* was revived on Broadway in 2008 in Jill Santoriello's *A Tale of Two Cities, A Musical*, which I will turn to in closing.

Before looking at the latest event in the series of reworkings, I want to suggest a way of understanding the multiple versions of this material as part a larger impulse to prolong the life of characters. In his encyclopedic reference of dramatizations drawn from Dickens's works, H. Philip Bolton writes that "it should come as no surprise that Oliver, the Artful Dodger, Little Nell, Smike, Little Em'ly, Little Paul, and Tiny Tim, Mr. Pickwick and Mr. Micawber, Uriah Heap, Fagin and Scrooge, Sarah Gamp, Mrs. Nickleby, and Lord Verisopht,—together with a long parade of other Dickens people—all should have been resurrected on the stage. In Dickens's time, this was one fate that fictional characters were born for" (12). Though the characters from *A Tale of Two Cities* don't appear in that list, many of its characters were born for resurrection, not only on the stage, but within the novel itself. *A Tale of Two Cities* is a novel preoccupied with the possibilities of resurrection from the recovery of Dr. Manette, long presumed dead and "recalled to life" from his extended imprisonment in the Bastille, to Jerry Cruncher's second job as a Resurrection Man, robbing graves for profit. *A Tale of Two Cities* was Dickens's experiment with the machinations of plot, each detail serving the larger design. Wilkie Collins calls it his "most perfect work of constructive art" (1860 Preface to *Woman* 644). But the construction relies on an overabundance of fake deaths and returns to life. It is not enough for Dr. Manette to be recalled to life or Charles Darnay to cheat death in the final moment by Carton's heroic exchange. The positive result of Jerry Cruncher's work as a resurrection man is his ability to identify that Roger Cly has "feigned death and come to life again" (292; bk. 3, ch. 7), information that gives Carton the necessary advantage over John Barsad, who is Solomon Pross reincarnated as an undercover spy.

The novel presents two opposing types of resurrection: a criminal violation (grave-robbing) and a redemptive recovery (Manette's reunion with his daughter, or Carton's self-sacrifice). Both types, Cruncher's criminal occupation and what Catherine Gallagher terms "benign Resurrection," stand as analogues for the act of narration (Gallagher 137). Gallagher draws attention to the less flattering connection for the novelist: between Cruncher's violation of the corpse's sacred resting place and the novelist's prying into the most private realm for subject matter to make his profit. Albert Hutter, however, draws a more positive connection, seeing the novelist as having "at least the illusion of breathing life back into the lifeless object, of a kind of fictive resurrection" (14). Through the narrative act, according to Hutter, the novelist gives life to his characters.

If resurrection in *A Tale of Two Cities* can serve as a double for the narrative act, I would argue that it also provides a model for thinking about the way in which characters come to exceed their part in a single work and be taken up in new texts, readings and performances, what I have called "intertextual resurrection." During the narrative time of the story, an author can breathe life into a fictional character, but after the story ends the character is laid to rest. If resurrection is already overly present within Dickens's novel, it is further multiplied in the adaptations. Intertextual resurrection allows the continuation of life after death.

The stage adaptations serve as resurrections themselves and further play with the possibilities of resurrection laid out in the novel. Tom Taylor's stage version begins with a sort of resurrection: this time of the woman, nameless in Dickens's version, whom Dr. Manette was called in to treat by the Marquis de St. Evrémond. Restored from second-degree textuality (appearing only in Manette's letter within the novel) and granted a name, Collette is brought on the stage in the prologue fully alive to tell her own story. Colette is also given a second life during the time of the play. After her death in the prologue she is resurrected in the character of her sister, Madame Defarge, both played by Madame Celeste. The novel has more than one pair of identical characters: Carton and Darnay, who are "sufficiently like each other to surprise ... everybody present" (71; bk. 2, ch. 3) at the trial, and the Marquis and Chevalier de St. Evrémond who were "greatly alike in stature, manner, voice, and, as far as I could see, face too," as Manette describes them in his Bastille letter (306; bk. 3, ch. 10). No mention of a similarity of appearance between Thérèse Defarge and her sister appears in the novel. In the play the two brothers are played by different actors, as are Carton and Darnay; only Colette and Therese are played by the same actor. Madame Celeste, the famed actress-manager, would have been highly recognizable in both roles especially since she had used the same practice before (Lawrence 406). Although Celeste's performance causes Thérèse Defarge to appear as a reincarnation of her victimized sister, which appears to have made her more sympathetic, Lawrence calls this a "stereotyped system of juggling with two roles," a comment that once again draws attention to the unoriginality of Taylor's work.[6]

Cooper's version borrows this same chronology (which would have made him liable to suit), but draws further attention to the resurrection by having the Marquis mistake Madame Defarge for her sister, this time called Lucille in a strange additional doubling of Lucie Manette. Madame Defarge confronts the Marquis during an attack on his home. He first hears her voice and mistakes it for the voice of the dead girl. When Madame Defarge appears before him, the Marquis exclaims, "Lucille! vision of horror! What sends you here to shake a heart that human peril never yet hath cowed?" (Cooper act 3, sc. 2).[7] If the burial of Dr. Manette in the Bastille does not prevent him from returning, here even the documented death of his patient cannot prevent her from returning to redress the violence inflicted on her by the man who was now the marquis. In each successive version examples of resurrection are multiplied and given greater emphasis.

The concluding scenes of Cooper's adaptation borrow directly from Dickens (via Taylor) in the prison scene where Carton drugs Darnay and assumes his place. However, in a departure from other versions, here the stage direction reads, "Carton is all but sinking with emotion as Barsad appears at the door—he advances to Carton, and beckons him off—Carton meets him, and with one movement passes the vial across Barsad's features, who falls insensible at his feet as the Scene is closed" (Cooper act 3, sc. 3). Unlike the novel, where Darnay remains unconscious at the conclusion, this additional substitution leaves Darnay conscious to discover what Carton has done. He frantically attempts to return to the guillotine "my friend to save" (Cooper act 3, sc. 5.) Darnay's efforts at heroism are unnecessary, though, for at that moment Carton returns dressed in Barsad's clothes. Informed that the victim sent to the guillotine was Barsad, Darnay shouts out, "Joy! joy! My friend yet lives, and is restored to us! Thank heaven! thank heaven!" Just before the curtain descends "the characters kneel in thankfulness to Providence, except Carton, who forms the centre of the tableau" (Cooper act 3, sc. 5).

This ending seems ridiculous and implausible. As unlikely as it is that Carton should bear such a striking resemblance to Darnay, here all characters seem interchangeable. Could Barsad look like both Carton and Darnay? The carefully laid demonstration of their physical likeness is rendered ineffective, as ultimately the switch depends mainly on a costume change. And while the ending tableau images Carton as the center of a new domestic bliss, as a profligate third wheel, there is no possible imagined future for him alive. Unlike the self-sacrifice of the novel, here Carton uses the vile of sedative fumes to force Barsad to take his place in order to escape. Despite Barsad's exaggerated malevolence in this stage version, Carton has essentially murdered him. This act of murder eliminates the self-sacrificing glory that would have immortalized Carton and incorporated him into the family through their memorial tribute to him. And yet, if Dickens anticipated Carton's resurrection both intratextually (through the family's remembrance and future generations bearing his name) and extratextually in his authorized stage production, Cooper simply grants an immediate resurrection rather than deferring it to the next performance. Just as Dickens's recreation of Wardour in *A Tale of Two Cities* leads to a new character that integrates both the character and the actor who played him, Cooper's ending writes in the return of Carton effected by Dickens through Taylor's staging. Both Cooper and Dickens participate in a similar impulse to recast characters and re-contemplate their endings.

For Dickens, we could trace the series of resurrections all the way back to the real-life antecedent of Sir John Franklin whose expedition to the Arctic inspired Dickens's contributions to *The Frozen Deep*. After a lengthy effort to locate Franklin and his missing crew, a report by Dr. Rae claimed to have found them and discovered evidence of their resorting to cannibalism. This statement was highly controversial: a public that had long anticipated the discovery and report of their heroic explorers was instead offered a tragic and savage conclusion. Dickens entered the public discourse on the subject and expressed his personal dissatisfaction with Rae's conclusions in a two-part article written for *Household Words* entitled "The Lost Arctic Voyagers." Critics like Erika Behrisch and John Kofron read Dickens's contributions to *The Frozen Deep* as another way he addressed the controversy. Appearing in the aftermath of this controversy, *The Frozen Deep*'s arctic setting would have conjured the famed expedition for the play's audiences.

Though the story of *The Frozen Deep* deviates significantly from the story of the Franklin expedition, in its final scene the play is able to offer audiences a new conclusion to the story that revises Rae's tragic ending. Kofron traces how "the idea of the self-sacrificing hero is found in 'the Lost Arctic Voyagers,' becomes Richard Wardour in *The Frozen Deep*, and then Sydney Carton in *A Tale of*

Two Cities. The self-sacrificing Englishman transmigrates from article to play to novel, the Arctic connection becoming subtler as the successive characters' moral foundations become stronger" (88). As we've seen, this is only part of the complex chain of interconnected texts and performances through which the "self-sacrificing Englishman transmigrates." Each adaptation allows the character to be returned to life and his ending to be made more heroic.

In her discussion of the undead in *Great Expectations*, Catherine Gallagher proposes that "part of the explanation for the replacement of the dead by the undead ... is that the novel can thus rehearse, in its fable, its imagery, and its rhetoric, a general function of novels: animating and suspending animation" (Gallagher and Greenblatt 188). *A Tale of Two Cities*, like *Great Expectations*, "invite[s] us to play with the difference between animate and inanimate beings." Gallagher suggests that this is related to larger questions in circulation in the Victorian period about the human afterlife and the possibilities of reanimation. Resurrecting characters in performance makes it possible to extend this time of play, never coming to an ultimate determination about the finality of death. Jean Ferguson Carr shows how "the metaphor of theatre also mitigates Dickens's ambivalence about the finality of self-expression, its tendency to freeze a person in only one role or posture, in an 'official' portrait or memorial. The play uses a script, but its text can be altered under performance; it eludes, to some extent, the awful finality of the word on a page" (33). The ability to return to the start through rereading or reviving in performance postpones the inevitable, unalterable end.

A Tale of Two Cities marks a critical moment in Dickens's career when he turned from the drama to public readings. Though I would argue that in this case there appears to be little difference between the pirate dramatizations Dickens decried and his own practices, he saw his adaptations (in public reading, novel, supervised dramatization) as achieving something different—a benign resurrection in opposition to the adaptors' grave robbing. With his death the opportunity for those approved resurrections ended, but the other kind (less desirable in his eyes) persists even to the present. In closing I turn to the most recent adaptation of *A Tale of Two Cities* to show how some of the issues that plagued Dickens concerning this text (the contestation over originality, the difficulty of bringing the text successfully to the stage) still persist.

Jill Santoriello's *A Tale of Two Cities, A Musical* marks the most recent event in a nearly continuous history of adaptation dating from just weeks after the novel was published. In the elapsed time, the controversy over the novel's sources has fallen from memory. But the desire to continue resurrecting these characters has remained long after Dickens's stake in such reworkings came to an end. Like the novel and early dramatizations, this most recent adaptation is prone to comparison with other works from the playwright's own time and from Dickens's. Santoriello's version can be placed in a direct lineage with Taylor's adaptation because it begins by staging the back-story: the Marquis' assault on the peasant girl and Manette's treatment of her and subsequent imprisonment. The musical invites comparison with other nineteenth-century novels, particularly those by the Brontës, via twentieth-century musical adaptations. Santoriello's Sydney Carton calls to mind the Brontë sisters' brooding heroes. This might be because Santoriello's first attempt to write a musical was an adaptation of *Wuthering Heights* or because James Barbour, the *Tale of Two Cities* star, played Rochester in *Jane Eyre, the Musical*, an adaptation of Brontë's novel that debuted on Broadway in 2000.

Even the Broadway playbill admits that "*A Tale of Two Cities* is also a tale of two shows," the other show being *Les Miserables* (Smith 46). The *Tale's* producers were both stars of the earlier show, which one reviewer calls another "tuneful epic of injustice and retribution played out against the backdrop of France in chaos" (Gurewitsch E3). Except for the performers playing Sydney Carton and Lucie Manette, most of the other actors in the Broadway version of *A Tale of Two Cities* also performed in *Les Miserables*. Though Victor Hugo's 1862 book is not one of the texts that I have placed in competition with Dickens's novel, Santoriello points out that he was "writing about the student uprising of 1832 at the same time Charles Dickens was writing about the French Revolution of 1789.... Dickens's *Tale* got to the market first, she says, and she has spent the past 22 years—from 1986 B.L.M. (Before *Les Miz*) to last week—musicalizing it" (Smith 46). As in the controversy between Dickens and Phillips (or Rivers and Taylor), Santoriello senses that her work will be compared to *Les Miserables* and makes a claim for having started her work before her competition came into being.

Like Taylor and Cooper, Santoriello picks up on the theme of resurrection in *Tale of Two Cities* by featuring Jerry Cruncher and his grave-robbing assistants throughout the musical, often with shovels in hand. When one of Jerry Cruncher's companions wonders how Carton knew they were "going fishing," another informs him that "shovels give it away every time" (Santoriello act 1, sc. 9).[8] Though in the novel Cruncher is only seen with a shovel at night when he goes "fishing" in Roger Cly's grave (152; bk. 2, ch. 14), the idea of burying and digging up recurs throughout the novel and early adaptations. In fact, "Buried Alive" was one of the titles Dickens considered for *A Tale of Two Cities*, but he feared it was "too grim" (*Letters* 8: 531). Perhaps a similar reason led to the elimination of a catchy song called "Resurrection Man" from the Broadway score of Santoriello's musical.

Santoriello's adaptation seems to relish the idea of grave-robbing and makes frequent reference to Cruncher's occupation. In the audience's first introduction to Sydney Carton, Cruncher tells Carton and Stryver directly that he's going to drop a body off at the medical center next door and drags a large burlap bag off stage. When Stryver criticizes Cruncher as a "graverobber," Carton casually replies, "Call him oversensitive, but he prefers the term 'resurrectionist'" (Santoriello act 1, sc. 4). For all the attention to his grave-robbing, its role as a plot device is eliminated in the musical. Other than drawing attention to the multiple types of resurrection in the story, Cruncher's occupation primarily functions as comic relief. The idea that Santoriello is herself a book-snatcher or a body-snatcher in adapting Dickens's novel may seem more comic than compelling 150 years after the novel's publication. But as a "resurrectionist," she once again animates characters caught in a continuous cycle of intertextual resurrections.

Superintending the dramatization of *A Tale of Two Cities* was one way Dickens tried to control the resurrection of his characters. Despite his partial success with this technique, its efficacy was limited in scope. Once Taylor's adaptation had left theaters and memories, new playwrights were able to produce their own version free from competition with any proclaimed "authorized" adaptation. Readers' persistent desire to see Dickens's characters on stage presents an ongoing demand that has continually been answered by dramatists seeking financial gain, popularity, or literary credibility. When copyright law proved insufficient, Dickens's persona, presented in prefaces, articles, public speaking engagements, public readings, and performances, as physical source for his multitude of characters established a relationship between himself and his works which, if it didn't prevent the widespread resurrection of his characters, framed Dickens as perpetual victim in constant struggle against aggressors. Though Cooper's or Santoriello's versions suggest the impossibility of Dickens's attempts to control the circulation of his works (in his own time or beyond), the fact that we consider *A Tale of Two Cities* his, that the debate over its relationship to Phillips's earlier work is forgotten, shows the power of both his role as author-celebrity and his self-mythologization as the body-snatched, book-snatched creator.

NOTES

1. See *Letters* 1: 304n. After Moncrieff's version appeared on 20 May 1839, Dickens responded with a scene between Nicholas and Mr. Snittle Timberry, "who had dramatised in his time two hundred and forty-seven novels as fast as they had come out— some of them faster than they had come out" (583). Nicholas firmly denounces his practice of adaptation.
2. I mean the term "intertextual" to encompass both printed works and performances. Both Jacky Bratton's useful term, "the intertheatrical" (37), and what has been called the "intermedial" are included in my understanding of intertextuality. My focus, however, is on the prefix, the relationship across various works rather than the particular medium of a given instance.
3. Cooper had already adapted *Master Humphrey's Clock* also for the Victoria in 1840, and *Hard Times* and *Little Dorrit* for the Strand in 1854 and 1856.
4. In his brief discussion of the adaptation history of *A Tale of Two Cities*, S. J. Adair Fitz-Gerald notes this odd publication and asks "Was Fox Cooper also Henry J. Rivers—or, what happened? I have never seen H. J. Rivers' name down as an author, while that of Fox Cooper is well known" (285). But there certainly was a person named Henry J. Rivers living at the time of this publication. George's preface claims he was an actor at

the Olympic, and E. L. Blanchard records his performance at the St. James's in 1854 (124n). Cooper's great-great-grandson, F. Renad Cooper, answers Fitz-gerald's question "clearly in the negative" (191) and offers several alternatives.

5. This staging occurred prior to and alongside the final three installments of 12, 19, and 26 November (book 3, chapters 12–15), from the period of Charles Darnay's second imprisonment to the novel's close.

6. In "Lyceum Theatre" (31 Jan. 1860), the *Times* reviewer recorded "a few sounds of disapprobation" (12) from the audience when Madame Defarge is killed, suggesting that audience members felt some sympathy for her not warranted by Dickens's novelistic treatment.

7. Just as all of the material included here appears to be circulating through multiple texts, this scene of Cooper's can be seen as a possible precursor to a similar scene in Mary Elizabeth Braddon's "Levison's Victim," in which the dead woman's sister appears before her murderer to provoke a confession.

8. My descriptions of the performance come from my attendance at the Broadway opening night on 18 September 2008. References to act and scene numbers are to the published edition of the play, which in some ways deviates from the performance.

WORKS CITED

Andrews, Malcolm. *Dickens and His Performing Selves: Dickens and the Public Readings*. New York: Oxford UP, 2006.

Behrisch, Erika. "On the Trail of an Arctic Tale: Tracing Sir John Franklin in Charles Dickens and Wilkie Collins's *The Frozen Deep.*" *Storytelling: Interdisciplinary and Intercultural Perspectives*. Ed. Irene Maria F. Blayer and Monica Sanchez. New York: Peter Lang, 2002. 58–71.

Blanchard, E. L. *The Life and Reminiscences of E. L. Blanchard*. Ed. Clement Scott and Cecil Howard. Vol. 2. London: Hutchinson, 1891. *Google Book Search*. Web. 13 Apr. 2011.

Bolton, H. Philip. *Dickens Dramatized*. Boston: G.K. Hall, 1987.

Braddon, Mary Elizabeth "Levison's Victim." *Victorian Tales of Mystery and Detection*. New York: Oxford UP, 1992. 69–83.

Brannan, Robert Louis, ed. *Under the Management of Mr. Charles Dickens, His Production of The Frozen Deep*. Ithaca: Cornell UP, 1966.

Bratton, Jacky. *New Readings in Theatre History*. New York: Cambridge UP, 2003.

Carr, Jean Ferguson. "Dickens's Theatre of Self-Knowledge." *Dramatic Dickens*. Ed. Carol Hanbery Mackay. New York: St. Martin's, 1989.

Collins, Philip, ed. Introduction. *The Public Readings*. By Charles Dickens. Oxford: Clarendon Press, 1975. xvii–lxix.

Collins, Wilkie. 1860 Preface to *The Woman in White*. Ed. John Sutherland. New York: Oxford University Press, 2008. 644–46.

Cooper, Frederick Fox. *The Tale of Two Cities*. London: Dick's, 1886. *Nineteenth-Century English and American Drama*. New Canaan, CT: Readex, 1985ff. Microfiche.

Cooper, F. Renad. *Nothing Extenuate: The Life of Frederick Fox Cooper*. London: Barrie and Rockliff, 1964.

Dickens, Charles. *David Copperfield*. Ed. Jerome H. Buckley. New York: Norton, 1990.

———. *The Letters of Charles Dickens*. Ed. Madeline House, Graham Storey, et al. Oxford: Clarendon, 1965–2002. 12 vols.

———. *Nicholas Nickleby*. Ed. Paul Schlicke. New York: Oxford UP, 1990.

———. *A Tale of Two Cities*. Ed. Andrew Sanders. New York: Oxford UP, 1999.

Dickens, Mamie. *My Father As I Recall Him*. New York: Dutton, 1900. *Google Book Search*. Web. 12 Nov. 2009.

Ferguson, Susan L. "Dickens's Public Readings and the Victorian Author." *SEL* 41.4 (2001): 729–49.

Fitz-Gerald, S. J. Adair. *Dickens and the Drama*. London: Chapman and Hall, 1910. *Google Book Search*. Web. 4 Apr. 2011.

Gallagher, Catherine. "The Duplicity of Doubling in *A Tale of Two Cities*." *Dickens Studies Annual* 12 (1983): 125–45.

Gallagher, Catherine, and Stephen Greenblatt. *Practicing New Historicism*. Chicago: U of Chicago P, 2000.

George, Daniel. "Remarks." In *A Tale of Two Cities a Drama in Three Acts and a Prologue*. London: Davidson's Actable Drama, 1862. *Nineteenth-Century English and American Drama*. New Canaan, CT: Readex, 1985ff. Microfiche.

Gurewitsch, Matthew. "Realizing a Musical Dickensian Dream." *New York Times* 17 Sept. 2008: E3.

Howe, Winona. "Charles Dickens and The 'Last Resource': Arctic Cannibalism and *The Frozen Deep*." *Cahiers Victoriens et Edouardiens* 44 (Oct. 1996): 61–83.

Hutcheon, Linda. *Theory of Adaptation*. New York: Routledge, 2006.

Hutter, Albert D. "The Novelist as Resurrectionist: Dickens and the Dilemma of Death." *Dickens Studies Annual* 12 (1983): 1–39.

Kent, Charles. *Charles Dickens as a Reader*. London: Chapman and Hall, 1872.

Kofron, John. "Dickens, Collins, and Influence of the Arctic." *Dickens Studies Annual* 40 (2009): 81–93.

Kreilkamp, Ivan. *Voice and the Victorian Storyteller*. Cambridge: Cambridge UP, 2005.

Lawrence, W. J. "Madame Celeste." *Gentleman's Magazine* 265 (Oct. 1888): 391–410. *British Periodicals Online*. Web. 11 Aug. 2010.

"Lyceum Theatre." *Times* [London] 31 Jan. 1860: 12. *The Times Digital Archive, 1785–1985*. Web. 1 May 2010.

Morley, Malcolm. "The Stage Story of *A Tale of Two Cities*." *The Dickensian* 51 (1954): 34–40.

Nayder, Lillian. *Unequal Partners: Charles Dickens, Wilkie Collins, and Victorian Authorship*. Ithaca: Cornell UP, 2002.

Phillips, Emma Watts. *Watts Phillips: Artist and Playwright*. London: Cassell, 1891.

Phillips, Watts. *The Dead Heart*. London: Thomas Hailes Lacy, 1858. *Nineteenth- Century English Drama*. Microfiche.

Reade, Charles. *The Eighth Commandment*. London: Trubner, 1860.

Santoriello, Jill. *A Tale of Two Cities, A Musical*. New York: Samuel French, 2010.

———. *A Tale of Two Cities, A Musical*. Dir. Warren Carlyle. Perf. James Barbour, Natalie Toro. Al Hirschfeld Theatre, New York. 18 Sept. 2008. Performance.

Smith, Cathy. "Back to the Barricades." *Playbill A Tale of Two Cities*. Al Hirschfeld Theatre. 18 Sept. 2008. 46–48.

Taylor, Tom. *A Tale of Two Cities*. London: Thomas Hailes Lacy, 1860. *Nineteenth-Century English and American Drama*. New Canaan, CT: Readex, 1985ff. Microfiche.

Tetens, Kristan. "Commemorating the French Revolution on the Victorian Stage: Henry Irving's *The Dead Heart*." *Nineteenth Century Theatre and Film* 33. 2 (2005): 36–69.

"Theatre Royal Lyceum." *Illustrated London News* 18 Feb. 1860: 150–51.

Vlock, Deborah. *Dickens, Novel Reading, and the Victorian Popular Theatre*. Cambridge Studies in Nineteenth-Century Literature and Culture: 19. Cambridge: Cambridge UP, 1998.

Bradley Headstone's Bad Example of Self-Help: Dickens and the Problem with Ambition

Rebecca Richardson

This essay explores Charles Dickens's vexed relationship to self-help. Popular self-help texts, such as Samuel Smiles's 1859 Self-Help, *offered hundreds of examples of men who succeeded through their perseverance and hard work. Dickens was himself an example of successful self-help, and readers since his death have seized upon this image, as the compulsive critical attention to his childhood stint at the Warren's Blacking factory demonstrates. In his novels, however, Dickens tends to condemn such ambitious characters. This essay argues that despite Dickens's personal history and political support for the institutions of self-help, he understood that the ambition to improve one's condition could also disrupt civil society. Some ambition is necessary if one is to succeed in industrial capitalism; Dickens reveals, however, that ambition and perseverance can become monstrous when developed in excess. Through close analysis of Dickens's speeches and his use of Bradley Headstone in* Our Mutual Friend, *this essay shows how Dickens translated the problem of ambition into narrative: Bradley's perseverance helps drive the plot, but it also leads him to monomania and suicide.*

On December 3, 1858, Charles Dickens gave a speech at the Institutional Association of Lancashire and Cheshire—an Association of mechanics' institutes and mutual improvement societies that offered classes and an itinerant library to

---

Dickens Studies Annual, Volume 44, Copyright © 2013 by AMS Press, Inc. All rights reserved.   DOI 10.7756/dsa.044.013.267-288

workingmen. In his speech, Dickens praised the hard work of some of the men who took classes through the Association and who would be recognized in that evening's prize-giving:

> There are two poor brothers from near Chorley, who work from morning to night in a coal-pit, and who, in all weathers, have walked eight miles a night, three nights a week, to attend the classes in which they have gained distinction.... There is a chain-maker, in very humble circumstances, and working hard all day, who walks six miles a night, three nights a week, to attend the classes in which he has won so famous a place. There is a moulder in an iron foundry who, whilst he was working twelve hours a day before the furnace, got up at four o'clock in the morning to learn drawing. (Fielding 281)

In the above passage, Dickens praises the incredible amount of time and effort these working-class men devote to self-improvement. Despite physically demanding jobs, they walk long distances to attend classes and forego sleep to study. In the examples above, we do not learn much about the classes that these particular men took—in fact, only one drawing class is mentioned—but rather, about their persevering desire to improve themselves.

In offering these examples, Dickens invoked a genre familiar to Victorians: the self-help story. The prototypical self-help story features a man who perseveres despite great obstacles—ranging from obscure working-class laborers who prop books on plows or spinning jennies, to famous figures such as George Stephenson, who overcame his early poverty to become "the Father of Railways." The genre includes such titles as *The Pursuit of Knowledge under Difficulties* (1830–31) by George Lillie Craik, and Samuel Smiles's bestselling *Self-Help; with Illustrations of Character and Conduct* (1859), which sold twenty thousand copies in the first year alone. Smiles was greatly influenced by Craik[1] and similarly stocked his volume with "examples of what other men had done, as illustrations of what each might, in a greater or less degree, do for himself" (Smiles 7). The biographies of great men, Smiles explains, are "most instructive and useful, as helps, guides, and incentives to others" (21). Smiles's book is inextricably intertwined with the history of working-class improvement, as he based it on a talk he gave in 1845 to the Leeds Mutual Improvement Society—a society not unlike the one that Dickens found himself in front of thirteen years later. Dickens was familiar with these collections of inspirational biographies, and showed a particular fondness for the awkward title of Craik's two-volume *The Pursuit of Knowledge under Difficulties.* Two allusions to this work nicely bookend Dickens's writing career: in *Pickwick Papers* (1836–37) Mr. Weller asks Sam, who is writing a Valentine, "wot's that, you're a-doin' of? Pursuit of knowledge under difficulties, Sammy?" (432; ch. 32); in *Our Mutual Friend* (1864–65) the narrator describes Mr. Boffin as "easily attired for the pursuit of knowledge, in an undress garment of short white smock-frock" (62; bk. 1, ch.5). In contrasting how Dickens uses self-help tropes in his speeches with how he uses them in his novels, I wish to suggest that, although in his politics Dickens supported the institutions of self-help, in his fiction he easily turns the self-help story to his own ends.

Of course, Dickens had even more intimate knowledge of self-help than these examples might suggest. Ever since John Forster's *Life of Dickens* (vol. 1, 1871) revealed his early poverty and work in a blacking warehouse, the self-help story has proved an irresistible narrative arc for explaining Dickens's success. For example, as early as 1906 G. K. Chesterton vividly described the young Dickens's ambition and his "resolution to rise which had glowed in him even as a dawdling boy, when he gazed at Gad's-hill" (57). Chesterton's Dickens sounds much like a self-help character, as Dickens "set to work, without any advice or help, to learn to be a reporter," working "all day at law, and then all night at shorthand" (58). This view of Dickens has so dominated our imaginations, in fact, that Alexander Welsh has claimed "[a]ny reasonably attentive student of literature believes that the single most important event in the life of Dickens was not the writing of any novel, or his attaining of independence, or his marriage and the births of his children, but the four months he spent in Warren's Blacking warehouse at the age of twelve" (*Copyright* 2). And despite Welsh's critique, this fixation shows no sign of receding: Michael Slater's 2009 biography of Dickens repeatedly invokes the "formidable" (232) and "phenomenal energy" (370) that drove Dickens's career and even his leisure.

Dickens, then, according to biographers and critics, was himself a self-help figure who succeeded by trying desperately—even angrily. By contrast, most of Dickens's main characters seem to succeed by *not* trying; characters such as Nicholas Nickleby and Oliver Twist end well without ever revealing ambitious desires. It is this dichotomy that I take as my focus in this article: why Dickens praises the ambition behind self-help when he speaks at a mechanics' institute—an ambition that his own biography suggests he shared—and yet never fully uses this narrative arc in his fiction. Even when he fictionalizes his own professional rise, Dickens shies away from representing this ambition; on the contrary, as John Jordan has argued, David Copperfield "tends to disavow his social ambition and aggression" (78), and condemns these qualities in Uriah Heep—a strategy that allows David to pursue "his own parallel course under the cover of moral superiority" (Jordan 78). Validated ambition is thus pursued "under cover" and made less visible, and, indeed, it does not seem as strong as the ambition associated with self-help. Instead, when critics have examined self-improvement or self-help tropes in Dickens they have tended to turn to *Great Expectations* and Pip's transformation into a gentleman, as Jerome Meckier does in "*Great Expectations* and *Self-Help*: Dickens Frowns on Smiles," and Robin Gilmour in "Dickens and *Great Expectations*." Although such readings have yielded productive discussions of how Dickens became disillusioned with the promise of upward mobility, I would suggest that Pip is not, strictly speaking, an example of self-help. Pip is bestowed money and status rather than exercising Smilesian hard work and perseverance to earn them himself. Perhaps more convincing, then, is George Orwell's reading of the novel as "an attack on patronage" (7), an attack Bruce Robbins explores further by revealing the "structural parallel" of Pip and Magwitch's meeting with those of Horatio Alger's boys and patrons (75). Dickens includes more examples of patronage than self-help in his novels, as he populates them with what Orwell famously called "that recurrent Dickens figure, the Good Rich Man (6)," and what Robbins might call benevolent "fairy godmothers." It is these men who dole out rewards to the deserving characters, as the Cheeryble brothers do in *Nicholas Nickleby*, the Boffins in *Our Mutual Friend*, or the rather disenchanting Magwitch in *Great Expectations*. To further this discussion, I would suggest that we do not find a true representation of the self-help ethos in Dickens's protagonists.

Instead, the only Dickensian characters that both desperately desire to better their socioeconomic condition and actively pursue upward mobility are the antagonists. But their ambition is not rewarded. In *David Copperfield*, Uriah Heep tries to rise from Wickfield's clerk to his partner, and ends in jail. Bounderby of *Hard Times* fraudulently claims to have overcome extreme poverty, and uses these claims to bully everyone around him; he is publicly shamed and his wife leaves him. In *Our Mutual Friend*, Bradley Headstone, who started as a pauper lad and worked his way up to schoolmaster, ends by committing murder and suicide. Here, I will focus on the ambitious lower-class characters who go unredeemed in Dickens's fiction—in other words, the bad examples of self-help. I argue that Dickens uses these characters in order to siphon off and punish ambition in his novels.[2]

As the last self-help character that Dickens imagines, Bradley will serve as my case study for how Dickens engages with the self-help narrative. Put simply, Bradley is the monstrous result of his ambition, which has warped him into an obsessively persevering character. His perseverance—that quality much revered by Smiles—served him well in his professional rise to schoolmaster. When applied to the current marriage plot, however, this perseverance takes a criminal turn as Bradley monomaniacally fixates on usurping Eugene Wrayburn's place in Lizzie Hexam's affections. I argue that Bradley is a character that models how excessive ambition troubles Dickens and his novels. Bradley is the site around which the problem of ambition, or, stated in another way by Welsh, the problem of "a culture that persistently reproves selfishness and rewards the selfish" (*Copyright* 40) is negotiated. We find this problem mirrored in the discrepancy between Dickens's fictional depictions of self-help and his speeches—or even his own history. In the first section, I will consider how Bradley functions as a self-help character, and how he consequently serves as a scapegoat for Victorian (and more specifically, Dickensian) fears of excessive ambition. In the second section, I will consider how Bradley's ambition works, and conflicts with, the novel: his perseverance-turned-monomania serves both to extend and suspend the narrative, as his character becomes defined by a repetition that is at odds with the forward movement of the plot. In the final section, I will situate my reading of Bradley Headstone and *Our Mutual Friend* in the context of Dickens's wider uses of the self-help story.

I. "Had toiled hard to get what it had won": Bradley Headstone and Ambition

> The ambition of intellectual excellence is, in truth, the same passion, by whichsoever of the many roads that lie open to it it may choose to pursue its object. The thing that is interesting and valuable is the purity and enduring strength of the passion.
>
> —George Lillie Craik

When Dickens introduces Bradley Headstone in the second book, he bases him on self-help characters, and suggests that such characters do not always fit the Smilesian model of the compulsive do-gooder. At the school where Charley Hexam is a student and Bradley Headstone is a teacher, the curriculum includes the self-help story of Thomas Twopence, which is described in the following passage: "unwieldy young dredgers and hulking mudlarks were referred to the experiences of Thomas Twopence, who, having resolved not to rob (under circumstances of uncommon atrocity) his particular friend and benefactor, of eighteenpence, presently came into supernatural possession of three and sixpence, and lived a shining light ever afterwards" (215; bk. 2, ch. 1). We quickly learn, however, that the students find this story inspiring for all the wrong reasons: "[s]everal swaggering sinners had written their own biographies in the same strain; it always appearing from the lessons of those very boastful persons, that you were to do good, not because it *was* good, but because you were to make a good thing of it" (215; bk. 2, ch. 1). These "young dredgers and hulking mudlarks" read self-help stories about boys—boys much like those in Dinah Mulock Craik's *John Halifax, Gentleman* and Horatio Alger's *Ragged Dick*—and subvert them into models for their own lives. By suggesting how easily readers can mistake a correlation between good behavior and financial success for a cause-effect relationship, Dickens comments on the adaptability of the self-help trope. In other words, stories of boys resolving to be good and achieving respectability might inspire the reader to straightforward imitation, or to a cynical imitation, where virtue is affected solely for the financial rewards these stories inevitably lead one to expect.

It is significant that Bradley Headstone enters the scene immediately after the passage describing Thomas Twopence. Like this fictional character, Bradley is an example of self-help. But Dickens's narrator treats him as anything but an inspiring figure:

> It was the face belonging to a naturally slow or inattentive intellect that had toiled hard to get what it had won, and that had to hold it now that it was gotten. He always seemed to be uneasy lest anything should be missing from his mental warehouse, and taking stock to assure himself. Suppression of so

much to make room for so much, had given him a constrained manner, over and above. Yet there was enough of what was animal, and of what was fiery (though smoldering), still visible in him, to suggest that if young Bradley Headstone, when a pauper lad, had chanced to be told off for the sea, he would not have been the last man in a ship's crew. Regarding that origin of his, he was proud, moody, and sullen, desiring it to be forgotten. And few people knew of it. (218; bk. 2, ch. 1)

In Smiles, we could imagine Bradley being held up for emulation because he began as a pauper lad, he has "toiled hard," and he is now a respectable school-master. But in Dickens it seems that this effort is somehow shameful and has marked Bradley's character in grotesque ways. Despite his upward mobility into the respectable lower-middle class, he still labors to maintain what he has acquired. This makes him compulsively self-interested, always inspecting his own storehouses. And, despite all his self-improvement, Bradley has not changed his essential nature, but merely suppressed it; he certainly does not exude the gentlemanly qualities that Smiles imagined hard work would produce in his self-help characters. Perhaps because Bradley is a schoolmaster rather than a ship-mate, his qualities are always in tension: a slow intellect opposes, and checks, a fiery passion. Further, we assume that it is the fieriness that is natural, while the slow intellect is what Bradley has cultivated in his schooling. Bradley becomes a negative example of self-help, as if Dickens's narrator were warning the reader that toiling hard to improve one's lot does not always improve one's character, but sometimes merely suppresses part of it, leaving it to smolder under cover of a civilized surface.

This need to punish certain types of ambition, and particularly excessive ambition, is a sign of the quality's ambiguous moral standing—particularly for Victorians, and even more particularly for Dickens. The word "ambition" can be used to positive or negative ends: the *Oxford English Dictionary* defines it as "[t]he ardent (in early usage, *inordinate*) desire to rise to high position, or to attain rank, influence, distinction or other preferment" (italics mine). Even in *Self-Help* Smiles uses the word in both senses, as a helpful, energizing force toward self-improvement, and as an overreaching hubris. He writes that, "if a working man have high ambition and possess richness in spirit,—a kind of wealth which far transcends all mere worldly possessions—he may not only help himself, but be a profitable helper of others in his path through life" (254). In this passage Smiles effectively equates ambition with the aspiration to help oneself and others. But elsewhere he states that Wellington's "great character stands untarnished by ambition, by avarice, or any low passion" (195), thereby aligning ambition with vicious characteristics. This is also true of George Lillie Craik's use of the word in *The Pursuit of Knowledge under Difficulties*, as he will modify it with "honourable" ("Considerable as this disadvantage must have been, we see how completely it was overcome by their perseverance and honourable ambition" [1:

60]), or with "immoderate" ("it was his own immoderate ambition that led this great man to his ruin" [1: 282]). Thomas Carlyle goes so far as to contrast ambition with earnestness in the following passage from *On Heroes, Hero-Worship, & the Heroic in History:* "Ah no: this deep-hearted Son of the Wilderness, with his beaming black eyes, and open social deep soul, had other thoughts in him than ambition. A silent great soul; he was one of those who cannot *but* be in earnest ..." (47).[3] As these examples show, the word "ambition" is strangely over-dependent on context for its meaning, rather than on essential connotations.

The uncertain value of ambition has much to do with how political economists understood self-interest. The Victorians inherited Adam Smith's model of the economy, which found great value in self-interest—when many individuals act according to their various interests, the economy grows and benefits everyone. But they also inherited Thomas Malthus's model of human reproduction outpacing agricultural production, with the many competing for fixed resources. These two models imagine self-interest as something that redoubles and produces value, or as something that produces conflict in a zero-sum game. Ambition seems to function in an analogous way: it is a necessary driving force behind the industrial economy, but it also threatens civil society.

In an attempt to reconcile these two conflicting models of how ambition works, the Victorians seem to have valued ambition according to its quantity; one should have some ambition, but not too much. When Frederic in *A Sentimental Education* claims to have no ambition, he is told, "Il faut en avoir un peu!" (126; ch. 5)—or, one needs a little. But the word carries vestiges of the early usage's association of ambition with "inordinate" desires, as it is a quality that easily slides into excess. Most of the ambitious characters produced in the nineteenth century go awry because of this excess, which makes social or economic success an end that justifies any means. This problem of ambition and its scale preoccupies *Our Mutual Friend*, with the novel offering two extremes for comparison. Bradley, as I have argued, will come to stand for excessive ambition. At the other extreme we find Eugene Wrayburn, the man who "abominates" talk about energy and argues against hard work (30; bk. 1, ch. 3). In the following passage, he takes offense to Mr. Boffin's praise of bees, and argues that bees overwork themselves:

"Ye-es," returned Eugene, disparagingly, "they work; but don't you think they overdo it? They work so much more than they need—they make so much more than they can eat—they are so incessantly boring and buzzing at their one idea till Death comes upon them—that don't you think they overdo it? And are human labourers to have no holidays, because of the bees? And am I never to have change of air, because the bees don't? Mr. Boffin, I think honey excellent at breakfast; but, regarded in the light of my conventional schoolmaster and moralist, I protest against the tyrannical humbug of your friend the bee. With the highest respect for you." (99; bk. 1, ch. 8)

Eugene here counters Isaac Watts's didactic poem on the "busy Bee" who improves "each shining Hour": Eugene channels Shakespeare's Sir Toby Belch to argue that bees should not serve as exemplary models for human behavior, but as cautionary tales—bees "overdo it." Although Bradley Headstone will not be introduced for another ten chapters, it is telling that Eugene associates the bee with his "conventional schoolmaster and moralist"—as if he were foreshadowing the introduction of this character that on the surface is a conventional schoolmaster, yet will indeed overdo everything. Further supporting such a retrospective reading is the fact that Eugene will insist upon calling Bradley not by his name, but by the title "Schoolmaster." By the end of the first few chapters of the novel, we have two extreme models for how energy and ambition work (or avoid working): the constantly laboring bee (associated with schoolmasters) and the laconic gentleman (Eugene).

Considering how Bradley and Eugene end, it seems that in Dickens too much ambition is more dangerous than too little. And it is excess that creates interest in nineteenth-century novels. One has only to think of Julien Sorel in *Le Rouge et le Noir* or Becky Sharp in *Vanity Fair* to recognize that this fascination with excessively ambitious characters is not limited to Dickens. In fact, Peter Brooks has argued that a defining characteristic of the modern novel may well be that "it takes aspiration, getting ahead, seriously, rather than simply as the object of satire ... Ambition provides not only a typical novelistic theme, but also a dominant dynamic of plot: a force that drives the protagonist forward" (Brooks 39). And yet, although ambition has great potential as a driving force, Victorian novels often do not value it. This finds a parallel in the larger debate about Dickensian energy and violence, those forces that provide so much interest in his novels, but which he cannot finally accommodate. This debate, best articulated in the work of John Carey and John Kucich, has led the latter to ask "[w]hy, then, this radical division: why does a culture that rewards self-assertion and dynamic energy simultaneously profess a dogma of moral or philosophical renunciation and a thematics of individual failure?" (9). To return to the problem of self-interest, and to borrow again Welsh's succinct summary of the problem, why does a culture that "rewards the selfish" so "persistently [reprove] selfishness"? (*Copyright* 40). I read these discrepancies as ultimately questions about ambition, which catalyzes energetic action and is necessary in moderation for the reproduction of the capitalist system, but, if taken to excess, has the potential to disrupt that same system. Not surprisingly, then, the Victorians simultaneously lionized and demonized the self-help figure. More specifically, ambitious self-help is rewarded in Victorian society, but punished in the stories that this society tells about itself.

The problem of ambition pervades Dickens's writing. Whereas Julien Sorel and Becky Sharp are both protagonists—and arguably very sympathetic protagonists—Dickens mutes ambition in his protagonists, and overloads it in the minor antagonists. Ambition, that quality that is finally taken seriously in modern fiction and which could motivate the movement of the plot, only indirectly drives the

Dickensian narrative and protagonist forward. This pattern relegates protagonists to passive reactors, and villains to active shapers, a pattern we see vividly in the contrast between David Copperfield and the overly driven Uriah Heep. In the next section, I will examine how the problem of ambitious desire surfaces in Dickens's last novel, and how Bradley Headstone's perseverance and erotic ambition indirectly drive the plot of *Our Mutual Friend*.

II. Bradley's Perseverance: Extending and Suspending the Plot of *Our Mutual Friend*

> Hence it happens that the men who have most moved the world, have not been so much men of genius, strictly so called, as men of intense mediocre abilities, and untiring perseverance; not so often the gifted, of naturally bright and shining qualities, as those who have applied themselves diligently to their work, in whatsoever line that might lie.
>
> —Samuel Smiles

> Do as I have done—persevere.
>
> —George Stephenson (qtd. in *Self-Help*)

We know from Bradley's introduction that he potentially has more psychological interest than the average Dickensian minor character—the suppression of something fiery would suggest depth, after all—but he also has the marks of a minor character when he is introduced in the Second Book with Charley at the National School. While talking to Charley in this scene, Bradley repeatedly looks at and bites his finger, the sort of easily spotted physical tic that one might expect Dickens to latch onto as an identifying characteristic. In fact, it is the sort of tic we would expect from a Dickensian minor character, and particularly from Bradley, who combines the qualities of "the functional worker and the deviant eccentric" (Woloch 161)—two major categories of the nineteenth-century novel's minor characters, as Alex Woloch has observed. But this tic does not resurface. Instead, Dickens introduces a new repetitive motion, Bradley's wiping of his brow, which is a tic that serves not only to identify Bradley, but also to suggest suppression and struggle. At points of high emotion in the plot we find Bradley breaking into a sweat. For example, when he argues with Eugene he "break[s] off to wipe the starting perspiration from his face" (290; bk. 2, ch. 6), and when he initially speaks to Lizzie he "[takes] out his handkerchief and wipe[s] his forehead and hands" (340; bk. 2, ch. 11). During Bradley's interview with Rokesmith-Harmon, he again wipes his brow with "a shaking hand" (381; bk. 2, ch. 14), and when asking Riderhood for information about Eugene's whereabouts, he requires "an effort at self-repression that force[s] him to wipe his face" (620; bk. 4, ch. 1). Bradley's effort is always showing itself.

In choosing to associate Bradley with sweat—that traditional mark of labor—Dickens both implies and elides Bradley's psychology. In other words, Dickens uses the tools of caricature to suggest exactly the opposite of caricature in Bradley's character: his tic signals that he is not all surface. We might read this as shorthand for psychology, as if Dickens were putting minimal effort into rounding out Bradley's character. But the progression of Bradley's tic from biting to sweating suggests that Dickens's ideas for this character evolved, and that he found he could do more with it than previous versions of the type, such as Uriah Heep. Instead, it is almost as if Bradley were struggling against becoming a caricature; he suppresses the inflated desires that threaten to overwhelm and define him, and yet, in so doing, he acts in ways that make those signs of suppression almost indistinguishable from the signs of caricature. Bradley's sweat is also at odds with the initial description of his character as "mechanical" (218; bk. 2, ch. 1)—Bradley's sweat marks him as anything but a mechanical automaton. In other words, Bradley's self-suppression is too visible to allow him to be relegated to the role of caricature: his interiority literally seeps out of his pores.

Bradley's interiority similarly shows itself too much in the marriage plot, where he repeatedly displays an excess of emotion and a tendency to volunteer too much information. When Bradley and Charley confront Eugene over the education of Lizzie, the common love interest, Eugene suggests that it is a "natural ambition" for Bradley to wish to teach Lizzie himself. In the following excerpt, Bradley escalates the argument:

> "A natural ambition enough," said Eugene, coolly. "Far be it from me to say otherwise. The sister who is something too much upon your lips, perhaps—is so very different from all the associations to which she had been used, and from all the low obscure people about her, that it is a very natural ambition."
>
> "Do you throw my obscurity in my teeth, Mr. Wrayburn?"
>
> "That can hardly be, for I know nothing concerning it, Schoolmaster, and seek to know nothing."
>
> "You reproach me with my origin," said Bradley Headstone; "you cast insinuations at my bringing-up. But I tell you, sir, I have worked my way onward, out of both and in spite of both, and have a right to be considered a better man than you, with better reasons for being proud." (290–91; bk. 2, ch. 6)

Eugene frames Bradley's desires in terms of ambition, a "natural ambition" to help Lizzie match in education the sphere she already matches in spirit. In other words, Bradley would help Lizzie to realize the same self-help narrative he followed in his education. Defending such a "natural ambition," Bradley here invokes a truism of self-help: that rising by one's own efforts is not only a source of pride, but also proof of character development. Bradley implies that, by "working his way onward" in the socioeconomic arena, he has also become a "better man" than the indolent gentleman who lounges before him. But, in presenting words from the mouth of this character, Dickens's narrator mocks rather than endorses these assumptions of self-help. Bradley is instead the monstrously self-centered, bad example of self-help: he is too self-conscious and self-aggrandizing, as he not only touts his own character but easily redirects a discussion of Lizzie into a discussion of himself. In other words, we see how self-involved Bradley's mind is, and how everything, even the shared goal of their love triangle, Lizzie, is about competing with rivals and beating them (literally, as the case turns out).

To better understand Bradley's rivalry, I suggest that Bradley is acting not in the marriage plot, but in the self-help plot. Of course, these plots overlap symbolically— the marriage plot easily becomes an analogy for the marketplace in Victorian fiction, and it is the arena in which women can improve their socioeconomic status—but Bradley's failures show where these plots diverge. Bradley has already acted out his self-help plot, yet he still seems trapped in it. He argues that because he is a "better man" in his self-help plot, this should translate into the marriage plot. For example, he refers to himself as a "man of unimpeachable character who had made for himself every step of his way in life" (381; bk. 2, ch. 14), and echoes this when he proposes to Lizzie: he has "in [his] way won a station which is considered worth winning" (388; bk. 2, ch. 15). And yet, as we see here and in many other Victorian novels, the marriage plot relies on what is ineffable, not on a list of character qualities.

As unlikely a candidate as Bradley seems in this marriage plot, however, we are not entirely able to take Eugene's side against him. Eve Sedgwick has noted the strange way in which "[t]he moral ugliness of Eugene's taunts against the schoolmaster is always less striking, in the novel's presentation, than the unloveliness of the schoolmaster's anxiety and frustration" (167). And Eugene does not acknowledge how he goads Bradley into this "unloveliness." Instead, he accuses Bradley of being overly sensitive about his origins: "A curious monomaniac.... The man seems to believe that everybody was acquainted with his mother!" (291; bk. 2, ch. 6). Dickens's narration eventually sides with Eugene's perspective. We realize the extent to which the narrator echoes Eugene in the following passage: the narrator observes that Bradley perfectly comprehends that he hates Eugene "with his strongest and worst forces," and that if he fulfills his perverse desire to see Eugene with Lizzie he will further incense himself (536; bk. 3, ch. 11). The narrator then hints that Bradley knows he will attack Eugene: "And he knew as well what act of his would follow if he did, *as he knew that his mother had borne him*. Granted, that he may not have held it necessary to make express mention to himself of the one familiar truth any more than of the other" (536; bk. 3, ch. 11; italics mine). Dickens's narrator transitions from a sympathetic description of Bradley's tortured state of mind, to an underhanded critique of how he knows

his own perversity without confronting it. The juxtaposition of such sympathy
with such criticism gets at a key way in which Bradley cannot win in this novel.
If he pays too much attention to his origins, he is a monomaniac. And if he does
not acknowledge the "one familiar truth" that his mother has borne him, he is
prideful. Although the narrator uses a commonplace phrase—"he knew that his
mother had borne him"—it echoes the only other mention of Bradley's mother in
the novel, which came from Eugene in their first confrontation ("The man seems
to believe that everybody was acquainted with his mother!"). Dickens's narrator
entertains a certain sympathy for Bradley—to the extent that Angus Wilson has
even imagined that when Bradley writhes in misery "Dickens feels as strong a
pity for him as David had felt for Steerforth" (90)—but in the end, he endorses
Eugene's assessment of him.

To some extent, of course, Eugene is right about Bradley in that initial confrontation scene: Bradley *is* a monomaniac. The repetition of "fixed idea" in relation
to Bradley invokes the French phrase for monomania: the idée fixe. In the passage quoted above, Bradley is possessed "in his jealousy by the fixed idea that
Wrayburn was in the secret" of where Lizzie has hidden herself (536; bk. 3, ch.
11). Earlier in the novel he walks with "a bent head hammering at one fixed idea"
(336; bk. 2, ch. 11). After the murder attempt he endures the "slower torture of
incessantly doing the evil deed again and doing it more efficiently" (690; bk. 4,
ch. 7), and he is "chained heavily to the idea of his hatred and his vengeance"
(691; bk. 4, ch. 7). Before the crime Bradley fixates on Eugene, after the crime
he obsessively reimagines the attack. Significantly, his ability to fixate on one
idea until he succeeds is intimately linked to his self-help story. When Bradley is
convinced that Eugene knows Lizzie's location, the narrator writes that "Bradley
was as confident of getting the better of him at last by sullenly sticking to him,
as he would have been—and often had been—of mastering any piece of study in
the way of his vocation, by the like slow persistent process" (536; bk. 3, ch. 11).
To get the better of Eugene, Bradley uses exactly the qualities he has developed
in his self-help story. He is not more innately intelligent than Eugene, but simply
persistent. Dickens's narrator, too, will not let us forget this: he describes Bradley's "slow and cumbrous thoughts" (542; bk. 3, ch. 11), "slow observation" and
"sluggish memory" (624; bk. 4, ch. 1), "slow conception" (689; bk. 4, ch. 7), his
"cumbersome way" (380; bk. 2, ch. 14) and "slowly labouring expression" (691;
bk. 4, ch. 7)—Bradley even speaks "doggedly" (380; bk. 2, ch. 14). Bradley is all
persistent, slow work; nothing comes naturally. And instead of inspiring us, as it
would in a Smilesian version of Bradley's rise from pauperism to respectability,
this perseverance repels us.

It is telling that Bradley's character is defined by repetition, as it gets at how
Dickens makes use of this character type. Bradley's persistence, translated into
the level of plot, extends scenes. He tends to draw out his encounters with other
characters, as evidenced by his postponed courting of Lizzie. As if knowing that
Lizzie will reject him, he delays proposing to her:

"Limit my meaning for the present," he interrupted, "to the whole case being submitted to you in another interview."

"What case, Mr. Headstone? What is wanting to it?"

"You—you shall be informed in the other interview." Then he said, as if in a burst of irrepressible despair, "I—I leave it all incomplete! There is a spell upon me, I think!" And then added, almost as if he asked for pity, "Good-night!" (341; bk. 2, ch. 11)

In this exchange Bradley delays submitting the "whole case" of his proposal, as if reluctant to open the possibility of Lizzie's refusal. What he leaves incomplete will create tension and uncertainty—in other words, it will make the most of an emotion and of a scene. The narrator uses a paratactic structure to describe Bradley's request ("Then he said ... And then added"), mirroring and emphasizing Bradley's awkward style of extension. Bradley even extends this scene at the micro-level of individual words, with his emotionally charged stutter. And when he does finally propose in a subsequent scene, he draws out that scene as well, requesting that Lizzie continue to walk with him in a circle around the cemetery: "I entreat of you let us walk round this place again ..." (389; bk. 2, ch. 15). He then again asks that Lizzie wait to give her answer: "Stop! I implore you, before you answer me, to walk round this place once more. It will give you a minute's time to think, and me a minute's time to get some fortitude together" (390; bk. 2, ch. 15). Bradley works to extend and repeat these scenes. But in both these passages we find suppression at odds with extension: Bradley's plea is for more time, but it requires that he cut off Lizzie's response. In other words, the desire to extend a scene involves, paradoxically, the suppression of the action.

I read this extension that results in suppression as analogous to the way in which the narrator both enters Bradley's consciousness and refrains from identifying with that consciousness, as explored above in relation to the narrator's comment about Bradley's state of mind. The narrator—although depicting a monomaniacal character who is defined by his habit of fixing on things, whether they be ideas, people, or habits—refrains from fully identifying with Bradley, as if Bradley might distract him from the story at hand. Indeed, Bradley repeatedly poses this threat to the plot. As the rival for Lizzie, he can be read as trying to insert himself into a marriage plot that is at odds with the actual self-help plot that he finds himself in. As Charley's teacher, he interferes with the Hexam family dispute. In order to attack Eugene and deflect suspicions, he dresses up as Riderhood, as if one role were not enough for him. Even at the level of individual scenes, Bradley takes more time than the other characters are willing to give him: he defers leaving Mortimer and Eugene's rooms, and refuses to let Lizzie put an end to the proposal scene. As if he were continually popping up where he was not needed, Bradley is also included in two scenes where his presence serves not to advance the plot, but to stress (even belabor) his fixation on Lizzie and Eugene— when Rokesmith-Harmon asks Bradley to take Sloppy on as a pupil, and when

Bradley meets the Milvey-Lightwood-Bella party, which is en route to Eugene's bedside. Bradley can be read as unsuccessfully trying to take over the novel, or as being repeatedly invited in, and then expelled.

Bradley's speech is similarly suggestive of depths beyond what we would expect to find in a caricatured minor character. Unlike so many of Dickens's characters—and particularly his minor characters—Bradley's speech is unmarked. He does not repeat certain phrases or give away his class origins, as Riderhood repeatedly does with his claims to being "nat'rally a honest man, and sweating away at the brow as a honest man ought" (355; bk. 2, ch. 12). Bradley speaks as correctly as any protagonist in Dickens. Readers and critics have long noted that characters like Oliver Twist or even Lizzie Hexam defy their backgrounds by speaking unaccented Queen's English, as if Dickens were signaling their true or future class status. But, unlike these characters, Bradley's unmarked speech is not a sign of authorial favor or his true nature, but a sign of his schooling. If he has a verbal tic, it is the stylistic equivalent of his perseverance—a patterned, repeating prose that verges on the eloquent. This prose style is particularly pronounced in the following speech Bradley makes to Lizzie: "You could draw me to fire, you could draw me to water, you could draw me to the gallows, you could draw me to any death, you could draw me to anything I have most avoided, you could draw me to any exposure and disgrace ... But if you would return a favourable answer to my offer of myself in marriage, you could draw me to any good—every good—with equal force" (389–90; bk. 2, ch. 15). Bradley's style relies on anaphora and parallel syntax for its rhetorical effect, gathering examples as if they were so many weapons. At root, anaphora and parallelism are structures that utilize repetition; we might understand them as the poetical equivalents of the school system that produced Bradley, and which required students to memorize and repeat lessons, as parodied in *Hard Times*. But, unlike straightforward repetition, Bradley's "mechanical poetics" make the case less rather than more clear. His language moves from precise imagery to abstractions: first his nouns are concrete (fire, water, gallows), then abstract (death), then downright vague ("anything I have most avoided," "any exposure and disgrace"). We would expect the reverse order in this sentence, with the examples moving from the abstract to the precise, but Bradley does the opposite. And his imagination seems to fail him completely when it comes to the sort of good that Lizzie could draw him to ("any good—every good"). Something about Bradley's suppression actually results in *more*: more difficulty in moving from one idea to another, and so repeating phrases and syntax, more difficulty in clarifying his terms, and so multiplying examples.[4]

Bradley's perseverance turned monomania thus works at both the level of plot and the level of style to extend scenes and dialogue, not by necessarily advancing the action, but by suspending a state—whether the state of silence before Lizzie's answer to his proposal, or the sense of a sentence. Perhaps the best illustration of Bradley's monomaniacal perseverance and its effect on the plot is Eugene's oft-quoted description of how he invites Bradley to—for lack of a better term—stalk him. As evidenced by the awkwardness of this phrase, the logic is counterintuitive: although Eugene imagines that he initiates the "pleasures of the chase," it is *Bradley* who stalks Eugene, hoping that Eugene will lead him to Lizzie's hiding place. Eugene admits that he "[goads] the schoolmaster to madness" with this game, first checking that the "schoolmaster [is] on the watch," then leading and tempting "him on, all over London" (533; bk. 3, ch. 10). Eugene seeks out "No Thoroughfares" so he can then "glide into them by means of dark courts, tempt the schoolmaster to follow, turn suddenly, and catch him before he can retreat" (533; bk. 3, ch. 10). Even here Eugene exploits the socioeconomic disparity between their positions, noting that he sometimes walks, but sometimes proceeds "in cabs, draining the pocket of the schoolmaster who then follows in cabs" (533; bk. 3, ch. 10).

The entire passage is strange, particularly in its length, considering that the laconic Eugene is the speaker—and strange in the action that Eugene somehow both inspires and is inspired to take. Eugene assumes the position of the hunted (the prey) here, but he actually depends on Bradley's following him; he depends on Bradley's monomaniacal attention. It is tempting to read this sadistic game of "tag" as analogous to Dickens's relationship with his readers, and in fact it has been read as such.[5] But it is particularly tempting if we consider the fact that Dickens has at this point in his career turned toward plots that rely more and more on secrets withheld from the reader, a trend that ends with his death in the midst of writing *The Mystery of Edwin Drood*. Of course, Eugene plays this game on the premise of knowing a secret that he actually does not yet know: Lizzie's location. The "pleasures of the chase" might never result in progress, but they are infinitely repeatable, in some way mirroring Bradley's tendency both to extend and to suspend action. It is action without the potential for development, which mirrors the dead end of Bradley's self-help plot.

Bradley shows this psychological tendency when he repeats the attack on Eugene rather than processing it. As Peter Brooks has argued in *Reading for the Plot*, characters like Pip repeat in order to work through their traumas;[6] with Bradley, however, Dickens gives us a character that seems stuck at repetition. After his crime, Bradley is "always doing the deed and doing it better.... He was doing it again and improving on the manner, at prayers, in his mental arithmetic, all through his questioning, all through the day" (691; bk. 4, ch. 11). Bradley is unable to process the event beyond the realization that he did not succeed in killing Eugene: he is stuck at imagining better ways to commit the same crime. And, as if unable to invent anything new, he recreates the earlier scene of "the pleasures of the chase." Now, it is Bradley who entices Riderhood to follow him, as he walks back and forth along the river. Bradley first leaves the Lock House in the direction of London, and Riderhood walks by him in silence for three miles before Bradley suddenly turns "to *retrace his course*" (779; bk. 4, ch. 15; italics mine). Bradley leads them back to the Lock House, and, an hour later, Bradley again leaves and starts walking in the opposite direction. Riderhood again follows, and this time, "as before, when he found his attendant not to be shaken off, Bradley suddenly [turns] back" (779; bk. 4, ch. 15). But this time, rather than going into the Lock House, Bradley heads to the Lock itself. Now Riderhood speaks: "Come, come, Master ... This is a dry game. And where's the good of it? You can't get rid of me, except by coming to a settlement. I am a going along with you wherever you go" (779; bk. 4, ch. 15). A few lines more of Riderhood's cajoling, and Bradley, "[w]ithout taking the least notice ... leans his body against a post, in a resting attitude, and there [rests] with his eyes cast down" (781; bk. 4, ch. 15). Bradley imitates Eugene's idle stance, as he replicates a past scene even as he helps forward the plot. He not only acts out "the pleasures of the chase"— and I would argue Dickens intends us to see this parallel, as Riderhood calls it a "dry game"—but Bradley also takes the composed, disdainful stance that Eugene adopted at their first confrontation (leaning against a post, rather than a chimneypiece). Despite adopting Eugene's stance, however, Bradley is doomed to his own type of repetition: another attack that ends in the river. Bradley's role as both a self-help character and as a suitor suggests that his ambition can let him rise only so far, to schoolmaster and respectability, to rival for Lizzie's love, before it is checked.

III. Industry and Idleness: The After Story of Self-Help

Alexander Welsh has argued that Eugene fairs better than previous idle loafers in Dickens—like Richard Carstone of *Bleak House*—because Dickens now has his own grown sons, who are also uncertain of how to tackle their careers (*The City of Dickens* 77). But I read Dickens's generosity toward Eugene as having less to do with Eugene, and more to do with Bradley. It is not that Eugene "wins," but that Bradley loses. Bradley's descent into murderous monomania is exactly what propels Eugene from his indecisive state right before the attack—a state which is aptly summed up by his soliloquy-like dilemma: "Out of the question to marry her ... and out of the question to leave her. The crisis!" (682; bk. 4, ch. 6)—into his decision to marry Lizzie after she saves his life. Put simply, Bradley here acts as the hand of the author, disciplining Eugene's desire so as to redirect the novel toward closure.

I have read Bradley's monomania as intimately linked to the perseverance he has practiced in his self-help story, yet as we can see in the "pleasures of the chase," there is something antithetical to development or improvement in this monomania. By revising (and extending) the typical self-help story's uncritical happy-ever-after, Dickens dramatizes the after-story of self-help and the limits to a pauper lad's desires. It is significant that, unlike Smiles, Dickens starts not with his character's poverty, but with his respectability. In other words, Dickens starts with Bradley having completed rather than just embarking upon his self-help story. And much like Shakespeare when he starts with a marriage rather than ending with one, the story shifts from comedy to tragedy. The persevering energy that took Bradley from pauper lad to schoolmaster is "smoldering" when we meet him, and it reignites into a failed love plot. The qualities that served him in his back-story lead him to murder and suicide in the present of the novel.

Dickens's take on self-help, then, is at odds with the received narrative. We can see just how far Dickens has deviated with Bradley if we compare him to earlier depictions of self-help. In Hogarth's *Industry and Idleness* prints (1747), Industry perseveres at his work, marries his master's daughter, and rises in the world, while Idleness sinks into dissipation and crime. Dickens wished to model Walter Gay of *Dombey and Son* on Hogarth's Idleness, to make of Idleness a "pathetic" character (Slater 257). Although Forster apparently persuaded Dickens against this plan (Slater 258), the narrative consequences of idleness and industry, and the problem of deciding how much sympathy each should garner, resurfaces in later work. Dickens and Wilkie Collins turn the narrative to comic ends when they adopt the characters of Francis Goodchild and Thomas Idle in 1857 for their "Lazy Tour of Two Idle Apprentices." (Fittingly, Dickens claimed the role of Goodchild.) In a more serious vein, *David Copperfield*'s depiction of self-help parallels that found in Hogarth's prints. Here, two young men start from similar positions, compete for a girl, and end in diametrically opposed socioeconomic positions: like Industry, David ends up with the daughter of an employer; like Idleness, Uriah ends up a criminal, despite his industry and ambition.[7] In such two-rival systems, both the girl and the upward mobility are competed for within a zero-sum game: there is one girl, and one successful position. In other words, as one character succeeds, the other fails.

In *Our Mutual Friend*, however, Dickens plays with this system. Here we have many young men trying to make their way in the world—John Harmon is industrious but not ambitious, Eugene Wrayburn and Mortimer Lightwood want gentlemanly careers but have just enough money to lack energetic ambition, and Bradley Headstone has achieved a position but wants the girl. If we take Bradley and Eugene as the analogous rival system to that found in *David Copperfield* between David and Uriah, then Bradley seems less capriciously malicious than Uriah, but more punished; and Eugene is much more idle than David, but equally rewarded. If we compare them to Hogarth's rivals, however, it is Industry (Bradley) who ends in crime, and Idleness (Eugene) who gets the girl.

This revision of the self-help story is even more extreme when compared with how Dickens invokes the traditional story—for example, in the quotation with which I began this essay, or in the following selection, which is taken from a speech Dickens gave in 1843 at the First Annual Soiree of the Athenaeum in Manchester:

The man who lives from day to day by the daily exercise in his sphere of hand or head, and seeks to improve himself in such a place as the Athenaeum, acquires for himself that property of soul which has in all times upheld struggling men in every degree, but self-made men especially and always. He secures to himself that faithful companion which, while it has ever lent the light of its countenance to men of rank and eminence who have deserved it, has ever shed its brightest consolations on men of low estate and almost hopeless means. It took its patient seat beside Sir Walter Raleigh in his dungeon-study in the Tower; and it laid its head upon the block with More. But it did not disdain to watch the stars with Ferguson, the shepherd's boy; it walked the streets in mean attire with Crabbe; it was a poor barber here in Lancashire with Arkwright; it was a tallow-chandler's son with Franklin; it worked at shoemaking with Bloomfield in his garret; it followed the plough with Burns; and, high above the noise of loom and hammer, it whispers courage, even at this day. (Fielding 48)

Here Dickens even more closely follows the model of self-help texts as he connects the work of the man who "seeks to improve himself" in the present day with the work of famously successfully men who also persevered to improve themselves (and their socioeconomic positions). Or, to offer an example from the end of his career, from his September 1869 address to the Birmingham and Midland Institute: "The one serviceable, safe, certain, remunerative, attainable quality in every study and in every pursuit is the quality of attention. My own invention or imagination, such as it is, I can most truthfully assure you, would never have served me as it has, but for the habit of commonplace, humble, patient, daily, toiling, drudging attention" (Fielding 406). I quote these passages to show the extent to which Dickens endorses and perpetuates the tropes of self-help: that inspiration should be taken from famous examples; that self-help is admirable in all struggling men, but particularly in those who are entirely "self-made;" and that the object is not riches or distinction so much as character, or "property of soul." Dickens even identifies himself as something of a self-help figure, as he owes his success not to his imagination or genius, but to his "toiling, drudging" attention—and these adjectives I think should rightly remind us of Bradley's "slow persistent process" (536; bk. 3, ch. 11). As Bradley would claim, such work gives one the "right to be considered a better man ... with better reasons for being proud" (291; bk. 2, ch. 6).

Why such a discrepancy between fact and fiction? John Carey has argued that by the time Dickens writes Bradley Headstone, "Dickens, formerly a hearty advocate of universal education, now sees it as the breeder of pedantry and social pretensions. Once educated, the lower classes get above themselves. In his decent black coat and waistcoat Headstone looks, Dickens says, like a workman in his holiday clothes" (28).[8] I would suggest, however, that if we consider the speeches Dickens delivered to mechanics' institutes and athenaeums throughout his professional life—for example the selections I have quoted from 1843, 1858, and 1869—we see a definite continuity in his political orientation toward self-help, rather than an evolution or break. Robin Gilmour has argued that when Dickens wrote *Great Expectations*, he was finally able to "understand the ironies of the great expectations which had inspired his own social rise" (109). To further elucidate *how* Dickens's ambivalence takes narrative shape, then, I suggest that Dickens sees two paths for ambition: how the excessive energy of self-help can be channeled toward the inspirational self-help anecdote, or toward the cautionary tale. The chain-maker and coal-pit workers are examples of how self-help works in the Dickensian anecdote, usually directed to the working or lower-middle class; Bradley illustrates how self-help works in the eight-hundred-page Dickensian novel, largely directed to the middle class. Even while he praises self-help in his speeches, in his novels he is aware of how such excessive energy can grow monstrous once it has attained, or been diverted from, its object. Or, perhaps more exactly, he is aware of how excessive energy can become dangerous to the status quo when it is translated into socioeconomic ambition.

As I have argued, however, this excessive ambition is useful for extending and suspending plots. Perhaps we do not find self-help characters such as the "chain-maker in very humble circumstances" or the "two poor brothers" working in a coal-pit in Dickens's novels because even their modest ambitions to improve themselves would, upon encountering the space of the Dickensian novel, grow to monstrous proportions and result in very different sorts of characters. Instead, as if always siphoning off and disciplining the excessive ambition that results in a Uriah Heep or a Bradley Headstone, or perhaps even a Charles Dickens, the Dickensian novel ends with Idleness getting the girl and Industry at the bottom of the river. Or, to increase the cast of characters, Idleness gets the girl, Ambition commits suicide, and Industry (in the form of John Harmon) is rescued from the river and goes on to find his happily ever after.

NOTES

1. This influence was not lost on Smiles's reviewers. In its notice of *Self-Help*, the *New Quarterly Review* observed that "[o]f all the works published by the Society for the Diffusion of Useful Knowledge, none was more popular than the little treatise on 'The Pursuit of Knowledge under Difficulties.' The present volume is written on a similar subject" (430).

2. To some degree this parallels the phenomenon John Carey has traced in Dickens, that, "[t]he savages and the cynics, the Quilps and the Scrooges, who have all the vitality, are, in the end, tritely punished or improbably converted" (Carey 16). I understand ambition to be an especially troubled category of vitality in Dickens, as it tends to lead to characters being punished or killed, without the chance to convert.

3. Carlyle similarly invokes negative connotations of "ambition" when he describes Cromwell: "A man of ability, infinite talent, courage, and so forth: but he betrayed the Cause! Selfish ambition, dishonesty, duplicity; a fierce, coarse, hypocritical

Tartufe; turning all that noble Struggle for constitutional Liberty into a sorry farce played for his own benefit: this and worse is the character they give of Cromwell" (179).

4. Bradley's character is the site for this tension between suppression and extension at the textual level as well. Joel Brattin, in "Dickens' Creation of Bradley Headstone," examines how Dickens overwrites, cuts out, and revises Bradley's character in the manuscript. When a number is short, Dickens adds more content to Bradley; occasionally he does this to excess and must cut extra scenes from the text. Even with sentence-level revisions, Brattin argues, many of Dickens's changes focus on finding the right expression of Bradley's character. I would suggest that this tendency Brattin has isolated has much to do with how Dickens's narrator identifies with Bradley and then retreats.

5. Robert Kiely, for example, has noted that "...[i]n tracing a meaningless design through the streets of the city, [Eugene] behaves like a contemptuous and cynical author baiting a gullible reader while refusing to deliver a message" (278).

6. Brooks writes that, whereas "the *Bildungsroman* seems to imply progress, a leading forth, and developmental change, Pip's story—and this may be true of other nineteenth-century educative plots as well—becomes more and more as it nears its end the working through of past history, an attempted return to the origin as the motivation of all the rest, the clue to what must else appears, as Pip puts it to Miss Havisham, a 'blind and thankless' life" (134). In contrast, Bradley repeats without the possibility of using his past history to develop; we have several clues to suggest that Bradley has not come to terms with his own rise from pauper lad to schoolmaster, most notably when he accuses Eugene of casting "insinuations at [his] bringing-up" (291; bk. 2, ch. 6).

7. As Jordan has observed, Uriah and David are in fact quite similar—from their social ambitions, to their love interests, to, most importantly for this argument, their industriousness (78). It would seem, then, that it is not industriousness and idleness that are being opposed in *David Copperfield*, but types of ambition: ambition that is pursued, as Jordan writes of David, "under the cover of moral superiority" (78), and ambition that is made too visible.

8. Carey's political reading of Dickens—that Dickens negates self-help without proposing a positive path by which such a pauper child might acquire an education—becomes more clear in the following full passage: "[Bradley] might have made a good sailor if, when a pauper child, he had taken to the sea instead of to learning. As it is, his learning is merely mechanically acquired. Needless to say, Dickens doesn't explain what the alternative ways of acquiring learning might be" (28). I read Bradley less as a representative of a true type, and more as a placeholder for the threatening excesses of ambition; less as a political statement against universal education, and more as a projection of Dickens's own ambition.

WORKS CITED

Brattin, Joel. "Dickens' Creation of Bradley Headstone." *Dickens Studies Annual* 14 (1985): 147–65.

Brooks, Peter. *Reading for the Plot: Design and Intention in Narrative*. Cambridge: Harvard UP, 1984.

Carey, John. *The Violent Effigy: A Study of Dickens' Imagination*. London: Faber, 1973.

Carlyle, Thomas. *On Heroes, Hero-Worship, and the Heroic in History*. Ed. Michael K. Goldberg. Berkeley: U of California P, 1993.

Chesterton, G. K. *Charles Dickens: A Critical Study*. New York: Dodd, Mead, 1907.

Craik, George Lillie. *The Pursuit of Knowledge under Difficulties*. London: W. Clowes, 1830–31. 2 vols.

Dickens, Charles. *Our Mutual Friend*. Ed. Adrian Poole. New York: Penguin, 1997.

———. *The Pickwick Papers*. Ed. Mark Wormald. New York: Penguin, 2003.

———. *The Speeches of Charles Dickens: A Complete Edition*. Ed. K. J. Fielding. Oxford: Clarendon, 1960.

Flaubert, Gustave. *L'Éducation Sentimentale*. Paris: A. Quantin, 1885.

Gilmour, Robin. "Dickens and *Great Expectations*." *The Idea of the Gentleman in the Victorian Novel*. London: George Allen and Unwin, 1981.

Hecimovich, Gregg A. "The Cup and the Lip and the Riddle of *Our Mutual Friend*." *ELH* 62.4 (1995): 955–77.

Jordan, John. "The Social Sub-Text of *David Copperfield*." *Dickens Studies Annual* 14 (1985): 61–92.

Kiely, Robert. "Plotting and Scheming: The Design of Design in *Our Mutual Friend*." *Dickens Studies Annual* 12 (1983): 267–83.

Kucich, John. *Excess and Restraint in the Novels of Charles Dickens*. Athens: U of Georgia P, 1981.

Meckier, Jerome. "*Great Expectations* and *Self-Help*: Dickens Frowns on Smiles." *Journal of English and Germanic Philology* 100.4 (2001): 537–54.

Orwell, George. *Dickens, Dali, and Others: Studies in Popular Culture*. New York: Cornwall Press, 1946.

Oxford English Dictionary Online. "Ambition." Oxford: Oxford UP, 2010. 10 June 2010 <www.oed.com>.

Robbins, Bruce. *Upward Mobility and the Common Good: Toward a Literary History of the Welfare State*. Princeton: Princeton UP, 2007.

Sedgwick, Eve Kosofsky. *Between Men: English Literature and Male Homosocial Desire*. New York: Columbia UP, 1985.

"Self-help, with Illustrations—Character and Conduct." *New Quarterly Review* 8.32 (1859): 430.

Slater, Michael. *Charles Dickens*. New Haven: Yale UP, 2009.

Smiles, Samuel. *Self-Help: With Illustrations of Character, Conduct, and Perseverance*. Oxford: Oxford UP, 2002.

Welsh, Alexander. *The City of Dickens*. Oxford: Clarendon, 1971.

———. *From Copyright to Copperfield: The Identity of Dickens*. Cambridge: Harvard UP, 1987.

Wilson, Angus. "The Heroes and Heroines of Dickens." *Bloom's Modern Critical Views: Charles Dickens*. Ed. Harold Bloom. New York: Chelsea, 2006. 83–90.

Woloch, Alex. *The One vs. the Many: Minor Characters and the Space of the Protagonist in the Novel.* Princeton: Princeton UP, 2003.

The Storm at the Lighthouse by Wilkie Collins, with an Introduction, Textual Notes, and Appendix

Robert C. Hanna

Wilkie Collins composed his first surviving original play, The Storm at the Lighthouse, *between September 1854 and May 1855. The original text of the play is published here for the first time. Sometime prior to June 1856, Collins shortened the play and retitled it* The Lighthouse. *This version was translated into French by Émile Forgues and is the only previously published edition. Textual notes compare these two versions, the only ones preserved entirely in Collins's hand. Collins's play is noteworthy in Dickens studies, as well. Charles Dickens was the first to recognize the play's dramatic possibilities, producing, directing, and acting in its premiere at Tavistock House in June 1855. An introduction includes a summary of* The Storm at the Lighthouse, *an examination of its themes of guilt and forgiveness in writings of both Collins and Dickens, influences of the 1827 play* Trente Ans *on both Collins and Dickens, a summary of major differences between Collins's 1853 short story "Gabriel's Marriage" and his reworking of that story into* The Storm at the Lighthouse, *and an examination of the four surviving manuscripts, including locales mentioned therein. An appendix contains the play's performance history during Collins's lifetime.*

Dickens Studies Annual, Volume 44, Copyright © 2013 by AMS Press, Inc. All rights reserved.   DOI 10.7756/dsa.044.014.289-364

Acknowledgments

The Storm at the Lighthouse by Wilkie Collins and textual notes based on his revision of the play as *The Lighthouse* are published here for the first time, owing to the generous permission of Mrs. Faith Clarke, great-granddaughter of Wilkie Collins. I am most grateful for her interest in and support of this project, from my very first contact with her through the project's completion.

The National Art Library of the Victoria and Albert Museum, The New York Public Library, and The British Library kindly granted permission for my examination of their respective holdings of the four surviving manuscripts.

Bethany Lutheran College in Mankato, Minnesota, once again made it possible for me to access original manuscripts. Specifically, I thank President Dan R. Bruss, Dean of Academic Affairs Eric K. Woller, and Bethany Lutheran College's Faculty Development Committee.

Stanley Friedman, one of the editors of *Dickens Studies Annual*, was exceptionally helpful in guiding my presentation of content, analysis, text, and textual notes. As always, it has been a great pleasure to work with him.

David Ramm, Editor-in-Chief at AMS Press, could not be more supportive and patient, each and every time I have the opportunity to work with him. I cannot adequately express my appreciation for his editorial assistance and expertise, but I am glad that I can acknowledge and thank him.

I dedicate this publication to Emily Hanna, who enthusiastically provided invaluable assistance, from deciphering manuscript text, to improving commentary wording, to proofreading all draft versions.

Introduction

Wilkie Collins was not yet widely known as an author when he first met Charles Dickens in 1851. His signed, published credentials then consisted of two short stories, a biography of his father, a novel, and a book of travel essays.[1] Dickens's desire to meet Collins was not based on these publications. Rather, Collins already had amateur theatrical acting experience,[2] and Dickens was in need of an additional amateur player for his acting company. Dickens had known Collins's father, and Augustus Egg was a mutual friend who arranged their first meeting (Dickens, *Letters* 6: 310). Collins readily accepted the minor role of the valet Smart to Dickens's character Lord Wilmot in Sir Edward Bulwer-Lytton's commissioned play *Not So Bad as We Seem* (Clarke 58).

In 1852, Collins began contributing to Dickens's journal *Household Words*, founded in 1850. By the end of 1854, Collins had published three short stories in *Household Words*[3] (Lohrli 235), and, independently of Dickens, a Christmas book and his second and third novels.[4] All this time, however, he retained his interest in drama, as is revealed in a letter to his friend Charles Ward, dated 10 September 1854:

> This smooth existence of mine will soon become as ruffled as yours—though in a different way. I have plenty of hard work in prospect—some of it, too, work of a new kind, and of much uncertainty as to results. I mean the dramatic experiments which I have been thinking of, and which you must keep a profound secret from everybody, in case I fail with them. This will be an anxious winter for me. If I were not constitutionally reckless about my future prospects, I should feel rather nervous [two erased words] just now in looking forward to my winter's work. (Collins, *Letters* 127)

Collins seems to have worked on assorted "dramatic experiments." One is referred to in a 21 January 1855 letter to another friend, Edward Pigott. He asked, "How about that ... Play of mine? Has it been sent?" (Collins, *Public Face* 1: 111–12). On 9 June 1855, Collins wrote again to Pigott, "The Play is in *five* acts—I have finished it ... The story is in many important respects altered from the book—and improved in the telling" (125). However, Collins's only surviving play between 10 September 1854 and 9 June 1855 is *The Storm at the Lighthouse*.

As this play has not previously been published, a detailed summary is provided below.

Summary of *The Storm at the Lighthouse*

Act I

Aaron Gurnock, his son Martin, and Jacob Dale are lightkeepers at Eddystone Lighthouse in 1748. A gale has been blowing relentlessly for four weeks, and the men have exhausted their food supply and are near starvation. Delirious and weak, Aaron has a confession to make, not only to ease his conscience, but also to fulfill the command of a ghost who has been haunting him in his dreams.

Aaron asks Martin if he recalls some seven or eight years ago when his mother was alive and the family lived on a farm on the coast of Cornwall. Martin remembers well, including being sent away with his mother to live with her relatives. Aaron explains that this was caused by debt so great that he was at risk of imprisonment. No sooner had his family departed, than an old companion, Benjamin Tranter, arrived and moved into the farmhouse. Tranter was equally poor, and the two men discussed how they might raise money.

One night, a lady arrived at the farmhouse, alone with her pony and saddlebags. Aaron describes her appearance in great detail, so vividly does he remember her. The lady explained that she had been riding in the misty fog from the sea, and had lost her servant. She now needed shelter for the night.

Aaron showed her to his wife's room, while Tranter took the pony to the stable. Tranter then apparently wanted to sleep and left Aaron sitting alone in the kitchen. Aaron himself soon dozed in his chair.

Suddenly, Aaron awoke to the sight of Tranter with a saddle bag and a bloody knife that dripped one drop of blood on the kitchen table, the same table before Aaron and Martin now. Tranter had cut her throat. Aaron refused to take any of the lady's money, but he did help Tranter place her body in Daw's Cave, used by smugglers and inaccessible during high tide. Tranter drove the pony off a cliff onto the rocks below and departed. When a party came searching for the lady, known as Lady Grace, only the pony was found. Daw's Cave was empty from the outgoing tide, and the people concluded that she had fallen off the cliff in the fog and had been washed out to sea. It is Lady Grace's ghost who has been speaking to Aaron in his dreams.

Martin is terrified by his father's participation in a murder, and angered by his father's protecting Tranter through his silence. Aaron reveals that Tranter was later killed in a public house fight and insists that he himself is innocent of murder. His words and behavior, however, make it clear that he has been living with a deep sense of guilt. Martin now feels so degraded by being Aaron's son that he believes he can no longer marry Phoebe Dale, Jacob Dale's daughter.

Jacob calls below that the fog is lifting and he sees a rescue boat arriving from shore. Pilot Samuel Furley is accompanied by fishermen, relief lightkeepers, and Phoebe. In a scene of comic relief, Furley prepares food for the starving men and has difficulty in making Jacob and Aaron eat slowly and safely. Furley also calls for a cheerful song from Phoebe, as all will now be well. Furley and the crew heartily join in the chorus.

Nonetheless, there is underlying tension during the rescue scene. Aaron is convinced that either someone has overheard his confession or Martin will reveal it to others. Martin keeps Phoebe away from Aaron, and then watches his father so intently that he seems not to care when she tells him about her own suffering while he was stranded.

Just after the food has revived Aaron, Martin, and Jacob, everyone hears an emergency gunshot from a ship in distress, soon seen bearing directly toward the rocks beneath the lighthouse. The only hope of saving any lives is from lowering rope from the lighthouse. Phoebe screams when she sees people engulfed by the waves, but Aaron shrieks in terror when Phoebe tells everyone the name she sees on the doomed ship: *The Lady Grace*.

Act II

The second act commences with another scene of comic relief. Between acts, only a few sailors and a lady passenger were rescued. Furley, the fishermen, and the rescued sailors discuss whom or what they have most to thank for the saved lives. Much of the debate centers on two different rope manufacturers, one from Falmouth and the other from Plymouth. This discussion permits the details of the offstage rescue to be explained.

Martin continues to shun Phoebe, which Jacob cannot but notice. Phoebe is quieter than usual and sad. Furley tries to cheer up all three with conversation but fails and cannot account for everyone's strange behavior. Furley has even noticed that Aaron is "looking as suspiciously at every man of our boat's crew, as if he thought we were all in league to rob and murder him before we go ashore."

Furley leaves for another room, and, in spite of Phoebe's protestations, her father decides to confront Martin with his unloving and unkind behavior toward his fiancée. Martin dares not confess what Aaron told him, but insists that he loves Phoebe just as much as ever. Jacob gives Martin half an hour to explain all, or he will end Phoebe's engagement to Martin. Offstage, Phoebe has been consulting with the rescued lady, while onstage Martin tries to avoid Aaron.

Aaron becomes angry and asks Martin for the meaning of his disrespectful behavior toward his parent. Martin reluctantly recounts details of Aaron's confession, all of which Aaron denies as he becomes enraged against Martin. Aaron finally calms down and explains that everything he supposedly confessed never occurred and that he must have been speaking of the dreams and visions of a starved man. Just when Martin is nearly convinced of his father's innocence, a woman approaches the father and son from behind. She is dressed precisely as Aaron had described the murdered lady. She reveals herself to them and announces that Aaron's original confession was true.

Aaron believes he is seeing the ghost of the woman whose murder he helped to conceal, and soon loses consciousness. The woman then tells Martin that she is Lady Grace, explains why the wrecked ship was named after her, and how she was placed in Daw's Cave still alive. She was found and rescued by smugglers, only to be captured with the smugglers by French sailors during the Seven Years' War. She spent her captivity helping her captured and wounded countrymen. She learned enough from Phoebe and from overhearing Aaron to pronounce Martin fit to marry Phoebe.

Aaron recovers from fainting, and when Martin relates the good news of the survival of Lady Grace, he asks, "Whose hand helped to lay her in the Daw's Cave where the cruel sea might take her? What atonement can my bitterest repentance offer to her? Forgive me? How can she forgive me?"

Lady Grace offers her hand to Aaron and replies, "Thus! Take it. I entreat, I command you to take it. The privilege of forgiving is a right, Aaron Gurnock, that we may all insist on." Everyone then prepares to take the boat back to shore. Jacob has apologized for having doubted Martin, and Phoebe and Martin are reconciled. The chorus from Act I is reprised by everyone who is offstage.

Dickens's Reaction to *The Storm at the Lighthouse*

Collins derived much of *The Storm at the Lighthouse* from his 1853 contribution to *Household Words*, "Gabriel's Marriage." When he completed this play, he had enough confidence as a playwright to write to Dickens[5] and ask him to read it, perhaps mentioning (or perhaps hoping that Dickens would recognize) its short story origin. On 11 May 1855, Dickens wrote back, "I will read the Play with great pleasure if you will send it to me—of course will at any time, with cordial readiness and unaffected interest, do any such thing. 'I am here' (to adopt [John] Forster's last sonorous form of speech), for that purpose" (Dickens, *Letters* 7: 616).

Dickens immediately recognized the play's dramatic possibilities, and on 20 May he shared with Clarkson Stanfield a proposed dramatic experiment of his own:

> I have a little Lark in contemplation, if you will help it to fly. Collins has done a Melo Drama (a regular old-style Melo Drama), in which there is a very good notion. I am going to act it, as an experiment, in the childrens' *[sic]* Theatre here—I, Mark [Lemon], Collins, Egg, and my daughter Mary.... I want to make the stage large; and shouldn't have room for above five and twenty spectators.[6] (7: 624–25)

Dickens further explained to Angela Burdett Coutts on 24 May that "Mr. Collins has written an odd Melo Drama, the whole action of which (of course it is short) takes place in a lighthouse. He shewed it to me for advice, and some suggestions that I made to him involved a description of how such a thing ought to be done in a Theatre" (7: 629).

By 31 May, Dickens was able to report to Collins:

> Lemon assures me that the Parts and Promptbook are to arrive to day. Why they have not been here two days, I cannot for the life of me make out. In case they *do* come, there is a good deal in the way of clearing the ground, that you and I may do before the first Rehearsal *[sic]*. Therefore, will you come and dine at 6 tomorrow (Friday) and give the evening to it? (7: 635)

Within about one month of Dickens's having first read *The Storm at the Lighthouse*, he enlarged the stage of his children's theater, commissioned scenery, cast the parts, rehearsed the play under the new title *The Lighthouse*, and invited select audiences to witness the play's dramatic effectiveness during the 15 June dress rehearsal and its 16, 18, and 19 June performances.

Guilt and Forgiveness in the Writings of Collins and Dickens

Collins's first literary examination of the themes of guilt and forgiveness is found in his 1852 novel *Basil: A Story of Modern Life*. Basil is the second son of a wealthy English gentleman who is overly proud of his ancestral heritage, which predates the Norman Conquest of 1066. The father teaches his children "that to disgrace our family ... was the one fatal crime which could never be forgotten and never be pardoned" (1: 6; ii). Nevertheless, Basil risks such a disgrace by secretly courting and marrying Margaret Sherwin, a linen-draper's daughter. In seeking Margaret's father's approval for the secret marriage, Basil reveals his strategy to overcome his own father's disapproval:

> "For instance, when the marriage was completed, past all hindrance or opposition, I might introduce your daughter to my father's notice—without disclosing who she was—and leave her, gradually and unsuspectedly, to win his affection and respect (as with her beauty, elegance, and amiability, she could not fail to do), while I waited until the occasion was ripe for confessing everything. Then if I said to him, 'This young lady, who has so interested and delighted you, is my wife,' do you think, with that powerful argument in my favour, he could fail to give us his pardon?" (1: 218–19; x)

Basil is so certain of his lack of any guilt in marrying the woman he loves, that he views his father's certain displeasure as a minor obstacle to be overcome through his certain granting of forgiveness.

However, Collins has more in store for Basil—and the reader—than is first realized. Margaret's love for Basil is a sham. Once their marriage is made public, she intends to live in luxury as a lady. Worse, she is under the influence of her father's chief clerk, who has designs on her virtue and is successful, even gaining her acquiescence, all of which Basil hears from a hotel room next to theirs. Basil now feels a real guilt that he has brought on both himself and his entire family.

Basil intends never to see Margaret again. However, he relents when he learns that she has contracted typhus and is calling for him on her deathbed. He hears her confession of guilt and sheds "tears that did not humiliate me; for I knew, while I shed them, that I had forgiven her" (3: 190; vii). Margaret hears no words of forgiveness from Basil. She murmurs that Basil should leave her forsaken, after which she dies.

At the novel's conclusion, the forgiveness that Basil receives from his father is clear but undeveloped. After Basil banishes himself from his family, he suffers a mental and physical breakdown, and is returned home unconscious and nearly dead. He is nursed back to health and simply relates of his father, after the fact, that "I never, to my own knowledge, gave him any course to repent the full and loving reconciliation which took place between us" (3: 287; Letters in Conclusion).

In 1853, Collins replaces the differing perspectives on guilt by a father and son in *Basil* with consequences of erroneously perceived guilt on three generations of a family in "Gabriel's Marriage." While the plot summary below will demonstrate a different and sustained examination of guilt and forgiveness, the specific quotations should be noted, as they contain wording Collins retains in his reworking of "Gabriel's Marriage" into *The Storm at the Lighthouse* in 1854 or 1855.

"Gabriel's Marriage" is set on the coast of Brittany during the early years of the French Revolution. A fisherman's family resides in a cottage: François Sarzeau, his ailing father (always called "grandfather"), his two sons (Gabriel and Pierre), and his even younger daughters. Gabriel is recovering from an injury, so that Pierre accompanies François to aid in fishing. A ferocious storm suddenly arises, and grandfather believes drops of water are falling at the foot of his bed, signifying his son and grandson's deaths at sea, as well as his own impending death.

Grandfather Sarzeau has a deathbed confession to make to Gabriel alone. Over ten years ago, just before Gabriel's mother died, a young man with a knapsack arrived at the cottage at night, seeking shelter until morning. François saw that the stranger kept banknotes in his pocketbook, and, grandfather says, François "looked at me in a way I didn't like" (152). Grandfather stepped outside the cottage for no more than ten minutes, only to see through a window that François was holding a knife over the sleeping stranger. Almost immediately, grandfather saw François carrying the stranger's body out of the cottage, only to be threatened with death if he did not help hide the body within Druid ruins known as "The Merchant's Table." Fearing his son, grandfather has never spoken of this to anyone. He tells Gabriel to seek the stranger's bones and bury them properly.

The next morning, François and Pierre return, unharmed by the storm. With what little strength remains, grandfather quickly tells Gabriel that last night's story was merely the result of a light-headed mind. He then dies, leaving Gabriel in doubt as to the truth, and in doubt as to his fitness to marry his fiancée, Rose. François demands to know what grandfather told Gabriel, but the latter speaks only vaguely of guilt from knowledge of a crime. François calls his father a fool, yet keeps a close eye on Gabriel, especially when Gabriel searches "The Merchant's Table." Finding no remains, Gabriel dismisses grandfather's story and ceases to worry about being "the son of an assassin and a robber" (184). He may now proceed to marry Perrine, because, as he exclaims, "I am the son of as honest a man as there is in Brittany!" (157). However, François renews Gabriel's doubts when he calls him a spy and tells him in anger, "An innocent man and a spy are bad company. Go and denounce me, you Judas in disguise!" (182).

Meanwhile, Perrine's father learns that his name is on the list of those denounced as enemies of the Revolution. He deems it essential for Gabriel to marry Perrine as quickly as possible, so that she will have a protector, should he be executed or taken away. Reluctantly, Gabriel agrees. Father Paul, a priest who has devoted himself to protecting the peasants from the Revolutionists, will perform the ceremony. However, Gabriel is so noticeably distressed that Father Paul takes him aside to learn what troubles him. Gabriel unburdens his conscience by revealing grandfather's story. Father Paul shows a scar on his neck and presents himself as the stranger whose life was attempted, but not actually taken, while he slept in the cottage.

Father Paul explains that when he regained consciousness at "The Merchant's Table," he was being searched by two smugglers, who used the location for storing goods and letters. He promised them a reward if they would spare his life, aid his recovery, and return him to Paris, all of which subsequently occurred. Gabriel can now marry Perrine as a fit husband.

Father Paul insists on meeting François after the marriage. Gabriel takes the priest to François, who violently trembles before the only other man alive who has firsthand knowledge of the robbery and attempted murder. Father Paul forgives François, but this is reported only after the fact, similar to Collins's treatment of scenes of forgiveness in *Basil*. It is not until Collins composes *The Storm at the Lighthouse* that he presents an actual scene of forgiveness, along with an explicit rationale for its bestowal.

In light of Dickens's enthusiastic response to *The Storm at the Lighthouse*, a few observations about his own literary treatment of the themes of guilt and forgiveness might prove of interest. Among Dickens's fifty-six sketches collected as *Sketches by Boz*, with such a wide variety of topics and themes, it should not be surprising to find examples of a literary treatment of any common themes, including guilt and forgiveness. Five examples demonstrate how differently Dickens was able to treat these themes in the short space of paragraphs within short sketches.

In "A Christmas Dinner," the arrival of "poor aunt Margaret" prompts grandmamma to become "rather stiff and stately; for Margaret married a poor man without her consent, and poverty not being a sufficiently weighty punishment for her offence, has been discarded by her friends, and debarred the society of her dearest relatives." Setting aside any consideration of grandmamma's guilt in causing her daughter to suffer, Dickens shows "happiness and harmony" restored after Margaret "throws herself, sobbing, on her mother's neck" (237–38).

Dickens presents a far more disturbing version of guilt and forgiveness in "A Visit to Newgate." He takes the reader to the condemned ward of the prison and focuses, in part, on a prisoner who has "neglected in his feverish restlessness the timely warnings of his spiritual consoler" and is now powerless to turn to "the Almighty Being, from whom alone he can seek mercy and forgiveness, and before whom his repentance can alone avail" (225). Unable to turn to God, the prisoner is glad to turn to his wife and "fall on his knees before her and fervently beseech her pardon for all the unkindness and cruelty that wasted her form and broke her heart!" (226). This, too, is impossible; his wife appears but in his final dream.

In what could have become another prison scene, Dickens, in "The Hospital Patient," describes a pale prisoner who is forced to accompany two magistrates to a hospital, for possible identification by a victim as her assailant. "'Jack,' she tells him, 'they shall not persuade me to swear your life away. He didn't do it, gentlemen. He never hurt me.'" She then whispers to Jack, "'I hope God Almighty will forgive me all the wrong I have done, and the life I have led'" (258). In a few seconds more, she dies.

Then, in what is similar to a dream scene, Dickens offers a series of stream of consciousness vignettes, examining clothing and populating the garments from his imagination in "Meditations in Monmouth Street." Yet in the midst of these pleasant speculations, he includes a "coarse round frock, with a worn cotton neckerchief" that must mean "banishment or the gallows." Dickens sees the man giving anything to be a boy once again, "restored to life, but for a week, a day, an hour, a minute, only for so long a time as would enable him to say one word of passionate regret to, and hear one sound of heartfelt forgiveness from, the cold and ghastly form that lay rotting in the pauper's grave!"—his mother (86).

Finally, in "The Drunkard's Death," Dickens captures the essence of Aaron Gurnock's confession to Martin in *The Storm at the Lighthouse*:

> It is a dreadful thing to wait and watch for the approach of death; to know that hope is gone, and recovery impossible; and to sit and count the dreary hours through long, long, nights—such nights as only watchers by the bed of sickness know. It chills the blood to hear the dearest secrets of the heart, the pent-up, hidden secrets of many years, poured forth by the unconscious helpless being before you; and to think how little the reserve, and cunning of a whole life will avail, when fever and delirium tear off the mask at last. Strange tales have been told in the wanderings of dying men; tales so full of guilt and crime, that those who stood by the sick person's couch have fled in horror and affright, lest they should be scared to madness by what they heard and saw; and many a wretch has died alone, raving of deeds, the very name of which has driven the boldest man away. (516–17)

Dickens more fully explores these themes in his novels immediately preceding Collins's composition of *The Storm at the Lighthouse* and its revision as *The Lighthouse*, as demonstrated by Dennis Walder in *Dickens and Religion*. Of *Dombey and Son* (1846–48), Walder writes:

> The challenging, broader implications of Mr Dombey's treatment of his daughter [Florence] are powerfully present in the narrator's last warning to the recalcitrant father: 'Awake, unkind father! Awake, now sullen man! The time is flitting by; the hour is coming with an angry tread. Awake!' (ch. xliii). Ruin follows. And yet there is hope, too, in Florence's infinite loving forgiveness, movingly expressed on her return to the lonely, broken figure (ch. lix). At last Mr Dombey feels 'oh, how deeply!—all that he had done,' and begs God for forgiveness (ch. lix). (137)

In *David Copperfield* (1849–50), Walder recounts Mr. Peggotty's initial reaction to his niece's elopement with Steerforth: "At first Mr Peggotty tries to rush out in wild pursuit of his niece, prepared even to drown her seducer" (152). However, when Mr. Peggotty is finally reunited with Emily, his response is "accepting back his 'dear child' in compassionate forgiveness," being reminded of the dust in which 'our Saviour' wrote 'with his blessed hand' (ch. li), as he carries out precisely the Christian demand implicit in John 8: 3–11" (153). And in *Bleak House* (1852–53), Walder relates how Esther Summerson's "mother, Lady Dedlock, in effect condemns herself to the 'earthly punishment' inflicted by contemporary mores, and must die, insisting on being 'beyond all hope, and beyond all help,' keeping her secret [of Esther's illegitimate birth] for the sake of Sir Leicester's honour, and not seeking help or forgiveness in her cold isolation (ch. xxxvi)" (168).

When Dickens directed *The Lighthouse* as a home theatrical production in June 1855, he premiered the role of Aaron Gurnock. By August, Dickens had already composed the first four chapters of *Little Dorrit* (Dickens, *Letters* 7: 692). David Payne, in *The Reenchantment of Nineteenth-Century Fiction*, argues convincingly that Dickens was significantly influenced by Collins's play. Just as Martin Gurnock is deeply troubled by his father's guilt in hiding what was believed to be a murder, so is Arthur Clennam deeply troubled by a perceived, but as yet unknown, wrong committed by his deceased father. According to Payne:

> The Clennam plot is a matter of the obstruction of the wishes of the Clennam testator, Arthur's great-uncle. But its specifics remain unknown to Arthur with the destruction of the codicil to that great-uncle's will, just as the story of that obstruction is difficult to reconstruct and virtually impossible to recall. The problem of recalling and construing the past, for which this inheritance plot has itself become a metaphor, is as intractable as remembering and knowing the many meanings of the paternal command "Do Not Forget"—a list that includes the existence of the codicil; Mrs. Clennam's judgment of her own guilt; [and] the relation between Arthur's father and biological mother. (74)

This leads to the interesting question of whether or not anyone influenced Collins himself.

Influence of *Trente Ans* on Collins

No one, as yet, has been able to date the composition of *The Storm at the Lighthouse* more precisely than between 10 September 1854 and 11 May 1855. An examination of the 1827 French play *Trente Ans, ou La Vie d'un Jouer* (*Thirty Years, or The Life of a Gambler*) by Victor Ducange and Dinaux [Jacques Félix Beudin and Prosper Goubaux] may allow a more precise dating of *The Storm at the Lighthouse*. Collins and Dickens attended a performance of *Trente Ans* in Paris on either 12, 13, or 14 February 1855 (Collins, *Letters*: 136–37; Dickens, *Letters* 7: 536), and four plot features are found in both Collins's play and *Trente Ans*, but not in "Gabriel's Marriage."

First, both Aaron Gurnock and Georges de Germany are approaching starvation and eat greedily when finally given food. Second, both men are dreadfully agitated over the appearance of blood. Third, Aaron has an evil companion, Benjamin Tranter, while Georges has an evil companion, Warner, and each pair works together to conceal a body. Fourth, debt contributes to each man's secret past. If Collins did adapt these plot elements from *Trente Ans*, then his own play's composition would be between 21 February and 11 May 1855, based on his manuscript's notation of his London residence of 17 Hanover Terrace, to which he returned home from Paris on 21 February (Collins, *Public Face* 1: 116).

Even if Collins composed *The Storm at the Lighthouse* prior to his seeing *Trente Ans*, making all four similarities between the two plays entirely coincidental, Collins was deeply impressed by the performance. He discussed the performance thirty-two years later with his friend Frank Archer. When Archer asked him if Dickens's account of the play in Forster's biography (100–01) was accurate, Collins replied, "Certainly. It is not one whit exaggerated. Dickens and I saw the play together, and at the end of one of the acts we were so utterly overcome that we both sat for a time perfectly silent!" (Archer 303).

Influence of *Trente Ans* on Dickens

Trente Ans premiered in Paris at Théâtre de la Porte Saint-Martin on 19 June 1827, with twenty-six-year-old Frédérick Lemaître in the lead role of Georges de Germany (Ducange 163). Georges is so addicted to gaming tables that he is heedless of the harm he brings to his father, wife Amélie, and children. His ongoing monetary losses lead him to theft and murder. The play portrays thirty years of Georges's life by placing Act 1 in 1790, Act 2 in 1805, and Act 3 in 1820.

When Dickens and Collins saw Lemaître reprise his role at Théâtre de l'Ambigu-Comique in February 1855, the actor was now fifty-four years old. Dickens wrote to John Forster:

Incomparably the finest acting I ever saw, I saw last night at the Ambigu.... Old Lemaître plays his famous character, and never did I see anything, in art, so exaltedly horrible and awful. In the earlier acts he was so well made up, and so light and active, that he really looked sufficiently young. But in the last two, when he had grown old and miserable, he did the finest things, I really believe, that are within the power of acting.... He said two things in a way that alone would put him far apart from all other actors. One to his wife, when he has exultingly shewn her the money [from a murder], and she has asked him how he got it—"I found it"—and the other to his old companion and tempter [Warner], when he was charged by him with having killed that traveller, and suddenly went headlong mad and took him by the throat and howled out, "It wasn't I who murdered him— it was Misery!" And such a dress; such a face; and, above all, such an

This photograph by Tourtin, from the collection of M. J. L. Croze, shows Frédéric Lemaître in costume as the gambler in *Trente Ans*, the role that inspired Dickens to act the role of Aaron Gurnock, borrowing from Lemaître's performance. The photograph is included by Frank Archer (the pseudonym used by Frank Bishop Arnold) in his book *An Actor's Notebooks* (London: Stanley Paul, n.d. [1912]).

extraordinary guilty wicked thing as he made of a knotted branch of a tree which was his walking-stick, from the moment when the idea of the murder came into his head! (Dickens, *Letters* 7: 536–37)

Either Dickens condensed part of Act III in relating it to Forster, or Dickens incorrectly recalled two memorable parts of Lemaître's performance as occurring back-to-back. The actor's lunge at Warner's throat is accompanied by his cry, "Hell has sent you here to deliver you to my revenge!" (Ducange 197). His words, "No! It is misery and despair. Come and help me hide it [the corpse]" are said after the two men are again plotting together (199). In either case, Dickens soon impressed others with his own interpretation of Lemaître's performance.

In 1879, Juliet Lady Pollock collaborated with her son Walter Herries Pollock (1850–1926) and published *Amateur Theatricals*. She reported, "Of all professional actors the one whom [Dickens] most resembled was Frédérick Lemaître, and those who have seen that great French player can form some notion of the leading characteristics of our English novelist as a dramatic performer" (13). However, it was not until 1902 that Frederic G. Kitton obtained and published further information from Walter:

> *Apropos* of "The Lighthouse," Mr. Walter Herries Pollock favours me with the following reminiscence: "My mother, Juliet Lady Pollock, wife of the second Baronet, congratulating Dickens most enthusiastically after the performance, presently said, 'There is one actor, and only one, I have ever seen of whom you sometimes remind me—that is Frédérick Lemaître.' Dickens replied, with a twinkle in his eyes, 'Odd you should say that. He is the only actor I have ever tried to take as a model.'" Mrs. [Elizabeth] Yates (herself a distinguished actress) also compared Dickens, in this part, to Lemaître in his best days. (414–15)

A comparison of *Trente Ans* and *The Storm at the Lighthouse* can explain Dickens's desire to premiere the role of Aaron Gurnock, modeled after Lemaître's performance as Georges de Germany. For instance, Warner convinces Georges that Rodolphe, a friend of his wife Amélie's uncle, has seduced her. Georges shoots Rodolphe and then must flee France, to escape apprehension and punishment. Georges becomes more and more suspicious of others, fearful of arrest for debt, theft, and now murder.

Aaron, nearly dead, eases his conscience by confessing to Martin his role in concealing what he believes was murder. As soon as Aaron understands that he and Martin are being rescued, Aaron becomes more and more suspicious of others, fearful of arrest as an accomplice to murder. Aaron's dialogue reveals his distrust of Furley, Phoebe, and finally Martin.

Georges responds with rage to Rodolphe, Amélie, and Warner. Aaron responds with rage to Martin when Martin accuses his father of making him unfit for marriage with Phoebe, as the son of an accomplice to murder. A wide range of facial and emotional responses are available to actors portraying either role, as each man has a terrible past with which to live.

Major Differences between "Gabriel's Marriage" and *The Storm at the Lighthouse*

Before examining major differences among the surviving "Lighthouse" manuscripts, it might be helpful to begin with a summary of major differences between the original short story "Gabriel's Marriage" and its dramatic reworking as *The Storm at the Lighthouse*. The setting shifts from a cottage on the Quiberon Peninsula in the province of Brittany during the 1790s to a lighthouse off the Ram Head Peninsula in the region of Cornwall in 1748.

The names, relationships, and occupations of comparable main characters are as follows:

"Gabriel's Marriage"	*The Storm at the Lighthouse*
François Sarzeau (father, fisherman)	Benjamin Tranter (unrelated, unemployed)
Grandfather Sarzeau (grandfather, retired)	Aaron Gurnock (father, lightkeeper)
Gabriel Sarzeau (son, fisherman)	Martin Gurnock (son, lightkeeper)
Rose Bonan (fiancée of Gabriel)	Phoebe Dale (fiancée of Martin)
Père Bonan (fiancée's father, farmer)	Jacob Dale (fiancée's father, lightkeeper)
Father Paul (Catholic priest)	Lady Grace (humanitarian and nurse)

In the original story, the supernatural element consists of Grandfather Sarzeau's perceiving water dripping into the family's cottage, as well as the White Women, who dig graves for those drowned at sea. In the revised version, Aaron Gurnock is visited in his dreams by the ghost of Lady Grace, who commands him to confess his role in her murder.

As for what is believed to have been an actual murder in both stories, Grandfather Sarzeau swears to keep secret both the murder and the disposal of the body under a Druid stone structure called "The Merchant's Table," used by smugglers. In the revision, Aaron Gurnock swears no oath, but rather chooses to keep secret both the murder and the disposal of the body in "Daw's Cave," used by smugglers.

After Gabriel hears his grandfather's confession and retraction, he seeks confirmation of the confession by examining "The Merchant's Table." He is concerned that he should not marry Rose, but he proceeds with her father's request that he do so. A different scenario occurs in the lighthouse. After Martin hears his father's confession and retraction, he has no means by which he can prove or refute the confession. His inability to act causes Phoebe's father to give him thirty minutes to account satisfactorily for his coldness toward Phoebe, or her father will end the engagement.

Finally, the motivations of the victims of attempted murder differ. Father Paul became a priest, specifically with the intention of serving in Brittany, finding his would-be murderer, and then giving him an opportunity to repent or else denouncing him. Lady Grace always performs charitable deeds during times of peace and serves as a nurse during a time of war. She has no desire to find either her would-be murderer, Benjamin Tranter (already deceased), or his accomplice in hiding the robbery and attempted murder, Aaron Gurnock. Rather, Lady Grace attributes the wreck of her boat on the rocks below the lighthouse to "the mercy of Heaven," in that Aaron can now repent, atone, and be forgiven.

Selection of Text for Publication with Textual Notes

The earliest manuscript of Collins's play seems to be *The Storm at the Lighthouse*, held by the Victoria and Albert Museum National Art Library (reference number Forster MS 115; pressmark Forster 48.D.9). On the inside front cover, Collins signed his name "W. Wilkie Collins" and recorded "17 Hanover Terrace, Regents Park," his residence from August 1850[7] to October 1855 (Gasson 73–74). There are two indications that this could be the original manuscript. First, it demonstrates the hesitations of a first draft, with expected emendations, additions, and deletions. Said deletions are rigorously obliterated with ink. Second, it contains dialogue deleted by thin, straight lines to accommodate Collins's inclusion of Dickens's "little ballad for Mary [Dickens, in the role of Phoebe Dale]—The Story of the Ship's Carpenter and the little boy, in the Shipwreck"[8] (Dickens, *Letters* 7: 628). Collins originally had Samuel Furley ask Phoebe for a cheerful song, to boost the spirits of the three rescued lightkeepers. Collins then added new dialogue to the manuscript, to explain the inclusion of Dickens's rather mournful ballad lyrics, both sung in the play and published in the playbill (Dickens, *Letters* 7: 920).

The Storm at the Lighthouse has been selected for publication, having no prior publication history in this full-length version. The manuscript is entirely in Collins's hand, making it an authoritative source of the text. The care with which Collins subsequently lined through certain dialogue suggests a possible intent to maintain a record of the original wording, now permitting a restoration of that wording here.

The textual notes following *The Storm at the Lighthouse* are based on Collins's revised, shortened version of the play, retitled *The Lighthouse*. This second manuscript is also entirely in Collins's hand, making it authoritative for documenting his alterations within textual notes. This manuscript is held by the New York Public Library (call number Berg Coll m.b. Collins 88p.) and is erroneously dated 1885 in the *Index of Literary Manuscripts* (Rosenbaum and White 676). The date of composition is likely between 20 May 1855, when Dickens wrote to Clarkson Stanfield about producing and acting in *The Storm at the Lighthouse*, as yet unaltered to accommodate Dickens's ballad lyrics (Dickens, *Letters* 7: 624–25), and 13 April 1856, when Dickens wrote to Collins from Paris, "I enclose a letter from Forgues. The book of the Lighthouse accompanies it, which I will bring with me" (8: 86–87).

In this latter letter, Dickens refers to Émile Daurand Forgues (1813–1883), who accurately translated to French the second manuscript, including all the stage directions, and then published the translation in four consecutive issues of *L'Ami de la Maison*, starting with the 3 July 1856 issue.[9] A page was subsequently pasted on the inside front cover of Collins's second manuscript, reading: "L F à H L E/Wilkie Collins [signature]/[obliterated line of text]/This was given by Wilkie Collins/to Emile Forgues his French/translator/Leon Forgues gave it to me in/1866/H L E/Collins [separated from the preceding text and found at the bottom of the page]." Collins's signature and the obliterated line of text are in black ink; all other wording is in pencil.

Léon Forgues was one Émile Forgues's four children. This suggests that Collins returned the manuscript to Forgues as a gift, sometime after 13 April 1856 and, perhaps, October 1859, when Collins dedicated his novel *The Queen of Hearts* to Forgues, writing, in part, "Your excellent translation of *The Lighthouse* had already taught me how to appreciate the value of your assistance" (1: ii).

Other Manuscripts

A third manuscript in an unknown hand is held by the British Library (Manuscripts Catalogue number Add. 52967 H). This manuscript contains the text submitted to the Lord Chamberlain's Office for examination and licensing. It bears a submission date of 31 July 1857 and a licensure for public performance date of 1 August 1857. This is not a fair copy, in that most stage directions are absent.

In contrast to Collins's first two manuscripts, this version contains a prologue written by Dickens, as well as the ballad lyrics Dickens composed for the play's song. The manuscript of the prologue is in the Beinecke Rare Book and Manuscript Library at Yale University (Gimbel Collection, identification number F15), while the manuscript of the ballad is in the University of Michigan's Special Collections Library (Dickens, Charles, 1812–1870. Letters and Miscellany, 1839–1873). The third manuscript also includes a concluding couplet absent from Collins's first two manuscripts. Lady Grace speaks these final words: "Great attribute of *Him* in whom we live / And who forgives us as we do forgive!"

A fourth surviving manuscript is of least importance. With the exception of the title page, the dramatis personae page, and twelve lines of the initial stage directions in Act I, the text is in the handwriting of an unknown amanuensis, who attempted and failed to create a fair copy. Collins's corrections in his own hand are recorded throughout, including making notations where stage directions were miscopied as dialogue.

While the date of the fourth manuscript in unknown, the *Index of English Literary Manuscripts* incorrectly dates the text c. 1855 (Rosenbaum and White 676), an impossibility, as Collins records and dates in his own hand the original 1857 cast from the Royal Olympic Theatre production. The text is basically that of the second manuscript, but with the retention of Lady Grace's concluding couplet from the third manuscript. The major differences are found among the stage directions. The fourth manuscript is also held by the New York Public Library (call number Berg Coll m.b. Collins 53p).

Locales Included in All Four Manuscripts

For the setting of *The Storm at the Lighthouse*, Collins utilized knowledge and experience obtained from his 1850 walking tour of Cornwall, published as *Rambles beyond Railways* in 1851. On 29 July 1850, he wrote to his mother, "You can trace out our route on the large map of England, if you like. From Plymouth we went to St Germans (in Cornwall) by a *boat*" (Collins, *Letters* 63–64). Although Plymouth is in Devonshire and is omitted from *Rambles beyond Railways*, Plymouth is mentioned in *The Storm at the Lighthouse* as the location of a rope-maker. In *Rambles*, Collins does mention walking through Falmouth (112), where he places another rope-maker in the play.

One of Collins's first stops in Cornwall brought him within sight of Eddystone Lighthouse. He writes in *Rambles*, "Not a ship was in sight; but out on the extreme line of the wilderness of grey waters there shone one red, fiery, spark— the beacon of the Eddystone Lighthouse" (43).

Central to the plot of *The Lighthouse* is the revelation of how smugglers rescued Lady Grace from Daw's Cave in Cornwall. Collins further reports in his travel book, "In reference to smuggling, many years have passed without one of those fatal encounters between smugglers and revenue officers which, in other days, gave a dark and fearful character to the contraband trade in Cornwall.... It is only the oldest Cornish men who can give you any account, from personal experience" (108–09). More specifically, Collins writes of "entering a cavern in the rocks, called 'Daw's Hugo' (or Cave). The place is accessible only at low water" (132).

Although not mentioned in *Rambles beyond Railways*, Ram Head, where the last boat had sailed with provisions for the three stranded lightkeepers, was also familiar to Collins. According to Arthur L. Salmon, in *The Cornwall Coast*, "[O]ne of the most frequent and popular trips of the Plymouth pleasure-steamers, and the picturesque spot, once haunted by smugglers, is now, during the summer months, a lively playground of the excursionist.... Southward is Penlee Point, and westward Rame or Ram Head. This is the most southern point of East Cornwall, and the nearest land to Eddystone" (25).

It is interesting to note, as well, that part of *Basil* takes place in Cornwall, and that a miner from Cornwall helps the ailing Basil return home for medical treatment. The miner is named William Penhale, and the only minor character in *The Lighthouse* who is ever called by name is the relief lightkeeper *Penhale*—perhaps a private joke by Collins, while he patiently waited for anyone to ask him about the onetime use of a name entirely unnecessary to his play.

Editorial Decisions Regarding Presentation of Collins's Manuscript's Text

In general, Collins places parentheses around his stage directions, underlines them once, and underlines twice the names of characters mentioned therein. Stage directions presented here are placed in *[italics within brackets]* for two distinct purposes. First, once the dialogue commences, underlined words now uniformly designate dialogue to be spoken with emphasis. Second, for performances of this play, it should prove helpful to both director and cast to see immediately the difference between spoken text and stage direction text. Collins's original spelling, capitalization, and punctuation within stage directions are retained.

As for the left margin names, which indicate who speaks which lines, Collins almost always underlines these names (once or twice), and he sometimes abbreviates them. Said names are here standardized and presented without underlines, for ease of reading. Lastly, in some instances, Collins names a speaker, followed by the speaker's dialogue and stage directions, followed by a renaming of the speaker and the speaker's concluding dialogue. As presented here, the unnecessary second identification of the same speaker is omitted.

Commentary on *The Storm at the Lighthouse* Manuscript

The manuscript is recorded within a hardcover notebook, with a height of 7¾ inches and a width of 5 inches. Leaves original to the notebook contain twenty-five preprinted lines on each side. Neither the cover nor the leaves indicate the notebook's manufacturer. The leaves themselves contain no watermarks.

Some leaves have been cut and removed from the notebook, including at least the first ten leaves. Some of the missing leaves retain evidence of writing on the thin strips of margins still attached to the binding and reused for pasting in new leaves. The notebook now holds sixty-four leaves, each being used on at least one side, with the last page of the play written on the inside back cover. Some leaves are of smaller size, having been partially cut and removed. Other leaves, from different stationery, have been pasted in. Of the sixty-four leaves, fifty-six are original to the notebook.

Text is typically recorded on the notebook's right-hand leaves, and these are usually the hand-numbered pages. However, some unnumbered left-hand leaves contain textual corrections or additions, while some numbered left-hand pages are entirely filled with text. Some page numbers are used twice, such as 29 ½ after 29, and 33b after 33a. The text is in black ink, with a few insertions and deletions in blue ink.

Commentary on *The Lighthouse* Manuscript Used in Textual Notes

The manuscript is recorded within a hardcover notebook, with a height of 6 inches and a width of 4 inches. The notebook is comprised of forty-six originally blank leaves, with no watermarks. Some of the leaves have become detached from the binding, so it is not possible to state with certainty that the binding initially held only forty-six leaves. Moreover, the inside spine of the binding contains a small slip of paper reading "Corlies, Macy & Co." This is the name of a Manhattan stationer on Nassau Street, in business at least as early as 1862. Accordingly, Corlies, Macy & Co. could have repaired the original binding or could have provided a new binding for the manuscript.

With the exception of the title page and corrected stage directions on the reverse of the title page, the remaining used pages are numbered consecutively, from page one through 65. Page 66 is then incorrectly numbered 65, resulting in pagination from the repeated page 65 through 86, instead of the correct identification of these pages as 66 through 87.

Text is recorded entirely in black ink on both sides of every leaf, with the exception of the back side of the forty-fifth leaf and the entirety of the forty-sixth leaf, these latter three pages being entirely unused.

The Storm At The Lighthouse.

A Play In Two Acts

Persons of The Drama.

<u>Aaron Gurnock</u> .	Head Lightkeeper at the Eddystone Lighthouse
<u>Martin Gurnock</u> .	His son. Second Lightkeeper
<u>Jacob Dale</u> .	Third Lightkeeper.
<u>Samuel Furley</u> .	A Pilot.
Fishermen. Sailors. Lightkeepers.	

<u>Lady Grace</u> .
<u>Phoebe Dale</u> .

<u>The Scene</u> is the interior of the second Eddystone
Lighthouse, built by John Rudyerd.
<u>Period</u>, The year 1748

<u>Act I</u> .

[Scene: The Kitchen-Chamber of the Lighthouse. Across the Flat, a Tarpaulin stretched on a line, and hanging to the ground. A Dutch clock just visible above it. On one side, a sliding shutter in the wall, with drawers and lockers below it, and oil cans, spare panes of glass, and strips of chamoy leather hanging about it. On the other side, a fireplace; and beyond that, a door. Before the fireplace a round table standing between a chair and a sea-chest. On the table a candle burning in a lanthorn; a jug of water, and a mug.

Jacob Dale is discovered seated in the chair with a slate on his knees, and his hands crossed listlessly over it. Martin Gurnock is on the sea-chest opposite, with his head and arms resting on the table. A Pause, after the rising of the curtain. Nothing is heard but the whistling of the wind outside, and the crash of the waves against the Lighthouse.]

Jacob   Martin! Martin Gurnock! Look up a bit, lad, I want to speak to you.
    Martin! *[Another pause.]* How the Lighthouse shakes! I thought there was a

lull in the storm an hour ago—now it sounds worse than ever. No hope! no hope of rescue! Before it is calm enough for the provision boat from shore to put off, we shall all have died of starvation on this lonesome rock.—Martin! Oh, Martin, look up and speak to me! *[Martin raises his head slowly.]* How is it with you, lad? You're young and strong: you ought to weather it out longer than your father and me—longer a good deal, Martin.

Martin   My head feels strange—light and dizzy, somehow. I've been dreaming; and yet I hav'nt been asleep. I suppose it's hunger, Jacob—hunger and weakness. *[Raises himself to an upright position on the chest.]*

Jacob   Aye, aye lad, that's the complaint with all three of us now. My   10
head is as dazed as your's. Here's our log-book *[Shows the slate]*—I ca'nt somehow steady my hand and clear my eyesight to make the entry for today—and it's not for want of trying: it is'nt indeed, Martin.

Martin   Today? It _is_ day again, then? Another day!

Jacob   *[Looking round at the clock.]* Just ten in the morning. Here's yesterday's entry:—"December Sixteenth, One Thousand, Seven Hundred, and forty eight"—I can make that out still; but I ca'nt manage to write even so much as:—"December Seventeenth. Wind still blowing a gale from the South West. No hope of relief from the shore."—I ca'nt write as much as that, this morning.   20

Martin   Let me try. *[Takes the slate.]* Any water left in the jug?

Jacob   Yes. Stop a bit; and I'll pour it out for you. *[gives the mug to Martin.]* Does it do you any good?

Martin   Not much. But I think I can write the line in the log for today. *[Writing]* "December 17th. Wind still blowing a gale from the South West. No hope of relief from the shore. Provisions all exhausted."—Has that been put down, Jacob?

Jacob   Two days ago. I wrote it myself. I did'nt say, "Provisions all exhausted"; I only said, "Divided our last morsel into three equal shares." But I suppose it do'nt matter much. When they find us all dead here, they   30
will know well enough what we died of.

Martin   How long is it today, since the boat made her last trip to the lighthouse from shore?

Jacob   Look back on the slate. I ca'nt reckon it in my head.

Martin   *[Reading]* "Eddystone Lighthouse. Monday, nineteenth November. Boat came from the Ram Head, and brought ten days' provision for the three lightkeepers." *[Counting with the slate pencil]* Monday nineteenth to Monday Twenty Sixth—one week. Monday third December—two weeks. Monday Tenth—three weeks. Monday seventeenth—four weeks.—Four weeks, today, Jacob!   40

Jacob   Four weeks of heavy gales on this lonesome rock, ten miles out at sea! Four weeks of weather that no boat could put off in! Four weeks alone here, and only ten days' provisions to stand it out on!

Martin   We ought to have saved more. We ought to have lived on quarter rations the first week.

Jacob   It will be all one soon, Martin. Our life's work in this world is pretty nigh over. A few hours more or less will end it.

Martin   A few hours may bring a lull in the gale—a few hours may bring the boat from shore. While there's life there's hope, Jacob! We've got a little brandy left, hav'nt we?

Jacob   A little better than half a wine-glass full. It's in the wicker bottle, locked up there. *[Points to the locker.]*

Martin   A teaspoonful apiece will keep us alive for today; and who knows   10
what may happen before tomorrow? *[Looks towards the Tarpaulin.]* Has father moved or spoke at all since I have been dreaming here on the table?

Jacob   Not that I have heard. I'm afraid our bringing his bed down here into the warmest room has'nt done much for him.

Martin   Hush! I think I hear him moving. *[Goes to the Tarpaulin: draws a corner of it aside, and looks in.]*

Jacob   How is he?

Martin   Bad, Jacob. Lighter in the head seemingly than either of us two. His eye is wandering; and he moans a kind of gibberish to himself. Can you measure out a spoonful of the brandy?   20

Jacob   I'll try. *[Goes to the locker, and, taking out the bottle, measures the brandy into a wine glass.]* Here! see if you can get him to swallow that.

Martin   *[Takes the glass, and stoops down inside the Tarpaulin; then returns to the table with the empty glass.]* It seemed to quiet him directly. I think he will get to sleep again now.

Jacob   *[Standing by the locker with the teaspoon in his hand.]* Shall we take our shares, before I put the bottle back?

Martin   Do as you like. I shall save mine till the last.

Jacob   So will I then. *[Puts away the bottle and spoon, and returns to his former place at the table. Another pause.]* You said you was a-dreaming,   30
just now, lad—what of?

Martin   Your daughter's cottage ashore, Jacob. I fell into a sort of doze thinking of Phoebe.—When you startled me up, I thought it was holiday-time with me, and that I was taking my pipe in the chimney-corner, and talking to her while she sat at work.

Jacob   A bitter thought, that, for Phoebe's old father away here in the lighthouse; and for you, her husband that was to be, come Christmas-time!

Martin   They must have put up our bans in Church yesterday, for the last time of asking. I fancy I can hear the parson a reading of it—"I publish the bans of marriage between Martin Gurnock, bachelor, and Phoebe Dale,   40
spinster, both of this parish."—I dare say the congregation thought of us, when they heard that.

Jacob   And prayed for us perhaps, lad.

Martin   Prayed for us, likely enough—prayed for old Aaron Gurnock and
          Jacob Dale—prayed for Martin Gurnock when they heard him asked in
          church, and remembered that he was starving out here, with ten miles of
          raging sea between him and his promised wife.
Jacob   And only a year, Martin, since she give you her promise.
Martin   Less: less by a good six weeks. Have you forgotten my getting
          leave on shore, and coming off, when it was over, with Phoebe in the boat?
Jacob   Forgotten? Not I!—I can call it to mind as easy as ever you can.
          I remember her taking me below into the storeroom, poor child. "Why,
          Phoebe," says I, "your two cheeks are as red as my old fishing-cap. What's   10
          Martin been saying to you in the boat?"—"He's been asking me,"—says
          she, and then stops short. "I know what he's been asking of you," says I;
          "and what's more, I know you have said Yes." She looks up at me with
          the tears in her eyes, and nods her head, and puts her arm round my neck,.
          and begins kissing of me. "I know how to come over poor old father," she
          whispers, and kisses of me again.—Ah, Martin! I can remember—I'm not
          past that yet!
Martin   I've got a keepsake of her's—it's only a bit of ribbon that she used
          to wear round her neck on Sundays. I did it up as well as I could, and wore
          it about me, tied by this string. *[Pulls it out of the breast of his jacket.]*—It   20
          is'nt much; but if the boat do'nt get off to help us till too late, I should'nt
          like it to fall into strangers' hands.
Jacob   Keep it hanging outside, as it is now.
Martin   Why? What good will that do?
Jacob   She'll see it; and the sight of it will speak plain enough to her, when
          we have done speaking forever.
Martin   How?
Jacob   How! You do'nt know my girl, Martin, as well as I do. The sea may
          run high; the gale may blow; but when the first boat puts off from shore for
          the lighthouse, whether it's day or whether it's night, safe or not safe, risk   30
          or no risk, my Phoebe will be one of the crew!
Martin   One of the crew! Suppose they should come too late! Suppose
          Phoebe—? Do'nt let's talk about it anymore, Jacob! It wo'nt bear talking
          of. Let's get to work at something, and stop thinking that way.
Jacob   How much strength have we got left to work with?
Martin   The brandy will help us, if we ca'nt do without it. *[Rises.]* Have
          you been up to the Crow's Nest to look out this morning?
Jacob   Yes, at eight oclock.
Martin   Did you see anything?
Jacob   Towards shore the drizzle was too thick. Out at sea the fog had   40
          lifted. I saw the waves running in from the Atlantic awful high. And when
          I looked through the glass, I thought I saw a ship.
Martin   Was she beating out to sea?

Jacob   That's more than I can tell you. If she was'nt, with such a coast as our's under her lee, her chance in this gale is not worth sixpence.

Martin   I wonder whether it keeps clear to windward still? *[Goes to the sliding-shutter.]*

Jacob   Mind what you're at! That window has not been mended since the sea-gull broke it the other night. Look out for the wash of the spray, Martin—look out!

Martin   I wo'nt keep the shutter back more than a moment. *[Mounts on the locker, and pulls back the shutter. The howling of the wind is heard with sudden violence. He closes the shutter again quickly, and descends from the locker wiping the spray from his face.]*   10

Jacob   Well?

Martin   It looks worse than ever. The fog has come down on us again. Stop here, Jacob, will ye? in case father should want help. *[Going out.]*

Jacob   Where are you going to?

Martin   Up into the Crow's Nest.

Jacob   What for?

Martin   Did I not tell you the fog had come down on us again?—You know what our orders are. "When the Lighthouse is hid in fog, the lightkeepers are to warn ships off the Eddystone rocks, by sounding the gong."—We   20 must do our duty to the last. You stop here with father, while I go up to the gong.

Jacob   Steady there, my lad! It's my turn to keep the gong going; and, as long as I've any life left in me at all, I'll work fair with my mess-mate, turn and turn about.

Martin   Thankee, Jacob—but your strength is'nt equal to it.

Jacob   My strength <u>is</u> equal to it, as long as I can lift my arm from my side. A child could strike upon our lighthouse gong; and I'm equal to child's work any day, famished as I am.—Sit down again, Martin, and let me have my own way! *[Goes to the door—then stops.]* You leave   30 the door open here; so that, if anything happens I can call down the stairs.

Martin   You had much better stop here, and leave the work with the gong to me. I'm fittest for it—I am indeed!

Jacob   No! no!—no more words about that. Give us your hand, lad, before I go. It may be goodbye forever with us two, sooner than we think for. When men have got all their strength pretty nigh starved out, a staircase between them is as bad as a gulph.—God bless you, Martin, and your poor old father too! He's as honest a man as ever stepped; and you are your father's son, every inch of you. It would have been a happy day for me, if   40 I could have seen my Phoebe your wife—

Martin   Do'nt let us despair of that day coming yet. Remember what I said just now—While there's life there's hope.

Jacob   Yes, yes. That's a good saying enough. The worst I know of it is
that it means a deal more to a young man than it does to an old one. Goodbye, Martin. *[Exit]*

Martin   Goodbye, Jacob. Poor old fellow! I wish he had let me do that
work for him. He's too weak for it—I know he's too weak. *[Looks
towards the Tarpaulin]* I do'nt hear father moving. The gong will disturb
him, I am afraid; but that ca'nt be helped—as long as the fog lasts, we are
bound to keep it going. *[Sits down in the chair by the table, turning his
back to the tarpaulin, but leaving the whole of it visible to the audience.]*
Phoebe's keepsake! *[Taking it up in his hand.]*—I ca'nt bear to look at it: 10
I must hide it away again. Poor dear Phoebe! I dare say she was in church
yesterday when the parson put up the bans! *[The first stroke of the gong
reverberates through the lighthouse.]* Brave old Jacob! he's as good as
his word—he's at work already. I wonder if father was much startled by
that first stroke? *[Turns again towards the tarpaulin.]* Shall I look?—
No! not unless he calls. He moans and murmurs about his hunger, whenever he sees me; and I hav'nt a morsel of food to give him.—Oh this
storm! this storm! When will the wind shift and the sea go down? *[Sec-
ond stroke of the gong. The Tarpaulin moves—a hand appears, clutching
at one side of it impatiently.]* I wo'nt give up hoping yet—I wo'nt, for   20
Phoebe's sake. There was a lull in the storm this morning: there may be
another before noon. *[The Tarpaulin is moved aside from behind, and
Aaron Gurnock appears in a sitting position on his bed. He has an old
boat-cloak wrapped round him, which falls to his feet. His face is pale,
his throat bare, his grey hair in disorder.]*

Aaron   *[calling faintly from the bedside.]* Martin! Martin!

Martin   *[not hearing or moving.]* If they come off in the boat in time to save
us; if Phoebe should really, as her father says, make one of the crew, what a
meeting it will be! My heart thumps again when I think of it! *[Third stroke
of the gong. Aaron starts as he hears it; then slowly rises, and advances   30
with difficulty to the back of his son's chair.]* How we shall talk of the
storm at the Lighthouse in after years! How much dearer this great danger
and distress will make us to each other!

Aaron   *[Laying his hand on his son's shoulder.]* Martin!

Martin   Father?—How you startled me!—Do you want to sit up? *[Aaron
nods his head.]* Take my chair then: it's nearest the fire. *[Places his father
in the chair]* Are you cold?

Aaron   No: not cold.

Martin   I thought you could not be, lying down in your clothes, with your
stuff jerkin on, and the great boat-cloak to cover you. Stop; let me get   40
your list shoes. *[Fetches them from the bedside, and puts Aaron's feet into
them.]* There! that's more comfortable now. Are you still hungry?

Aaron   No: not hungry.

Martin There was a lull in the storm, this morning, father—there may be another before long; and then we may look out for the boat. Do you hear?—for the boat—for rescue from the shore.

Aaron No rescue for <u>me</u>.

Martin Yes, yes—for you and for me and for Jacob.

Aaron Where is Jacob?

Martin Up in the Crow's Nest. The sea-fog has come down on us; and he is keeping the gong going. *[Fourth stroke of the gong.]* There! Do you hear? He's as old as you; and yet, you see, he's strong enough for his work still. Do'nt be down-hearted father—hope to the last, like me.   10

Aaron I've done with hope, Martin. I'm dying.

Martin No, no. You're only weak with long fasting.

Aaron I'm dying—dying hard—dying with the horrors on me, to make death dreadful!

Martin *[aside]* His mind wanders.

Aaron *[overhearing him.]* Yes! My mind—that's it. How did you know it was my mind?

Martin I did not know it. I spoke at random—do'nt be angry!

Aaron *[Vacantly.]* That's what comes of being a scholar. My son is a great scholar; and he knows it's my mind.—Martin! do'nt tell Jacob.   20

Martin Do'nt tell what?

Aaron It's on my mind: it's eating of me away by inches. I ca'nt think for it—I ca'nt say my prayers for it—I ca'nt die for it. But do'nt tell Jacob!

Martin *[aside.]* What can he mean?

Aaron Jacob is an honest fellow in his way; but he ca'nt keep a secret. He'd tell upon me. He'd get frightened, and go ashore to the magistrate. Him and me are friends; but he'd hang me for all that.—Do as I bid you, Martin. When I'm dead, it do'nt matter; but while I'm alive, do'nt tell Jacob! *[Fifth stroke of the gong. From this time, the strokes grow gradually fainter; and succeed each other, during the scene between Aaron and* 30 *his son, at longer and longer intervals; so as to convey the impression of increasing weakness in the person making the strokes.]*

Martin What is it I am not to tell Jacob?

Aaron Hav'nt I told you?

Martin No.

Aaron I ca'nt die without telling it to somebody. You're fond of me, Martin. You wo'nt go to the magistrate, for my sake. I'll tell <u>you</u>; and then it will be <u>your</u> secret.

Martin Secret? Magistrate?—Father! do you know what you're saying?

Aaron It's a load on my soul—I must rid my soul of it before I die—I—   40 *[lays his hand on the table, and starts.]*—What's this? Blood?

Martin Hush! hush! Nothing.

Aaron Blood?

Martin   No, no, no. I drank some water a little while ago—it's only a drop
           spilt out of that mug—a drop of water.

Aaron   Water? Ah! Water now: years ago, it was blood.

Martin   [aside.] How strangely he returns to that!

Aaron   Is'nt this my old table?

Martin   Yes.

Aaron   My old table that I had when I was a farmer ashore?

Martin   Yes.

Aaron   My old table that I bought when I got married; that I've kep' by me
           ever since?   10

Martin   Yes, yes.

Aaron   Water now, Martin, if you like; but blood once.—There! there's the
           place where he put the knife—there was blood on the blade, and a drop
           dripped off it.

Martin   [aside.] Again! [To Aaron, who still steadfastly points to the wet
           place on the table.] Father! do'nt point like that.—He does'nt hear; his
           senses seem gone. What can I do for him?—The brandy! my share of the
           brandy—I have got that still left to give him, and he shall have it. [Goes to
           the locker.]

Aaron   Martin! Where are you going? Oh, Martin, do'nt tell Jacob!   20

Martin   No, no. I'll stop here with you. [Measures out the brandy.] Half for
           father, and half for Jacob.—Here, father, drink this. It will make you feel
           stronger: it will steady your head.

Aaron   Will it? [Drinks.] Aha! good. I shall last a little longer after that.

Martin   It makes you feel steadier and clearer, does'nt it?

Aaron   Steadier and clearer—yes. Happier—no. What did I say last, before
           you got the brandy?

Martin   Oh, not much to matter. Strange words as if you were hardly awake.

Aaron   Son Martin, answer me honestly. What did I say?

Martin   You said you had something on your mind; and you said that spot   30
           of wet on the table was blood. But now you feel stronger and better—

Aaron   Now I feel stronger and better, I can go on and end it. Sit near
           me—sit near, and let me speak. Last evening when you wished me good
           night,—did you feel my hands trembling?

Martin   Yes.

Aaron   The secret lay very heavy on my soul last night. I could'nt get to
           sleep for it. I heard Jacob go to his bedplace up above—I heard you fall
           off to sleep—I heard the clock ticking over my head—I heard the rush
           of the wind, and the heavy wash of the sea outside. I was'nt sleeping and
           dreaming—I was awake—and I saw her ghost.   40

Martin   Whose ghost?

Aaron   The tall woman, with the black hood, and the long white sleeves,
           and the red scar on her throat. She come close up to my bedside; and spoke

to me. I could'nt hear you sleeping, or the clock ticking, or the rush of the wind, or the heavy wash of the sea.—I could only hear <u>her</u>. "Tell it," she says, "tell it, Aaron Gurnock, before you die".

Martin   *[shrinking away from the table.]* Father, do'nt look so! do'nt talk so! There's a dread stealing over me—there's a thought coming into my mind.—Oh, go back! go back to bed, and say no more!

Aaron   I must say on to the end.—It was in your mother's life time. You remember seven or eight years ago, when I had the farm house on the Cornish shore?

Martin   Yes.

Aaron   You remember the autumn time, when things went wrong with me, and I got into debt?—When you went away with your mother, to stay along with her relations for a little while?

Martin   I do remember.

Aaron   When you two left the house I was alone in it, true enough; but you had'nt been gone a day before I had some one come to keep me company. An old mate of mine, before I was married—by name, Benjamin Tranter. Your mother always hated him, and said he was fit company for no honest man. So he skulked till her back was turned; and then he came and kept me company at the farm-house. Did I tell you it was autumn-time then?

Martin   Yes! yes!

Aaron   A heavy, hot, misty autumn-time. Benjamin and me kept together in the farm house—low enough both of us. I had debts gathering behind me, and prison threatening before. And he had'nt a shilling left in the world. One night we sat by the kitchen hearth, grumbling about the hard times, and rummaging our brains for ways of raising money. I remember the sea-fog had been gathering over the moor all round us, ever since the afternoon.—All of a sudden, my old sheep-dog jumps up and growls; and then we hear a knock at the door. I go and open it; and, under the porch, I see a lady.

Martin   A lady! A lady alone on the moor at night!

Aaron   There she stood, holding a stout Devonshire pony by the bridle; and no servant or anybody with her: There were saddle-bags on the pony's back. "I've lost my servant, miles away, in this white sea mist;" she says; "and I want shelter for myself and my pony tonight." I asked her in; and Benjamin, he took off the saddle-bags. They weighed heavy, and he give me a look, as he hefted them, that I did'nt like. *[Martin shudders.]* What are you shivering about?

Martin   *[Turning away his head.]* I'm cold.

Aaron   I took the saddle-bags from Benjamin, and showed her into the kitchen. She wore a black hood lined next the face with white, and a black gown, and long hanging white sleeves. She was a fine woman, with bright eyes, and a kind comely face. "We are poor," says I; "my wife's away; and

I hav'nt much to eat in the house."—"Never mind that: it's rest I want,"
says she. "You do'nt come from our parts?" says I. "No," says she; "I'm
not from your south Cornish coast—I'm from North Devon. Have you
got a bed for me to lie down on?"—"Yes," says I; and showed her the
room; and took her saddle-bags upstairs for her. "We will talk more about
you and your poverty, tomorrow morning," says she.—Those were all the
words we had together: all I said to her; all she said to me.

Martin All! You mean "all", for that night?—Father! father! I hope you
mean "all," for that night!

Aaron "All," for ever! [Martin starts to his feet, and draws back a step or   10
two, in horror.] Sit down again, and hear me out. [Martin obeys.] When
I got back to the kitchen, I had time to fill a pipe and smoke it out, before
Benjamin came in from the stable. "You've been a long time littering
down the pony," says I. He gave me no answer: he would not even look at
me. "The strange lady is up in my wife's room," says I. "And where are
the saddle-bags?," says he very quick. "Up with her, of course", says I.
He laughed, after that. "Why do you laugh?", says I. He would'nt answer
again. He seemed to want to go to sleep. I soon got drowsy myself, with
nothing to do, and nobody to talk to; and dozed in my chair. I was'nt quite
asleep, for I heard the dog restless; and I saw, in a sort of half dream-   20
ing way, Benjamin get up softly, and take a turn or two backwards and
forwards in the room, and then go out suddenly. After that my head got
heavier, and I fell off into a sleep.—Sit nearer! What are you shrinking for?
What is there in me to frighten you?

Martin [sternly.] Everything. Remember that you are speaking to your son!

Aaron I do'nt know how long I slept, or why I woke; but I did wake all of
a sudden. The dog was crouched down on my feet, trembling and whining
and there was a smell of burning that I could'nt account for. The candle
was guttering; but there was light enough for me to see that Benjamin was
in the kitchen. He had a knife in one hand, and a heavy leather bag in the   30
other; and, when I opened my eyes, I met his, staring straight at me. He
stood by the side of this table that we are sitting at; and when we looked
at each other, he put the knife down here. I got up and saw something drip
off the blade. It was blood. And there's the place it dripped on.—There,
Martin—there! [Rises a little and reaches across the table to enforce Martin's attention by touching his arm.]

Martin [Shrinking away.] Do'nt touch me!

Aaron [angrily.] Martin!

Martin [hiding his face.] Do'nt touch me!

Aaron I did'nt kill her.   40

Martin Did you give up the guilty man?

Aaron No.

Martin Did you—? I ca'nt say it! I ca'nt speak the words.

Aaron   I helped him to hide her dead body.

Martin   Oh, my God!

Aaron   Hush! or Jacob may hear you.

Martin   *[To himself]* Jacob! Jacob, who took my hand not half an hour ago, and told me I was the son of an honest man!

Aaron   We carried her, dressed as she was, all in black, with her hood and her long white sleeves, down the cliff path from the edge of the moor—down, down to the sea beach. We never said one word to each other all the way. The mist was gone, the tide was at the ebb, and the sand was shining under the harvest moon. Without a word passing between us, we took her   10
into the Daw's Cave. The tide leaves it at the ebb, and fills it at the flow. We left her against a heap of shells and seaweed high up in the cave, and went back to the farm house. And still we never said so much as one word to each other all the way! Benjamin—

Martin   *[Eagerly.]* Where is he now?

Aaron   Where I am going to soon—he was killed in a fight at a public house. Benjamin, I say, went into the stable, and took the pony out, saddled, to the cliff-side; and I went after him because I was afraid to be alone. He drove the pony over the cliff on to the rocks below. Then, he turns to me and says:—"It's all safe now: I burnt the bed linen while you were   20
asleep. How much do you want?", he says; and takes the leather-bag out of his coat-pocket. "Nothing," says I: "it's blood-money, and I wo'nt touch it." He did'nt speak another word, and we parted company on the spot. He went his way over the moor; and I went mine back to the farm. In two days the Hue and Cry came after the lady; but the Flood Tide was beforehand with the Hue and Cry; and the Daw's Cave was empty when the constable and his men looked into it. They only found the pony jammed in among the rocks. And the next day they traced her servant, who had gone astray in the mist to the shaft of an old mine. After that, everybody knew that she had fallen over the cliff-side in the fog. *[Here the sound of the gong is heard*   30
faintly, for the last time.]

Martin   And you never dropped a word of the truth?

Aaron   Never to any living soul from that day to this.—People came all the way, Martin, from where she lived, to know if her body had been found—poor people, who said she had fed, clothed, and taught them, as if they had been her own children. They cried when they talked about her. They said, since her husband died, she always kept to that black dress of her's, always lived alone, always spent her time in doing good. They cursed the fogs and the mists of Cornwall, and the day when she heard that our poor were suffering and set forth to help them with her money and her kind words. The   40
very children the strangers brought with them fretted and cried too; and asked when Lady Grace was coming back. That was the only name they gave her—Lady Grace.

Martin   And you let the man escape who had murdered her!—you helped
him to hide her corpse—!

Aaron   Do'nt be hard on me, Martin—I'm dying. Keep the secret till I'm
gone. I did'nt kill her, mind that! *[Relapsing into incoherency.]* The children called her Lady Grace. They cried, and said, when will Lady Grace
come back?—This is my old table that I had at the farm-house; and here's
where the blood dropped on it from the blade of the knife.—Be a good son
to me, Martin; be a good son to me, till I'm gone!

Martin   Good! Your son good to his father! *[Takes the keepsake from his
breast.]* Oh, Phoebe! Phoebe! Is the son of Aaron Gurnock worthy to wear   10
your keepsake!

Aaron   The death of Lady Grace lay so heavy on my soul, Martin—I
could'nt die till I'd told the secret to somebody. But I did'nt kill her—it
was'nt my hand made that scar on her throat.—Hark! I hear something.
Was it the wind?

Martin   *[starting to his feet.]* The wind? It sounded like a cheer from the
sea. Hush!

Jacob   *[calling from above.]* Martin! Martin!

Aaron   It's Jacob! He's heard us talking! he's heard the secret!

Jacob   *[from above.]* Martin! The fog's lifting towards shore.   20

Aaron   Do'nt let Jacob come in here! do'nt let him!

Martin   Silence! he's calling again.

Jacob   *[from above.]* Martin! The boat—the boat from shore! *[A distant
hail is heard:—"Lighthouse ahoy!". Jacob answers it faintly from above.
A distant cheer follows.]*

Aaron   Oh, Martin, keep Jacob away from me! I know he's heard us—I
know he's heard the secret!

Martin   *[Not noticing.]* The boat from shore!—And Jacob said Phoebe
would make one of the crew!—Can I look her in the face, after all that I
have just heard? *[Jacob Dale hurries into the room.]*   30

Jacob   Food! Food!

Aaron   *[shrinking back in his chair.]* Martin, do'nt desert me!

Jacob   Cheer up, Aaron! They're here. The boat has put off at last, in spite
of the storm.—Martin! They will have a hard job of it to land. Come and
lend a hand to help them. *[Exit.]*

Martin   How can I meet her eye! How can I take her hand!

Aaron   Do'nt go, Martin! Jacob wants to come back when I am alone. He
wants to charge me with the murder of Lady Grace.

Martin   She knows my whole heart and soul. She'll see the horrid secret in
my face—she'll hear it in my voice! *[Noise and confused voices outside.*   40
Martin starts, and goes to the door.]

Aaron   Stop! stop with me! *[Phoebe speaks outside:* "Oh, father, father!
thank Heaven we are in time"!*]*

Martin   *[Drawing back into the room]* Her voice! Phoebe has come!
Aaron   That's right!—stop with me. *[Enter Jacob.]*
Jacob   This way, Phoebe: here they are.
[Enter Phoebe. She runs to Martin and throws her arms round his neck. Furley, and the Fishermen and Lightkeepers who have manned the boat, follow her into the room. They carry hampers, baskets, and jars with them, which they arrange in a corner at the back of the stage. Jacob goes to help them.]
Phoebe   Martin! dear, dear Martin! *[Drawing back a little and looking at him.]* Oh, how pale you are! how lost and sad you look! I have suffered too, dear. The last four weeks have almost broken my heart.—And your   10
father, Martin? I do'nt see him. *[Turns round to where Aaron sits looking suspiciously from person to person.]* How awfully he is altered! He seems as if he hardly knew me. *[Tries to go to Aaron.]*
Martin   *[Stopping her.]* Your cloak, Phoebe—let me take it off. It is wet through with the salt water.
Phoebe   Wet through indeed! and my hood almost washed off my head. Oh, we have had such a gale to pull through, such a sea to fight with! *[Tries to go to Aaron again. Martin catches her by the hand]*—Why, Martin! wo'nt you let me shake hands with your father? *[whispering and casting down her eyes demurely.]* My father that is to be, one of these days!   20
Martin   *[aside.]* Her father! Benjamin Tranter's accomplice her father!
Phoebe   I do'nt hear you, dear.
Martin   *[constrainedly.]* My father is hardly fit to be spoken to just now. He wanders a little in his mind. It is only weakness from long want of food.
Phoebe   Want of food! How dreadful to think of at his age, and at poor old father's! *[Turning towards the back of the stage]* Oh! Master Furley, master Furley, how long you are unpacking the hampers. Shall I come and help you?
Furley   No, no, my lass. You had better a deal sit down and rest yourself, after the pull we have had in the teeth of the gale.   30
Jacob   Yes, yes. Do as Furley tells you. Rest yourself, my love—rest yourself.
Martin   *[Drawing her away to the locker, with an uneasy look at his father.]* Come and sit by me, Phoebe.
Phoebe   Ah, Martin! This time yesterday I was thinking of you in Church— thinking whether I should ever sit by your side again. *[They seat themselves on the locker. Furley comes forward with a saucepan in his hand]*
Furley   *[Putting the saucepan on the fire.]* Jacob! Where's the cloth and the crockery? *[Jacob puts them on.]* Now, my men! *[addressing the boat's crew.]* bustle about; and let's have the table ready in no time. *[Two of the   40
men move the table to the middle of the stage.]* Friend Aaron—
Aaron   Martin! he's going to take me ashore—stop him Martin, stop him!
[Martin rises from the locker]

Furley   Leave him to me! Jacob told me his poor storm beaten wits had been woolgathering I'll bring him round—never fear! *[To Aaron]* Take you ashore? And why not? It's your turn to go ashore.

Aaron   No!

Furley   But I say, yes—your turn, and Jacob's, and Martin's. Of course we've brought the three extra lightkeepers off in the boat to relieve you. And we're going to take you all ashore, as soon as we have fattened you up again with something to eat.

Aaron   Something to eat!

Furley   Yes! good broth with lots of taturs and barley in it. The right sort of   10
stuff, friend Aaron, for the stomachs of half-starved men

Aaron   Give it me now! Now! now! I wo'nt wait!

Furley   Oh, wo'nt you though! Here, Jacob, take him out of sight of what I'm doing till I've got the broth heated

Jacob   *[Advancing with one of the fishermen.]* Come along, Aaron;—sit down a bit on your bedside, till the broth's ready.

Aaron   Martin! do'nt let them take me away!

Jacob   *[Leading him to the bed with the fisherman's help.]* Lord help him! Where are his poor wits wandering to?

Phoebe   Has your father been like that many days, Martin?   20

Martin   *[confusedly.]* No, not many—one or two days—I hardly know how long.

Phoebe   Well, as I was telling you just now, I bore it pretty well till our bans were put up. Then, when I heard your name and mine, I burst out crying before all the people in church. *[Martin looks away uneasily after his father.]*—He does'nt listen! Martin!

Martin   Yes, Phoebe.

Phoebe   You do'nt seem to be listening to me.

Martin   Oh, yes! I was listening indeed. You were saying—?

Phoebe   *[rather sadly.]* Oh, nothing!   30

Martin   I was listening, Phoebe—I was indeed.

Phoebe   It was only a word or two about what happened to me in Church. *[Taking his hand.]* For days before I had been so weak and broken down with fright and anxiety about you, that I was'nt fit to bear much.—You can fancy what I must have suffered, Martin, hearing the pitiless wind blow as if it would blow forever—seeing the white raging surf always the same, morning, noon, and night—asking Furley and the fishermen every day when the boat could put off to rescue you, and always getting the same cruel answer:— "No boat, lass, that ever was built, could live in such a sea as that."—*[Martin again looks uneasily after his father.]*—Oh! I cried at night, Martin, and   40
woke with the heart-ache in the morning, till I thought I should die too, and wondered whether they would bury us together, in the same grave!—Not listening again! What makes him look so anxiously that way?

Furley   *[calling from the fireplace]* The broth's ready! Jacob, come to the
table, and settle old Aaron down comfortably alongside of you.—Martin!
leave off courting Phoebe, and come and make love to a good basin-full of
broth.—Give us hold of the ladle. *[Ladles out the broth into basins placed
before Aaron, Martin, and Jacob.]* Now then, whatever you do, do'nt be in
a hurry!

Jacob   Oh Lord! it's a pleasure only to smell it.

Furley   A regular nosegay, is'nt it? Steady there, friend Aaron; I'm not
going to let you have too much, or swallow too fast. I was one of a starving boat's crew once myself; and I know the danger of letting a famished   10
man over-eat himself. Slower, Jacob, or you'll scald your throat. Look
at Martin—he's the only one of the three who swallows his broth like a
gentleman.

Aaron   *[Handing his basin to Furley]* More!

Jacob   *[Doing the same.]* More!

Furley   More? Do you call that manners? Wait a bit and take breath. Do
you think I'm going to let men in your condition swallow a whole sauce-
pan-full of broth among you at once?

Phoebe   Oh, give them a little more, Master Furley!—a little more ca'nt
hurt them. Look! here's Martin's basin empty.   20

Furley   Ah! I dare say. Let you alone, young woman, for looking after Martin's basin. No! it's no good trying to wheedle me. *[Aaron snatches at the
saucepan.]* And it's no good trying to snatch at the saucepan either. I've
made up my mind to keep you waiting a little for your own good, and I
wo'nt alter it.

Aaron   More! more!

Jacob   Oh, Furley, give us some more!

Furley   Only wait a bit; and you shall have more. You ca'nt hurry me. I'm
one of the sort that have wills of their own. When I was at school, they
called me pig-headed Sam—and I did'nt get that name for nothing, I can   30
promise you!

Phoebe   Do you feel better, Martin?

Martin   Yes, Phoebe—better already.

Phoebe   I'll make Master Furley give you some more *[aside]* He looked
at me in the old way then—perhaps I was wrong in thinking him altered
towards me, after all?

Aaron   More! more!

Jacob   Only another spoonful!

Phoebe   *[handing Martin's basin.]* Yes, only one other spoonful!

Furley   Will you all promise to take a long time over it?   40

Jacob   Yes.

Aaron   Yes, yes.

Phoebe   Martin deserves a double share for eating so slowly the first time.

Furley   Does he, Miss?—I believe if you had the feeding of him, he'd be a
dead man in half an hour! *[Ladling out the broth.]* Now, here's a second sup
for you—and let it slip down gently, or you wo'nt get a drop more. Stop! I
wo'nt trust you. *[Elevating the ladle]* Steady, and take your time from me.

Aaron   Let us alone!

Jacob   Yes—do let us alone!

Furley   Silence there; and stop directly, or I'll pitch all the rest of the broth
out of window. *[They drop their spoons in terror.]* Aha! I thought I should
get the upper hand of you: I thought you'd give in at last to pig-headed
Sam! Now! *[Flourishing the ladle.]* Take your time properly from me, and   10
you shall have a third help. One, two, three—take a spoonful! Four, five,
six—take another!—Stop; or, by the Lord Harry, the broth shall go into
the sea!—Seven, eight, nine—third spoonful! Ten, eleven—Hullo! basins
empty again! I gave you four spoonfuls—where's the fourth?

Jacob   *[patting his stomach.]* Where it ought to be!

Furley   Ha! ha! ha!—What you've plucked up your spirits again already?
Wait a bit; and, if you're all good boys, you shall have another spoonful.—
Look up, Aaron! How do you feel, Martin!—Now's the time, I think, to
throw in the Dutchman's strong water. There, my lads, drink away, and
be happy!—Give me a toothful of liquor for myself—Here's all our good   20
healths!—Martin, drink!—Phoebe! You do'nt look half happy enough!
Jump up, lass—and sing us a song. Sing, Phoebe, or I shall never get them
to wait long enough for their third course.

Phoebe   Sing, Master Furley?

Furley   Aye, to be sure! Why not? We have cheered them up with hot broth
and brandy and water—now let's cheer them up with a song.

Phoebe   What song shall it be?

Furley   Any you like. Pipe away, my little girl, like a skylark; and leave me
and the boat's crew to give you a roaring chorus!

*[Song and Chorus. Furley beats time with the ladle—while the first verse is   30
being sung, Martin and Aaron exchange glances; then look away from each
other. Aaron tries faintly to join in the chorus. Martin makes no attempt to
sing. During the next chorus, Phoebe observes his silence: her face grows
serious, and she sings the last verse in a lower tone and with some appearance of effort.]*

Furley   Is that all, Phoebe? Why it is'nt half as sung! I'll give you one
that's twice as long.

Jacob   Give us some more broth.

Aaron   Yes, more broth!

Furley   All in good time. You shall have the last of it, I promise you. *[ladles   40
out more broth]*

Phoebe   *[aside.]* Something <u>has</u> altered Martin! He was the only one of
them who did not join in the chorus.

Furley   There! Make the most you can of it, for there is'nt a drop more. And now for my song. *[Goes up the stage to put the saucepan away]*

Phoebe   *[aside.]* He never so much as looked at me while I was singing! he wo'nt notice me now!—Why does he look so anxiously after his father?

Furley   Clear your pipes, my lads.

Jacob   I shall be ready directly.

Phoebe   *[aside.]* He does'nt eat as he ought—he keeps strangely silent—his face seems to have a downcast look on it that I never saw there before. If I did'nt know all his secrets, I should think he had something on his mind, and that he wanted to hide it from me.   10

Furley   Now for my song!

Jacob   *[Finishing his basin. The distant report of a gun is heard. They all start.]*

Aaron   What's that?

Jacob   Hush! *[A second report.]*

Martin   A ships gun!

Phoebe   Martin! are you certain of that? *[A third report.]*

Jacob   A ship in danger—Stop!—I know what ship it is.

Aaron   You!

Furley   What do you mean?   20

Jacob   Do'nt you remember, Martin, my telling you I sighted a ship this morning from the Crow's Nest?

Martin   True!—a ship far off.

Jacob   I'm afraid she's nigh enough now. I forgot to tell you of it in the hurry and pleasure of seeing the boat from shore—but when I last looked out, after sounding the gong, I thought I saw that same ship, under bare poles, running straight down on us.

Martin   I'll go up to the Crow's Nest.

Furley   No, no. Let one of the fresher men do that work.

Aaron   Yes—you stop here with me, Martin—mind you stop here with   30 me!

Furley   *[To one of the extra Lightkeepers]* Penhale—you have the keenest eyes of all of us—go up, and see what you can make out. If there really is a ship in danger, signal it down here by striking on the gong. *[Exit Lightkeeper.]*

Martin   You are quite sure you made out a ship this morning?

Jacob   I ca'nt be downright certain, because my eyesight's not as good as it used to be; and there was a little fog still hanging to seaward.

Aaron   *[Beckoning to his son.]* Martin! *[Martin goes to him]*

Phoebe   If the ship should strike on these rocks, father, can we save the crew?   40

Aaron   *[whispering]* Whatever happens, Martin, do'nt tell the secret— do'nt say a word to anybody about the death of Lady Grace! *[Several loud strokes in quick succession on the gong.]*

Jacob   I was right—the ship is in danger!

Furley   Martin, have you got a speaking trumpet here?

Martin   Yes.

Furley   Get it; and wait for me till I come back from the Crow's Nest.
         [Exit.]

Aaron   I'm cold—I'm all of a tremble—how low the fire has got! *[Turns
         aside and crouches over the fire]*

Phoebe   Father, can I be of any use? do make me of some use!

Jacob   Stop a bit, Phoebe. Have you found the trumpet, Martin?

Martin   I've got it. *[Goes to the sliding shutter and draws it back. The*   10
         *increased sound of wind and sea which is heard immediately, continues until
         the end of the Act.]* The fog is lifting every moment—I can see the ship!

Jacob   Near?

Martin   Awfully near.

Phoebe   What will become of the poor souls on board!

Aaron   Cold, cold, cold. What about the ship, son Martin? What more
         about the ship?

Jacob   Do you make her out large?

Martin   No. A brig with her foretopmast carried away, and her storm-jib in
         ribbons. She's driving right down on us at the mercy of wind and sea.   20

[Enter Furley.]

Furley   Ropes! ropes! In less than ten minutes that brig will be wrecked on
         the rocks below us. The only chance of saving the crew is to have the ropes
         handy before the ship strikes.

Jacob   The ropes are all in the store-room.

Martin   Let me go—

Furley   No: I want you at the window to give orders to the men below,
         while I am in the gallery. *[To the Lightkeepers &c]* Get the ropes out of the
         store room. Take some up into the gallery—bring some in here—and keep
         the rest below. *[Exit the Lightkeepers.]*   30

Phoebe   Make me of some use—do make me of some use!

Jacob   Yes, yes. Let's move this table and chest out of the way to begin
         with.

Aaron   What are you all deserting me for? Why am I left alone here doing
         nothing?

Martin   *[To Furley.]* Shall we veer a rope of out this window?

Furley   Yes; in case the other rope fails. Come here; and I'll show you what
         I mean. *[Takes him to the window.]*

Phoebe   Oh, father! if we can only save the crew from death.

Aaron   Death? Who set you talking of death? What have you been listen-   40
         ing to?

Furley   *[At the window.]* Look at the brig now! look how she's driving
         down on us!

Martin   *[Hurrying across to the door.]* Lively there! lively with the ropes!
[The Lightkeepers enter with a coil of rope.]
Furley   Martin, set them to work. It's time I was in the gallery. Now, my
    men, up to the gallery after me. *[Exit. Followed by Lightkeepers]*
Martin   Jacob, get that coil unbent; and give me the end to veer out of the
    window.—Phoebe, all the spare blankets we have are rolled up in that
    chest—get them out, and spread them before the fire. *[Phoebe opens the
    chest. Martin goes to the window]*
Jacob   Now, Aaron, lend a hand here with the rope!
Aaron   Yes, yes. My hands! my hands! What makes them tremble so?—   10
    Jacob! What set your girl talking of death just now?
Jacob   Do'nt talk—put out your strength, and help me with the rope.
Martin   *[Hailing the ship through the speaking trumpet]* Brig ahoy!
Phoebe   What is it?
Aaron   What do you see?
Martin   They're launching a boat over the brig's quarter. It's madness—
    it's throwing away their lives. *[Hailing.]* Brig ahoy! do'nt trust to the
    boat!
Jacob   They ca'nt hear you—the wind's too high.
Martin   The rope, Jacob—quick with the rope. *[Jacob carries the free end*   20
    of the rope to Martin.]
Aaron   *[aside to Phoebe.]* Do'nt you talk about death again—I do'nt like
    it! *[Phoebe does not appear to hear.]*
Martin   *[Paying out the rope.]* Steady, Jacob—that's enough for the pres-
    ent. *[Hailing below]* Below there! Send a man with the largest block and
    two pulleys up into the gallery.
Jacob   *[Keeping with Martin at the window.]* Clear away the other end,
    Aaron—right out to the door ready for use.
Aaron   My hands shake—how my hands do shake! What am I trembling
    for? There's nothing to be frightened of!   30
Phoebe   The boat, Martin—What are they doing now with the boat?
Martin   They have manned her and got her clear of the brig—Gallery ahoy!
    We can spare you another man up there.
Jacob   *[Looking out.]* Look at that wave!—Oh, the boat! the boat!
Phoebe   What of her?
Jacob   Capsized. *[Phoebe screams.]* The wave took them amidships.—
    Lord help their poor souls! The best part of that brig's crew have gone to
    their account already!
Phoebe   Father! look out again. Can you see how many are left alive in the
    ship?   40
Jacob   Three or four only, huddled together on the deck.
Aaron   Give me something more to do! I ca'nt stop idle. I tremble so. More
    to do! more to do!

Martin   *[Looking round.]* Some body put a fresh bit of candle in the lanthorn. They want more light down in the storeroom.

Aaron   Leave it to me—I'll do it! *[prepares to light the lanthorn.]*

Martin   *[Hailing out of the window.]* Man wanted in the gallery. Lanthorn
for the storeroom ready directly.—*[looking into the room.]* Quick with the
light! Stand ready for every thing, Jacob: the brig will be a wreck now, in
a few minutes.

Jacob   *[Looking out.]* Another wave! and the empty boat coming on like a
straw on the top of it. The next sea will bring the brig on the rocks.

Aaron   *[Lighting the lanthorn.]* Oh, the awful time! the awful time!   10

Phoebe   *[Turning the blankets.]* If we can save them—if we can only save
them from that horrible death—!

Martin   *[Hailing.]* Below there! Take a turn with a rope round that man's
waist before he goes out on the steps.

Jacob   The boat! The boat is washed up on the high rock beneath us. Look
down, Martin—There's the name of the ship painted in white on the boat's
stern. Use your young eyes, and try if you can read it.

Martin   Read it? Yes, yes, I can. "The—

Jacob   Well?

Martin   *[Jumping off the locker.]* Lord save us! Can that really be the name   20
of the brig? Or am I not in my right senses?

Jacob   The name, Martin—you hav'nt said what the name is.

Phoebe   *[Hurrying to the locker.]* I can read it father!

Jacob   Quick! before the waves wash the boat away again!

Phoebe   *[Looking out.]* Oh the ship! how awfully near us!—I can see the
poor lost people huddled together on deck.

Jacob   The boat! What is the name on the boat?

Phoebe   I can read it easy, father. The name painted on the boat's stern is,
"The Lady Grace."

Aaron   *[starting forward with the lighted lanthorn in his hand.]* What?   30

Jacob   The brig is on the rocks—the brig is striking!

Aaron   *[Loudly.]* What name?

Phoebe   "The Lady Grace" *[Crouches on the locker, and hides her face.]*

Aaron   Martin! The Lady Grace!! *[Drops the lanthorn with a scream of
terror. Martin springs forward to quiet him. The instant after the crash of
the striking vessel is heard on the rocks outside. The Act drop falls.]*

Act II .

[Scene. The same as in the preceding Act, except that the Tarpaulin and the bed are removed, and the bare stone wall of the room appears at the back. Furley, the fishermen, and three sailors are discovered in the middle of the stage, coiling ropes. Jacob Dale and Phoebe sit together on the locker. Martin occupies the chair, on the opposite side, by the table; and keeps his head turned from the place where Phoebe is sitting. Jacob is occupied in splicing a rope.]

Furley   Now, my lads!—those ropes have had plenty of time to get dry since yesterday. Coil them up as neat as you can; and let's have them all put back in their places in the Lighthouse Storeroom.

1st Sailor   Trust us to take care of them, Master Furley. These ropes saved our lives; and—after you and the fishermen here—I look on them as the best friends we have in the world

1st Fisherman   Give all the credit, brother, where the credit is due—to Martin Gurnock there, and to Master Furley. We should never have got the first rope aboard your brig, if it had'nt been for them.

Furley   And how much do you think we should have done, if it had'nt been for the man who got out on the brig's bowsprit, and risked his life to catch the rope?

1st Sailor   Aye, aye—all very well—but who cast the rope so that I could catch it?—No! no! I give the credit to the men at the Lighthouse—that's what I do.

Furley   *[Pointing to a rope in the sailor's hand.]* And I give it to that rope—the rope that held firm and saved you.

1st Fisherman   A regular good bit of stuff, that rope! Thoddy of Plymouth made it.

1st Sailor   Did he now? *[Slaps the rope.]* Thoddy of Plymouth is the friend for my money!

Furley   *[Taking up another rope.]* And, mind you, here's one that ought'nt to be forgotten. If I was asked to name which rope saved the lady passenger on board the brig, I should say this here.

1st Fisherman   And that's even a better bit of stuff than the other! Tinkler of Falmouth made that.

1st Sailor   Tinkler of Falmouth may be the lady's friend—but Thoddy of Plymouth for my money!

1st Fisherman   *[Pointing to the rope in Furley's hand.]* How do you make out that it was Tinkler of Falmouth saved the lady-passenger on board the brig?

1st Sailor   *[holding up his rope.]* When Thoddy of Plymouth was made fast between the Lighthouse and the wreck!

Furley   Stop a bit. First, you on board the brig lashed this same lady-passenger
safe in the arm-chair—did'nt you?

1ˢᵗ Sailor   Yes—but what did the arm-chair run upon to the Lighthouse?
Thoddy of Plymouth!

Sailors and Fishermen   Aye, aye—Thoddy of Plymouth sure enough!

Furley   Stop a bit. Thoddy of Plymouth bore the weight, I grant you. But
when we wanted to haul in the chair from the brig to the lighthouse, and
when we wanted to steady it at the bottom while we were hauling, what did
we lay our hands on?—Tinkler of Falmouth!

1ˢᵗ Fisherman   Right, Master Furley—quite right. Tinkler of Falmouth it was.   10

Sailors and Fishermen   Aye, aye—Tinkler of Falmouth.

1ˢᵗ Sailor   *[catching up his coil of rope doggedly.]* I do'nt care—Thoddy of
Plymouth for my money! *[Exit.]*

1ˢᵗ Fisherman   *[Taking the rope from Furley.]* And I do'nt care either!
This rope's the best bit of work of the two—Tinkler of Falmouth for my
money! *[Exit. The sailors and fishermen follow.]*

Furley   Well! well! whichever rope did it, you three men and the lady-
passenger are safe in the lighthouse, at any rate. And that's something to
say, now the brig has gone to pieces on the rocks. *[Turns to Phoebe.]* Why,
my lass, you look but downhearted this morning!—Have you been up to   20
see how the lady is getting on after her night's rest?

Phoebe   *[sadly.]* Yes. She has slept well, and talks of going on shore in the
boat this morning.

Furley   That's right. Have you found out anything about her yet?

Phoebe   Nothing—except that she is the kindest lady I ever met with.
We had such a long talk together, and she seemed to be so interested in
everything that interested me, that we got to be like old friends directly.
[Innocently.] I answered all her questions, and I'm afraid I told her all
my secrets.

Furley   Nothing remarkable in that, my girl! You would'nt be half a woman   30
if you could keep your secrets to yourself!

Jacob   *[looking up for the first time from his work.]* What did you tell the
lady, Phoebe?

Phoebe   *[glancing at Martin.]* I would rather not say, father, just
now.

Furley   Well, whoever the lady may be, this I will say of her—she's the
bravest woman I ever clapped eyes on. To see her yesterday, with her life
hanging on the strength of a rope—with the sea yawning for her below—
and the wind howling at her above—never screeching out, never fainting
away, never saying so much as one useless word—was the bravest sight I   40
ever saw. You were with us, Jacob, when we saved her? Did you ever see
the like of it in a woman before?

Jacob   *[shortly]* No.

Furley   *[To himself.]* "No"!—that's rather a short answer, friend Jacob. *[Turns to Martin.]* Martin, you hav'nt seen the lady yet, have you? You were down here alone with your father all the time, were you not?

Martin   *[shortly.]* Yes.

Furley   *[To himself.]* Another short answer! "No," on one side, and "Yes," on t'other!—Something seems to have gone wrong among the three light-keepers. Here are these two, sulky and silent without any reason for it— and there is old Aaron, alone down stairs, looking as suspiciously at every man of our boat's crew, as if he thought we were all in league to rob and murder him before we go ashore.   10

Phoebe   *[overhearing the last words.]* When did you say the boat was going back to shore, Master Furley?

Furley   In half an hour, if the lady is ready. The sun's shining, and the sea's smoothing. We shall have a regular holiday pull of it back to land.

Phoebe   *[aside.]* A holiday pull back! There will be little enough of the holiday in it for <u>me</u>!

Furley   What did you say, my girl?

Phoebe   Nothing, Master Furley—nothing.

Furley   *[To himself.]* She's in the conspiracy too! I'm in the way here, that's plain enough. Better be off before I get told to go.—Martin! I'm   20 away to look after the boat.—Ecod! I ca'nt get an answer at all, this time. *[Exit.]*

Martin   *[aside.]* What must Phoebe think of me?—Oh, that secret! that shameful, fearful secret!

Phoebe   *[glancing at Martin.]* He has not once spoken to me—he has hardly looked at me since we have been in the room! What can I have done? What can have happened to change him so?

Martin   If I could only venture to trust her with my father's horrible confession! She sees the change it has made in me; and yet I dare not open my heart to her—   30

Jacob   *[Looking up from his work.]* Phoebe, another bit of cord.

Martin   Suppose I try and sound her father?

Phoebe   *[cutting off the cord.]* Is this long enough?

Martin   Jacob, I want to ask you a question.

Jacob   *[shortly.]* Well?

Martin   When one man commits a crime, and another helps him to escape answering for it, is it true that the Law thinks that other man a criminal, and punishes him as such, whenever it can lay hands upon him?

Jacob   *[ungraciously.]* I do'nt know.

Phoebe   *[timidly.]* What makes you ask such a strange question?   40

Jacob   *[aside to Phoebe.]* Do'nt speak to him!—After the way he's behaved to you, I wo'nt have you speak to him!

Phoebe   Oh, father!

Martin   I was reading about it in a book, and I did'nt know—I mean, I
wanted to know whether the book was right. *[Turns away again.]*

Jacob   *[To Phoebe.]* I say again, do'nt speak to him. What did you tell the
lady upstairs?—Furley's gone now—what did you tell her?

Phoebe   *[lowering her voice.]* She was so good to me, and so interested in
what little I said to her about myself—and, oh father! She has such a sweet
smile when she speaks to you—

Jacob   But how came she to ask you about your secrets?

Phoebe   I do'nt know how she came to see it; but she said I looked a little
sad, and asked if I had any sorrows of my own, and if she could help me—   10

Jacob   Yes, yes, likely enough. But what has this got to do with those
secrets you told her?

Phoebe   I only mentioned it, because—

Jacob   Because what?

Phoebe   Because she told me afterwards that she suspected I must have a
sweetheart; and then—

Jacob   Well?

Phoebe   And then she asked if he was kind and true to me.

Jacob   Aye, aye—I begin to understand now.

Phoebe   *[Laying her head on Jacob's shoulder.]* She looked at me so ten-   20
derly with her clear, kind eyes that—I hardly know how it happened—but
I told her all.

Jacob   All I made you tell me this morning?

Phoebe   Yes—all about Martin and me, and how strangely he had altered
towards me, without ever saying what I had done to change him. She spoke
to me about it as kindly as if she had been my own mother; and said, if I
liked, she would speak to Martin before we left the lighthouse.

Jacob   *[Throwing aside his work.]* She speak to him!—Well, well, she
means kindly, I dare say. But it's your father's business, Phoebe, to speak
to him—and speak I will, this very minute. Martin Gurnock!   30

Phoebe   Oh, not now! pray, pray not now!

Jacob   Yes, now. Martin Gurnock, turn this way and listen to me. I have
something to say to you.

Martin   I am ready to hear it, Jacob.

Phoebe   *[Rising.]* Let me go, father—let me go first!

Jacob   Go? Why?

Phoebe   Ca'nt you guess!

Jacob   *[looking from her to Martin.]* I think I can. Yes, yes, my child—go
away.

Phoebe   Do'nt speak harshly to him, father!   40

Jacob   Why not? Has he behaved kindly to you? *[Phoebe bursts into
tears.]* Come, come, child—none of that! I'd rather see you scold him
than cry about him—There! dry your eyes, and leave us alone for a little

while. *[Takes her to the door.]* Go, now—and whatever you do, do'nt cry anymore. *[Exit Phoebe. Jacob returns to Martin.]* Did you hear what my girl said to me, just now?

Martin   No.

Jacob   She told me not to speak harshly to you. Stand up, and face me like a man; and tell me honestly which you deserve—harshness, or kindness?—You do'nt answer.

Martin   I ca'nt answer.

Jacob   You must, if you mean to marry my girl. What has altered you towards her?—Do'nt you fancy she's been telling tales to me! I noticed   10
you last night, after all the confusion of that shipwreck was over: I noticed you again this morning—and I wrung the confession out of her that she had noticed you too. You do'nt talk to her as you used—you do'nt look at her as you used—you keep out of her company as if you were ashamed of her—you make her heart ache with silence and secrecy and sad looks.— What does it mean? Have you lost all your liking for her?

Martin   I love her more dearly than ever.

Jacob   You take a strange way of showing it. Any man with eyes in his head, who saw how you have been treating her since last night, would say you wanted an excuse for breaking your marriage-promise. You have   20
behaved as if you were ashamed of her—as if you were ashamed of taking my Phoebe for your wife!

Martin   Ashamed! No such thought ever entered my heart. Say, afraid— and you may be nearer the truth.

Jacob   Afraid of taking her for your wife! Why?

Martin   Because she might be ashamed of taking me for her husband.

Jacob   On my word as an honest man I begin to think she might too!— And since when, pray, has this fear got into your head? Since you were talking to me about her yesterday?

Martin   Yes.   30

Jacob   Did any of Furley's crew bring you news in the boat from shore?

Martin   No—not a word of news.

Jacob   Not a word—eh? Then, again I say it; what has altered you since yesterday? We are not on shore, where visitors come and go, and changes may happen with every hour. We are shut up, three men alone in a light-house—three men who ought to know each other's secrets by this time, if ever men did yet since the world began. What has happened to change you? Make a clean breast of it. Speak out like an honest man!

Martin   I have told you that I ca'nt speak out—at least, not yet.

Jacob   And why not yet?   40

Martin   Because I have another person to consult—another person whom I am obliged to be careful of—who might suffer, if I spoke out too hastily.

Jacob   What other person? *[Martin hesitates.]* What other person?

Martin   Oh, Jacob, have some confidence in me! Show some pity for me! I
have a fearful trouble to fight against—I have been tried as never man was
tried before: I have indeed, Jacob! Whichever way I turn, whatever I do,
the chance that I may commit some dreadful error, or be guilty of some
unmanly deception, terrifies me into silence.—Give me a little time longer
to think what I ought to do; and trust in me mercifully till that time arrives.
Surely, surely my past conduct to you and to Phoebe gives me the right to
ask that much!—Another day, Jacob—only one other day, to think what I
ought to do!

Jacob   I will give you half an hour—in half an hour, Furley's boat will   10
be ready to go ashore. I'm a plain man; and I do'nt understand all these
ins and outs, and ugly mysteries and strange necessities for silence. I give
you the half hour before the boat goes back—If by that time, you ca'nt
speak a little plainer than you speak now,—if you ca'nt make it right
with Phoebe and right with me—all is over, Martin Gurnock, between
you and her! I, her father, tell you so: and you know me for a man who
sticks to his word. *[Exit.]*

Martin   Half an hour! Half an hour to decide on the future of my life, and
of Phoebe's life as well—my head swims when I think of it. If I trust the
horrible secret to Jacob, how do I know that he may not think it his duty   20
to deliver my father up to Justice?—And, even if he is willing to keep
silence, would he give me his daughter, after he knows the secret? Would
he marry Phoebe to a man whose father helped the hiding and shared the
guilt of a murder?—I know him too well to hope it.—Oh, my head, my
head! The minutes slip away; and still it burns and swims—still I see nothing between confession that would be ruin, and deceit that would degrade
me in my own estimation for ever!

[Enter Phoebe.]

Phoebe   Martin!

Martin   Phoebe here now!—It wanted but that to make the trial complete!   30

Phoebe   Martin, I have heard all.

Martin   *[Affrightedly.]* All?

Phoebe   All that passed between my father and you.—What is this dreadful
secret that threatens to separate us?—Oh, Martin! are you really true to me
still?

Martin   True in my heart of hearts—never truer, Phoebe, than at this
moment.

Phoebe   Then trust me with the secret! Whatever it is, I will take all the risk
of telling it to my father.

Martin   *[Aside, and moving from her towards the table.]* Trust <u>her</u> with it!   40
Soil her pure heart with that foul secret?—oh, never! never!

Phoebe   You turn away! Wo'nt you tell me?—Have you decided to tell my
father? let me know that, at least—our time is short—in less than half an

hour the boat will put off for shore.—Martin! all that we two have to hope
for in this world is at stake. Have you decided?—Yes? or No?

Martin *[Sinking back into the chair.]* No!

Phoebe And yet I heard you tell my father that you loved me more dearly
than ever!

Martin Oh, Phoebe! do you too distrust me?

Phoebe No, Martin! I trust in you with all my heart—and if the whole world
doubted you, I would trust just the same. I spoke hastily—do'nt think of
what I said—think of nothing, but that our time is short, and that the half
hour which is to decide everything is slipping fast away.   10

Martin If I only knew where to turn for advice!—I am not fit to decide for
myself; and here, in this lighthouse, there is no one to help me—

Phoebe No one? *[Reflects for a moment.]*—Yes, yes!—there is!

Martin Ah! You mean Furley the Pilot—a man who has no more book-
learning, Phoebe, than I have.

Phoebe *[aside.]* Book-learning?—he wants someone with book-learning to
advise him?—

Martin Furley is as hearty a friend and as good a pilot as ever stepped; but
he would be no help to me now.

Phoebe *[aside]* I know who would be—the lady—the lady, upstairs,   20
who offered of her own accord to speak to Martin. She has book-
learning to help him with—more book-learning than all of us here
put together. If she could only be got to talk to Martin as she talked
this morning to me—! I'll speak to her: I'll go up and speak to her
this very moment. *[Goes to the door—then stops, looks at Martin,
and returns.]* Have you forgiven me those hasty words I spoke just
now?—My heart trusts in you, Martin, whatever my lips may say.
[offers him her hand.]

Martin My own Phoebe! My own generous, true-hearted girl! *[Turns
from her]*   30

Phoebe Now to see the lady! My last hope of help is the hope I have in her.
[Exit.]

Martin How can I decide? How can I so much as think, with such a
prospect as lies before me, look which way I will?—Phoebe! *[Looks
round.]* She is gone—gone perhaps never to return again.—Father!
father! better I had died in my cradle than have grown up to hear what
you told me yesterday—better I had never been born than have lived to
suffer for your sin!

[Enter Aaron Gurnock.]

Aaron Son Martin, the boat is going back to shore. Why are you stopping   40
here alone?

Martin *[rising.]* Who am I fit company for? What honest man's face am I
worthy to look at?

Aaron   That is a strange way of answering. Why do you speak these words
to me?

Martin   You know well enough. Do you mean to stop here?—If you do,
let me go. I may forget what is due to my father if I stay. There are more
rooms than one in the lighthouse. Let us keep apart.

Aaron   *[Placing himself before the door.]* Wait! You have spoken to me as
if I was the worst enemy you had on earth. What have I done?

Martin   Let me go!

Aaron   I say again, what have I done? You shall answer me before you
leave this room. Reach out your hand, and drag your father from the door-   10
way—you wo'nt pass him without doing that!

Martin   You want no answer. You know the meaning of what I said just
now as well as I do.

Aaron   I say I do'nt.

Martin   No?

Aaron   No!

Martin   What should you say of a man who stood between me and my marriage with Phoebe Dale? Should you say that man was my enemy?

Aaron   I am not that man.

Martin   Not! Remember what you told me yesterday!   20

Aaron   Yesterday? There was a brig wrecked on the rocks below us, yesterday.

Martin   Remember what happened before that shipwreck! Who told me
the horrid secret of the murder of Lady Grace? *[Aaron starts.]* Who
degraded me in my own eyes and unfitted me for the eyes of others, by
telling me that my father had been the accomplice of an assassin and a
robber? Who?

Aaron   Who?

Martin   You echo my words!

Aaron   No: I ask who told you your father had been the accomplice of an   30
assassin and a robber?

Martin   You ask that?

Aaron   Yes—I ask it.

Martin   *[aside]* Is he going to deny his own words?

Aaron   Who told you? *[A pause. They look at each other, then advance to
the front of the stage—Aaron on the side next the table: Martin on the side
next the locker]* I am waiting for an answer.

Martin   It is mockery to ask for one. Have you forgotten yesterday?—
before the boat came to rescue us from starvation?

Aaron   No.   40

Martin   Have you forgotten your getting out of bed, and sitting there,
almost where you're standing now?

Aaron   I do'nt remember getting out of bed, or sitting there.

Martin   You do'nt! There is the very chair you sat on—there, the very place on the table where the drop of water was spilt—the drop of water that you took for a drop of blood. *[Aaron immediately crosses from the table to the locker, without answering. Martin crosses to the table.]*

Aaron   *[Seating himself.]* I'm not as strong as I ought to be yet—I must sit down.

Martin   Why not here in your usual place?

Aaron   I like the locker for a change.

Martin   *[aside.]* For a change?—How suddenly he left the table when I said that about the spot of blood! 10

Aaron   What are you muttering about? Out with it! What do you suspect me of?—You talked about blood, just now. Is it murder?—Ha! ha! You're a dutiful son! You honor your father's grey hairs! Ha! ha! ha! Ten years ago I should have doubled my fist and knocked you down for looking at me like that. Now I'm old and fit for nothing but to laugh at you. Ha! ha! ha! Damn your suspicious looks! I hate a spy: I curse a spy with all my heart and soul. What do you suspect? Out with it, Spy—out with it!

Martin   *[aside]* Is he in his right senses?

Aaron   What do you suspect? 20

Martin   I suspect nothing: I know what your own lips told me yesterday.

Aaron   And what was that? Come! let's hear it all from beginning to end.

Martin   To what purpose? You were famished and in fear of death yesterday—and you spoke. Food has given you back your strength and your hope of life today—and you deny your words. Why should I repeat the infamous story of the murder of Lady Grace? Why remind you again of the spot that you talked of at this table? You have forgotten yesterday—would to Heaven that I had lost my memory of it as well!

Aaron   The murder of Lady Grace! What story-book have you been reading that in? *[Looks away.]* Lady Grace? A pretty name! Who was Lady 30 Grace? I never heard of her before.

Martin   *[aside.]* He looked away from me while he said that!

Aaron   I never heard of her before.

Martin   You had heard of her yesterday—for when you knew that the name of the wrecked brig was "The Lady Grace," you gave a scream that rang through the lighthouse.

Aaron   *[Turning round angrily]* How dare you suspect your father!

Martin   I would give my right hand to know that he was innocent.

Aaron   Innocent of what?

Martin   Of all share in the crime which began in the farmhouse bedroom, 40 and ended in the Daw's Cave.

Aaron   The Daws' Cave? A famous place for smugglers. What about the Daws' Cave?

Martin   Did you never stand in it with Benjamin Tranter—one night, when
a woman's corpse lay between you? One night when the tide was at the ebb
and the sand was shining under the harvest moon?

Aaron   [starting up.] How dare you bandy questions with your father?

Martin   I will ask no more: they are worse than useless.

Aaron   [angrily approaching the table.] How dare you talk about yesterday? You were not in your right senses yesterday! You were so weak
with hunger yesterday that you wandered in your mind! How dare you sit
there, with your cursed, suspicious, Judas-face, and talk about yesterday?
[Strikes his fist passionately on the table.]   10

Martin   [pointing to the place.] Your hand was on it again then!

Aaron   On what?

Martin   On the place where the drop of water was, which you said was a
drop of blood. [Aaron suddenly turns from the table, and goes back to his
seat on the locker. Martin watches him anxiously. There is another pause.]

Aaron   [with a sudden change to gentleness in his voice and manner.]
Martin, we are getting over hot and angry about this. I am a little too hasty
with you; and you are a little too hard on me. Let us talk about it quietly. I
was nigh dead with hunger and weakness yesterday; and Jacob told me this
morning I was wandering in my mind. Is that true?   20

Martin   It is true.—[aside.] What can be the meaning of this sudden
change?

Aaron   Wandering in my mind—as Jacob says. Famished and in fear of
death—as you yourself said a minute ago. Now tell me, Martin, is it fair
to expect a man in that state to speak sense and truth? Is it fair to suspect a
man on the strength of what dropped from him when he was light-headed?

Martin   I ca'nt tell—I know nothing for certain. [aside] Can it be? Can
that horrible confession have sprung only from the dream of a wandering
mind?

Aaron   I have heard say, Martin, that starved men, when the weakness gets   30
to their heads, have dreams and visions. I dreamed; and all the night long I
had dreadful visions. Did I get up from my bed, and sit there, and talk? It's
well I did no worse—well for both of us—you must own that, Martin?

Martin   [aside.] He spoke confusedly and wildly, yesterday, when he
began—but then he went on and mentioned names and places—he spoke
of the least things—he stopped to tell the smallest particulars—

Aaron   You own that, do'nt you?

Martin   [aside.] The time of the year—the talk between himself and the
murderer—the old sheep-dog whining and trembling—the leather bag
of money—the crying of the poor people and the children after the kind   40
friend they had lost—the very dress that the lady had on—he mentioned all
those things, and more. Are men who wander in their minds ever as exact
as that?

Aaron   Do'nt keep on muttering to yourself, Martin. Talk to me.

Martin   *[aside]* That scream too, when Phoebe told him the name of the brig! My memory, my reason, my conscience, all tell me but too plainly that when he spoke yesterday he must have spoken the truth.

Aaron   Tell me all the wild words I said, when I was in that lightheaded state. You have told me nothing yet, except that I spoke about somebody I never heard of before. *[Looks away again.]* Somebody named Lady Grace. How came I to talk about Lady Grace?

[Enter Lady Grace. She is dressed, in the fashion of a century ago, exactly in accordance with Aaron's description of her in the first Act. She enters   10 *noiselessly, and stands close against the wall of the room, so that Martin and Aaron, who sit with their backs to it, cannot see her.]*

Martin   You told me you had seen her ghost. You told me her ghost called you by your name; and, reminding you of a dreadful secret, said, "Tell it, Aaron Gurnock; tell it before you die." *[Lady Grace starts, and looks earnestly towards Aaron.]*

Aaron   *[in low tones.]* Dreams, son Martin—dreams of a wandering mind.

Martin   *[also lowering his voice.]* You described the very dress she wore:— A black hood, with white next the face—a black gown—and long, hanging white sleeves.   20

Aaron   *[Faintly.]* Dreams! dreams!

Martin   Oh, would to Heaven they were!

Aaron   *[in a whisper.]* Dreams!

Martin   Is it a dream that Lady Grace was once a living woman? A dream that she came to your farm-house for shelter? A dream that she was murdered for the money she had with her by Benjamin Tranter? A dream that you allowed him to escape, and helped him to hide her corpse?—Oh, father, if all this is a dream; if you are innocent of all share in the guilt of blood, give me proof of it, and make my life happy again! Give me proof of it; and let me marry Phoebe with a clear   30 conscience!—Father, do you hear me? Will you doubt and question and dispute with me no longer? Will you tell me, in one honest word, whether all you said at this table yesterday, when you spoke of Lady Grace, is true or false? *[Lady Grace advances towards them down the middle of the stage.]*

Aaron   *[hiding his face.]* False!

Lady Grace   *[standing between them]* True!

Aaron   *[Looking at her and sinking to his knees.]* Mercy! mercy!

Martin   *[starting up.]* Lord save us! The figure my father saw—the very dress that he described as the dress of Lady Grace!   40

Aaron   *[stretching out his hands towards Lady Grace.]* You found me in the night-time—you came stealing on me with your ghostly step—you said, "Tell it,"—and I told it! Oh, why did I ever speak again? why, why

bring you back to surprise me, with the false thought in my heart and the
false word on my lip? Spare me—spare me! Remember how I was tempted
when I denied my words! Remember that the shame of my guilt was
exposed before my son!—Oh, it is hard to hold to the truth; when the truth
makes a man despised by his own child.—Spare me, for I have repented!
Leave me, and let me die in peace!

Martin   *[crossing to Aaron.]* Father! there was a lady saved from shipwreck
yesterday—

Aaron   Martin! on your knees—on your knees before a spirit from the
dead!   10

Martin   There was a lady saved from shipwreck while you and I were down
here alone. That lady—

Lady Grace   *[To Martin.]* Hush! let me speak. *[To Aaron.]* Aaron Gurnock, Lady Grace lives—she stands before you and speaks to you now.

Aaron   The ghost spoke to me in the night—but not in that voice.

Lady Grace   Rise from your knees and touch me.

Aaron   The ghost looked at me in the night—but not with those eyes.

Martin   *[looking earnestly at Lady Grace.]* She lives! who could have
dared to hope it? She stands before us and speaks to us—I can hardly
believe it even yet!   20

Lady Grace   *[To Aaron.]* Touch me; and be sure that I am mortal as yourself. Rise from your knees—or, if you kneel at all, kneel in thanksgiving.
The mercy of Heaven that saved me, has saved you also from the commission of a deadly sin. The chances of repentance and atonement are yet
your's. Touch my hand—touch it, and be assured that I am alive. *[Aaron
affrightedly obeys her, and starts thunderstruck to his feet the instant he
touches her. Lady Grace clasps his hand firmly.]*

Aaron   Alive? *[Looks intently at her for a moment—then reels back in a
swoon towards the locker. Lady Grace keeps him grasped by the hand
and shoulder as he sinks on the seat. Then places herself by his side and*   30
supports him.]

Lady Grace   He has only fainted. Leave it to me to recover him.

Martin   To you!

Lady Grace   Yes—this is woman's work. *[supports Aaron's head on her
shoulder.]* How he has suffered! It is not Time only that has traced these
furrows on his face! *[Passes her handkerchief over his forehead—then
begins to loosen his neckcloth.]*

Martin   Oh, Madam, to see your kind hand stretched out to help him; and
then to think—!

Lady Grace   Hush, Martin! In the wrecking of the brig on these rocks, and   40
in the saving of my life from the walls of this lighthouse, there is more
than mere Chance. The Mercy to which I owe my existence has saved me
to succour and forgive! *[Loosens the collar of Aaron's shirt.]* So: that is

better.—Is it not true that he confessed all to you, yesterday? I overheard your last words together on my entry into this room.

Martin   He confessed all, Madam, that he could know.

Lady Grace   And the rest it is fit that you should hear from my lips. The last thing I remember at the farm-house is seeing a man shorter and darker than your father by my bedside, with a knife in his hand. Does he still live?

Martin   He is dead, or come what might of it, I would have gone to the ends of the earth to make him answer for his crime.

Lady Grace   *[Bending over Aaron.]* See! he is less pale already. *[Puts back his hair from his face; then fans him with her handkerchief while she goes* 10 *on speaking.]* My next remembrance is of waking, as it seemed to me, on board a ship, and of being questioned by strangers in a foreign tongue. In a few days more I knew that I had been found by smugglers in the Daw's Cave—that they had taken me away in their vessel—and that we had been chased and captured by a French privateer—

Martin   You must be weary of supporting him, Madam—Will you let me take your place?

Lady Grace   No, no—in a few minutes he will be well again. *[Touches Aaron's wrist.]* His pulse is beating more firmly every moment.—We were among the first prisoners whom the French took—it was then the begin- 20 ning of the Seven Years' War—my wound was long to heal—exile too was heavy to bear at first—but in making myself helpful among my coun- trymen who were taken prisoners—in comforting the downhearted and the sick—I learnt patience, and bore with my hard lot. The articles of peace were signed only a few months back—I embarked for Plymouth in the vessel which was lost yesterday—

Martin   And that vessel was called "The Lady Grace"!

Lady Grace   Called so after my name. My fellow prisoners had a grate- ful remembrance of what little I had done to help them; and they begged that the first English ship despatched from the foreign port after the 30 war, might be called The Lady Grace. *[Points to Aaron.]* Hark! he is breathing more audibly: his senses are coming back. Take him from me now, Martin; for it might be dangerous if he saw me when he first opens his eyes again. *[Martin takes Lady Grace's place.]* One word more before he recovers. There is a young girl here who has been very kind to me since my rescue from the wrecked ship. Her name is Phoebe—is it not?

Martin   Yes, Madam—Phoebe Dale.

Lady Grace   Fan his face a little still. *[Points to Aaron, and gives her hand- kerchief to Martin.]* Phoebe has been speaking to me of an obstacle to your 40 marriage and of a change in your conduct towards her.

Martin   A change in my conduct, it may be—but none in my love. The misery of hearing my father's confession—

Lady Grace   Let us not refer to it again. *[Points to Aaron.]* He is trying to
lift his head. Raise it for him a little. I heard what you said, Martin when
you spoke of your father's confession and of your own marriage. You have
a true heart: and your courage and honour shall meet with their reward. I—
who of all persons living have the most right to say it—I tell you that you
may marry Phoebe with a clear conscience now; and I promise to make
your happiness and her's my care.

Martin   Oh, Madam! how can I thank you? how show myself worthy—?

Lady Grace   Silence! your father is recovering. Let us say no more.—Be
gentle in recalling him to what happened after I came into this room. Wait   10
here till my return. I go to tell Phoebe that all her troubles are at an end. Be
careful with your father, Martin—be careful with him at first. *[Exit.]*

Aaron   *[recovering.]* Where am I? What has happened?

Martin   Nothing to hurt us, father—everything to make us grateful and
hopeful for the rest of our lives.

Aaron   Am I right in my mind? Did I see her?—Was it long ago, or only
lately?—Did I really see her alive?

Martin   Alive!—a living, breathing woman—an angel of mercy and forgiveness!

Aaron   Forgiveness?—Let me be!—my head whirls—let me be for a min-   20
ute by myself. *[Martin leaves him. Enter Phoebe.]*

Phoebe   Martin! Martin! I said the lady would help us—I knew it would all
end well if we only trusted to her!

Martin   Do you know <u>how</u> it has ended, Phoebe?

Phoebe   No. I could wait to ask nothing—I was too happy. First the lady
came to me, and said, all my anxieties might be at an end—Then my father
followed her, and told me he had done you wrong—and then I suppose I
must have flushed up red in the face with joy; for they both smiled at me;
and I ran away to you here. I can wait patiently to know <u>how</u> it has ended,
Martin.—It is enough for me now to know that it has ended well.   30

Martin   Enough? Think again, Phoebe—are you sure that it is enough?

Phoebe   Quite sure. What more can I want to know at such a moment as
this?

Martin   My conduct seemed strange to you. You might want to know that I
was not to blame.

Phoebe   I always knew that.—Martin! Martin! did I not say that if all the
world doubted you, I would trust you still?

[Enter Lady Grace and Jacob.]

Lady Grace   *[To Martin.]* Is your father composed enough yet to be spoken
to?   40

Martin   I will prepare him, Madam, to hear you. *[Lady Grace takes Phoebe
aside and speaks to her.]*

Jacob   Martin, my lad, I ask your pardon for ever having doubted you.

Martin   Do'nt name it, Jacob. Do'nt let us ever name it again. *[Goes to Aaron. Enter Furley, and the three extra lightkeepers.]*

Furley   The boat for shore!—Jacob, here are the three lightkeepers of the relief all ready for duty. Aaron, Martin, look alive! The boat is manned for shore. *[Lady Grace leaves Phoebe, and approaches Aaron and Martin.]*

Phoebe   *[To Jacob.]* The boat for shore! How the sound of those words has altered for the better, father, since we heard them last!

Aaron   *[To Martin.]* Whose hand helped to lay her in the Daw's Cave where the cruel sea might take her? What atonement can my bitterest repentance offer to her?—Forgive me?—how can she forgive me?   10

Lady Grace   *[advancing between them, and offering her hand to Aaron.]* Thus! *[Aaron hides his face with a gesture of despair. Lady Grace touches him on the shoulder.]* Take it.—I entreat, I command you to take it. The privilege of forgiving is a right, Aaron Gurnock, that we may all insist on. *[Aaron bends forward and kisses Lady Grace's hand.]* Rise now; and let us embark. The boat is ready for shore—the boat that takes me back to my poor peasant-neighbours who love me: the boat that takes you to your son's wedding. *[Aaron slowly rises.]*

Martin   *[approaching.]* He is still weak—he wants an arm to lean on.

Lady Grace   Let it be mine then. Your place is by Phoebe. Remember, this   20 is your first step on the way to church; and in a wedding-procession the bride and bridegroom walk together. *[Martin joins Phoebe. The chorus of the song in Act I is heard from outside. Furley and Jacob place themselves nearest the door. The three lightkeepers are ranged against the Flat. Lady Grace turns again to Aaron, and takes his arm in her's]*

Furley   *[to Jacob]* The boat's crew are getting tired of waiting for us.

Jacob   And they're wiling away the time with a snatch of Phoebe's song.

Lady Grace   *[To Aaron.]* Come! that is not a face for a marriage—You must learn to look happier on the wedding-day. Hark! The stout rowers remind us that we keep them resting idly on their oars. *[waving her hand   30 towards the door.]* To shore, friends—to shore!

[As they all move to go out, the curtain falls.]

TEXTUAL NOTES

Sometime between the composition of *The Storm at the Lighthouse* and April 1856, Collins revised the play into a shorter version titled *The Lighthouse*. Although *The Lighthouse* was published in French during Collins's lifetime, neither version of the play has ever been published in English. Therefore, the textual notes below are based entirely on a comparison of each version's sole surviving manuscript entirely in Collins's hand. The textual notes consist of changes to wording, and dialogue transferred from one character to another. Variations in spelling, capitalization, and punctuation are not included, except when they occur within changes to wording.

The abbreviations used in the textual notes are as follows:

D = dialogue
rev. = revised to
canc. = canceled
add. = added
trans. = transferred

309.1
The Storm At The Lighthouse. **rev.** *The Lighthouse.*
309.4
A Play In Two Acts **rev.** *A Drama In Two Acts.*
309.8
Add. Men **beneath** *Persons of the Drama.*
309.9–10
Head Lightkeeper at the Eddystone Lighthouse **rev.** *(The Head Lightkeeper)*
309.11
Second Lightkeeper **rev.** *(The second Lightkeeper)*
309.12
Third Lightkeeper **rev.** *(The Third Lightkeeper)*
309.14
Fishermen. Sailors. Lightkeepers. **rev.** *Lightkeepers of the relieving party. Sailors. &c. &c.*
309.16
Add. Women.
309.17
Lady Grace **rev.** *The Shipwrecked Lady.*
309.29–40
Description of entire opening scene rev. *[Scene: A Chamber in the Lighthouse. On the left, a door. Nearer to the audience a window closed by a shutter, and a locker. On the right, a bed, hollowed in the wall, with an old curtain hanging before it. A fire-place, a chest, and a stool, with a table between them. On the table a jug of water, an hour-glass, and a slate. Jacob Dale is discovered, sitting by the table, looking down at the slate. Martin Gurnock, is on the other side of the table, lying asleep on the floor, with his head*

on the chest. A pause after the rising of the curtain. Nothing is heard but the whistling of the wind outside, and the crash of the waves against the Lighthouse.]
309.43
Canc. *Martin!* **before** *[Another pause.]*
310.1
Canc. *now it sounds worse than ever.*
310.9
Canc. *[Raises himself to an upright position on the chest.]*
310.11
log-book **rev.** *log*
310.11–12
I ca'nt somehow **rev.** *It's as much as I can do to*
310.13
Canc. *and it's not for want of trying: it is'nt indeed, Martin.*
310.14
Add. *[rising]* **before D**
310.14
It is *day again, then? Another day!* **rev.** *Another day come then! How long is it past midnight?*
310.15
[Looking round at the clock.] **rev.** *[turning the hour glass]*
310.15
Just ten in the morning. Here's **rev.** *One in the morning. Here is*
310.17–18
I can make that out still; but I ca'nt manage to write even so much as **rev.** *I'm just a-going to make today's entry now. [Writing]*
310.19–20
I ca'nt write as much as that, this morning **rev.** *Provisions all exhausted."*

310.21–31
Canc. *Let me try ... they will know well enough what we died of.*

310.34
Canc. *Look back on the slate. I ca'nt reckon it in my head.*

310.35–40
D trans. to Jacob

310.36
provision **rev.** *provisions*

310.40
today, Jacob! **rev.** *today, Martin!*

310.41–42
Canc. *ten miles out at sea*

311.5–6
Canc. *A few hours may bring a lull in the gale— a few hours may bring the boat from shore. While there's life there's hope, Jacob!*

311.6
We've **rev.** *We have*

311.8–9
A little better than half a wine-glass full. It's in the wicker bottle, locked up there **rev.** *A little better than a dram left. It's in the bottle there.*

311.10
teaspoonful **rev.** *drop*

311.11
[Looks towards the Tarpaulin.] **rev.** *[Looks toward the curtain over the bed]*

311.12
on the table? **rev.** *by the table?*

311.13–14
Canc. *I'm afraid our bringing his bed down here into the warmest room has'nt done much for him.*

311.15–16
[Goes to the Tarpaulin: draws a corner of it aside, and looks in.] **rev.** *[Goes to the bed, draws aside a corner of the curtain, and looks in. Jacob puts the hour glass away in the locker.]*

311.18
Add. *[Returning to the table]* **before D**

311.18
Lighter in the head seemingly than either of us two. **rev.** *Light in the head.*

311.19–30
Canc. *Can you measure ... Another pause.]*

311.30
a-dreaming **rev.** *dreaming*

311.37
come Christmas-time! **rev.** *come this next blessed Christmas time!*

311.39–41
Canc. *I fancy ... of this parish."*

311.42
when they heard that **rev.** *when they heard it.*

312.5
give **rev.** *gave*

312.10–11
What's Martin **rev.** *What has Martin*

312.11
He's been **rev.** *He has been*

312.12
he's been **rev.** *he has been*

312.13
what's more **rev.** *what is more*

312.18
it's only **rev.** *a lock of her hair tied in*

312.19–20
Canc. *I did it ... this string*

312.20
[Pulls it out of the breast of his jacket.] **rev.** *[Takes it out of his cravat.]*

312.23
Keep it hanging outside, as it is now. **rev.** *Do'nt put it back—tie it to your coat.*

312.24
Canc. *Why? What good will that do?*

312.28
Canc. *Martin*

312.28–29
sea may run high **rev.** *sea may run mountains high*

312.29
the gale may blow **rev.** *the wind may blow Heavens hard*

312.29–30
for the lighthouse **rev.** *to the Lighthouse*

312.31
After *one of the crew!* **add.** *[A Pause. The storm, which has been heard under the speakers' voices throughout, now grows louder.]*

312.32–36
Canc. *One of the crew! ... [Rises.]*

312.36–37
Have you been up to the Crow's Nest to look out this morning? **rev.** *When was you up in the Crow's Nest last?*

312.38
Yes, at eight oclock. **rev.** *At ten o'clock.*

312.40
Add. *[rising]* **before D**

312.40–41
the fog had lifted **rev.** *there was a break and a strip of moon.*

312.42

through the glass, I thought I saw a ship. **rev.**
*through the night-glass, I thought I made out
a ship.*

313.2

is not worth sixpence. **rev.** *is not worth that!
[Snaps his fingers]*

313.3–4

[Goes to the sliding-shutter.] **rev.** *[Goes to the
closed window]*

313.8

I wo'nt keep the shutter back **rev.** *I wo'nt keep
it open*

313.8–11

*[Mounts on the locker, and pulls back the shut-
ter. The howling of the wind is heard with
sudden violence. He closes the shutter again
quickly, and descends from the locker wiping the spray from his face.]* **rev.** *[Opens the
shutter. The howling of the wind is heard
with sudden violence. The spray flies in at
the window. He closes the shutter and returns to the table, wiping the spray from his
face]*

313.13–14

Canc. *Stop here, Jacob ... [Going out.]*

313.15

Add. *[Jacob rises]* **before D**

313.15

D trans. to Martin

313.16

D trans. to Jacob

313.17–18

Canc. *What for? ... down on us again?*

313.18–20

*You know what our orders are ... sounding the
gong."* **trans. to Jacob**

313.20–22

Canc. *We must do our duty to the last. You stop
here with father, while I go up to the gong.*

313.23–30

Canc. *Steady there ... then stops.]*

313.33–314.2

Canc. *You had much better ... to an old one.*

314.5–6

[Looks towards the Tarpaulin] **rev.** *[Puts the
water jug away in the locker; then looks towards the bed]*

314.8–9

*[Sits down in the chair by the table, turning his
back to the tarpaulin, but leaving the whole
of it visible to the audience.]* **rev.** *[Sits down
by the table, turning his back to the bed, but
leaving it visible to the audience.]*

314.10

[Taking it up in his hand.] **rev.** *[Pressing the ribbon to his lips.]*

314.10–11

Canc. *I ca'nt bear to look at it: I must hide it
away again.*

314.15

Canc. *[Turns again towards the tarpaulin.]*

314.19–20

*[The Tarpaulin moves—a hand appears, clutch-
ing at one side of it impatiently.]* **rev.** *[A
hand appears, moving the bed-curtain.]*

314.21

this morning **rev.** *last night*

314.22–24

*[The Tarpaulin is moved aside from behind, and
Aaron Gurnock appears in a sitting position on his bed. He has an old boat-cloak
wrapped round him, which falls to his feet.*
rev. *[The curtain is torn aside, and Aaron
Gurnock appears from the bed.*

314.26

[calling faintly from the bedside.] **rev.** *[speaking
faintly from the bed.]*

314.29

when I think of it! **rev.** *as I think of it!*

314.30–31

*Aaron starts as he hears it; then slowly rises,
and advances with difficulty to the back of
his son's chair.]* **rev.** *Aaron starts—then advances to the back of his son's chair.]*

314.34

[Laying his hand on his son's shoulder.] **rev.**
[touching his son's shoulder]

314.35–36

[Aaron nods his head.] **rev.** *[Aaron nods.]*

314.36

Take my chair then: it's nearest the fire. **rev.**
*Sit down on the chest: it is nearest to the
fire.*

314.36–37

Canc. *[Places his father in the chair]*

314.39–40

Canc. *your stuff jerkin on, and*

314.40

to cover you. **rev.** *over you.*

314.40–42

Canc. *Stop ... more comfortable now.*

315.1

this morning **rev.** *last night*

315.12

You're only weak **rev.** *You are only weak*

315.19–20

Canc. *My son is a great scholar; and*

315.20
Martin! Do'nt tell Jacob. **rev.** *Martin! [with terror.] Do'nt tell Jacob!*
315.21–24
Canc. *Do'nt tell what? ... What can he mean?*
315.27–28
Canc. *Do as I bid you, Martin. When I'm dead, it do'nt matter; but*
315.29–32
Canc. *From this time, the strokes grow gradually fainter ... the person making the strokes.]*
315.36–39
Canc. *I ca'nt die without telling ... do you know what you're saying?*
315.42–43
Canc. *Hush! hush! ... Blood?*
316.1–2
I drank some water a little while ago—it's only a drop spilt out of that mug—a drop of water. **rev.** *Jacob drank some water a little while ago—it's only a drop spilt on the table.*
316.12
Canc. *Water now, Martin, if you like; but blood once.—There!*
316.12–13
there's the place **rev.** *[pointing] There's the place*
316.18
Add. *[Fetches the liquor.]* **after** *my share of the brandy*
316.18–22
Canc. *I have got ... half for Jacob.*
316.26
Canc. *last*
316.28–29
Canc. *Oh, not much ... What did I say?*
316.39
Canc. *outside*
316.42
The tall woman **rev.** *The woman*
316.43
She come **rev.** *She came*
317.1–2
Canc. *I could'nt hear you sleeping ... I could only hear <u>her</u>.*
317.4
[shrinking away from the table.] **rev.** *[shrinking away.]*
317.7
Add. *Sit down.* **after** *I must say on to the end.*
317.14
I do remember. **rev.** *I remember.*

317.30
Add. *[Sixth stroke of the gong.]* **after** *I see a lady.*
317.33–35
anybody with her: There were saddle-bags on the pony's back. "I've lost my servant, miles away, in this white sea mist;" she says; "and I want shelter for myself and my pony tonight." **rev.** *any body with her. "I've lost my servant, miles away in this white sea mist," says she, "and I want shelter for myself and my pony tonight." There were saddle-bags on the pony's back.*
317.36
give **rev.** *gave*
317.42
fine **rev.** *pretty*
318.10–11
[Martin starts to his feet, and draws back a step or two, in horror.] **rev.** *[Seventh stroke of the gong.]*
318.11
Canc. *Sit down again, and hear me out. [Martin obeys.]*
318.23
into a sleep.—Sit nearer! What are you shrinking for? **rev.** *into a sleep.—[Martin rises.]—What are you shrinking for?*
318.25
Canc. *[sternly.]*
318.25
Canc. *Remember that you are speaking to your son!*
318.27
on my feet **rev.** *at my feet*
318.32
this table that we are sitting at **rev.** *this table that we are standing by now*
318.34
Canc. *It was blood*
318.35–36
[Rises a little and reaches across the table to enforce Martin's attention by touching his arm.] **rev.** *[Touches Martin's arm to attract his attention.]*
318.39
Canc. *[hiding his face.]*
319.3
Canc. *Hush! or Jacob may hear you.*
319.4–5
Canc. *[To himself] Jacob! Jacob, who took my hand not half an hour ago, and told me I was the son of an honest man!*
319.28
her servant **rev.** *the servant*

319.29
everybody knew **rev.** *everybody believed*
319.30
[Here the sound of the gong **rev.** *[The sound of the gong*
319.39
she heard that our poor **rev.** *she heard our poor*
319.41
strangers **rev.** *strange people*
319.43
Add. *[Throws himself on the table with a cry of despair, and with his face hidden in his hands. A pause. Nothing audible but the storm.]* **after** *That was the only name they gave her—Lady Grace.*
320.1–10
Canc. *And you let the man escape ... [Takes the keepsake from his breast.]*
320.10
Add. *Father! [Tries to raise Aaron from the table; then shrinks away.]* **before** *Oh, Phoebe! Phoebe!*
320.10
Add. *Can I look you in the face after all that I have just heard?* **after** *Oh, Phoebe! Phoebe!*
320.12–14
Canc. *The death of Lady Grace ... on her throat.*
320.14
Hark! I hear something. **trans. from Aaron to Martin**
320.15
Canc. *Was it the wind?*
320.16
Canc. *[starting to his feet.] The wind?*
320.16
It sounded **rev.** *It sounds*
320.17
Canc. *Hush!*
320.19
Add. *[starting up in terror.]* **before D**
320.20–23
Canc. *The fog's lifting towards shore ... Martin! The boat—*
320.24–25
Jacob answers it faintly from above. A distant cheer follows.] **rev.** *Jacob answers faintly from above. A cheer follows.]*
320.26
Canc. *I know he's heard us—*
320.29-30
Can I look her in the face, after all that I have just heard? **rev.** *Dare I look at her after all that I have heard?*

320.30–39
Canc. *[Jacob Dale hurries into the room.] ... She knows my whole heart and soul.*
320.40–41
[Noise and confused voices outside. Martin starts, and goes to the door.] **rev.** *[Noise and speaking outside.]*
320.42
Canc. *Stop! stop with me!*
320.42
[Phoebe speaks outside: **rev.** *[speaking outside.]*
321.1–2
Canc. *[Drawing back into the room] ... stop with me.*
321.4–7
Furley, and the Fishermen and Lightkeepers who have manned the boat, follow her into the room. They carry hampers, baskets, and jars with them, which they arrange in a corner at the back of the stage. **rev.** *Samuel Furley, and the Extra Lightkeepers who have manned the boat, follow her. They carry hampers, baskets, and jars with them, which they arrange at the back of the stage.*
321.8–9
Canc. *[Drawing back a little and looking at him.]*
321.11
[Turns round to where **rev.** *[Turns to where*
321.19–20
Canc. *and casting down her eyes demurely.*
321.26
Canc. *[Turning towards the back of the stage]*
321.31–32
Canc. *Yes, yes. Do as Furley tells you. Rest yourself, my love—rest yourself.*
321.33–34
[Drawing her away to the locker, with an uneasy look at his father.] Come and sit by me, Phoebe. **rev.** *[Fetching two stools, while the Lightkeepers set the table.] Come and sit by me, Phoebe. [Casts an uneasy look at his father.]*
321.36–37
[They seat themselves on the locker. **rev.** *[Seats herself by Martin.]*
321.37
Canc. *Furley comes forward with a saucepan in his hand]*
321.38
[Putting the saucepan on the fire.] **rev.** *[advancing with a saucepan]*
321.38–39
Canc. *Jacob! Where's the cloth and the crockery? [Jacob puts them on.]*

321.39–40
[addressing the boat's crew.] **rev.** *[To the boat's crew.]*
321.40
let's have the table ready **rev.** *let us have dinner ready*
321.40–41
Canc. *[Two of the men move the table to the middle of the stage.]*
321.42
Add. *[starting.]* **before D**
321.43
[Martin rises from the locker] **rev.** *[Martin rises.]*
322.1
Add. *[To Martin.]* **before D**
322.5
Canc. *Of course*
322.7
And we're going **rev.** *And we are going*
322.11
Add. *[Warms the broth over the fire.]* **after** *half-starved men*
322.12–19
Canc. *Give it me now! ... Where are his poor wits wandering to?*
322.25–26
after his father.] **rev.** *towards his father.]*
322.29
Canc. *Oh*
322.30
[rather sadly.] **rev.** *[Sadly.]*
322.33
Canc. *[Taking his hand.]*
322.34
I was'nt fit **rev.** *I was not fit*
323.1
[calling from the fireplace] **rev.** *[From the fireplace]*
323.1–4
Canc. *Jacob, come to the table ... Give us hold of the ladle.*
323.4–6
[Ladles out the broth into basins placed before Aaron, Martin, and Jacob.] Now then, whatever you do, do'nt be in a hurry. **rev.** *Now then whatever you do, do'nt be in a hurry.—[Ladles out the broth. Aaron and Jacob take it at the table. Phoebe takes Martin's basin to him.]*
323.19
Canc. *Oh*
323.21–22
looking after Martin's basin. **rev.** *looking after Martin!*

323.22–31
Canc. *No! it's no good ... When I was at school, they called me pig-headed Sam—and I did'nt get that name for nothing, I can promise you!*
323.37–39
Canc. *More! more! ... one other spoonful!*
323.40
Will you **rev.** *Now, will you*
324.1
he'd be **rev.** *he would be*
324.2
Now, here's a second sup **rev.** *Now there's a second sup*
324.4
[Elevating the ladle] **rev.** *[Raising the ladle.]*
324.9–10
Canc. *I thought you'd give in at last to pig-headed Sam!*
324.14
where's the fourth? **rev.** *where is the fourth?*
324.16–18
Canc. *What you've plucked up your spirits ... How do you feel, Martin!*
324.18–19
Now's the time, I think, to throw in the Dutchman's strong water. **rev.** *Now's the time to throw in the Dutchman's strong waters.— [Produces a bottle of Hollands.]*
324.20–21
Here's all our good healths! **rev.** *Here's all your good healths!*
324.22–41
Canc. *Jump up, lass—and sing us a song ... [ladles out more broth]*
324.42–325.2
Canc. *He was the only one of them who did not join in the chorus ... [Goes up the stage to put the saucepan away]*
325.3–4
[aside.] He never so much as looked at me while I was singing! he wo'nt notice me now! **rev.** *He does'nt notice me: he does'nt seem to know that I am near him.*
325.5–11
Canc. *Clear your pipes, my lads ... Now for my song!*
325.12
Canc. *[Finishing his basin.*
325.14–15
Canc. *What's that? ... [A second report.]*
325.16
Add. *[A second report]* **after** *A ships gun!*
325.17
Canc. *Martin! are you certain of that? [A third report.]*

325.18
A ship in danger **rev.** *A ship in danger!—[A third report.]*
325.19
Canc. *You!*
325.20
D trans. to Martin
325.21
Canc. *Martin*
325.24–25
Canc. *I forgot to tell you of it in the hurry and pleasure of seeing the boat from shore—but*
325.26–27
I thought I saw that same ship, under bare poles, running straight down on us **rev.** *I saw that same ship, under bare poles, bearing straight down on us*
325.28–33
Canc. *I'll go up to the Crow's Nest ... Penhale—you have the keenest eyes of all of us—*
325.33–34
go up, and see what you can make out. If there really is a ship in danger, signal it down here by striking on the gong. [Exit Lightkeeper.] **rev.** *Furley! Go up and see what you can make out. Signal it down here by striking on the gong. [Exit Furley, followed by Lightkeepers]* **with D trans. to Jacob**
325.35
You are quite **rev.** *Are you quite*
325.36–37
I ca'nt be downright certain, because my eyesight's not as good as it used to be; and there was a little fog still hanging to seaward. **rev.** *Yes, though there was a little fog still hanging to seaward.*
325.38–42
Canc. *[Beckoning to his son.] ... the death of Lady Grace!*
325.42–43
[Several loud strokes in quick succession on the gong.] **rev.** *[Loud strokes are heard on the gong.]*
326.1
Add. *[Aaron turns aside and crouches over the fire.]* **after** *in danger!*
326.2–7
Canc. *Martin, have you got a speaking trumpet here? ... crouches over the fire]*
326.9
Stop a bit, Phoebe. Have you found the trumpet, Martin? **rev.** *Wait a bit, Phoebe.*
326.10
Canc. *I've got it.*

326.10–12
[Goes to the sliding shutter and draws it back. The increased sound of wind and sea which is heard immediately, continues until the end of the Act.] **rev.** *[Martin goes to the sliding shutter, and draws it back. The increased sound of wind and sea is heard immediately, and continues until the end of the Act. The whole of this scene, from the time when the first report of the gun is heard, must be played with the greatest rapidity.]*
326.12
Add. *[At the window.]* **before** *The fog is lifting every moment—I can see the ship!*
326.15
What will become **rev.** *Oh, what will become*
326.16–17
Canc. *Cold, cold, cold. What about the ship, son Martin? What more about the ship?*
326.22
that brig will be wrecked **rev.** *she'll be wrecked*
326.23
The only chance of saving the crew **rev.** *The only hope of saving the crew*
326.24
Add. *[Calling off at the door.]* **after** *before the ship strikes.*
326.25–28
Canc. *The ropes are all in the store-room ... while I am in the gallery*
326.28
[To the Lightkeepers &c] **rev.** *[Calling off at the door.]*
326.30
Canc. *[Exit the Lightkeepers.]*
326.32–327.1
Canc. *Yes, yes ... [Hurrying across to the door.]*
327.2
[The Lightkeepers enter with a coil of rope.] **rev.** *[Enter Lightkeepers with a coil of rope.]*
327.3
Canc. *Martin, set them to work. It's time I was in the gallery.*
327.4
[Exit. Followed by Lightkeepers] **rev.** *[Exit, followed by the Lightkeepers.]*
327.5–7
Canc. *Jacob, get that coil unbent ... spread them before the fire.*
327.7–8
[Phoebe opens the chest. Martin goes to the window] **rev.** *[Phoebe opens the chest, and gets out the blankets.]*

327.9–12

Canc. *Now, Aaron, lend a hand here ... help me with the rope.*

327.13

[Hailing the ship through the speaking trumpet] **rev.** *[Returning to the window, and hailing the ship through a speaking-trumpet.]*

327.15

Canc. *What do you see?*

327.20–21

[Jacob carries the free end of the rope to Martin.] **rev.** *[Jacob and Martin pass the rope out of the window.]*

327.22–24

Canc. *[aside to Phoebe.] ... [Paying out the rope.]*

327.25–26

Send a man with the largest block and two pulleys up into the gallery. **rev.** *send a man up into the gallery.*

327.27–30

Canc. *[Keeping with Martin at the window.] ... There's nothing to be frightened of!*

327.32

Add. *[Hailing above.]* **after** *clear of the brig*

327.34

Oh, the boat! the boat! **rev.** *The boat!—the boat's capsized!*

327.35

Canc. *What of her?*

327.36

Canc. *Capsized.*

327.36–38

Canc. *The wave took ... gone to their account already!*

327.42–328.12

Canc. *Give me something more to do! ... horrible death—!*

328.13–14

[Hailing.] Below there! Take a turn with a rope round that man's waist before he goes out on the steps. **rev.** *[calling at the door.] Show your blue lights below, there! The next sea will bring the brig on the rocks. [The blue lights are burnt outside]*

328.15

Add. *[At the window: to Phoebe]* **before D**

328.15

Canc. *The boat!*

328.15–16

Canc. *Look down, Martin—*

328.16–17

There's the name of the ship painted in white on the boat's stern. Use your young eyes, and

try if you can read it. **rev.** *There's the name of the ship painted in white on the stern. Use your young eyes—read it.*

328.18–22

Canc. *Read it? ... what the name is.*

328.23

[Hurrying to the locker.] **rev.** *[getting on a chair to look out]*

328.24

Canc. *Quick! before the waves wash the boat away again!*

328.25

Canc. *[Looking out.]*

328.25–26

Canc. *I can see the poor lost people huddled together on deck.*

328.27

The boat! What is the name on the boat? **rev.** *Quick! quick!*

328.30

[starting forward with the lighted lanthorn in his hand.] **rev.** *[starting forward.]*

328.31–32

Canc. *The brig is on the rocks ... What name?*

328.33

Add. *[Louder]* **before D**

328.33

Canc. *[Crouches on the locker, and hides her face.]*

328.34–36

Martin! The Lady Grace!! [Drops the lanthorn with a scream of terror. Martin springs forward to quiet him. The instant after the crash of the striking vessel is heard on the rocks outside. The Act drop falls.] **rev.** *[With a scream of terror.] Martin! The Lady Grace!!! [The crash of the striking vessel is heard on the rocks outside. Phoebe crouches on the ground and hides her face. Martin springs forward to quiet his father. The Act-drop falls.] End of Act I*

329.4–10

Description of entire opening scene rev. *[Scene: The same as in the preceding Act. Furley, the Lightkeepers, and three sailors, are discovered in the middle of the stage, coiling ropes. Jacob is seated to the right on the chest, splicing a rope's end. Phoebe sits at work on a stool near him. Martin stands alone on the left, looking out of the window.]*

329.12–13

Canc. *Coil them up as neat as you can; and let's have them all put back in their places in the Lighthouse Storeroom.*

329.15
fishermen **rev.** *lightkeepers*

329.17
D trans. to First Lightkeeper

329.19
had'nt **rev.** *had not*

329.28
D trans. to First Lightkeeper

329.30–31
Thoddy of Plymouth is the friend for my money! **rev.** *Thoddy of Plymouth's the man for my money!*

329.32
ought'nt **rev.** *ought not*

329.35
D trans. to First Lightkeeper

329.39
D trans. to First Lightkeeper

330.5
D trans. to Sailors and Lightkeepers

330.10
D trans. to First Lightkeeper

330.11
D trans. to Sailors and Lightkeepers

330.12
Canc. *doggedly*

330.14
D trans. to First Lightkeeper

330.15
work of the two **rev.** *stuff of the two*

330.16
[Exit. The sailors and fishermen follow.] **rev.** *[Exit. The sailors and Lightkeepers follow]*

330.17
Add. *[Looking after them.]* **before D**

330.28
Canc. *[Innocently.]*

331.1
[To himself] **rev.** *[aside]*

331.2–3
Martin, you hav'nt seen the lady yet, have you? You were down here alone with your father all the time, were you not? **rev.** *Martin, neither you nor your father have seen the lady yet?—Am I right?*

331.5
[To himself.] **rev.** *[aside]*

331.7–10
Canc. *Here are these two, sulky and silent without any reason for it—and there is old Aaron, alone down stairs, looking as suspiciously at every man of our boat's crew, as if he thought we were all in league to rob and murder him before we go ashore.*

331.11
Canc. *[overhearing the last words.]*

331.11–12
When did you say the boat was going back to shore, Master Furley? **rev.** *Do you know when the boat is going back to shore, Master Furley?*

331.15
Canc. *enough*

331.19
[To himself.] **rev.** *[aside]*

331.19
Canc. *She's in the conspiracy too!*

331.20
Canc. *Better be off before I get told to go.*

331.23
Canc. *What must Phoebe think of me?—*

331.25–33
Canc. *[glancing at Martin.] He has not once spoken to me ... Is this long enough?*

331.34
Add. *[Looks round.]* **before D**

331.36
Add. *[still at the window.]* **before D**

331.38
lay hands upon him **rev.** *lay hands on him*

332.2
[Turns away again.] **rev.** *[Looks away again.]*

332.3
[To Phoebe.] **rev.** *[Removing Phoebe, and seating her with her back to Martin.]*

332.5–6
in what little I said to her **rev.** *in what little I told her*

332.20
Canc. *[Laying her head on Jacob's shoulder.]*

332.21
Canc. *but*

332.28
Canc. *[Throwing aside his work.]*

332.29–30
But it's your father's business, Phoebe, to speak to him **rev.** *But it is your father's business to speak to him, Phoebe*

332.35
Canc. *[Rising.]*

332.36-38
Canc. *Why? ... I think I can.*

332.38–39
Yes, yes, my child—go away. **rev.** *Well, well, my child, perhaps you are right—go, if you like.*

333.5
Canc. *Stand up, and*

333.10
she's been telling tales **rev.** *she has been telling tales*

333.16–20
Canc. Jacob: *What does it mean? Have you lost all your liking for her?* Martin: *I love her more dearly than ever.* Jacob: *You take a strange way of showing it. Any man with eyes in his head, who saw how you have been treating her since last night, would say you wanted an excuse for breaking your marriage-promise.* **[Collins erroneously retains Phoebe's assertion at 335.4–5 that she overheard these canc. lines.]**

333.20–21
You have behaved as if **rev.** *You have behaved, I say, as if*

333.23
Canc. *No such thought ever entered my heart.*

333.34
where visitors come and go **rev.** *where visitors can come and go*

333.36–37
Canc. *three men who ought to know each other's secrets by this time, if ever men did yet since the world began.*

333.38
Canc. *Make a clean breast of it.*

333.39–40
Canc. *I have told you ... And why not yet?*

333.41
Canc. *Because*

334.7–9
Canc. *Surely, surely my past conduct to you and to Phoebe gives me the right to ask that much!—Another day, Jacob—only one other day, to think what I ought to do!*

334.19–25
Canc. *my head swims ... it burns and swims*

334.25–26
still I see nothing between confession that would be ruin **rev.** *Half an hour to choose between confession that would be ruin*

334.29–30
Canc. *Martin! ... to make the trial complete!*

334.36
Canc. *Phoebe*

334.40–41
Canc. *[Aside, and moving from her towards the table.] ... oh, never! never!*

335.3
Canc. *[Sinking back into the chair.]*

335.13
Add. *[aside.]* **before D**

335.13–19
Canc. *[Reflects for a moment.] ... no help to me now.*

335.20
Canc. *[aside] I know who* <u>would</u> *be—the lady—*

335.21–23
Canc. <u>She</u> *has book-learning to help him with—more book-learning than all of us here put together.*

335.23
If she could only be got to talk to Martin **rev.** *If she would only talk to him*

335.25–26
[Goes to the door—then stops, looks at Martin, and returns.] **rev.** *[goes to the door; then returns to Martin]*

335.28
[offers him her hand.] **rev.** *[Gives him her hand.]*

335.29–30
Canc. *[Turns from her]*

335.31
Add. *[aside]* **before D**

335.31
My last hope of help is the hope I have in her. **rev.** *My last hope of help is in her!*

335.35
She is gone—gone perhaps never to return again. **rev.** *She's gone—gone, never perhaps to return again!*

335.36
have grown up to hear **rev.** *have lived to hear*

335.37–38
Canc. *better I had never been born than have lived to suffer for your sin!*

335.42
Canc. *[rising.]*

336.1
speak these words **rev.** *speak those words*

336.3–4
Canc. *You know well enough. Do you mean to stop here?—If you do, let me go. I may forget what is due to my father if I stay.*

336.6
Canc. *[Placing himself before the door.]*

336.8–16
Canc. *Let me go! ... No!*

336.17
What should you say of a man **rev.** *Done? What should you say of a man*

336.20
Remember what you told me yesterday! **rev.** *Remember what you said to me yesterday!*

336.21–23
Canc. *Yesterday? ... before that shipwreck!*

336.24
Canc. *[Aaron starts.]*
336.34
Canc. *[aside] Is he going to deny his own words?*
336.35–37
[A pause. They look at each other, then advance to the front of the stage—Aaron on the side next the table: Martin on the side next the locker] **rev.** *[A pause. They look steadfastly at each other]*
336.37
Canc. *I am waiting for an answer.*
336.38–40
Canc. *It is mockery ... No.*
336.41–42
Have you forgotten your getting out of bed, and sitting there, almost where you're standing now? **rev.** *Have you forgotten your getting out of bed and sitting there? [Points to the place]*
337.1–2
There is the very chair you sat on—there, the very place on the table where the drop of water was spilt **rev.** *Here is the very place where you sat, and where the table stood on which the drop of water was spilt*
337.3–4
[Aaron immediately crosses from the table to the locker, without answering. Martin crosses to the table.] **rev.** *[Aaron moves away abruptly. Martin and he cross each other.]*
337.5–8
Canc. *[Seating himself.] ... the locker for a change.*
337.9
Canc. *For a change?—*
337.9
How suddenly he left the table **rev.** *How suddenly he changed*
337.22–25
Canc. *And what was that? ... Why should I repeat*
337.26–28
Canc. *Why remind you again of the spot that you talked of at this table? You have forgotten yesterday—would to Heaven that I had lost my memory of it as well!*
337.32–37
Canc. *[aside.] ... How dare you suspect your father!*
337.38
I would give my right hand to know that he was innocent. **rev.** *Never? I would give my right hand to know that you were innocent!*

338.1–2
when a woman's corpse lay between you? **rev.** *when the body of a lady lay between you?*
338.4
Canc. *[starting up.]*
338.4
How dare you bandy questions with your father? **rev.** *How dare you ask such questions?*
338.5–6
Canc. *I will ask no more ... [angrily approaching the table.]*
338.8–9
How dare you sit there **rev.** *How dare you stand there*
338.10
[Strikes his fist passionately on the table.] **rev.** *[Seizes him by the arm]*
338.11–12
Canc. *[pointing to the place.] ... On what?*
338.13–14
On the place where the drop of water was, which you said was a drop of blood. **rev.** *Take your hand away! I ca'nt bear that hand! I see it pointing again to the drop of water on your old round table—the drop of water that you said was a drop of blood!*
338.14–15
[Aaron suddenly turns from the table, and goes back to his seat on the locker. Martin watches him anxiously. There is another pause.] **rev.** *[Aaron suddenly turns away up the stage. Martin and he cross each other again.]*
338.16
[with a sudden change to gentleness in his voice and manner.] **rev.** *[After a pause, suddenly changing his voice and manner]*
338.19–20
Canc. *this morning*
338.21–22
It is true.—[aside.] What can be the meaning of this sudden change? **rev.** *[surprised] It is true!*
338.23–24
as Jacob says. Famished and in fear of death—as you yourself said a minute ago. **rev.** *as Jacob said—famished and in fear of death as you saw with your own eyes.*
338.27
Canc. *Can it be?*
338.32–37
Canc. *Did I get up ... You own that, do'nt you?*
338.42
those things **rev.** *these things*
338.42–43

ever as exact as that? **rev.** *ever so exact as that?*
339.2
That scream too **rev.** *That cry, too*
339.3–4
Canc. *My memory, my reason, my conscience,
all tell me but too plainly that when he spoke
yesterday*
339.5–7
Canc. *Tell me all the wild words I said, when I
was in that lightheaded state. You have told
me nothing yet, except that I spoke about
somebody I never heard of before. [Looks
away again.]*
339.9–12
*[Enter Lady Grace. She is dressed, in the fashion
of a century ago, exactly in accordance with
Aaron's description of her in the first Act. She
enters noiselessly, and stands close against
the wall of the room, so that Martin and
Aaron, who sit with their backs to it, cannot
see her.]* **rev.** *[Enter the Shipwrecked Lady.
She is dressed in the fashion of a century ago,
exactly in accordance with Aaron's description of Lady Grace in the first Act. She enters
noiselessly, and stops close against the wall
of the room, so that Martin and Aaron who
stand with their backs to it, cannot see her.]*
**[Collins designates Lady Grace as "The
Shipwrecked Lady" and "The Lady," so
that readers of the published French translation will not learn her true identity earlier than an audience would learn the same.]**
339.15–16
*[Lady Grace starts, and looks earnestly towards
Aaron.]* **rev.** *[The Lady starts, and looks
earnestly towards Aaron.]*
339.17
Canc. *[in low tones.]*
339.18
Canc. *[also lowering his voice.]*
339.21
Canc. *[Faintly.]*
339.22
Canc. *Oh*
339.23
[in a whisper.] **rev.** *[Faintly.]*
339.24–28
Canc. *Is it a dream ... to hide her corpse?*
339.28–29
*Oh, father, if all this is a dream; if you are inno-
cent of all share in the guilt of blood* **rev.** *Oh,
if all this dreadful story is really a dream; if
you are innocent of all share in the murder
of Lady Grace*

339.31–32
Canc. *Father, do you hear me? Will you doubt
and question and dispute with me no longer?*
339.32–33
*Will you tell me, in one honest word, whether all
you said at this table yesterday* **rev.** *Father!
father! tell me in one honest word, whether
all you said yesterday*
339.34–35
Canc. *[Lady Grace advances towards them
down the middle of the stage.]*
339.36
[hiding his face.] **rev.** *[Loudly and with an effort.]*
339.37
Lady Grace **rev.** *The Lady*
339.37
[standing between them] **rev.** *[Stepping between
them.]*
339.39
Canc. *[starting up.]*
339.39–40
the very dress that he described **rev.** *the very
dress he described*
339.41
[stretching out his hands towards Lady Grace.]
rev. *[On his knees, stretching out his hands
towards The Lady.]*
340.2
false word on my lip? **rev.** *false word on my lips!*
340.7
Canc. *[crossing to Aaron.]*
340.9
Martin! on your knees **rev.** *On your knees, Martin!*
340.11–12
Canc. *There was a lady saved from shipwreck
while you and I were down here alone. That
lady—*
340.13
Lady Grace **rev.** *The Lady*
340.13
[To Martin.] **rev.** *[To Martin, who tries to speak
again.]*
340.18–20
Canc. *[looking earnestly at Lady Grace.] She
lives! who could have dared to hope it? She
stands before us and speaks to us—I can
hardly believe it even yet!*
340.21
Canc. *[To Aaron.]*
340.25–27
*[Aaron affrightedly obeys her, and starts thun-
derstruck to his feet the instant he touches*

her. *Lady Grace clasps his hand firmly.]* **rev.**
*[Aaron affrightedly obeys her—then falls
back in a swoon. Martin catches him and
supports him towards the chest. He sinks to
the ground there, at Lady Grace's feet.]*
340.28–31
Canc. *Alive? ... and supports him.]*
340.32
Add. *[Signing to Martin to lay Aaron's head on
her lap.]* **before D**
340.34–35
[supports Aaron's head on her shoulder.] **rev.**
[Supports Aaron's head on her lap.]
341.7–8
Canc. *or come what might of it, I would have
gone to the ends of the earth to make him
answer for his crime.*
341.9–10
[Puts back his hair **rev.** *[Puts back Aaron's hair*
341.27
And that vessel was called "The Lady Grace"!
rev. *The Lady Grace!*
341.29
of what little I had done **rev.** *of the little I had
done*
341.31
Canc. *Hark!*
341.33–34
*it might be dangerous if he saw me when he first
opens his eyes again.* **rev.** *it might be dangerous if he saw me on first opening his eyes
again—*
341.40
Phoebe has been speaking **rev.** *She has been
speaking*
341.41
Add. *I understand it now.* **after** *a change in your
conduct towards her.*
341.42–342.2
Canc. *A change in my conduct ... Raise it for him
a little.*
342.2–4
*I heard what you said, Martin when you spoke
of your father's confession and of your own
marriage. You have a true heart: and your
courage and honour shall meet with their reward.* **rev.** *I heard what you said, when you
spoke of your father's confession and of your
own marriage. You have a true heart, Martin; and your honour and courage will meet
with their reward.*
342.9
Canc. *Silence!*
342.9–11

Canc. *Be gentle in recalling him to what happened after I came into this room. Wait here
till my return.*
342.11–12
*I go to tell Phoebe that all her troubles are at
an end. Be careful with your father, Martin—be careful with him at first.* **rev.** *I will
tell Phoebe that all her troubles are at an
end.—[Looking at Aaron.] Be careful with
him at first.*
342.20
Add. *[Turning away, and seating himself on the
chest.]* **before D**
342.29–36
Canc. *I can wait patiently ... I always knew that.*
342.37
I would trust you still? **rev.** *I would trust in you
still!*
342.42
Canc. *and speaks to her.*
343.7
Add. *[Turning to Lady Grace.]—Oh dear Lady!
dear Lady!* **after** *since we heard them last!*
343.10
Add. *[Hides his face.]* **after** *how can she forgive
me?*
343.11–18
Canc. *[advancing between them, and offering
her hand to Aaron.] Thus! [Aaron hides his
face with a gesture of despair. Lady Grace
touches him on the shoulder.] Take it.—I
entreat, I command you to take it. The privilege of forgiving is a right, Aaron Gurnock,
that we may all insist on. [Aaron bends forward and kisses Lady Grace's hand.] Rise
now; and let us embark. The boat is ready
for shore—the boat that takes* me *back to my
poor peasant-neighbours who love me: the
boat that takes* you *to your son's wedding.*
(add. and trans. to 343.29)
343.18
Canc. *[Aaron slowly rises.]*
343.19
*[approaching.] He is still weak—he wants an
arm to lean on.* **rev.** *Father, can you rise?
The lady wishes to speak to you.—[To Lady
Grace.] He is still weak, Madam: he wants
an arm to lean on.*
343.20
Let it be mine then. **rev.** *Let it be mine, Martin.*
343.22–25
Canc. *[Martin joins Phoebe. The chorus of the
song in Act I is heard from outside. Furley
and Jacob place themselves nearest the*

door. The three lightkeepers are ranged against the Flat. Lady Grace turns again to Aaron, and takes his arm in her's]

343.26

Canc. *[to Jacob] The boat's crew are getting tired of waiting for us.*

343.27

Canc. *And they're wiling away the time with a snatch of Phoebe's song.*

343.28

Canc. *[To Aaron.] Come!*

343.28

Add. *Phoebe, dear!* **before** *that is not a face for a marriage—You must learn to look happier on the wedding-day.*

343.29–31

Hark! The stout rowers remind us that we keep them resting idly on their oars. [waving her hand towards the door.] To shore, friends— to shore! **rev.** *[Signs to Martin to join Phoe-*be. Then touches Aaron on the shoulder, and offers her hand.]—The boat is waiting for us: the boat that takes* <u>me</u> *back to my poor peasant-neighbours who love me: the boat that takes* <u>you</u> *to your son's marriage.— Take my hand; I entreat, I command you, to take it.—[Aaron kneels and kisses Lady Grace's hand.]—The privilege of forgiving, Aaron Gurnock, is a right that we may all insist upon!*

343.32

[As they all move to go out, the curtain falls.] **rev.** *[As they move towards the door, the Lightkeepers of the relieving party settle themselves in their places in the room, and the Curtain falls slowly.]*

343.33

Add. *The End.*

APPENDIX

PERFORMANCES OF *THE LIGHTHOUSE* IN COLLINS'S LIFETIME
Locations, Dates, Attendees, Cast

I. Tavistock House, Tavistock Square, London

15 June 1855 (Friday)   Dress rehearsal, with audience

16 June 1855 (Saturday) Audience included John Forster; Rebecca Stanfield (Dickens, *Letters* 7: 650)

18 June 1855 (Monday) Audience included Eliza Becher; John, 1st Baron Campbell; John Forster; Douglas William Jerrold; Thomas Carlyle; John Leech; Thomas Longman; Anne Thackeray; Harriet Thackeray; Edmund Yates; Elizabeth Yates (7: 650–51); unknown attendance date for Juliet Lady Pollock[10]

19 June 1855 (Tuesday) Audience included Charles Cowden Clarke; Mary Cowden Clarke (Cowden Clarke 332); Sir Charles Beaumont Phipps (7: 653; 9: 376); probably Benjamin Webster (7: 652); and possibly Marion Bell, née Shaw and widow of Sir Charles Bell[11]

Campden House, Kensington

09 July 1855 (Monday) Dress rehearsal, with audience

10 July 1855 (Tuesday) Charity performance, in aid of the Bournemouth Sanatorium for Consumption (also known as the Hospital for Consumptive Patients)

Cast

Prologue[12]	John Forster
Aaron Gurnock	Charles Dickens
Martin Gurnock	Wilkie Collins
Jacob Dale	Mark Lemon
Samuel Furley	Augustus Egg
Relief Lightkeepers	Charles Dickens, Junior
	Edward Hogarth
	Alfred Ainger
	William Webster
Shipwrecked Lady	Georgiana Hogarth
Phoebe Dale	Mary (Mamie) Dickens

[note: Tavistock House performances followed by Dickens's acting company in *Mr. Nightingale's Diary* by Mark Lemon; Campden House performances followed by *A Wonderful Woman* by Charles Dance, not performed by Dickens's acting company.]

II. Royal Olympic Theatre, Strand, London

10 August through 17 October 1857

19, 20, 21 November 1857[13]

Cast

Prologue	Mr. George James Vining
Aaron Gurnock	Mr. Frederick Robson
	[Thomas Robson Brownbill][14]
Martin Gurnock	Mr. Walter Gordon
	[William Aylmer Gowing]
Jacob Dale	Mr. Edward Phillips Addison
Samuel Furley	Mr. George Boughey Cooke
Shipwrecked Lady	Miss Louisa Swanborough
	[later Mrs. Lyons]
Phoebe Dale	Miss Wyndham
	[Emily Clara Turner;
	Mrs. Henry William Compton]

III. Laura Keene's New Theatre, 624 Broadway, New York
21–23, 25–26 January 1858

Aaron Gurnock	Mr. Charles Wheatleigh
Martin Gurnock	Mr. G. W. Stoddart
	[James Henry Stoddart]
Jacob Dale	Mr. James G. Burnett
Samuel Furley	Mr. Charles Peters
Shipwrecked Lady	Miss Laura Keene[15]
	[Mary Frances Moss]
Phoebe Dale	Miss Charlotte Thompson

IV. New Royalty Theatre, London
21 November 1862 Charity performance, in aid of the Distressed Lancashire Operatives

Cast

Aaron Gurnock	John Palgrave Simpson

V. Royal Bijou Theatre, London
3 May 1865 Charity performance, in aid of the Lambeth School of Art

Cast

Aaron Gurnock	Paul Grave [John Palgrave Simpson]
Martin Gurnock	Mr. J. A. Courtland
Jacob Dale	Mr. Garton
Samuel Furley	Mr. Claude Andrews
Shipwrecked Lady	Miss Aylmer [Blake]
Phoebe Dale	Mrs. Garton

VI. [unidentified theatre]
3 July 1866[16]

Cast

Aaron Gurnock	John Palgrave Simpson

VII. Private Theatre, Boscombe Place [renamed Boscombe Manor 1873 (Jacob 1)], Bournemouth
30 April and 2 May 1867
Cast

Aaron Gurnock	John Palgrave Simpson
Martin Gurnock	Mr. C. L. Tupper
Jacob Dale	Captain Wingfield
Samuel Furley	Sir Percy Florence Shelley
Shipwrecked Lady	Jane Lady Shelley
Phoebe Dale	Miss Ricketts

VIII. Private Theatre, Boscombe Place, Bournemouth
13–14 April 1871
Cast

Aaron Gurnock	John Palgrave Simpson
Martin Gurnock	Mr. Herbert Gardner
Jacob Dale	Captain Wingfield
Samuel Furley	Mr. Harcourt Popham
Shipwrecked Lady	Jane Lady Shelley
Phoebe Dale	Mrs. Scarlett

IX. Private Theatre, Boscombe Place, Bournemouth
3 February 1872
Cast

Aaron Gurnock	John Palgrave Simpson
Martin Gurnock	Mr. Herbert Gardner
Jacob Dale	Captain Wingfield
Samuel Furley	Sir Percy Florence Shelley
Shipwrecked Lady	Jane Lady Shelley
Phoebe Dale	Miss Anna Felix Smith

NOTES

1. "Volpurno—or the Student." *The Albion: A Journal of News, Politics and Literature* 8 July 1843: 2, 27; "The Last Stage Coachman." *The Illuminated Magazine* Aug. 1843: 209–11; *Memoirs of the Life of William Collins, Esq., R.A.* 2 vols. London: Longman, 1848; *Antonina; or, The Fall of Rome. A Romance of the Fifth Century.* 3 vols. London: Richard Bentley, 1850; *Rambles Beyond*

Railways; or, Notes in Cornwall Taken A-foot. London: Richard Bentley, [January] 1851.

2. "Amateur performances of plays by Oliver Goldsmith and Richard Brinsley Sheridan were staged in the back drawing-room. Collins also translated [only Act 3 is in Collins's hand] a French play, *A Court Duel*, which was given a charity [Female Emigration Fund] performance by the Collins brothers and their friends on 26 February 1850" (*Oxford Dictionary of National Biography*. 12: 735). The manuscript of *A Court Duel* is held by the British Library, manuscript number Add 43024 (Vol. 160), ff. 1000–25. *A Court Duel* is a translation of *Un Duel sous le Cardinal de Richelieu, drame en trois actes* by Monsieur Lockroy [Joseph Philippe Simon] and Monsieur Edmond Badon (Paris: Jules Didot L'Aîné, 1834). Catherine Peters reports that Collins also acted in the farce that followed *A Court Duel*, *Raising the Wind* by James Kenney (84).

3. "A Terribly Strange Bed." *Household Words* 24 Apr. 1852: 129–37; "Gabriel's Marriage. Chapter the First." 16 Apr. 1853: 149–57; "Gabriel's Marriage. Chapter the Second." 23 Apr. 1853: 181–90; "The Fourth Poor Traveller" Christmas 1854: 19–26.

4. *Mr. Wray's Cash-Box; or, The Mask and the Mystery: A Christmas Sketch*. London: Richard Bentley, 1852 [1851]; *Basil: A Story of Modern Life*. London: Richard Bentley, 1852; *Hide and Seek; or, The Mystery of Mary Grice*. 3 vols. London: Richard Bentley, 1854.

5. Untraced. If retained by Dickens, the letter was most likely included among the letters he burned on 3 September 1860, "the accumulated letters and papers of twenty years" (*Letters* 9: 304).

6. According to the Dickens *Letters* editors, "Stanfield designed the interior and painted a frontdrop showing the lighthouse in a storm" (7: 625). The frontdrop is held by the Charles Dickens Museum, London.

7. Baker dates Collins's move to Hanover Terrace September 1850 (40).

8. For additional information regarding the shipwreck on which Dickens based his ballad, see John Suddaby's "The Wrecked Dying-Child Near Natal: Its Lifelong Effects on Dickens" in the *Dickensian* 7 (1910): 92–98.

9. "Le Phare." *L'Ami de la Maison: Revue Hebdomadaire Illustrée* 3 July 1856: 1–6; "Le Phare (Suite)." 10 July 1856: 17–22; "Le Phare (Suite)." 17 July 1856: 33–37; "Le Phare (Suite et fin)." 24 July 1856: 49–53. The first installment begins with an introduction by Forgues, followed by his translation of a 1 June 1856 introduction by Collins. Collins acknowledges a "deep appreciation" to Dickens for offering to produce the play in Tavistock House, an offer which Collins "accepted immediately." Collins discusses the play's plot and performance history, as well as his unsuccessful attempts to secure a professional London premiere. In all four installments, Forgues divides the play's two acts into various scenes. Each installment includes three pen-and-ink illustrations.

10. Kitton (414–15) does not provide the actual date of the performance attended by Lady Pollock. Elizabeth Yates also commented on Dickens's similarity to French actor Frédérick Lemaître, perhaps a topic of conversation on the same evening.

11. A presentation copy of *The Hand; Its Mechanism and Vital Endowments as Evincing Design* (sixth edition) by Sir Charles Bell (London: John Murray, 1854) is inscribed, "To Charles Dickens Esq With kind regards, from Marion Bell [signature]" and dated 19 June 1855, the date of the final Tavistock House performance, perhaps presented in person before or after the performance. Content is from personal examination of presentation copy, privately held.

12. Alfred Ainger, who had performed as one of the relief lightkeepers, wrote in 1870 (182) that he "can recall as if it were yesterday the impressive elocution of Mr. John Forster, as he spoke behind the scenes the lines which follow" (190–91). Ainger provides from memory fourteen of the prologue's twenty-one lines, with a remarkably high level of accuracy. According to the Dickens *Letters* editors, "C[harles] D[ickens] spoke the Prologue, but did not say he had written it" (8: 394).

13. Collins was partly misinformed when he wrote to John Palgrave Simpson on 17 October 1857, "The run of *The Lighthouse* will be stopped after this week, until Robson returns to London from his country trip—after which it will appear again in the bills" (Collins, *Public Face* 1: 153). After the 17 October 1857 performance of *The Lighthouse*, Frederick Robson continued performing at the Royal Olympic Theatre in six performances of the burlesque *Masaniello*, by Robert B. Brough. He did not perform again at this theatre until he reprised his role as Aaron Gurnock on 19 November. The theatre placed the following notice in the London *Times*: "Royal Olympic Theatre— To-night (Thursday), Mr. F. Robson, having partially recovered from a severe hoarseness, will re-appear in Wilkie Collins's drama of THE LIGHTHOUSE" (19 Nov. 1857: 6). The London *Sunday Times* reported under "Olympic":

> On Thursday evening, Mr Robson made his re-appearance on the boards of his own favourite little theatre, in Wych Street, in Mr Wilkie Collins's drama of *The Lighthouse*, and received a hearty welcome from his assembled friends. It was intended that Mr Robson should have also resumed his part in the burlesque *Masaniello*, but recent indisposition, arising from a severe cold, of which the traces were observable in his voice, obliged him to limit his exertions to the performance of his original character in *The Lighthouse*. (22 Nov. 1857: 3)

14. The incorrect spelling *Brownhill* is commonly found. For authoritative spelling, see *Oxford Dictionary of National Biography* and John Camden Hotten's introductory tribute, written and published the month of Robson's death, in Sala's *Robson: A Sketch* (3–28).

15. On 15 October 1858, Laura Keene performed as Florence Trenchard in the premiere of Tom Taylor's *Our American Cousin*. She reprised the role in the Washington, DC, production at Ford's Theatre when President Abraham Lincoln, in the audience, was assassinated by actor John Wilkes Booth on 14 April 1865.

16. On 3 July 1866, Collins wrote to Simpson, "There *is* a fatality against my seeing you in 'The Lighthouse.' This morning, I woke with an attack of gout in my right foot—and

the doctor threatens me with being 'laid up'—if I don't take the necessary physic and keep quietly at home for the next three or four nights. My foot pains me enough to back the doctor—so here is *another* chance lost! Think of me, and pity me, when 'Aaron Gurnock' is bringing the house down tonight" (Collins, *Public Face* 2: 40–41). Apparently, Collins had yet to see one of Simpson's amateur productions from November 1862 through July 1866.

WORKS CITED

Ainger, Alfred. *Lectures and Essays, Volume II*. London: Macmillan, 1905.

Archer, Frank. *An Actor's Notebooks: Being Some Memories, Friendships, Criticisms and Experiences of Frank Archer*. London: Stanley Paul, 1912.

Baker, William. *A Wilkie Collins Chronology*. Basingstoke, Hampshire: Palgrave Macmillan, 2007.

Clarke, William. *The Secret Life of Wilkie Collins*. London: Allison & Busby, 1989.

Collins, Wilkie. *Basil: A Story of Modern Life. In Three Volumes*. London: Richard Bentley, 1852.

———. "Gabriel's Marriage." *Household Words* 16 Apr. 1853: 149–57; 23 Apr. 1853: 181–90.

———. *The Letters of Wilkie Collins*. Ed. William Baker and William M. Clarke. New York: St. Martin's, 1999. 2 vols.

———. *The Public Face of Wilkie Collins: The Collected Letters*. Ed. William Baker et al. London: Pickering & Chatto, 2005. 4 vols.

———. *The Queen of Hearts. In Three Volumes*. London: Hurst and Blackett, 1859.

———. *Rambles beyond Railways; or Notes in Cornwall Taken A-foot*. London: Richard Bentley, 1851.

Cowden Clarke, Charles, and Mary Cowden Clarke. *Recollections of Writers*. London: Sampson Low, 1878.

Dickens, Charles. *The Letters of Charles Dickens*. Pilgrim Edition. Ed. Madeleine House et al. Oxford: Clarendon, 1965–2002. 12 vols.

———. *Sketches by Boz: Illustrative of Every-day Life and Every-day People*. London: Chapman and Hall, 1839.

Ducange, Victor, and Dinaux. *Trente Ans, ou La Vie d'un Jouer: Mélodrame en Trois Journées*. In *La France Dramatique au Dix-Neuvième Siècle, Choir de Pièces Modernes*. Ed. C. Tresse. Paris: Barba et Bezou, 1845.

Forster, John. *The Life of Charles Dickens, Volume the Third*. London: Chapman and Hall, 1874.

Gasson, Andrew. *Wilkie Collins: An Illustrated Guide*. Oxford: Oxford UP, 1998.

Jacob, W. L. *Sir Percy Shelley's Theatre: Boscombe Manor 1866–1877*. Bournemouth: Russell-Cotes Art Gallery and Museum, 1982.

Kitton, Frederic G. *Charles Dickens: His Life, Writings, and Personality*. London: T.C. & E.C. Jack, 1902.

"Laura Keene's New Theatre." *New York Times* 22 Jan. 1858: 4.

Lohrli, Anne, comp. *Household Words: A Weekly Journal 1850–1859 Conducted by Charles Dickens*. Toronto: U of Toronto P, 1973.

"Olympic." *Sunday Times* [London] 22 Nov. 1857: 3.

Oxford Dictionary of National Biography. Ed. H. C. G. Matthew and Brian Harrison. Oxford: Oxford UP, 2004. 60 vols.

Payne, David. *The Reenchantment of Nineteenth-Century Fiction: Dickens, Thackeray, George Eliot, and Serialization*. New York: Palgrave Macmillan, 2005.

Peters, Catherine. *The King of Inventors: A Life of Wilkie Collins*. Princeton: Princeton UP, 1991.

Pollock, Walter Herries, and Lady Pollock. *Amateur Theatricals*. London: Macmillan, 1879.

Rosenbaum, Barbara, and Pamela White, comps. *Index of English Literary Manuscripts* vol. 4, part 1. London: Mansell, 1982.

"Royal Olympic Theatre." *Times* [London] 19 Nov. 1857: 6.

Salmon, Arthur L. *The Cornwall Coast*. London: T. Fisher Unwin, 1910.

Sala, George Augustus. *Robson: A Sketch*. London: John Camden Hotten, 1864.

Suddaby, John. "The Wrecked Dying-Child Near Natal: Its Lifelong Effects on Dickens." *The Dickensian* 7 (1910): 92–98.

Walder, Dennis. *Dickens and Religion*. London: George Allen & Unwin, 1981.

Recent Dickens Studies: 2011

Elizabeth Bridgham

*This essay surveys Dickens scholarship in the year 2011, summarizing and
commenting on nearly 150 critical articles and books. While the body of
work produced in this year has been wide-ranging and diverse in its interests, some scholarly trends emerge. Particularly vibrant fields of study are
life writing about Dickens, no doubt in anticipation of his bicentennial year;
Dickens adaptations, particularly in performance; and Dickens's relationship to economics. These common interests reflect our contemporary preoc-
cupations, and the extent to which Dickens's life and works are relevant
to these current concerns. The scholarship surveyed is organized into the
following categories: Life Writing; General Studies; Influences on Dickens,
Dickens's Influence: Intertextualities; Performance and Adaptation; Places
and Spaces: Geography, Internationalism, and the Urban Imagination; Material Culture and Publication; Reading, Writing, Textuality; Inner Lives:
Psychology, Philosophy, Religion; Social Institutions and Issues: Capitalism, Law, Politics; Science and Technology; and Gender and Sexuality,
Family and Children.*

Writing this survey of Dickens studies has felt at times like being the opening
act for a major concert: because this essay examines work published just before
Dickens's bicentennial year, it begs to be read in the context of the celebrations
and conferences during that year, and with reflections on where we are currently
in Dickens studies. The marvelous and expansive body of scholarship produced
in 2011 is thus interesting in two ways: each individual study is significant in its
own right, and in what it contributes to our understanding of (with apologies to

Dickens Studies Annual, Volume 44, Copyright © 2013 by AMS Press, Inc. All rights
reserved.   DOI 10.7756/dsa.044.015.365-490

Matthew Arnold) the function of Dickens criticism at the present time. As I have spent time steeped in a year's worth of scholarly contributions to Dickens studies, I have been impressed and, at times, nearly overwhelmed by the sheer volume of material, and by its consistently excellent quality. Clearly, nearly 200 years on from his birth, we continue to have much to say about Dickens, and Dickens has much to say to us.

Unsurprisingly, a large amount of the scholarship produced just before the bicentenary has been biographical. Several new full-length biographies of Dickens and members of his circle were published in 2011, encouraging fresh examinations of Dickens's life and relationships. Interestingly, a number of specialized studies of distinct periods and friendships in Dickens's life also appear in this survey: it seems that by breaking Dickens's biography into its smaller component parts, we are able to put each under the microscope and to study it in minute detail. However, one of the most substantial contributions to our understanding of Dickens's biography in 2010 (published just before the date parameters of this survey and included here) was Duane DeVries's two-volume bibliography of autobiographical and biographical studies of Dickens; this valuable macro-level study synthesizes life writing by and about Dickens to this point and allows us to situate new scholarship in the context of what has come before.

Two other trends emerge in the Dickens scholarship of 2011: an attention to adaptations of Dickens's fiction, and a consideration of the relevance of capitalist economics to his writing. In this, I would argue, we see reflections of our own age. By studying ways in which Dickens's work translates to other media (the theater, opera, cinema, sound recording) or to contemporary narratives (post-colonial literature, in particular), we can gauge Dickens's portability and relevance beyond his own time, and beyond the covers of a book. Such criticism also allows us to draw comparisons between adaptations in Dickens's time and in our own, noting differences and similarities, and theorizing about the reasons for them. In terms of economic criticism, since a worldwide recession occupied our consciousness in 2011, it makes sense that Dickens scholars should turn to Dickens's perspectives on and reflections of his own economic climate. Indeed, not only scholars have been tempted to do so; recent articles in the popular press have looked to such texts as *A Christmas Carol* and *Little Dorrit* to make sense of contemporary economic crises. Dickens's own social criticism thus continues to extend beyond the nineteenth century, proving its enduring relevance.

The sheer amount of scholarly productivity in 2011 has required me to confine my attention, in this survey, to critical studies, rather than imaginative works inspired by Dickens; I have, unfortunately, not had space to examine directly the many intriguing fictional and television adaptations of Dickens produced that year. Nor have I included reprintings of Dickens's own works or reflections on Dickens by his contemporaries. By focusing my attention on scholarship alone, I have attempted to be comprehensive in this survey, though, perhaps inevitably, some works may have been omitted; my apologies to any scholars whose work has been left out inadvertently. For ease of use, I have divided the works in this survey into the following eleven categories: Life Writing; General Studies; Influences on Dickens, Dickens's Influence: Intertextualities; Performance and Adaptation; Places and Spaces: Geography, Internationalism, and the Urban Imagination; Material Culture and Publication; Reading, Writing, Textuality; Inner Lives: Psychology, Philosophy, Religion; Social Institutions and Issues: Capitalism, Law, Politics; Science and Technology; and Gender and Sexuality, Family and Children. These categories, of course, frequently overlap and are, perhaps, most interesting when they do. A virtue of 2011's Dickens scholarship—and perhaps of Dickens scholarship more generally—is its diversity of interest and inquiry, and its forays into cross-disciplinary subjects.

Life Writing

"He left a trail like a meteor, and everyone finds their own version of Charles Dickens" (416). With this comment, Claire Tomalin's *Charles Dickens, a Life*, draws to a close. This biography, which spans the whole of Dickens's life and career, offers several versions of Charles Dickens the man and author, most often presenting him as a mercurial, difficult, wildly energetic, and strong-willed figure, one whose very "strength of will became the agent of his own destruction" (405), both in terms of his domestic relationships and of his physical health.

Tomalin divides her biography into three parts: the first covering Dickens's origins to the writing of *The Old Curiosity Shop*; the second treating the composition of that novel through that of *Little Dorrit*; and the third concerning the breakup of Dickens's marriage, his relationship with Ellen Ternan (of which Tomalin has written extensively, in *The Invisible Woman*), and the end of his writing career and his life—which, indeed, concluded simultaneously. Tomalin also includes apparatus useful to the reader: the biography is preceded by three maps tracing Dickens's movements in Gad's Hill and Rochester, Central London, and North London, respectively. It also includes a helpful "Cast List" of major and minor figures in Dickens's life—as extensive a list of characters as is to be found in any Dickens novel. Three sections of black-and-white photos and reproductions of paintings allow readers to pair faces with names, and street views with places, and Tomalin offers useful glosses of several of these images. For example, she describes Frith's 1859 portrait of Dickens as showing "a man with angry eyes staring out as though to defy the world" (305). Lest we think this is only Tomalin's idiosyncratic reading of the portrait, she adds the comments of a variety of sources: "Dickens himself acknowledged ruefully that [Frith] had done well when he was presented with the portrait. It was hated by Georgina. When it was shown at the Royal Academy, Landseer observed, 'I wish he looked less eager and busy, and not so much out of himself, or beyond himself'" (305). The accretion of reactions here teaches us how Dickens and his contemporaries saw the portrait, and by Tomalin's extending the technique through the biography, the world.

Charles Dickens: A Life is strong in several areas, most notably in its portrayal of Dickens the shrewd businessman, the friend, and the legend whose story continues to be transmitted long after his death. Tomalin insightfully writes that "leaving out the women in Dickens's life made appreciation [of his character] easier" (408). Tomalin does not omit Dickens's scandalous behavior to Catherine in the late 1850s, nor his compromised and compromising relationship with Ellen Ternan, nor the possibility that he himself patronized prostitutes even as he strove to redeem them at Urania Cottage. She explains this contradiction thus: "it may be that he reckoned he was unlikely to end prostitution single-handed, and that men would always find what they wanted in one way or another" (203), refusing to excuse the hypocrisy inherent in such an "inconsistency" while explaining it in the context of the wider Victorian double standard, from which Dickens did depart to a degree. Still, she shows Dickens's relationships to be most solid and secure among men, detailing his friendships with John Forster, Wilkie Collins, and George Dolby, among many others, as affectionate and lasting, even to the grave. Tomalin does make an error in including in the biography the apocryphal story of Dickens's meeting with Dostoevsky (321–22); however, since this has been noticed elsewhere and will be amended in future editions of the biography, I will not dwell on it here.

Another inconsistency in Dickens's life can be found, of course, in the ways in which Dickens alienated men who criticized his behavior, dissented from his opinions, or compromised what he perceived as his interests. Thus Tomalin describes carefully Dickens's fallings out with Bradbury and Evans, Mark Lemon, and H. K. Browne, each motivated by wrongs that Dickens felt had been done him. Dickens's penchant for mixing business with friendship was no doubt partially responsible for what volatility existed in his friendships with men; writing of an early financial dispute with his publishers, Tomalin calls attention to the complications of doing so:

> Dickens's habit of reneging on contracts was not morally defensible as business practice—even his friends said so—but it has been argued that, since no one had foreseen his spectacularly rising sales, which meant his publishers made thousands out of his work while his rewards remained relatively modest, he had a case. In these circumstances, he felt entitled to insist on adjustments to the contracts, and Forster backed him. Chapman & Hall were prepared to be generous ... with the result that Dickens regarded them as friends, while Bentley became "the Robber." (85–86)

This paragraph occurs in a section of the biography primarily devoted to Dickens's intimate relationship with Forster, yet it also reveals a good deal about his loyalties and friendships within the publishing world, along with the difficulty his friends and publishers had staying on Dickens's good side.

Less satisfying than the portrayal of male relationships in the biography is Tomalin's portrait of Catherine Dickens, one that too often falls back on conventional critical attitudes. Her version of Catherine, while often sympathetic with her plight as the cast-off wife, shows her to be passive (and occasionally passive-aggressive), inferior in intellect and physical prowess to Dickens, and disengaged from the administration of the household. Of Catherine, Tomalin writes, "She was incapable of establishing and defending any values of her own, of making her own safe situation from which she should rule within the home, let alone taking up any other interest. So little of her personality appears in any eyewitness account of the Dickens household that it seems fair to say there was not much more there to describe" (66). Such a dismissal seems, in the wake of Lillian Nayder's *The Other Dickens*, to be unconscionable; while the two books must have crossed in the press, one could wish that Tomalin had engaged in a bit more rigorous research into the life, friendships, and personality of Catherine before so glibly writing her off.

Tomalin's literary criticism is equally problematic, and more pervasive in the biography. Although she offers a complex if critical view of Dickens's life, she has a tendency to describe the novels and Christmas books in terms of black and white, good and bad, and she occasionally suggests a more autobiographical reading of the novels than they are likely to support. In an instance of this latter point, she writes of the passage in *Dombey and Son* in which Mr. Dombey insists that Polly Toodle renounce her children and change her name while working in the Dombey household: "reading this chapter makes you wonder about the wet nurses who came to work for the Dickens family year after year, and what sort of conversations Dickens may have held with them" (192). If this chapter in any way endorsed Mr. Dombey's behavior, Tomalin might have a fair point; however, the clear critique implicit in the portrayal of his high-handedness to a kind character of a good family invalidates her insinuation, without further evidence. An example of the negative value judgments that Tomalin frequently makes on the works relates to several of Dickens's later minor efforts. Writing of "George Silverman's Explanation," Tomalin offers more flat dismissals:

> Although some critics have struggled to find psychological interest in it, it is one of his failures. He also produced some slight stories for children, 'Holiday Romance', for the American market. Further, he collaborated with Wilkie Collins on a crudely melodramatic tale, *No Thoroughfare*.... All these works show diminished power and poor judgment and are read today only because they are by Dickens: but they brought in money, and he kept going. (361)

Such a string of insults to the works, though they may not represent Dickens's best, is nevertheless unhelpful to Tomalin's readers. Those familiar with these shorter fictions do not need such cursory commentary, and those unfamiliar with them are unlikely to engage with them after reading it. While Tomalin instructively reports on Dickens's contemporaries' receptions of his work for good and bad, the biography might have done better to offer a more nuanced approach.

The final chapter of Tomalin's book is, however, a tour de force. Like a Dickens novel, it follows the fortunes of Dickens's friends and family members after his death, offering the reader narrative closure in this sense. But it also opens up Tomalin's own narrative of Dickens's life by discussing some of the early versions of it published and spoken by those who knew him. Tomalin considers Forster's biography briefly, probably because its story is so well known. More interesting is her reflection on Ellen Ternan's version of her life with Dickens, and her reinvention of herself in relationship to it. Not only did Ternan lie about her real age, claiming to be twelve years younger, but she also revised her relationship: "Nelly put it about that she had been a god-daughter of Dickens and a mere child when she knew him. She must have had nerves of steel in case Mamie or Georgina let drop any remark that undermined her story, but it was in all their interests to protect his reputation" (406). Tomalin also includes in the chapter some consideration of Georgina Hogarth and Mamie Dickens's edition of Dickens's letters (413) and Gladys Storey's *Dickens and Daughter*, based on Katey [Dickens] Perugini's frank recounting of her life with her father (414). The incorporation of other versions of Dickens, each of which contributed to Tomalin's own, in this final section of the biography reinforces the multitude of lives the author led, and leads, for his acquaintances and his readers.

One of these lives, of course, is that of "a little laboring hind" in Dickens's youth. Michael Allen's *Charles Dickens and the Blacking Factory* is an idiosyncratic biographical study focused minutely on the world of the blacking factory that shaped Charles Dickens's childhood experience as we know it. Allen meticulously inspects and transcribes documents from the British National Archives that elaborate on Dickens's autobiographical fragment and the account of it in John Forster's biography, clarifying the relationships among those who operated the several competing Warren's Blacking factories. Citing court cases and trial records, affidavits, newspaper articles, and intricate family trees, Allen also clarifies Dickens's own memories of his work at the blacking factory and how it was originally arranged. Allen points out that in considering Dickens's experience in the factory Dickens scholars have been "entirely in [Dickens's] hands—there has been nobody to challenge him. He exercised supreme control over the history of his own childhood and of his time at Warren's Blacking. Yet, inevitably, it was not the complete story" (1). Allen's narrative seeks to fill the gaps in Dickens's account and to contextualize Dickens's experience. In so doing, Allen zeroes in on a heretofore understudied branch of the Dickens family tree: that of his cousin by marriage, George Lamerte.

In the Autobiographical Fragment, Dickens references a "James Lamert," who managed the blacking factory and who suggested that "I should go into the blacking-warehouse, to be as useful as I could, at a salary" (qtd. in Allen 85). The historical record, however, shows no James Lamert associated with the blacking business; rather, George Lamerte, a cousin ten years Dickens's senior, who for a time lived with the Dickens family, was the factory manager, and was probably responsible for Dickens's presence there (89). Allen traces the record of Lamerte's employment with the firm to determine a new possible set of dates for Dickens's employment. He proposes "that young Charley started at Hungerford Stairs in September 1823, that he was moved to Chandos Street in January 1824 when the business was relocated, and that his father removed him from Warren's Blacking [after quarreling with George Lamerte] in either September or October 1824" (94). Such a timeline means that Dickens would have started work at the age of eleven, earlier than most Dickens scholars—and perhaps even Dickens himself—had imagined.

Dickens's relationship with George Lamerte opens the door to some intriguing but admittedly speculative theories within Allen's narrative. Lamerte was the son of Matthew Lamerte and his first wife; Matthew Lamerte entered Dickens's life when he married Dickens's aunt, Mary Allen (née Barrow, Dickens's mother's sister). Lamerte and his first wife were of German-Jewish descent, and Michael Allen theorizes that George Lamerte, while living with Dickens's family, may have taken Dickens along on visits to his mother's side of the family, in the east end of London (Allen suggests that George Lamerte may even be the "Somebody" referenced in Dickens's 1853 essay, "Gone Astray" [15]). If so, Dickens may have encountered George's uncle, Henry Worms, a Jewish "broker of household goods," and later, a marine-store operator in Fox Court, an area to which Dickens would frequently refer in his writings (25–27). Allen suggests that Fox Court may have formed the basis for *Bleak House*'s Tom-all-Alone's (29–30), and that Henry Worms, who was a receiver of stolen goods eventually transported to Van Diemen's Land for his crimes, may have served as the original for *Oliver Twist*'s Fagin, *Great Expectations*'s Magwitch, or both. (36). Allen writes, "The young Dickens may well have been in very much closer proximity to Henry Worms than he ever was to Isaac Solomons, [another possible original for Fagin], standing next to him in his shop in Fox Court, observing his German-Hebrew accent, a man in his late fifties, just 5'3" tall—an old Jew, as Dickens described Fagin. Taken there by his Cousin George Lamerte" (37). Such claims are necessarily inconclusive, but Allen juxtaposes them with detailed documentary evidence that supports their plausibility.

Much of this documentary evidence is provided, in full, in the final chapters and appendices of Allen's book. Transcribing for the first time many documents relevant to the several Warren's Blacking operations in competition in the nineteenth century, Allen makes them widely available to the select audience anxious to delve further into the contextual details of Dickens's child labor, or indeed into the realities of business history. In so doing, Allen performs a true service to scholarship. The documents include Chancery proceedings in court cases between the various owners and operators of the Warren's Blacking factories; transcripts from Henry Worms's criminal trials at the Old Bailey; an account from *The Penny Magazine* of "A Day at Day and Martin's," detailing the activities which Dickens might have performed or witnessed at his own workplace; newspaper accounts providing clearer, truncated versions of the Chancery proceedings among the Warren's Blacking litigants; and family trees clarifying the sometimes perplexing connections among the Lamerte, Worms, and Dickens (Barrow) families. Allen himself, in the introduction to his book, acknowledges that reading the court documents, in particular, and "working through the never-ending flow of words is a bit like reading Joyce's *Ulysses* without the imagination, insight, and humour" (2), but he manages to craft a narrative from them that exhibits at least the first two of these qualities.

Another biography that focuses on a specific period of Dickens's life—this time on his young adulthood and beginnings as a writer—is Robert Douglas-Fairhurst's *Becoming Dickens: The Invention of a Novelist*. Focusing largely on the 1830s as the decade marking Dickens's early development as a writer, *Becoming Dickens* resists the biographical attitude that sometimes takes Dickens's remarkable success to have always been a foregone conclusion. Doing so, Douglas-Fairhurst argues, allows us to understand Dickens's "life as it was lived: ambitiously, uncertainly, and full of loose ends" (14). The result is a compelling and often conversational account of Dickens's early years, one which takes seriously the alternate career and life paths that Dickens might have taken, which imagines the results of these through the examples of Dickens's contemporaries who did take these paths, and which considers the impact of historical events and coincidence on shaping the genius and opportunities of the emerging writer.

Douglas-Fairhurst's narrative begins traditionally, with Dickens's childhood experience in the Warren's Blacking factory, calling the autobiographical fragment "the response of a successful writer to a set of circumstances that nearly prevented him from becoming a writer at all" (29). More time is spent than usual, though, on Dickens's education at Wellington Academy and employment as a junior clerk at Ellis and Blackmore, a job that ranked the not-yet inimitable Dickens with the "growing army of clerks" that Douglas-Fairhurst characterizes as "difficult to tell one from another" (54). From here, his next job, as a free-lance stenographer in Doctors' Commons, was a step up: "it rewarded precisely the talents he had been most assiduous in cultivating: accuracy, patience, and a willingness to listen closely to other people" (66). Though these qualities are obviously central to Dickens's later success as a novelist, Douglas-Fairhurst hesitates to draw a direct line from stenography to creative composition; instead, he stresses the fact that as late as 1855, Dickens considered entering the legal profession. Douglas-Fairhurst ascribes this to the "security and status" which the law could afford and to which writing, despite Dickens's meteoric rise to success, offered less certain access (68).

In Dickens's next position as a gallery reporter for *The Mirror of Parliament*, he achieved a status "considerably higher than that of ordinary hacks" (71), yet the chapter "Up in the Gallery" refers both to Dickens's time as a parliamentary reporter and to his love of the theater. "Theaters are places where high culture knocks up against far lower urges," writes Douglas-Fairhurst; "they are an expression of civilization and its discontents" (82). This chapter addresses the performances from each venue that Dickens witnessed and wrote about, keeping the question of social class firmly at the fore. Dickens's own class status continues to be important in the next chapter, "Mr. Dickin," which continues to address Dickens's journalistic work while considering his failed courtship of Maria Beadnell. Comparing the way in which Dickens saw his relationship with Maria as the stuff of romance with Pip's attitude to Estella, Douglas-Fairhurst points out the wisdom that came of this relationship: "Dickens would later show just how dangerous it was to think that life fell into the reassuring patterns of old stories" (94). More potential careers arise for Dickens in this chapter, which shows Dickens considering emigrating to the West Indies (97) and, alternatively, becoming an actor (99). Ultimately, a timely introduction kept Dickens in journalism; John Payne Collier, of *The Morning Chronicle*, was instrumental in Dickens's procuring his next position. Without diminishing Dickens's talent, Douglas-Fairhurst makes consistently clear the roles that contingency and luck played in the trajectory of Dickens's life.

The next few chapters consider Dickens's burgeoning career as a writer, first of sketches, then of *The Pickwick Papers*, and on to *Oliver Twist*. A strength of the biography is the extent to which it discusses and analyzes Dickens's minor writings from this period. "A Dinner at Poplar Walk," Dickens's first story, which Douglas-Fairhurst admits is "the ugly duckling of Dickens's career" (111), receives substantial attention for its connection to pantomime and "to the fine calibrations of class" (115). While the focus here is certainly on the early years of Dickens's career, Douglas-Fairhurst offers some helpful leaps forward in time, explaining how ideas explored in early stories and sketches came to be developed in Dickens's later works. "The Boarding House," for instance, was the story in which the name "Boz" first appeared (133); this was, of course, the pen name that Dickens would retain until the volume-publication of *Oliver Twist*, the point at which Douglas-Fairhurst ends his biography. Douglas-Fairhurst describes Boz as "amateur detective, but also anthropologist, sociologist, tour guide, and master of ceremonies" (158), reflecting the many sides of the city of London and of Dickens himself.

"Pickwick Triumphant" dwells on the development of *The Pickwick Papers* from a collection of sketches into an episodic novel. The first installment, which Douglas-Fairhurst calls "a selection of highlights from [Dickens's] back catalogue" (192), was unpopular, and Dickens and the illustrator, Robert Seymour, were at odds over whose work was to be preeminent in the serial. The uncertainty over the fate of *Pickwick* is emphasized here: Seymour's suicide, the lagging popularity of the serial, and its ambiguous form all had the potential to derail Dickens's progress. Douglas-Fairhurst persuasively argues that Sam Weller saved *Pickwick*, and that "the novel's fortune turned on a single scene": that in which

Weller first appeared (199). With Weller, *Pickwick*'s sales picked up, and Dickens's serial became recognizably a novel; Douglas-Fairhurst credits Dickens and Chapman and Hall with "invent[ing] the modern paperback" (202).

Dickens was still unsettled in his self-definition of a career, however. "Transforming himself from sketch writer to novelist, and from reporter to editor, were only two of the possible futures he was contemplating for himself," writes Fairhurst. "A third was as a playwright" (225). Dickens kept his options open, recognizing the instability of a writing career, and diversifying his talents and skills. The chapter "Novelist Writer" considers the marketing of Boz as a public figure and commodity, by Dickens himself, by his publishers, and by those who pirated his works. It also considers John Forster's role in Dickens's development, arguing for the significance of Forster to Dickens's understanding of himself as a literary and popular artist, and that Forster "was Dickens's critical conscience" (236).

The next two chapters of Douglas-Fairhurst's biography trace the intersections of Dickens's domestic life with his work, giving particular attention to his relationship with Mary Hogarth and its influence on the Rose Maylie plot of *Oliver Twist*. His readings of this novel, in particular, are fascinating for the parallels Douglas-Fairhurst draws between the development of Dickens's career and the novel's plot. *Oliver Twist* presents "a world in which every action is surrounded by a cluster of ghostly alternatives, signaled by an insistent counterfactual grammar of 'could have,' 'would have,' and 'might have'" (277). This statement could equally apply to the version of Dickens's life set forth in *Becoming Dickens*, which demonstrates how easily Dickens could have pursued other paths in his life, could have written differently, or not at all. That we have and know the works of Charles Dickens today, this biography makes clear, should be a source of wonder, and Douglas-Fairhurst ably encourages us to look at the creations—and their creator—anew.

Another biographical work paying substantial attention to Dickens's early writing career is the section of Nikki Hessell's *Literary Authors, Parliamentary Reporters* devoted to Dickens. Hessell uses information about parliamentary reporting practices at the major publications, what we know of Dickens's own experience and prowess at parliamentary reporting, and, ingeniously, Dickens's letters to Catherine Hogarth before their marriage to make some tentative attributions of anonymous parliamentary reports to Dickens himself. Hessell acknowledges that these attributions must, of necessity, be speculative while building a compelling case for her attributions, and for applying higher standards of scholarship to this area of literary studies.

Dickens reported on Parliament's proceedings for both the *Mirror of Parliament* and *The Morning Chronicle* from 1834–36, but the two publications had very different sets of standards and practices. The *Mirror* required shorthand of its reporters and valued a direct transcript of parliamentary speeches, but its practice "of allowing MPs to correct their speeches" after delivering them was controversial (134). On the other hand, like most other newspapers, *The Morning Chronicle*

did not favor verbatim accounts of the speeches, preferring paraphrase and interpretation; "the daily papers did not have the space, nor the inclination, to cover
the debates in full" (136). In analyzing a speech that Dickens himself claimed to
have covered, Hessell argues, "The relationship between the *Mirror*'s text and
those of other publications demonstrates the complicated mixture of accuracy and
abbreviation that was prevalent in 1830s reporting and that influenced Dickens's
style" (149).

Hessell attributes the coverage of other speeches to Dickens based on the dates
and times in letters that Dickens wrote to Catherine while serving as a parliamentary reporter. By cross-referencing dates when he told Catherine he would be
at the House late with the speeches and debates on the floor, and with the shift-
system for newspaper reporters in Parliament, Hessell builds plausible evidence
to attribute particular reports to Dickens. She finds a subtly unique style in these
reports, arguing that "the splash that he made, in a profession that valued judi-
cious reportage, would have involved both an unusually high level of accuracy
and an ability to pick and choose when to deploy it" (165).

In her conclusion, Hessell expands her consideration of the relevance of parliamentary reporting to literary criticism, suggesting that the authors she discusses
"should be viewed primarily as journalists" (168). The authors' relationship to
print culture and to literary collaboration, she argues, was in part shaped by their
experience as journalists and is worthy of further study.

Michael Slater's *The Genius of Dickens* reprints and revises Slater's 1999 publication, *The Intelligent Person's Guide to Dickens*, for the bicentenary. It serves
as a useful guide to Dickens's life and works for a non-specialist audience of
Dickens readers. Slater's introduction considers contradictions in the term "Dickensian," an adjective paradoxically used to signify conviviality and wretchedness
in different contexts (9–10). The book goes on to trace Dickens's engagement
with Victorian concerns, anxieties, and values. Chapters are arranged themati-
cally around the subjects of Fancy, Innocence, Responsibility and Earnestness,
Progress, Home, and Faith.

Fancy, Slater argues, was one of Dickens's own favorite words and concepts,
despite the fact that it became unfashionable during the Victorian era. Dickens, he
explains, uses fancy and imagination to reshape the city of London time and again,
borrowing from "legends, fairy tales, folklore, and popular literature generally"
(17). Fancy is also critical to Dickens's notion of childhood; a childhood without
a strong dose of imaginative play is a warped one, likely to produce a warped
adult (18). Slater distinguishes fancy from wonder at the natural world, all the
while arguing for the connection between the two experiences. Although Dickens
critiques a system of education based solely on "facts" in *Hard Times*, his works
show a belief in the usefulness of facts to inspire a sense of wonder (20). Indeed,
the mundane world, for Dickens, benefits from fancy, which can "bring the exotic
and fabulous to bear on the mundane, everyday life in nineteenth-century England" (24). Not all uses of fancy, however, are beneficial; Slater opposes benign

fancy to "malign fancy," present in the novels' schemers and hypocrites, who "rearrange factual reality to suit their purposes" (30). *Bleak House*'s Harold "Skimpole is Fancy's Traitor, manipulating the faculty of imagination for sordid ends" (31). Likewise, moralizing, didactic literature was suspect, for Dickens, who criticized the use of imaginative stories for narrow-minded purposes in his essay "Frauds on the Fairies" (38). Despite the negative purposes to which Fancy could be employed, however, Dickens believed it to be an ultimate good, putting his money and his advocacy where his beliefs lay by tirelessly supporting his fellow artists and writers in their efforts to share their fancies with the public.

Innocence, the natural province of children, makes a natural successor to the theme of fancy in Slater's book. Slater sums up the complexity of Dickens's attitude to childhood thus: "It's a pity—we have to grow up" (47). The loss of childhood innocence is a serious thing for Dickens, but to attempt to arrest our development unnaturally is very wrong, whether through the false childhood of Skimpole or the pitiable perpetual childhood of *Little Dorrit*'s Maggie. Slater does not, however, dwell on the literal innocence of children in this chapter, but interestingly turns to manifestations of innocence in Dickens's fictional adults. A number of adult males in the fiction embody child*like* innocence while functioning with various degrees of success in the adult world: Pickwick, the Cheerybles, Tom Pinch, Mr. Dick, and Joe Gargery are some examples (48–49). Dickens's essay, "Where We Stopped Growing" draws a line between unhealthy arrested development and the preservation of a sense of childlike wonder at the world. Slater explains the difference: "Childhood may survive beneficently in the adult through the vivid memory of particular stories, scenes, people or things that made so big an impact on the child's imagination that no amount of subsequent mundane experience of the same subject has been able to efface it" (50). The Christmas books provide evidence that Christmas is an appropriate time to cultivate such memories. While innocence in men is generally a positive trait in Dickens's works, for his good women, it is required, a fact that Slater and many other readers find problematic. Despite the many threatened or fallen women in the fiction, Dickens had an "essentialist belief in the innate moral and spiritual superiority of women" (54). Sexuality provides the litmus test that permanently divides innocence and its absence in Dickens, particularly for women, and this raises challenges that, perhaps, give rise to his childish portrayals of young wives.

Although innocence is a positive quality in Dickens's adult characters, it does not suffice for Dickens's male protagonists. Rather, Slater claims that "responsible" is the adjective most appropriate to describe Dickens's heroes in his chapter, "Responsibility and Earnestness" (66). To explain this, Slater turns to Dickens's biography, positing that the privileging of responsibility probably stems from the early age at which Dickens took on adult responsibilities as a child worker in the Warren's Blacking factory (70). "'Earnestness' underpins responsibility" in Dickens's works, "but he also uses the word, like his contemporaries, to express emotional honesty and energy" (89). Slater highlights Dickens's personal senses of responsibility and earnestness here, considering the responsibilities he felt to his public, to the poor, and to children, in both his writing and charitable work (74). However, he may give too much credit to Dickens in claiming that "a strong sense of responsibility towards his public as much as any more turbulent emotion ... in 1858, caused Dickens to take the sensational and very ill-advised step of publicising his marital difficulties in the press, in the same statement repudiating the scandalous rumours that had begun to circulate about his sex life" (72). A consideration of Dickens's sense of responsibility in marriage might usefully accompany such an assertion.

The next chapter, "Progress," highlights Dickens's belief in technological and moral progress, which Slater calls a "progressive view of history" (105). "Dickens was always roused to fiercely satirical wrath by any talk of the 'good old days', or any movement such as Disraeli's 'Young England' party in politics, or the Oxford movement in the Church of England, or Pre-Raphaelitism in the world of art, that seemed to be looking back nostalgically to past times or even attempting to restore some aspects of them" (114). Impediments to progress, in Dickens's view, included autocracy and Roman Catholicism, both of which he associated with England's past. Although many of Dickens's own novels are set in the recent past, Slater reads this not as a generalized nostalgia for an idealized history, but rather as a specific interest in the past of his own childhood, a nostalgia, perhaps, for his own innocence (124).

Slater next turns his attention to "Home," focusing on the domesticity and the virtues of the hearth with which "Dickensian" has become synonymous. While domesticity is celebrated and promoted in all of Dickens's fiction, it is perhaps most prominent in the Christmas books, in which the redemption of the central character involves a reintegration with the family virtues that Dickens believed to be essential to the individual and the nation (127). However, home is a "precarious institution" in the fiction. From *Dombey and Son* on, "Dickens seems to be more concerned with domesticity frustrated, or with the destruction or subversion of domestic havens and the ideal of Home, either by outside enemies or by failure within the walls" (131). Thus homelessness and vagabondage, the inverses of domesticity, are continual threats.

The final chapter of *The Genius of Dickens*, "Faith," tackles the perennial problem of understanding Dickens's relationship to religion. Slater acknowledges the difficulty of pinning Dickens down on this issue, writing that the "*flavour* of religion ... is found throughout all his writings" (154) and that the reader gets from Dickens's works a "strong impression of a generalised Christian message" (155). It is, perhaps, easier to address what Dickens's version of religion or positive faith did *not* involve, rather than what it did: "Dickens was against an overemphasis on the form, rather than the content of religious belief; he opposed religion that interfered with individual freedom or engaged in classist oppression; he found the notion of eternal damnation both morally offensive and somewhat ludicrous" (175). Unsurprisingly, Dickens celebrated humane Christianity and focused on the humanity rather than the divinity of Christ in *The Life of Our Lord* (168). The most interesting segment of Slater's chapter concerns Dickens's relationship to the scientific discoveries of his day, and the impact of these discoveries on his faith. Whereas many of his contemporaries were moved to doubt by Darwinism, Dickens's faith doesn't seem "to have been shaken by the great Science v. Religion debate that was so much a feature of the intellectual life of his day, having a strong belief in Nature as the Book of God in which geologists, chemists, physicists and other scientists gradually learn to read more and more" (169). To return briefly to the first chapter of *The Genius of Dickens*, "Fancy," it seems that Dickens lived his philosophy that the natural world and scientific fact should inspire one with wonder.

Several biographical studies of 2011 examine Dickens's relationships, the most extensive and groundbreaking of which is Lillian Nayder's *The Other Dickens: A Life of Catherine Hogarth*. The title highlights a central concern of the book: the tension between its subject's identity as the wife of Charles Dickens and the versions of her self that are defined by other relationships, especially those with other members of the Hogarth family that shaped her development and her life during and after her marriage. Nayder explains:

> Over the course of her sixty-four years, Catherine defined herself in various ways and adopted varied personae in writing to correspondents. A member of female communities, she tells other women of childbirths, marriages, and engagements; a faithful Christian, she offers condolences and prayers, and resigns herself to God's will; mistress of a middle-class household, she expresses concern for the welfare of former servants, recommending them for jobs and offering advice. Writing as a Hogarth, Catherine commiserates with her father's niece about her sister Mary's death, and as a Thomson [Catherine's mother's family], describes her life at Gloucester Crescent to her mother's sister. (10)

Nayder's biography provides its readers with a lucid and enjoyable account of Catherine's life, experiences, and relationships from—insofar as is possible—the perspectives of Catherine and of those whose sympathy with and close relationships to her allow them to speak and write on her behalf.

Beyond this central purpose, *The Other Dickens* performs a number of concomitant tasks. It offers a counternarrative to Charles Dickens's characterizations of Catherine and of the twenty-two-year marriage that preceded the Dickens's separation in 1858, one that "forces [Charles Dickens] to the margin" and explicitly sympathizes with Catherine (1). In so doing, Nayder's book urges its readers to resist Charles Dickens's single, self-serving perspective, which scholars have, Nayder argues, been too often willing to accept unquestioningly. Throughout the volume, Nayder returns to instances where the scholarly or editorial record misrepresents or undervalues Catherine, taking the opportunity to correct this record.

Discussing the attribution and significance of Catherine's letters, for instance, Nayder questions the attribution to Dickens, in the definitive Pilgrim edition of Charles Dickens's letters, of third-person letters on behalf of the couple: it "is regrettable because it obscures the experience and person behind them. Catherine's invitations and replies to invitations illuminate her responsibilities as hostess and domestic manager" (224), responsibilities that Dickens would later accuse her of shirking. Further, "equating the joint marital identity of the Dickenses with that of the husband, these misattributions reinforce the logic of coverture while promoting Dickens's claims, as literary genius, to texts authored by subordinates" (225). By periodically returning to questions of bias and to gaps in the scholarly record, Nayder encourages her readers not only to approach her particular subject, Catherine Dickens, with fresh eyes, but also to reexamine their own scholarly practices and assumptions.

The Other Dickens also offers, in its portrait of Catherine, a broader understanding of her life's experiences in their Victorian legal and social context. While in some respects being married to "the Inimitable" Charles Dickens placed Catherine in a unique position, in others Catherine's experience was emblematic of that of many Victorian wives. Under the legal restrictions of coverture, Catherine's legal identity became subject to that of Dickens when she married; Dickens himself, though, added further to her subjugation by grooming her for submission in marriage during their engagement, "authoring the terms of their marriage" (61), and by micromanaging the household after the wedding, taking "an unusually active part in household matters" (65). As the mother of ten children, Catherine spent a significant portion of her married life pregnant, and Nayder devotes considerable attention to the realities of family planning, pregnancy, childbirth, and confinement for Victorian women. But Nayder also reaches some surprising conclusions about these realities for Catherine, particularly in the argument that as a mother, "Catherine came closer to achieving parity with Dickens than she did as his wife—not because they cared for the children together but because the care of infants and toddlers largely fell to her in a sphere that was uncontested" (107). At once limiting and liberating, Catherine's role as mother was thus both relational and independent.

The complexity of motherhood for Catherine also applies to her role as sister to Mary, Georgina, and Helen Hogarth. As elsewhere in her biography, Nayder looks beyond Dickens's characterizations of these women and their relationships, examining closely the record of letters among and about these sisters describing their activities and attitudes. She finds that Mary's relationship with Catherine, instead of being mediated through Dickens, was Mary's first concern when she lived with the Dickenses, and that "free from obligation to a husband, often irreverent or arch in her dealings with men and full of admiration for and fellow feeling with her older sister, Mary gave Catherine a sense of herself that was difficult to sustain after Mary's death" (85). After Catherine's separation from Dickens, Helen would step into Mary's place in her fierce loyalty to and support of her sister (299). Even Georgina, who would later echo Dickens's critiques of Catherine, lived in a collaborative, rather than competitive relationship with her sister while both formed part of the Dickens household (197).

Just as Nayder opens her biography by considering Catherine *Hogarth* before the marriage to Dickens, she continues it through the twenty-one years of her life following their 1858 separation, filling in blanks that many scholars have left empty. Not only did Catherine survive the separation, but she also outlived Dickens by nine years and, Nayder insists, "to do justice to Catherine and her story, we need to rethink its ending and pluck her from the flames of her husband's funeral pyre" (340). Acknowledging that the marital separation "placed Catherine on the margins" (275) of her own family, restricting Catherine's access to her children and perpetuating her dependency on male authority in the form of the male trustees named by the "Deed of Separation," Nayder keeps Catherine's experience squarely at the center of her narrative, focusing on the relationships that Catherine maintained and established from her own household. "Her life was much busier and happier than critics acknowledge. Far from reclusive, she equipped herself to entertain" (289), and she carried on lively and engaged correspondence with many friends, even including Charles Dickens's one surviving sister, Letitia Austin. After Dickens's death in 1870, Catherine's social status improved still further; "it was considerably more prestigious to be Dickens's widow than to be his jilted wife" (323). And while Nayder's biography treats the scathing terms of Dickens's will in detail, the narrative closes with Catherine's own will, in which Catherine left keepsakes and heirlooms to numerous named legatees:

> Catherine uses these objects to redefine the very idea of worth. Describing the origins or provenance of many of the items she bequeaths, she gives her heirs a sense of family history and interconnection.... Representing herself as a Hogarth daughter, sister, and aunt, and as the loving mother and grandmother of the Dickenses, Catherine reminds her relations of their ties to the woman her husband wished to forget. (337)

By closing her biography with the significance of Catherine's will, and by inscribing it with narrative weight of its own, Nayder reads the document as a kind of autobiographical fragment to be read—in combination with Catherine's other acts of authorship, including her letters and her recipe book, *What Shall We Have for Dinner?*—as part of the story of a fascinating life, valuable beyond its intersection with that of Charles Dickens.

Nayder turns her attention to Dickens's relationship with another woman in his life in "'The Omission of His Only Sister's Name': Letitia Austin and the Legacies of Charles Dickens." Her point of departure is Dickens's will, in which he left legacies to Ellen Ternan, Georgina Hogarth, and Catherine Dickens, but neglected even to mention his only surviving sister, who was a widow and struggling financially at the time of Dickens's death. Nayder seeks to explain this omission, offering plausible hypotheses for this unbrotherly behavior. Most likely is that Dickens was upset by Letitia Austin's continued relationship with Catherine after she and Dickens separated in 1858. Nayder rightly points out that this would be sufficient grounds for estrangement between the siblings, since Dickens had cut off communications with former friends when they showed support for Catherine. And though Letitia herself was an uncontroversial Victorian woman, her financial difficulties after her husband's death made her wish for greater independence and made her understand the precarious position of women who found themselves without male protectors. While Nayder acknowledges that her conclusions are speculative (in fact, they must be, since Dickens burned all of Letitia's letters to him), they are consistent with Dickens's behavior in other relationships and with the circumstances of Letitia's situation, and they shed new light on this hitherto underexamined relationship.

Anne Isba's *Dickens's Women* synthesizes and condenses much of the known biographical information about the relationships Dickens maintained with the women in his life. Explaining that "it is not within the scope of this book to map the characteristics of the real women in Dickens's life onto the female characters in his novels" (xiii), Isba confines her attention to the historical record, considering, in turn, Dickens's relationships with his mother, Maria Beadnell, the Hogarth sisters, Angela Burdett-Coutts, and Ellen Ternan. Surprisingly, although Isba regularly cites Katey Dickens's opinions about Dickens's relationships with other women, she does not devote a substantial section of the book to Dickens's daughters.

Little new information is contained in *Dickens's Women*, though Isba's account of the relationships she includes is clear and concise, and she does provide useful contextual information. For example, the chapter "Philanthropist," dealing with Dickens's work with Coutts at Urania Cottage, provides useful detail about prostitution and the condition of the "fallen woman" in the Victorian period. Readers looking for fresh analysis of Dickens's relationships may, however, be disappointed by, for instance, Isba's repetition of the conventional wisdom about Catherine Dickens "being of a retiring and nervous disposition" (44), particularly in light of Lillian Nayder's reconsideration and suspicion of Dickens's accounts of his wife in *The Other Dickens*, a biography of which Isba shows some awareness. Some statements, too, are perplexing from a historical perspective: when Isba writes, without further critical comment, that Augusta de la Rue's ailments were "possibly hysterical" (57), is she referring to a Victorian diagnosis or reflecting on de la Rue's condition from a twenty-first century perspective? If the latter, then certainly more commentary and clarification is needed. By the same token, further citation would help to clarify unattributed assertions like "there has been a suggestion that Georgy's illness was psychosomatic as a result of being upstaged by Nelly" (117); readers would benefit from a more concrete attribution of this suggestion, as well as further explanation of its meaning. Isba's biographical account will serve as a brief, though necessarily incomplete, introduction for readers who wish to learn more about Dickens's relationships with women.

Miriam Margolyes and Sonia Fraser's *Dickens's Women*, a one-woman stage show first performed by Margolyes in 1989, was reissued by Hesperus Press in 2011 with a new introduction by Margolyes. In it, Margolyes argues that "more than any other writer, [Dickens's] life was in his work" (7), and she reads the representations of women in Dickens's novels through the lens of his relationships with women in his life. The introduction assumes a basic familiarity with the events of Dickens's life story; Margolyes's intent is to illustrate how these events can be brought to bear on an interpretation of the way that Dickens writes women. Drawing on Michael Slater's *Dickens and Women*, as well as Claire Tomalin's biography of Ellen Ternan and Lillian Nayder's biography of Catherine Dickens, Margolyes argues "that [Dickens] never portrayed a woman whom we would recognise as a mature sexual and emotional partner for his heroes. And I venture to suggest this was because his own relations with women were all damaged, incomplete, or destructive" (12). This claim is uncontroversial, though the same cannot be said for Margolyes's more debatable statement that "never was he able to draw a complete, believable, fully realized female—because the women in his life never offered him the opportunity" (16). Margolyes dwells on the representations of Dickens's comic women, his childlike ingénues, and his mothers and daughters, particularly those of *Dombey and Son*, all of whom are represented in her play.

The fabric of *Dickens's Women* itself weaves together monologues developed from Dickens's dialogue, anecdotes from Dickens's life, and accessible literary criticism that offers context for the characters that Margolyes portrays. For instance, Margolyes explains the age and innocence of Dickens's young heroines by relating the story of Mary Hogarth's death, Dickens's reaction to it, and the reaction of other critics (like Oscar Wilde and G. K. Chesterton) to the idealized female characters (34–35). Explanations of the biographical origins of Mrs. Pipchin (37), Florence Dombey (38), Mrs. Micawber (38–39), Mrs. Lirriper (40), and others follow in the performance. Margolyes goes beyond assertions of biographical inspiration to claim definitively that "David Copperfield meeting Dora Spenlow is Charles Dickens meeting Maria Beadnell" (42), proceeding to explain the latter's subsequent transformation into *Little Dorrit*'s Flora Finching (44).

After an interval, *Dickens's Women* considers the novels' female caricatures. "It's with his grotesques, with the women that he didn't want to take to bed, that he erupts into life" (51), write Fraser and Margolyes, saying a mouthful with this statement about Dickens's relationships to his female characters. Mrs. Skewton, Miss Mowcher, and "the lesbian, Miss Wade" (57) all come in for consideration here. Following these outliers are the wives and would-be wives of Dickens's fiction, in the biographical consideration of whom Fraser and Margolyes include Ellen Ternan and Georgina Hogarth. The final monologue of *Dickens's Women* is Miss Flite's, which the writers call "his tenderest portrait" (67).

An afterword of sorts follows the main sections of Fraser and Margolyes's text and discusses Betsey Trotwood, "Philanthropic Ladies," "Urania Cottage," Mrs.

Bardell, Dickens's actresses, and, finally, Madame Defarge. The authors suggest that Betsey Trotwood's constancy to her abusive husband may complicate Kate Perugini's assessment that Dickens did not understand women (75), but that Mme. Defarge confirms it: she is not "a real woman" but "an iconic distillation of feminine power, misdirected and distorted" (94). *Dickens's Women* is a fascinating document: it integrates Dickens's language, the writers' language, biography, and literary criticism in performance into a new genre. Miriam Margolyes's one-woman show seems very much in the spirit of Dickens's own public readings, in that it involves an actor embodying the voices of Dickens's characters onstage. The final irony the text of the show communicates is that, despite its unabashed critique of Dickens's relationships to and rendering of women, it is ultimately celebratory of Dickens's art and its ability to move and to entertain.

Though a number of studies in 2011 examine Dickens's relationships with women, fewer turn their attention to his relationships with men. One of these is Holly Furneaux's "Inscribing Friendship: John Forster's *Life of Charles Dickens* and the Writing of Male Intimacy in the Victorian Period." Responding to critiques of Forster's *Life of Dickens* that fault the biography for dwelling too much on Forster's relationship with Dickens, Furneaux construes this feature of Forster's *Life* its main strength. Rather than conforming to the conventions of biographies that trace the subject's life from birth, through marriage and reproduction, and then to death, Forster's biography focuses on literature and friendship. "This friendship," Furneaux argues, "rewrites biology as Dickens becomes Forster's brother, bound 'by ties as strong as ever nature forged', and reworks the legal ties of the marriage ceremony to cement a life-long fidelity" (254). She links this privileging of friendship to Boswell's *Life of Johnson* and also to the elegy, "one of the dominant literary conventions for acceptably expressing the intensity of feeling between men" (250). Furneaux situates Forster's *Life* with respect to Tennyson's elegies "Break, Break, Break" and *In Memoriam, A. H. H.,* and also with respect to the ways in which Dickens describes intimate friendship in novels like *The Pickwick Papers* and *Our Mutual Friend.* Though he glosses over Dickens's relationships with women and omits Ellen Ternan from the biography entirely, "Forster's careful scrutiny of Dickens's work allows him to present an intertextual inscription of male friendship in *The Life*, which closely imitates Dickens's strategies for expressing male intimacy to describe the relationship between biographer and subject" (253).

Tracing lines of connection between Thackeray's career, politics, and personal life and those of Dickens, Jeremy Tambling's "William Makepeace Thackeray: A Bicentennial Tribute" reminds those of us engaged in Dickens's 2012 bicentenary to celebrate that of Thackeray in 2011. Tambling considers the vexed relationship between Dickens and Thackeray, including biographical details such as Dickens's rejection of Thackeray's pictures for *The Pickwick Papers*, the "antagonism between Thackeray and Forster," and the "mutual mistrust" between the two novelists that led to Dickens's unflattering "partial portrait" of Thackeray in

Little Dorrit and their eventual falling out in a personal dispute (124). Tambling explains the distance between the two writers as stemming from "three matters which both writers highlighted: Thackeray as the gentleman and amateur, as the realist novelist, and (in the eyes of his enemies) as the 'cynic,' *versus* Dickens as the professional writer, as the 'idealist' in his fiction, and as bohemian in his inclinations" (124). Still, Thackeray admired Dickens's novels, and they shared a mutual attachment to eighteenth-century fiction and its freedoms (124–25). Even Thackeray's class position may have been closer to Dickens's than it seemed: "He was exceptional ... in being an intellectual amongst an upper class that was not. He was close to Dickens's class of professional writers, yet aware of class difference, which made him caricature his own position" (125). Tambling applauds Thackeray as a triple threat: a novelist, journalist, and illustrator of the first order, and he encourages scholars undertake "serious studies ... of *Vanity Fair* with the contemporary *Dombey and Son*, and of *Pendennis* with *David Copperfield*" (125).

Turning from Dickens's relationships with people to his relationships with places, Ruth Richardson chronicles her role as a historian in achieving the preservation of a historic London building with Dickensian connections in "Charles Dickens and the Cleveland Street Workhouse." Tracing the workhouse's significance from the memoirs of Dr. Joseph Rogers, a workhouse doctor whose efforts at reform were supported by Dickens, Richardson moves back through time to examine Dickens's more personal proximity to the Cleveland Street Workhouse. While at the Warren's Blacking factory as a child, Dickens was located within the parish of St. Paul Covent Garden and may have worked alongside boys familiar with the inside of the Cleveland Street Workhouse (102). Moreover, Dickens himself lived at 10 Norfolk Street, now 22 Cleveland Street, for four non-consecutive years in his youth. Richardson has learned that his address on Norfolk Street, now renamed, was only nine doors from the Cleveland Street Workhouse (103). From this historical information, Richardson goes on to build a case that Dickens may indeed have had Cleveland Street in his imagination when describing the workhouse of *Oliver Twist*: the age of the Cleveland Street Workhouse fits the way that Dickens sets his fictional workhouse back in time; the nearness of the Cleveland Street Workhouse to a pawn shop is also consistent with the pawning and redemption of the important locket in Dickens's novel (106, 107). While Richardson acknowledges that there are also differences between the historical and fictional workhouses, and that the parallels between the two are not definitive, she makes a compelling argument for Cleveland Street's influence on *Oliver Twist*, one that she elaborates in her 2012 book *Dickens and the Workhouse*.

Following in the footsteps of Charles Dickens's 1866 journey to Portsmouth, Geoffrey Christopher establishes in "Dickens and the Southsea Pier Hotel: A Note" that Dickens stayed at this hotel with his traveling retinue on the nights of 24 and 25 May while on his reading tour (113). Although the original structure was bought by Portsmouth Polytechnic University, renamed Rees Hall, and rebuilt in 1995 to accommodate students, it retains the "frontal 'Scottish Baronial' features" of the hotel built in 1865 (113). Christopher adds that Dickens "Fellowship Branches are negotiating with the University to have a plaque placed on the wall of the Hall, and it will then be added to the city's Dickens Trail" (114). This discovery fills a small gap in our ability to trace Dickens's movements on his reading tours and travels.

Dickens helps record his own life in the annual supplements to the Pilgrim edition of *The Letters of Charles Dickens*, edited by Angus Easson, Margaret Brown, Leon Litvack, and Joan Dicks. "Supplement XV" includes several personal letters accepting or declining social engagements, some fragmentary letters of which the import is not entirely clear, and a few letters concerning working instructions to correspondents including Hablot K. Browne and Camilla Toulmin (127, 128). Dickens's involvement with charitable and social concerns is evident here from his 1841 letter to Sir Martin Archer Shee regarding the sanitorium at Devonshire House (129) and from his 1851 letter to Thomas Batson regarding Batson's pamphlet *How to Improve the Condition of the Agricultural Labourer* (141). Of particular interest are two letters that Dickens wrote in 1842 to the Rev. George Armstrong, declining the opportunity to write a tribute to the Unitarian minister William Ellery Channing, who had recently died. Dickens writes with regret, claiming that *Martin Chuzzlewit* would occupy him entirely, and saying, "I really have so deep a sense of his immense usefulness in such a land as America, that I think I should, at the best, feel it almost presumptuous to write of such a man" (132). Upon Armstrong's request to reprint this very letter, Dickens again declined, repeating, "I so honestly feel the presumption of trumpeting *my* opinion of such a man as Dr. Channing, who is immortal in the hearts of all good men, that I shrink involuntarily from the idea of having my letter to you published" (133). If a single theme repeats in the letters in this supplement, it is Dickens's need to draw boundaries by declining or strictly limiting his response to the many requests made of him.

"Supplement XVI" finds Dickens energetic as ever and pressed for time; the early letters, from 1852, find him declining invitations and opportunities, pleading his work schedule as an excuse. However, an 1852 letter from F. O. Ward alters this pattern; Dickens replies to his request, bearing on what the editors call "sanitary subjects," thus: "I seem to be under a kind of spell when you propose anything" (229). Still, because of his full calendar, Dickens deputizes W. H. Wills to stand in for his own presence and to be with Ward for a meeting at the Board of Health. Other letters of interest in this supplement include one from 1854 expressing Dickens's approbation of the "proposed treaty of Copyright with America," a document with which he found some minor flaws, but which he ultimately thought "to be decidedly advantageous to English authors" (232). The treaty, however, was not to be ratified by the U. S. Senate. The warmest letter in the supplement was written in October 1858 to Mrs. Thomas Whitford, a friend of the Dickens family, and expressed regret that Dickens was unable to see her when his reading tour took him to Leeds (239). From "August down to this time," Dickens laments,

"I have set foot in no friend's house and have eaten or drunk at no friend's table. The 'very grand folks' and the very plain folks everywhere have been equally shut out from me" (240). A letter from 1860, written in French to Dickens's French publishers Hachette et Cie, expresses his delight at the upcoming translation of *A Tale of Two Cities*; in it, Dickens claims "que cette ouvrage soit connue en France … [est] un de mes espoirs les plus ardents, en l'ecrivain" (241).

Dickens scholars seeking information of any kind about Dickens's life and the ways that it has been described need look no further than Duane DeVries's *Autobiographical Writings, Letters, Obituaries, Reminiscences, Biographies*, the second volume of his planned mammoth four-volume set of annotated bibliographies of Dickens studies.[1] Reading DeVries while preparing this survey for *Dickens Studies Annual* has been, for me, both an inspiring and a daunting process. Focused as it is on life writing by and about Dickens, this comprehensive two-book set covers 1,568 pages with knowledgeable summaries and evaluations of relevant publications up to 2010. In addition to these exhaustive bibliographic entries, DeVries begins the first section of the volume with a 130-page introduction highlighting major studies, trends, and topics in Dickensian biography. DeVries rightly points out in this introduction that "by 2010 … Dickens's life has been analyzed, canonized, demythicized, anathematized, codified, psychoanalyzed, and deconstructed, among other biographical practices" (cxxix). That in this annotated bibliography he catalogues, makes sense of, explicates, and evaluates each available instance of these practices is a feat worthy of praise and wonder.

DeVries has organized this second volume of his annotated bibliographies into five parts, continued on from his first volume, *Bibliographies, Catalogues, Collections, and Bibliographical and Textual Studies of Dickens's Works*. Part 8 covers Dickens's own autobiographical writings, including the "Autobiographical Fragment," selected letters, speeches, and diaries. Part 9 is devoted to Dickens's letters; Part 10 addresses "obituaries and eulogies … and reminiscences and recollections of Dickens" (xviii); Part 11 zeroes in on major biographies; Part 12 which, together with the author and subject index for the volume merits an entire book to itself, is devoted to shorter biographies, sketches, and studies of Dickens's relationships (xviii–xix). In all, Volume 2 comprises 6,686 discrete bibliographic entries, ranging in length from one cursory sentence to multipaged analytical considerations. In his introduction, and in each entry, DeVries helpfully distinguishes substantial and scholarly studies from slighter ones, and makes clear which biographical works have been most influential in Dickens criticism. Indexing the entries alone must have been a Herculean task: the author index begins with fifteen pages of listings for anonymous sources, each catalogued alphabetically by title; this section is followed by a more traditional author listing. The subject index is exhaustive and usefully divided into sections for Dickens's Works and Subject Headings, a category that includes subheadings for works dealing with major figures in Dickens's life such as his father, his wife, and other members of the Dickens family.

While most Dickens scholars will find DeVries's annotated bibliography of life writing most useful as a reference book to be consulted on specific subjects relevant to their own work, its introduction is a marvelous essay on the state of the field, interesting in its own right and certainly important for any scholars embarking on biographical studies of their own. In it, DeVries surveys major and minor texts concerning Dickens's life, pointing out gaps in the scholarship (for example, "little of any significance has been written about the autobiographical elements in [Dickens's nonfiction], though excerpts from many of them have been included in small collections of Dickens's autobiographical writings" [xxvi]) and pointing out major contributions. In so doing, DeVries engages with and in metacriticism, particularly in the section that concerns "Surveys of Dickensian Biography and Biographical Studies" (xxvii–xxx). The section on "Pre-Forster Biographical Writings" details the fascinating ways in which Dickens's contemporaries attempted to get to know the often-elusive author, from attempts to establish the identity of "Boz" before it was well-known, to efforts to read his life through the novels: "The early details that emerged in the press about Dickens's life were generally sparse, inaccurate, or, where descriptions of him were concerned, based on published reproductions of portraits rather than on personal knowledge" (xxxv). DeVries recounts Dickens's own reactions to some of these press reports, including Thomas Powell's *Living Authors of England* (1849), which "aroused Dickens's ire, since Dickens knew that Powell was a liar and a forger and, one suspects, had come a little too close to truths about his life that Dickens did not want revealed" (xxxvi). This comment is representative of DeVries's readable and occasionally witty commentary; even a forger can tell the truth sometimes, and Dickens's dual objections to both the lies and truths told about him in this case seems representative of his desire to guard his privacy and his reputation closely throughout his life.

DeVries devotes considerable space in the introduction to biographies, memoirs, and letters published by those who knew Dickens, the chief among these being John Forster, volumes of whose *The Life of Charles Dickens* were published in 1871, 1872, and 1873, and of which DeVries comments that "it was a biography as much of the friendship of the two men as it was a biography of the more famous one" (xliv). This establishes a pattern in DeVries's summaries of the biographical writings; he ably and succinctly highlights the main concerns of each, thereby distinguishing one from another and explaining the significance of each. Later biographies through the end of the nineteenth century DeVries reads mainly as supplements to Forster (xlviii), though he finds much interest in memoirs of Dickens published in this period, especially those by Dickens's own children, and in select critical works with "strong biographical component[s]," particularly those by Leslie Stephen and George Gissing (xlix). "At the turn of the century," DeVries writes, "Dickens's literary reputation was high, and through *Forster* and the carefully-selected *Hogarth-Dickens Letters* and Wilkie Collins letters, his personal reputation remained largely untainted.... And yet, when one compiles it, at least in bibliographical form as here, there was far more information published about Dickens in the nineteenth century than would ever make its way into a biography of Dickens" (li).

As the introduction progresses, DeVries devotes attention to how emerging and controversial information about Dickens's life made its way into the canon of Dickens biography. As new letters came to light in the early twentieth century, especially those between Dickens and Maria Beadnell, biographers came to understand more about Dickens's early life and about his relationships with women (lii–liii). New information about Dickens's relationships with W. H. Wills was also published in the early twentieth century, making public additional knowledge about Dickens's editorial work, and "reminiscences of Dickens abounded in the first three decades of the century" (lv). DeVries praises the 1928 edition by J. W. T. Ley of Forster's biography, which made use of new information to update the original and to provide "extensive notes that ... reflected then-current research into Dickens's life" (lviii). On the other hand, he criticizes Edward Wagenknecht's *The Man Charles Dickens: A Victorian Portrait* (1928), which emphasizes Dickens's personality through "psychography," a study that DeVries regards as "ultimately an unbalanced work" (lix). Wagenknecht, in this biography and thereafter, resisted evidence suggesting that Dickens had an affair with Ellen Ternan. Another biography, however, Thomas Wright's *The Life of Charles Dickens* (1935), "would change the face of Dickensian biography forever in elevating Ellen Lawless Ternan to a prominent place in the last decade and a half of Dickens's life" (lxi). Thereafter, all biographies would grapple with the status and significance of this relationship.

In citing biographical works from the 1930s and 40s, DeVries highlights *The Letters of Charles Dickens* (*Nonesuch Letters*, 1938), which "would remain an essential source of biographical information from Dickens's own hand until 1965, when the first volume of the *Pilgrim Letters* was published, and continue to be useful until the final volume was published in 2002" (lxix). The three volumes, edited by Walter Dexter, included many previously unpublished letters, though the edition was "not reliable, since the majority [of the letters] had not been checked against originals" (lxix). Also published in this period as *Dickens and Daughter* (1939), Gladys Storey's account of Kate Dickens Perugini's memories of Dickens sheds light on "Dickens's relationships with women—his wife and two daughters, Georgina Hogarth and, most notably, Ellen Ternan.... With its revelations about Dickens's relationship with Ellen Ternan, this was a highly controversial book" (lxxii).

DeVries's highest praise for a general biography of Dickens goes to Edgar Johnson's *Charles Dickens: His Tragedy and Triumph* (1952). Of Johnson, he writes, "no biographer since has matched Johnson's scholarship, professionalism, and insight" (lxxv). Johnson treats both Dickens's professional success and the dark side of his personality and life, arguing that the latter helped to produce the former by deepening "'his insight and sharpen[ing] his criticism, spurr[ing] him to a continued intellectual and artistic growth'" (lxxxvi). DeVries mentions in this section that "as the volume of Dickens studies proliferated in the 1950s (and later), Dickens became the author most frequently written about—after Shakespeare, of course. Between 1952 and 1965 twenty-three full-length biographical studies and innumerable critical works were published" (lxxviii). In the midcentury, the twelve-volume *Pilgrim Letters* also began to be published; new volumes would appear from 1965–2002, and supplements continue to appear in *The Dickensian* (the latest is "Supplement ·XVI," considered elsewhere in this essay). DeVries calls the *Pilgrim Letters* "the major scholarly event in Dickens biography bar none. It is authoritative and as definitive as anything can be" (lxxxvii). Calling attention to the methodology of the compilation and its editors, DeVries points out that, in 2010, some 14,252 letters by Dickens had been identified and published (lxxxviii), providing all future biographers with an overwhelming amount of material on which to draw.

In his considerations of recent biographies of Dickens, DeVries also devotes substantial attention to Fred Kaplan's *Dickens: A Biography* (1988), Peter Ackroyd's *Dickens* (1990), and Michael Slater's *Charles Dickens* (2009), "the first major biography of Dickens of the twenty-first century and the first to take full advantage of the completed publication of all twelve volumes of the *Pilgrim Letters*" (xcii). DeVries appreciates all three of these biographies, praising the latest the most, noting Slater's attention to detail, reluctance to speculate, and consistency of approach. "It is a *writer's* life that Slater gives us," DeVries writes, "and it is a full life indeed" (xciii). In addition, DeVries highlights Rosemarie Bodenheimer's *Knowing Dickens* (2007), "a perceptive investigation into what Dickens knew, starting with, in chapter 1, a 'look at the special kinds of knowledge he cultivated and practiced'" (xcv). This work focuses on Dickens's inner life, the life of the mind, and the intellectual strategies that he used in his life and work (xcvi).

The final pages of DeVries's introduction to his bibliography expand outward from Dickens's life proper to scholarship that addresses and documents the lives of those close to him: his family members (parents, brothers, and children), the Hogarth family, and particularly Catherine Hogarth Dickens, and, of course, Ellen Ternan. "Post-1965 studies of Dickens's relationships with friends, colleagues, and acquaintances abound" (cxi), suggesting that the field of Dickens studies is an ever-expanding one, with scholars seeking new avenues for information about Dickens and his work. In looking over the past century and a half of biographical studies, DeVries finally asks,

> Will we learn more? Probably not a great deal more, though the raw material in the last six volumes of the *Pilgrim Letters* remains to be further processed and understood.... Yet I suppose we must ask the question how much more do we want or really need to know, after all?... The Dickens we already know is many-sided, complex, deep, often an enigma, someone we can sometimes love and sometimes deplore, sometimes respect and sometimes censure. (cxxx)

As we have seen, the year 2011 did indeed produce several more considerations of Dickens's biography, detailed in this survey, and the bicentennial year will no doubt produce still more, which will supplement and expand DeVries's annotated bibliography.

General Studies

The June 2011 issue of *Partial Answers*, edited by Leona Toker, is devoted entirely to Dickens and his works, with a particular emphasis on *Our Mutual Friend*. The essays are unified, Toker explains in her introduction, "Uneasy Pleasures," by the attempt to bridge or elide the gap between the novels' social consciousness and the enjoyment that their artistry evokes in their readers (216). In "Reading Dickens Writing London," Murray Baumgarten locates the "uneasy pleasures" we experience when reading Dickens in the fact that we move vicariously through the Dickensian city. Beginning with scenes of arrival in London in *Oliver Twist*, *Nicholas Nickleby*, *Little Dorrit*, and *Great Expectations*, Baumgarten emphasizes the mixture of anticipation and anxiety that we experience along with the characters who face opportunities and dangers in their new locale (220–21). We are able to enjoy the risks that these characters confront because "their experiential difficulties are not ours. The aesthetic distance between the reader and the characters maintains the pleasure of our reading of their dis-ease" (225). The theoretical framework of Baumgarten's essay combines the Bakhtinian chronotope, which determines how readers understand "urban space-time" (222), and Bernard Harrison's understanding of meaning "as a relationship [among] linguistic expressions, items or aspects of reality, and socially devised and maintained practices" (226). Dickens's style combines all three in what Baumgarten calls "his urban and linguistic palimpsest" (227). The complexity of the narrative space-time in Dickens's novels, exacerbated by the constantly shifting boundaries and landmarks of the modern city, is combined with the literal and symbolic significances of Dickens's language, creating an interpretive uncertainty in the reader, an uncertainty that the reader experiences along with the novels' characters.

Elsie B. Michie locates the "uneasy pleasures" of the social-problem novel in the difficulty fiction writers faced, in the 1830s, of balancing critiques of social ills with their narrative art. In "Morbidity in Fairyland: Frances Trollope, Charles Dickens, and the Rhetoric of Abolition," Michie argues that Dickens modeled *Nicholas Nickleby* on the structure and ideas of Frances Trollope's 1836 anti-slavery novel *Jonathan Jefferson Whitlaw* (233). However, Dickens learned from the reviews garnered by Trollope's novel that too explicit a social critique in fiction could provoke a negative critical—and, perhaps, popular—reaction. The denunciation of slavery that Michie reads in *Nicholas Nickleby* is, then, encoded in the abuses of Dotheboys Hall, where students are mercilessly flogged (replicating one of the most publicized abominations of slavery) and punished for running away (237). Nicholas's immediate and successful opposition to Squeers offers readers the satisfying suggestion "that one can fight back against oppression and injustice," an impossibility in Trollope's antebellum Southern setting, where an outraged individual could do nothing against the systematic horrors of slavery (240). The positive critical response to *Nickleby*, in contradistinction to the reviews of *Whitlaw*, suggests to Michie that "mid-1830s readers were not yet ready for the social-problem novel in its fullest form" (249).

Goldie Morgentaler's contribution to the volume, "Dickens and Dance in the 1840s," examines depictions of dance in the Christmas books in their Victorian social, cultural, and medical contexts. In so doing, she shows that dances, in these and other works "are more than simple exercises of bravura writing in the service of conveying exuberance and good fellowship; they also merge with the social criticism that played so large a role in [Dickens's] fictional writing" (253). Beginning with the intersection of dance and race in Dickens's *American Notes*, Morgentaler goes on to argue for the democratizing features of Fezziwig's ball in *A Christmas Carol*. Despite the good cheer and freedom associated with the dances there, she points out the fact that the ephemeral nature of dance undercuts the happiness that it achieves (258). In considering another example of the dark side of the dance, Morgentaler turns to the runaway success of the ballet *Giselle* in the 1840s, a culturally influential ballet that both introduced many popular European folk dances to England and "taps into earlier beliefs in the *danse macabre*, [linking] dance to the morbid and the deadly" (259). In some ways, this link was literalized in the period, with doctors arguing over whether dancing was a healthy activity, particularly for women's reproductive health (260–61). Still, Morgentaler points out that dancing was crucial to the marriage market and was seen as an opportunity for women to take exercise and a modicum of control. Dickens, in *The Battle of Life*, offers readers an image of young women dancing on a former battlefield that had claimed many men's lives, thus combining notions of dance as an innocent, healthy pleasure with the *danse macabre*, and introducing unease into the scene.

The next essay in the volume, Géza Kállay's "'What Wilt Thou Do, Old Man?'—Being Sick Unto Death: Scrooge, King Lear, and Kierkegaard," turns from Morgentaler's study of physicality in Dickens to a philosophical perspective. Opposing the comedy of *A Christmas Carol* to the tragedy of *King Lear*, Kálly questions why tragedy has the power to give pleasure, ultimately deciding that it structures and gives meaning to suffering (281). The explanation of Kierkegaard's relevance to Shakespeare and Dickens would benefit from elaboration beyond the fact that Dickens and Kierkegaard were contemporaries (274). By using the latter's "interpretation of sickness, death, and despair: 'the self is in sound health and free from despair only when, precisely by having been in despair, it is grounded transparently in God'" (274), Kállay is able to explore the function of (essentially nonexistent) religion, selfhood, and the efficacy of free will in both texts. Explaining that, in Danish, "despair" can be read as "intensified doubt," Kálly shows that this emotion is "a means to make the protagonists see the limits of love: the comedy from the positive, creative side, the tragedy from the negative, destructive one" (281).

David Paroissien takes on the question of the critical reputation of Dickens's literary art in "Subdued by the Dyer's Hand: Dickens at Work in *Bleak House*." Because Dickens rarely commented on his own craft or aesthetic philosophy, many years passed before he was fully credited for having a deliberate literary method. But Paroissien argues that "three interrelated convictions shape all his work: that fiction has a serious purpose; that writers have an obligation to entertain their readers; and that poems or novels ... should allow the textual details themselves to provide a model for the kind of reader response the product itself seems to expect" (286). *Bleak House* is Paroissien's case study, his example of a novel which must grapple with the difficulty of communicating the harsh truths that Dickens discovered as a journalist with pleasure for "the sweet-toothed reader" (288). The latter aim is achieved in the novel by the aesthetics of Dickens's prose, and by the pacing of the plot: carefully provoked suspense, combined with periodically satisfied curiosity, carries attentive readers through the novel. Add to this the "perspective of the crow" which the reader gains by reflecting on what s/he has read and the emotional attachment to the characters that grows with extended contact with them (292), and Dickens demonstrates that the strategy of dwelling "on the romantic side of familiar things" is an effective one for combining narrative pleasure with inconvenient truths.

Like Baumgarten, Elana Gomel draws inspiration from Bakhtin in "'Part of the Dreadful Thing': The Urban Chronotope of *Bleak House*." In the novel's two narrators, Gomel believes, Dickens collapses the unnecessary division between two approaches to urban space-time: those of the flâneur and the social reformer. Gomel reads what she calls the "extra-diegetic narrator" as a sociologist, with a vertical perspective on the geography of London, "in which the urban space is envisioned as a ladder of precisely defined social and gender stations, which is hard to climb and easy to fall off from" (302). Esther Summerson, on the other hand, experiences urban space horizontally; she is part of the body of the city, which has the ability to infect her body, as well (305). Though Esther is not precisely a flâneur, Gomel's essay argues that "there is a structural similarity between Dickens's own ambiguous attitude toward London, composed as it is of the reformer's indignation and the flâneur's pleasure, and the trajectory of Esther's urban perambulations" (306).

In a commentary on Dickens's imaginative metafiction, Efraim Sicher's "Dickens and the Pleasures of the Text: The Risks of *Hard Times*" argues that instead of merely opposing Fact to Fancy, *Hard Times* uses Fancy to fight Facts—or at least a utilitarian ethos which dismisses Fancy as useless (313). In this reading, Coketown becomes an imaginative dystopia, while the circus suggests a positive model for combining imaginative play with work. Like some of his colleagues in this issue of *Partial Answers*, Sicher invokes Bakhtin, but rather than the chrono-tope, the point of reference here is the carnivalesque, elements of which, Sicher argues, replace strict narrative structure and control with a subversive narrative playfulness (322). The combination of narrative pleasure with social criticism in *Hard Times* "argues that reading for pleasure *is* an agent of change" (327).

Turning from *Hard Times* to *Little Dorrit*, Regenia Gagnier offers a new take on uneasy pleasure in "Freedom, Determinism, and Hope in *Little Dorrit*: A Literary Anthropology." Reflecting on the 150-year anniversaries of *The Origin of Species* and *On Liberty*, Gagnier focuses (as did many Victorians and present-day scientists) on what we can learn from a combined study of science and culture, nature and nurture. "We should celebrate," she writes, "the uneasy pleasures of knowing we are both nature and culture, free but only within limits" (332). *Little Dorrit* is a novel that demonstrates Dickens's interest in how scientific matters enter into and affect our social and cultural lives. The novel elides distinctions between humanity and animality, anthropomorphizing the animal and locating animalistic qualities in characters like Blandois. It portrays both human psychology and "mechanical culture," a combination that constitutes "realism" for a Victorian world that was, on the one hand, interested in forces that could overcome the individual will (institutional "red tape," mesmerism, etc.), and on the other, fascinated by "the moral springs of action" (334–36). Human technologies and their ability to transform the natural world also dominate the novel and suggest "that things can and will change. Hope is the natural consequence of the genetic under-determination of the human phenotype" (341). The novel thus considers many cultural and scientific aspects of humanity, showing us what we are and hinting at what we perhaps can be.

Adina Ciugureanu's "The Victim-Aggressor Duality in *Great Expectations*" applies a psychological lens to the novel's female characters. Ciugureanu suggests that Mrs. Joe, Miss Havisham, and Molly (and, to an extent, Mr. Jaggers) all suffer from narcissistic personality disorders which lead them to see themselves as victims and, subsequently, to victimize others. Most persuasive where it addresses the case of Miss Havisham, the essay contends that this character, frequently associated with a looking glass, "maintains an alienated relation of self to its own image" (353). This alienation began when Miss Havisham was left at the altar and results in a failure to love that is matched only by Miss Havisham's desire for love. This desire, Ciugureanu argues, combined with a drive toward revenge, results in "the victim-aggressor duality, which overlaps with the narcissistic pattern. It is always the other side, the other image of her ego that Miss Havisham continually misses" (356).

While Ciugureanu makes a number of intriguing points about the characters of Mrs. Joe and Molly (for instance, that Mrs. Joe's narcissism elevates her from a mere grotesque to a character of psychological depth [351]), she sometimes neglects to provide compelling evidence for her claims. Diagnosing illness—and particularly mental illness—in characters from a period that does not share our psychological vocabulary is always tricky, and is occasionally unconvincing here. Not only is Mrs. Joe a narcissist, Ciugureanu argues, but she is also psychotic, particularly when she abuses Pip and Joe. Further, the essay suggests that Mrs. Joe's narcissistic desire for attention extends to her docile, post-attack personality: "her wish to see Orlick daily, her enjoyment of the company of the people whom she had victimized, and her eagerness to be reconciled with them … can … be read in psychological terms as a Narcissistic attempt to embrace, through the others, her ideal self, the object of her real love" (352). Without more support, this reading of Mrs. Joe's character seems merely cynical. One also wonders why Estella is not given more space in Ciugureanu's article; the omission is conspicuous, given the argument's focus.

Sally Ledger's contribution to the issue focuses more directly on unease than on pleasure. In "Dickens, Natural History, and *Our Mutual Friend*," Ledger studies the impact of science, and particularly of Darwinian science, on the novel's worldview. The concept of natural selection influences the novel's response to political economy, the Malthusian version of which had long been the subject of Dickensian critique. The scope of the problem shifts, however, in *Our Mutual Friend*:

> Whereas Dickens's initial assault against the New Poor Law in *Oliver Twist* is aimed at a very specific legal and social wrong that he believed could be remedied, his later invective, in 1864–65, needs to be understood, firstly, as part of a wider social-Darwinian account of the struggle for existence, and, secondly, in terms of the ontological shift effected by Darwin which, in the end, removed the possibility of Providential design. (367)

Characters in *Our Mutual Friend* succeed or fail owing to their adaptability to change; Bradley Headstone is never comfortable in his schoolmaster's clothes or life, but Lizzie Hexam, for instance, is able to adapt to several new phases of life and to social advancement. Toward the end of her argument, Ledger argues that the novel anticipates Darwin's *The Descent of Man* (1871), in which Darwin argued for evolution without the intervention of a God. *Our Mutual Friend* expresses a fear that the order and comfort of "ethical design" is absent both from the human worlds of private and public affairs and from "the wider post-Darwinian world" (376).

Turning from Dickens's approach to science toward Victorian pseudoscience, Angelika Zirker's "Physiognomy and the Reading of Character in *Our Mutual Friend*" ably explains how the novel "can be seen as testing Lavater's theory of physiognomy" (388). Dickens's characters read and misread one another's countenances throughout the novel, and the narrator invites the reader to attempt the same through its detailed descriptions of many of the characters' faces. Using the examples of Fascination Fledgeby, who is legible by Riah mainly through the lens of the latter's prior knowledge, and Mrs. Wilfer, who wrongly fancies herself "a physiognomist" (381), Zirker shows that reading a countenance is a complicated matter, improved by depth of acquaintance or by a sympathetic outlook. She also dwells on those characters whose features are difficult to read, like Mr. Boffin and Bella Wilfer; Dickens describes each as having ambiguous features that suggest their susceptibility to change.

Continuing the consideration of "uneasy pleasures" that structures the volume, Jeffrey Wallen's "Twemlow's Abyss" argues that aesthetic pleasure and social critique cannot be divided in *Our Mutual Friend*. Beginning with the example of Twemlow, who not only experiences but also causes confusion at the Veneerings' dinner table (Is he a person? Is he a piece of furniture?), Wallen locates pleasure in the reader's resolution of this confusion. But he also points out that in *Our Mutual Friend*, "confusion is the sign of a social problem" (394). Although the reader's impulse is to solve the problem by clarifying that which confused him or her, and thereby separating pleasure from social critique, Wallen warns that this is not always a strategy endorsed by the novel. Sometimes, "the social critique requires our learning *not* to pull apart that which has become aesthetically entangled.... Social critique is here based on empathy rather than reason" (396). In either case, whether our confusion, or that of the text, is resolved or no, "the initial confusion of the reader—which is essential to the aesthetic pleasure—does not finally produce a moral confusion" (397). Wallen closes his argument by considering the disintegration of the body in *Our Mutual Friend*, and its ability to be both a person and a material object of exchange, sometimes simultaneously (as in the case of Wegg). This causes another kind of confusion, which is not readily resolved. Speculation (in the senses of prediction, of financial risk, and of vision), might offer a possibility. The novel offers examples of all three kinds of speculation, but it suggests that aesthetic and moral vision "possess the power to displace and rearrange the social—and metaphysical—order" (401).

Bernard Harrison's "Always Fiction? The Limits of Authorial License in *Our Mutual Friend*" closes the *Partial Answers* special issue with a linguistic consideration of Dickens's realism. Calling attention first to the fantastical elements of Dickens's multiplot novel, many of which rely on fairy-tale tropes, Harrison locates realism (or the place where authorial license reaches its limit) at the level of Dickens's language. For Harrison, literary discourse intersects with reality in terms of language practices: "it is concerned with words as the signs and tools of the multifarious practices by means of which we continually recreate ourselves, and by which we were in the first place created as participants in the particular human world into which each of us was born" (414). The essay's central examples are the discussions of self-promotion among Bradley Headstone, Charley Hexam, and Lizzie Hexam; Dickens uses these to demonstrate the manipulative uses of language and particularly to interrogate the discursive concepts of "getting up in the world" and "making the best of oneself" (425). Harrison goes on to show how the novel uses such moments of language-as-practice as part of its social criticism: through the examples of Headstone and Charley Hexam (among other characters in *Our Mutual Friend*), Dickens suggests that status-seeking as an end in itself is corrupt: "By contrast, what unites the 'good' characters in the novel is that they either care nothing for, or eventually relinquish,... the supposedly glittering prize of social standing" (427). Again the aesthetic pleasure—and power—of language is linked to Dickens's social criticism.

Sally Ledger and Holly Furneaux's edited collection, *Charles Dickens in Context*, provides incisive short essays on a variety of cultural issues by a who's who of Dickens scholars. Furneaux's preface explains that the volume was the brainchild of Sally Ledger, to whom it is dedicated and who passed away before its publication. Furneaux writes in the preface that "this book seeks to illuminate the contexts—social, political, economic and artistic—in which Dickens worked, as well as the ways he has been read and rewritten from the nineteenth century to the present" (xix). This is a tall order for any single book, and this one makes no claim to be exhaustive; rather, the entries in *Charles Dickens in Context* offer snapshots of Dickens's life, work, influence, and critical reception: they are focused and discrete, geared toward readers who already have a basic understanding of Dickens and pointing the way toward further research on their given topics.

The book is divided into two parts: "Life and Afterlife" and "Social and Cultural Contexts." The former begins with a very brief biography, in two parts, by John Bowen; the point of division between the parts is the beginning of Dickens's relationship with Ellen Ternan, clearly a turning point in Dickens's life. These are followed by Michael Slater's "Dickens's Lives," a summary of major biographies of Dickens from John Forster's (1870) to Peter Ackroyd's (1990). From these stories of Dickens's life, essays on the afterlives of his works begin. Examples of these include Anne Humpherys's look at Victorian adaptations of the novels for stage and page, John Drew's examination of Dickens's reception history, and Michael Hollington's "The European Context," which argues against notions that Dickens is quintessentially British, claiming that "Dickens is the least parochial of Victorian novelists, most particularly because of his affinities with Fyodor Dostoevsky, Nikolai Gogol, and Honoré de Balzac,... but also because of his revered standing with more 'classic' realists such as Tolstoy, Benito Pérez Galdós, Alphonse Daudet, and Alexander Kielland, all of them unquestionably and avowedly indebted to him" (44). These are followed by several essays addressing twentieth- and twenty-first century adaptations of Dickens's works in a variety of media, ending with Cora Kaplan's "Neo-Victorian Dickens." This essay selects respected novels by Sarah Waters, Peter Carey, and Lloyd Jones, explaining that the latter novels, in particular, ask "the reader to reflect on the power relations of writing and reading that reach across centuries and continents" (87). Perhaps controversially, Kaplan groups Ackroyd's biography, *Dickens*, with these fictional works, arguing that "in a clever amalgam of the biographer's meditative voice and Dickens's own, Ackroyd seems at times to take on the discursive identity of the man he is describing, and with it his authority" (82). Latter-day afterlives of Dickens, then, blend—and bend—Dickens's voice and works into a variety of media and genres, creating hybrid texts in neo-Dickensian contexts.

Part 2 of *Charles Dickens in Context*, "Social and Cultural Contexts," is quite broadly defined, with issues ranging from the generic (Florian Schweizer's "The *Bildungsroman*," Ian Duncan's "The Historical Novel," Mary Elizabeth Leighton and Lisa Surridge's "The Illustrated Novel") to the geographic (Ruth Livesey's "Europe," Ella Dzelzainis's "The Victorians and America," Anne Humpherys's "London") to the socio-political (Grace Moore's "Empires and Colonies," Priti Joshi's "Race," Janis McLarren Caldwell's "Illness, Disease, and Social Hygiene," Catherine Waters's "Gender Identities"). Although a clearer rationale for the order of these essays could be helpful to the reader, and perhaps some subdivisions could serve as subject-matter signposts, the material in this section is, again, broad in scope and rich in detail. Joss Marsh's "The Rise of Celebrity Culture" makes a strong case for dating the concept of celebrity to the Victorian period; Marsh points out that "the very word 'celebrity,' in its current meaning (a celebrated person; a public character; someone who is much talked about) dates from the later 1840s" (98), and that "the Victorian celebrity ... was also an idol whose sway depended on performance" (99). This is, indeed, a useful context for our understanding of Dickens as a literary celebrity, one who built theatrical performance into his very identity as author. "His experience of celebrity," Marsh writes, "was diagnostic, foundational, premonitory. For years, its sheer extent made him critically suspect; the celebrification of Anglo-American culture has dramatically reinstated his relevance and importance" (102).

Kate Flint's "Visual Culture" considers the new visual technologies of the Victorian period, particularly daguerreotypes and photographs, as well as new trends and topics in the visual arts, including "representations of social issues" (149).

> Yet the Victorians were fascinated not just with *what* they saw but with *how* they saw: by the mechanics and reliability (or otherwise) of the human eye; by the connection between the physiological fact of seeing and the way in which the psychology of perception influenced one's interpretation, and memory, of what they saw; by the instruments and toys ... that altered one's normal way of seeing, and by the type of seeing that took place inwardly, in the mind's eye—in the imagination, in dreams, or in hallucinations. These forms of unbidden vision recur across Dickens's fiction. (151)

The kinds of links that Flint draws between these varieties of ways of seeing are representative of this volume, which seeks to unite multiple contexts and cultural lenses through which to see Dickens and his works clearly and to see them whole. Ledger and Furneaux end *Charles Dickens in Context* with an extensive and helpful "Further Reading" section, subdivided into the topics of the volume. In so doing, they offer yet more context for the individual essays within, encouraging readers to expand their understanding of Dickens's world.

In the run-up to the bicentenary, it is appropriate that Eugene Goodheart's edited collection, *Critical Insights: Charles Dickens*, offers several opportunities

to reassess the criticism that has shaped readers' understandings of the major novels to this point: it brings together essays from such venerable scholars as Lionel
Trilling and Monroe Engel and juxtaposes them with offerings from newer critics
like Elizabeth Gumport and Matthew J. Bolton. The essays compiled here form
an idiosyncratic collection from which there is much to learn, but which raises
several unanswered questions.

As the title of this volume promises, each essay within offers valuable scholarly perspectives into Dickens's life and work. The book's apparatus is also well
designed: its "Resources" section contains a chronology of Dickens's life, a dated
list of Dickens's works (including minor works, such as the plays), and a comprehensive bibliography. In addition, the fact that the entire volume is available
online to purchasers is useful to readers who may wish to access it on the go.

The book, however, lacks a holistic sense of purpose as a collection. Goodheart
offers a brief introduction to the volume containing one-sentence summaries of
its contents, without any overarching explanation as to how the collection was
assembled, or how the essays might usefully be put in dialogue with one another.
Although threads of connection exist among some of the essays (several allude
to Dickensian fall narratives; several link Dickens's Victorian style and subjects
with the eighteenth or twentieth centuries), no overarching theme, idea, or critical
perspective emerges from the volume. This book may have been more coherent
with a well-articulated editorial vision, to clarify for the reader how essays dating
from the 1950s through to the present day speak to one another and to us.

Even without such guidance, however, readers of Dickens will find much to
interest them in the three sections of Goodheart's collection: "Career, Life, and
Influence," "Critical Contexts," and "Critical Readings." The first of these begins
with an essay by the editor surveying Dickens's techniques and thematic concerns. A condensed "Biography of Charles Dickens," originally published in 2001
by Patricia Marks, appears next. This overview of the author's life, and its influence on the novels, is impressive in its elegance and economy, but it inevitably
engages in some reductive and incomplete interpretations. Overall, this brief portrait of Dickens is useful to new students of his work. Elizabeth Gumport's 2011
appreciation of Dickens, written for the *Paris Review*, rounds out the first section
of *Critical Insights*. Taken together, these three essays introduce the author for
general readers seeking to situate their readings of Dickens in their own world
and experiences.

The "Critical Contexts" section provides an overview of some major issues
in Dickens studies. Shanyn Fiske, in "Charles Dickens in His Times," considers
Dickens in relation to child abuse and labor, prostitution, crime and sensationalism, and imperialism. By discussing how Dickens confronted these issues in his
life and work, Fiske lucidly shows how the author influenced and was influenced
by his social environment. Laurence Mazzeno's essay "Charles Dickens's Critical
Reputation" traces the influence of the times on Dickens from a different perspective: that of literary evaluation. Mazzeno is right that "the circuitous path of Dick-

ens criticism is noteworthy not only for what it says about the novelist but also for what it reveals about the path of literary criticism in the nineteenth and twentieth centuries" (41). Given its brevity, Mazzeno's essay covers an impressive array of material, and its summaries and bibliography are helpful to any readers looking to begin or broaden their critical reading of Dickens. Finally, Nancy M. West's 1989 *South Atlantic Review* essay, "Order in Disorder: Surrealism and *Oliver Twist*," counters critiques of the novel that disparage its departures from realism or its incoherent structure by arguing that, in fact, these effects are deliberate and anticipate surrealist techniques. Drawing on examples from across Dickens's career, and from the surrealist canon, West argues that Dickens "used his art to explore the role that dreams and fantasy play in our understanding of external reality and what lies beyond it" (60).

The final and longest section of the volume, "Critical Readings," offers deeper engagement with individual Dickens novels. Some highlights merit individual mention. The first of two essays primarily devoted to *David Copperfield*, Alan P. Barr's "Mourning Becomes David: Loss and the Victorian Restoration of Young Copperfield" (*Dickens Quarterly*, 2007) sees an elegiac portrayal of the loss of childhood innocence as central to our understanding of David's *Bildung*. Using Freud's "Mourning and Melancholia" as a lens through which to examine loss in Dickens's novel, Barr considers David's eventual success a result of his successful mourning of his own loss of innocence (123). Julia F. Saville's "Eccentricity as Englishness in *David Copperfield*" (*ELH*, 2002) establishes a national connection to the novel's eccentric characters. Saville argues that "... to be *a character* in the sense of feeling free to assert one's individuality was simultaneously to participate in defining the *national character* as free" (126). However, the freedom to be personally unique must always be in tension with the need to conform to a civic nation (126–27).

G. Robert Stange's "Expectations Well Lost: Dickens' Fable for His Time" (*College English*, 1954) also takes up the tension between the individual and society by examining the evolving question of criminality in *Great Expectations*. Pip's initial sense of guilt, Stange reasons, comes from "a natural bond ... between the child and the criminal; they are alike in their helplessness; both are repressed and tortured by established society, and both rebel against its incomprehensible authority" (148). Concluding that "the last stage of Pip's progression is reached when he learns to love the criminal and to accept his own implication in the common guilt," Stange's essay effectively delineates the novel's versions and extenuations of this guilt.

Michele S. Ware, in one of the volume's two treatments of *Bleak House*, suggests that Dickens's mythopoeia presents an insufficient alternative to the suffering and social injustice represented by Chancery. In "'True Legitimacy': The Myth of the Foundling in *Bleak House*" (*Studies in the Novel*, 1990), Ware argues that Dickens builds on the foundling narratives of eighteenth-century novels with Oliver Twist and Esther Summerson. Unlike most eighteenth-century foundlings, however, Dickens's are not restored to any proper place in society once their true identities are discovered. Esther's virtues may be alternatives to the corruption of her society, but they cannot overpower this corruption.

The volume's capstone essay—and one of its strongest—is Matthew Bolton's "Charles Dickens, James Joyce, and the Origins of Modernism." Like Nancy West's consideration of *Oliver Twist*, Bolton's argument traces lines of influence between the nineteenth and twentieth centuries. Bolton examines the influence of *Little Dorrit* and *Our Mutual Friend* on *Ulysses* and urges us "to think of the relationship between the two novelists [and perhaps the two literary periods] as evolutionary rather than revolutionary" (256).

Shari Hodges Holt's "Recent Dickens Studies and Adaptations: 2009," published in the 2011 volume of *Dickens Studies Annual*, provides an excellent—and, to me, inspiring—guide to the publications in Dickens criticism for that year. Holt divides her survey into the following categories: "Intertextual and Cross-Cultural Influences; Gender, Sexuality, Marriage, and Children; Science, Religion, and Philosophy; Law, Economics, and Politics; Victorian Media and Spectacle; Geographical Spaces; Studies of Adaptations in Fiction and Film; Studies of Individual Works; Biographies and Reference Works; and Recent Adaptations: Graphic Novels, Films, and Fiction" (331). Perhaps most fascinating is this final section, which requires Holt not only to examine critical but also creative texts from 2009. These include such diverse productions as graphic novel versions of Dickens's most popular works, BBC heritage adaptations of *Oliver Twist* and *Little Dorrit*, and such literary reworkings of Dickens's texts as Richard Flanagan's *Wanting* and Dan Simmons's *Drood*. Holt's perspectives on these works constitute valuable literary criticism in their own right and are significant contributions to our understanding of contemporary neo-Victorianism.

Influences on Dickens; Dickens's Influence: Intertextualities

Influences on Dickens

Dickens's interactions with other texts and authors resulted in a substantial number of contributions to Dickens studies in 2011. Beginning with the influence of other authors *on* Dickens and his works, three separate texts study Dickens's qualifications as a Shakespearean. Daniel Pollack-Pelzner's engaging "Dickens and Shakespeare's Household Words" examines Dickens's reasons for employing Shakespearean allusion and technique, as well as the surprising phenomenon of reverse influence. Dickens's use of language, particularly in the speech of some of his most memorable characters, like Sam Weller and Wilkins Micawber, is self-consciously quotable and performable, in the manner of Shakespeare's lines. Pollack-Pelzner parses the formula for a Wellerism: "a commonplace phrase, as a surprisingly menacing figure said, when he performed a vile action completely at odds with the original context of the utterance. With over fifty instances in *Pickwick*, they became the novel's most quotable and portable phrases" (538). In fact, Weller himself may have been inspired by *Lear*'s Fool, who adheres to a similar formula when speaking home truths to his master (542). By writing quotable dialogue that makes sense both in and out of context, Dickens extends his words beyond the page, putting them into spontaneous circulation in the mouths of his readers and the culture more broadly. In so doing, he achieves the explicit goal of the journal *Household Words*, which takes its name from a previously little-known quotation from *Henry V*'s St. Crispin's Day speech: "Familiar in their mouths as Household Words." This quotation, too, is significant; before Dickens used it as the tagline for his weekly serial, it was seldom quoted out of context, and the phrase "household words" was not commonplace. As Pollack-Pelzner points out, since articles in *Household Words* were published anonymously, "Dickens's and Shakespeare's were the only names that appeared on the masthead" (547). Casting himself as a kind of collaborator with Shakespeare, then, would burnish Dickens's literary reputation, "and Shakespeare ... posthumously profited from the association as well" (552). Thus the Victorian Dickens cast light back on his Elizabethan influence, influencing later readers' and critics' associations with and appreciations of Shakespeare himself.

Adrian Poole's "Dickens and Shakespeare's Ghost(s)" contends that Dickens is the "major writer in English [most] obsessed by Shakespeare" (322). Dickens is, he argues, haunted by Shakespeare the writer, as well as specifically by manifestations of the supernatural in Shakespeare's plays. Focusing mainly on the influence of Shakespeare's tragedies and histories upon Dickens's novels and essays, Poole begins his article with a consideration of parody and comedy: the ways in which Dickens alludes to and transforms Shakespearean language for comic effect. "Parody, travesty, burlesque, caricature, cartoon: these depend on readers or audiences recognizing what is being mockingly impersonated, and this recognition creates a certain sociability" that includes some and excludes others who do not get the joke (325). Shakespeare's familiarity makes his writing an easy choice for such allusions, which expand the community of the audience. Poole also suggests that Shakespeare's melodramatic touches (the heightened and intensified language of some of Hamlet's speeches, for instance, and the juxtapositions of high and low, tragic and comic, etc.) may have appealed to Dickens in the manner of the "streaky bacon" which Dickens defends in *Oliver Twist* (327).

Poole's argument next settles into a deeper discussion of the archetypal functions of Shakespeare's tragedies for Dickens. References to *Hamlet* and *Macbeth* appear most often in Dickens's works, although *King Lear* is also important. *Hamlet*, Poole suggests, is the *ur*-text for Dickens's bildungsromans: *David Copperfield* and *Great Expectations* (332). *Lear*, "concerned with unhousing, exiling, and humbling the father so that he can be redeemed by the 'daughter-wife,' [is] a story we find in *The Old Curiosity Shop*, and perhaps most prominently in *Dombey and Son* and *Little Dorrit*" (332). *Macbeth* is a major source for Dick-

ens's notions of "criminality and guilt" (333). Perhaps some of Dickens's ghostly
Shakespearean allusions are unconscious, while others are clearly intentional and
call attention to themselves within the text. In any case, Poole concludes, "to the
nightmares of loneliness, guilt, and despair that give Dickens's fiction its enduring credibility,... Shakespeare's ghost made a royal contribution" (335).

   Poole further considers the topic of Dickens and Shakespeare in his collaboration with Rebekah Scott on *Scott, Dickens, Eliot, Hardy: Great Shakespeareans*. Each author receives a stand-alone chapter, and Poole and Scott consider
Dickens's debt to Shakespeare from a variety of angles. Beginning generally,
they offer categories of understanding Shakespeare in Dickens's work, including
"Popularity," "Pretensions," and "Allusion." The first of these points out that,
in Dickens's early life, only two theaters were licensed to perform Shakespeare;
others had to make do with parodies and variations on Shakespearean themes.
Dickens himself, as a novelist, participates in this activity of "making fun *out
of* Shakespeare," drawing on what Poole and Scott call "this popular property, a
vocabulary of well-known characters and stories, not primarily a matter of words
but of visual and theatrical icons and tropes" (55). Dickens's and Shakespeare's
most important commonality, they argue, is their use of the grotesque, the juxtaposition of that which should be kept separate (different social classes, tonal
registers, moralities or the lack thereof, etc.). In "Pretensions," Poole and Scott
focus on the issue of Shakespearean performance and its appearances in Dickens's novels. Citing "Mrs Joseph Porter, 'Over the Way,'" *Nicholas Nickleby*,
and *Great Expectations* in particular, they point up examples of Shakespearean
tragedies turning comic in bad performances by amateur actors, the "misprisions
of Shakespeare distinguished by their shallowness, condescension, and opportun-
ism" (63). Dickens discriminates, they argue, between professionalism and dilet-
tantism in performance (61), raising questions along the way of the compatibility
of gentility and the theater. Shakespeare's plays, it seems, lend themselves to
pretentious adaptation. The last of the general sections, "Allusion," raises intriguing questions of "what counts as an allusion," and to what uses Dickens puts allusions to Shakespeare (67). Ranging from direct quotation to comic misquotations
to ironic Shakespearean comments on the characters, Dickens's deployment of
Shakespeare is varied and complex. It does essentially claim "a kind of sportive
fraternity with his great predecessor: they are in the same game" (70).

   From such generalized meditations on Shakespeare in Dickens, Poole and Scott
go on to discuss the appearance of three specific plays in Dickens's novels: *Hamlet*, *King Lear*, and *Macbeth*. *Hamlet*'s emphases on words and performativity
are treated extensively, as is the theatricality of Dickens's novels, notable in that
they demonstrate a consciousness of their audience. The *King Lear* section of the
essay doubts that Dickens's vexed novels of (grand)fathers and daughters (*OCS,
D&S, LD*) derive directly from the *Lear* narrative, and raises the interesting point
that "there is a way of being a 'great Shakespearean' that does not involve specific
bequests so much as the independent treatment of common materials with a depth

and complexity that warrant comparison" (84). Thus we can learn from reading *Little Dorrit* side by side with *Lear*, even if the one is not a deliberate rewriting of the other. The authors do raise the possibility that *Lear* influenced Dickens's "passion for justice, for the redressing of injury and the recognition of true need" (87), though doubtless the same is true for many other influential texts. Finally, in the essay's treatment of *Macbeth*, Poole and Scott see in this play a source of the darkness that pervades Dickens's oeuvre. "Unendurable guilt" (87), "a contemporary urban world of squalor, poverty, and crime," and "the abuse of innocent victims" (89) are subjects that provoke invocations of the play in Dickens's novels. Although the novels also offer antidotes, generally in the form of selfless love, to *Macbeth*'s nihilistic violence, the play recurs with such frequency as to suggest that the darkness is never fully vanquished.

The next few critics to examine Dickens's influences look to texts and authors a bit closer to Dickens's own period. Rodney Stenning Edgecombe's brief note, "Keats, Hood, Dickens, Crones, and Little Boys," follows a motif knitting together "The Eve of St. Agnes," "Plea of the Midsummer Fairies," and *Dombey and Son*. The poets' work, Edgecombe argues, influences Dickens's portrayal of the relationship between little Paul Dombey and Mrs. Pipchin, since each poem features the image of a boy seeking or gaining knowledge from a more experienced, or even magical, crone. Dickens, Edgecombe suggests, modifies the conceit, investing Paul with his own uncanny wisdom, even as he "[studies] Mrs. Pipchin, and the cat, and the fire ... as if they were a book of necromancy, in three volumes" (82). Edgecombe draws no further conclusions from this line of influence, allowing this interesting connection to be a potential line of study for a future scholar.

Jeremy Tambling's "Lamb, Hogarth, and Dickens" connects the three writers as urban artists (including Blake and Chaucer along the way). Using Lamb's defense of Hogarth, "On the Genius and Character of Hogarth," as a central document, Tambling argues that this essay, influenced by Blake's discussion of Chaucer in his 1810 Exhibition's "Descriptive Catalogue," in turn influenced Dickens's appreciation and understanding of Hogarth's art. Dickens's critiques of George Cruikshank's prints, *The Bottle* and *The Drunkard's Children: A Sequel to the Bottle*, compare them negatively with Hogarth's satirical prints. "Like Lamb," Tambling argues, "Dickens goes 'beyond.' His critique of Cruikshank, is that he does not do this, but reads drunkenness too literally, as a thing in itself.... Dickens shows ... that the trace of the past is in the present, and that causes are to be read from the visible scene, but this does not yield itself to an eye that does not work at the detail, as Dickens does. As Lamb said, everything *tells*, in Hogarth or Dickens" (112–13). Lamb's and Dickens's appreciations of Hogarth, then, point to a visual technique in Hogarth that is also present in Dickens's fiction: "investigation of invisible causes" (113). The imagination, or "the eye of the mind," in Lamb's language (114), is provoked by the art to seek for these causes, and to find the story behind the story.

Another critic to take up the influence of Lamb on Dickens is Peter Rowland, in *Dickensian Digressions: The Hunter, the Haunter, and the Haunted*, an engagingly-written, idiosyncratic examination of several of Dickens's heretofore insufficiently studied influences. Lamb is the subject of what Rowland calls "Bout No. 1: The Irrepressible v. the Inimitable." Rowland carefully traces the potential influence of Elia's essays on Dickens's own work, paying special attention to their effects in *Sketches by Boz*, *The Pickwick Papers*, and *The Uncommercial Traveller*. Dickens knew Lamb's essays well and commented on his appreciation of them in letters of the 1830s and early 1840s (11). Although occasionally the connections that Rowland draws between Lamb's subject matter, themes, and style and those of Dickens seem tenuous, *Dickensian Digressions*, on the whole, makes a compelling case for the deep impression that Lamb's work would have made on Dickens. This is especially true where Rowland considers the potential influence of *Mrs Leicester's School*, written mainly by Mary Lamb with contributions from her brother, on Dickens's novels. Though Rowland cannot prove outright that Dickens read this book in his childhood, the connections between its plots and characterizations and those in several Dickens novels seem too close for coincidence. Rowland wisely calls the parallels he finds between the Lambs' stories and Dickens's "tentatively suggested" (40), but they remain richly fascinating.

Rowland's discussion of Lamb's influence on Dickens is followed by what he calls an "Interlude": "What's in a Name? Fagin and Araminta." This brief chapter contains two brief *Notes and Queries*-style investigations of echoes of Dickens's biography in his writing. The first attempts to track down the original Bob Fagin of Warren's Blacking, to whom Dickens refers in the autobiographical fragment. Rowland's research into Victorian death registers leads him to conclude that Dickens's Bob Fagin would actually have been Bob Fag*a*n, or possibly Bob *Fegen*, because the latter names were far more common in England and Wales, and because his research led him to a Robert Fegen who may well have been Dickens's young colleague (45). Rowland next turns his attention to Maria Beadnell, adding to the fictional Dora Spenlow and Flora Finching another representation of her in *Household Words*. Rowland argues that "Gone to the Dogs," written and published by Dickens in 1855, refers to the aging Maria Winter as "Araminta," a name that combines "an anagram of Maria" with an "echo" of the name Winter (48).

Next in Rowland's study is a consideration of the relationship—or rather the surprising lack of relationship—between Dickens and historian Thomas Babington Macaulay. Though both writers moved in the same circles and sometimes enjoyed one another's work, they seldom met and never became close. As Rowland puts it, their relationship "was of such a subtle, subterranean nature that it has scarcely been noticed" (53). Rowland points up interesting coincidences between the lives of the two men, including the fact that Macaulay was an MP at the time when Dickens was a reporter in the House of Commons (59), and explains how Dickens imitated and critiqued Macaulay by turns (65, 73–74). Likewise, he mines Macaulay's journal for references to Dickens's novels, which Macaulay read and reread. Speculating that "Macaulay must surely have seemed, to Dickens, the embodiment of complacency," and that, to Macaulay, "Dickens was vulgar," Rowland offers some potential reasons why the two writers may not have formed a friendship. Yet the lack of a relationship provides small matter for a sixty-eight-page chapter, and like the relationship itself, Rowland's meditation on the pair provides "an anti-climactic end to what had been a curiously unsatisfactory relationship" (115).

A second "Interlude," called "Hauntings, Hunters, and Howitt," uses the correspondence between William Howitt and Charles Dickens on the subject of spirits and the supernatural, as well as information from *All the Year Round*'s Christmas number for 1859 and from the March 1863 number to establish definitively "that Charles Dickens—all protestations of having an open mind on the subject notwithstanding—did *not*, never had and never would, believe in ghosts or haunted houses" (125). From this brief argument, Rowland turns to *The Mystery of Edwin Drood* in the final "Bout" of his *Digressions*: "John Jasper v. Sherlock Holmes." Rowland, who has written his own ending to *The Mystery of Edwin Drood*, reveals his to be the fifth in a line of six twentieth-century conclusions to Dickens's unfinished novel that have employed Sherlock Holmes to crack the case. After relating the anecdote of Conan Doyle's spiritualist "conversation" with the late Charles Dickens about the intended ending of the novel, Rowland summarizes the versions of other Sherlockian conclusions before offering his own theory: that Drood is alive, and that Datchery is a disguise for Dickens himself. Finally, in his "Epilogue," Rowland discusses another reviser of Dickens: H. G. Wells, whose *Tono-Bungay* rewrites the opening of *David Copperfield*. "Wells, having picked up a familiar pack of cards, has shuffled them afresh, discarded one or two and dealt them out in a fashion that dazzles us with its apparent freshness" (144). With this comment, Rowland concludes his *Dickensian Digressions*, a critical-creative work that stresses the indebtedness—to and by Dickens—of the interconnected literary tradition.

Tracing the influence of Francis Jeffrey as a friend and editor on Dickens's personal and professional life, and chiefly on Dickens's role as the "Conductor" of *Household Words* is Iain Crawford's project in "'Faithful Sympathy': Dickens, The *Edinburgh Review*, and Editing *Household Words*." Dickens was friendly with most of the editors of the *Edinburgh Review*, but especially with Jeffrey, thirty-nine years his senior, with whom he formed a kind of filial bond. The friendship with "Jeffrey was unique, explains Crawford, "in its combination of warm affection and unmatched counseling over the deeply sensitive issue of the connection between professional success and personal finance" (51).

Jeffrey also served as an editorial role model for Dickens. Though the weekly serial *Household Words* might initially seem very different from the quarterly *Edinburgh Review*, both journals shared a desire for uniformity of ideology and mission, and both established "a fixed and hierarchical relationship between the editor and his writers" (56). The editors paid all of their contributors, thereby avoiding the pitfalls of creating a divide between genteel amateurs and professional hacks. "The *Edinburgh* thus took a crucial first step towards professionalizing journalism and endowing it with the secure social status of being a respectable activity for a gentleman" (55), and *Household Words* followed suit. Likewise, the editors of both journals insisted on the creation of a recognizable and consistent editorial voice.

Dickens's editorial choices differed from Jeffrey's in two respects: despite his direct intervention into many of *Household Words*'s publications, "the younger man consciously developed a team of regular contributors and ... divided up editorial responsibility between himself and Henry Wills," thus allowing himself time for other concerns (57). Dickens also cultivated many female contributors to *Household Words*, contrasting with the "resolutely masculinist character of the *Edinburgh*" (63). But, despite their differences, the *Edinburgh Review* and *Household Words* share "a commitment to a progressive social-political agenda and a sense of the importance of imaginative literature in cultural formation" (62).

Dickens's Influence

Turning to the influence of Dickens himself on other writers, but continuing to focus on Dickens's role as editor, Simon Cooke's "'A Regular Contributor:' Le Fanu's Short Stories, *All the Year Round*, and the Influence of Dickens" makes the case that Sheridan Le Fanu, in an effort to increase his earning power, to appeal to a specifically English audience, and to partake in the reputation enjoyed by Dickens's prominent literary journal, deliberately crafted his story submissions to *All the Year Round* to appeal to its editor's practical, aesthetic, and thematic concerns. As the former editor of the *Dublin University Magazine*, Le Fanu understood the "social and cultural orientation" of *ATYR*, and his stories "embody the editor's demand that his busy readers should be offered an intense reading experience." Through close readings of "The Child that Went with the Fairies," "The Vision of Tom Chuff," and "Green Tea," Cooke demonstrates the ways in which Le Fanu drew on Dickens's interests (or, perhaps more fairly, the two writers' joint interests) and elaborated specifically on Dickens's shorter fiction in his own narratives. "The Child that Went with the Fairies" and "The Vision of Tom Chuff" draw, in particular, on the Christmas Books, whereas "Green Tea," in its treatment of hallucination and suicide, corresponds with the same concerns in "The Signalman." The latter two stories form a central part of Cooke's argument, and Cooke convincingly demonstrates that despite the central characters' outward differences, each is plagued by guilt and fear, and may be suffering from a psychological disorder. "Viewed in these terms," Cooke writes, "the spectral beings they witness are the logical embodiment of their innermost anxieties." Couching such anxieties in fairy tales and stories of the supernatural, Le Fanu follows Dickens's lead, and Cooke suggests that his stories of hauntings are indeed haunted, "with uncanny persistence, by the ghost of Charles Dickens."

Moving from the ghost story into the mystery, LeRoy Lad Panek considers the role of Charles Dickens in the development of the detective genre, as well as the way that Dickens's own treatment of the detective story evolved across his career, in *Before Sherlock Holmes: How Magazines and Newspapers Invented the Detective Story*. Beginning with the treatment of crime and its discovery in *Oliver Twist* and *Barnaby Rudge*, Panek locates the punishment of crime in the actions of Providence and conscience (90, 94). While human agency may play a role, as in Mr. Brownlow's search for evidence in *Oliver Twist*, the bringing of a criminal to justice in these novels, which draw heavily on the Newgate novel for inspiration, is foreordained. *Martin Chuzzlewit*, however, marks a shift in Dickens's technique. In this novel, Jonas Chuzzlewit is pursued by a private detective, the mysterious Mr. Nadgett, whose powers of observation allow him to collect damaging evidence against Chuzzlewit (97). Dickens also uses the element of surprise to mislead his readers as to the cause of Anthony Chuzzlewit's death, thus heightening suspense in the novel.

Although *Oliver Twist*, *Barnaby Rudge*, and *Martin Chuzzlewit* evince suspicion of official law enforcement officers, Dickens's admiration for Detective Inspector Charles Field caused him to portray *Bleak House's* Mr. Bucket in a generally positive light. Prior to the novel's publication, Dickens's portrayal of Field in *Household Words* "made [him] into a star" (99). Bucket has a sinister edge but is generally professional, friendly, and insightful (101–02). Panek's characterization of him as "middle-class" may be somewhat inaccurate, but his overall reading of Mr. Bucket as an early example of a detective who springs a surprise on the novel's characters and readers alike establishes Bucket as a progenitor of later detectives in the genre. Panek goes on to consider "Hunted Down" and "To Be Taken with a Grain of Salt," before finishing his study of Dickens with *The Mystery of Edwin Drood*. He makes the interesting case that the novel's largest contribution to the detective genre is its unfinished quality, which has prompted readers and writers to attempt to read the novel for clues and evidence as to its eventual ending. Little new ground is broken in Panek's study of Dickens, but placed as it is in a broader consideration of the detective genre, this chapter provides useful context for understanding Dickens's role in its development.

The representation of London in the works of Charles Dickens is a familiar subject, given fresh life by Rosemarie Bodenheimer's "London in the Victorian Novel." While she touches briefly on Thackeray's, Trollope's, and Eliot's versions of the metropolis, construed mainly as collections of disconnected addresses with which the authors' readerships would be familiar, and which connoted status, class, and ethnic distinctions, Bodenheimer does so mainly by point of contrast with the more totalizing versions of the city in Dickens's novels. Beginning with the bold claim that "mid-nineteenth-century London acquired its breadth, depth, and density as a fictional space almost entirely through the work of Charles Dickens" (142), Bodenheimer builds her case by concentrating on how Dickens's works convey and make sense of the city's chaos. Her essay provides examples of Dickens showing the city as practiced space, through which characters moved alone, encountered one another, and formed connections. Bodenheimer also demonstrates that Dickens acknowledged and dwelt on the complexities of the cityscape, in which new buildings are crowded in next to old, private moments are possible in very public space, and crowds may or may not give rise to mobs. Dickens's novelistic reaction to change within the city, often spurred by technological advancement, is also shown to be a mixed one, and Bodenheimer examines the railway of *Dombey and Son* and Todgers's boarding house in *Martin Chuzzlewit* as examples of the Dickensian "border between modernity and nostalgia" (150). The city can be transformed by mood, as well, whether by a particular narrative perspective, by the attitudes of the characters experiencing urban life, or by the changing weather that gives the city literal and metaphorical atmosphere. The final segment of Bodenheimer's essay focuses on the legacy of Dickensian London in the fin-de-siècle. Stevenson and Conan Doyle are heirs to Dickens's use of mood and atmosphere, and Holmes's and Watson's movements through the city resemble those of Dickens's characters (153). Conrad modifies Dickens's renderings of the London underworld in *The Secret Agent* (154). But "George Gissing," Bodenheimer argues, "was the only late-century novelist to take on London as a full-time job," pessimistically representing a dismally fragmented city without the connections and "imaginative play" of Dickens's work (154, 157). Like Conrad, Gissing revises Dickens's version of Victorian London.

Taking as its premise that "[George] Gissing's works use, rewrite, respond to, filch from the novels of the man he grew up thinking the archetypal great English novelist and great man, the writer in whose footsteps, presumably, in the innocent and terrible early London years he aspired to follow" (21), M. D. Allen's "'The Knight of the Simple Heart'; Twemlow into Tymperley" traces the influence of *Our Mutual Friend* on Gissing's 1899 short story "The Poor Gentleman." Gissing's title character, Tymperley, resembles Twemlow in his retiring manner, in his difficulty navigating the complex social world of London, and in the fact that he falls into "dire financial straits through lack of worldly experience and unwise trust in a friend" (16). Both Twemlow and Tymperley are, according to Allen, resolutely gentlemen despite their reduced financial circumstances, and, in fact, the title of Gissing's story, "the poor gentleman," appears twice in *Our Mutual Friend* to describe Twemlow. Allen points out that Gissing, in his *Charles Dickens: A Critical Study*, dissented from "'the common judgment that Dickens never shows us a gentleman," and that Twemlow, though not specifically mentioned by Gissing in this context, surely qualifies to be counted among "John Jarndyce, Mr. Crisparkle, Sir Leicester Dedlock, and Cousin Feenix" (17–18). Unlike Dickens, however, Gissing "insists," in his short story, "on the demoralizing effects of poverty on the sensitive and ... decries a sentimental attitude to the working classes" (20). Allen's article is brief and convincingly makes the case for the influence of *Our Mutual Friend* on "The Poor Gentleman," but it could benefit from an expanded treatment of this important difference between the two linked works.

Thinking ahead to Dickens's latter-day influence, Maria Teresa Chialant's "Dickensian Resonances in the Contemporary English Novel" surveys the neo-Victorian novel of the past fifty or so years, categorizing its genres and concerns, and pointing out its intersections with Dickens's style and techniques. The historical novel, research novel, and novel of the self-made woman are the major foci of Chialant's essay, and she considers direct adaptations of Victorian novels, fictionalized biographies of Dickens, and novels that "invoke the Dickens world" (44–45). Chialant touches on contemporary examples of the multiplot novel and of a neo-Dickensian narrative persona, and of London's underworld as a setting, before arriving at the strongest segment of her essay: a consideration of the frank sexuality in neo-Victorian novels like Michel Faber's *The Crimson Petal and the White* and Sarah Waters's *Fingersmith*. The eroticism of these novels "expose[s] details that Dickens and his fellow authors knew but couldn't or wouldn't write about" (48), describing Victorian realities from a twentieth-century perspective. The several points that Chialant's essay offers are each interesting in their own right but do not contribute to a single, coherent argument; rather, they amount to a compilation of the ways in which "the Victorian novel offers [contemporary authors] a rich field for exploitation" (50).

Complex Intertextualities
Several critical studies in 2011 consider Dickensian intertextuality in ways not easily categorized as "influenced by" or "influence on." Instead, they consider complex webs of connections between Dickens's works and those of other writers and critics. Jonathan Arac's *Impure Worlds: The Institution of Literature in the Age of the Novel* connects essays published across his career to date, from the 1970s to the 2000s. Three of the book's ten chapters concern the relationships between Dickens novels and other works of literature. The first of these, "*Hamlet*, *Little Dorrit*, and the History of Character," suggests that the common twentieth- and twenty-first-century view of Shakespeare as a master of individual characterization "became available only in the nineteenth century" (34). That is, we read Shakespeare through the lens of "cultural formations since his own" (35). Arac examines the relationship between *Hamlet* and *Little Dorrit*, "further[ing] the project of new literary history by paying attention to the reception history of works after their time of initial production, by concern with their cultural afterlives" (35). Hamlet influences Arthur Clennam's characterization and the situations to which he must respond: the watch paper with the initials "D. N. F.," signifying the sentence "Do not forget," alludes to the instructions given to Hamlet by his father's ghost. "Paradoxically," writes Arac, "by using his memory, he should whet his purpose for future action, rather than remaining tied to the past" (40). Arthur, like Hamlet, is stymied by the paradox. But *Hamlet* is not only a direct influence on *Little Dorrit*; the novel is also influenced by the Gothic tradition that can be traced back to Shakespeare's play, and "between *Hamlet* and *Little Dorrit* there intervened a series of cultural shifts mediated by the romantic

critics of Shakespeare, who staged him in their writings" (45). Thus, three levels
of intertextuality link the Shakespearean text with the Dickensian, the early modern period with the Victorian. Along the way, Romantic readings of Hamlet as a
universal individual have been transmitted through novelists like Dickens to academic critics of the present day, who read this individuality back to Shakespeare.

Arac's next chapter, "The Struggle for the Cultural Heritage: Christina Stead
Refunctions Charles Dickens and Mark Twain," argues that Stead's 1940 novel
The Man Who Loved Children deploys the cultural power of both nineteenth-
century writers in a "conscious revisionary polemic" (50). Stead created, in her
title character, "Samuel Clemens Pollit," a middle-class, patriarchal socialist. His
name and passions point to Dickens and Twain, questioning their relevance to the
world of 1930s politics. "The Popular Front," which Stead satirizes in her novel,
"relied upon the belief that change could happen without a painful struggle against
existing values.... Her criticism of the Popular Front is inscribed ... in her critique
of humanism through Dickens and Twain" (54). Instead of specifically revising or
referencing particular works by the canonical writers, Stead relies instead on the
broader cultural understanding of these figures' books and biographies, allowing
the *idea* of Dickens and Twain to function as synecdoche for a set of cultural values (55). Arac reads Stead's use of the images of Dickens and Twain through the
lens of gender, as a feminist critique, and considers its exposure of how "fascinating and attractive ... patriarchal power can be" (57). Stead "refunctions the critical
Gestalt of Dickens and Twain. Refusing to validate them either by showing their
continuing relevance ... or by decrying their contemporary degradation..., instead
she criticizes them. Her tone refunctions the very 'irreverence' that characterized
the masculine comic philistine humanist genius of Dickens and Twain and makes
it into a woman's weapon against them" (60).

Arac's next consideration of Dickens is chapter 6 of *Impure Worlds*: "Narrative Form and Social Sense in *Bleak House* and *The French Revolution*." At
the outset, Arac disrupts readers' expectations, explaining that his goal is not to
trace "Carlyle's influence on Dickens," but rather to "consider Carlyle's work
in its public role in the institution of literature, as the first book to embody and
articulate a mode of writing ... that became dominant in early Victorian England"
(79). Arac finds parallels between the literary strategies of Dickens and Carlyle
for sustaining long volumes of text: "The mode of writing in *Bleak House* and
The French Revolution combines shared techniques of narrative unity and variety
with a similar plot of social action" (83). Each also employs Gothic conventions
and scientific references (particularly to disease and contagion) as part of its social
criticism. These strategies, taken together, provide an alternate model of social
change to that of violent revolution:

> The gothic language in both expresses the fear that people are prey to
> incomprehensible forces of the past, but gothic appearances are reduced to
> social and psychological processes in the present. Naturphilosophie provides

a synecdochal view of the world, by which the works assert that human energies are at one with the forces of nature and that human beings can therefore change the world. The spatializing power of narrative overview demonstrates the human ability to comprehend the world. (93)

Though it seems that this chapter does, because of Carlyle's importance to Dickens, in fact enumerate Carlyle's influence on Dickens, it also has a broader purpose: to use these two influential writers as models of fictional and nonfictional Victorian social writing, genres which shared a common method and a common purpose.

In "The Reference to the Year 1793 in *A Tale of Two Cities, Ninety-Three* and *The Devils*," Sarah Boudant traces threads of connection among the portrayals of what she calls "the myth of 1793" (76) in Dickens, Hugo, and Dostoevsky. While calling attention to the mutual admiration between Dickens and Hugo, and to the admiration of Dostoevsky for Dickens, Boudant provides largely persuasive arguments *against* direct influence as an explanation for the similarities among the three writers' portrayals of and references to 1793, the year in which the Reign of Terror began in France. She reads 1793, the year in which the French Revolution turned from "*Liberté, Egalité, Fraternité*" to "*Mort*," as a reference point that each author uses to measure the political and social realities of his present day. Hugo sets *Quatrevingt-Treize* just before the Terror begins, "since the desperate situation in which the Third Republic finds itself in [1871], at the mercy of Prussia and the Commune, calls to mind the threat England and the *Vendée* posed to Revolutionary France in 1793.... Hugo isolates from the [historical] events a single principle, violence, on which he then reflects" (81). Dostoevsky also draws a connection between present-day politics and the references to 1793 in *The Devils*, which concerns a corrupt Russian revolutionary group. Dostoevsky "makes it clear ... that the practical application in Russia of European ideas leads inevitably to disaster" (86). Boudant's discussion of *A Tale of Two Cities*'s interest in the Terror is somewhat less compelling than her analysis of the other two authors considered here; though her analysis of the function of the slogan "Liberty, Equality, Fraternity ... or Death" as "a despotic injunction" contrasted with Sidney Carton's mantra, "I am the Resurrection and the Life," is convincing (89, 91), her explanation of Dickens's use of the historical novel as a way "to denounce certain characteristics of his own society without offending his contemporaries' sensibilities" (84) fails to account for the many instances across Dickens's career where he directly criticized present-day institutions and abuses.

Finally, in this section focusing on Dickens, literary influence, and intertextuality, two new biographies of G. K. Chesterton consider the content and impact of his Dickens criticism: *Charles Dickens: A Critical Study* (1906), and the introductions to the Everyman Library editions of Dickens's novels (1911). Kevin Belmonte's *Defiant Joy: The Remarkable Life and Impact of G. K. Chesterton* calls *Charles Dickens* "a catalyst" for further Dickens studies and credits Ches-

terton's books with the twentieth-century's revival of interest in Dickens's work
(97). Characterizing Chesterton's criticism as "free-ranging," Belmonte traces its
consideration of Dickens's mythmaking as potentially influencing other religious
literary critics, including C. S. Lewis and J. R. R. Tolkein (101–02). Belmonte
closes his discussion of Chesterton's Dickens criticism with a brief reception history, citing two *New York Times* reviews, one of which was mixed in its estimation of the book, and the second of which, a direct reply to the first, praised
Chesterton's use of paradox and humor (107–08).

While Belmonte's biography is written for a popular audience, Ian Ker takes a
more scholarly approach to Chesterton's Dickens criticism. Delving more deeply
into the specifics of this criticism, Ker cites idiosyncrasies that demonstrate Chesterton's unique spin on Dickens's texts while concurring with Belmonte that
"Chesterton's unfashionable defence of [Dickens] is also his finest tribute to the
despised, recently departed Victorian era" (164). Ker argues that "for Chesterton,"
who often wrote in paradoxes, "the central paradox of Dickens's life was that the
hated blacking factory of his unhappy boyhood 'manufactured also the greatest
optimist of the nineteenth century,' so that, if (as his critics complain) 'he learnt to
whitewash the universe, it was in a blacking factory that he learnt it'" (166). Ker
also considers Chesterton's paradoxical claims about Dickens: that despite Dickens's disdain for the Middle Ages, much of his writing (including his celebration
of Christmas) is medieval in spirit (171) and that despite Dickens's suspicion of
Roman Catholicism as superstition, the novels are also Catholic in spirit. Such
assertions confirm Chesterton's attitude to literary criticism: that "it exists to say
the things about [authors] which they did not know themselves" (173). Factual
inaccuracies, brought to Chesterton's attention by Dickens's daughter, Kate Perugini, were acknowledged by Chesterton but never corrected (182–83). Still, Ker
persuasively shows Chesterton's *Charles Dickens* to be a fascinating and influential work of criticism, in spite or because of its quirks: it "is criticism where the
critic becomes as much a creator as the subject of his criticism" (181).

Performance and Adaptation

Influence and intertextuality are, of course, necessary to the process of adaptation, and the critical studies that follow are primarily concerned with theatrical,
literary, and cinematic adaptations of Dickens's fiction, and with Dickens's own
theatrical connections.

Dickens's Performances

Dickens's twelve prefaces to his novels form the subject of Mario Ortiz-Robles's
essay, "Dickens Performs Dickens." Ortiz-Robles here examines the genre of the
preface, which he calls an unstable form, occupying a liminal position between

fiction and non-fiction, depending for its existence on the fictional work to follow, and generally preceding a work with a full knowledge of what is to appear in the subsequent narrative (since nearly all prefaces, and all of Dickens's, are written after the composition of the work they introduce). Dickens uses the odd genre of the preface to present himself as what Ortiz-Robles calls "a thoroughly modern novelist": he is both a professional writer with the ability to act independently on his text and in the world, and he creates art that can also be "put ... to work in the service of political action" (460). In so doing, he constructs the identity of "Dickens" in five forms, enumerated thus in the essay: "the Friend, the Truth-Teller, the Advocate, the Professional Writer, and the Famous Author" (464). Out of these five categories, a surprisingly coherent persona emerges: Dickens's prefaces progress toward a self-construction as "a great Author" (473) and thus make a case for authorial legitimacy. At the same time, Ortiz-Robles claims, the ephemeral nature of a preface, which is always subject to revision and is more contingent than the work which follows it, suggests an "impulse towards self-less-ness and self-effacement" which, in the novels, is linked to ethical behavior (475). Thus Dickens's prefaces, though they do not programmatically nor extensively discuss Dickens's literary philosophy nor methods, together make a case for the agency and power of both author and text.

Authorial power is also the subject of Amanda Adams's "Performing Ownership: Dickens, Twain, and Copyright on the Transatlantic Stage," a transatlantic consideration of the authors' approaches to the absence of international copyright. Adams argues that Dickens and Twain, without legal or economic recourse when their works were pirated by publishers overseas, asserted their authorial rights by directly demonstrating their authorship in the form of public readings in America and England, respectively. Public performances cemented their position that they alone should have the right of ownership over their works in two ways: "on the one hand, they performed an authorial persona that stressed the author-as-source; on the other, they achieved an embodied intimacy with the published work from which the reading came" (224). Dickens, who altered substantially the portions of his novels that he performed in public, claimed the exclusive right to make such alterations, writing that "there was no printed version which would approximate his readings 'save in my copies: and there it is made, in part physically, and in part mentally, and no human being but myself could hope to follow it'" (229). In performance, however, Dickens would often seem to disappear into the roles of the several characters he would portray, illustrating for his audiences how intimately the characters and stories were intertwined with his imagination (230). Mitigating the authorial disappearance, however, was the author's dress: by appearing in evening clothes, rather than the costumes of his characters, Dickens exhibited a constant visual reminder of his status as author, even as his voice and body transformed into the roles he portrayed (233).

Twain used some of the same strategies in performance as did Dickens, whose American public reading of *Martin Chuzzlewit* Twain attended in 1867. Instead of reading from a prepared text, however, Twain used sketched notes, indecipherable to anyone but himself, and told his stories seemingly extemporaneously, sometimes changing their order or content: "All that unifies them and authorizes them is the author" (235). Like Dickens, Twain shifted, in performance, between his own authorial persona and that of his "innocent" character or narrator, each of which he embodied personally. By placing their authorship and intimate, personal connection with their works before their audience's eyes, Adams suggests, both writers "challenged the gap between author and text with which nineteenth-century readers ... at times seemed comfortable" (238).

The purpose of Robert C. Hanna's "Selection Guide to Dickens's Amateur Theatricals—Part 1" is to recommend celebratory performances for the 2012 bicentenary, by branches of the Dickens Fellowship worldwide, of the plays in which Dickens himself participated. Doing so would, he argues, provide "an opportunity for all fellowships to introduce Boz to new audiences in a unique and highly visible manner" (220). To promote this project, Hanna provides in his article a brief overview of Dickens's own enthusiasm for amateur theatricals and a detailed listing and description of each play in which Dickens performed. To make the article less cumbersome, he splits the listing over two issues of *The Dickensian*, only the first of which appeared in 2011. This portion of the listing, which proceeds alphabetically by play title, begins with *Amateurs and Actors* by Richard Brinsley Peak, in which Dickens performed as Mr. Wing on 27 April 1833 at Bentinck St., London (221), and ends with *Fortunato and His Seven Gifted Servants*, by James Robinson Planché, in which Dickens performed several roles on 8 Jan. 1855, at Tavistock House (227). Hanna includes a brief plot summary for each play, as well as highly useful explanatory notes. For instance, he contextualizes the listing for *The Elephant of Siam and the Fire Fiend*, performed in a "toy-theatre version," thus: "Charles Dickens, Jr., wrote how his own toy theatre 'fascinated my father,' who 'set to work to produce the first piece ... the "Elephant of Siam," which included designing and painting landscapes and architecture of Siam. Dickens's documented time, work, and enthusiasm as the play's producer may very well have led to his operating and speaking for some of the numerous minor characters when they appeared on stage" (224). Such detailed notes and information about each of the plays are valuable not only to their potential producers and performers, but also, of course, to scholars who can use the concise information that Hanna provides as a springboard for further research.

Novels into Novels: *Great Expectations*

Surprisingly, few articles in 2011 addressed specifically literary adaptations of Dickens's fictions directly. Chialant's essay, in the "Intertextualities" section, above, is an exception, as are the following two articles, both of which address post-colonial adaptations of *Great Expectations. Mister Pip*, Lloyd Jones's 2006 novel that reimagines *Great Expectations* in the setting of Bougainville's civil war, is the focus of Monica Latham's "Bringing Newness to the World: Lloyd

Jones's 'Pacific Version of *Great Expectations.*'" Latham examines the several ways in which Jones's novel intersects with and revises Dickens's novel, making a hypertext of Dickens's "hypotext." From oral retellings and approximate remembrances to memoirs that are a hybrid of Dickens's story and lived events, *Great Expectations* appears in a variety of formats in Jones's novel, offering its characters, variously, an imaginative escape from their traumatic circumstances; an opportunity to experience Dickens's England, and through it, other parts of the world; a new way to communicate with their families; and a new way of understanding their own identities. Latham calls Mr. Watts, the teacher who initiates his students into the world of Dickens's novel, "a *bricoleur* who makes a new story out of Dickensian materials" and the stories of the Pacific islanders among whom he lives (34–35). Of course, Jones himself is also a *bricoleur*, whose novel "suggests we also have an impact on books, [and] ... the endurance of classics such as Dickens's *Great Expectations* is largely tributary to numerous tellings, retellings, adaptations, and the creation of spin-offs" (39).

Erik Martiny argues, in his brief article "*Jack Maggs* and *Mister Pip*: the Empire Strokes Back: Commonwealth Bibliophilia in Australasian Responses to *Great Expectations*" that these two novels signify a "second phase of postcolonial literature ... in which writers from former imperial colonies view the work of English masters as part of a literary common-wealth, not to be necessarily subverted or struck down but to be celebrated" (2). Both Peter Carey's *Jack Maggs* and Lloyd Jones's *Mister Pip* are, in Martiny's view, more "sentimental than *Great Expectations*," softening the analogues to Dickens's grotesque characters before delivering violent shocks at the end. While Martiny is right that both contemporary novels demonstrate their own and their authors' bibliophilia and attest to the power of Dickens's novel, his argument could benefit from a more extended and complex treatment, which would allow him to elaborate and better support his claims. For example, the assertion that *Jack Maggs*'s Ma Britten, an abortionist and thief who brutally beats and humiliates the central character, then forces his young lover to abort her baby, is a "watered down version of Mrs. Joe" is a clear misreading of Carey's text (3). Likewise, the notion that, in the claustrophobic atmosphere of dread occasioned by the blockade of Bougainville, an island torn apart by civil war, "Joe's saucer of gravy has, at it were, been poured over everyone and everything" (4) offers a misleadingly simplistic reading of *Mister Pip*. Perhaps a more effective strategy would have been to examine the ways in which bibliophilia and "counter-discursive politics" coexist in Carey's and Jones's neo-Victorian novels (5).

Dickens Spoken and Sung: Drama, Musicals, Opera, and Sound Recordings
Stage adaptations of *David Copperfield* since its initial publication have struggled to reconcile the bildungsroman plot of the novel with its fallen woman plot, argues Karen E. Laird in "Adapting the Seduction Plot: *David Copperfield*'s Magdalens on the Victorian Stage." Most such adaptations in the 1850s took David as their

central figure but, to allow Dickens's widely-ranging plot to fit the constraints of the Victorian stage, they all but omitted the details of David's childhood. "It seems," writes Laird, "that adaptors of the bildungsroman form doubted whether the appeal of childhood scenes was worth the logistical headaches of casting child actors or young women in the requisite youthful parts" (196). Thus, adaptations like George Almar's *Born with a Caul*, J. Courtney's *David Copperfield the Younger of Blunderstone Rookery,* and John Brougham's American production of *David Copperfield*, all staged in 1850, limited their treatment of David's early life while expanding their attention to the sensational seduction plot, a staple of Victorian melodrama. Brougham even gives David increased agency in the reclamation of Emily, denying "the sentimental father-figure [Peggotty] any power of action" while allowing David to direct the response to Emily's disappearance and return (200).

In the 1860s, David's plot is further deemphasized in stage adaptations of the novel, which focus entirely on Little Emily's plot. F. C. Burnand's 1863 dramatization, *The Deal Boatman*, which played at Drury Lane to critical success (201), omits David entirely while reinventing the Peggottys. "By keeping the novel's Emily-Ham-Steerforth love triangle perfectly intact—but by reimagining the characters as Mary-Matt-Edward—Burnand asserts his authority as a playwright qualified to rewrite significantly Dickens's celebrated novel" (202). Mary, in Burnand's reimagined version of the tale, turns out (in keeping with the sensational demands of melodrama) to be the daughter of an aristocrat and a Jamaican woman. Perhaps surprisingly, her racial origins do not impede her class ascension in this play, and she assumes her social role as a lady fit to marry Edward, her seducer. Laird explains this change from the novel thus: "this urge to forgive the seducer should be viewed as a group of adapters' rewriting of an element of the source text that they thought would perhaps be not wholly acceptable to an audience" (204). Laird also considers Andrew Halliday's 1869 adaptation, *Little Em'ly*, "the only staged version of *David Copperfield* to enjoy the novelist's official seal of approval" (205). In this version, Mr. Peggotty is reinstated to his sympathetic heroic role, Emily and Martha are both portrayed (according to Dickens's recommendation) as sympathetic figures, and, as in the novel, Rosa Dartle's cruel treatment of Emily encourages the audience to side with the latter.

Finally, Laird addresses Dickens's own stage adaptation of *David Copperfield*: not for a play, but for his public readings. Like other adapters, Dickens struggled with the format, eventually deciding "to structurally juxtapose the 'child wife' Dora ... with Emily, the perpetually-reproduced fallen woman. His completed reading, first performed on October 28, 1861, consists of six chapters that cross-cut between the Emily/Peggotty plot and the Dora/David plot." Significantly, "Emily never once speaks" (209). While Laird leaves her readers to draw their own conclusions from this detail, her argument would give greater insight into the public readings of *David Copperfield* by explicating it more fully. The final adaptations to which she turns her attention, however, are those written and performed after Dickens's death and the publication of John Forster's biography, which revealed the parallels between David's and Dickens's childhood labor. Mr. Peggotty is prominent in these adaptations which, like the 1850s stage versions of the novel, shy away from David's childhood, but for different reasons: "Completing a final cycle of correction via adaptation, the productions of *David Copperfield* staged in the wake of Dickens's death steer clear of any biographical allusions that might humble their fallen hero" (210).

Detailing the American theatrical performances of "John Brougham's *Little Dorrit*" in 1874 and 1875, Allan Sutcliffe explains the process and the product of this stage adaptation of the Dickens novel. Theatrical manager F. B. Dobson took out a copyright on the play on 29 Nov. 1873, which was described as "a Drama ... founded upon Chas. Dickens's story, by John Brougham, Esq." (214). Dobson also hyped the play, before its performances, with extensive publicity, including lithograph posters and a "newspaper-style publication ... entitled *The Wallace Sisters' Pictorial 1874–5*," a title that emphasized the theatrical troupe that would perform the play (214–15). Though the publicity and the copyright gave credit to Dickens as the source of the play's story, they also freely admitted that the adaptation took great liberties with the novel, "'for in the original the dramatic element being almost totally disregarded, [Brougham] was obliged to call on his invention to supply the deficiency, and endeavor to satisfy the popular demand for the sensational by the introduction of new scenes and situations'" (215–16). It is amusing to imagine how these new scenes would play on stage: they include a cross-dressing Flintwitch [*sic*], a ruse in which Amy Dorrit is imprisoned and nearly drugged by Rigaud and Flintwitch after being tricked into thinking "that Arthur Clennam has been run over by an omnibus." After the villains unwittingly reveal their plan to her, the building in which Amy is locked catches fire, and Maggie and Arthur rescue her (216). Certainly, the play aimed to please crowds by adding these melodramatic elements, and it also added additional popular entertainments, including "'Songs and Dances, Clog Dances, Banjo Solos and Hornpipes' of the Wallace Sisters" (217). Most press reports praised the adaptation, which was performed in Pennsylvania, New York, Ohio, Indiana, Michigan, and Rhode Island (217).

Turning to musical theater in "Making Music with the Pickwickians: Form and Function in Musical Adaptations of *The Pickwick Papers*," Marc Napolitano compares two such adaptations across the centuries: W. T. Moncrieff's *Sam Weller, or The Pickwickians* (1837) and Leslie Bricusse and Cyril Ornadel's *Pickwick* (1963). The former, which Dickens despised, draws on the tradition of the English ballad opera, using stage music to divert the audience, but not to advance the plot of the play nor to enhance the audience's understanding of the characters. Napolitano is insistent on the "random" placement and generic meanings of the songs in Moncrieff's play, arguing that "so superfluous are all of these airs to the overall narrative of the play that the scenes would play out in entirely the same way even if the songs were excised from the libretto" (37). While this point may be true, it is interesting that Napolitano is able to cite with precision which specific songs would be sung by which characters, and at set times in the play, circumstances that throw into some question whether the songs can really be said to be "placed indiscriminately throughout the adaptation" and that seem to call for further analysis.

Pickwick, by contrast, an American-style British-penned musical, draws on the twentieth-century theatrical tradition in which songs are fully integrated into the meaning of the musical; were the songs in *Pickwick* to be excised, the play would lose much of its sense. While this form of musical is more satisfying to modern audiences than that of Moncrieff's play, Napolitano suggests that the latter is more authentic to the form of Dickens's episodic novel, in which the Pickwickians' adventures appear to occur by happenstance. Napolitano also calls attention to the national valences of the two musical forms: Moncrieff's play is specifically British in form and content, whereas Bricusse and Ornadel's musical situates a British story in an American genre (42). Napolitano ends his article with an intriguing speculation: he proposes that the most satisfying theatrical adaptation of *The Pickwick Papers* might take the form of a concept-musical like Rupert Holmes's choose-your-own-adventure music-hall-style adaptation of *The Mystery of Edwin Drood* or Stephen Sondheim's non-chronological *Company*, which is structured around a theme (of marriage) rather than a plot (50–51). Such a concept-musical could, Napolitano argues, accommodate the "chaotic yet comical structure of Dickens's original novel" while allowing "the easier reconciliation of the divergent British and American qualities of any musical adaptation of *The Pickwick Papers*" (52). We can hope that a contemporary musical team attuned to *Dickens Studies Annual* will pick up Napolitano's idea.

Sondheim makes an appearance in the 2011 edition of *Dickens Studies Annual*, in Sharon Aronofsky Weltman's "Boz versus Bos in *Sweeney Todd*: Dickens, Sondheim, and Victorianness." Following the strands of influence which link the anonymously published Victorian melodramatic fiction *A String of Pearls* to Stephen Sondheim's musical *Sweeney Todd* on stage and on screen, Weltman finds that the original source has little resemblance to Sondheim's version of the story. Instead, Sondheim reaches back to a major influence on the author of *A String of Pearls*: Charles Dickens. *A String of Pearls* was likely written by Thomas Peckett Prest, a Dickens imitator who sometimes styled himself "Bos," and, in his novel, parallels to *Oliver Twist* appear. Sondheim, Weltman argues, makes these parallels still more explicit, adding a Dickensian class consciousness to the story of the murderous barber (63) and giving Todd a sympathetic backstory in which he revenges himself against abuses of the law which have destroyed his family (64). More specific echoes of Dickens appear in the play: Sondheim provides a stock bumbling beadle, perhaps derived more from the musical *Oliver!* than from Dickens's novel, and his Mrs. Lovett sings about "hard times" (67, 65). Tim Burton's film adaptation of *Sweeney Todd* adds still more elements from Dickens, making an adolescent character into a vulnerable child resembling Oliver Twist

(68). The conclusions that Weltman draws from following Dickens's influence on twentieth- and twenty-first-century Sweeney Todds are fascinating and stretch well beyond the specific material she mentions here. She argues:

> Sondheim and his collaborators intensify the Victorianness of his play derived from a Victorian novel *not* by closely following the source but by inserting details chiefly inherited from Dickens's *Oliver Twist* and, perhaps more surprisingly, from Bart's musical adaptation. Sondheim's reworking of Bos's imitation of Boz yields a powerful locus for representations of Victorianness and the Dickensian, which audiences now read as the same thing. (69)

If Weltman is right that "Dickensian" and "Victorian" are now synonymous adjectives, then this compression of contemporary understandings of the nineteenth century may be tested against present-day costume dramas and literary adaptations. It may, indeed, account for the many neo-Dickensian novels that have arrived on the literary scene in the recent past.

Beginning with *The Village Coquettes* (1836), Dickens's one personal foray into writing for the operatic stage, David Haldane Lawrence's "Charles Dickens and the World of Opera" investigates what he sees as the general lack of success that Dickens's works have met with on the operatic stage. *The Village Coquettes*, subtitled "a Burletta," may have been made possible by Dickens's sister Fanny, who could have introduced Dickens to his collaborator, the composer John Pyke Hullah (6). Lawrence describes the work as "a compromise between spoken drama, ballad opera and comic opera" (7–8); this hybrid genre privileged the words of "Boz" over the songs of Hullah. The opera met with mixed reviews that reflected the priority of the play's writing, some of which criticized its lack of originality while others praised the "'lightly told'" tale (7). In any case, *The Village Coquettes* closed after nineteen performances, with sporadic single revivals (7).

Despite the many well-known, often unauthorized theatrical adaptations of Dickens's novels, Lawrence points out the absence of operatic adaptations, "probably due to the lengthy and complicated plot structures of his novels," and the contemporary local settings, which ran counter to the fashion for exotic locales (9). The late nineteenth and early twentieth century, however, marked a change in taste, and a desire to adapt Dickens for the opera. *A Christmas Carol* is Dickens's most-often adapted work for the operatic stage (10), but operatic adaptations, in Italian, German, and English, have been created from many of the novels and Christmas books. Lawrence points out a number of liabilities that attend operatic adaptations from Dickens: a tendency to over-sentimentalize already sentimental works (Karl Goldmark's *Das Heimchen am Herd* [*The Cricket on the Hearth*], 1896); a lack of cohesion or focus (Albert Coates, *Pickwick*, 1936); excessive length (Arthur Benjamin, *A Tale of Two Cities*, 1951), and an inability to "accommodate [Dickens's] distinctive style or his social commentary" (16). The strongest operatic adaptation discussed in Lawrence's essay is Thea Musgrave's *A*

Christmas Carol, first performed in 1979 (16). This adaptation takes great liberties with Dickens's text, including only one Christmas "spirit," adding two scenes not in Dickens's original, and using "God Rest Ye Merry Gentleman" as a leitmotif (16–17). Still, 1981 marks the most recent revival of this opera.

In closing his article, Lawrence briefly contrasts the many failed examples of Dickensian operas with Lionel Bart's 1960 musical *Oliver!*, which continues to be performed today. Despite the imperfections of Bart's adaptation, it seems to strike a chord that operatic adaptations of Dickens do not; Lawrence's argument would benefit from a more thorough explanation of why this should be so.

Jason Camlot considers a different medium of adaptation in "The Three-Minute Victorian Novel: Remediating Dickens into Sound": the phonographic recording. Using Dickens as his case study, Camlot examines the uses of and theories behind late-nineteenth- and early-twentieth-century sound adaptations of literature. Initially intended as entertainment, recordings that excerpted performances by Dickens impersonators like William Sterling Battis and Bransby Williams promised to provide "corporeal realization of ... 'real living personalities' found in [Dickens's] fiction, with 'all their little idiosyncrasies,' 'sayings and doings,' and 'temperaments.'... They were nothing less than enactments of the reader's experience of immersion in a feeling of intimate encounter with the 'people' of Dickens's brain" (34). In the second and third decades of the twentieth century, however, recordings of Dickens were produced for educational purposes, as producers of phonographs and records came to see schools as markets (29). Harold D. Smith, who produced the education catalogue for Victor Records, argued that listening to records was a social activity which "allows 'the bond of sympathy' to be 'established between [English students] and the character in [a] story'" (35). Nonetheless, the educational effects of the recordings were limited by the medium by which they were transmitted. "So," writes Camlot, "whereas the recordings may have been marketed as providing a more immediate, transparent, and 'real' experience of a fictional character [than reading can],... the fixed action pattern of the Victor record, the fact that it must turn in one direction at the correct speed and that its grooves are uniformly spaced to play only one set of audible vibrations again and again—betrays its inflexible materiality as a medium. The same might be said of the fact that these records based on Dickens novels were short, only about three minutes long" (38). The new medium fundamentally changes the experience of the Dickens character, even as the fact that it is auditory presents that character as if it were just what was initially imagined by Dickens, *un*mediated.

Dickens on Film

U. C. Knoepflmacher undertakes an intertextual study of Dickens and Robert Louis Stevenson in "Boy-Orphans, Mesmeric Villains, and Film Stars: Inscribing *Oliver Twist* into *Treasure Island*." Knoepflmacher does briefly make a case that Stevenson's 1882 novel revises Dickens's text, in that "Stevenson not only extricated Long John Silver from a hostile mob as deadly as that which drives Sikes to his death, but also freed him from the very gallows to which Dickens condemns Fagin" (6): "the closure of Stevenson's pirate narrative all but mocks the final note of respectability that Dickens provided for his Newgate novel" (6). But because no direct evidence to prove such a connection between the two works exists, Knoepflmacher devotes the majority of his article to resonances of the two works in the many film adaptations of each. While David Lean's 1946 *Oliver Twist* preserved Dickens's punitive purging of its villains from the end of the story, Carol Reed's 1968 musical, *Oliver!*, and Roman Polanski's 2005 *Oliver Twist* allow for more sympathy between Oliver and Fagin, and therefore, Knoepflmacher argues, "bring their films closer to *Treasure Island*" (6). Likewise, film adaptations of *Treasure Island* ranging from the 1920s through 2003 have borrowed elements from and made reference to *Oliver Twist*, both by recalling elements from Dickens's text and, perhaps still more often, by referencing earlier film adaptations of the Dickens novel, sometimes by casting the same actors. Knoepflmacher cites examples like the 1920 Paramount *Treasure Island*, which cast a girl in the role of Jim, and which set a precedent for feminized versions of Jim in later film versions that brought the character closer to Oliver's age and level of helplessness (9). After the second World War, however, more masculine versions of *Treasure Island* were dominant, including the 1950 Disney version that cast Robert Newton, David Lean's Bill Sikes, as Long John Silver (12). Jim is able to hold his own against Newton's Silver, in this version, and thus, Knoepflmacher argues, in this film "*Oliver Twist* [serves as] an unacknowledged textual foil" (15). His essay continues to follow the cross-pollination of the two narratives through the 1996 *Muppet Treasure Island*, which Knoepflmacher praises as a mélange of "humans and muppets who mix song with action, earnestness and irreverence, traditional morality with a delight in anarchy, to form a narrative that also recombines Dickens and Stevenson as components of a new hybrid 'family'" (22). The persistence of these two influential narratives, and their association in the minds of filmmakers and audiences, demonstrates a continuing fascination with their shared Victorian themes of orphanhood, family, transgression, and redemption.

Another object of such continuing cinematic fascination, *A Christmas Carol* was adapted by the Victorians as plays and stories long before twentieth-century film and television adaptations exponentially increased the public awareness of Dickens's tale. Natalie Neill's "Adapting Dickens's *A Christmas Carol in Prose*" engages in an analysis of the *Carol* as metafiction, a myth that builds into itself the practices it advocates. Its status as a consumer object, ideal for gift-giving, connects it to Scrooge's conversion to generosity at Christmas (71). Likewise, as a story that lends itself to adaptation and to seasonal retelling each year, *A Christmas Carol* becomes a ritual in itself, one that encourages and permits readers and audiences "'to keep Christmas well'" (81). Neill traces trends in adaptation since the *Carol*'s first publication in 1843, from Victorian spin-offs and pirated versions, including the adapted public readings in which Dickens himself engaged

(73), through essentially faithful film adaptations that "trade on the high cultural cachet of the original text," to barely-recognizable adaptations like Frank Capra's *It's a Wonderful Life* and Dr. Seuss's *How the Grinch Stole Christmas* (75). The accretion of these adaptations, she argues, has made "the original text [recede] in importance for both adapters and audiences. Gradually, it became just one of hundreds of versions" (80). While this assertion may seem heretical to devoted readers of Dickens, it accounts for the cultural prominence and familiarity of Scrooge's conversion story even among those who have never read the *Carol*, and Neill even suggests that in writing a *carol* for Christmas, Dickens builds in the likelihood of repeated and transformed iterations of his story, all of which suggest to readers and audiences alike "the potential of transformation in every person" (82).

Places and Spaces: Geography, Internationalism, and the Urban Imagination

Dickens's significance within and engagement beyond England is the topic of several important studies of 2011. Belonging to this category, and to the previous category of adaptation, Rebecca Soares's "Literary Graftings: Hannah Crafts's *The Bondswoman's Narrative* and the Nineteenth-Century Transatlantic Reader," seeks to move beyond critical speculation about Crafts's authorial identity and to consider her narrative from a different angle: as the product of an astute reader of Dickens's *Bleak House*, possibly as it was serialized in *Frederick Douglass's Paper*. The winner of the 2010 VanArsdel Prize, awarded each year by the Research Society for Victorian Periodicals, Soares's essay acknowledges that it is, necessarily, itself speculative, since so little is known about Crafts, her intentions for her narrative, or her process of writing it. For example, in a somewhat self-contradictory paragraph, Soares suggests both that Crafts seems to have intended *The Bondswoman's Narrative* to be "for private edification solely" and that Crafts wrote in the style of serials, with frequent suspenseful chapter endings, as if the narrative were instead intended for serial publication (11). Both possibilities are open and, it seems, insufficient evidence exists to argue definitively for either. Soares thus examines Crafts's adaptation of *Bleak House* in her narrative from the perspective of nineteenth-century readership and print culture, seeing Crafts's borrowings from Dickens as analogous to scrapbooking, a popular nineteenth-century practice that involves both appropriation from others' sources and the creativity of the scrapbooker (12). If Crafts did indeed encounter *Bleak House* in *Frederick Douglass's Paper* (another speculation), then her "scrapbooking" becomes still more intriguing: *Bleak House* was serialized alongside critical arguments about *Uncle Tom's Cabin*, thus enacting, in the periodical, "an amalgamation of Stowe's tale of slavery and Dickens's depiction of the London poor" (15).

The Bondwoman's Narrative, Soares argues, can be read as a fictional version of this amalgamation; thus "Crafts can be viewed as the 'ideal' reader ... that Douglass envisioned when he decided to reprint the British text" (15). Because so many questions raised in Soares's essay cannot be definitively answered, the argument is not wholly satisfying, but it provokes consideration of the relationship between periodical print culture and fiction, about the relationship between transatlantic texts and authors, and about the relationship between author and reader.

Two articles examine Dickens's relationship with readers of specific nationalities: Norwegian and Japanese, respectively. "Dickens in Norway," Ivar Johannessen and Fred-Ivar Syrstad's brief account of the author's reputation in that country, inquires as to why there have been few translations of Dickens's novels into Norwegian since the 1930s. One reason, they suggest, is that, despite the popularity of British television adaptations of Dickens in Norway, Dickens is considered there to be mainly a children's author. Johannessen and Syrstad go on to offer examples of two Norwegian translations of *The Pickwick Papers*, from 1912 and 1956, respectively. Though they point out several translation errors and oddities, no sustained analysis of the two translations is included in the article, which ends by pointing out the coincidence of the Dickens bicentenary and the centenary of the first Norwegian edition of *The Pickwick Papers*.

Highlighting the joys and headaches of Dickens's international appeal, Toru Sasaki's "Translating *Great Expectations* into Japanese" explains the complexities of his project. Beginning with the obvious challenges, Sasaki illustrates the changes that must be made when transferring Roman letters into the Japanese writing system, which "runs vertically and moves from right to left, mixing Chinese characters with [Japanese] syllabary" (198). Puns and other such figures of speech are often impossible to translate from one language to another, and in the case of *Great Expectations*, even the title proves problematic: "It is not possible in Japanese to express the meanings of 'great hope' and 'expected great fortune' in one phrase" (197). Sasaki solves the problem by following the Japanese tradition of calling the novel *Ooinaru Isan*, or "'great legacy'" (197). Other challenges to the translator involve the many levels of formal address in the Japanese language that have no correspondents in English. This becomes particularly difficult to Sasaki when he must decide how Pip is to address Joe. "I simply cannot imagine what kind of 'you' Pip would use when addressing Joe!", writes Sasaki. "He is Pip's intimate friend, an equal, and also a senior person who ought to be respected. He is a gentle Christian man, I know, but he has given me a hard time" (200). Ultimately, Sasaki explains that he must negotiate the tension between what Julian Barnes calls "'smoothness ... and authenticity'" (200), aiming at all times for both, but sometimes, of necessity, privileging or sacrificing one or the other.

Dickens in the City; Dickens in the World
Dickens's own writing about geographical space is the subject of a number of critical studies this year. Piracy provides a method by which Dickens and Col-

lins displace and complicate their reactions to the "Indian Mutiny" in *The Perils of Certain English Prisoners*, argues Garrett Ziegler in "The Perils of Empire: Dickens, Collins, and the Indian Mutiny." The collaborative narrative, written for the 1857 Christmas number of *Household Words*, encodes Dickens's reaction to the mutiny, to which he responded with outrage and a generalized racist desire to "'raze [the Indians] off the face of the Earth'" (150). Ziegler acknowledges Dickens's assertion, as the "conductor" of *Household Words* and, later, *All the Year Round*, that all of the material therein conformed with his opinion; then, Ziegler complicates this narrative, as well as that of *The Perils of Certain English Prisoners*, by analyzing Collins's contribution to the Christmas number. Embedded as part 2 of the three-part narrative, this contribution moderates Dickens's thinly veiled indictment of the Sepoys, defusing the threat that they present the prisoners in the story by making it comic. In so doing, Collins "actually undermines the imperial ideologies and anxieties present in the Dickens pieces by blunting and obscuring the aims of British imperial power in the months following the Indian uprising" (151).

The central trope that Dickens uses to indicate the urgency of the threat to be faced from the pirates in *The Peril of Certain English Prisoners* is that of rape. Although Dickens never directly names this threat, "the spectre of it drives the action of the noble British soldiers, who are bound by duty to do anything they can to protect the sanctity of their women" (158). Violence is justified, in the narrative, in order to prevent the shattering of the domestic ideal that rape represents, and there is a direct line between this value in Dickens's story and the ideology that emerged from the Indian Mutiny, after which rumors of the rape of English women drove the brutal retribution of the British. Collins, however, defuses this threat in his portions of the narrative. He suggested to Dickens that the Indians be replaced, in the story, with pirates, thereby removing "the nationalist tenor of Dickens's response to the Mutiny" (154)—though not removing, as Ziegler points out, the racial otherness of the villains in Dickens's sections (156). Moreover, Collins's central section of the narrative removes the sexual threat expected from the pirates, especially by "queering [the pirate captain]; any threat to British women is negated by the Pirate Captain's implied homosexuality" (160). The Pirate Captain's flamboyant behavior and dress draw surprise and laughter from the English prisoners, suggesting that they are not indeed as imperiled as they had feared, "and the sexual ambivalence associated with pirates allow[s] Collins to redirect the anxiety of heterosexual rape and thus to dampen the motivation that so ignited Captain Carton in Dickens's initial section. If it is men these pirates are after, instead of women, then Carton's belief that Englishmen are obligated 'to exterminate these people from the face of the earth' is no longer so compelling" (161). Surprisingly, Ziegler does not comment extensively on the new implied threat of homosexual rape—though he does mention a brief moment of homosexual panic on the part of one English character. Still, his argument that Collins was able to undermine the political import of the collaborative narrative in Dickens's own journal is compelling and suggests that Collins was able "to eradicate some of the difference and distance that Dickens had put" (164) between the pirates and the colonists, the Indians and the British.

Turning to the urban experience and juxtaposing the representation of space with that of time in Dickens's novels, Sue Zemka's *Time and the Moment in Victorian Literature and Society* explores the changing representations of time's significance in rapidly industrializing Victorian society. She identifies in her study an increased fascination with the ability of a moment, a unit of time that becomes both more measurable and more instantaneous in this period, to create "sudden, remarkable changes.... The moment is a punctualist form; it is over in a flash, though its effects may linger" (1). Chapter 4 of the book, titled "Dickens's Peripatetic Novels," links Dickens's well-known practice of taking lengthy urban walks with the passing of time. Zemka argues that "the myth of Dickens as a writer with a symbiotic dependency on walking cannot be dismissed as a biographical fallacy because it is consciously built into the overall fictive project at every level" (111). Physical movement through a city often structures the pacing of Dickens's narratives, Zemka explains, and momentary epiphanies, generated by encounters on the street, are but stops along the way. Drawing examples from *Master Humphrey's Clock*, "Night Walks," and *Bleak House*, Zemka suggests that Dickens refrains from placing too much symbolic weight on the experience of a moment; rather, the moments of encounter that she calls "intersubjective moments of humanity" (114) become failed or ambiguous epiphanies. The processes of walking, of literary creation, and of narrative itself supersede the lightning-strikes of the moment in Dickens's writing.

Tanya Agathocleous's *Urban Realism and the Cosmopolitan Imagination in the Nineteenth Century: Visible City, Invisible World* is also concerned with the links between space and time, the national and the international. By focusing on the narrative forms of the sketch and the panorama in nineteenth-century literature, Agathocleous selects two techniques central to Dickens's body of work, and by considering these techniques and the relationship of the urban to the global landscape, she selects two subjects of interest in nearly every Dickens novel. For the purpose of her study, which spans writers from Wordsworth to Woolf, the Dickens novel that Agathocleous examines most closely is *Bleak House*.

"Cosmopolitan realism" is the term which Agathocleous coins to describe the ways in which Victorian writers combined the sketch and panorama, "not merely reflect[ing] a new global consciousness..., but us[ing] the city to shape it—and to relate it to quotidian experience" (xvi). Sketches could be transformed by "three epistemological contexts" into cosmopolitan documents: "one moral-allegorical [demonstrating the universality and interconnection of fragmentary portraits], one transnational-comparative [often providing a kind of 'panoramic breadth' in the aggregate of many sketches (83)], and one artistic-anthropological [both engaging in 'cultural voyeurism' and creating social-scientific taxonomies (87)]" (45). Although the panorama, which seems to provide a 360-degree perspective on the world, seems to be diametrically opposed to the slightness of the individual sketch, Agathocleous argues that sketches, taken together, form a kind of panoramic vision, and that both techniques are "deeply ambivalent formation[s], complex enough to be read as both conservative and progressive; adaptable enough to serve as imperial propaganda-tool[s] or as champion[s] of cosmopolitan democracy" (91).

Bleak House, a novel that privileges national over international concerns, incorporates both the sketch and panorama, casting suspicion on the uses of both forms while, perhaps, suggesting how they might best be put to use. Agathocleous suggests that the sketchy cosmopolitan character of Harold Skimpole, whose many unfinished works of art can be read as sketches, is used to satirize "the artistic-anthropological context of the sketch tradition by highlighting its connection with idle privilege, imperialistic exploitation, and self-indulgent entertainment. In doing so, [Dickens] necessarily calls into question his own use of the genre, particularly in such works as *Sketches by Boz*" (109). Though Agathocleous may overstate her case here, the argument is on firmer ground as it examines Dickens's use of the panorama, the 360-degree vision of which is obscured, in *Bleak House*, by the ever-present urban fog. Dickens suggests that no overarching, dominant vision of the city is possible by offering an alternative form of panorama, knitted together by the slowly-emerging relationships among the novel's characters (111): "The novel also insists that the sympathetic imagination … must extend beyond the details of city life to embrace a universalist conception of humanity" (112). It is in this universalism that *Bleak House*'s cosmopolitanism consists.

The metropolitan experience in *David Copperfield* is the subject of Rosemarie Bodenheimer's "Copperfield's Geographies," which attempts to understand why Dickens's most overtly autobiographical novel, and the one that contains a version of Dickens's childhood experience working at the Warren's Blacking factory, contains what she calls "no urban vision" (177). David travels extensively in the novel and spends significant time in London, yet his urban experience is often hazy, especially compared with the important events that take place in the novel's other settings, including Yarmouth, Canterbury, and Highgate. Yarmouth, described by Dickens as "'the great wide level' proves to be a child's field of dreams, delusions, and portents" where, Bodenheimer argues, David is oblivious to the class distinctions that separate him, and later Steerforth, from the Peggottys (180). Still, David's personal ambition takes him to higher ground than Yarmouth; as his fortunes rise, so does his physical geography: to the cliffs of Dover, a top floor apartment in London, and then Highgate, which overlooks the city (180). Canterbury, the site of David's education and early development, becomes what Bodenheimer calls "a holy site," associated as it is with Agnes Wickfield (181–82), though it is temporarily under threat. Interestingly and rightly, Bodenheimer argues that David's London workplace, the casually corrupt Doctors' Commons, "acts as Canterbury's double, a place to put Dickens's more usual skepticism about aging bureaucracies stuck in some earlier period of time" (183). Though his time at Doctors' Commons focuses the novel on a London institution, it is hardly one that is central to the bustle and modernity of London as Dickens knew it.

Part of David's—and perhaps Dickens's—hesitancy to focus on London as a location is intimately related to memory: both author and character see the respective warehouses in which they have worked as "saturated ... in punishment, humiliation, parental abandonment, isolation, and shame" (184). On David's return to London, he overtly recollects little of his childhood experience there. Yet Bodenheimer finds some intriguing details in the way that David does describe the city. David remarks upon "sites that are autobiographically significant to [Dickens] in ways that his fictional character does not comprehend"; many of these sites are located around Buckingham Street (186). Still more provocatively, David associates London with fallen women—particularly with Martha Endell and with Little Em'ly's seduction, which, of course, happened elsewhere: "Dickens maps a story of sexual seduction, which takes place entirely offstage, onto markedly dreamlike or nightmarish London scenes" (188). In this way, Dickens shows that Little Em'ly's

> story is all about David. It's about his unconfessed guilt at having brought Steerforth into her life, about his need to compensate ..., and about his need to hide behind a door to see her punished for stealing Steerforth away from him. In the end, it's about the shame of unspeakable class and sexual conflict, which gets its dream-expression in figures that emerge like specters of unfinished business from London streetscapes. (188)

This shame encompasses David's experience at Murdstone and Grimby's, as well as Dickens's experience at the Warren's Blacking factory.

While Bodenheimer is primarily concerned with the representation of urban space in *David Copperfield*, Dickens's blending of urban and rural idealities of space is the subject of David Wilkes's "The Mudworm's Bower and Other Metropastoral Spaces: Novelization and Clashing Chronotopes in *Our Mutual Friend*." Beginning with an example from *The Uncommercial Traveller*, Wilkes argues that in "Arcadian London" "Dickens collapses Arcade and Arcadia into one ideographic space that becomes 'entirely new' to the weary traveler" (296). This new hybrid space is what Wilkes calls "metropastoral," and he uses Bakhtin's chronotopes to explain its parameters. Dickens goes on from *The Uncommercial Traveler* to employ the same kind of blended space in *Our Mutual Friend*, wherein "the 'idyllic chronotope' squares off with the 'chronotope of theatrical space' almost immediately" (298). Wilkes argues that in these hybrid spaces, teaching and learning can occur, problems can be solved, and transformations take place.

Wilkes identifies a number of key settings in the novel as metropastoral: these include Gaffer Hexam's windmill, Boffin's Bower / Harmony Jail, the Six Jolly Fellowship Porters, Riah's rooftop garden, and the Wren's Nest. The natural elements of many of these (their situations on the Thames, for example, or their embodiment of the ideal of a garden) suggest the "bucolic-pastoral-idyllic chronotope," while the presence of rogues and tricksters within them signal what Wilkes calls the "theatrical chronotope" (299). Wilkes adds that "each metropastoral space in *Our Mutual Friend* [also] contains ... a pedagogue who seeks to inculcate his or her truth" (304). Truth in this case may be interpreted widely: it applies to Gaffer Hexam's attempt to teach his daughter to embrace the livelihood they get on the Thames, to Silas Wegg's attempt to con Noddy Boffin in Boffin's Bower (306), to Miss Abbey's efforts to make Lizzie Hexam—and indeed all of her customers—respectable (310), and to the various attempts to teach Lizzie and Jenny Wren to read (311). Wilkes includes in this process Mr. Boffin's and John Harmon / Rokesmith's "pious fraud," designed to test and promote Bella Wilfer's values (318). He describes the urban pedagogues as counterparts of the pastoral shepherd, leading their flocks through the complexities of London life. The article also finds precedents for several of Dickens's characters and their behavior in pastoral literature: Wegg is likened to Shakespeare's Autolycus; his trap for Mr. Boffin—and indeed, Mr. Boffin's trap for Bella, resemble Robert Greene's "cony-catching trick" (305, 318).

The metropastoral spaces of the novel, then, become proving grounds for its characters. Some have more potential than others for these positive transformations: Wilkes makes a distinction between the dangerous cellar spaces of Hexam's dwelling and, to some extent, Boffin's Bower, and the more positive attic spaces of Riah's garden and the Wren's Nest. Within these spaces, if the characters learn their lessons and are transformed for the good, then they are rewarded. Thus Wilkes sees in *Our Mutual Friend* "a Bakhtinian twist" on the pastoral tradition: "it is the city-dwellers, and not the simple rustics, that incarnate the virtues of the locus moralis. It is the novelized pastoral, and not the 'pastoral novel' as a mode" (320).

Dickens's fascination with the city has now, of course, provoked our fascination with the Dickensian city, a subject that Alexis Easley treats in detail. In *Literary Celebrity, Gender, and Victorian Authorship*, Easley devotes a chapter to the subject of literary tourism and, specifically, the attempt to recapture or recreate an experience of the London portrayed in Dickens's novels. In an ever-changing, unstable, and often incomprehensible urban environment, Easley argues, literary tourism allowed Dickens's readers to imagine the city as a locus of "coherence and meaning" constructed by the novels' narratives (29). Easley focuses for much of the chapter on late-nineteenth-century literary tourism in an era of rapid urban renewal that threatened to demolish many of the original sites on which Dickens based his London settings. Photography provided a method of preserving some of these locations, and to "make permanent the literary significance of London's urban geography and preserve the cultural markers of the past—the moral vision of Dickens himself" (31). The purchase, in the early twentieth century, of No. 48 Doughty Street by the Dickens Fellowship, and its eventual opening as a museum and site of literary pilgrimage, also promoted "the literary tourism industry, which

relied not only on nostalgic representations of Dickens's London but also on idealized accounts of Dickens's domestic performances" (43). Easley's consideration of Dickens tourism ends with a reading of Dickens World, the Chatham
theme park opened in 2007. As an indoor reconstruction of Dickensian London
located outside of London itself, Dickens World is entirely a fictional representation of sites and scenes from Dickens's fiction, and it points up the fact that
Dickens's "London ... had, after all, always been a kind of fiction.... Dickens
World thus acts as a literalization of a long-standing imaginative practice among
Dickens enthusiasts, which involved superimposing narrative upon narrative as
a way of understanding and interpreting an increasingly fragmented urban landscape" (46–47).

Material Culture and Publication

The link between artistic production and commodity culture was of interest to
numerous Dickens scholars in 2011, who explore in their research Dickens's
participation in and awareness of the tension between aestheticism and commercialism. Juliet John's *Dickens and Mass Culture* examines Dickens's enduring
popularity as a function of a deliberate aesthetic and marketing strategy on the
author's part. Dickens's exploitation of new and wide-ranging forms of media, his
engagement with popular entertainment, his concern with international distribu-
tion of his works, and his attention to the business side of his career demonstrate
his commitment to generating "numbers of readers" (9). Dickens himself, John
argues, created what Laurence Mazzeno has called the "Dickens industry," and
his self-fashioned literary celebrity informs readers' response to his works from
the Victorian period through today. John begins her study with a consideration of
Dickens's class consciousness, claiming that Dickens "destabilized the familiar
idea of a binary opposition between high and low culture, and subverted established cultural hierarchies" (39). Advocating "Amusements of the People," Dickens defined "people" as broadly as he could, championing forms of culture that
could bridge the gap between social classes and build community, in a form that is
comprehensible but not pandering to audiences without the advantages of extensive education (43). Dramatic performance was an avenue that Dickens seemed
to find best suited to such a project; his love of the theater and engagement with
performance as an actor and public reader correspond with this preference. In an
effort to explain the politics of Dickens's cultural popularity, John acknowledges
the difficulty in defining Dickens's political outlook. Dickens himself "often sublimated or translated politics into moral, cultural, or humanist discourse.... The
view of Dickens as radical by temperament rather than by political affiliation was
widespread in his own day and would no doubt have pleased Dickens" (57–58).
Yet the very popularity of Dickens across social classes can be read as radical;

John points out that being what Trollope called "Mr. Popular Sentiment" was radical "in an era when 'popular sentiment' was newly powerful and potentially dangerous" (59). Instead of provoking "class consciousness," though, Dickens's writing builds "a consciousness of other classes," and suggests "a desire for a world where class ceases to matter" (71–72).

An ironic exception to this democratic impulse occurs in Dickens's writings from and about America, including *American Notes for General Circulation.* Disturbed by the fact that, in America, he experienced the downside of his celebrity, feeling that he was "turned into a commodity whose exploitation was outside his control" (87), Dickens took refuge among the intellectual elite of the United States. His intimate circle there comprised Harvard academics, including C. C. Felton, and the lines between high and low culture were, for Dickens, temporarily redrawn in stark terms. Not only was Dickens discomfited by his own transformation into a commodity, but he was also disturbed by American commodity culture writ large. "Not fully conscious of the ways in which he could be seen to be exploiting America [in his writing], Dickens is nonetheless critically observant of the ways in which America exploits its own people and the ways in which 'mass', commercialized culture seems to corrupt relationships between people" (92). This commercialism infects art and intellectual engagement, displacing idealism in an attention to more sordid realities: "In *American Notes*..., the fear haunting the text is that America embodies a kind of post-civilization in which capitalism and materialism provide the new laws of the jungle" (100). Dickens participated in the very system he feared; his works were and are popular commodities as well as works of art, and in America, Dickens was confronted with the potentially negative implications of this dual role.

The next few chapters of *Dickens and Mass Culture* examine the ways in which Dickens sought to engage productively and personally with his reading public. "'Personal' Journalism: Getting Down into the Masses" discusses Dickens's editorial philosophy and its evolution from *The Daily News*, through *Household Words*, to *All the Year Round*. In each case, Dickens sought a mass audience that included the working classes, and in each case he made a distinction between popular appeal and pandering to the lowest common denominator. In Dickens's desire to reach the broadest audience possible while upholding high journalistic standards was a reform agenda: he was motivated "by a sense of the need to elevate and 'purify' the popular press, which Dickens saw as debasing rather than improving readers" (110). Dickens rejected sensational material for his journals while pricing them so as to be affordable to a broad range of readers. He also "conducted" these journals in a personal voice, adopting an intimate persona with whom his readers could form a bond. Dickens required his anonymous writers to conform, more or less, to this generalized personal voice, thereby creating what John calls a "cultured community" of writers and readers. "In a 'wholesale' commercial culture, Dickens wanted to influence the greatest number of readers to remember the importance of the personal and the communal" (112).

"'Coming Face to Face with Multitudes': The Public Readings" explores Dickens's relationship with the public from another angle. Here, too, commodity culture is relevant: Dickens charged money for the readings and turned a comfortable profit from them. He was also concerned to attract the largest crowds possible to the readings. Yet the profit margin was not Dickens's only—nor even primary concern. John argues that Dickens was as concerned with his reputation as he was with his pocketbook on his reading tours, and that to raise ticket prices, especially on his second American tour, would mean "profiteering rather than profiting from the readings" (142). Instead, "Dickens wanted to rise above the moral malaise of the market by making sure that his own behavior was above reproach. Though he no longer seemed to believe in his own ability to control the market, he wanted to limit the extent to which the market controlled him" (143). Though Dickens did want to attract as many audience members to the readings as he could, John points out that, in describing the reading tours, "Dickens writes of his special relationship with 'the public' rather than 'the people'" (147). Marking a difference from his journalism, Dickens's primary object in performing his readings was not to achieve reform nor to equate the social classes (149). Rather, Dickens's attempts to "humanize the market" by creating a sense of personal relationship and community between himself and his (paying) audience remained in the realm of the personal and the emotional.

The final chapter in Part 1 of John's book, "Culture, Machines, and Cultural Industry," takes issue with the common criticism of Dickens's writing as being mechanistic, "formulaic and repetitive" (157). Instead, John argues, "Dickens occupies a threshold position in cultural history, his works and philosophies formed by both a mechanical *and* an organicist conception of art" (158). Using examples from *Hard Times*, *Bleak House*, and *Little Dorrit*, John disrupts an easy dichotomy between the industrial and the natural, claiming that even in *Hard Times*, the most mechanistic of Dickens's novels and that which is most directly concerned with the machine age, machines themselves are not the problem. Characters like Stephen Blackpool and Rachael, who work long days with machinery, retain their humanity, while the masters at a remove from the machines are deprived—or deprive themselves—of theirs: "The problem is not so much machines, then, but the idea that mechanical or 'wholesale' relations between people should replace personal or emotional relations instead of complementing them. For Dickens, machines ... can function productively in industrial society if used to further community and intimacy between people" (169). Machinery, "as opposed to the 'Mechanical Philosophy,'" (183) is also linked to others among Dickens's values: the work ethic, social progress, and invention.

Part 2 of *Dickens and Mass Culture* shifts the book's focus from Dickens's own cultural practices to his cultural "afterlives." The first two chapters here analyze Dickens's influence on the cinema and, conversely, the cinema's impact on how we now understand Dickens. Using Sergei Eisenstein's seminal essay, "Dickens, Griffith, and Ourselves," John examines "the ideological importance of the relationship between aesthetics, the mass market, and the 'dull people' said to comprise it" (189). Dickens's fictional juxtapositions of the stylistics of melodrama and the conventions of realist narrative predict the cinema's use of montage, John argues, "a form of parallelism, scenic alteration, or, at its most accomplished, dialectical juxtaposition, which Griffith consciously borrowed from Dickens" (192). Dickens himself not only practiced this technique but was aware of it; the "streaky bacon" passage from *Oliver Twist* describes and defends the use of such "dialectical juxtapositions."

John attributes the number of Dickens adaptations in popular cinema to the way that "Dickens's texts straddle the realist and the anti-realist," (206) allowing filmmakers to emphasize one aspect or the other of his writing. She illustrates this by charting the history of *Oliver Twist* adaptations, from the silent cinema through the highly influential (and sometimes controversial) adaptations by David Lean and Carol Reed, through to recent cinema and television adaptations from Roman Polanski and the BBC. *Oliver Twist* is Dickens's novel most often translated to the cinema (210), and it has become so pervasive that it is now what John calls a "cultural myth" (211). This makes the job of tracing Dickens's impact on the cinema more complicated: "a process of intertextuality operating between screen adaptations, as well as between screen and novel, has created shared yet shifting constructs of the 'original' story, whilst undermining the notion of originality" (227). Moreover, historical context changes audience responses to narrative, as John explains when discussing the violent post–World War II reactions against the perceived anti-Semitism in David Lean's *Oliver Twist*. The fact that many audiences first (or *only*) encounter Dickens on screen also gives the cinema power to shape what is a "Dickens" narrative: mainstream adaptations of Dickens novels tend to keep to Victorian settings, only rarely updating and revising their stories. Cinema has reified Dickens's "association with Englishness and his Victorianness," (239) mining Dickens for his position as a classic novelist while ensuring that this is the primary image of him in the present culture.

John's final chapter, "Heritage Dickens; or, Culture and the Commodity," enquires into this phenomenon. From the Dickens ten-pound note to knickknacks and other versions of Dickensiana, to Dickens-inspired tourism, John considers the ways in which Dickens's image or memory is used or associated, in the present day, with the mass-market. "The Dickens ten-pound note captures much about the way in which his image has been used posthumously: it works to promote an association between Dickens and an idea of Englishness which combines cosy communality with reminders of England's cultural, political, and historical 'greatness'" (240). The nostalgia that this and other examples generate ignores the harsher realities of this historical greatness, including the imperial violence that made England what it was. John locates the origins of our nostalgia for Dickens in Dickens's own deliberate shaping of his image and legacy (246), a legacy celebrated in the tourist industry and in the association of Dickens with home and Christmas. "The ability of *A Christmas Carol* to appear to elevate morality over money whilst simultaneously generating wealth, to rise above a historical moment whilst remaining steeped in it, captures in miniature the story of heritage Dickens," John argues (272). Yet the final example she offers of Dickens in the heritage industry, the Dickens World theme park, complicates this point. By "Disneyfying" Dickens, the attraction removes the author from the ether of the highbrow, repopularizing Dickens for the contemporary moment. As John rightly points out, "the idea that the business of popular culture could benefit the community as well as taking the individual on an imaginative journey is true to Dickens's cultural and social vision" (274). Though critics object to the commercialism of Dickens World and its commodification of Dickens's legacy, John shows in *Dickens and Mass Culture* that Dickens and his works have always partaken of the tension between art and commerce, and that Dickens World, by continuing this tradition, is authentic in its own way.

While John's consideration of Dickens World focuses on both British and American popular responses to Dickens and his works, the extent of and reasons for Dickens's impact on the American common reader is the subject of Robert McParland's "Material Production and Circulation of Charles Dickens, 1837–1870." McParland actually extends the time period of his study beyond what his title indicates, into the 1890s, to explore how "the wide consumption and reproduction of Dickens's work by American audiences contributed to shaping the development of American literature and culture by launching imitations, circulating socially shared themes and caricatures, promoting business, and fostering shared sentiment" (90). The essay examines discussions of Dickens in readers' letters and autobiographies; the use of Dickens in American "reading circles," early book clubs that focused on reading aloud and discussing common texts; the circulation of Dickens's books from American lending libraries, including one 1857 Mormon library in Utah, indicating the western trajectory and wide appeal of the novels (93); and competition among American publishers for the rights to print and distribute Dickens's works (though McParland makes little mention of the absence of international copyright). Amid these material concerns, McParland also offers examples and interpretations of *how* Dickens's books were read in America: Mr. Micawber's refrain "something may turn up" became a cliché; McParland explains, "for America, Dickens's phrase echoed a kind of cultural expectancy, a sense of the promise of the vast continent" (94). The essay also cites repeated examples of negative American reactions to Oliver Twist as a greedy or grasping character. McParland rightly suggests that such a use of Oliver in the popular parlance may suggest that many Americans had a general cultural familiarity with the character's asking for "more" without having read the novel itself (95). Perhaps Dickens's greatest achievement in America was creating a "field of discourse" which united a people divided by physical distance, the urban experience, and even a civil war.

Dickens's creative productions, as we have seen, stretch far beyond his original texts, to theatrical and cinematic adaptations, and even to theme parks. They also inspire and create markets for physical, saleable objects. Brian Maidment's "*Pickwick* on Pots—Transfer Printed Ceramics and Dickens's Early Illustrated Fiction" turns to Dickens's place in material culture, examining the reasons why images from Dickens's works seldom appear on ceramic wares produced between 1830 and 1850. Using archaeologist Gavin Lucas's work on the subject as a starting point, Maidment introduces legal reasons for the absence to supplement and, in some cases, refute the cultural reasons that Lucas offered. The 1839 Copyright of Designs Act and Design Patents Act and the 1842 Ornamental Designs Act created regulations for intellectual property that may have inhibited the use of *The Pickwick Papers*'s illustrations on consumer goods; Maidment points out that these acts created a registry for copyrighted designs, acknowledged the original qualities of these designs, and created separate categories for industrial invention and ornamental designs. "After 1842," he writes, "the use of images derived without permission from other sources became technically illegal, and ... in the previous decade, there had been clear attempts to discourage unacknowledged or informal borrowing" (117). There are, however, some exceptions to the otherwise surprising absence of Dickens illustrations from ceramicware: Maidment cites the example of J. & R. Godwin's "Pickwick" mugs, some of which portray convivial scenes from Phiz's illustrations on two-handled "loving-cups." These items suggest a marriage of form and function: mugs made for social celebration eschew images from more "genteel" subjects and literature for lively Dickensian caricatures that share the same convivial spirit.

Not only did Dickens characters and scenes appear on nineteenth-century ceramicware, but Dickens himself wrote about material objects in interesting and significant ways. The multiple meanings of headgear form the subject of Mark M. Hennelly, Jr.'s exhaustive article "Dickens's Immaterial Culture of Hats and *The Pickwick Papers*." The first half of the article considers the symbolic, synecdochic, and metonymic value of hats across Dickens's oeuvre, drawing on Peter Brooks's theories of melodrama and Mikhail Bakhtin's *carnivalesque*. Hats in Dickens, argues Hennelly, are more than material; they are (melo)dramatic; "their real relevance actually transcends their materiality and becomes 'immaterial'" (85). That is to say, hats act in Dickens's fiction to provide a proverbial shorthand (86); to signify "Victorian class, gender, and social (if not moral) standards" (89); to emphasize or demonstrate astonishment, especially when thrown peremptorily to the ground (95); and to "reflect but also fashion selfhood in Dickens's fiction" (96). This selfhood is not necessarily merely personal; Hennelly argues that it can apply to national identity as well: "In *Martin Chuzzlewit*'s satire of America, headgear signifies the cruelly pretentious and clownishly hypocritical psychology of an entire culture" (99).

After providing a taxonomy of hats and bonnets, and their fictional uses to Dickens, Hennelly turns his attention to *The Pickwick Papers*. The first of three scenes that he examines is Sam Weller's use of his "lost" hat in a stratagem to woo Mary the housemaid:

On the one hand, the understated narrative plays out like a sublimated and egalitarian, courtly-love match-making, in which a 'below stairs' servant-class couple genuflects to each other and so previews higher class couples ... in finding pretexts for ingenious but innocent foreplay under the nose of the panoptic father.... On the other hand, the overstated narration seems to recount a bawdy, carnivalesque tryst featuring lower-body functions.... In the first scenario Sam's hat serves as a prophylactic prop, both directing and deflecting desire; in the second, it serves as a Rabelaisian codpiece, a metonym for the phallus. (102)

The hat is here made to bear a great deal of symbolic weight; perhaps more than it can support effectively in Hennelly's reading.

More convincing is the next Pickwickian hat considered in the article: the nightcap which Mr. Pickwick fears exposing to Miss Witherfield after preparing for bed in the wrong room. Hennelly finds the source for this farcical scene in Henry Fielding's *Joseph Andrews*, arguing that Dickens's chapter "looks before and after—back to Parson Adams and Slipslop's madcap comedy of terrors, and forward, as a dress rehearsal, to Pickwick's tragicomic nightcap encounter with Smangle and the Zephyr," in which his nightcap will be subjected to further indignities (104). The nightcap here becomes a fool's cap, reflecting the innocence and lack of judgment that Mr. Pickwick should have shed in his youth (as Sam Weller reminds him).

The first major hat scene in *The Pickwick Papers* forms the subject of Hennelly's final example, the chase scene in which Mr. Pickwick pursues his hat: "Pickwick's 'ludicrous distress' pursuing 'his own hat' prefigures his episodic, romance pursuits, particularly his unself-conscious quest for 'his own' selfhood, throughout the text" (108). Hennelly reads this passage closely, emphasizing Mr. Pickwick's relentless pursuit of his goal and invoking D. W. Winnicott's *Playing and Reality* to conclude that the hat chase can teach Pickwick this lesson: "he can't change a changing world; he can only change himself in trying to keep up with it, and so Pickwick 'puffed' with the puffing wind, inhaling its carnivalesque jeu d'esprit. Such successful adaptation to his changing environment allows Pickwick to crown himself as Alice ultimately is crowned in *Through the Looking Glass*" (109). In this, Hennelly concludes, Pickwick comes into a new self-awareness, a process that will need to be repeated throughout the novel. Though Hennelly makes a number of compelling points in this essay, it may ultimately overread Dickens's comic hats by taking them so seriously.

Handmade craft objects in *Our Mutual Friend* are the subject of Talia Schaffer's fourth chapter, "Salvage: Betty as the Mutual Friend," in *Novel Craft: Victorian Domestic Handicraft and Nineteenth-Century Fiction*. In a novel dominated by the trope of dust and refuse, Schaffer argues, Dickens endorses today's ethic of "reduce, reuse, recycle": as Schaffer puts it, "the type of work Betty [Higden] does—restoring, recycling, purifying, transforming—is fundamental to Dickens's vision of a viable England and, more specifically, a humane economy" (119). Betty Higden knits in order to make a living, and she is not alone in attempting to survive on the fruits of her own personal labor; Jenny Wren uses scraps of material to fabricate elaborate dresses for dolls, and Mr. Venus uses scraps of former humans to articulate the skeletons for sale in his own and in West End shops. These characters stand for values that seem to be slipping away in *Our Mutual Friend*, a phenomenon that Schaffer explains thus: "Dickens felt that the qualities for which domestic handicraft stood—imagination, affection, decorative pleasure—were under attack in a modern world that had quite different values" (123). That none of the three characters above thrives by the production of his or her wares suggests how far the values of the modern world supersede those of handicraft.

Schaffer points out that, with the exception of Betty Higden, the working-class characters who try and fail to make a living by their crafts are actually engaged in tasks more common to middle-class women, who were encouraged to engage in embroidery, other decorative arts, and even taxidermy within the home (124). These tasks were seen by Victorians as fitting for the amateur but not viable as remunerative work, which, no doubt, explains Jenny Wren's and Mr. Venus's lack of financial success. Betty Higden's knitting is a task appropriate to a working-class character (125), yet the manner by which she attempts to sell her wares is outdated. By seeking sales in open markets and private homes, Betty operates outside the economic trends of her time, which saw most sales occurring in shops (129). It is telling that Betty dies in the attempt to market her work, collapsing behind a paper mill: "Thus Betty's lifetime of textile labor, mangling and laundering and knitting, painstakingly managing rags and cloth, ends at the factory" (129). Yet Dickens's plan here is not so pat as it might seem. Schaffer points out the fact that the paper factory is not the destructive, machine-driven factory of *Hard Times*; instead, it provides Betty with a fitting place to die, in the community of factory workers, and allows for Betty to meet and connect with Lizzie Hexam, who, through Betty, in turn meets the Boffins, Bella Wilfer, and John Rokesmith. In this sense, Betty Higden becomes the true "mutual friend" of the novel's title, suggesting that emotional ties supersede economic ones in the world of the novel (131).

Schaffer goes on to consider the relationship in the novel between craft and capitalism, arguing that Dickens opposes material craft to the characters in the novel—Fledgeby, Veneering, Lammle, and Podsnap—who make their living strictly on the exchange of capital and shares. Such an economy signifies "a new financial world in which the previous rules are upside down: a debt is worth money, a friend can sell your interests, and nothing is what it seems to be. What makes Dickens uneasy ... is the way value fluctuates, unfixed, depending on the circulation of scraps of paper that represent other transactions in process" (135). Certainly this is true of Pubsey and Co., the front for Fledgeby's money-lending business, in which the Jewish character, Mr. Riah, works. Riah, Schaffer argues, is an attempt to bridge the gap between the new, disorienting capitalist economy and the craft-based world for which Dickens is nostalgic: "by day, Riah manages debts; by night, Riah provides beads" and other salvage for Jenny Wren's dolls' dressmaking (139). The Jewish community in this novel is a hybrid of industrial and craft values (the paper factory, too, is run by Jews), and Schaffer suggests that the ambiguities of Jewishness, for the Victorians, make this choice appropriate, if ultimately unsatisfactory. For Dickens, as many critics have argued, does not fully realize the character of Riah: "the 'Jew' has no content: no community, no doctrine, no moral code" (140). Riah fades from the novel in its final chapters; he is inessential to its resolution, and, ultimately, the ethic of craft that he and several of *Our Mutual Friend*'s other characters try to embrace is superseded by the ethic of money.

Taking a unique approach to refuse in Dickens's novels, Leslie Simon's "*Bleak House, Our Mutual Friend*, and the Aesthetics of Dust" uses postcolonial and postmodern theory and literature to understand the complexities of meaning in Dickens's recurring trope of dust. Noting that postcolonial literature tends to use "dust as a metaphor for historical displacement and the fragmentation of cultural identity" (218), Simon reads this usage back to Dickens, suggesting that "rather than simply conveying notions of waste, expenditure, or disuse, dust in Dickens suggests that modern life might be reinterpreted through structures of fragmentation, miscellany, and dynamic interrelation" (219). To understand dust in this way, Simon acknowledges the need to discern the negative from potentially positive connotations of dust. The deck, in Dickens, seems to be stacked on the negative side: in response to her rhetorical question "does [Dickens], in a sense, endorse disorder?", Simon reacts with an initial, seemingly definitive "no" (220). *Bleak House,* for instance, presents Esther's character and narrative as a potential corrective to the chaotic disorder of the third-person narrator's portion of the story; *Our Mutual Friend*, too, dwells on the disorienting and dangerous side to the disintegration of material objects, human bodies, and human personalities. However, Simon also offers examples of the potential for positivity in dust's entropic disorder. Looking to *Hard Times*, she recalls that this novel shows it to be "better to engage in moderated forms of spiritual anarchy than fall like mute objects into the machinery of industrial culture" (223); in *Bleak House* and *Our Mutual Friend*, the dust heap "works structurally to articulate modern selfhood according to the principles of difference and divergence that characterize the modernizing world" (224). Simon links this function of the dust heap to the genre of the realist novel, arguing that this form, as heterogeneous as the dust heaps themselves, seeks to reproduce the complexity and mutability of lived experience while ordering and making sense of that experience: "Dickens, that master-writer of the home-myth, reflects in his novels the unsettled nature of the nineteenth century[,] and ... he registers this unsettledness as the real stuff of life, finding in the patterns of the dust-pile a way to express the heterogeneity, bagginess, liminality, and chaos of the world around him" (229).

Architecture and the arts are themselves part of the Victorian marketplace and, in this capacity, influence both Dickens's imagination and his critical reception.

Michael Hollington, in "Dickens, Sala and the London Arcades," takes up the recently popular subject of Dickens and *flânerie*, opposing the arcades or, as Hollington points out, more accurately *passages* of Paris with the arcades of London. Architectural history forms the first part of the article; Hollington explains the genesis of the first Paris arcades just before the French Revolution as spaces that combined the public with the private, creating a "new safe space for pedestrians and shoppers and diners and idlers" (274). Though construction of new *passages* halted in Paris by mid-century, the spirit of competition caused arcades to be built in London following the Napoleonic wars. The neoclassical Royal Opera Arcade was the first constructed; the Burlington Arcade was the best known. Following this explanation of the arcade and how it came to be, Hollington turns to literary reactions to the architectural innovation. Looking at the writings of Albert Smith (the British *flâneur* who first punned on arcade/Arcadia), George Augustas Sala, and Dickens, Hollington demonstrates "the pretty caustic ironic tone adopted in all three" (279). Sala's "Arcadia," published in *Household Words* in 1853, demonstrates a suspicion of the arcade's classism, critiquing its trade in aristocratic wares. Dickens's 1860 *All the Year Round* essay "Arcadian London" also treats the arcades with suspicion, contrasting their innocence in summer, when their usual patrons are away, with the corruption of what Hollington calls "ultra civilisation" (282). Hollington also suggests a visual correspondence between Burlington Arcade and Pentonville Prison, a similarity first noted by Henry Mayhew, as a potential reason for Dickens's dislike of the arcade. Dickens's sensitivity to prisons may have made this "'dream palace' of modernity" (283) into a nightmare.

Dehn Gilmore's "Terms of Art: Reading the Dickensian Gallery" points out the converging worlds of Victorian art and literary criticism, noting the widespread practice of using terminology from the visual arts to analyze and interpret literature of the period. While contemporary critics have been attentive to such juxtapositions with regard to other Victorian writers, they have largely overlooked them when it comes to Dickens, probably because of Dickens's own lack of expertise in or theory of the visual arts. This leaves, however, a gap in our criticism, and in our understanding of Dickens's reception in his own time, by neglecting the prominence in which "terms of art" are placed in Victorian reviews of Dickens, and particularly in their discussions of the *reader's* experience of the novels. Gilmore makes a strong case for understanding the Dickensian space of the novels as akin to "the space of a commercial gallery of art" (6).

Gilmore attributes the increasing critical attention to the visual arts to the expansion of the market for paintings and reproductions to the commercial classes, and to the corresponding boom in artistic production and exhibition, in which "modern works and Old Masters squared off" for public attention (11). Galleries were literally crowded with pictures and patrons alike, stimulating—and overstimulating—the Victorian aesthetic imagination with chance juxtapositions of works from different periods and genres, and requiring "a new eye, or a new focus" (14). Dickens both commented on this atmosphere in his writing and was commented on; throughout his career, Dickens's critics linked him with Hogarth (17). Comparisons of Dickens with visual artists went much further, however, and were often negative: though some critics positively linked his penchant for detail to "Dutch painting" (18), others disparaged his "Pre-Raphaelite" tendencies (surely an insult to Dickens) and compared his "sketches" with the paintings of "the great masters" (19), and most sought to categorize Dickens with one aesthetic taste or another. The main interest of Gilmore's argument, however, comes from its attention to reviews that situated Dickens as a kind of curator, using the language of the gallery to refer both to individual novels and to Dickens's oeuvre more broadly (22). The variety of and within Dickens's works lent itself to such analogies, suggesting a museum space with many rooms (24). This heterogeneity was often frustrating to critics (though not, perhaps to the wide variety of Dickens's readers): "what seemed often most irksome about Dickens was how bad 'draw[ings]' and good ones hung side by side ... and somehow you had to find a way to evaluate it all together" (25). Like the crowded wall of a Victorian gallery, Dickens's novels confront their critics with abundance and require a new focus.

Reading, Writing, Textuality

This section of the survey concerns practices of reading Dickens, and the narrative techniques and strategies that shape our reading experiences. Dawn Potter's "Dickens the Novelist: A Love Letter" dares to ask the question that perhaps every literary critic should ask himself or herself: "why should we bother to read or write about *David Copperfield* when we could just reread *David Copperfield*?" (423). Far from an anti-intellectual retreat from meaningful engagement with literature, Potter's essay, which she calls a "love letter," considers closely Dickens's rhetorical style, explaining how "what Dickens does so blithely ... to ignite a distinct physical reality by means of an outlandish, even silly, comparison becomes, in his major novels, a sleight-of-hand so deft and miraculous and sensitive that words fail me" (421). But Potter also unabashedly argues for the value of Dickens's novels, and particularly, for her, *David Copperfield*, as literary comfort food, worth returning to not for further critical dissection of the novel, but because "word by word, sentence after sentence, reading upon reading upon reading—you, *David Copperfield*, have invented my vision of the world" (424). This assertion makes a grand claim for the value of Dickens's literature and reopens a largely forgotten space in literary criticism itself for enjoyment and appreciation.

Grahame Smith joins with Potter in calling for further appreciation of Dickens, this time for his artistic achievements. *Contra* the received wisdom that Dickens was and is, primarily, a popular writer rather than a high artist, "Earth, Air, Fire, and Water: The Struggle for Pip's Soul in *Great Expectations*" makes the case that Dickens's novels deserve a critical reconsideration of their artistry: "It is no part of my purpose here to sweep away entirely the gains in understanding that have flowed from the historicist and materialist readings of Dickens," Smith explains. "But there is another Dickens to be placed beside these, the *artist* passionately addicted to his art" (148). For Smith, an example of this artistry is Dickens's deployment of the elements in his narrative of Pip's transformations in *Great Expectations*. While essentially glossing over air and earth, Smith dwells on Pip's formative experiences with water on the marshes, at the beginning and end of the novel, and with the Thames, in his attempt to save Magwitch at the novel's end. He also examines Pip's "ordeal[s] by fire" in his encounters with Orlick at the forge and with Miss Havisham at Satis House" (151). By structuring Pip's struggle toward maturity and goodness as "elemental," Dickens signals its depth and high seriousness.

Two articles consider Dickens's representations of the act of reading. Focusing on the character of Tom Pinch and his relationship to reading, Yael Maurer's "Rubbing 'that wonderful lamp within': Reading *Martin Chuzzlewit*" considers fiction as a force for good and ill in the novel. Although Tom is a book-lover, he is also "the most gullible and deluded character of the novel" (120), leading Maurer to inquire into the relationship between reading and dangerous naivety. Because Tom is unable to read accurately the characters of those around him, he is unwittingly complicit with Pecksniff's hypocrisy, allowing his own good name to be used to support his employer's frauds. Once enlightened as to Pecksniff's true character, Maurer argues, Tom still does not change; his innocence and inability to read people seem to be intertwined (125). This may be unsatisfying to the reader, who could wish, as Ruth Pinch does, for Tom's virtue to be rewarded, and for him to become the hero of his own life. But, Maurer points out, Tom understands his secondary role in textual terms, realizing that poetic justice is not for him, and adjusting his expectations and pleasures accordingly. While Maurer identifies an important thread in *Martin Chuzzlewit* by examining Tom's relationship to textuality, her argument could elaborate on the differences between the types of reading Tom engages in: that of literal books, of other characters, and of his own life. Doing so would allow Maurer to explain more clearly the interrelationships among the novel's various acts of reading, and would allow her own readers to understand her argument more fully.

Little Dorrit is a novel that goes beyond telling a remarkably complex and intricate story, argues Robert Tracy in "*Little Dorrit*: The Readers Within the Text." Indeed, story itself is central to the plot and themes of this novel. Arthur Clennam, seemingly the protagonist of *Little Dorrit*, is a character without a story, who compensates for his own lack of agency and imagination by eagerly consuming the stories of others, hoping to have an opportunity to intervene in them. Other characters, like Mrs. Clennam, Flintwinch, Rigaud, and Miss Wade, wield power through telling and withholding stories and the information within them. This power, Tracy suggests, is analogous to that of the novelist, and it sometimes seems to rebel against the novelist's craft (139). Tracy offers the example of Miss Wade's narrative, "The

History of a Self-Tormentor," a kind of autobiographical fragment that disrupts the central stories of *Little Dorrit*. It is "Dickens's effort to supplement the main narrative of *Little Dorrit* by presenting the novel's 'idea' in a different but auxiliary narrative—as a more diseased part, perhaps, of contemporary society" (140). In her story, Miss Wade reveals her jealousies and desire for control and power to Arthur Clennam, and to Dickens's reader, temporarily seizing control over the novel with her interpolated tale: "She interrupts Dickens' novel, to become the hero, or at least the protagonist of her own life" (143). In so doing, Miss Wade achieves a narrative control that many others in the novel attempt to assert.

Dickens's historical novel becomes a postmodern text in Jim Barloon's essay, "Cryptic Texts: Coded Signs and Signals in *A Tale of Two Cities*." Arguing that the novel "interrogate[s] the very bases—language and identity—upon which we build our representations of our world and ourselves" (262), Barloon offers many examples of the ways in which communication in the novel is indirect, mediated, encoded, or goes astray. Indeed even the individuals communicating in these cryptic ways are indeterminate: they change names, identities, and countries, adopting aliases and disguises as they go. Among Barloon's examples of the slipperiness of language in the novel are Jarvis Lorry's use of code in the novel's second chapter to refer to the rescue of Doctor Manette, and the encoded knitting of names and crimes into Madame Defarge's shrouds (262, 264). Both examples of code are used for a "two-fold purpose: [to] illuminate ... meaning ... while keeping those outside its ambit in the dark" (262), but Madame Defarge's knitting goes deeper. Barloon calls Madame Defarge "an underground 'historian' [who] spins a text that is revolutionary on many fronts.... In its deeply, deliberately problematic symbology, Madame Defarge's register inscribes the leveling, chthonic program—one that wants to conserve nothing—that she and her fellow conspirators are plotting" (264).

The encodedness of language and meaning are both a means for the revolutionaries to gain power and an indication of how little power they have, at least at the beginning of the novel and the revolution. Without the safety to speak freely, they must resort to "their own language—gestural, devious, and coded—which both speaks and elides" (265). The same is true of their adoption of a communal name, "Jacques," in which there is both community and anonymity, and in which any personal identity is replaced with a number. "Numbers in this novel," writes Barloon, "have the kind of stability, of accountability, normally ascribed to names" (267), and this becomes true at the end of the novel, when Sidney Carton replaces Charles Darnay in the execution rolls, which must always add up to "Fifty-Two." Names become interchangeable and essentially meaningless in the whirlwind of the revolution, though not in the individual characters' minds: Barloon dwells on Carton's final vision of Lucie's future, in which he sees "'that child who lay upon her bosom and who bore my name, a man, winning his way up that path of life which once was mine.... I see him ... bringing a boy of my name, with a forehead that I know and golden hair, to this place.'" As Barloon rightly points out, the symbolic conflation of Darnay and Carton that began with their shared appearance will end with their shared name: "The son of Lucie and Charles might be named Sydney, perhaps even Sydney Carton, but his official surname would be 'Darnay': Sydney Carton Darnay" (269). In this sense, words, or names, will speak to a deeper truth about identity by clearly demonstrating the lines of connection between the characters. Yet this can only be true if Carton's vision is accurate, a point which the novel allows to remain ambiguous: "Carton's words, like the bright future he foresees, are forever prospective, forever inconclusive" (270). Ultimately, Barloon claims, "communication [in *A Tale of Two Cities*] functions like a one-way mirror, a means of exchange that disguises or obscures what is passed from one to another" (271).

Jerome Meckier and David Paroissien both consider Dickens's narrative practices in *Great Expectations*, examining specific textual details to emphasize the precision in Dickens's technique. In "Installment 33 of *Great Expectations*: the 'Masterpiece' Chapter," Meckier offers a close reading of the chapter in which Pip and his accomplices attempt to help Magwitch escape England and are thwarted. Dickens's friend and biographer, John Forster, called this single-chapter installment of the novel "a masterpiece," praising its suspense, its parallelism with Magwitch's capture in chapter 5, and its setting's correspondence with reality (196). Meckier first focuses on this verisimilitude, showing through such details as the descriptions of the tides in installment 33 that "there probably exists no comparable stretch of a Dickens novel that conforms more precisely to an actual locale than chapter 54 of *Great Expectations*" (197). The realism of the setting, however, contrasts with the stretches of credibility in Pip's escape plan (no foreign-bound vessel would stop if hailed to pick up unknown and suspicious passengers) (201); Meckier posits the possibility that Dickens was punctilious in his descriptions of the Thames journey in order to cover over the breaches of plausibility in the plot. Still, such hair-splitting seems to be beside the point; in the broader scheme of things, chapter 54 serves to "complete" the father-son relationship between Pip and his benefactor and puts an end to Pip's expectations once and for all, while signaling Pip's deeper transformation. These factors combined make it, in Forster's and in Meckier's estimations, "the finest one-chapter installment that Dickens ... ever wrote" (204).

Paroissien's "Clarriker, Pocket, and Pirrip: The Original Tale of Dickens's Clerk," reconsiders the two endings of the novel, arguing that the first, discarded ending is, based on evidence from the text, the only one that is consistent with and appropriate to the time frame and narrative voice of the novel as a whole. Critics have not sufficiently considered these issues when discussing the value of each ending, Paroissien argues, and if they had, they would see "that the revised ending breaks the integrity of a narrative Dickens planned, stuck to, and executed flawlessly" (277). Dickens wrote *Great Expectations* quickly and with a sense of the coherence of the whole; Paroissien makes much of a letter that Dickens wrote to Forster in spring of 1861, in which he includes the following lament:

It is a pity that the third portion cannot be read all at once, because its purpose would be much more apparent; and the pity is the greater, because the general turn and tone of the working out and winding up, will be away from all such things as they conventionally go. But what must be, must be. As to the planning out from week to week, nobody can imagine what the difficulty is, without trying it. But, as in all such cases, when it is overcome, the pleasure is proportionate. (282)

This letter both signals the meticulous attention that Dickens gave to the consistency of his narrative and the fact that he deliberately meant to break with convention in its ending. Paroissien reads this as meaning that Dickens intended to avoid "the conventional use of a wedding to signal narrative closure, and the use of horror, thrills, and excitement to enliven the narrative pace" (282). The original ending is consistent with the former aspect, at least; though other couples are paired off by the end of *Great Expectations*, Pip remains a bachelor, and "the original ending represents the logical conclusion to the story told by Dickens's elderly, unmarried hero" (283).

Paroissien concludes that the retrospective narrator of the novel is elderly through a careful consideration of the novel's time frame, deciding that Pip is likely to be "just over sixty" (284). For evidence, he draws on specific time markers in the novel: Pip's coming of age and the "many" years that pass before Pip becomes a partner in Clarriker and Co., which mark time within the fictional world of the novel, Paroissien reads in combination with its real-world, time-specific referents. For example, he uses the fact that Pip offers Magwitch two one-pound bank notes, a form of currency discontinued in 1821, to date Magwitch's return from Australia (287). He also finds a reference to Darwin's *On the Origin of Species* in the opening lines of the novel, where Pip seems to allude to his dead siblings' having "given up 'trying to get a living, exceedingly early in that universal struggle'" (288). Since Darwin's text was not published until 1859, then several decades must have elapsed between the experiences that Pip narrates, largely occurring in the 1820s, and the time at which he narrates them (288). If this is so, then the last line of the second ending to the novel ceases to make sense. The older narrator Pip has no reason to withhold from his readers whether or not he and Estella remain together beyond the boundaries of the story; as Paroissien puts it, "Is he [Pip] trying to convince us of his not knowing what happened after an interval of another thirty years? Such questions ... originate in a common source: a revised ending grafted onto a narrative whose chronology and retrospective telling time had been decided upon right from the novel's inception" (289). Dickens's intentions, therefore, are thwarted by the second ending, which disrupts the coherence of the final third of the novel—indeed of the novel as a whole—and threatens his desire to craft an unconventional ending for Pip and Estella.

The next several essays in this section turn from investigations of individual novels to Dickens's technique across the Dickens canon. The example of Dickens is somewhat incidental to Kent Puckett's "Some Versions of Syllepsis," whose argument responds to Garrett Stewart's 2010 article, "The Ethical Tempo of Narrative Syntax: Sylleptic Recognitions in *Our Mutual Friend*." Puckett explains that

> Stewart's article is ... a larger argument about syllepsis as the textual meeting point of rhetoric, ethics, and time. Stewart understands syllepsis as having an ethical charge because it reveals a temporal gap between a semantic reading that urges us on towards a readerly end and a syntactic reading that encourages us to get caught up in the material writerly means of prose narrative. Syllepsis thus nudges us into a position of critical and ethical openness. (178)

Dickens's writing does this, in *The Pickwick Papers*, for example, when Pickwick, "'after rising to his legs to address the company in eloquent speech,... fell into the barrow, and fast asleep, simultaneously'"(178). The "textual come-again" that such a turn of phrase creates disrupts the rhythm of our reading, argues Stewart, and "syllepsis is thus a highly concentrated version of that moment when life as disorderly remainder breaks into, exceeds, and shatters forms that would otherwise seek to control that life" (179).

Puckett builds on and further complicates Stewart's reading of syllepsis by proposing another possibility for the figure of speech's literary function. "I wonder, though," he muses, "if the force of syllepsis is best understood in terms of an ethics of delay, an ethics of 'keeping things going'" (182). Not only can syllepsis prompt critical and ethical openness on the part of the reader, but it can also, argues Puckett, quash such unexpected freedom of interpretation:

> There is also a bad version that, instead, helps to support the flattening effects of social convention. Syllepsis in Dickens *either* functions as a critically effective answer to the law of the excluded middle (falling asleep and down) *or* it shores up bourgeois pieties at the level of the rhetorical figure ("welcome to your house and home"). (182)

These theoretical complexities are, in Puckett's essay, finally placed in the context of William Empson's *Some Versions of Pastoral* (1974), which claims the pastoral is a genre that attempts comprehensively "to represent life" (184). For Empson, "the reader faced with the pastoral is put in the apparently impossible position of both believing in the capacity of literary form to suggest a syntheses [*sic*] between things that would not otherwise fit together and knowing that the belief in those syntheses is at best provisional and at worst foolish.... One must *temporarily* accept a set of conventions in order to be able to act critically on them" (186). In the final analysis, Puckett sees in the juxtaposition of Stewart's and Empson's theoretical analyses an escape, of sorts, from theory that Dickens might have approved: the ethical space that the sylleptical temporal pause opens for readers not only affords the opportunity to understand and interpret in multiple ways, but also to *act* on these new understandings.

Identifying humor as a surprisingly rare subject in Dickens studies, Malcolm Andrews's "Dickens, Comedy, and 'Biosocation'" begins to fill what he identifies as this "gap" (185). Attending to the techniques by which Dickens elicits laughter, Andrews identifies the phenomenon of "bisociation," a term coined by Arthur Koestler to describe the laughter that derives from incongruities. When we hear a joke or read a line of prose that juxtaposes the high and the low, the spiritual and the profane, the profound and the trivial, "having to hold the two in bisociative relation (recognizing the incongruity at the same time as a grotesque logical continuity)—constitutes a kind of shock: the laugh is the physical expression of that shock" (187). Andrews cites examples of such imaginative incongruities from across Dickens's career, from *Sketches by Boz* to *Great Expectations*, dwelling on the many sophisticated incongruities in the example of Mr. Wopsle's *Hamlet* in the latter text. Here, the attempted high seriousness of the play contrasts with its reality in performance, and with the audience's raucous deflation of Mr. Wopsle's pretensions. Pip, as narrator, "mediates between" the two (192). Andrews's analysis is especially interesting in its connection of Dickens's use of bisociation for comic effect to Dickens's more general ability to juxtapose the seemingly incongruous, and to see often-overlooked analogies. Thus, Dickens's formal techniques for generating humor correspond to his methods of social criticism.

Umberto Eco's *Vertignine della Lista* provides the inspiration for Francesca Orestano's "Charles Dickens and the Vertigo of the List: A Few Proposals," which applies several critical theories of the list, including Eco's, to the works of Charles Dickens. Hearkening back to classical rhetoric, which organized the device of the list into the categories of enumeration and accumulation, Orestano considers how both strategies of listmaking appear in Dickens's work. Like Eco, she begins with the opening of *Bleak House*. Here, the accreting sites of London accumulate seemingly without structure, the fog which obscures them providing the only organizing principle. However, as Orestano points out, the third-person narrator will "[assert] a degree of control over lists and disparate objects, characters, and places, thus connecting the device of the list to his command over the whole story" (207). She examines the lists of objects in *The Old Curiosity Shop* and in Mr. Venus's shop, wherein seemingly jumbled, disordered objects are given purpose and a tenuous coherence by the list: "This transformative power, conferring a new potential value unto objects is, according to Eco, 'either typical of a primitive society which has not yet fixed its hierarchies of genus and species, or ... of a very mature society, perhaps at ... a period of crisis, when all previous definitions are called into doubt'" (209). Orestano sees Victorian England as such a mature society. To Eco's perspective on lists and list-making, Orestano adds that of Francesco Orlando, who believes that objects have emotional afterlives, and that of Gibert Weiss and Ruth Wodack, whose interest in lists stems from the regulatory power (after Foucault) involved in the compilation and composition of lists. In listing so many theoretical perspectives herself without delving deeply into any, Orestano's argument cannot be fully developed here; rather, this article can serve as a scholarly jumping-off point to call attention to the many significant lists in Dickens's oeuvre.

Inner Lives: Psychology, Philosophy, Religion

The books and essays in this category consider Dickens's rendering of interiority in his writing. Psychology is the perspective most often taken in this criticism, though it intersects in intriguing ways with philosophy and literary theory. The final entries in this section consider the interior experience of Victorian religion, and its outward expression in Dickens's works.

Sarah Winter's *The Pleasures of Memory: Learning to Read with Charles Dickens* seeks to understand the relationship between Dickens's serial novels, his reading audience(s), and the social and pedagogical uses of literature. Using the Victorian psychological theory of associationism, Winter explains that "Dickens's project [was] to shape the reception of popular serial fiction into a means of gathering readers into a new constituency with democratic, participatory potentials" (6). To achieve this goal, Dickens's novels must serve an educational purpose, urging readers to civic engagement by informing and instructing them about the stakes of and reasons for such participation. Winter distinguishes such instruction from political indoctrination, claiming that Dickens's project was distinct from party politics or pat ideologies: "reading audiences could form some kind of constituency, even if temporary, toward shared [humanitarian] social and political goals that would not have to assimilate or express every aspect of any given reader's social or individual identity" (11). Permanent conversion to a particular point of view, then, was not Dickens's plan, according to Winter. Instead, temporary communities of readers united by their engagement with and memories of Dickens's fiction could be moved to positive action.

Winter's book spends considerable time discussing the origins of the theory of associationism, which "came to serve as a crucial means to articulate the relations among politics, social conditions, and human nature in the period from roughly 1714 ... to circa 1870, when the physiological approach to psychology began to take hold" (34). While Winter cites philosophers including Locke, Hobbes, Bacon, David Hartley, and the Utilitarians, the philosophy of David Hume, combined with the educational writings of Henry Mayhew, seems to be most important for her discussion of associationism in Victorian pedagogy. "As an epistemology, associationism posits the train of thought, or the concept of relation itself, as its principle of possibility and coherence, and its implications are so sweeping because it also affords a *common explanation* through a theory of serial memory for both mental and social order and connection" (48). As a pedagogy, associationism suggests that learning happens through an association of ideas and feelings, allowing new ideas to be assimilated with associations in the memory. Dickens knew Hume's work, but Winter points out that, since the theory of associationism was very much in the Victorian ether, Dickens "more probably" adopted associationist techniques "from other literary works that develop a Humean notion of fictionality and, most important, from Samuel Rogers's [poem,] *The Pleasures of Memory*" (57).

How, then, is associationism manifest in Dickens's writing? In her second chapter, Winter examines the self-conscious formation of Dickens's celebrity, claiming that Dickens used his fame and popularity to create "a particular relationship to his working-class readers by supporting their social inclusion ... while envisioning a more intimate role for his fiction in providing pleasurable and instructive reading" (81). At the same time, Victorian reviews of Dickens's early novels used "associationist terminology" to describe "Dickens's originality, the reality effects of his descriptions of London life, and the reader's retention of his memorable scenes and characters" (81). By studying these early reviews, Winter forms a sense of Victorian readers' reception of Dickens's works, and of the psychological connection between author and reader. Other chapters in *The Pleasures of Memory* investigate how Dickens uses *The Old Curiosity Shop* to inculcate secular methods through contrary methods to those of religious didactic fiction: "In reconceiving the kind of moral lesson that a child heroine like Nell could teach, *The Old Curiosity Shop* also disassociates the new medium of serial fiction from an Evangelical providentialist epistemology, with its view of literacy as a means of social control and of reading as a means of conversion" (147). Curiosity, Winter argues, replaces conservative ideology as a new form of teaching through literature (148). She goes on to offer a compelling reading of Dickens's associationist techniques in *Nicholas Nickleby*, arguing that "Dickens combines his journalistic investigation with a carefully constructed analogy between the collective neglect of glaring social problems and the failure of memory or its reduction to mere unthinking habit" (179). However, Winter also points out that *Little Dorrit*, whose Miss Wade is damaged and made cynical by her memories, may seem to undercut the link between memory and social progress (182). Winter coins the term "epitaphic reading" to describe Victorian churchyard scenes, "pivotal for forging thematic connections among death, kinship, and personal identity" (196); the mnemonics of headstones provide a means of association between the present and the past, and the process of reading them permits the association. Readers—of a headstone, or a novel, or a headstone *in* a novel—then draw connections of their own. Dickens's novels draw "attention to the transition between reading and being immersed in one's own straying thoughts—a transition that also constitutes the very mundane Victorian practice of reading fiction in parts.... This understanding of reading as an activity that crosses over into everyday life affords a means of instigating the reader's 'good deeds' as Dickens envisions them" (222).

The final chapters of *The Pleasures of Memory* turn their attention directly to schools—as they are represented in *Our Mutual Friend*, and as they came to incorporate Dickens's writing into their curriculum. *Our Mutual Friend*'s fascination with literacy actually celebrates the imaginations of the novel's poor and illiterate (or at least un- or undereducated) characters, while condemning the educational model of rote learning represented by Bradley Headstone and Charley Hexam. Mercenary motives for education, combined with the misuse of memory for strict memorization, threaten to undermine the social progress that the novel advocates; Dickens uses them as negative examples that contrast with those of the unorthodox and creative Jenny Wren and Mr. Venus. Lizzie Hexam, Winter argues, is Dickens's ideal reader: she is "newly literate, but with her street smarts still intact." Perhaps more importantly, her moral compass remains intact, and she is able to combine "practical wisdom and activity" (265) in ways that Dickens would endorse.

Winter ends her study with a consideration of Dickens's ability to teach through literature in the classroom itself. In the latter part of the nineteenth century and early decades of the twentieth, Winter argues, "English as a school subject becomes 'Dickensian,' since Dickens's canonical image seems to personify not just the effects of reading his own novels in the literature classroom but also the effects of the English curriculum more generally within a system of public education meant to train children to practice classroom cooperation and consideration for less fortunate others as models for civic participation" (271). This chapter, then, joins the others in *The Pleasures of Memory* in demonstrating how Dickens's texts, by provoking memory and by being remembered, form democratic communities of readers and train them to participate in these communities. Though Winter's study is occasionally marred by a hesitancy to pin down definitions of its own terms of art, it is an interesting consideration of the nexus of authorial intent, reader response, psychological, and pedagogical theories. A strength in the argument is that, seeking to understand Dickens—and Victorian writers more broadly—on their own terms, it takes nineteenth-century theories as seriously as it does contemporary ones.

The first chapter of Rebecca N. Mitchell's intriguing *Victorian Lessons in Empathy and Difference* is devoted to the question of the empathetic imagination in Dickens's novels. Mitchell's argument starts from the seemingly paradoxical notion that empathy can best be achieved, in Victorian literature, through a recognition of alterity; that is, only by appreciating other individuals' fundamental difference from the self can characters—and, presumably, people—reach an understanding of and serve the needs of others. Mitchell opens her consideration of Dickens by examining the many instances in his work of the ineffable: his first-person narrators' (including that of the autobiographical fragment) desires and failures to articulate their emotions and explain themselves. Mitchell sees in these repeated examples a "limitation [that] inscribes alterity, as it insists that the self must always be a mystery to the other, and the other always a mystery to one's self. Yet that limit is in constant tension with the nearly compulsive drive to overcome it" (28).

As case studies, Mitchell uses *A Tale of Two Cities*, in which the most effectively empathetic characters are the ones who insist most on their outsider status: Jarvis Lorry and Sydney Carton; *Great Expectations*, in which Pip's advances in literacy are countered by his failure to read other people, except through the lens of his own desires; and *Bleak House*, in which Lady Dedlock's inability to imagine that others might react to her past more empathetically than she herself does leads to tragedy. The chapter concludes with an analysis of Scrooge, who is moved to empathetic action only after confronting his own death: "It is a spectacle that Scrooge refuses, in doing so recognizing that as death is the one unknowable instantiation of the self, so too is the human other" (47). Recognizing what cannot be known in himself thus brings Scrooge closer to the unknowability of others and allows for what Mitchell calls "movement outside of oneself" (47). In both Winter's argument and Mitchell's, then, reading (books or people) can lead the reader to a deeper social consciousness, and even to social action.

John Gordon's *Sensation and Sublimation in Charles Dickens* is an unusual and compelling work of criticism, and a "good read" in the tradition of John Sutherland's books. Like Sutherland, to whom this book sometimes refers, Gordon sets out to solve some literary mysteries; the "book's methodology," writes Gordon, is "to go with what I don't yet get" (5). Specifically, *Sensation and Sublimation* seeks to understand the subtexts and sources of three Dickens novels: *Oliver Twist*, *Dombey and Son*, and *Bleak House*.

Gordon's fascinating chapter on *Oliver Twist* argues that the opposition between the devilish Fagin and Christ-like Oliver "is a fairy tale in modern dress, and the tale in question is the blood libel" (34). Evidence for this assertion is, in Gordon's estimation, everywhere in the novel: *Oliver Twist* may be gallows-haunted, but it is also haunted by the specter of infanticide, "a policy of killing children because they *are* children" (11). The bureaucratic institutions Oliver encounters, the abusive and murderous apprenticeship opportunities available to him, the eventual fate of little Dick, and that of the child-thieves Fagin sends to their deaths all support this claim, as does the historical evidence Gordon provides that infanticide rates increased around the time that *Oliver Twist* was written and published (13). Given these instances of infanticide, the fact that the blood libel is built on accusations of infanticide, and the possibility that a widely-known story, "the medieval tale of Little Saint Hugh of Lincoln is [the] main model" for the blood libel plot in *Oliver Twist*, Gordon makes a strong case. The argument is more interesting yet: Gordon goes on to argue that Fagin comes to stand in for all of the other infanticidal forces in the novel.

> Fagin is an ogre who creeps out of the shadows to snatch and dispatch little boys, and such figures do not exist: they are, as Mr. Grimwig would say, the matter of 'lying story books.' But, Mr. Grimwig, see here: the board, the

Beadle, Mrs. Mann, Gammidge, and the Sowerberrys exist. They exist to
hang, flog, starve, burn up, box up, and bury little boys.... Fagin's extinction
at book's end is classic scapegoating. (42)

Though Gordon acknowledges that Dickens "was never much of an anti-Semite
himself, his storytelling instincts sensed how anti-Semitism's legacy would add
juice" (46). Perhaps the harsh words Dickens's narrator reserves for the mob that
lusts for Fagin's blood at the novel's end suggest an uneasy awareness of his
complicity with the anti-Semitic narrative.

As Gordon turns to *Dombey and Son*, he focuses on the novel's sublimated
sexuality and politics—or rather, perhaps, its politics of sexuality. The novel "is,"
for Gordon, "all about how what matters has been occulted, marginalized, and,
especially, pushed under" (56). He examines many instances of how Dickens represents the subconscious: with the sea, with naming, with word association, highlighting in his argument the difficulty, for both readers and characters, of making
coherent sense of the novel's subtext (91–92). Zeroing in on the many repetitions
of female breasts in *Dombey and Son*, from Paul's wet nurse to Florence's bruise
from her father's assault, Gordon argues that "the figure of the nursing woman is
the center toward which the concentrically arrayed approximations of *Dombey
and Son* gravitate. In that capacity the mediator of life, she is also the mediator of
meaning, of the subterranean, fountain-and-geyser kind this book identifies with
the overlooked" (109).

Gordon's treatment of *Bleak House* also examines the intersections between the
subconscious and conscious mind in both the characters' apprehensions of reality
and the reader's. Beginning his third chapter with a consideration of the novel's
mythopoeia, he finds allusions to several classical myths underlying the action:
the Daedalus/Icarus, Perseus/Medusa, and Orpheus/Eurydice stories (116). Each
of these is reflected in the examples of *Bleak House*'s characters who overreach,
who cannot bear to face reality or their own reflections, and whose ultimate desire
is forbidden them. The chapter also investigates Esther's "women's intuition";
Gordon argues that "when at the beginning of her narrative she allows that she has
'rather a noticing way,' she is being, as usual, absurdly modest. She can also put
together what she has noticed" (141). Esther intuits, dreams, and has premonitions
that often bring her—and the reader—closer to the truth. "*Bleak House*," in Gordon's estimation, "repeatedly shows itself to be a psychological puzzle palace,
one in which mental mechanics are at issue as much as externals. The mystery's
central mystery is the mind" (153).

In the next chapter, Gordon pursues ten other mysteries of *Bleak House,* posed
in the form of questions. Ranging from "Where does [Esther's] dream [about
Boythorn and her godmother] come from?" to "if Tulkinghorn is so attentive to
everything going [on] around him, how can he be careless enough to get murdered?" to "is Esther pretty?"—all of the questions hinge on issues of consciousness and epistemology: how do characters and readers reach their conclusions?

While Gordon's answers to these questions are largely speculative, they do tend to be plausible. For example, in response to the question "what does Guppy know and when does he know it?," Gordon suggests "a puzzle in a puzzle": how does he fall in love with Esther? The response is this: "I suggest that he discerned within Esther's form, face, and bearing what Blake calls 'the lineaments of gratified desire'—that with his sharpened social climber's eye he was ... able to spot what he pined for: a real lady, however obscured by circumstance" (171). Perhaps. But Occam's Razor suggests that Guppy may simply have found Esther lovely and ladylike, and his affection may later have led him to Lady Dedlock and further mysteries of Esther's birth. Gordon acknowledges that reading can become over-reading (186), and this book flirts with the dividing line as its arguments develop. But in part, at least, trying to discern the division is the project of the book: *Bleak House*, Gordon writes, requires readers to discern meaning obliquely, "like the activity of a sleeper trying to make, distinguish, and coordinate what the mind has made of the world when most sealed off from it and what the same mind has made of the world when, to be sure, problematically, awake to it" (187).

Another book deeply concerned with psychology in *Bleak House* is John O. Jordan's very personal study, *Supposing Bleak House*. The first chapter focuses on Esther Woodcourt's retrospective narrative voice. Esther the narrator may be expected to know already all the details that she reveals to the reader chronologically, and therefore gradually, but Jordan argues that her narration is more complex than this: "there are things about her past that Esther knows but does not understand; there are things she is unaware that she knows and that she is therefore incapable of telling; and there are things that she knows but does not *want* to know" (5). Esther's narration sometimes, then, reveals or hints at more than it may overtly mean, requiring the reader to perform what Jordan calls a "voice-oriented reading" (15), with special attention to Esther's relationship to "the figure of the absent mother that she relentlessly pursues through the pages of her text" (12). With this focus, the reader recognizes that Esther controls the voices of herself and of the other characters in her sections of *Bleak House*, meaning that these characters also reveal important truths about her psyche. Using psychoanalytic theory to delve into the potential unconscious of Esther, Jordan focuses on several key scenes in the novel, including Esther's witnessing of the death of the brickmaker's baby, her encounter with Lady Dedlock in the thunderstorm, and the onset of her illness.

Jordan next turns his attention to *Bleak House*'s illustrations, reading them through Mieke Bal's "narratological concept of focalization" (27). Focalization suggests that images are often shaped by an "interaction of different perspectives," and Jordan identifies three intriguing perspectives shared by many of *Bleak House*'s plates. One of these is external: the perspective of a viewer who is not a character in the novel. The corresponding perspectives are, perhaps obviously, internal: those of characters within the story and usually within the frame of the plate itself. A third, more complicated perspective, combines the external and internal. Jordan explains that a number "of the illustrations can be read as if seen from outside the image by an observer whom we know from inside the verbal text. Usually, but not always, the invisible viewpoint belongs to Esther" (31). This phenomenon parallels Esther's retrospective narration: as narrator, she is able to serve as both participant in and observer of the illustrations in her narrative.

The next chapter, "Psychoanalysis," traces the relevance of psychoanalytic theory to Jordan's readings of the novel. Beginning with trauma studies, Jordan discusses Freud's *Nachträglichkeit*, or "deferred action" as a way of understanding retrospective trauma, and he also explains Robert Stolorow's "biphasic, relational model of trauma" (45), in which trauma is caused not by a painful event but by an inadequately supportive response to this event by those who surround the victim. Under this interpretation, Esther's childhood trauma was caused not by separation from Lady Dedlock, but by Miss Barbary's coldness to her pain (47). Cathy Caruth's "emphasis on voice and on the ways in which trauma speaks belatedly and from displaced sites of articulation" (46) is also important to Jordan's understanding of Esther's narration. And André Green's "The Dead Mother" applies to Lady Dedlock's emotionless behavior, which masks the traumatic past that she and Esther share (48–52). The second part of this chapter is concerned with the mythic subtext of *Bleak House*, which Jordan traces to the Persephone and Orpheus and Eurydice tales (58–60): "What is most extraordinary in the novel's handling of the myth is that Dickens allows the story to be told by and from the perspective of Eurydice. Or," writes Jordan, "to press my psychoanalytic analogy still further, *Bleak House* is the story of a psychoanalysis, complete with episodes of extreme dissociation and even psychosis, narrated by the patient" (61).

In Jordan's estimation, Inspector Bucket performs a psychoanalysis of sorts on Esther in chapter 59 of the novel, in which Esther discovers her dead mother. In the chapter "Endings," Jordan concludes that this analysis has been unsuccessful (71), as has Esther's later attempt to psychoanalyze herself by writing her narrative (74). The ending of the novel reinforces Esther as a character in the plots of others (particularly of John Jarndyce), without agency of her own. But Jordan finds an escape in Esther's "supposing," a last word that "retains at least the possibility of recovering the voice [Jordan finds] missing from her final chapters" (79). A more appropriate ending to her story may exist, Jordan suggests, "Down in Lincolnshire," in the penultimate chapter of the novel. Jordon proposes—or perhaps supposes—that in the Gothic plot of the novel, and at the family plot of the Dedlocks, Esther functions as a kind of ghost, even potentially appearing in the illustration of "The Mausoleum at Chesney Wold" (84), a point that Jordan elaborates in the book's appendix. If the shadowy image that appears before the crypt does represent Esther in some way, then that might suggest an alternate ending for her character.

Although much of Jordan's consideration of narrative voice in *Bleak House* avoids the issue of authorial intention and intervention in the text, his fifth chapter, "Dickens," tackles the novel's intersections with Dickens's biography. After

discussing some of Dickens's potential avatars in the novel, including Harold
Skimpole, as a potential fulfillment of the hardworking Dickens's wish for idleness (93), and Inspector Bucket as a master of his craft (95), Jordan also notes an
abundance of metafictional self-reference in the novel. Above all, he argues, "the
juxtaposition [of novel and author's biography] may help to shed light on the fictionality of the so-called life and on previously unrecognized personal dimensions
in the fiction—perhaps also on a mutually constitutive dynamic between the two"
(98). Toward this end, Jordan focuses on the sad events in Dickens's life leading
up to and overshadowing the writing of *Bleak House*: the deaths of his father and
of his daughter, Dora, each of which influences details of *Bleak House* in complex, perhaps unquantifiable ways: "Esther's descent into the world of her unconscious," Jordan claims, "is also Dickens's descent into a personal past" (112).

Broadening his perspective to a historical consideration of *Bleak House*, the
final full chapter of Jordan's study, "Specters," reads the novel through the lenses
of Dickens's *A Child's History of England* and Derrida's *Specters of Marx*. The
former text, written during the same years as *Bleak House*, takes as its climactic
moment the English Civil War, the same period from which dates the ghost of
Chesney Wold's ghost walk. Jordan argues that "the original ghost of Chesney
Wold is a figure of resistance that continues to haunt the house of England and
that returns from time to time whenever the original injuries of the civil war are
reactivated in a new historical context by the struggle between established power
and the needs of the people" (122). In these returns, the historical subtext of the
novel resembles the psychological traumas of its central characters. The heroes
of *A Child's History* are champions of the people, including Wat Tyler, who
appears prominently in *Bleak House*, whereas the villains are monarchs who act
against the people's interests. Jordan goes on to show that the same is true of
Bleak House, wherein what he calls "ghosts" of the historical peoples' champions
appear in such characters as Watt Rouncewell, Hortense, Jo, and the disembodied
"Tom-all-Alone," all of which represent "popular values" (138).

Supposing Bleak House concludes with an epilogue in which Jordan juxtaposes the novel, which lacks a Christmas chapter, with Dickens's Christmas story
for 1851, "What Christmas Is As We Grow Older." This story stresses loss and
change, yet it ends with what Jordan calls "an expanded social vision of Christmas as a feast" to which all will be invited, regardless of social position, time
or place (145). This unifying vision serves as a final commentary on the novel
that brings so much and so many characters, emotions, and ideas together, giving the novel and Jordan's book a contingent happy ending to, perhaps, complete
Esther's unfinished sentence.

The psychology of trauma is the subject of Menalcus Lankford's "*Bleak
House*: A Tale of Two Retreats." In his article, Lankford argues that Lady Dedlock and John Jarndyce are each scarred by a traumatic experience from the past:
in Lady Dedlock's case, the losses of her lover and daughter, combined with
cruel treatment by her unforgiving sister, Miss Barbary; in Jarndyce's case, the

suicide of his uncle, Tom Jarndyce, resulting from despair induced by the lawsuit of Jarndyce vs. Jarndyce. Each character responds to trauma with a retreat from the world: Lady Dedlock chooses "to hide it as far as possible and radically to withdraw into the apparent safety of marriage to a much older man, a member of the aristocracy," while Jarndyce "withdrew himself completely from further involvement in the suit from which his family had long suffered" but remained open-hearted and charitable to others (102). Lankford makes a distinction in the two cases, acknowledging that Jarndyce's trauma is not caused by him personally, while Lady Dedlock takes on a good deal of blame and guilt for becoming a fallen woman and giving birth to an illegitimate child. This allows his retreat to be of a different kind from hers: "not destructive of the self but saving and enlarging of the best within him" (107). Not only does Jarndyce's retreat from the lawsuit save him personally, but it also allows him to lift his family's "curse" by refashioning Bleak House into a place of community and love, as opposed to the cold, haunted atmosphere of Chesney Wold; Lankford calls Jarndyce's Bleak House "a benign shelter for all" (110), and he claims that in offering this shelter to Esther Summerson, "he becomes her true father" (111), nurturing her in a way that her mother, Lady Dedlock, cannot. While Lankford's argument is generally persuasive, it could be made still more so by pointing up the difference not only in *kind*, but also in *degree*, of the kinds of traumas that Lady Dedlock and John Jarndyce suffer. Though Jarndyce is deeply troubled by his uncle's suicide, Dickens does not give us a sense of an especially close personal relationship between these two relatives. Lady Dedlock, by contrast, lost all of her loved ones essentially at once, abandoned by her lover, rejected by her sister, and bereft of her child. Complete emotional retreat, in such a case, may be the only option for this character.

Psychological trauma plays a key role, too, in "The Locked Compartment: Charles Dickens's 'The Signalman' and Enclosure in the Railway Mystery Story." In this chapter, Michael Cook specifies a subgenre within the detective genre of the "Locked Room Mystery." Citing the many horrific railway accidents that occurred in the 1850s and 60s, a sensational murder committed in a railway car in 1864, and the claustrophobic atmosphere of Victorian railway cars and tunnels, Cook explains that trains became sites of anxiety for Victorian travelers and reading audiences. In his 1866 story, "The Signalman," Dickens explores these cultural anxieties (and probably his own personal trauma from the 1865 Staplehurst train accident), linking the external, physical trappings of rail travel with psychological distress (29). The signalman himself, Cook argues, seems to be personally haunted by a ghost, but since he is the only character to see the ghost, it is more likely that psychological trauma provokes a hallucination. He is thus entrapped both in the physical confinement of his signalman's box in the railway trench, and within the pathology of his own mind (33). Cook supports his reasoning with close readings of Dickens's text and with reference to Freudian psychology and psychoanalytic literary theory. The implications of his findings are impressive, in terms of the influence he claims for Dickens's story: "in this reading of 'The Signalman,' what emerges is a view from the locked room; the fact that this particular space is the psyche does not lessen the sense of entrapment, the only outlet for which is death. As such it becomes a model for the reading of mystery from the alternative standpoint of the victim" (33).

Alan Palmer applies a psychological and narratological perspective to characters' relationships in "The Mind Beyond the Skin in *Little Dorrit*." Arguing that most narratological criticism focuses on an "internalist" version of the mind, one which is represented through such literary techniques as free indirect discourse, interior monologues, and streams-of-consciousness, Palmer shifts the focus to what he calls an "externalist perspective" that examines the social, relational mind (80). Identities are situated; that is, they do not depend solely on each individual's self-definition, but also on the interpretations and definitions of others. To understand fully the representation of identity in fiction, then, critics must examine both its representation of "intermental thought," or shared cognition, and its representation of private, "intramental thought" (82). The essay's title derives from the disciplines of psychology and philosophy, which recognize "that mental functioning cannot be understood merely by analyzing what goes on inside the skull but can only be fully comprehended once it has been seen in its social and physical context" (83).

Little Dorrit is Palmer's case study, and he uses Dickens's novel to examine the many combinations and permutations of social minds in fiction. Indeed, Palmer claims that "social minds in this particular novel are more important than the solitary or private ones" (98). By examining the interactions of Mrs. Clennam and Arthur Clennam; Clennam and Flora Finching; Mrs. Clennam, Flintwinch, and Affery; Clennam, the Meagleses, and Gowan; Little Dorrit and Pet Meagles; and Miss Wade and Tattycoram; Palmer creates a kind of taxonomy of intersubjectivity. Arthur Clennam and his mother, for instance, though they know each other's characters, cannot really read one another's thoughts ("mind-reading" is, for Palmer, a frequent metaphor). Mrs. Clennam and Flintwinch, however, the "clever ones," according to Affery, have "minds [that] are transparent to each other" (90). These minds are used to scheme, bully, and manipulate, as is clear from the oppressed situation of Affery; thus, intermental thought is not always a positive thing, but can be competitive or confrontational. Opposed to such uses of intermental thought are the elective affinities of Little Dorrit and Pet Meagles, who feel an instant "sympathetic understanding" toward each other (95). While Palmer's application of psychological theory to his reading of *Little Dorrit* raises the fascinating subject of social thought in this and other novels, some questions go unanswered in his essay. More of a distinction between social cognition and social emotion would be useful, as would a clarification of the difference (if any) between reading another's mind through understanding body language and other non-verbal cues, and the event of thinking-together with another.

Another psychological study, Jeremy Tambling's "*Little Dorrit*: Dickens, Circumlocution, Unconscious Thought," seeks to explain the digressive nature of

Little Dorrit, arguing that digression is central to the strategy of the narrative, which centers on the inherently digressive Circumlocution Office. Tambling catalogs the varieties of digressions in the novel, from Mr. Plornish's "puzzlement and frustration" and Mr. Dorrit's repression "of the shameful nature of what is being said" (39), through Flora Finching's and Mr. F's Aunt's different strains of logorrhea, the latter of which may express the sublimated anger of the former (42). The essay also notes the digressive nature of London, which "offers no direct routes, and the city's existence constructs a memory, and an unconscious, and so a narrative, for its walkers" (43). The essay ends with a consideration of Miss Wade's "History of a Self-Tormentor," a self-contained narrative which, Tambling argues, we read as digressive to our cost:

> To consider Miss Wade's story as digressive, even exaggerative, could suggest a fear that it yields too many discomforts, and supplements the main text in the same way that Adorno says that "in psychoanalysis, nothing is true except the exaggerations." The remark tips *Little Dorrit* towards being seen as a psychoanalysis of "Society"; and the logic of psychoanalysis knows neither "digression," nor single plot, nor single subject. (46)

The subtext, then, to which *Little Dorrit*'s digressions tend suggests a very conscious narrative strategy on Dickens's part; one which reveals the unconscious of his characters, his city, and his culture.

Sara Dehghanzadeh Sahi's psychoanalytic approach to Pip's development in "The Relationship Between Selfhood and Otherness in *Great Expectations:* A Lacanian Reading" posits that "the theme of *Great Expectations* is the attempt to find some integration of an individual Self into social life. Throughout most of the narrative, Pip mistakes 'Otherness' for himself, remolding people and events in order to have them conform to his private fantasy." Using Lacan's notion of the Other as that powerful "structural position in the symbolic order ... that every one [*sic*] is trying to reach, to merge with, in order to get rid of the separation between 'Self' and 'Other,'" Sahi's argument treats in turn the characters in the novel that represent the Other for Pip. These include Magwitch and Mrs. Joe, two problematic parental figures that provoke identification and horror in Pip. "Magwitch and Mrs. Joe inspire the same feelings—fear and guilt—it is this parallelism between them which explains the fact that Pip, against all reasons, sees Magwitch's second appearance as the return of the dead Mrs. Joe," Sahi claims. She also opposes Magwitch to Miss Havisham; though each molds a child for his and her own purposes, Miss Havisham, for Pip, represents the fairy-tale figure who will allow him to achieve his desires; this is, of course, his fantasy. Magwitch, on the other hand, represents a harsh reality: "Pip's misinterpretation can be seen as a representation of the heart's desire to escape from the world of reality into the world of pure imagination and fantasy, a desire which is crushed by the inevitable discovery that such an escape is impossible." So, too, is Lacan's desired merging of self and

Other impossible: "the desire [to be the Other] can never be fulfilled." Sahi sees this doomed desire as represented in the relationship of Pip and Estella. Estella provokes Pip's desire to be transformed by showing him his imperfections, and Sahi argues that, in so doing, Estella comes to seem perfect (by contrast) in Pip's eyes. Possessing her would mean achieving perfection himself, but, of course, this is never to be. Toward the end of her argument, Sahi addresses other objects of Pip's desire: money and gentility. "Money, in *Great expectations* [*sic*],... is the principal system whereby relations between the individual Self and society are established" and, of course, in this novel, "Dickens merges the motif of money and gentility with the passion of love." That Pip is largely disappointed in his expectations of all three demonstrates the degree to which the achievement of desire, the possibility of merging with the Other, is itself certain to disappoint.

Maia McAleavey's "The Discipline of Tears in *The Old Curiosity Shop*" turns from a strict concern with psychological interiority to a concern with emotional or sentimental self-expression. Responding to the large body of criticism that dismisses or shows contempt for the sentimentality in Dickens's novels, McAleavey argues that, contrary to stereotype, the sentimentality of this novel is carefully and deliberately calibrated, constituting Dickens's own philosophy of sentimentality. McAleavey counters reactions that find crying in *The Old Curiosity Shop* to be cheap or manipulative, demonstrating that despite the heroine's (and others characters') relatively frequent tears, Nell most often represses them or hides them from view. The occasions on which she does give vent to her grief publicly have serious consequences: they leave her vulnerable to the persecutions of Quilp and open to the observation of spectators either sympathetic or dangerous: "*The Old Curiosity Shop* advocates tears not as easy escape or self-deceiving wallowing, but as a rare release from the social strictures it more frequently emphasizes" (124).

Unsurprisingly, given Dickens's emphasis on communal emotion and social action through empathy, shared moments of crying appear at key moments in *The Old Curiosity Shop*. McAleavey suggests that in these moments "of mutual tears, the dangers of observation are transformed into the pleasures of recognition" (131). Such pleasures differ from the "pleasurable sorrow" of ordinary sentimentality (133) in that "benevolence is motivated by identification and transference.... For the appropriately sympathetic, crying must be contagious" (134). Dickens's characters model such shared moments of emotional release, drawing the reader into communion with them as we shed tears for the characters in the novel, and this is, perhaps, the most significant aspect of the book's perspective on sentiment. Grief, transferred and shared one to another, can have "an ethical impact" (137), and thus the right kind of tears, both within the text and provoked by it, can move us to act.

Howard Eiland briefly considers *Great Expectations*, alongside fuller readings of *Hamlet*, *King Lear*, and Kafka's works, in his meditative belletristic essay, "Allegories of Falling." This philosophical (even at times theological) reconsideration of fall narratives is suggestive rather than conclusive, but it raises some interesting ideas about Pip's story. Linking Pip with *Hamlet*, both in *Great Expectations*'s comic descriptions of Mr. Wopsle's performance and in the novel's more subtle allusions to Shakespeare, Eiland proposes that in both works, "the struggling lost soul of man is redeemed only after the ideal of purity is simultaneously relaxed and tempered in exposure to evil" (181). Pip's suffering and disillusionment transform and redeem his character. Ultimately, Eiland's argument seems less about how to read fall narratives in literature, and more about how literature translates and reflects philosophical and religious concepts of fallenness; Dickens's novel is one means toward his argument's end.

Surprisingly, only two articles in 2011 look directly to interpret spirituality and religion in Dickens's works. Keith Hooper's "The 'Our Parish' Curate" painstakingly detects in this 1835 sketch Dickens's awareness of and engagement with his contemporary ecclesiastical realities. Arguing that the curate is of the Evangelical branch of the Established Church, Hooper notes his involvement with the abolitionist cause and with charity (both associated with Evangelicalism), his extemporaneous style of preaching, his "practice of reading prayers" (which marks him as a moderate Evangelical), his administering communion (infrequent in the Established Church, except among Evangelicals), and his leading afternoon service, "synonymous with Evangelicalism" (115–16). After building his case for the curate's affiliation, Hooper attributes his Evangelicalism to the prevalence of this party in London at the time of Dickens's writing (117). He then goes on to address the curate's working conditions: he likely presides over the parish church as a substitute for the parish's non-resident clergyman, who would draw most of the parish's salary. The curate also finds himself competing for parishioners with the new "chapel-of-ease," erected "by public subscription or, more frequently, by wealthy private benefactors" to provide a more convenient place for parishioners to worship (118). Though Hooper points out that Dickens likely meant a "proprietary chapel" rather than "chapel-of-ease," (118) he rightly demonstrates that Dickens is concerned with illustrating the practical side of religious business, which is subject to professional difficulties and competition like any other. As part of this practicality, Dickens shows the curate participating in direct acts of charity, caring for the poor, using his own money to provide for their needs, and sacrificing his own convenience and health to do so (120). Hooper suggests that "Dickens's historic religious content and his use of specific characters to express his personal beliefs" are two subjects deserving of further study (121), and this essay, combined with other recent work on Dickens's portrayal of ecclesiastical matters, shows that the former assertion, at least, is certainly true.

Dickens's relationship to Roman Catholicism has long been known to be vexed, yet Louis J. Oldani, S. J., argues in "Dickens, Roman Catholicism, and the Jesuits" for a more nuanced understanding of Dickens's views. Juxtaposing critical commentary in *Pictures from Italy* about Catholicism in general and Jesuits in particular with the more balanced and even sometimes supportive attitudes to

Catholics expressed in *Barnaby Rudge*, Oldani suggests that "hindsight seems to allow ... not a settled position, but a creative tension of opposites in Dickens's response to Roman Catholicism" (203). The most useful sections of Oldani's article situate Dickens's anti-Catholicism within the context of Victorian values and judgments, particularly with respect to Thomas Babington Macaulay's influential *The History of England*, which juxtaposes what Macaulay estimates as the virtues of Jesuits alongside their more prevalent vices (205). Oldani concurs with Douglas Jerrold's comment "that in the middle of the nineteenth century Macaulay's view has been and 'will remain the view of the ordinary citizen'" (206) and was likely the view of Dickens.

The centerpiece of this article is a lengthy consideration of Dickens's 1861 reprinting of "Secret Instructions of the Jesuits" in *All the Year Round*. This document, now known to be a forgery, is emblematic of anti-Jesuit sentiment and literature in its "allegations about strategies and tactics of Jesuits—to gain power and wealth through use of such deception as pretended friendship and exploitative spiritual directions" (207). The article includes a selection of the *All the Year Round* article, noting that Dickens's reprinting "omit[s] the most damning accusations contained in the full text of the ['Secret Instructions of the Jesuits']" (208). Oddly, Oldani then spends substantial space refuting or contextualizing most of its contents in a way that sheds little light on Dickens's understanding of them. Still, Oldani does return to Dickens, commenting that his publication of the document "attests ... to the topicality of the centuries-old anti-Jesuit themes and to one long-standing source of their credibility" (210). Oldani suggests that we read the *All the Year Round* article in the context of Dickens's "aggregate of statements on Catholicism," which he claims attempt an accuracy and balance grounded in Dickens's "passion for fairness, his condemnation of oppression, and his transcendent gift of sympathy" (211).

Social Institutions and Issues: Capitalism, Law, Politics

The nexus of capitalism, the law, politics, and social issues forms the broad subject of this category, to which all of Dickens's works are relevant. The studies in this section share a concern with Dickens's representations of institutional power and individual powerlessness.

Capitalism and Class

Deborah Epstein Nord's "Dickens's 'Jewish Question': Pariah Capitalism and the Way Out" tracks the well-known transformation of Dickens's Jewish characters from the irredeemable Fagin of *Oliver Twist* to the saintly Riah of *Our Mutual Friend*, contextualizing these characters with respect to the cultural rhetoric linking Jewishness and economics. Karl Marx's "On the Jewish Question" (1844) blames "Jewishness—or Judaism ... [for] the very mentality from which modern capitalist society suffers," and Nord connects this anti-Semitic sentiment to Fagin, who "is to the Christian society of *Oliver Twist* what Marx's Jew is to modern society writ large and in almost exactly the same way. Fagin is ... the embodiment of rampant individualism. Dickens uses him ... as a mouthpiece and symbol for the misguided, soul-destroying political and economic philosophies of his day" (32). Also relevant to our understanding of Dickens's characterizations of Jewish characters are Matthew Arnold's notions of Hebraism, which suggest that Judaism inclines to self-interest, and Max Weber's *Protestant Ethic and the Spirit of Capitalism*, which argues that "speculation and usury characterize Jewish modes of capitalism, whereas Protestant forms are marked by rational organization and ... dedicated labor" (34). Without claiming direct influence of the texts on Dickens's novels (each was published after the novel that corresponds to it in Nord's argument), Nord cites Marx, Arnold, and Weber to illustrate the persistent associations between Judaism and rapacious, self-interested capitalism. Although Dickens inverts these associations in *Our Mutual Friend*, in the figure of Mr. Riah and in the novel's critique of its anti-Semitic characters, Nord argues that Riah is made to stand in for all Jewish people, and that he must essentially "undergo conversion" by the novel's end: "He acknowledges that he must atone not for profiting from others' debt ... but for encouraging the world to think ill of Jews by his apparent misdeeds" (40). Nord's assertion that Riah in so doing embraces essentially Christian values is undermined by the novel's demonstrations of greed and self-interest in its purportedly "Christian" characters, and by the fact that Riah remains part of a solidly Jewish community throughout the novel, but the case she builds for the division, in the Victorian imagination, between "the Jewish realm of pariah capitalism and ... the Christian world of rational and redemptive labor" (43) is convincing and troubling. Even in rewriting and redeeming the character of Fagin with that of Riah, Dickens cannot escape this paradigm.

Two critics explore the relevance of Malthusian political economy to *A Christmas Carol*. The prologue of Sylvia Nasar's *Grand Pursuit: The Story of Economic Genius* frames the economic debates of the Hungry Forties as an ideological and generational clash between the political economy of Thomas Malthus and the humane optimism of Charles Dickens's *A Christmas Carol*. While the link between Malthus and Scrooge has often been discussed by critics, Nasar directs her attention to the images of plenty in Dickens's first Christmas book. Nasar argues that, influenced by the abundance he had seen on his recent sojourn in America, Dickens imports it: "the England of Dickens's story is a vast Fortnum & Mason where the shelves are overflowing, the bins are bottomless, and the barrels never run dry" (7). Though she overstates the "groaning board" (8) of the Cratchit Christmas dinner, Nasar's conclusion that Dickens "hoped to convert political economists as the Ghost of Christmas Future had converted Scrooge" (10) is accurate and helps to set the stage for the wide-ranging economic history that follows in her book.

Challenging readings of *A Christmas Carol* that see the ending as fundamentally conservative, since the reform in the text is personal to Scrooge rather than systemic, Jessica Kilgore's "Father Christmas and Thomas Malthus: Charity, Epistemology, and Political Economy in *A Christmas Carol*" argues that this ending is more radical than it may seem. Kilgore focuses on the text's privileging of emotion at the expense of the pure rationalism of Malthusian political economy. "To accomplish his own divorce from economic 'fact,'" she writes, "Dickens chooses to appeal to his audience scientifically in early sections of his book, and then, through a series of textual maneuvers, to encourage them to abandon the strict position of the political economists" (143). For instance, as the story progresses, readers accept more and more readily the appearance and behavior of the novella's four ghosts, embracing the fictional (as opposed to the factual), and, as Scrooge softens to the scenes he is shown, embracing the emotional along with him. Kilgore focuses on the figures of Ignorance and Want, noting that "Dickens's privileging of Ignorance as the greater evil stands directly in opposition to Malthus, whose theory rests on the overwhelming power of famine" (151). Although she follows this strong point with a more questionable reading of Ignorance as representing "the middle class ignorance of the poor" (152), Kilgore rightly stresses the significance of these embodiments of the social ills that Dickens seeks to correct. To refute the allegation of textual conservatism, Kilgore argues that Scrooge's charity, to the Cratchits and to the charitable gentleman whom he had initially turned away, results from "a spontaneous overflow of benevolence" (155). He gives generously to the gentlemen, but Dickens conceals the amount of his gift, a detail which Kilgore reads in two ways. First, the absence of a set amount allows readers to imagine an appropriate gift for themselves, thus encouraging their own charitable giving; second, "the absence of an amount forces the scene to hinge on feeling, rather than money" (156). This emphasis on emotion changes the terms of the predominant discourse surrounding poverty in the early 1840s, from the facts and statistics of political economy to the common humanity of all.

In "Consuming the Family Economy: Disease and Capitalism in Charles Dickens's *Dombey and Son* and Elizabeth Gaskell's *North and South*," a chapter in Katherine Byrne's broader study, *Tuberculosis and the Victorian Literary Imagination*, the author argues that, in Dickens's novel, Paul Dombey's "illness is represented ... as a result of the capitalist way of life, and hence functions as a condemnation of consumerism, as well as an indication of its physical dangers" (48). In its deadly attack on Mr. Dombey's only male heir, Paul's disease both deprives Mr. Dombey of a son and of future economic success for his firm. For Paul himself, however, who, at least as a child, does not wish to participate in his father's mercantile enterprise, death may be a release, "as the only way of escaping from the demands of mechanical time and the capitalist world it represents" (52). Tuberculosis, a likely candidate for Paul's disease, is thus able to intervene in and negatively affect business, on which capitalism depends; it is also, in the fact that it often affects middle- and upper-class patients, a disease which, for the Victorians, was sometimes associated with consumerism itself. This creates a cyclical process of consumption and destruction: "if industrialism and capitalism, as a consequence of their inherent pathogenicity, produce tuberculosis, and tuberculosis interrupts and undermines the system, then society is, of course, the agent of its own destruction" (60). Byrne's chapter also considers Bessy Higgins, who dies of lung disease in Gaskell's *North and South*, as a working-class analogue for Paul Dombey, but one who is directly, not symbolically, made sick by the process of industrial production and capitalist consumption. More could be done in the chapter to distinguish tuberculosis from Bessy's ailment, which arises, as Bessy says, because "the fluff got into my lungs, and poisoned me," and is thus likely byssinosis, or brown lung disease. However, since the two diseases produce similar symptoms, the parallel is worth drawing, and Byrne effectively demonstrates the multiple levels on which "consumption ... defeats capitalism" (68).

Continuing an examination of Dickens's critiques of capitalism, two chapters of Eleanor Courtemanche's *The 'Invisible Hand' and British Fiction, 1818–1860* concern the tense relationship between Dickens's novels and Adam Smith's laissez-faire political economy. Courtemanche considers *Bleak House*'s double narrative structure as an attempt to reconcile the "bird's-eye" vision of society (represented by the omniscient narrator) with the "worm's eye" view that is able to consider only its own needs (represented by Esther Summerson's limited perspective). She argues the relevance of a comparison between Smithian economics and Dickensian narrative thus: "formal shapes of novels, the boundaries of nations, and the imagined cosmopolitan dynamics of transnational economic systems like capitalism ... are all related fantasies about spatial relations that cannot be completely seen with the naked eye" (77). In *Bleak House*, the fog obscures some of the interconnectedness of social systems and characters while, at the same time, uniting all of London and, more broadly, England, in its opacity. At the center of the fog is, of course, Chancery, whose inaction (which might be compared to that of the noninterventionist sovereign advocated by Smith) is condemned by both of Dickens's narrators. Courtemanche suggests that Dickens "sees [laissez-faire] as a nightmare of deferred agency rather than a utopia" and that he also "inverts the moral conclusions of invisible hand social theory" (108). Instead of individual selfishness producing the public good, for which Smith argued, *Bleak House* demonstrates the ways in which public institutions like Chancery corrupt individuals like Richard Carstone. The novel also prefers Esther's ethos that "virtuous actions lead to virtuous effects," even when these actions do not succeed, to "Smith's comic view of vice leading to virtue" (109).

Courtemanche next explores the ways in which *Hard Times*, Dickens's most explicit critique of political economy, responds to and refutes Harriet Martineau's *Illustrations of Political Economy* (1832–34), even as *Hard Times* is influenced by Martineau's "defence ... of fiction's power to reveal social truth" (144). Whereas the preface of Martineau's stories explains that they all serve one goal, "to teach Political Economy" (129), *Hard Times*'s "goal was both to invert the determinism of political economy's narratives by means of a wicked cynicism and a sentimental narrative of decline, and to undercut its determinism by pointing out the vast gulf between the social scientist's Facts and Laws and the real unpredictability of experience" (139–40). There is an irony in the contradiction between this didactic purpose and the novel's suspicion of didacticism, which may account for the genre-bending of *Hard Times*: by blending elements of realism, fairy tale, and moral fable, the novel attempts to portray life as it is and to suggest what it should be.

Ayşe Çelikkol's book chapter, "The Compression of Space in Charles Dickens's *Little Dorrit*," in her *Romances of Free Trade: British Literature, Laissez-Faire, and the Global Nineteenth Century*, examines the novel's intense focus on and suspicious attitude toward global commerce. Examining the Gothic associations with commerce and cosmopolitanism in *Little Dorrit*, Çelikkol first considers the silence around Arthur Clennam's activities in China, which hints at an involvement with the opium trade. "The Clennams' and the narrator's reticence about their dealings in China intimates past acts of injustice committed by the family in particular and the nation in general" and makes what Çelikkol calls "an apt Gothic secret" (127).

The bulk of Çelikkol's analysis, however, centers on the sinister cosmopolitanism of Rigaud, who seems able to appear and disappear at will, to travel long distances in moments or, indeed, seconds, to escape prisons in which he rightly belongs, and to be, and be from, "'here and there and everywhere'" (132). Rigaud (and, to a less melodramatic extent, Merdle) "presents a dystopic vision of free trade in which the uncontainable flow of commodities turns into a nightmare. He effectively transports the one commodity whose portability indexes the fluidity of capital in a globalized economy: information" (130). As a blackmailer, Rigaud engages in activities that carry overtly Gothic implications; not only can he, and the information that he wants to sell, cross spatial and temporal barriers, but by trading in secrets, they also cross the imagined and literal thresholds between the public and the private. "Privacy," suggests Çelikkol, "stands in tension with capitalism, whose inherent expansionism [after Marx] entails permeation.... The tension between economic liberalism and individual privacy accounts for the perpetual failure of the separate spheres model in Victorian culture" (131). Dickens uses Gothic conventions of trespass and transgression to illustrate the personal and cultural threats of global commerce.

James Carker and Walter Gay are the foci of Suzanne Daly's "The Clerk's Tale: Characterizing the Middle in *Dombey and Son*." The role of the clerk in Victorian society and fiction was an ambiguous one, Daly argues. Because the opportunity for advancement meant that clerks theoretically could enjoy class mobility, they could be seen as "social and economic climbers" (130) who "would adopt the superficial appearance of middle-class businessmen and, what was worse, begin to aspire above their station" (132). This mobility could threaten the stability of the middle class, "a state one inhabits without having to attain it" (130). Although

Dickens complicates questions of class in *Dombey and Son*, locating, for instance, values traditionally considered to be middle-class in the novel's working-class characters, the malevolent and destructive character of James Carker embodies Victorian concerns about what ambitious clerks could enact. Carker's villainy problematizes the role of Walter Gay, another clerk successful in his ambitions— indeed, more successful than Carker, in that Walter eventually marries Florence Dombey and inherits his father-in-law's firm. Dickens solves the problem of Walter's prosperity by locating his rise off-stage in the novel's narrative middle. We do not witness Walter's ambition coming to fruition; rather, after he is lost at sea and much later returns to England, Daly argues, "what little Dickens reveals about Walter's change in fortune ... is framed merely as virtue rewarded" (139). Stripped, then, of potentially threatening ambition, Walter achieves class mobility in an essentially passive way; though his fortunes change, his character does not.

Class mimicry, rather than class mobility, is the subject of Lauren Watson's "Mimics, Counterfeits, and 'Other' Bad Copies: Forging the Currency of Class and Colonialism in *Great Expectations.*" Applying the lens of Homi Babha's post-colonial theory to Dickens, Watson claims that "mimicry is shown to be both a mode of—and a threat to—power" (493). This dual function of mimicry appears most clearly in Magwitch's attempt to manufacture a gentleman, but it is also apparent in the novel's portrayal of criminality: *Great Expectations*'s criminals engage in forgery and counterfeiting, which Watson calls "the perceived subaltern inversion of legitimate commercial activity. Comparable to the status of treason only a century before, such acts held a special horror for the capitalist society. Both were perceived as attacks on the 'sovereign' state" (494–95). Authenticity is thus at issue in the novel, and the stakes of inauthenticity are high: not only do they signal individual misbehavior or betrayal, but they also threaten to dismantle seemingly stable categories of personal, class, and national identity.

Watson first considers the figure of what Babha has called the "'mimic man': the split colonial subject who occupies the liminal space between self / other and is—in his 'sly civility'—both an agent of discipline and disorder" (494). Both Compeyson and Magwitch fulfill this role in different ways: by mimicking the standard of bourgeois gentility, Compeyson takes "the position of the 'good copy', of quietly cooperating in the dynamics of hegemony" (496). However, Magwitch appears the more criminal, and in embodying the role of the other, defines by contrast the innocent (497). Yet Magwitch, too, has an opportunity to perform the role of the "mimic man" after his transportation to Australia; he becomes "a model prisoner whose irrevocable separation from England renders his partial approximation of colonial / bourgeois identity acceptable (indeed, desirable) to imperialist / capitalist authority" (497). While this lasts—that is, while Magwitch remains in Australia—he is an agent of discipline; however, on his unauthorized return to England, Magwitch becomes a disorderly element, and his attempts to position Pip in the role of gentleman extend the threat of this mimicry to another character in the novel.

Not only is Pip's transformation to the status of a gentleman problematic, involving as it does Magwitch's transgressions of traditional class boundaries and the law, but "the convict's attempt to incite his protégé to ever more ostentatious displays of consumerism reveals gentility's position as a material spectacle," calling bourgeois class values into question (499). Pip, who has always been uneasy in his class advancement, becomes more so once he realizes that his new status has its origins in what he considers to be an illegitimate source of wealth and power: that which originates in a criminal—and a transported felon, at that. But Watson suggests that at least some of this unease comes from the fact that this very illegitimacy throws the class hierarchy, and the system of power in nineteenth-century England, into question: "Pip's exposure to the laboured mimicry of Magwitch has instilled in the young gentleman an uncomfortable theoretical awareness of the mechanics of colonial / bourgeois identification, where heterogeneity is revealed to be the ironic condition of the apparently homogenous power of capitalism and imperialism" (501). If Pip's wealth and status come from a convict, what might that say about the legitimacy of the wealth and status of others? Watson sees in the two endings of *Great Expectations* "a parallel anxiety about the text's own integrity" (504). Knowing that there is a shadow ending behind the official version opens up *Great Expectations* when the reader expects closure; instead of receiving definitive answers about the way the novel ends, the ending "appear[s] inconclusive" (504).

The end of Watson's argument turns its attention from *Great Expectations* to the theory through which she has been reading the novel. Homi Babha, she argues, "like the 'mimic man' he so adroitly describes—arbitrarily adopts the different (and often contradictory) ideas contained within / by the theoretical category of 'post-structuralism' and brings them into conflict within his 'self'.... His pluralistic discourse simultaneously repeats and undermines the philosophical ideas that have influenced post-colonial criticism" (505). Both novel and theory, then, make problematic the relationship between self and other, the oppressor and the oppressed, systems and their adherents. This being so, Watson's own argument, which relies on both novel and theory to make its case, is enmeshed in the same ambiguities and ambivalences that it flags in the texts that it interprets. This is, perhaps, intentional: it seems impossible to escape what Watson calls "the repeated attempts of power (in its various personal, political, and discursive forms) to negotiate this problematic position and rearticulate itself" (506).

Criminality and the Law
In "Making Crime Pay in the Victorian Novel Survey Course," Lisa Rodensky invites literature professors to encourage their students to view Victorian novels through the prism of criminality, and "to investigate how these novels enact the relation between mental state and action, the two elements that define a crime" (126). The Dickens novel that primarily concerns Rodensky here is *Oliver Twist*, though one could imagine her argument applying to many works in the Dickens

canon. Rodensky puts *Oliver Twist*, whose title character passively consorts with criminals, yet whose narrator, by always clarifying Oliver's state of mind for the reader, saves him from guilt by association, in conversation with *Middlemarch* and *Tess of the D'Urbervilles*, novels in which criminality, agency, and morality are more ambiguous terms. In each of the novels she considers, Rodensky focuses on the question of intent, and on the ways in which the novelists complicate this question: in the example, for instance, of the half-asleep Oliver's witnessing Fagin's self-incrimination, or of Fagin himself hanging for being an "accessory before the fact" to Nancy's murder, intending that she die, but leaving the action (as he so often does) to others (128–29). Using these instances of ambiguous responsibility as points of comparison, Rodensky goes on to consider Bulstrode's indirect responsibility for Raffles's death in *Middlemarch*, and Tess's murder of Alec d'Urberville while seemingly in a dissociative state. Ultimately, Rodensky argues, "taking up questions of criminal responsibility in these Victorian novels gives students a very specific way into thinking about elements, both formal and thematic, central to the texts" (135).

Kieran Dolin's "*Bleak House* and the Connections between Law and Literature," on the other hand, approaches the Dickens novel from an interdisciplinary perspective, applying to it "the founding principle of the law and literature movement..., that both fields structure reality through language and both have more or less formalized practices of reading and writing" (289). While acknowledging that law wields more direct and enforceable power in the external world than does literature, Dolin argues that "Dickens's passionate criticism was generated as part of a larger reform movement. The novelist aimed to bring about legal change" (291). *Bleak House* uses formal innovation, through the use of two narrators, both to accuse the corrupt, inactive system of Chancery law and to propose limited, domestic solutions to it.

The legal and emotional meanings of "trust" as "both an *interest* in property ... and a *relationship* between two persons" (3) permeate Phoebe Poon's "Trust and Conscience in *Bleak House* and *Our Mutual Friend*." Jarndyce vs. Jarndyce is the obvious case in which trustees and equity are concerned, but Poon's argument is more interested in alternative, interpersonal forms of trust in the novel. Jarndyce delegates his position as trustee of Richard to Esther, who, as an individual disinterested in the court case, is able to exert influence outside the power of Chancery (7). Esther expands her trusteeship to Allen Woodcourt, extending her personal ties and exerting a specifically feminine and positive influence over both Woodcourt and Richard. This influence contrasts sharply with the masculine, legal trusteeship abused by Vholes and Tulkinghorn. Turning her attention to *Our Mutual Friend*, a novel more concerned with finance than law, Poon applies the logic of a "Law and Literature reading" to the novel (12–13). After briefly commenting on the ways in which *Our Mutual Friend*'s financial speculators manipulate the notion of trust, using it as "a commercial façade" (14), she devotes the remainder of the argument to interpersonal trustees who use their positions in untrustworthy ways. The Boffins and John Harmon, who conspire to reform Bella, whom they take in trust, engage in morally suspect dishonesty; likewise, Eugene Wrayburn, who uses a variety of strategies to take Lizzie Hexam in trust, has mixed motives for doing so. Finally, in a reversal of roles, Lizzie (like Esther) takes the maimed Eugene in her trust as both his wife and caretaker. Poon argues that these examples of female trustees demonstrate the need for stronger feminine trusteeship in both the legal and domestic spheres. Though it occasionally makes broad but insufficiently supported claims (that Esther "progresses towards the achievement of a legal status for herself by proving her own [metaphorical] capabilities as a trustee" [8–9], for instance), Poon's overall argument convinces and brings a fresh perspective to critical examinations of law in *Bleak House*.

Oliver Twist contains the first of many violent deaths in the Dickens canon, and Annette Federico examines the aesthetic form and thematic significance of Nancy's, Bill Sikes's, and Fagin's deaths in "The Violent Deaths of *Oliver Twist*." Beyond sensationalism or shock value, Federico argues that "the scene of death acquires transformative potential when violence is introduced; vivid, sometimes graphic, description of the event replaces moral instruction; confronted with a violation of normalcy without the comfort of religious belief or the soothing voice of the narrator, the Victorian reader is forced to ask, 'What does this death *mean*?'" (365). Dickens's portrayals of murder, violent accident, and execution cause the reader to sympathize with both victim and perpetrator, and to confront what Federico calls the "radical transformation" of each through the process of violence (367). Nancy, for example, is transformed by her murder from a sentient being, a character with whom it is possible to identify, to an object, a wholly alien thing. Confronted with this transformation, the character that caused it, Bill Sikes, himself transforms "from a monster into a trapped and terrified man. By focusing the murder on a dark interiority, on Sikes, Dickens opens 'the immeasurable gulph' that separates the murderer 'from the ordinary tide and succession of human affairs'" (375). Most interesting in the article is Federico's attention to Fagin's transformation, through the reader's experience of his interiority during and after his trial. Whereas Sikes becomes monomaniacally obsessed with the image of Nancy's eyes after the murder, Fagin, while on trial, is distracted by a multitude of seemingly insignificant details of the living world around him; he cannot focus on the proceedings because of his attention to "the concrete and objective world, the world that will continue to exist after his execution" (379). Instead of moralizing about the wages of sin, Dickens's use of violence allows the reader access to experiences on either side of the threshold between life and death and creates a concrete awareness of life in the moment. Federico's concluding argument, one of the article's most intriguing, is unfortunately one of the least developed: she suggests that "Dickens purposefully uses the focusing power of violence to address a political, moral, and psychological situation: modernity's threat to the metaphysical integrity of the self" (382).

The title of Neil Davie's "History Artfully Dodged? Crime, Prisons, and the Legacy of 'Dickens's England'" promises, perhaps, a focus on the subject of crime in Dickens's works. However, Davie offers instead a fascinating metacommentary on the uses to which Dickens's novels, and particularly their descriptions of Victorian social conditions, are put by present-day academics. Social historians are of particular interest here; traditionally, many have been suspicious of literary evidence as source material and have shown a tendency to conflate, and dismiss, Dickens's fiction and journalism on this score. However, there has also been a contrary tendency to take what Davie calls a "'Dickens's England' approach to history," in which Dickens's writings are seen to "offer something resembling a photographic snapshot of Victorian social life" (265). These approaches, alongside a parallel tendency for historians to accept "non-fiction" sources like Henry Mayhew's *London Labour and the London Poor* at face value as a historical source, should be scrutinized, Davie suggests, in order to better understand the relationship between literary representation and historical fact. Dickens's approach to crime and punishment provides an opportunity for literary critics and historians alike to re-evaluate their views of the "cultural significance in Dickens's work" (269).

The Body Politic and Body Politics

In "What's in *The Daily News*? A Re-evaluation—Part 2," John Drew and Michael Slater attribute a previously unknown set of articles to Dickens's authorship. Published 7 Feb. 1846 and 28 Feb. 1846, the satirical "Special Commission: Indictment of Robert Peel, John Russell, and John Tyrell, Severally, for the Murder of Mrs. Food Monopoly Price—Before the Lord Chief Justice People" parodies a recent trial for attempted murder in Ireland, applying the style and methods of court reporting to "the countrywide debate over the repeal of the Corn Laws, and in particular the question of which of three political agencies should be held responsible for the imminent demise of the various forms of price protection for British wheat" (22–23). Drew and Slater reprint the whole of the witty satire, which caricatures Peel, Russell, and Tyrrell's mannerisms and relationships to one another, as well as their political records.

The articles' attribution to Dickens is grounded in Dickens's role as literary editor of the *Daily News*, in their particular comic style, and in each piece's length, all of which suggest that Dickens took responsibility for the contributions. Drew and Slater cite Dickens's 1843 satire on sectarianism in the Church of England, "Report of the Commissioners Appointed to Inquire into the Condition of the Persons Variously Engaged in the University of Oxford," as a precedent for the satirical method of the "Special Commission" articles and find further examples of Dickens's allegorical political satires in *Household Words* (32). The smoking gun, though, is likely a burlesque that Dickens wrote for a January 1846 mock-up of the *Daily News*, which "took the form of an account of a mock trial, reporting on the indictment at the Old Baily of '[a] person named *Jones* ... for that he wilfully and maliciously had occasioned the death' of his workforce" (32). Dickens's legal and journalistic experiences also contribute to the frequent satirical courtroom scenes in his fiction, which share commonalities with the *Daily News* pieces.

From the attribution, Drew and Slater go on to consider what insight the article in the *Daily News* provides about Dickens's political attitudes. "From one angle," the authors argue, "the article ... continues Dickens's practice of reading individual judicial decisions against the wider political context" and reinforces his position against capital punishment (33). "From another angle, Dickens reveals an opinion on the matter of Free Trade that he is not known to have published elsewhere" (33). It is predictable that Dickens would side with The People in his satire, who judge that "the Corn Laws thoroughly deserve to be repealed" (34). However, the article suggests that the end of the Corn Laws would prove "inevitable" (34) and "shows signs ... of warming to a Tory leader [Peel] whom he had openly despised on his coming into office in 1841" (35). Finally, Dickens's "powers of political analysis are on full display in these newly-identified pieces from the *Daily News*" (36); Drew and Slater argue that the "Special Commission" can be read alongside the political satires embedded in *Bleak House* and Dickens's other novels.

Jennifer Esmail's fascinating article, "'I Listened With My Eyes': Writing Speech and Reading Deafness in the Fiction of Charles Dickens and Wilkie Collins," takes up Harriet Martineau's observation that while blindness is a disability compatible with heroism in fiction, deafness seldom is. From the perspective of disability studies, Esmail investigates whether and why this statement is true in nineteenth-century novels, using two exceptions to the rule as case studies: Charles Dickens's "Doctor Marigold" and Wilkie Collins's *Hide and Seek*. Distinguishing between the categories of Deaf (which refers to individuals who identify as deaf, belong to a non-hearing community, and use sign language) and deaf (which refers to those who have hearing loss, often from aging), Esmail finds that characters fitting the latter category appear often in Victorian fiction, often as figures of fun, whereas those in former are quite rare. The reasons for this, she suggests, are complex: perhaps because we can all expect, as we age, to participate in deafness, "the universality of the aging process" allows us to relate to and laugh at these future versions of ourselves (994). Novelists also have difficulty, Esmail argues, in representing a fully characterized Deaf individual because of their reliance upon dialogue and dialect as instruments of characterization. Even when representing the writing of their characters (in letters, personal narratives, and the like), writers like Collins and Dickens tend to transcribe dialogue.

Collins and Dickens also wrote in the midst of a cultural conflict between the Oralists, hearing people who decried the use of sign language as "primitive" and advocated that Deaf people learn to speak and read lips, and those who supported the use of sign language. While both authors sided, in their texts, with sign language supporters, neither was able to represent meaningful communication through sign language in his narrative. Collins generally replaces "Madonna's language of the body" with her "body language," describing appearance, facial expressions, gestures, and behavior in detail. The expression "seemed to say" also appears often in both texts, allowing the narrators to interpret and "ventriloquize" their Deaf characters' language (1003, 1008). Dickens's representation of Deafness is still more complicated, since, Esmail points out, he performed "Doctor Marigold" in his public readings frequently between 1866 and 1870, visually embodying the communication between his Deaf and hearing characters. In the final analysis, though, Esmail finds that absence of Deaf characters in Victorian fiction and even the secondary role that Deaf characters play in the rare instances when they are seemingly central characters is attributable to "the Victorian fictional paradigm ... that so often constructs fiction as a transcription of what characters have said and heard.... A disability that effaces speech, then, is a disability that resists integration into this fiction" (1014).

Science and Technology

The works in this section concern Dickens's engagement with Victorian scientific and technological developments, along with one consideration of how present-day technology can help us to understand Dickens's works further. Anna Neill puts scientific history, and particularly the connections between evolutionary and medical science, to work for her argument in "Evolution and Epilepsy in *Bleak House*." This article argues that Dickens's interest in scientific progress, particularly in the treatment of mental illness, and his cultural awareness of the evolutionary theories of Lamarck, Chambers, and Spencer, combine presciently in *Bleak House*'s descriptions of altered states of consciousness, anticipating John Hughlings Jackson's work on epilepsy in the 1870s. Jackson drew upon Spencer's counter-evolutionary theory of "dissolution to describe changes in nervous organization," explaining the "dreamy state" of epileptic experience as a lowered awareness of one's present experience and heightened awareness of former experience (808, 810). At times, these altered states of consciousness could even manifest as a kind of clairvoyance. Neill argues that while Guster is the only overtly epileptic character in *Bleak House,* Esther, and even the third-person narrator, experience such altered states of consciousness, in which (in Esther's case), visions or (in the third-person narrator's case) atmospherics like the fog distance them from immediate events and allow them to perceive more phantasmagoric realities. In such a state, for instance, Esther begins to grasp the family connection between herself and Lady Dedlock. Although Neill's thesis makes intriguing connections between Dickens's fiction and contemporary scientific discussions, its suggestion of Esther-as-epileptic is insufficiently supported. This is particularly true since, in the course of her argument, Neill references Jackson's quotation from *David Copperfield* in which the narrator describes the nearly-universal experience of déjà-vu (810). Neill calls this "an everyday manifestation of the dreamy state" but does not differentiate such common experiences from the more particularized experiences associated with epilepsy.

Drawing on the field of forensic anatomy which, in the 1830s, was becoming more public and prominent, Andrew Mangham's "Anatomical Sketches by Boz" suggests that, instead of being disengaged from the scientific issues of his day, Dickens was intimately aware of and interested in medical forensics. Mangham sees the influence of forensic anatomy on Dickens particularly in *Sketches by Boz* and *The Mudfog Papers*, which draw upon and transform contemporary cases from the popular press. "Before the days of photography,... the dead body became, in itself, a snapshot of the violence enacted upon it," Mangham explains, arguing that Dickens's sketches function in a similar way: "The camera metaphor is a useful one, but not the one that Dickens could have had in mind when writing *Sketches*. What the author was more likely to have been influenced by were the various forensic ideas and images working their way into popular culture via the notoriety courted by criminal trials" (45). This nexus of the professional and the popular appeals to Dickens, who adapts forensic descriptions of dead bodies to his description of London in "The Streets—Morning," wherein London is "pervaded by a sense of motionlessness and expiration; yet the very fact that there is a lull in activity speaks volumes about the intense action that takes place at other times of the day" (46). The essay continues into a discussion of medical imagery in *Sketches by Boz*, claiming that "in images of disease, pathology, and trauma, the author discovers a language of unevenness and interrupted regularity which allows him to present a new and uncomfortable picture of nineteenth-century urban life" (47).

Mangham continues his discussion to address the potential commentary that a work like *Sketches by Boz* makes on the practice of forensic anatomy, a discipline strictly dependent on factual analysis. Because *Sketches* adopts many of the methods of medical examiners yet blends "fact and fancy," it raises questions about the ability of medical science to stick solely to fact (51). These questions about the reliability of forensic science were exacerbated by the notoriety of the "'body-snatching' and 'Burking' scandals of the 1820s and 30s" (52), cases that interested Dickens and found their way into his writing. *The Mudfog Papers* present an ambivalent attitude to medical science; its "scientists cannot even agree whether they are looking at a coconut or the skull of a man, woman, or monkey.... What this suggests is that science may be guilty of overestimating the value of its evidence" (56). Mangham makes a strong and original case for Dickens's early investment in scientific concerns, but it is surprising that the argument does not extend to the novels, and particularly to *Our Mutual Friend*, in which the significance of cadavers and anatomical articulation play so central a role.

Revisiting the critical attention to the literary figure of the double, Goldie Morgentaler's "The Doppelganger Effect: Dickens, Heredity, and the Double in *The Battle of Life*" argues that Dickens's use of this device "is analogous to his use of heredity, which he understood as a process of unending duplication from one generation to the next. For Dickens, doubling erases death in much the same way as the repetitions of biological heredity nullify the irreversible impact of extinction" (162). This style of doubling departs from more traditional kinds of doubles, of which Morgentaler offers a critical taxonomy, including doubles that are moral opposites, doubles that are circumstantial opposites, and the categories that Maria Cristina Paganoni defines as "'the hypocrite, the Doppelgänger, and the split self'" (160). Morgentaler also traces the use of the double through the literature of the nineteenth century, considering its psychological use by the Romantics alongside its social application by the Victorians, who, by strictly dividing "private life and public domain," simultaneously divided public persona from private personality (161). In turning to Dickens, however, she also takes into account historical understandings of heredity, especially those which read heredity "as a process of engendering resemblance" (162). Beginning at the macro-level, Morgentaler examines Classical and Biblical versions of heredity, passing on to medieval theories of hereditary resemblance, before examining the concept of "preformation," which "posited that all generations that ever were or ever would be, were created by God at the dawn of time, one encapsulated within the other, like Russian dolls" (163–64). Dickens, however, was generally more up to date in his notions of heredity, using the relatively new term "reproduction" in his novels, which "conferred a past on living things by implicitly linking them to their forebears, to their producers" and which links the reproduction of a person to the reproduction of a work of art. In Dickens's fiction, this link is significant, as Dickens often revealed the heredity of his characters through their resemblance to portraits (165).

At this point in her argument, Morgentaler helpfully asks, "But what has all of this to do with the double? The answer is that doubles—at least in Dickens's work—are manifestations of the hereditary phenomenon of resemblance translated into horizontal terms" (166). Heredity is vertical: traits are passed down through generations, whereas in doubling, "peers and contemporaries" share the same traits. "Sameness implies not only similarity, but also rebirth and renewal," Morgentaler argues, offering as a central example the case of Charles Darnay and Sidney Carton (166). She then extends this argument for literary resurrection to *The Battle of Life*, the Christmas book whose opening pages describe the transformation of a bloody battlefield into a fertile pasture resplendent with new life. In the story, through many iterations of doubles, and especially through the doubling of two self-renunciatory sisters, Dickens illustrates "his understanding of heredity as a force that is endlessly repetitive—and one that is governed by resemblance and reiteration" (169). The sisters, both of whom are in love with the same man, overcome this sibling rivalry through self-sacrifice; however, each sister is then rewarded with essentially indistinguishable happiness. Morgentaler writes,

the similarity between the sisters means that it hardly matters which sister marries each man.... The simultaneous birthdays and anniversaries indicate the extent to which all elements in the story melt into each other without meaningful distinction or difference.... Thus, in *The Battle of Life*, battles of any kind, both the bloody and the bloodless, have no determining effect on the course of the action. They are merely spokes in the wheel of renewal. (171)

Such adherence to a conceptual theme undermines the effectiveness of Dickens's plot, Goldentaler acknowledges; the stakes for the reader in the cause and effect of the story are limited by its "insistence on repetition, renewal, resurrection" (172). Still, Dickens's use of doubling to reinforce this theme opens new possibilities in literary technique and for our understanding of the figure of the double.

Wayne Melville and Philip Allingham explain, in their brief essay, "Faraday, Dickens, and Science Education in Victorian Britain," the collaboration between scientist and popular author in the early 1850s. Connecting the passion that both men shared for education reform, and pointing out that "a salient aspect of Dickens's reform agenda in the 1850s was the necessity to broaden the Government's education mandate, especially with a view to useful and contemporary educational curriculum practices" (122), the article's authors show that *Household Words,* which they call "Dickens's primary organ for championing the cause of parliamentary, social and education reform [in the 1850s]" (122), was also an ideal platform for Faraday to expand his own audience and thus educational influence. Dickens employed Percival Leigh, a writer and physician, to translate Faraday's scientific lecture notes into readable popular narratives on subjects including "The Chemistry of a Candle" and "The Chemistry of a Pint of Beer" (123). In so doing, the three collaborators brought the practicality of science home to *Household Words*'s middle-class readership. Melville and Allingham see in this not only a fascinating historical marriage of literature and science, but also "interesting strategies for promoting an understanding of science for all people" today (123).

Turning from medical science and chemistry to technology in Dickens, several scholars focus on the relevance of machinery to Dickens's fiction in 2011. Tamara Ketabgian delves deeply into the resonances of Dickens's expression for factory machinery in *Hard Times*—the "elephant in a state of melancholy madness" (54)—in her book, *The Lives of Machines: The Industrial Imaginary in Victorian Literature and Culture*. This unusual combination of industrial, animal, and emotional imagery suggests that these categories are not as distinct as we often like to believe, and that Victorians were coming to an awareness of their conflation. Ketabgian cites evidence from Victorian medicine, which sometimes compared the human body to a factory (51); from Victorian psychology, which explained melancholy as "'intensity of idea,'... an emotional effect born of accretion ... [that] gains its greatest extremity through repetition and monotony" (56), but which can burst out into demonstrations of rage (57); and from the Victorian imperial understanding of elephants, animals whose docility is a result of tyrannical human oppression and which can transform to "murderous vengeance" at any unpredictable moment (59). Synthesizing these ideas, she reads Dickens's description of the factory machinery as a metaphor for the explosive potential of the anger that accumulates in otherwise docile factory "hands" and products of the factory system, like Stephen Blackpool and Louisa Bounderby. Machines, animals, and people mirror one another, in the novel and elsewhere in Dickens's and the Victorian consciousness.

Many critics have commented on the importance of the visual imagination to Dickens's works, and Susan Cook's "Season of Light and Darkness: *A Tale of Two Cities* and the Daguerrean Imagination" participates in and expands this tradition, drawing parallels between Dickens's historical fiction and the technology of the daguerreotype. Cook draws on scholars including Georg Lukacs, Nancy Armstrong, and Roland Barthes for their perspectives on the historical and realist novel, and particularly on the realist novel's relationship to the rise of photography (239). Although the daguerreotype, in particular, was outmoded technology by the time Dickens wrote *A Tale of Two Cities* in 1859, its unique interplay of light and darkness and complex mediation between the present and past are, Cook argues, particularly relevant to Dickens's narrative strategies in that novel. Like all photographs, daguerreotypes are dependent on light for the images they bear; however, they must be viewed in relative darkness: "Placed in direct light, daguerrotypes vanish; they are paradoxically seen most clearly when surrounded by darkness" (242). In direct light, in fact, the metal plates on which daguerreotypes are printed become mirrors, reflecting the present-day viewer, rather than a fixed image from the past. Cook suggests an awareness of this in the ways that Dickens employs metaphors of light and shadow in *A Tale of Two Cities*, and in that novel's juxtaposition of revolutionary Paris with a London more recognizable to his modern readers.

The binary oppositions with which the novel commences create what Cook calls an "economy of contradiction [that] is central to Dickens's engagement with the historical novel form: this is, after all, a tale of *two* cities as well as two times, and in that respect, it is a commentary on 1850s London as much as it is about 1790s Paris. This is not, in other words, a novel about merely two locations, but about two temporalities as well" (247). Dickens uses spatial distinction between the two cities to vacillate between the time periods of the novel's setting and its composition (248). Although Dickens's portrayal of these cities is "affective," and "more impressionistic than realistic, neither city ... is described in a way that seems particularly descriptive in a photo-realistic sense of the term" (249). However, the temporal slippage of the daguerreotype allows us to understand the type of this novel's realism. Cook focuses on the high contrast between light and dark in Phiz's illustrations for *A Tale of Two Cities* and offers a close reading of Dickens's description of the Manettes' street in London to illustrate her point. In describing the Manettes' corner, in which shadow displaces light in the heat of the afternoon, Dickens's narrator

could be describing a photographic process: what is light becomes dark, as a light space on a negative will become dark once it is printed. This imaginary image is more akin to a daguerreotype than a collodion print, however: like a daguerreotype held in the light, the darkness is eclipsed by "a glare of brightness."... Read in conjunction with daguerreotype technology, the light in the Manettes' street that becomes shadow revealing light introduces us to a spatial and temporal indeterminacy that is both particular to the Manettes and part of the novel's larger historical frame. (253)

For Dickens to create a historical novel that travels between light and darkness, France and England, the past and the present does not require the technology of the daguerreotype. Rather, Cook suggests, this increasingly obsolete photographic medium "lends the discourse [of historical truth and representation] a particular vocabulary" (255). By complicating the kinds of binaries with which Dickens begins his novel, blurring the lines between light and dark, present and past, the daguerreotype provides a particular model for and parallel to realist fiction.

Although *Mugby Junction* is a collection of stories by several authors, Tamara Wagner argues in "Dickens's 'Gentleman for Nowhere': Reversing Technological Gothic in the Linkages of *Mugby Junction*" that it is held together by its frame tales and by its invocation of the Gothic in new and unexpected ways. The "Barbox Brothers" sections of the story, written by Dickens, provide the sense of a consistent narrator, one who instills the collection with a sense of coherence. Moreover, this narrator, the "gentleman from nowhere," "settles near the junction, endorsing it as a place of convergence and joining" and disrupting the more traditionally Gothic aspect of the railway as a technology of danger and division (59). Although Dickens's best-known story from the collection, "The Signalman," is founded on failed communication and the "spectralization of the everyday," an element of technological and urban Gothic (57), Wagner suggests that we interpret this story as part of a larger whole, and that we move away from a reductive biographical reading of "The Signalman" as the product of Dickens's trauma in the Staplehurst accident. Indeed, she finds in *Mugby Junction* an inversion of the usual Gothic approach to technology and, specifically, to railways: "the death-imagery that a solitary, directionless traveler associates with the crossroads at which he finds himself is converted into metaphors of joining" (62). This joining is both thematic and generic, suggesting the railway's potential for connection while linking the various lines of the *All the Year Round* Christmas number for 1866.

Rounding out this section on technology is an article that draws on critical interpretation and computer models to achieve the difficult task of attributing an anonymous article to Dickens. This is John Drew and Hugh Craig's project in "Did Dickens Write 'Temperate Temperance'?" Because no office book for *All the Year Round* survives, and because the only existing record of Dickens's own authorship is second-hand and uncertain, the authors explain, the attribution cannot be definitive. Until recently, attributions have depended on the 126-item list of Dickens's contributions compiled by Frederic G. Kitton before March 1900, which Kitton drew from what he called "a complete 'office' set of *All the Year*

Round." However, this set does not seem to survive, and Kitton did not account, in his list, for the other contributions and contributors to the journal (268). Looking beyond this partial source, then, is necessary to make any new attributions.

Using a combination of "internal clues" and computer analyses, Drew and Craig make a compelling case that Dickens did, indeed, author "Temperate Temperance." The short article is consistent with Dickens's point of view on the subject of temperance; indeed, Dickens himself elsewhere used the phrase "temperate temperance" in his essay on the same theme, "The Poor Man and His Beer" (*AYR* 1, 30 April 1859) (273). Additionally, it is likely that Kitton's catalogue of Dickens's contributions to *AYR* is incomplete; Drew and Craig point out that Dickens authored or co-authored fifty-seven percent of the contributions to *Household Words*, but according to Kitton and a contributor list compiled by E. A. Oppenlander in 1984, he appeared in only twenty-two percent of the attributions (270). This suggests, but does not prove, that some of his contributions are thus far unaccounted for.

Because the above evidence is compelling but circumstantial, Drew and Craig turn to the "Burrows method" of computational statistics to build their case further. This method of computer analysis allows cross-testing of anonymous texts against an author's known writings in order to determine whether the anonymous text bears the "authorial 'signature'" of his or her vocabulary. The Burrows method examines "the very common words of English, the 'function' words, [which vary] significantly between texts by different authors, while remaining comparatively consistent within a single author's work" (270). Based on testing of "Temperate Temperance" against other Dickens texts and against articles written by other *AYR* contributors, the Burrows method suggests that "Temperate Temperance" is likely a Dickens contribution. It is "as Dickensian in style as 'The Poor Man and His Beer' or 'The Boiled Beef of New England' on these measures, and ... more so than 'Refreshments for Travellers'" (280). While acknowledging that the attribution is not absolutely certain, and that "Temperate Temperance" could be a collaboration or a contribution by an extraordinarily effective Dickens imitator, the authors argue that these explanations are unlikely and that it is "a perfectly genuine piece of vintage Dickens editorial." This discovery opens up the possibility that more heretofore unattributed Dickens works may be discovered in the journalism, and it strongly suggests that Kitton's list "present[s] a probable margin of error" (284).

Gender and Sexuality, Family and Children

Surprisingly few works were published in 2011 that deal specifically with issues of gender and sexuality in Dickens from a nonbiographical perspective. One of these is Laurie Garrison's *Science, Sexuality and Sensation Novels: Pleasures of*

the Senses. Here Garrison argues that *Great Expectations*'s Estella is an unconventional sensation heroine, in that what shocks the reader most in her character
is "her conditioned lack of sensation" (124). Estella's almost inhuman coldness,
instilled in her and perpetuated by Miss Havisham, is likewise chilling to the
reader. Garrison reads Estella's conditioning—and the class-conscious conditioning of Pip—as compatible with nineteenth-century social theory, and particularly
with Herbert Spencer's notion of human adaptation. Yet Dickens also demonstrates the complexity and unpredictability of social conditioning in that Estella
and Pip are eventually able to resist and rebel against their conditioning. Estella's
marriage to Bentley Drummle is, as Garrison argues, "the ultimate act of self-
sacrifice;" Estella marries Drummle in order to spare more deserving suitors, and
particularly Pip, the punishment of being married to one who has, in her estimation, no heart to give. "By confronting her own inability to feel," Garrison
explains, "Estella unwittingly reveals that she can feel" (135).

Approaching the significance of gender and sexuality to the media for which
Dickens wrote, Jacky Bratton investigates why "no drama that survived unquestioned in the canon of English literature through the twentieth century was written
and staged in London between ... 1877 and ... 1895" (87). Bratton wonders why
a writer like Dickens, who loved the theater and both wrote and performed for
theatrical productions, did not devote a serious part of his literary career to being
a playwright, rather than focusing on novels and journalism. The class and gender
positions of the creative writer help to explain, she argues, why writers invested
in the "Dignity of Literature" debate could not write exclusively or mainly for
the stage (90). In an era that privileged "separate spheres of home and work" for
women and men, and which, for the middle-class man, also privileged the world
of "commerce and conquest," the writer, who generally worked from home, was
in a difficult position (89). Because the theater was, for some time, associated with
questionable sexuality, was considered less professional than other avenues for
work, and involved working closely with working women, it was to be avoided
by writers who wanted to secure their status as successful, bourgeois men. Dickens, who did engage frequently with the theater in the forms of amateur theatricals, collaborating on plays, and public readings, "had to present himself with
great care for the boundaries of class and status" (93). Even those fiction writers
who practiced a very English version of Bohemianism tended to create a reimagined, masculine domestic sphere outside their homes, at the club. This masculine
"artistic / domestic world" existed in contradistinction to a more theatrical side to
Bohemianism, one which was often presided over by aristocratic patronesses who
held salons, and one in which women therefore played a central role.

Thanks to Natalie McKnight's valuable collection *Fathers in Victorian Fiction*, four articles focusing on Dickens's fathers appeared in 2011. McKnight's
own "Dickens's Philosophy of Fathering" synthesizes examples of fathers, both
biological and surrogate, from across his fiction, along with examples from his
own biography, to compile a consistent selection of Dickensian parenting do's

and don't's. The stern stereotype of the Victorian heavy father is, of course, to be avoided, as *Dombey and Son* and *David Copperfield* show us, as is the neglectful behavior of fathers in *Barnaby Rudge* and *Nicholas Nickleby* (53–54). A smothering father, however, goes too far in the opposite direction, as John Willet of *Barnaby Rudge* demonstrates (54).

A quality that Dickens values in his fictional and real-world fathers is playfulness—both in language and in sport. "Since language shapes our perceptions of reality," McKnight explains, "playful language encourages more creative, light-hearted attitudes toward our own failings and sorrows" (55). Domesticity and order are also important to Dickens's concept of a good father, a point that McKnight illustrates with examples from Dickens's own home life. In a time in which the public and domestic spheres were culturally conceived as quite separate, and in which the domestic sphere was generally seen as the domain of women, Dickens's prescription for a good father thus suggests a measure of androgyny (57). Not only are these qualities evident in both Dickens's writing and his personal life, but McKnight goes on to connect them with Dickens's version of religion: "In *Life of Our Lord* Dickens stresses the aspects of Jesus and God that most match his fictional depictions of good fathers" (60). Dickens's philosophy of fathering, then, is an all-encompassing one that may indeed extend to a cosmic vision.

Michael Hollington explores the significance of the unconventional Jupe family in "Dickens's *Hard Times*; The Father as Tragic Clown." Situating the absent Signor Jupe in the European tradition of the melancholic Pierrot, Hollington reads *Hard Times* both as a realist portrayal of the "circus families [that] are notable for strong bonds of affection inside and outside the family" (36), and as an allegory for the figure of the tragic father that is part of "the European panorama of the tragic clown as a major motif of nineteenth- and early twentieth-century art" (39). In this allegorical tradition, the melancholy Pierrot can be made to serve a Christ-like role, and Hollington, following Peter Conrad's description of another sad clown, Charlie Chaplin, calls Jupe a "'dejected saviour'" who "dies off stage" (45). Using examples from European painting and poetry, he reads the figure of the tragic clown "as an icon ... of everyman in modernity, faced with a bewilderingly complex world that has apparently lost all semblance of purpose and meaning" (46). Thus, at the end of *Hard Times*, Mr. Gradgrind, whose systems of belief have failed him, steps into the role of humiliated "father as tragic clown" (47).

In "Buried Secrets: Lost Fathers in *Bleak House*," Monica Young-Zook applies a psychoanalytic lens to the absent or failed fathers in this novel. Considering the roles of the biological father (Nemo), surrogate father (Jarndyce), and the nationally symbolic patriarch (Sir Leicester Dedlock), Young-Zook finds all wanting, yet she notes a failure to mourn the loss of such comforting father-figures in the novel, as well. Invoking the theories of Nicolas Abraham and Maria Torok, Young-Zook calls this failure a "psychic crypt, a mourning of an unmournable loss blocked because of a guilty secret" (125). The secret in question varies, depending upon the father-figure who has failed; it is, perhaps, most obviously recognizable in the case of Nemo, whose illegitimate parentage of Esther, shared with that of Lady Dedlock, casts a pall over Esther's life. Jarndyce's "guilt" consists in his interest in blurring of the roles of father and husband, essentially depriving Esther, with his proposal of marriage, of her second father (137). "In the figure of Sir Leicester Dedlock, and his broader social deadlock in relation to the rest of a national infrastructure, Dickens encrypts the absent fathers of an entire nation" (145). Young-Zook's essay also considers what she calls the Oedipal rivalry between Richard Carstone and his cousin/father Jarndyce, as well as the novel's shift from an emphasis on the importance of fathers to the future of a son and "symbolic daughter" in the second Bleak House (150).

Regina Hansen's "Victorian Fathers on Film" uses examples from film adaptations of Dickens's *A Christmas Carol*, *David Copperfield*, and *Great Expectations* to build a case that Dickens's "intimate," or "maternal" father-figures, those that affectionately overlap with the traditional domestic role of Victorian motherhood, prefigure twentieth- and twenty-first century parenting values. *Great Expectations*'s Magwitch, for instance, "[takes] on the qualities expected of Victorian mothers in general, as his priorities evolve from violent self-preservation early on to ultimate self-sacrifice and quiet suffering" (209). *Great Expectations*'s Joe, like *David Copperfield*'s Clara, is more childlike than paternal, "but Joe is both forgiven and rewarded" for his failures to protect Pip, and comes into his own as a father-figure after Mrs. Joe's death (213). Hansen cites gender role reversal in the case of *A Christmas Carol*'s Bob and Mrs. Cratchit as another instance of a "maternal" father in Dickens; Bob is more demonstratively emotional, and Mrs. Cratchit is more outwardly "tough" in both the novella and in its film adaptations. Although she does examine David Lean's 1946 adaptation of *Great Expectations*, Hansen's argument draws film examples mainly from the past twenty years, focusing on a trio of adaptations from 1998–99. A more thorough explanation of the particular film selections quoted in the article might have strengthened the argument and helped to account for earlier or a wider variety of film adaptations of Dickens's work.

The focus of Barry McCrea's *In the Company of Strangers: Family and Narrative in Dickens, Conan Doyle, Joyce, and Proust* is mainly on modernist revisions of the family plot; however, the book's first chapter, "Queer Expectations," acknowledges Dickens's disruptions of "the dynastic family plot of the nineteenth-century English novel" (25) as anticipating the modernists. In this, McCrea's argument accepts the traditional division between modernist experimentation and Victorian convention, citing Dickens as a kind of exception that proves the rule.

Oliver Twist is the first novel that McCrea examines, emphasizing the significance of Oliver as an orphan. This status "highlights a ... basic conflict between inherited and acquired connections" (27), setting up a competition between Oliver's "romance-genealogical" family, to which the plot eventually restores him, and his "queer," or non-genealogical family encountered in Fagin's den. While McCrea's point that "the alternative family supplies the deviation from the genealogical plot and thus is rendered as criminal itself; outside the laws of narrative continuity and natural identity" (30) is an important one, the argument makes too much of the possibility that the consistently innocent Oliver must shed his criminality in his restoration to Brownlow and the Maylies. McCrea calls this Oliver's "de-Twisting" (32); however, Oliver's name has always carried this irony: no matter how abusers like Bumble, Fagin, and Sikes attempt to twist Oliver, he remains on the straight-and-narrow.

Bleak House is another novel that creates competition between the genealogical family and what McCrea calls the "queer" constructed connections formed in an increasingly powerful city environment. Here, the family plot cannot extricate itself from the complexities of London without what McCrea calls "outside help," in the form of Mr. Bucket. The need for a detective suggests the waning power of the "genealogical plot,... the whole point [of which] is that it is natural and unforced, that it happens automatically" (47). Coincidence and nature cannot, alone, unravel the mysteries of Esther's birth and George Rouncewell's estrangement from his family: "At stake in *Bleak House*, the reason a law enforcer is necessary, are the relative statuses of legitimacy and illegitimacy themselves.... The law in *Bleak House* functions as an allegory for the family, the system that provides for inheritance, control, and legitimacy. As a policeman, Bucket is a guarantor of legitimacy and the rule of law, the enemy of criminal conspiracy" (49). Family alone cannot maintain order in this novel; a professional is needed. The case of Jarndyce and Jarndyce is also concerned with legitimacy and inheritance; "it is the job of the Chancery suit to sort out from among a tanged mass of pretenders who is legitimately connected to whom and how and what the rightful, natural links between present and past are" (51). However, the end of the case, pointless and unilluminating, suggests that the "automatic links of the knowable, family universe no longer hold" (53), and that the queer urban connections that replace them are insufficient.

Finally, McCrea argues that the competition between genealogical family and queer outsider connections "as centers of narrative coherence is decisively resolved in favor of the criminals in *Great Expectations*" (54). The family fails as Pip's primary bond, from his misconstrual of his own name (from Pirrip to Pip) to his inability to understand his relationship to the gravestones in the churchyard. Magwitch, on the other hand, "usurps the role of the family in the novel" (57); the illegitimate father is the most important one. Pip's other extra-familial relationships—with Herbert Pocket, for instance, also give structure and coherence to the narrative. When *Great Expectations* does reveal an intricate family plot, the relationship between Estella, Magwitch, and Molly, this "yet remains irrelevant to the novel's meaning and structure" (61); the reader's expectations of the family plot are "dead ends." McCrea draws a parallel between Fagin and Magwitch, suggesting a reversal has occurred between Fagin's failure to replace Oliver's genealogical family structure and Magwitch's success in doing so. However, this reversal is complex. Pip's family relationship to Joe and Biddy is still important, but, as McCrea rightly points out, "Pip remains very much extraneous to this settled domestic world, on the outside looking in, and neither he nor the novel as a whole ever looks to the future, remaining quite outside the rhythms and promises of everyday life" (63). Joe and Biddy show us what Pip might have had and hoped for, if *Great Expectations* followed a conventional genealogical family plot, and Miss Havisham's story provides a failed instance of the marriage plot (65–66). The genealogical family, in *Great Expectations*, is a thing of the past.

The final three articles consider the role of children and childhood in Dickens's canon. Taking its title from a line of Charles Olson's 1987 poem "As the Dead Prey Upon Us," Ian Brinton's "*Great Expectations*: Untangle the Nets of Being" traces the theme of the inescapability of the past in *Great Expectations*. Brinton has two foci: Pip's development, and the infusion of Charles Dickens's own development into Pip's story. According to Brinton, "The nostalgic quality which haunts the opening pages of *Great Expectations*, accompanied by a sense of both fear and loss, registers the way in which Dickens felt about his early life before the shattering experience of imprisonment in the Blacking Warehouse," and Brinton hears echoes of the "secrecy and sense of shabby shame" that Dickens experienced as a child laborer in Pip's humiliations at Satis House (137). Close readings of the introduction and reintroduction of Magwitch in Dickens's novel demonstrate specific connections between Pip's childhood encounter and adult experience, supporting the notion that "we can never rid ourselves of those subtle strands which go to make up who we are" (140). Brinton's article draws clear parallels between the present and past of both author and character.

In the first chapter of Richard Locke's *Critical Children: The Use of Childhood*, the author revisits what he calls three of Dickens's most prominent "heroic victims": Oliver Twist, David Copperfield, and Pip. Each abused child, he suggests, conveys a different response to the Romantic ideal of the child. Oliver Twist, who ceases to perform any independent action by chapter 7 of his novel, "functions like a stone thrown into a pond that changes everything but is itself unchanged" (22); the character's purpose is a propagandistic one, engineered to spark social reform by provoking readerly sympathy (49). David Copperfield, by contrast, does turn out to be the hero of his own bildungsroman, in the Carlylean sense of "The Hero as Man of Letters" (24): "Rather than making the usual opposition between irresponsible, dreamy, romantic literary fancy and hard, realistic, Victorian practical material action, David describes his literary vocation as the ultimate—and heroic—civilizing force in modern England and its empire" (39). Pip, then, is a reversal of this style of heroism; in fact, it is precisely his propensity to invent a fairy-tale narrative for his life and to attempt to plot his own story that results in his self-victimization. One of the most interesting points in Locke's argument concerns Jaggers, whose own "plot manipulations have brought destruction to all his characters—including the child Estella," whom he had tried to save (46). In *Great Expectations*, Locke argues, "all plot is childish fantasy ... [and] no child can save us" (47).

Although Dickens is well known to have championed the cause of neglected and abused children in his fiction and nonfiction writings across his career, Galia Benziman, in "The Split Image of the Neglected Child: Dickens," makes the case that his attitude to child neglect was more ambiguous than critics often acknowledge. Characters like Oliver Twist, David Copperfield, and Esther Summerson (and indeed, like Dickens himself, in his autobiographical fragment), often have darker doubles. Benziman categorizes Dickens's wholeheartedly sympathetic portrayals of neglected children as embodying the trope of what she calls child-as-self; critical, stereotyped portrayals of neglected children, and especially of poor, neglected, marginal children, she categorizes as child-as-other (148). "At bottom," Benziman argues, "the notion of child-as-self in Dickens is shadowed by the anxiety of becoming that other" (149).

Some markers of the child-as-self / child-as-other dichotomy are the degree of interiority Dickens grants to the character, and its degree of individuality. The child-as-self suffers privately and deeply personally; the child-as-other tends to be a minor character who suffers on behalf of a larger class, whose mind the reader does not know, and who may "undergo a massive process of othering by being represented as [a] repellent or threatening figure" (151). Benziman cites examples from across the Dickens canon, including the Christmas books, the autobiographical fragment (in which Dickens focuses intently on his own suffering at the blacking warehouse, but not on that of his fellow child-laborers), *David Copperfield*, and *Bleak House*. This last example is one of the more interesting; Benziman investigates Dickens's treatment of Jo and finds that, despite offering a more sympathetic portrait of Jo than of many of his most impoverished and degraded child-as-other characters, "*Bleak House* again reproduces the impression that the poor child is deformed or repulsive, either because of the corrupting environment into which he was born, or because the poor are all too often much less attractive than 'their betters'" (182). Jo's infection of Esther with smallpox represents the fear and ambivalence Benziman finds throughout Dickens's many representations of children: that "the child-as-other threatens to swallow the child-as-self, erase his individuality, and turn him into the social other whose proximity he dreads" (170).

Although the preceding point ends the 2011 survey of recent Dickens studies on an ominous note, the prospect for future Dickens studies is nothing but bright. After having spent the productive bicentennial year looking back at and reading deeply the productions of 2011 myself, I look forward to the 2012 survey with interest. It is an honor to be part of such a vibrant and active scholarly community as Dickensians provide, and it has been a privilege to engage with a year's worth of important work in the field.

NOTE

1. Because Volume 2 (*Autobiographical Writings, Letters, Obituaries, Reminiscences, Biographies*) of Duane DeVries's comprehensive bibliography *General Studies of Charles Dickens and His Writings and Collected Editions of His Works: An Annotated Bibliography*, although officially published at the end of 2010, was not available in time to be considered by Nancy Aycock Metz in "Recent Dickens Studies: 2010" (in volume 43 of *DSA*), the work is reviewed in this survey.

WORKS CITED

Adams, Amanda. "Performing Ownership: Dickens, Twain, and Copyright on the Transatlantic Stage." *American Literary Realism* 43.3 (2011): 223–41.

Agathocleous, Tanya. "The Sketch and the Panorama: Wordsworth, Dickens, and the Emergence of Cosmopolitan Realism." *Urban Realism and the Cosmopolitan Imagination in the Nineteenth Century: Visible City, Invisible World.* Cambridge: Cambridge UP, 2011. 69–114.

Allen, M. D. "'The Knight of the Simple Heart': Twemlow into Tymperley." *The Gissing Journal* 43.3 (2011): 15–21.

Allen, Michael. *Charles Dickens and the Blacking Factory.* St. Leonards, UK: Oxford-Stockley, 2011.

Andrews, Malcolm. "Dickens, Comedy, and 'Bisociation.'" *Dickens Quarterly* 28.3 (2011): 185–94.

Arac, Jonathan. *Impure Worlds: The Institution of Literature in the Age of the Novel.* New York: Fordham UP, 2011.

Barloon, Jim. "Cryptic Texts: Coded Signs and Signals in *A Tale of Two Cities*." *Dickens Studies Annual* 42 (2011): 261–73.

Belmonte, Kevin Charles. "Mr. Dickens's Champion." *Defiant Joy: The Remarkable Life and Impact of G. K. Chesterton.* Nashville, TN: Thomas Nelson, 2011. 97–109.

Benziman, Galia. "The Split Image of the Neglected Child: Dickens." *Narratives of Child Neglect in Romantic and Victorian Culture.* Basingstoke, UK: Palgrave Macmillan, 2011. 142–85.

Bodenheimer, Rosemarie. "Copperfield's Geographies." *Dickens Studies Annual* 42 (2011): 177–91.

———. "London in the Victorian Novel." *The Cambridge Companion to the Literature of London.* Ed. Lawrence Manley. Cambridge: Cambridge UP, 2011. 142–59.

Boudant, Sarah. "The Reference to the Year 1793 in *A Tale of Two Cities, Ninetythree* and *The Devils*." *Other Voices: Three Centuries of Cultural Dialogue Between Russia and Western Europe.* Ed. Graham H. Roberts. Newcastle upon Tyne, UK: Cambridge Scholars P, 2011. 76–93.

Bratton, J. S. *The Making of the West End Stage: Marriage, Management and the Mapping of Gender in London, 1830–1870.* Cambridge: Cambridge UP, 2011.

Brinton, Ian. "*Great Expectations:* Disentangle the Nets of Being." *Use of English* 62.2 (2011): 134–43.

Byrne, Katherine. "Consuming the Family Economy: Disease and Capitalism in Charles Dickens's *Dombey and Son* and Elizabeth Gaskell's *North and South.*" *Tuberculosis and the Victorian Literary Imagination.* Cambridge: Cambridge UP, 2011. 45–68.

Camlot, Jason. "The Three-Minute Victorian Novel: Remediating Dickens into Sound." *Audiobooks, Literature, and Sound Studies.* Ed. Matthew Rubery. New York: Routledge, 2011. 25–43.

Çelikkol, Ayşe. "The Compression of Space in Charles Dickens's *Little Dorrit.*" *Romances of Free Trade: British Literature, Laissez-Faire, and the Global Nineteenth Century.* New York: Oxford UP, 2011. 123–42.

Chialant, Maria Teresa. "Dickensian Resonances in the Contemporary English Novel." *Dickens Quarterly* 28.1 (2011): 41–51.

Christopher, Geoffrey. "Dickens and the Southsea Pier Hotel: A Note." *The Dickensian* 107.2 (2011): 113–14.

Cook, Michael. "The Locked Compartment: Charles Dickens's 'The Signalman' and Enclosure in the Railway Mystery Story." *Narratives of Enclosure in Detective Fiction: The Locked Room Mystery.* New York: Palgrave Macmillan, 2011. 21–42.

Cook, Susan. "Season of Light and Darkness: *A Tale of Two Cities* and the Daguerrean Imagination." *Dickens Studies Annual* 42 (2011): 237–60.

Cooke, Simon. "'A Regular Contributor': Le Fanu's Short Stories, *All the Year Round*, and the Influence of Dickens." *Le Fanu Studies* 6.2 (2011). <http://www.lefanustudies.com/dickens.html>.

Courtemanche, Eleanor. *The "Invisible Hand" and British Fiction, 1818–1860: Adam Smith, Political Economy, and the Genre of Realism.* Basingstoke, UK: Palgrave Macmillan, 2011.

Crawford, Iain. "'Faithful Sympathy': Dickens, the *Edinburgh Review*, and Editing *Household Words.*" *Victorian Periodicals Review* 44.1 (2011): 42–68.

Daly, Suzanne. "The Clerk's Tale: Characterizing the Middle in *Dombey and Son.*" *Narrative Middles: Navigating the Nineteenth-Century British Novel.* Ed. Caroline Levine and Mario Ortiz-Robles. Columbus: Ohio State UP, 2011. 128–41.

Davie, Neil. "History Artfully Dodged? Crime, Prisons, and the Legacy of 'Dickens's England.'" *Dickens Quarterly* 28.4 (2011): 261–72.

DeVries, Duane. *General Studies of Charles Dickens: An Annotated Bibliography.* Vol. 2, Sections 1–2. New York: AMS, 2010.

Dolin, Kieran. "*Bleak House* and the Connections between Law and Literature." *Teaching Law and Literature.* Ed. Austin Sarat, Cathrine O. Frank, and Matthew Anderson. New York: MLA, 2011. 288–95.

Douglas-Fairhurst, Robert. *Becoming Dickens: The Invention of a Novelist.* Cambridge: Harvard UP, 2011.

Drew, John, and Hugh Craig. "Did Dickens Write 'Temperate Temperance'? (An Attempt to Identify Authorship of an Anonymous Article in *All the Year Round*)." *Victorian Periodicals Review* 44.3 (2011): 267–90.

Drew, John, and Michael Slater. "What's in *The Daily News*? A Re-evaluation—Part 2." *The Dickensian* 107.1 (2011): 22–39.

Easley, Alexis. "The Virtual City: Literary Tourism and the Construction of 'Dickens's London.'" *Literary Celebrity, Gender,and Victorian Authorship, 1850–1914*. Newark: U of Delaware P, 2011. 27–47.

Easson, Angus, Margaret Brown, Leon Litvack, and Joan Dicks, eds. "The Letters of Charles Dickens: Supplement XV." *The Dickensian* 107.2 (2011): 126–44.

———. "The Letters of Charles Dickens: Supplement XVI." *The Dickensian* 107.3 (2011): 228–44.

Edgecombe, Rodney Stenning. "Keats, Hood, Dickens, Crones, and Little Boys." *Keats-Shelley Review* 25 (2011): 81–82.

Eiland, Howard. "Allegories of Falling." *Telos* 155 (Summer 2011): 175–90.

Esmail, Jennifer. "'I Listened with My Eyes': Writing Speech and Reading Deafness in the Fiction of Charles Dickens and Wilkie Collins." *ELH* 78.4 (2011): 991–1020.

Federico, Annette. "The Violent Deaths of *Oliver Twist*." *Papers on Language and Literature* 47.4 (2011): 363–85.

Furneaux, Holly. "Inscribing Friendship: John Forster's *Life of Charles Dickens* and the Writing of Male Intimacy in the Victorian Period." *Life Writing* 8.3 (2011): 243–56.

Garrison, Laurie. "*Great Expectations:* Estella's Subtle Sensations." *Science, Sexuality, and Sensation Novels: Pleasures of the Senses*. New York: Palgrave Macmillan, 2011. 123–36.

Gilmore, Dehn. "Terms of Art: Reading the Dickensian Gallery." *Dickens Studies Annual* 42 (2011): 1–32.

Goodheart, Eugene, ed. *Critical Insights: Charles Dickens*. Ipswich: Salem, 2010. [Contents: Eugene Goodheart, "On Charles Dickens": 3–7; Patricia Marks, "Biography of Charles Dickens": 8–14; Elizabeth Gumport, "The *Paris Review* Perspective": 15–17; Shanyn Fiske, "Charles Dickens in His Times": 21–40; Laurence W. Mazzeno, "Charles Dickens's Critical Reputation": 41–58; Nancy M. West, "Order in Disorder: Surrealism and *Oliver Twist*": 59–79; Joseph M. Duffy, Jr., "Another Version of Pastoral: *Oliver Twist*": 83–104; Alan P. Barr, "Mourning Becomes David: Loss and the Victorian Restoration of Young Copperfield": 105–24; Julia F. Saville, "Eccentricity as Englishness in *David Copperfield*": 125–44; G. Robert Stange, "Expectations Well Lost: Dickens's Fable for His Time": 145–58; Monroe Engel, "The Sense of Self": 159–77; Robert A. Donovan, "Structure and Idea in *Bleak House*": 178–207; Michele S. Ware, "'True Legitimacy': The Myth of the Foundling in *Bleak House*": 208–20; Patricia E. Johnson, "*Hard Times* and the Structure of Industrialism: The Novel as Factory": 221–34; Lionel Trilling, "*Little Dorrit*": 234–47; Matthew J. Bolton, "Charles Dickens, James Joyce, and the Origins of Modernism": 248–63; "Chronology of Charles Dickens's Life": 267–70; "Works by Charles Dickens": 271–72.]

Gordon, John. *Sensation and Sublimation in Charles Dickens*. New York: Palgrave Macmillan, 2011.

Hanna, Robert C. "Selection Guide to Dickens's Amateur Theatricals—Part 1." *The Dickensian* 107.3 (2011): 220–27.

Hansen, Regina. "Victorian Fathers on Film: Dickens's Fathers as the Precursor of the Modern Sensitive Dad." McKnight 207–16.

Hennelly, Jr., Mark M. "Dickens's Immaterial Culture of Hats and *The Pickwick Papers*." *Dickens Studies Annual* 42 (2011): 77–122.

Hessell, Nikki. *Literary Authors, Parliamentary Reporters: Johnson, Coleridge, Hazlitt, Dickens.* Cambridge: Cambridge UP, 2011.

Hollington, Michael. "Dickens's *Hard Times*: The Father as Tragic Clown." McKnight 35–50.

———. "Dickens, Sala and the London Arcades." *Dickens Quarterly* 28.4 (2011): 273–83.

Holt, Shari Hodges. "Recent Dickens Studies and Adaptations: 2009." *Dickens Studies Annual* 42 (2011): 331–446.

Hooper, Keith. "The 'Our Parish' Curate." *The Dickensian* 107.2 (2011): 115–23.

Isba, Anne. *Dickens's Women: His Great Expectations.* New York: Continuum, 2011.

Johannessen, Ivar, and Fred-Ivar Syrstad. "Dickens in Norway." *The Dickensian* 107.1 (2011): 40–42.

John, Juliet. *Dickens and Mass Culture.* New York: Palgrave Macmillan, 2011.

Jordan, John O. *Supposing Bleak House.* Charlottesville: U of Virginia P, 2011.

Ker, Ian. "Dickens." *G. K. Chesterton: A Biography.* New York: Oxford UP, 2011. 159–94.

Ketabgian, Tamara. *The Lives of Machines: The Industrial Imaginary in Victorian Literature and Culture.* Ann Arbor: U of Michigan P, 2011.

Kilgore, Jessica. "Father Christmas and Thomas Malthus: Charity, Epistemology, and Political Economy in *A Christmas Carol*." *Dickens Studies Annual* 42 (2011): 143–58.

Knoepflmacher, U. C. "Boy-Orphans, Mesmeric Villains, and Film Stars: Inscribing *Oliver Twist* into *Treasure Island*." *Victorian Literature* 39.1 (2011): 1–25.

Laird, Karen E. "Adapting the Seduction Plot: *David Copperfield*'s Magdalens on the Victorian Stage." *Dickens Studies Annual* 42 (2011): 193–215.

Lankford, Menalcus. "*Bleak House*: A Tale of Two Retreats." *The Dickensian* 107.2 (2011): 101–11.

Latham, Monica. "Bringing Newness to the World: Lloyd Jones's 'Pacific Version of *Great Expectations*.'" *Dickens Quarterly* 28.1 (2011): 22–40.

Lawrence, David Haldane. "Charles Dickens and the World of Opera." *The Dickensian* 107.1 (2011): 5–21.

Ledger, Sally, and Holly Furneaux, eds. *Charles Dickens in Context.* Cambridge: Cambridge UP, 2011. [Contents: John Bowen, "The Life of Dickens I: Before Ellen Ternan": 3–10; John Bowen, "The Life of Dickens II: After Ellen Ternan": 11–17; Michael Slater, "Dickens's Lives": 18–26; Anne Humpherys, "Victorian Stage Adaptations and Novel Appropriations": 27–34; John Drew, "Reviewing Dickens in the Victorian Periodical Press": 35–42; Michael Hollington, "The European Context": 43–50; Toru Sasaki, "Major Twentieth-Century Critical Responses": 51–58; Tony Williams, "Modern Stage Adaptations": 59–66; Toru Sasaki, "Modern Screen Adaptations": 67–73; Juliet John, "The Heritage Industry": 74–80; Cora Kaplan, "Neo-

Victorian Dickens": 81–87; Paul Schlicke, "Popular Culture": 91–97; Joss Marsh, "The Rise of Celebrity Culture": 98–108; John Drew, "The Newspaper and Periodical Market": 109–16; Florian Schweizer, "Authorship and the Professional Writer": 117–24; Marty Gould, "The Theatre": 125–32; Juliet John, "Melodrama": 133–39; Florian Schweizer, "The Bildungsroman": 140–47; Kate Flint, "Visual Culture": 148–57; Ian Duncan, "The Historical Novel": 158–65; Mary Elizabeth Leighton and Lisa Surridge, "The Illustrated Novel": 166–77; Sally Ledger, "Christmas": 178–85; Holly Furneaux, "Childhood": 186–93; Martin Danahay, "Work": 194–202; Ruth Livesey, "Europe": 203–10; Ella Dzelzainis, "The Victorians and America": 211–38; Patrick Brantlinger, "Educating the Victorians": 219–26; Anne Humpherys, "London": 227–34; Michael Sanders, "Politics": 235–42; Paul Young, "Political Economy": 243–51; Andrew Sanders, "The Aristocracy": 252–59; Priti Joshi, "The Middle Classes": 260–67; Josephine McDonagh, "Urban Migration and Mobility": 268–75; Francis O'Gorman, "Financial Markets and the Banking System": 276–83; Grace Moore, "Empires and Colonies": 284–91; Priti Joshi, "Race": 292–300; Anne Schwan, "Crime": 301–09; Jan-Melissa Schramm, "The Law": 310–17; Emma Mason, "Religion": 318–25; James Mussell, "Science": 326–33; Jonathan H. Grossman, "Transport": 334–42; Janis McLarren Caldwell, "Illness, Disease, and Social Hygiene": 343–49; Catherine Waters, "Domesticity": 350–57; Holly Furneaux, "Sexuality": 358–64; Catherine Waters, "Gender Identities": 365–72.]

Locke, Richard. *Critical Children: The Use of Childhood in Ten Great Novels.* New York: Columbia UP, 2011.

Maidment, Brian. "Pickwick on Pots—Transfer Printed Ceramics and Dickens's Early Illustrated Fiction." *Dickens Quarterly* 28.2 (2011): 109–18.

Mangham, Andrew. "Anatomical Sketches by Boz." *The Dickensian* 107.1 (2011): 43–57.

Margolyes, Miriam, and Sonia Fraser. *Dickens's Women.* London: Hesperus, 2011.

Martiny, Erik. "*Jack Maggs* and *Mister Pip*—the Empire Strokes Back: Commonwealth Bibliophilia in Australasian Responses to *Great Expectations.*" *Notes on Contemporary Literature* 41.3 (2011): 2–5.

Maurer, Yael. "Rubbing 'that wonderful lamp within': Reading *Martin Chuzzlewit.*" *Dickens Quarterly* 28.2 (2011): 119–27.

McAleavey, Maia. "The Discipline of Tears in *The Old Curiosity Shop.*" *Dickens Studies Annual* 42 (2011): 123–41.

McCrea, Barry. *In the Company of Strangers: Family and Narrative in Dickens, Conan Doyle, Joyce, and Proust.* New York: Columbia UP, 2011.

McKnight, Natalie. "Dickens's Philosophy of Fathering." McKnight 51–62.

———, ed. *Fathers in Victorian Fiction.* Newcastle upon Tyne, UK: Cambridge Scholars P, 2011.

McParland, Robert. "Material Production and Circulation of Charles Dickens, 1837–1870." *Readings on Audience and Textual Materiality.* Ed. Graham Allen and Carrie Griffin. London: Pickering and Chatto, 2011. 89–106.

Meckier, Jerome. "Installment 33 of *Great Expectations*: The 'Masterpiece' Chapter." *Dickens Quarterly* 28.3 (2011): 195–204.

Melville, Wayne, and Philip V. Allingham. "Faraday, Dickens, and Science Education in Victorian Britain." *School Science Review* 92.340 (March 2011): 121–24.

Mitchell, Rebecca N. "Mysteries of Dickensian Literacies." *Victorian Lessons in Empathy and Difference.* Columbus: Ohio State UP, 2011. 27–48.

Morgentaler, Goldie. "The Doppelganger Effect: Dickens, Heredity, and the Double in *The Battle of Life.*" *Dickens Studies Annual* 42 (2011): 159–75.

Napolitano, Marc. "Making Music with the Pickwickians: Form and Function in Musical Adaptations of *The Pickwick Papers.*" *Dickens Studies Annual* 42 (2011): 33–53.

Nasar, Sylvia. "Mr. Sentiment vs. Scrooge." *Grand Pursuit: The Story of Economic Genius.* New York: Simon & Schuster, 2011. 1–10.

Nayder, Lillian. "'The Omission of His Only Sister's Name': Letitia Austin and the Legacies of Charles Dickens." *Dickens Quarterly* 28.4 (2011): 251–60.

———. *The Other Dickens: A Life of Catherine Hogarth.* Ithaca: Cornell UP, 2011.

Neill, Anna. "Evolution and Epilepsy in *Bleak House.*" *SEL* 51.4 (2011): 803–22.

Neill, Natalie. "Adapting Dickens's *A Christmas Carol in Prose.*" *Victorian Literature and Film Adaptation.* Ed. Abigail Burnham Bloom and Mary Sanders Pollock. Amherst, NY: Cambria P, 2011. 71–88.

Nord, Deborah Epstein. "Dickens's 'Jewish Question': Pariah Capitalism and the Way Out." *Victorian Literature and Culture* 39.1 (2011): 27–46.

Oldani, Louis J., S. J. "Dickens, Roman Catholicism, and the Jesuits." *The Dickensian* 107.3 (2011): 202–11.

Orestano, Francesca. "Charles Dickens and the Vertigo of the List: A Few Proposals." *Dickens Quarterly* 28.3 (2011): 205–14.

Ortiz-Robles, Mario. "Dickens Performs Dickens." *ELH* 78.2 (2011): 457–78.

Palmer, Alan. "The Mind Beyond the Skin in *Little Dorrit.*" *Current Trends in Narratology.* Ed. Greta Olson. Berlin: de Gruyter P, 2011. 79–100.

Panek, LeRoy Lad. "Charles Dickens." *Before Sherlock Holmes: How Magazines and Newspapers Invented the Detective Story.* Jefferson, NC: McFarland, 2011. 89–108.

Paroissien, David. "Clarriker, Pocket, and Pirrip: The Original Tale of Dickens's Clerk." *Dickens Studies Annual* 42 (2011): 275–94.

Partial Answers 9.2 (2011). [Contents: Leona Toker, "Introduction": 211–17; Murray Baumgarten, "Reading Dickens Writing London": 218–31; Elsie B. Michie, "Morbidity in Fairyland: Frances Trollope, Charles Dickens, and the Rhetoric of Abolition": 233–51; Goldie Morgentaler, "Dickens and Dance in the 1840s": 253–66; Géza Kállay, "'What Wilt Thou Do, Old Man?'—Being Sick Unto Death: Scrooge, King Lear, and Kierkegaard": 267–83; David Paroissien, "Subdued by the Dyer's Hand: Dickens at Work in *Bleak House*": 285–95; Elana Gomel, "'Part of the Dreadful Thing': The Urban Chronotope of *Bleak House*": 297–309; Efraim Sicher, "Dickens and the Pleasure of the Text: The Risks of *Hard Times*": 311–30; Regenia Gagnier, "Freedom, Determinism, and Hope in *Little Dorrit*: A Literary Anthropology": 331–46; Adina Ciugureanu, "The Victim-Aggressor Duality in *Great Expectations*": 347–61; Sally Ledger, "Dickens, Natural History, and *Our Mutual Friend*": 363–78; Angelika Zirker, "Physiognomy and the Reading of Character in *Our Mutual Friend*": 379–90; Jeffrey

Wallen, "Twemlow's Abyss": 391–403; Bernard Harrison, *"Always* Fiction? The Limits of Authorial License in *Our Mutual Friend"*: 405–30.]

Pollack-Pelzner, Daniel. "Dickens and Shakespeare's Household Words." *ELH* 78.3 (2011): 533–56.

Poole, Adrian. "Dickens and Shakespeare's Ghost(s)." *Shakespeare Without Boundaries: Essays in Honor of Dieter Mehl.* Ed. Christa Jansohn, Lena Cowan Orlin, and Stanley Wells. Newark: U of Delaware P, 2011. 322–36.

Poole, Adrian, and Rebekah Scott. "Charles Dickens." *Scott, Dickens, Eliot, Hardy: Great Shakespeareans.* Ed. Adrian Poole. London: Continuum, 2011. 53–94.

Poon, Phoebe. "Trust and Conscience in *Bleak House* and *Our Mutual Friend.*" *Dickens Quarterly* 28.1 (2011): 3–21.

Potter, Dawn. "Dickens the Novelist: A Love Letter." *Sewanee Review* 119.3 (2011): 419–27.

Puckett, Kent. "Some Versions of Syllepsis." *Partial Answers* 9.1 (2011): 177–88.

Richardson, Ruth. "Charles Dickens and the Cleveland Street Workhouse." *Dickens Quarterly* 28.2 (2011): 99–108.

Rodensky, Lisa. "Making Crime Pay in the Victorian Novel Survey Course." *Teaching Law and Literature.* Ed. Austin Sarat, Cathrine O. Frank, and Matthew Anderson. New York: MLA, 2011. 126–35.

Rowland, Peter. *Dickensian Digressions: The Hunter, the Haunter, and the Haunted.* Bethesda, MD: Academica P, 2011.

Sahi, Sara Dehghanzadeh. "The Relationship Between Selfhood and Otherness in *Great Expectations:* A Lacanian Reading." *Consciousness, Literature, and the Arts* 12.2 (2011). <http://blackboard.lincoln.ac.uk/bbcwebdav/users/dmeyerdinkgrafe/archiv/sahi.html>.

Sasaki, Toru. "Translating *Great Expectations* into Japanese." *The Dickensian* 107.3 (2011): 197–201.

Schaffer, Talia. "Salvage: Betty as the Mutual Friend." *Novel Craft: Victorian Domestic Handicraft and Nineteenth-Century Fiction.* Oxford: Oxford UP, 2011. 119–44.

Simon, Leslie. *"Bleak House, Our Mutual Friend,* and the Aesthetics of Dust." *Dickens Studies Annual* 42 (2011): 217–36.

Slater, Michael. *The Genius of Dickens.* London: Duckworth, 2011.

Smith, Grahame. "Earth, Air, Fire, and Water: The Struggle for Pip's Soul in *Great Expectations.*" *Dickens Quarterly* 28.2 (2011): 144–53.

Soares, Rebecca. "Literary Graftings: Hannah Crafts's *The Bondswoman's Narrative* and the Nineteenth-Century Transatlantic Reader." *Victorian Periodicals Review* 44.1 (2011): 1–23.

Sutcliffe, Allan. "John Brougham's *Little Dorrit.*" *The Dickensian* 107.3 (2011): 214–19.

Tambling, Jeremy. "Lamb, Hogarth, and Dickens." *Charles Lamb Bulletin* 154 (Autumn 2011): 100–14.

———. *"Little Dorrit:* Dickens, Circumlocution, Unconscious Thought." *Digressions in European Literature: From Cervantes to Sebald.* Ed. Alexis Grohmann and Caragh Wells. New York: Palgrave Macmillan, 2011. 36–48.

———. "William Makepeace Thackeray: A Bicentennial Tribute." *The Dickensian* 107.2 (2011): 124–25.

Tomalin, Claire. *Charles Dickens: A Life*. London: Penguin, 2011.

Tracy, Robert. "*Little Dorrit*: The Readers Within the Text." *Dickens Quarterly* 28.2 (2011): 128–43.

Wagner, Tamara. "Dickens's 'Gentleman for Nowhere': Reversing Technological Gothic in the Linkages of *Mugby Junction*." *Dickens Quarterly* 28.1 (2011): 52–64.

Watson, Lauren. "Mimics, Counterfeits, and 'Other' Bad Copies: Forging the Currency of Class and Colonialism in *Great Expectations*." *Textual Practice* 25.3 (2011): 493–511.

Weltman, Sharon Aronofsky. "Boz versus Bos in *Sweeney Todd*: Dickens, Sondheim, and Victorianness." *Dickens Studies Annual* 42 (2011): 55–76.

Wilkes, David. "The Mudworm's Bower and Other Metropastoral Spaces: Novelization and Clashing Chronotopes in *Our Mutual Friend*." *Dickens Studies Annual* 42 (2011): 295–330.

Winter, Sarah. *The Pleasures of Memory: Learning to Read with Charles Dickens*. New York: Fordham UP, 2011.

Young-Zook, Monica M. "Buried Secrets: Lost Fathers in *Bleak House*." McKnight 129–52.

Zemka, Sue. "Dickens's Peripatetic Novels." *Time and the Moment in Victorian Literature and Society*. Cambridge: Cambridge UP, 2011. 102–21.

Ziegler, Garrett. "The Perils of Empire: Dickens, Collins, and the Indian Mutiny." *Pirates and Mutineers of the Nineteenth Century: Swashbucklers and Swindlers*. Ed. Grace Moore. Burlington, VT: Ashgate, 2011. 149–64.

Index

(Page numbers in italics represent illustrations)